A Companion to World Philosophies

Blackwell Companions to Philosophy

This outstanding student reference series offers a comprehensive survey of philosophy as a whole. Written by today's leading philosophers, each volume provides lucid and engaging coverage of the key figures, terms, topics, and problems of the field. Taken together, they provide the ideal basis for course use, representing an unparalleled work of reference for students and specialists alike.

Published

1 A Companion to Ethics
Edited by Peter Singer

2 A Companion to Aesthetics
Edited by David Cooper

3 A Companion to Epistemology
Edited by Jonathan Dancy and Ernest Sosa

4 A Companion to Contemporary Political Philosophy
Edited by Robert E. Goodin and Philip Pettit

5 A Companion to the Philosophy of Mind
Edited by Samuel Guttenplan

6 A Companion to Metaphysics
Edited by Jaegwon Kim and Ernest Sosa

7 A Companion to Philosophy of Law and Legal Theory
Edited by Dennis Patterson

8 A Companion to Philosophy of Religion
Edited by Philip Quinn and Charles Taliaferro

9 A Companion to the Philosophy of Language
Edited by Bob Hale and Crispin Wright

10 A Companion to World Philosophies
Edited by Eliot Deutsch and Ron Bontekoe

Forthcoming

11 A Companion to Continental Philosophy
Edited by Simon Critchley and William Schroeder

12 A Companion to Feminist Philosophy
Edited by Alison Jaggar and Iris Young

Blackwell
Companions to
Philosophy

A Companion to World Philosophies

Edited by
ELIOT DEUTSCH
and
RON BONTEKOE

Advisory editors
Tu Weiming (Chinese)
J. N. Mohanty (Indian)
Ninian Smart (Buddhism)
Marietta Stepaniants (Islam)

BLACKWELL
Publishers

First published 1997

2 4 6 8 10 9 7 5 3 1

Blackwell Publishers Inc.
350 Main Street
Malden, Massachusetts 02148
USA

Blackwell Publishers Ltd
108 Cowley Road
Oxford OX4 1JF
UK

Library of Congress Cataloging in Publication Data

A companion to world philosophies / edited by Eliot Deutsch and Ron Bontekoe.
p. cm. – (Blackwell companions to philosophy)
Includes bibliographical references and index.
ISBN 0-631-19871-7 (hardcover: alk. paper)
1. Philosophy, Oriental. 2. Philosophy, African. I. Deutsch, Eliot. II. Bontekoe, Ronald, 1954– . III. Series.
B121.C664 1997
109 – dc20 96-36179
CIP

British Library Cataloguing in Publication Data

A CIP catalogue record for this book is available from the British Library.

Typeset in $10^1/_2$ on $12^1/_2$pt Photina
by Best-set Typesetter Ltd, Hong Kong
Printed in Great Britain by TJ International Ltd, Padstow, Cornwall

This book is printed on acid-free paper

Contents

Contributors

Tamara Albertini is a professor of philosophy at the University of Hawaii at Manoa.

Roger T. Ames is a professor of philosophy and Director of the Center for Chinese Studies at the University of Hawaii at Manoa.

David Bastow is a professor of philosophy at the University of Dundee, Dundee, Scotland.

John Ross Carter is a professor at Chapel House, Colgate University, Hamilton, New York.

Arindam Chakrabarti is a professor of philosophy at the University of Delhi, India.

John Charlot is a professor of religion at the University of Hawaii at Manoa.

Amita Chatterjee is a professor of philosophy at Jadavpur University, Calcutta, India.

Chung-ying Cheng is a professor of philosophy at the University of Hawaii at Manoa and Editor of the *Journal of Chinese Philosophy*.

A. S. Cua is professor emeritus at the Catholic University of America, Washington, DC.

Carine Defoort is a professor of sinology at the Katholieke Universiteit Leuven, Belgium.

Majid Fakhry is emeritus professor of philosophy at the American University of Beirut, Lebanon.

Segun Gbadegesin is a professor of philosophy at Howard University, Washington, DC.

Edwin Gerow is professor emeritus at Reed College, Portland, Oregon, and Editor of *The Journal of the American Oriental Society*.

Stephen J. Goldberg is a professor of art at the University of Hawaii at Manoa.

Bina Gupta is a professor of philosophy at the University of Missouri, Columbia, Missouri.

David L. Hall is a professor of philosophy at the University of Texas at El Paso.

Kenneth K. Inada is a professor of philosophy at the University of Buffalo, State University of New York.

P. J. Ivanhoe is a professor of philosophy at Stanford University, California.

Knut A. Jacobsen is a professor in the Department of Cultural Studies at the University of Oslo, Norway.

Matthew Kapstein is a professor of Buddhism at Columbia University, New York.

Thomas P. Kasulis is a professor of philosophy in the Department of East Asian Languages and Literature at the Ohio State University, Columbus, Ohio.

John M. Koller is a professor of philosophy at Rensselaer Polytechnic Institute, Troy, New York.

Daya Krishna is chairman of the Indian Council of Philosophical Research, Delhi, India, and formerly professor of philosophy and Ex-Pro Vice-Chancellor at the University of Rajasthan, Jaipur, India.

Gerald James Larson is the Tagore Professor of Religious Studies at Indiana University, Bloomington.

D. A. Masolo is a professor of philosophy at Antioch College, Yellow Springs, Ohio.

J. N. Mohanty is a professor of philosophy at Temple University, Philadelphia, Pennsylvania.

Josep Puig Montada is a professor in the Dpto. de Estudios Arabes e Islámicos at Ciudad Universitaria, Madrid, Spain.

Shigenori Nagatomo is a professor of religious studies at Temple University, Philadelphia, Pennsylvania.

Seyyed Hossein Nasr is University Professor of Islamic Studies at the George Washington University, Washington, DC.

G. C. Pande is chairman, Allahabad Museum Society, Allahabad, and formerly Vice-Chancellor of the Universities of Rajasthan and Allahabad.

Stephen H. Phillips is a professor of philosophy at the University of Texas at Austin.

P. D. Premasiri is a professor of philosophy at the University of Peradeniya, Sri Lanka.

Henry Rosemont, Jr is a professor of philosophy at St Mary's College, Maryland.

Shun Kwong-loi is a professor of philosophy at the University of California, Berkeley.

Ninian Smart is the J. F. Rowny Professor of Comparative Religions at the University of California, Santa Barbara.

Andrey Smirnov is a professor at the Center for Studies in Oriental Philosophies at the Institute of Philosophy, Moscow.

Marietta Stepaniants is Director, Center for Studies in Oriental Philosophies at the Institute of Philosophy, Moscow.

Tu Weiming is a professor of Chinese philosophy and Director of the Harvard-Yenching Institute, Harvard University.

Mourad Wahba is a professor in the faculty of education at the Goethe Institute in Cairo, Egypt.

John Walbridge is a professor of religious studies at Indiana University, Bloomington.

Michiko Yusa is a professor in the Department of Foreign Languages at Western Washington University, Bellingham, Washington.

Preface

When Stephan Chambers, then philosophy editor at Blackwells, invited me to edit a volume on non-Western philosophies for their Companion series, my first reaction was a rather vehement "no thank you." I argued that the whole idea simply betrayed the sort of "orientalism" that comparative philosophy has for some time striven to overcome – by and large successfully. This "orientalism" presumed that all philosophical traditions that were not defined as Western constituted an identifiable something simply in virtue of their being non-Western. But what, after all, does classical Chinese philosophy have in common with, say, traditional African thinking or, for that matter, with much of classical Indian philosophy that would warrant their being presented together within a single grouping? Mr Chambers's response was sympathetic, but he offered the counter-argument that this way of thinking was all very fine for those philosophers and students who were already knowledgeable about other traditions, but the actual state of affairs in the field as a whole was still such that the vast majority of philosophers and students, although now very interested in cross-cultural encounters, knew very little about traditions other than their own. An introduction to other traditions, at a rather high level, was still very much needed. Well, as is obvious, Mr Chambers won the argument.

In a general description of the project that was given to the invited contributors, I stated that

> The purpose of this work is to provide a sophisticated, one-volume companion to the study of select non-Western philosophical traditions. It has become increasingly evident to many teachers and students of philosophy as well as to general readers that philosophy is not the exclusive province of the West; that indeed other traditions have a depth and range comparable to Western thought and exhibit distinctive features, the knowledge of which can enrich philosophical understanding and creativity wherever it occurs. This volume will strive at once to introduce some of the finest thinking within and about non-Western traditions to teachers, students and general readers, and to offer interpretations and insights relevant to the work of other scholars in the field.

I would emphasize several points made in this "general description." First, that this Companion volume deals with *select* non-Western philosophical traditions, for it should be quite obvious that it is impossible to cover in any depth all of the various traditions in the world in a single volume. We have selected – and how could they possibly be excluded? – the great Indian and Chinese traditions, separating out the Buddhist as a kind of pan-Asian phenomenon. We have included the Islamic tradition, for although many of us still see it primarily as embedded in the Western experience (as providing a transition from the classical Greek to the medieval Christian world), it has come to be recognized as having a distinctive character of its own, and it is reasserting itself in a variety of ways at the present time. We have also included, by way of historical perspectives, something of the richness of traditional African and Polynesian thinking. The question is often raised whether largely oral traditions should in fact be counted as "philosophical" or be treated rather anthropologically as belief-systems of native peoples. We will not get into the debate here of what should count as a philosophical tradition, but note only that it seems quite clear that these and other, say, Amerindian cultures, did certainly develop a number of ideas (cosmological, social) and attempts to justify them that fit most definitions of what philosophy is, and that in any event these ideas are beginning to attract considerable attention among many persons not directly associated with these cultures.

The second point I would stress has to do with the *depth and range* of the selected traditions, by which I want to call attention to the extraordinary diversity within each of them. It is quite natural, hermeneutically speaking, for one to assume at first that the thought of another culture has a clear unity and simplicity in contrast to the multifarious character of one's own. It does not take long, however, before one discovers – and the many essays here will drive home the point quite effectively – that, for example, the Indian and the Chinese traditions have explored many of the same basic questions that have been dealt with in Western thought and have articulated in their own ways kinds of answers to them which can, without severe damage, be categorized within the "isms" of philosophy (realism, naturalism, idealism, materialism . . .) familiar to us. In short, that these traditions are as richly diverse (and inherently contentious) as our own. But this is not as important, I think, as the need to recognize what is genuinely distinctive in the contributions that have been made – which is to say that one's primary concern in the exploration of other traditions ought not to be that of simply finding more of oneself and what is familiar to one, but of learning about other possibilities of philosophical experience that can be opened up to one through cross-cultural encounter. In short, and this leads to the final point I would emphasize from the "general description," the philosophical explorer of other traditions needs to perform a dual role, which are two sides of the same coin. She needs first of all to *understand* as best she can the basic presuppositions, styles of argument, and the rest that are associated with other cultures, an understanding that does seek finally to locate what is truly distinctive in these traditions and to identify what can be contributory to enriched and enhanced philosophical possibilities. This leads quite naturally into the second role or task, which is the *creative* one of appropriating, in an unself-conscious way, those distinctive contributing elements so as to make them an inseparable part of one's own ground of thought and being. The second task, then, is simply that of becoming better philosophers in the light of the understanding of other cultures.

This Companion volume is organized in a way that will give the reader some knowledge of the historical background and contemporary situation with respect to each of the selected traditions. It will also show some of the distinctive ways of thinking developed within those traditions, by focusing on a number of specific topics: namely, conceptions of reality and divinity, of causality, of truth, the nature of rationality, of selfhood, of humankind and nature, ideas of the good, social and political ideas, and aesthetic values. These topics, while covering a broad range, do not, of course, come near to exhausting the philosophical content of these traditions.

The accounts given in this volume are all in English. The traditions themselves, needless to say, were developed within their own indigenous languages and it is extremely important for us not to assume that all basic ideas and concepts translate readily from one language to another. Many of the presentations will make that clear, but one must always be on one's guard to note that the usage of certain similar-sounding terminology (as given in translation) does not guarantee that the same philosophical issue is being addressed. When Western philosophers today worry about the nature of the self, say in terms of the problem of other minds, they occupy a quite different philosophical space than did the classical Chinese, who understood personhood as socially grounded, or the Indian philosophers in their speculations concerning the nature of human consciousness. But it is precisely these complexities that make the comparative philosophical enterprise so exciting.

One last note: reading secondary accounts about a tradition is no substitute for the harder work of studying the primary texts themselves – and indeed, of coming to an understanding that a philosophical *text* itself may mean different things in different traditions. For example, in the Indian tradition the major philosophical work is presented within commentarial traditions identified with the various schools rather than, with some notable exceptions, separate treatises with a distinctive authorial style of the sort that we are familiar with in the modern Western context. Philosophical truth itself was not something so much discovered as recovered within the framework of a given school of thought.

I am exceedingly grateful to the many distinguished contributors to this volume for their willingness to take time away from their own creative research to accept the difficult task of introducing in a sophisticated manner something of the splendor of other "world philosophies." My special thanks to Tu Weiming, J. N. Mohanty, Ninian Smart and Marietta Stepaniants, who served as advisory editors respectively for the Chinese, Indian, Buddhist, and Islamic areas. They were of immense assistance in helping me to identify some of the best people working in these areas. I want also to thank my co-editor, Ron Bontekoe, for his help in the organization of this work and for his tireless effort to bring it editorially into a coherent – and one trusts highly readable – shape and form.

Eliot Deutsch

Guide to pronunciation

Sanskrit (and Pāli)

Vowels

a	a in America or o in come
ā	a in far or in father
i	i in pit or in pin
ī	ee in feel or i in machine
u	u in put or in pull
ū	u in rule
ri(ṛ)	properly ur, but by modern Hindus as ri in river
e	ay in say or a in made
ai	i in rite or ai in aisle
o	o in go
au	ou in loud

Semivowels

y	y in yonder
r	r in ram
l	l in luck
v	v in clover

Consonants

Consonants are pronounced approximately as in English, except:

g	g in gun or in get (i.e., always "hard")
ch	ch in church
sh (ś, ṣ)	sh in sheet or in shun

When h is combined with another consonant (e.g., th, bh), it is aspirated: th as in boathouse; ph as in uphill, etc. The palatal ñ is like the Spanish señor (jña, however, is pronounced most often by modern Hindus as "gyah," with a hard g).

Accent

The general rule is to accent the next to final syllable, if it is long, or the nearest long syllable preceding it. If none is long, the first syllable is accented. (A long syllable is one which contains a long vowel or one in which a vowel is followed by two or more consonants.)

Chinese

This work employs for the most part the *pinyin* system recently introduced in China, which generally follows English rules of pronunciation and which is now widely used in contemporary scholarship. The older Wade–Giles system of romanization – which we give below, followed by the *pinyin* equivalents – has traditionally been used in English transliteration of Chinese terms and is employed most frequently in the titles and translations of classical texts.

Vowels

a	a in father
ai	to rhyme with why
ao	to rhyme with now
e	e in wet
ē	as the u in but
ei	to rhyme with stay
yi, i	as the e in me
ieh	to rhyme with (Oh) yeh
o	o in tore
ou	to rhyme with know
u	u in duty
ü	as in German

Consonants

When aspirated, pronounce as in English: e.g., k' – as in king, and ch' as in church. When unaspirated as:

ch	j in jam
eh	j in job
f	f in faint
h	h in how
j	r in ran
k	g in got
l	l in lake
m	m in moon
n	n in no
p	like b in bad
r	like r in rare
s	s in snow
sh	sh in shoulder
t	d in dub
ts	dz in adze

tz	ds in words
w	w in water

pinyin	*Wade–Giles*
a	a
b	p
c	ts
ch	ch
d	t
e	e
f	f
g	k
h	h
i	i
j	ch
k	k
l	l
m	m
n	n
o	o
p	p
q	ch
r	j
s	s, ss, sz
sh	sh
t	t
u	u, ü
v	–
w	w
x	hs
y	y
z	ts, tz
zh	ch

Arabic

Vowels

a	a in again (in unaccented syllables)
a	a in father (in accented syllables)
ā	a in attention
e	e in egg
ē	ay in way
i	ee in meet
ī	ee in see

o	o in OK
ō	o in so
u	oo in doom
ū	ue in sue

Consonants

b	b in baton
ch	ch in church
d	d in dam
dh	th in there
ḍ	emphatic dull palatal d
f	f in father
gh	g in agua
h	h in hot
j	j in Jane
k	k in kind
kh	h in horror
l	l in like
m	m in moon
n	n in not
q	k in Luke
r	r in row
s	s in saw
sh	sh in shower
ṣ	emphatic sharp palatal s
t	t in total
th	th in thick
ṭ	emphatic dull palatal t
w	w in waste
z	z in zebra
ẓ	emphatic dull palatal z
ʻ	explosive guttural sound, tonal counterpart to ḥ
ʼ	strong vocal inflection

PART I

HISTORICAL BACKGROUND

1

Chinese philosophy: a synoptic view

TU WEIMING

The ideal Chinese thinker is a scholar-official who is informed by a profound historical consciousness, well seasoned in the fine arts of poetry, lute and calligraphy, and deeply immersed in the daily routine of government. If philosophy is loosely defined as disciplined reflection on insights, Chinese philosophy is distinguished in its commitment to and observation of the human condition. It is a disciplined engaged reflection with insights derived primarily from practical living. The Chinese thinker, unlike the Greek philosopher, the Hebrew prophet, the Indian guru, the Christian priest, or the Buddhist monk, is engaged in society, involved in politics, and dedicated to the spiritual transformation of the world from within.

We can find some striking similarities between the idea of the Chinese thinker as a scholar and the modern Western intellectual, but the vision which informs each is different. The modern Western idea of the intellectual, which has its origins in the Russian conception of the intelligentsia, is the product of the Enlightenment, a form of secular humanism. The Chinese thinker, by contrast, is inspired by a cosmological as well as an anthropological vision and is, therefore, not at all anthropocentric. In Max Weber's conception, the two appropriate "callings" for the modern Western intellectual are science and politics. The Chinese scholar, while politically concerned and socially engaged, must also be dedicated to mediating cultural structures through education so that society and polity will not be dominated by wealth and power alone. Disenchanted with the magic garden or universal brotherhood, the modern Western intellectual overwhelmed by the demands of science, technology, and professionalism became, as Weber acknowledged he himself was, unmusical to religious matters and, we may add, unmindful of particularistic local knowledge. Yet in the light of the upsurge of interest in ethnicity, gender, language, land, class, and faith in academic circles in North America and Western Europe in recent decades, Weber's modernistic ideas, rooted in abstract universalism and instrumental rationality, seem anachronistic.

A modern counterpart of the Chinese thinker would likely be a critic of the Enlightenment, because the unintended negative consequences of this powerful ideology of the modern West have marginalized the spiritual resources of the Chinese tradition, destroyed the core values of the Sinic world, and made the viability of the human species problematical. Yet, since the Enlightenment mentality has become a defining characteristic of modern Chinese consciousness, the criticism would be intended to broaden, deepen, and enrich rather than to deconstruct the Enlightenment project.

The emergence of the Sinic mind

Chinese philosophy began when the Chinese mind first reflected upon the meaning of being human in antiquity. The earliest Chinese written records, the oracle bones of the Shang dynasty (1766?–1046? BCE), clearly show that the Chinese cultural elite, by posing questions covering such matters as the weather, crops, hunting expeditions, and sacrifice to the deities, were self-consciously engaged in forecasting and negotiation for the purpose of understanding and improving their human condition. Some scholars may question the assertion of Berkeley historian David Keightley to the effect that Shang diviners self-reflexively used divination to "charge" the ancestral spirits to be responsible for matters the king deemed beneficial to the well-being of the realm, and corresponding imperial actions that he had decided to undertake, as well as the health of his own physical body. But the messages of the oracle bones, together with those in the bronze inscriptions, do convey the sense of a sophisticated worldview governed by an elaborate ritual system, a complex bureaucracy, an economy based on the division of labor, and a stratified society.

The Harvard archaeologist K. C. Chang has challenged the "grand theory" of the origins of human civilizations. He maintains that the Chinese experience seems to suggest that polity and religion, rather than economy and technology, provided the primary impetus for the emergence of Chinese civilization. Surely, economic activities, such as the mechanism of the market, and technological advances, such as the invention of tools for fishing and agriculture, were instrumental in the advent of "civilization" in Neolithic China, but the need for political order and the desire to communicate with the Lord-on-High were particularly compelling for the ruling minority as they developed the institutional structures necessary for the emergence of what may be called the Sinic civilization in ancient China.

However, the assumption that Chinese civilization began in a core area, the Wei valley of the Yellow River, and then radiated outward to cover the area of present-day China has been seriously challenged by recent archaeological discoveries. The thesis that China came into being through the gradual interaction of several comparable Neolithic civilizations (from Painted Pottery and Black Pottery to the Bronze age) seems to have more persuasive power. Conceptually, it is convenient to use "dragon," the mythic symbol of potency, creativity, and transformation, to signify this process of integration. As a composite totem, the dragon possesses at least the head of a tiger, the horns of a ram, the body of a snake, the claws of an eagle and the scales of a fish. Its ability to cross totemic boundaries and its lack of verisimilitude to any living creature strongly suggest that from the very beginning the dragon was a deliberate cultural construction. The danger of anachronism notwithstanding, the modern Chinese ethnic self-definition as the "dragon race" indicates a deep-rooted sense that Chineseness may derive from many sources.

Chinese reflection on the meaning of being human may have predated the emergence of the idea of Chineseness by several centuries. This, at the first blush, seems odd. But if we make clear that our understanding of "Chinese" reflection, based on oracle bones and Bronze inscriptions, is not predicated on the prior emergence of a Chinese consciousness or a communal self-awareness of being Chinese, we may be justified in giving an account of what that reflexivity entails without prematurely addressing what actually constituted Chineseness in a historical sense.

David Keightley, in his "Reflections on How it Became Chinese", identifies seven features which, in his view, permeated the cultural tradition, later characterized as Chinese, from the Neolithic to the early imperial age in the Han Dynasty (206 BCE–220 CE):

1 hierarchical social distinctions;
2 massive mobilization of labor;
3 an emphasis on the group rather than the individual;
4 an emphasis on ritual in all dimensions of life;
5 an emphasis on formal boundaries and models;
6 an ethic of service, obligation, and emulation;
7 little sense of tragedy and irony.

The myth of Yu, a functional equivalent of the Biblical story of Noah, gives us a glimpse of what Keightley may have in mind. The story of Yu presents a Chinese version of the worldwide flood legend. This Chinese cultural hero confronted the natural calamity with human ingenuity. He managed to control the flood waters through great coordinated efforts on many levels. First, he inspired people through exemplary teaching. He is said to have worked on the project for nine years without visiting his family once. Second, his spirit of self-sacrifice was augmented by a charismatic leadership that enabled him to mobilize thousands of people to work at gigantic irrigation systems. Third, unlike his father who failed to contain the flood by constructing dams, Yu studied the terrain, understood the nature of the disaster and developed a comprehensive and practical plan to overcome it. As a result, he drained off the flood waters of the North China Plain, divided the empire into nine regions and, according to the quality of the land, equitably distributed the natural resources among all the feudal lords. Thus legend has it that Yu started the first Chinese dynasty, Xia (2205?–1766? BCE).

Human self-reflexivity

Understandably, the human factor, as it was manifested in the social order, the mobilization of labor, the ritual system, the work ethic, group spirit, artistic decor, and faith in the improvability of the conditions of existence, featured prominently in Chinese consciousness. Viewed in this context, Wing-tsit Chan's straightforward characterization of Chinese philosophy seems self-evidently true:

> If one word could characterize the entire history of Chinese philosophy, that word would be humanism – not the humanism that denies or slights a Supreme Power, but one that professes the unity of man and Heaven. In this sense, humanism has dominated Chinese thought from the dawn of its history.

Critical scholars may find too strong a Confucian flavor in this statement. They may argue that the classical Chinese thought which flourished in the Spring and Autumn period (722–481 BCE) was noted for its intellectual diversity. The so-called "Hundred Schools" represented such an array of life-orientations that "humanism", as the Confucians would have it, seems too narrow a concept to accommodate the whole range of philosophical horizons that the Chinese mind unfolded. For example, among the seventy or so masters assembled in the capital of the state of Qi, Jixia, in the third century BCE, there were naturalists, cosmologists, sophists, logicians, physiocrats, military strategists, proto-Legalists and Mohists as well as Confucian humanists.

However, if we use "humanism" to signify a strong commitment to the world, an emphasis on social relations, and the primacy of the political order, the world of ideas in ancient China was humanistic to the core. Besides the legendary sage-kings, Yao, Shun and the aforementioned Yu, the cultural heroes, vividly portrayed in ancient history, were all statesmen with profound insights into the human condition. The case of Prime Minister Zichan (active ca. 535 BCE) of the state of Zheng merits special attention. In a well considered political move to pacify the wandering ghost of Poyu, a high official who had undeservedly died a violent death and who, it was feared, was haunting the people of Zheng, Zichan had Poyu's son appointed as his father's successor, offering the following explanation: "When spiritual beings have a place to return to, they will not become malicious." He then suggested why Poyu had become a malicious spiritual being:

> In man's life the first transformations are called the earthly aspect of the soul (*po*). After *po* had been produced, that which is strong and positive is called the heavenly aspect of the soul (*hun*). If he has had an abundance in the use of material things and subtle essentials, his *hun* and *po* will become strong. From this are developed essence and understanding until there are spirit and intelligence. When an ordinary man or woman dies a violent death, the *hun* and *po* are still able to keep hanging about men and do evil and malicious things. How much more would be the case of Poyu [the descendent of ministers engaged in the government of Zheng for three generations]. (Wing-tsit Chan, pp. 12–13)

There are at least three implications in this anecdote: (1) the human world is intimately intertwined with spiritual beings; (2) the human soul is a complex mixture of earthly and heavenly forces; and (3) human intervention is often necessary to harmonize the cosmic process. Needless to say, hierarchy, work, the group, boundaries, ritual, obligation, and destiny all feature prominently in the Zichan story.

The anthropocosmic vision

Confucius (551–479 BCE) greatly admired Zichan. The minister's reasonable way of handling the malicious spirit must have struck a sympathetic resonance in Confucius' own ethico-religious thinking. When the Master was asked about "serving the spiritual beings," he retorted, "If we are not yet able to serve human beings, how can we serve spiritual beings?" When he was asked about death, he responded, "If we do not yet know about life, how can we know about death?" (*Analects* 11:11; Chan, p. 36 with modifications). Often the modern interpreter takes this to mean that Confucius was exclusively interested in life and human beings, and that he was oblivious to death and spiritual beings. This is, I surmise, a serious misreading of a profoundly meaningful statement about the relationship between life and death and between human beings and spiritual beings in Confucian humanism. The assertion that knowing life is a precondition for knowing death by no means implies the rejection of the need for knowing death. On the contrary, precisely because one cannot know death without first understanding the meaning of life, a full appreciation of life entails the need for probing the meaning of death. Similarly, it is impractical and, indeed, implausible to imagine that we can know spiritual beings without a prior knowledge of the human condition. Yet a full appreciation of the meaning of being human demands that we try to understand spiritual beings as well.

Modern scholars, impressed by Confucius' apparent pragmatism and atheism, have difficulty explaining the Confucian dictum that filial piety is characterized by our ability to serve our parents while they are alive, bury them when they die and continuously offer sacrifice to them as if they are always present, all according to the appropriate ritual practice. In fact, the Confucian tradition is noted for its rich repertoire of elaborate death rituals and its extensive literature on the remembrance and veneration of ancestors. How can the anthropologists characterize the ancestral cult as a defining characteristic of Confucian religiousness, if the Master was interested in neither death nor spirits? There is a wealth of material on death and spirits in the *Analects*:

> When Confucius offered sacrifice to his ancestors, he felt as if his ancestral spirits were actually present. When he offered sacrifice to other spiritual beings, he felt as if they were actually present. He said, "If I do not participate in the sacrifice [in person], it is as if I did not sacrifice at all." (*Analects* 3:12; Chan, p. 25)

> Wang-sun Chia [Jia] asked, "What is meant by the common saying, 'It is better to be on good terms with the God of the Kitchen [who cooks our food] than with the spirits of the shrine [ancestors] at the southwest corner of the house' "? Confucius said, "It is not true. He who commits a sin against Heaven has no god to pray to." (*Analects* 3:13; Chan, p. 25)

> Confucius was very ill. Tzu-lu [Zilu] asked that prayer be offered. Confucius said, "Is there such a thing?" Tzu-lu replied, "There is. A Eulogy says, 'Pray to the spiritual beings above and below.' " Confucius said, "My prayer has been for a long time." (*Analects* 7:34; Chan, p. 33.)

The human form of life envisioned by Confucius is not anthropocentric. Rather, it is anthropocosmic in the sense that there is implicit mutuality, constant communication, and dynamic interaction between the anthropological world and the cosmic order. Confucian humanism, as an inclusive organismic vision of human flourishing, involves life, death, and spiritual beings.

Human nature as lived concreteness

The Confucian assertion that "Human beings can enlarge the Way" and that "the Way cannot enlarge human beings" (*Analects* 15:28) is not the equivalent of the Greek idea that man is the measure of all things and that man has the will-power to change the natural course of action. Surely, as the myth of Yu implies, human beings, through diligent work, collaborative effort, charismatic leadership, knowledge, determination, and sacrifice, are capable of transforming chaos (for example, the flood) into order (for example, the well irrigated "nine regions"), but the Confucian human agent, endowed with rich inner resources for self-transformation, is a servant, partner, and co-creator of Heaven. As a servant, the Mandate of Heaven works through the human agent for its own realization; as a partner, the human agent, by self-cultivation, transmits the culture willed by Heaven; and, as a co-creator, the human agent joins Heaven in a collaborative enterprise to bring to completion the cosmic process: "Heaven engenders, humanity completes" (*tiansheng rencheng*). Our ability to enlarge the Way makes us humble servants, responsible partners, and reverential co-creators. Precisely because we are empowered by Heaven to be an anthropocosmic rather than an anthropocentric being, we cherish the virtues of humbleness, responsibility and reverence.

Implicit in this idea of the human is a non-reductionist conception of human nature. Perhaps Confucius' unique contribution to human self-understanding is his assertion that the concrete living person here and now is the basis for human self-reflexivity. A person so conceived is a dynamic process rather than a static structure, inevitably changing and deliberately transforming. The *Book of Change*, a major source of inspiration for Confucian teaching, articulates the linkage between the Heavenly course and the human way in terms of renewal: "Heaven marches forward vigorously; the profound person [emulating it as model] makes unceasing efforts for self-strengthening." The process of human self-renewal, individually and communally, is symbolized by three interconnected activities: poetry, ritual and music. Aesthetic sensitivity enables us to experience sympathetic resonance with nature; ritual practice helps us to find our proper niches in society; and the harmonization of self and other in both nature and society provides a sustainable manner of human flourishing.

The concrete living person is not viewed as an isolated individual but as a center of relationships. I am at the same time a son, a father, a husband, a brother, a son-in-law, a father-in-law, a student, a teacher, a friend, a colleague, a client, a patron, a partner, an uncle, a nephew, and a cousin. Strictly speaking, I do not assume social roles; I am what sociologists, for conceptual convenience, assign as my social roles. Yet I am not the sum total of my social roles. As a *center* of relationships, my dignity as a person is never reducible to my useful functions in society. Surely, I am obligated and willing to serve as a contributing member of my community, but I am not a tool for an external purpose or a means to achieve an outside goal. Learning, as character-building, is an end in itself; it is for my own sake, not for fame, profit, social utility, or parental approval. However, as a center of *relationships*, I am forever interconnected with an ever-expanding network of human-relatedness. My "learning for the sake of the self" is a personal task, but it is tantamount to the realization of communal well-being rather than a quest for private self-interest.

It is commonly assumed that, from an etymological point of view, the cardinal Confucian virtue in the *Analects*, humanity (*ren*), presupposes a dyadic relationship, for the character *ren* seems to consist of the ideogram for "human" and the sign for "two." The Berkeley Sinologist, Peter Boodberg, impressed by the significance of this combination, ingeniously rendered *ren* as "co-humanity." Indeed, humanity, in the Confucian context, is understood as co-humanity. Although this by no means suggests that the dignity of a person is reducible to its sociality (nor does it imply that human worth is externally determined), it emphasizes communication, dialogue, and conversation as proper ways of learning to be human.

As concrete living persons, we learn to become human through the ritual act. We can define the Confucian process of humanization as ritualization. We learn to drink, eat, stand, sit, walk, talk, see, listen, smell, and touch by personal knowledge of our environment mediated through the basic caring of those around us. No human being can survive without the constant involvement of the other. The Confucian practice of building an elaborate cultural code on the biological reality of the parent–child relationship is predicated on the belief that the loving care of the parent for the child and the emotional attachment of the child to the parent is the most immediate and natural expression of human feelings. These feelings are primordial sources for moral strength; they are also basic causes for aggression and self-destruction. It is, therefore, of paramount importance that elementary education begins with the gradual transformation of the biological necessity of the child's dependence on the parent into the ethics of filial piety. In psychoanalytical terms, the art of sublimating the Oedipal situation so that ego-strength can be developed must begin at an early age.

Self-cultivation as embodiment

Self-cultivation, the Confucian *raison d'être*, involves the full recognition that the body is the proper home for self-realization. The six arts – ritual, music, archery, charioteering, calligraphy, and counting – are all mental exercises rooted in the discipline of the body. Self-cultivation (*xiushen*, literally "nourishing the body") is a form of personal knowledge acquired through the refinement of the six senses. The proper ways to drink, eat, stand, sit, walk, talk, see, listen, smell, and touch are serious matters of elementary education, which teaches us to embody these basic ritual acts in our practical daily living.

Indeed, Confucius sees humanity as returning to "ritual" through self-cultivation and enjoins his students to talk, see, listen, and act in accordance with ritual (*Analects* 12:1). Through ritualization of the body, we appropriate the civilized mode of conduct. As we learn to express ourselves through the bodily constitution, we become embodied in it. This art of embodying our body as the result of a rigorous discipline of *tizhiyushen* ("to embody it [the experience of each of the six senses] in the body") is precisely the process of learning to be human.

Building upon this Confucian insight, Mencius (371–289? BCE) straightforwardly envisions the sage, the most authentic manifestation of humanity, as the "full realization of the bodily form" (*jianxing*). However, as a disciple of Confucius' grandson, Zisi, Mencius stresses the spiritual resources inherent in human nature as both the theoretical ground and the practical process of self-realization. He focuses his attention on the embodiment of the heart-mind (*xin*) as the spacious dwelling and the broad highway of profound persons (*junzi*). Those who aspire to become profound persons take as their ultimate concern the realization of humanity and rightness in the world through self-cultivation. In the process of actualizing their ultimate concern, profound persons consider all external conditions secondary. They tap their own internal strength to accomplish the task.

Like the spring about to gush forth or the fire beginning to burn, every human being is endowed with feelings that are necessary and sufficient for self-realization. Among them, the most precious is commiseration (a combination of sympathy and empathy) which characterizes the essential nature of humanity. The inability to bear the suffering of our most beloved kin (parent, child, sibling, or spouse) is an expression of commiseration. There is no guarantee that commiseration cannot be depleted, but, as long as the spring is not yet dried up or the fire extinguished, regeneration is always a possibility. Human beings as sentient beings can never be totally reduced to wood or stone. On the contrary, if this feeling is extended through cultivation, it can embody an ever-expanding network of human relationships.

Learning to be human is primarily the extension of sympathy and empathy. Since commiseration is boundless, it can, at least in principle, fill up the distance between Heaven and earth. We can, as human beings, embody the myriad things in our sympathy and empathy. When Mencius says that the way of learning is none other than the quest for the lost heart-mind, he means that the recovery of our depleted commiseration takes precedence over all other forms of education.

"Full realization of the bodily form," as Mencius understands it, entails the whole process through which profound persons acquire the personal knowledge to fully embody all dimensions of commiseration in their hearts and minds. Specifically, Mencius envisions six stages of self-transcendence – involving respectively, goodness, truth, beauty, greatness, sageliness, and spirituality. Goodness means tender-mindedness; truth refers to the inner resources of sympathy and empathy; beauty suggests the feeling of commiseration richly endowed; greatness implies that the inner qualities of being kind shine through brilliantly; sageliness entails the transformative power of caring; and spirituality conveys the mysterious efficaciousness of how such transformation works in the world. We learn to be good, true, beautiful, great, sagely, and spiritual by enhancing the germs and sparks of humanity (tender-mindedness, sympathy, empathy, commiseration, and kindness) inherent in our nature. Through the cultivation of the seeds of humanity in our hearts and minds, we learn to fully realize our bodily form.

Similarly, Mencius asserts that if we can completely realize the capacities of our heart-mind, we will understand our nature, and if we understand our nature, we will know Heaven. This faith in the human potential for understanding Heaven through self-knowledge and the human capacity for self-knowledge through the cultivation of the heart-mind is predicated on the sensitivity of the body, both as a spacious dwelling and as a broad highway for our ultimate personal realization.

Body politic: beyond collectivism and individualism

In Mencian thought, the unfolding of a holistic humanist vision involves four dimensions of personal experience – those of the self, the community, nature, and Heaven. They are interconnected by a threefold quest – involving respectively, mutuality between the self and the community, harmony between the human species and nature, and unity between Heaven and Humanity. The middle path espoused by Mencius was offered in response to two influential intellectual currents: Mohist collectivism and Yangist individualism. The thinker Mozi insisted that, for the sake of peace and love as willed by Heaven, people ought to sacrifice their private interests. Music and ritual should be simplified. A tight organization based upon a strict hierarchical order should replace the family, and the Will of Heaven should serve as a guiding principle for action. Furthermore, universal love and the establishment of peace by militant resistance against aggressive warfare are the main concerns of the Mohists. The opposite view was held by Yang Zhu, an advocate of radical individualism. Yang argues that since nothing is more valuable than what we are as individuals, the preservation of what we are endowed with ought to be the highest guiding principle for action. Mencius finds fault with both approaches. Mohist universal love thwarts the establishment of the parent–child relationship and Yangist self-centeredness makes the maintenance of political order impossible. The Confucian alternative is a middle path in which the self as a center of relationships can serve as a foundation for the politics of community.

Understandably, the *Great Learning* specifies that self-cultivation ("nourishing the body") serves as the root for the regulation of the family, the governance of the state, and peace throughout the world. The same logic that makes for human flourishing as a moral agent is applied to the body politic as well. Xunzi (active 298–238 BCE) has insightful observations to make in this regard. While he is critical of Mencius' theory that human nature is intrinsically good, he shares Mencius' faith in the improvability of the human condition through self-effort. Xunzi envisions self-cultivation as a cumulative process of moral transformation. He sees humanization as ritualization and underscores the importance of exemplary roles of significant social agents for the task: parents, teachers, elders, officials, and friends. Yet he considers the active participation of the students themselves in their own moral education the single most important factor in bringing about an ordered society.

Xunzi's systematic inquiries into the rectification of names, the wealth of nations, the way of the king, the way of the minister, the recruitment of officials, military affairs, ritual, music, government service, and Heaven indicate that his political concerns are extensive. To him, politics as rectification involves the correct use of language, the proper conduct of rulers, the appropriate methods of governance, and the right social ethos. Yet the smooth functioning of the body politic, like a well integrated body, requires constant attention and rigorous discipline. The mind of the profound person is receptive, unified and tranquil. There is always room for new information, capacity for integration, and aptitude for balance. Like the master of the house, the cognitive faculty of the mind transforms fragmented, conflicting, and chaotic information into intelligent patterns. While human nature, characterized by insatiable desires and unruly passions, tends to lead to social disharmony, the mind is endowed with the ability to know what is right and the will-power to act accordingly. Since human beings can only survive in groups, the right action is to sustain and enhance social harmony.

A salient feature of Confucian thinking, as interpreted by Xunzi, is the primacy of the political order. Politics is seen as an integral part of the ritual process through which the moral community comes into being. The purpose of politics is to provide a wholesome environment for human flourishing. The way of the sage-kings, as contrasted with the dictatorship of the hegemon, is openness to new ideas, receptivity to different voices, and hospitality to all human beings. Its political style is communal, participatory and democratic. The underlying tone, vibrating with the sympathetic resonance of contented people, is poetic. The hegemon may appear to humanity and rightness as justification for authoritarian control, but for him politics is a mechanism by which wealth and power are acquired. Nevertheless, as long as hegemonic politics maintains law and order, despite its moral hypocrisy, it performs a useful function in society. In Confucius' time, however, the hegemonic system had already collapsed. The new contenders for wealth and power were by and large oblivious to moral principles. By the time of Mencius and Xunzi, at the height of the Warring States Period, rulers did not feel any need to appeal to humanity and rightness. Indeed, brute force was the most effective, if not the only, *modus operandi* in politics.

A different voice

While Mencian moral idealism may have prevailed over Mohist collectivism and Yangist individualism, the Confucian project, despite its having a formidable defender in Xunzi, was seriously challenged by the Daoists. In the *Analects* Confucius is reported to have encountered hermits, such as the Madman from Chu, who urged him to abdicate his social responsibility, sever relationships with the human community, and abandon the world. Since the disintegration of the political system, like the torrential flood sweeping the entire world, could not be stopped, any attempt to change the inevitable process of history would be an exercise in futility. What the hermits proposed was in fact a course of action advocated by virtually all major ethico-religious traditions: to cultivate a spiritual sanctuary outside the lived world here and now. The Christian kingdom of God or the Buddhist "other shore" are exemplifications of this universal transcendental breakthrough. Confucius' existential choice to try to repossess the Way by working through the human community as it was constituted represents an anomaly.

The Daoist diagnostic reading of the situation was not at variance with the Confucians', but their approach was radically different. Laozi opted for a fundamental re-examination of the value system which was thought to have sustained the human community. He questioned not only the unintended negative consequences of humanism, but also the reasons underlying great humanist ideas such as humanity and rightness. He believed that not only does power corrupt, but even the most refined culture corrupts the true nature of being human. Inherent in all positive values (for example, truth, beauty, and goodness) is a self-destructive mechanism. Yet Laozi was neither cynical nor relativistic. He directed our attention to nature, the cosmic process, *Dao*. He invited us to transcend mental apparatuses, to resist verbalizing the *Dao* through conceptualization, and rather to see, listen, and experience it.

Laozi created a new linguistic strategy to evoke the ineffable *Dao*. It cannot be talked about, but since it is omnipresent, it can be directly experienced. The grammar of action, or in Daoist terms non-action, employs seemingly negative values – weakness, lowliness, yieldingness, backwardness, retreat, lostness, submission, ugliness and feebleness – to depict the subtle, incipient functions of the *Dao*. Images of water, valley, ravine, baby, womb, clay, and the uncarved block give the impression that the *Dao* as primordiality is fecund and inexhaustibly potent. The art of living is to emulate those natural processes that are consistent, steady, and enduring. A precondition for such a way of life is the spiritual discipline to transform our body into a vehicle of the *Dao*.

Liberation and spontaneity

Zhuangzi, in his philosophy of liberation and spontaneity, insightfully captures the Daoist spirit with a new literary genre, style of argumentation, epistemology, and metaphysics. Language is not used for discursive purposes. It does not say anything; nor does it intend to convey propositional truths. Rather, it is ingeniously manipulated to shock, provoke, stir, amuse, suggest, direct, guide, or deconstruct. Although Zhuangzi's writings reveal a wholesome measure of skepticism and a great deal of relativistic rhetoric, he is neither skeptical nor relativistic. The *Zhuangzi* is a profoundly spiritual text laden with delightful anecdotes, penetrating analyses, and keen observations. The parable of the dream, for example, (I once dreamt that I was a butterfly, but am I absolutely sure that I am not now a mere butterfly dreaming that I am a man?) tackles the issue of "material transformation" (*wuhua*) which, at least in part, is a critique of anthropocentrism. Similarly, the exchange with the logician, Huizi, on the River Hao, concerning the happiness of fish, seems to suggest that communication through experiential understanding is not confined to our subjective world. If we can rise above our self-imposed human condition, we can roam with the spirit of Heaven and Earth.

Liberation and spontaneity are spiritual attainments. They cannot be acquired without self-cultivation. The art that Cook Ding perfected in dissecting a bull with the natural grace of a ritual dance was the result of a long-term commitment to a form of life which has to be practiced daily for years. The process of unlearning (forgetting), much more rigorous than the pursuit of knowledge, requires mental intentness that only the most dedicated can endure. On the surface, Zhuangzi's *Dao* transcends humanity, rightness, ritual, and music and is definitely anti-humanist and unConfucian, but in a deeper sense what Zhuangzi aspires to is true enlightenment, in which all formalistic structures are relegated to the background to make room for great knowledge and profound virtue. This is perhaps the main reason why Confucian scholar-officials throughout Chinese history have found Zhuangzi's self-image a standard of inspiration:

> Alone he associates with Heaven and Earth and spirit, without abandoning or despising things of the world. He does not quarrel over right or wrong and mingles with conventional society. . . . Above, he roams with the Creator, and below he makes friends with those who transcend life and death and beginning and end. In regard to the essential, he is broad and comprehensive, profound and unrestrained. In regard to the fundamental, he may be said to have harmonized all things and penetrated the highest level. However, in his response to change and his understanding of things, his principle is inexhaustible, traceless, dark and obscure, and unfathomable. (Chan, p. 177)

Daoism was ostensibly a critique of Confucian humanism but, since it was taken absolutely seriously by the Confucians, it became gradually absorbed in the Confucian responses themselves. As a result, we witness the Daoist transformation of the Confucian tradition and the emergence of a tender-minded Confucian humanism. It may not be far-fetched to characterize the Zisi-Mencian line as an exemplification of this. Among the Confucian disciples, the thought and action of Confucius' most beloved disciple, Yanhui, seemed to have had the strongest Daoist flavor. It is not accidental that he features prominently in Zhuangzi as a truly accomplished master of the *Dao*. There may have been a Confucian transformation of the Daoist discourse as well.

The disputers of the way

A. C. Graham, in his thought-provoking account of classical Chinese thought, characterizes the shapers of the ancient Chinese world of ideas – the Confucians, Daoists, Mohists, Yangists, Cosmologists, and Legalists as "disputers" of the *Dao* (Way). While there is a general impression that the Chinese thinkers, unlike their counterparts in ancient Greece and India, did not develop elaborate epistemological systems with fully developed deductive methods, Graham persuasively shows that the art of argumentation based on sophisticated logical reasoning was a common practice among ancient Chinese thinkers. Epistemological questions such as how we know what we know, what criteria must be established for judging the truth claims of a proposition, and the standards of verifying the validity of a statement were raised and discussed. Indeed, some Chinese thinkers, notably the Mohists, became virtuosos in dealing with technical aspects of argumentation. They were intrigued by the problem of knowledge and absorbed in what F. W. Mote, in his *Intellectual Foundations of China*, refers to as "questions about the sources of knowledge, uses of names, and methods of inference."

The Confucian preoccupation with the relationship between name (term) and reality (content) in the thesis of the rectification of names and the Daoists' rejection of sophistry clearly indicate that the main thrust of ancient Chinese thinking was ethical and metaphysical, but epistemological issues remained relevant and, occasionally, central to the ongoing philosophical discourse. Actually, skepticism was a major challenge to Confucians and Daoists. Furthermore, thinkers in the nominalist and dialectical schools experimented with fascinating paradoxes reminiscent of those of Zeno the Eleatic. The linguistic and logical ingenuity of these "professional word-jugglers" suggests the great potential or, at least, the rejected possibility of a distinct Sinic style of abstract thinking. As Joseph Needham notes, the Chinese preference for algebraic rather than geometric mathematics and equatorial rather than ecliptic astronomy shows a style of theorizing significantly different from the West. However, the Chinese emphasis on empirical and observational aspects of "scientific" investigation suggests that the focus of the Chinese thinkers was the lifeworld and the human condition. Understandably, they were politically concerned about, socially engaged in, and culturally sensitive to the currents of thought that had a direct bearing on the livelihood of the people and the well-being of the human community.

State ideology and syncretism

The Confucianism that later triumphed in the Han dynasty (206 BCE–200 CE), however, was a tough-minded state ideology under the influence of Legalism. Historically, the Legalism of the brilliant scholar-official Han Fei (d. 233 BCE) grew out of Xunzi's Confucianism. Although Han Fei's intellectual genealogy could be traced to powerful statesmen such as Guan Zhong (d. 645 BCE) and Lord Shang (d. 338 BCE), and influential thinkers such as Shen Buhai (d. 337 BCE) and Shen Dao (350–275? BCE), he was Xunzi's disciple. His ability to synthesize three previous currents of Legalist thought – concerning law, statecraft, and power – seems also to have been influenced by Xunzi. Yet the confluence of ideas that made Han Fei a great Legalist thinker was anti-Confucian and his argumentation is predicated on a set of principles Confucians consider amoral and antithetical to humanism. Ironically, despite the predominance of Confucianism as the official Han ideology, it was the Legalized Confucian orthodoxy rather than the tender-minded Daoist Confucian humanism that was favored in the court.

Surely, statecraft is an integral part of Confucian learning. The Confucian ideal of "inner sagehood and outer kingliness" specifies that social service and political participation are natural outcomes of self-cultivation. The Confucian intent to transform society into a moral community through the political process compels all scholars to become officials and all bureaucrats to become teachers. Han ideology can be seen as a tug-of-war between the scholars who tried to moralize the political order and the officials who politicized Confucian morality as a mechanism of symbolic control. The canonization of Confucian classics, the inclusion of Confucian values in the recruitment and evaluation of high officials, the incorporation of Confucian practices in the legal system, and the implementation of Confucian education at local, regional, and state levels were all indications that the Confucian method was widely used in Han political culture. Nevertheless, the rulers unabashedly acknowledged that the principle that guided their governance was a mixture of "king" (Confucian) and "hegemon" (Legalist).

A defining characteristic of Han intellectual history is synthetic modes of thinking. Virtually all Han thinkers were action oriented. The most impressive Han synthetic philosophy was Dong Zhongshu's attempt to develop a comprehensive vision of mutuality between Heaven and Humanity. Drawing freely from Legalist, Daoist, *yin yang* Cosmologist, Mohist, and folk resources, Dong's *Luxuriant Gems of the Spring and Autumn Annals* is a coherent theological argument for a constitutional framework of political action based on an implicit covenant between the ruler and the Mandate of Heaven. It is primarily a transcendent worldview, critical of the status quo, rather than a metaphysical justification for the supreme authority of the "Son of Heaven." If Dong's work symbolizes Han syncretism based on Confucian morality, the *Huainanzi*, a collection of essays composed by the entourage of Prince An of Huainan, is an excellent example of Daoist syncretism. By analogy, the Huang-Lao classics in the Mawangdui silk manuscript, discovered in 1972, can be characterized as a case of Legalist syncretism.

Especially noteworthy is the prevalence of prognostication, divination, and numerological speculation in these syncretic texts. They clearly reflect the Han thinkers' preoccupation with the interaction between human affairs and the Way of Heaven. The Grand Historian, Sima Qian (died ca. 85 BCE), claims that his own ultimate concerns in writing the *Historical Record*, a rich repertoire of Chinese humanist wisdom, were "to probe the overlapping boundaries between Heaven and Humanity, to comprehend the transformation between past and present, and to complete the family tradition of a distinctive style of transmission."

The Book of Change as profound learning

By the time of the period of disunity (third to sixth century), *The Book of Change* with Wang Bi's (226–249) commentary, the classic that offers the paradigmatic anthropocosmic vision in Chinese philosophy, re-emerged as the core text for Profound Learning (*xuanxue*). If one book were to be singled out as the crystallization of the Chinese mind, the *Change* would be a compelling choice. As an evolving tradition, the hexagrams (a method of divination) had already exerted considerable influence on Chinese religion and politics for more than a millennium prior to Confucius' birth. The Confucian appropriation of the text through philosophical interpretation made the *Change* a rich fund of metaphysical insight. At the same time, its popularity as a repository of folk wisdom among prognostigators, diviners, and geomancers substantially increased. It is indeed rare for a book to be studied and consulted simultaneously by the most sophisticated scholars as well as the least educated peasants. The very fact that *The Book of Change* was shared as a source of inspiration by the erudite as well as the illiterate speaks of its symbolic richness. The elegant simplicity of its overall design (the 64 hexagrams) and the fruitful ambiguity of each of its component units (the precise position of a solid or broken line within each hexagram) as a thick sedimentation of interpretive scholarship has made it the most annotated, explicated, and studied, yet least understood classic in the history of Chinese thought.

The Book of Change, the *Laozi* (both with Wang Bi's commentaries), and the *Zhuangzi* with Guo Xiang's (d. 312) commentary constituted the Three Mysteries for the adherents of the "Pure Conversation" movement, a counter-cultural protest against social conventions and worldly values. Immersing themselves in fundamental philosophical ideas such as being (*you*) and nothingness (*wu*), the participants of Pure Conversation, notably the Seven Worthies of the Bamboo Grove, advocated a vision of cosmic unity through personal knowledge by transcending all distinctions: right/wrong, good/bad, beautiful/ugly, rich/poor, powerful/humble, and famous/unknown. Their willingness to ask challenging questions and their ability to address basic metaphysical issues substantially extended the Chinese intellectual horizon, making possible an unprecedented explosion of aesthetic creativity. As a result, some of the most original studies of the human personality and analyses of literary genres were composed.

Reconfiguring the Sinic mind

Philosophically, Pure Conversation also prepared the Chinese mind to appreciate the subtlety of the Buddhist message from India. Never in inter-civilizational communication have we encountered the same breadth of involvement and depth of absorption as in the Chinese transformation of Indian Buddhism. The story, eight centuries in length, included kings, ministers, scholars, traders, artisans, and farmers. People from all walks of life, all social strata, and all regions of China proper were profoundly affected. The Chinese physical landscape as well as the intellectual scene was forever altered. Yet the so-called "Buddhist conquest of China" was a peaceful voluntary conversion. Some of the most brilliant minds in China traveled thousands of miles on land and by sea to India to seek the true *dharma* for saving the world as well as for personal salvation. The very fact that nowadays the number of translated Buddhist sūtras available in Chinese surpasses that of the extant original in Sanskrit and Pāli by a wide margin clearly indicates the scope of the cumulative effort undertaken by the Chinese monk-scholars.

The massive translation projects initiated by Central Asian teachers such as Kumārajīva (344–413) and continued by erudite Chinese masters such as Xuanzang (596–664) were symptomatic of a nation-wide campaign to make the Buddhist message available to the literary class. However, Buddhist thinkers were instrumental in transforming the message into distinctive styles of articulating the *dharma* from varying Chinese perspectives. The monk-scholar Sengzhao (384–414), through inquiries into the "immutability of things" and the "emptiness of the unreal," established his interpretation of the "middle doctrine," which resembles the Confucian and Daoist claim that one can realize sagehood in one's life because

"Reality is wherever there is contact with things" (Chan, p. 356). Another monk-scholar, Jizang (549–623), compelled the organic monistic Chinese mind to confront the radical dualism of the two levels of truth. Born of a Parthian father and a Chinese mother, Jizang expounded the profound meaning of the "middle doctrine" in the true spirit of Nāgārjuna's (ca. 100–200) theory of the Mādhyamika, specifically the idea of *śūnyatā* ("emptiness"). While his "eightfold negations," critical spirit, and nominalism stimulated and inspired the iconoclastic minds of the Wei-Jin times (220–420), the main thrust of his dualistic argumentation, so alien to the Chinese mode of thinking, was not persuasive.

Similarly, Xuanzang's herculean efforts to make the Consciousness-Only School (Yogācāra) the main Buddhist tradition in China failed. Despite the allure of mystical enlightenment through metaphysical speculation, the elaborate technical analysis of layers of selfhood in the theory of "eight consciousnesses" fascinated but did not convince the Chinese mind. In fact, the three thoroughly Sinicized Buddhist schools, Tiantai, Huayan and Chan, have fully integrated the core values of the Chinese intellectual tradition – ultimate self-transformation through personal effort in this life, a holistic worldview, interconnected networks of perception, embodied thinking, experiential understanding, and commitment to the world here and now – into their syntheses.

The Tiantai School, named after the native place of its founder Zhiyi (538–597), approaches the *dharma* phenomenologically. It employs a threefold method to perceive the true nature of all *dharmas* – involving emptiness, temporality, and the middle. All *dharmas* are by nature empty, yet their temporary existence is real. Being both really empty and temporarily real, they can only be adequately comprehended by the middle. Through concentration and insight, we learn to grasp the perfect harmony of all three levels of truth. This enables us to understand that all three thousand worlds are immanent in an instant of thought and that every color, fragrance, or sound is a manifestation of the middle path.

The Huayan School, founded by Fazang (643–712), opts for an experiential embodiment of the *dharma* realms. By focusing on the emergent states of nature itself, Huayan masters, following the insight developed in the *Dachengqixinlun* (*Treatise on the Awakening of Faith in the Mahāyāna*) advocate that the one heart-mind can simultaneously open two gates: *tathāgatagarhba* (the Buddha-Mind) and *ālaya* ("storehouse consciousness"). The inseparability, mutuality, and harmony of these two gates of the same heart-mind enable Huayan thinkers to develop the paradox philosophy of "absoluteness and rounded harmony" in which not only is the oneness and purity of principle (*li*) melted in the multiplicity and mixture of things (*shi*) but the particularities of things themselves are totally harmonized. This provides the ontological justification for the realization of Buddhahood in our ordinary daily practical living.

Chan (Zen), the distinctively Sinic style of *dharma* practice, deconstructed Buddhist teaching, scriptural tradition, and monastic order. Whether or not we witness in the Chan cultural movement a revolution in which the Chinese mind reasserted itself, it significantly shaped the contour of the Chinese religious landscape with profound philosophical implications. If we do not take an essentialist interpretive position, the dichotomy of the Chinese mind reasserting itself against Indian influence is misleading. Huineng (638–713), the alleged illiterate, through oral transmission and exemplary teaching, captured the essence of Chan spirituality as follows:

> *Bodhi* (perfect wisdom) originally has no tree.
> Nor has the bright mirror any stand.
> Buddha-nature is forever clear and pure.
> Where is any dust?

Huineng's verse was a response to a different but reasonable formulation of Chan self-cultivation:

> The body is like the tree of *bodhi*.
> The heart-mind is like the stand of a bright mirror.
> Day after day diligently wipe it.
> Do not allow it to become dusty.

This approach, which locates perfect wisdom in the body and analogizes heart-mind as a bright mirror, is in accord with the Confucian and Daoist perceptions of personal knowledge. The idea of daily practice as a ceaseless reenactment of the ritual of self-renewal is also consistent with the emphasis that Mencius, Xunzi, and Zhuangzi place on the importance of cumulative effort in spiritual self-transformation. Huineng's outright rejection of essentialism, gradualism, ritualism, literalism, and scholasticism may have been rooted in Daoist iconoclasm, but it was a radical departure from the main stream of Chinese thought. Without sinification of the Indian praxis of *dhyāna* (contemplation) and *prajñā* (wisdom), this would not have been possible.

China, by the time of Huineng, was already a well-seasoned Buddhist country. By implication, Chinese philosophy as manifested in Chan thinking was indebted to imported Indian concepts as well as to indigenous Daoist and Confucian ideas. The Buddhist transformation of the Chinese mind provides a necessary background for understanding the revival of Confucianism in the eleventh century. Without the challenge of Sinicized Buddhism, and the Chan phenomenon in particular, it is difficult to imagine what shape the Confucian revival could have taken – indeed, difficult to imagine that there could have been a Confucian revival at all.

Embodied thinking

Neo-Confucianism, or the Second-Epoch of Confucian Humanism, was a creative transformation which substantially reconstituted the classical tradition in terms of basic scripture, core curriculum, styles of writing, educational institutions, political participation, and social meaning. The Neo-Confucian masters strongly believed that they had repossessed the *Dao*, revitalized the spirit, re-enacted the method of the heart-and-mind, and re-experienced the form of life envisioned by Confucius and Mencius. In comparative civilizational studies, it is rare to observe the representation of a seemingly outmoded symbolic universe with such philosophical originality and intellectual dynamism. Actually, the Song (960–1279) Confucian revival generated such creative energy that it flowed beyond China proper and eventually became a manifestation of East Asian civilization encompassing Ming (1368–1644) and Qing (1644–1912) China, Choson Korea (1392–1910), Later Le dynasty Vietnam (1428–1777), and Tokugawa Japan (1600–1868).

Zhou Dunyi (1017–1073) articulates the relationship between the great transformation of the cosmos and the moral self-realization of the person through a holistic cosmogonic interpretation of the *Book of Change*. The uniquely Sinic idea of trinity – Heaven, Earth, and Humanity – provides the ontological grounding for Zhou's philosophical anthropology. According to Zhou, human nature is endowed with humanity, rightness, propriety, wisdom, and faithfulness. And sagehood, as the most authentic expression of humanity, is a source of spiritual creativity which, like Heaven, gives ultimate meaning to human existence. The underlying moral metaphysics, as embodied in Zhang Zai's (1020–1077) *Western Inscription*, characterizes human beings as filial children of the cosmos:

> Heaven is my father and Earth is my mother, and even such a small creature as I finds an intimate place in their midst. Therefore that which fills the universe I regard as my body and that which directs the universe I consider my nature. All people are my brothers and sisters, and all things are my companions.

This assertion about human consanguinity with Heaven and Earth is predicated on: (1) the continuity of being; (2) the organismic unity of all things; and (3) the boundlessness of human sensitivity. Accordingly, Cheng Hao (1032–1085) defines humanity as embodying Heaven, Earth, and the myriad things.

While Zhu Xi (1130–1200) was critical of characterizing humanity in terms of undifferentiated and all-embracing sensitivity, he did not question that all modalities of being are endowed with vital energy (*qi*), that humanity is the "virtue of the heart-mind, and the principle of love" is all encompassing, and that, in principle, there is no limit to human sympathy and empathy. In his famous "Treatise on Humanity," he presents his observations in naturalist terms:

> The moral qualities of the heart-mind of Heaven and Earth are four: origination, flourishing, facility, and firmness. And the principle of origination unites and integrates them all. In their operation they constitute the course of the four seasons, and the vital energy of the spring permeates all. Therefore, in the human heart-mind there are four moral qualities – humanity, rightness, propriety, and wisdom – and humanity embraces them all. In their emanation and function, they constitute the feeling of love, the attitude of respect, the sense of appropriateness, and judgment of right and wrong – and the feeling of commiseration pervades them all.

Following Cheng Yi's (1033–1107) instruction that "self-cultivation requires reverence; the pursuit of learning depends on the extension of knowledge" (Chan, p. 562), Zhu Xi proposes a balanced incremental approach to education. He vigorously opposes Chan-like sudden enlightenment as an easy way that never really works.

His intellectual rival, Lu Xiangshan (1139–1193), however, forthrightly declares that "the universe is my heart-mind, and my heart-mind is the universe." He further asserts that the ontological unity between Heaven and Humanity is the reason that Mencius instructs us to "first build up the nobler part (the 'great body') of our nature." Indeed, he maintains that the affairs of the universe ought to be our personal affairs precisely because the universe is embodied in our humanity.

Wang Yangming's (1472–1529) "Inquiry on the Great Learning" offers an elegantly simple anthropocosmic vision to substantiate Lu Xiangshan's claim:

> The great man regards Heaven, Earth and the myriad things as one body. He regards the world as one family and the country as one person. . . . That the great man can regard Heaven, Earth and the myriad things as one body is not because he deliberately wants to do so, but because it is natural to the humane nature of his heart-mind that he do so. Forming one body with Heaven, Earth and the myriad things is not only true of the great man. Even the heart-mind of the small man is no different.

Yangming elucidates how, in practical terms, our sensitivity connects us with all modalities of being through concrete examples of differentiated human responses to the suffering and destruction of others (children, birds and animals, plants, and stones). Learning to be human, in this sense, is to extend from what we care about the most (our children, parents, and spouse) to all the realms of existence that we do not even imagine we are intellectually connected to.

Challenge of the Enlightenment mentality

Catholicism was introduced to the Chinese intellectual community by Matteo Ricci (1552–1610) and his fellow Jesuits. Although, as an expediency, they presented their Christian message in terms palatable to the Mandarin ethos, their underlying message was a radical dualism totally incompatible with Neo-Confucian modes of thinking. As a strategy, they urged the scholar-officials to rediscover their classical Confucian sensibility and reverence for the Lord-on-High or Heaven (a functional equivalent of God or the Father in Heaven). They contended that Neo-Confucian thinkers, corrupted by the Mahāyāna Buddhist doctrine of salvation by self-effort, alienated themselves from their primordial connectedness with the transcendent. Christian missionary work in China flourished, especially among the high officials of the court, in the half century after Ricci's death. However, the controversy over the ritual performance in veneration of ancestors before the family altar (that is, concerning whether this was a civil rite or pagan worship) split the Catholic community and severely damaged the reputation of the Jesuits. Despite the "Rites Controversy," which boiled along for a full century (ca. 1640–1742), the Christian community (estimated at 300,000 in the early part of the eighteenth century) survived in China.

An unintended consequence of the Jesuits' China experience was the Chinese intellectual contribution to the Enlightenment in Europe. Through missionary reports, French, British, Italian and German intellectuals became aware of the humanistic splendor of Chinese civilization. Montesquieu, Voltaire, Quesnay, Diderot, the philosophes, the physiocrates, and the Deists were fascinated by the Chinese worldview, cosmological thinking, benevolent despotism, and ethics. Yet the vogue for things Chinese that overwhelmed eighteenth-century Europe was more a craze for *chinoiserie* than a quest for philosophical insight. Ironically, the Enlightenment mentality, especially in its nineteenth-century Eurocentric incarnation, has become the most devastating disputation that the Chinese mind has ever encountered.

The modern West's dichotomous mode of thinking (spirit/matter, mind/body, physical/mental, sacred/profane, creator/creature, God/man, subject/object) is diametrically opposed to the Chinese habits of the heart. Informed by Bacon's knowledge-as-power and Darwin's survival-through-competitiveness, the Enlightenment mentality is so radically different from any style of thought familiar to the Chinese mind that it challenges all dimensions of the Sinic world. The Enlightenment faith in instrumental rationality, fueled by the Faustian drive to explore, know, subdue, and control, made spectacular progress in the fields of science, technology, industrial capitalism, nation-building, the democratic polity, legal systems, educational institutions, multinational cooperation, and military hardware. As the international rules of the game, defined in terms of wealth and power, were superimposed on China by gunboat diplomacy, Chinese intellectuals acknowledged the inevitability of Westernization and acted accordingly.

The sense of urgency that prompted May Fourth (1919) generation Chinese thinkers to advocate wholesale Westernization as a precondition for cultural survival was disorienting and self-defeating. The deliberate choice to undermine their own rich spiritual resources and to embark on a materialist path to save the nation led to revolutionary romanticism and populist scientism. The demand for effective action and demonstrable results was so compelling that the life of the mind was marginalized. As a consequence, there was little room for reflection, let alone meditative thinking. For philosophy, the outcome was disastrous. In this regard, the modern fate of Chinese intellectuals was much worse than that of their Indian counterparts. While centuries of colonization did not break the backbone of Indian spirituality, the semi-colonial status prompted the Chinese intelligentsia to reject *in toto* and by choice all the spiritual traditions that defined China's soul. We have only just begun to see indications that Chinese thinkers are recovering from this externally imposed and internally inflicted malaise.

With all of its boundless energy and creative impulse, the Enlightenment mentality is incapable of reflecting on things at hand, oblivious to the "holy rite" of human-relatedness, and ignorant of self-cultivation as an art of living. The collapse of the former Soviet Union may have destroyed the Chinese Communist faith in the inevitable historical process precipitated by the revolutionary vanguard in the strategy of class struggle for universal equality. However, the assumption that human beings are rational animals endowed with inalienable rights and motivated by their self-interest to maximize their profit in the marketplace is hardly an inspiring ideology. The market economy, democratic polity, and individualism, perceived by Talcott Parsons as the three inseparable dimensions of modernity, are likely to loom large in China's philosophical discussion. The more encouraging style of self-reflexivity may take the form of a humanist critique of the Enlightenment.

The Chinese, especially the Confucian, idea of the intellectual – politically concerned, socially engaged, and culturally sensitive – seems to have special relevance for contemporary professionals in the academy, government, mass media, business, and civic organizations who are anxious about the affairs of the world, involved in social praxis, and dedicated to the efficacy of mediating cultural institutions. In this sense, the Confucian scholar, in both spiritual self-definition and social function, can be a source of inspiration for the modern intellectual. Furthermore, given the need for a global ethic to address the crises of the human community in dealing with ecological degradation, social disintegration, and the lack of distributive justice, Confucian inclusive humanism seems more compatible with the spirit of our time than does the anthropocentric secular humanism of the Enlightenment.

An important implication is that Plato's allegory of the cave can be enriched, if not replaced, by the Mencian dictum that the sage is simply the one who has obtained (realized) the sameness of my heart-and-mind before me. The philosopher so conceived is an organic intellectual who shares his or her profound personal knowledge with all members of the human community through dialogue and conversation.

Bibliography

Chan, Wing-tsit 1963: *A Source Book in Chinese Philosophy* (Princeton: Princeton University Press).

Graham, A. C. 1989: *Disputers of the Tao* (La Salle: Open Court).

Hall, David L. and Roger T. Ames 1995: *Anticipating China: Thinking through the Narratives of Chinese and Western Culture* (Albany: State University of New York).

Hansen, Chad 1992: *A Taoist Theory of Chinese Thought* (Oxford: Oxford University Press).

Mote, F. W. 1971: *Intellectual Foundations of China* (New York: Alfred A. Knopf).

Needham, Joseph 1956: *Science and Civilisation in China*, Vol. 2 (Cambridge: Cambridge University Press).

Owen, Stephen 1992: *Readings in Chinese Literary Thought* (Cambridge: Council on East Asian Studies, Harvard University).

Schwartz, B. I. 1985: *The World of Thought in Ancient China* (Cambridge: Harvard University Press).

2

A history of Indian philosophy

J. N. MOHANTY

Origins

According to the Hindu tradition, the origin of the various philosophical ideas that were developed in the philosophical systems lies in the Vedas, a body of texts that seem to have been composed around two thousand years Before the Common Era (BCE). While the Vedas contain a myriad of different themes, ranging from hymns for deities and rules of fire sacrifices to music and magic, there is no doubt that one finds in them an exemplary spirit of inquiry into "the one being" (*ekam sat*) that underlies the diversity of empirical phenomena, and into the origin of all things. ("Was there being or non-being at the beginning?") One finds also predelineations of such concepts of *ṛta* (truth or moral order), *karma* and the afterlife, and the three qualities (or *guṇas*: *sattva*, *rajas*, and *tamas*) constituting nature (*prakṛti*). It is in the Upaniṣads (a group of texts composed after the Vedas and ranging from 1000 BCE to the time of Gautama, the Buddha), that the thinking, while still retaining its poetic flavor, develops a more strictly philosophical character. While still concerned with many different themes belonging to cosmology ("How did the one being become many?") and psychology ("What does the empirical person consist of?"), the Upaniṣads contain attempts to reinterpret, in symbolic terms, the elaborate Vedic sacrifices, and to defend, in many different ways, one central philosophical thesis – that is, the identity of *Brahman* (the highest and the greatest, the source of all things) and *ātman* (the self within each person). With this last identification, a giant step was taken by the authors of the Upaniṣads, a step that was decisive for the development of Indian philosophy. The Vedas had already decided, famously in the Nāsadiya Sukata, that at the beginning of things there must have been being and not non-being (for something cannot come out of nothing); now this primeval being was said to be the same as the spirit within. The highest wisdom was intuitively realizing this identity of subject and object (*tat tvam asi*). *How* to know it was the issue. Suggestions ranged from contemplative meditation to austere self-mortification. The idea of yoga and a picture of the *yogin* make their appearance – possibly having a different origin – and blend with the central thesis of the Upaniṣads. If the reality underlying outer appearance is the universal spirit within, is then the world merely phenomenal appearance (like the magician's creation, *māyā*), or is the *brahman-ātman* to be construed as the indwelling spirit of all things? These become the leading disputational questions amongst the commentators on the Upanisads, and amongst the various schools of the Vedānta philosophy.

Rise of the anti-Vedic, naturalistic, and skeptical thinking

Towards the end of the Upaniṣadic period, most probably when the major Upaniṣads had been composed, in the north-eastern Gangetic plains at the foothills of the Himalayas, in the present state of Bihar, there was born a most remarkable person, Gautama, the Śākya, of the Licchabi clan (ca. 560 BCE) as the son of the elected chief of a small republican country. Stories about Gautama's life are many, and few things are known with certainty. The story of his experiences with old age, sickness, and death – experiences of existential anguish – that led him to renounce his princely and worldly life and set him on the tortuous path to enlightenment, is rather well known. Upon reaching enlightenment, the wisdom containing his answer to the question of how to escape suffering, Gautama preached, in his first sermon, the fourfold "noble truths," which remain the central belief of Buddhism through all its exuberant growth of sects, schools, rituals, and practices. The noble truths are: the truth of suffering (existence is marked by suffering), the truth that suffering has a cause (which is craving, *tṛṣṇā*), the truth that there is an end to suffering (that is, *nirvāṇa*), and finally, the truth that there is a path (*mārga*) by which to reach that end (the eightfold right path). This path, described as the middle way – avoiding the extremes of sensuous indulgence, which is vulgar, low and unspiritual, and of self-torture, which is painful, useless and also unspiritual – consists of eight components: right views, right intention, right speech, right action, right livelihood, right effort, right mindfulness, and right concentration. In his sermons and conversations, Gautama avoided metaphysical questions, and insisted only on teaching the path to deliverance from suffering. But Buddhism, very early on, was committed to certain philosophical beliefs: the rejection of the Upaniṣadic thesis of *ātman*, the rejection of any permanent substance (of which the no-self doctrine may be regarded as a specific application), belief in a strict principle of causal dependence (called "dependent origination") to which all existence is subject, belief in *karma* and rebirth, and belief in eventual deliverance. Thus Gautama did not totally reject the Upaniṣadic theses. Rejecting the fundamental metaphysics of *ātman*, he still adhered to the other major components: rebirth and *karma* and *mokṣa* (called *nirvāṇa*).

Gautama represented a growing revolt against Brahmanism as it spread eastwards along the Gangetic valley. The revolt was as much against religious theory and practice as against the monarchical state which the Hindus glorified, a society ridden with priest-craft and caste. But Gautama was not the only, nor was he the first, rebel. The Vedic literature already bears evidence to much skeptical self-criticism. There were skeptics such as Saṁjaya who, when questioned as to whether there was an afterlife, said "I do not say there is an afterlife and I do not say there is no after life," thus using "illocutionary negation" in contrast to "propositional negation." This sort of skepticism seems to have had some influence on Buddhism. Among pre-Buddhistic philosophies, one text, *Sutrakṛtānga*, mentions 363 schools – of which 180 were *kriyāvādins* (believing in the efficacy of action), 84 were *akriyāvādins* (rejecting the efficacy of action), 67 were *ajñānikas* (skeptics, claiming not to know), and 32 were *vainayikas* (believing in salvation through good conduct). These numbers may be exaggerated, but they certainly show intense intellectual ferment. Among the skeptics, besides the famous Saṁjaya, there were those who refused to accept any claim to knowledge because of the many contradictory conclusions on offer and lack of general agreement, those who questioned the concept of omniscience, and those who emphasized the difficulty of knowing the other's mind. The Buddha, in the *Sangārava Sūtra*, classifies his predecessors and contemporaries into the traditionalists (*anussanika*), the rationalists (*takki*) and the metaphysicians (*vīmamsi*), and the experimentalists who appeal to a personal higher knowledge of the truth. Gautama regarded himself as belonging to this last group.

Of the pre-Buddhistic philosophers who rejected the Brahmanic belief, especial mention must be made of the Ājivikas whose leading member was Makkhali Gosala. He believed in strict determinism, rejected freedom of the will, advocated an atomistic cosmology, and practised austere asceticism. Other members of the school were Purāṇa Kassapa, Ajita Kesamkambali, and Pakudha Kaccāyana. These intellectual rebels had their influence on Gautama as well as on Mahavira (599–527 BCE) who founded Jainism. All of these intellectuals rejected sacrificial rituals, Upaniṣadic monism, and all recognized the rule of natural law; they were concerned with the efficacy of *karma* and were skeptical about another world. The two heretical views – *yadṛcchāvāda*, according to which the world is contingent, and *svabhāvavāda*, for which the world is determined by the nature of things and natural laws – contrast with *adṛṣtavāda* and *adhyātmavāda*. Both of these, in conjunction with tradition, believed in supernaturalism and the spiritual nature of reality.

Of all of these, besides Buddhism and Jainism, the one heretical school which is reckoned with in the doxographic literature is Lokāyata, originally one of the branches of Vedic learning, but later surviving as an anti-Vedic materialism. Some trace the origin of Lokāyata to the *dehātmavāda* (the thesis that the self is the body) found in Chāndogya Upaniṣad VIII 7–8 (attributed to Virocana). The Jaina author Haribhadra explains the position of Lokāyata to be: "this world extends only to the limits of possible sense perception."

Founded by Mahavira, an older contemporary of the Buddha, who is regarded as the last of the perfected men recognized in the school as prophets, Jainism denied the existence of a creator of the universe, looked upon the world as consisting of infinite souls and matter, construed the embodiment of souls as being due to karmic matter (thus presenting a completely new, materialistic, theory of *karma*), and believed in the possibility of the individual attaining perfection through austere practices and contemplative knowledge. Several very sophisticated positions characterize Jaina philosophy: first, the belief that things have infinite aspects, so that no philosophical conceptualization can exhaust its nature. For example, Buddhism is right in its view that things change, but wrong in not recognizing that they also have an aspect of permanence. This led the Jains to develop an elaborate metaphilosophical theory of different possible standpoints (*nayas*), and also a logical theory that rejected the usual two-valued logic and replaced it by a theory of "sevenfold predication" (*saptabhaṅginyāya*). For the latter theory – which may be regarded as one of the most outstanding achievements of ancient Indian thought – every judgment, its negation, as well as the conjunction of the two, has an element of truth. Prefix every judgment, the Jain recommends, with "maybe" (*syāt*), which is meant to convey that there must be a standpoint from which it is true and one from which it is false, another from which it is both, still another from which it is inexpressible. Three more possible "truth values" arise from various combinations of these basic four.

The philosophers and the philosophies reviewed in this section were anti-tradition – that is, anti-Vedic (although some of them, such as the Jainas, admitted the existence of an eternal self in each living being). To these, we must add another philosophy which was Vedic, but atheistic, naturalistic in an important sense, but admitting an eternal self, one for each individual. This is the Sāṃkhya of Kapila, a legendary figure widely respected for his wisdom even within the Vedic tradition. Already in the Upaniṣads – besides the *ātman-brahman* theory which later blossomed into the Vedānta school – there was another line of thinking which regarded the world as evolving out of three elements – water, fire, and earth. Even in the technical language of the Sāṃkhya, the Śvetāśvatara Upaniṣad (V.7.8.12; IV.5.1.3) describes nature (*prakṛti*) as being three-colored (red, white and black, standing for *rajas*, *sattva* and *tamas* respectively). It is quite possible that this ancient naturalism was a source of ideas for Buddhism and Jainism. In its mature form, it developed a theory of the evolution of the empirical world out of the original, undifferentiated nature. The three *guṇas*, rendered "qualities," but actually affective components, originally were in a state of equilibrium. This equilibrium was disturbed by contact with *puruṣa*, the self. The evolution of nature consists in progressive heterogeneity, in unequal distribution of the three components, and attachment of the self arising out of not distinguishing itself from the psychophysical complex which is a product of nature. Freedom or *mokṣa*, called "isolation," *kaivalya*, arises from the knowledge that the self is different from nature. While the influence of Sāṃkhya on the religious life is minimal, Sāṃkhya ideas go into other systems as their components; the distinction between the three gunas continues to be an important part of the Hindu view of things, and the Sāṃkhya became the foundation of much of Hindu science, especially of medicine, competing with Vaiśeṣika atomism.

Rise of the systems: a historical chronology up to 900 CE

The Imperial Mauryas ruled from 322 to 183 BCE. This is the time of the composition of the *Dharmaśāstras*, more famously of Manu's, also of Kautilya's, *Arthaśāstra*. In all of these books, the orthodox Brahmanism sought to preserve and strengthen itself against the anti-Vedic philosophies and their onslaughts. Philosophically more important is Pāṇini's grammar and Patañjali's commentary thereon. It is possible that no other Hindu intellectual achievement has been able to surpass Pāṇini. With the epic *The Mahābhārata*, the conception of four ends of life came to be established as an important part of the Hindu view of life. These four ends are *artha, kāma, dharma,* and *mokṣa,* meaning wealth, sensuous pleasure, righteousness and freedom from bondage respectively. The Hindu thinkers then sought to systematize thought about each of these ends, which consisted in defining the goal, laying down the means for achieving it, and classifying the various components as well as the types of relevant ends and means. Thus arose the *Arthaśāstras,* or sciences of wealth, the *Kāmasūtras,* or aphorisms on erotic pleasure, the *Dharmaśāstras,* or scientific treatises on *dharma,* and *Mokṣaśāstra* or the scientific treatise on *mokṣa.* Among the latter two, Jaimini's aphorisms on *dharma* and Bādarāyaṇa's Vedānta or *Brahmasūtras* remain the major works, bearing testimony to the Hindu determination to bring order and scientific exposition to unwieldy material in each case. Thus arose the two parts of the Mīmāṃsā system; the system which undertook to interpret the Vedic texts, giving rise to Pūrvamīmāṃsā and Uttaramīmāṃsā (or Vedānta) respectively.

It is noteworthy that a new style or genre of philosophical systematization began, one that is very uniquely Indian. This is the genre of the *sūtras* or aphorisms. Out of the disorganized motley of ideas already prevalent, a systematizing genius "formed" a system by composing neatly, systematically and scientifically, a number of aphorisms, brief formulae as they were, easy to memorize and keep one's grip on, however, too cryptic to make clear sense without the aid of explanatory expositions which soon were bound to follow. It was only natural that whereas the body of aphorisms laid down the general framework of a system, the explanatory expositions or commentaries (*bhāṣya*) made use of and exploited the ambiguity of the aphorisms in order to interpret them in new ways and to let the texts "show" new meanings and interpretive possibilities. Within such adventures, the "systems" or *darśanas,* loosely but misleadingly translatable as "ways of seeing," came into being, seemingly almost from nowhere save the everpresent appeal to the *śruti* or the "heard" texts. Thus we have: the *Nyāyasūtras* of Gotama (second century CE), the Commentary of Vātsyāyana (450–500 CE); the *Vaiśeṣikasūtras* of Kaṇāda (?), the Commentary of Praśastapada (fifth century CE); the *Mīmāṃsāsūtras* of Jaimini (200 BCE), the Commentary of Bādari (lost), and the Commentary of Śabara (sixth century CE); the *Sāṃkhyasūtras* of Kapila (lost); the *Vedāntasūtras* of Bādarāyaṇa (200 BCE), the Commentary of Śaṃkara (650–700 CE); the *Yogasūtras* of Patañjali (200 BCE), the Commentary of Vyāsa (500 CE).

Apart from the rise and systematization of the *darśanas,* the period of Imperial Mauryas also witnessed the rise of the *bhakti* or devotional religions. The Greek traveler Magasthenes of the fourth century BCE refers to the worship of Vāsudeva-Kṛṣṇa. The *pāśupata, Bhāgavata,* and *Tantra* systems come into being. The gods Śiva, Śakti, and Viṣṇu come to the forefront from their minor, sometimes latent, presence in the Vedas. The *Bhagavadgītā,* the song of God, containing Kṛṣṇa's discourse to Arjuna of the Pāndava dynasty, grows in stature, being viewed no longer merely as a chapter of the epic *Mahābhārata,* but rather as a major text of Hindu philosophy and religion.

Further development of the systems had to wait several hundred years to take place. What intervened was the Buddhist challenge in the centuries preceding and after the beginning of the Common Era, during the reign of the Kushāna dynasty (first to second century CE) and the Imperial Guptas (320–540 CE). During the Kushāna era, the most significant event philosophically was the rise of Mahāyāna Buddhism under the towering genius of Nāgārjuna. Building upon the skeptical questioning of Saṁjaya, Nāgārjuna may be said to have deconstructed the metaphysical and epistemological concepts and theories of both the Hindus (Nyāya, Vaiśeṣika, Sāṃkhya) and the early Buddhists. His complex dialectical arguments claimed to demonstrate, for one thing, that metaphysics and epistemology presuppose each other, that you cannot begin a metaphysics without assuming an epistemological theory, nor can you initiate an epistemological theory without assuming a metaphysics, so that there is no escape from this hopeless circularity. For another, he showed how metaphysical concepts such as rest and motion, part and whole, permanence and change presuppose each other and how each of such concepts involves self-contradictions. The result is a "destruction" of the philosophical–conceptual project *from within*, of philosophy and logic by using their own resources (as a disease is cured by the same poison that causes it, or a thorn is taken out by a thorn). He was circumspect enough to concede that if his thesis is valid, his own philosophy will suffer the same fate. What will remain is the cognizance of the true intent of Gautama's "silence," of the ineffability of true wisdom, and at the same time of the truth that *nirvāṇa* does not change anything, so that *saṁsāra* (being-in-the-world) and *nirvāṇa* are the same.

The age of the Imperial Guptas was a period of intense intellectual activity. In Buddhist philosophy, the Yogācāra school was founded by the two brothers Asaṅga and Vasubandhu (fourth century CE), Dignāga laid the foundation of Buddhist logic at the end of the fifth century CE. In his commentary on the *Nyāyasūtras*, Vātsyāyana (400 CE) not only elaborated the Nyāya doctrines, but replied to Nāgārjuna's criticisms of the epistemological project. The *Sāṃkhyakārikā* of Īśvarakṛṣṇa took the place of the not extant *sūtras* of Kapila. Pantañjali's *Yogasūtra* came into being. The systems were being consolidated in self-defense.

The seventh and the eighth centuries saw the continuation of creative work on the foundations laid. In Buddhism, the high point was reached in the works of Dharmakīrti (580–650 CE); in Mīmāṃsā, Kumārila's (600–700 CE) *Ślokavārttika* made a valiant attempt to meet the Buddhist challenge by defending realism (as opposed to the Yogācāra idealism) and the validity of the scriptures. The period culminated with Śaṃkara (650–700 CE), who established his non-dualistic Vedānta by interpreting the scriptural texts as much as by systematically refuting the Nyāya-Vaiśeṣika, Sāṃkhya, Buddhist, Jaina, and other competing philosophies. At the same time, Dharmakīrti's logical and epistemological challenges were taken up by Uddyotakara (about 650 CE) of the Nyāya school. Vācaspati (900–980 CE) and Udayana (1050–1100 CE) led eventually to the rise of Navya-Nyāya in Mithila under the leadership of Gaṅgeśa Upādhyāya (about 1320 CE).

Disputational issues and the development of the systems: theory of knowledge

The skeptical arguments against the validity of the Vedic texts, especially the Buddhist onslaughts, gave rise to a determined effort to intellectually safeguard, and establish, the foundation of Brahmanic religion, thereby making it necessary to develop a systematic epistemological theory. It must be emphasized, however, that although the origin of the Hindu epistemological theory must have been occasioned by the need to meet the skeptical attacks, the theory took up its own autonomous life. It gradually separated itself from the religious context and exhibited a remarkable theoretical autonomy. The epistemological project arose as much to ensure the possibility of the knowing of the mundane entities (through perception and inference) as of the knowing of such transmundane (*pāralaukika*) entities as moral law, *karma* and rebirth, and the absolute reality underlying all appearances, which was none other than the Brahman of the Upaniṣads. For this two-fold purpose, the Cārvāka claim that sensuous perception alone is a source of valid knowledge, and the arguments of all anti-Vedic thinkers to prove that mere *śabda*, that is, words, cannot be a source of true cognition, had to be met. At the same time, the claim of inference by which we acquire much of our knowledge of the world had to be legitimized and a sound logical theory of inference developed. All of this led to the rise of the so-called *pramāṇavāda*, or theory of *pramāṇas* or of the means of true cognition. A major part of this theory consisted in giving a list of irreducible sources of true cognition, defining each, and classifying each into its proper sub-types and arguing for its irreducibility to any other. Other topics, within the theory of *pramāṇa*, are: a theory of *prāmāṇya* or truth (with its three sub-parts: definition of truth, origin (*utpatti*) of truth, and cognition (*jñapti*) of truth), a theory of *apramā* (types of cognitions that are not true, such as error and doubt), and a theory of error or false cognition (*khyātivāda*). In developing all of these theories, the philosophers not only sought to argue against the skeptics and the Buddhists, but members of each school of Hindu philosophy argued, equally mercilessly, against the other schools subscribing to the Vedic orthodoxy. By this process of mutual criticism, the Indian thinkers were able by the sixteenth century, to develop a spectrum of highly sophisticated and theoretically well grounded epistemological theories, which form a most glorious part of Indian thinking.

In this spectrum, the Cārvākas held that perception is the only *pramāṇa*, the Buddhists and the Vaiśeṣikas recognized perception and inference, the Nyāya would have perception, inference, comparison (*upamāna*), and verbal instruction (*śabda*); and Vedānta added two more to the last four, namely, non-perception (*anupalabdhi*) and "impossibility of accounting for a fact otherwise" (*arthāpatti*). Several other candidates for this status seem to have been around, with their advocates and defenders, some of these being: memory, tradition (*aitihya*), and possibility (*sambhava*), but none of the major schools appear to have accepted the claim of any of these. Of all of these, perception, inference, and verbal instruction received the utmost attention.

(i) Perception

All schools of Indian philosophy accepted perceptual cognition as valid, though they did not quite agree as to its definition and its object. Early on, two opposed views seem to have laid down the parameters for the discussion of perception: on the one hand, the Buddhist view that only that perception deserves to be regarded as valid which is non-linguistic, non-conceptual and whose object is the pure particular, the *sva-lakṣaṇā* with no admixture of universal features; and, on the other, the view of the Grammarian, especially of Bhartṛhari (460–520 CE), that since no object is without a name and no cognition without "penetration" by language, all perception is linguistic. For Hindu philosophers, there is no pure particular as the Buddhist conceives it. The particular entity instantiates universal features; it is a this-there, but also a such-and-such. The Nyāya was quick to recognize that perception itself must be of two kinds, each corresponding to a stage of its unfolding: at first a non-conceptual non-linguistic taking-in of whatever is presented to the senses, and then a conceptual, linguistic, predicative cognition in which the entities presented to the senses are knit together as qualifier and qualified. If perception is to be a cognition that is brought about by contact of the sense organs with their respective objects (as the Nyāya held), how could one perceive anything besides the particular thing? How could the senses come in contact with properties and universals, as the Buddhists argued? In order to reply to this difficulty, Uddyotakara introduced what became an important part of the Nyāya theory: the contact of the sense organs with their objects can be of various orders of complexity, depending upon the nature of the object contacted. Thus the contact of the eyes with a material substance is one of conjunction (*samyoga*), which is a proper relation between two substances. But the color of that substance involves inherence-in-what-is-conjoined (*samyukta-samavāya*), while the color-universal which that color instantiates involves inherence-in-what-inheres-in-what-is-conjoined, for the color-universal inheres in the color, which, on its part, inheres in the substance.

(ii) Inference

Now, as regards inference (*anumāna*), Dignāga laid down the foundations of Buddhist logic while Dharmakīrti further advanced it, both stimulating the further development of the Nyāya theory already laid down in the *Nyāyasūtras* and in Vātsyāyana's Commentary. Inference was looked upon as a cognitive means, rather than merely as formally valid thinking. In order, therefore, to rule out of purview those inferences that are formally sound but materially false, it was necessary to stipulate – for the acceptability of an inference advanced in a dialogical disputational context – a requirement that the universal major premise adduced in favor must be shown, by the proposer, to be instantiated in a case agreed upon by both the proposer and the opponent, in the absence of which the inference cannot even get off the ground. This requirement of an example (*dṛṣtānta*) assured material truth and yet did not conflict with formal validity. Nor could the logician, interested as he was in inference as a means of cognition, keep out all psychological talk, for he had to give an account of the psychological process by which – outside the disputational and dialogical context – a person comes to infer-for-himself. Thus a distinction was made between inference-for-oneself (*svārtha anumāna*), which is a psychological process corresponding to an enthymeme, and inference-for-the-other (*parārtha anumāna*) in which all the constituent propositions are to be explicitly formulated so that – including the instance cited and the thesis proposed – one arrives at five constituents (*pancāvayava*) of the resulting structure. Common to both, in addition to the example, is the universal major premise (*vyāpti*) which was construed as co-occurrence of the middle (*hetu*) and the major (*sādhya*), being of the form "wherever F, there G." Much intellectual acumen was exercised on how precisely to formulate this relationship, broadly speaking whether affirmatively, as just given, or negatively, as "to whatever possesses the absence of G, F does not belong." Note that in neither of these formulations is a modal concept used – such as "necessarily" or "impossible," or "must" or "must not" – so that the Nyāya concept of *vyāpti* remains extensional, again in opposition to the Buddhist conception, especially of Dharmakīrti, who understood *vyāpti* to be based either on the relation of essential identity (*abheda*), in which case the universal relation of copresence is analytically necessary ("this is a tree, because it is an elm"), or on the relation of causality ("this possesses fire, because it has smoke"), in which case it is synthetic and contingent.

It is to be noted that while Dharmakīrti believed in the nature of things, Nāgārjuna denied that things have any intrinsic nature. Thus within Buddhist philosophy, Nāgārjuna and Dharmakīrti developed different logical systems. Nāgārjuna gives a new form of the *reductio* argument (*prāsaṇga*), a notoriously difficult "four-cornered negation," and a logic of self-referential statements (for example, "I have no proposition" and "everything is void").

Both the topics of perception and inference were developed by schools other than Buddhism and the Nyāya. The Nyāya defined a means of cognition generally by referring to the method, or mode, of its causal production. Thus perception was caused by sense-object contact, and not caused – in its first phase of non-conceptual perception – by any other cognition. Inference was caused by previous *knowledge* of *vyāpti* and its *remembrance* upon one's *perceiving* the middle (for example, smoke) in the minor (for example, the hill over there). Likewise, hearing sentences uttered by a speaker known to be competent, one knows that something is the case, and such knowledge is caused by, among other things, knowledge of the meanings of the component words of the utterance. Before briefly discussing the third *pramāṇa* (that is, *śabda*), I would like to mention here that the Jaina and Vedānta schools do not define perceptual cognition by its causes, but rather by some intrinsic and distinguishing feature of that cognition. The Jainas take this feature to be "clarity" (*vaiśadya*), so that perception is defined as cognition that is clear (*viśadam pratyakṣam*). The Vedāntin of the Advaita school follows another route: for them, as formulated by Dharmarajādhvarindra (sixteenth century CE) in his *Vedānta Paribhāṣā*, consciousness itself is perceptual taken in the broadest sense, but then, when one perceives a material object, there is an identity achieved between the consciousness of the knower and the consciousness underlying, and limited by, the object (for, after all, on the Vedānta metaphysics, all is superimposed upon an underlying ubiquitous consciousness.)

(iii) Śabda

Let me now briefly refer to *śabda* as a means of knowing that something is the case simply on the basis of hearing a person, who is known to be competent (*āpta*), utter a sentence. One of the distinguishing features of the Indian epistemologies is to have devoted a lot of attention to this kind of cognition, which recently has been termed "word-generated knowledge." Since "competency" was defined in terms of the speaker's knowing the subject matter and his moral integrity (so that he would not want to lie or mislead), a certain scope for being in error is definitionally ruled out. In the case of the Vedic scriptures, either the speaker is fault-free or there is no speaker; so, in either case, the possibility of error (which is due to a fault in the speaker) is excluded. The rest of the discussion then consists in arguing: first, that such word-generated knowledge is irreducible to inference (contrary to the Vaiśeṣikas); second, that there is no other way of knowing, save through verbal instruction, about moral rules (*dharma*); and, third, in the Advaita Vedānta School, the identity of *brahman* and *ātman* can only be ascertained on the basis of the texts of the Upaniṣads. Common to all these claims and their defense, is a philosophical discussion of language including a theory of how word-meanings connected together by contiguity, as well as semantic and syntactical appropriateness, generate or simply manifest sentential meaning. In all this discussion, one important issue comes to the forefront: is the sentential meaning composed of prior word-meanings, or if the original home of the word is in the sentence, is not the word-meaning derivative from sentential meaning? On this issue, the Nyāya and the Mīmāṁsā schools differed, the latter tending towards a holistic theory of meaning (for example, the entire Vedas may be looked upon as constituting one sentence), the former towards a "logical atomism." In between these extremes, the Advaita Vedānta held a third view, separating sentences about what is the case from those that recommend courses of action, and among the former demarcating a group of sentences that assert identity between two terms. It is this last-mentioned group which, for Advaita Vedānta, holds the key to opening the door to metaphysical wisdom. The identity sentences of the Upaniṣads, such as "thou art that" (*tat tvam asi*) and "I am He" (*so'ham*), are to be so construed that the differences in meanings of the terms, in each case, have to be excluded, thereby leaving a residue of pure identity which, in the case of the sentences, or the *mahāvākyas*, of the Upaniṣads, is nothing but the pure *ātman*. Thus identity sentences are not relational sentences, and so refer not to a relational state of affairs, but to a pure non-relational identity. The Advaita philosophy of language has one more feature which is connected with the above. Whereas in all other systems, the cognition generated by language is only mediate and conceptual and stands in sharp contrast to the immediate and intuitive grasp of a thing in perception, on the Advaita epistemology this contrast does not hold good. Under certain circumstances and in certain contexts, the cognition generated by an identity sentence may give rise to an immediate and intuitive knowledge of oneself, which holds good not only in mundane contexts, such as when a man counting a group of ten to which he also belongs and, missing the tenth person (which is he himself), is told by an onlooker that he himself is the tenth person (*daśamaḥ tvamasi*) realizes, intuitively, that he is indeed the missing member, but also, in the transmundane context, when a person seeking to know the Brahman is instructed that he is Brahman. The linguistic instruction followed by understanding, reflection, and meditation may bring about an intuitive apprehension of the truth.

Thus the opposition that Buddhism set up between, on the one hand, true knowledge of the nature of things and language, on the other, is denied by the Hindu philosophies, although in many different ways. The Nyāya and Mīmāṁsā denied this opposition by making reality as internally differentiated as language requires. The Advaita does the same by ascribing to language the ability to refer beyond itself by a series of negations ("not this, not this") or by identity sentences the understanding of which demands transcendence of the differences. Language still refers, although not by naming. As Bhartṛhari said, even to call reality "unspeakable" (*avācya*) is still to use language to talk about it. The use of negation is also a linguistic resource.

(iv) Prāmāṇyavāda

With the development of the theory of *pramāṇa*, the concept of *prāmāṇya* or truth inevitably received attention. Whereas in the early scriptural literature, the word for truth was *satyam*, which appeared in the Upaniṣadic description of Brahman as "*satyam, jñānam, anantam*" (truth, knowlege [and] infinite) and in the moral exhortation "*satyam vada*" (speak the truth), in the philosophical literature the word *prāmāṇya* replaces it. This replacement may well signify a gradual shift to intellectual inquiry. An early account of truth as *prāmāṇya* is given by Vātsyāyana in the commentary on *Nyāyasūtra* II.1.36: "true cognition is knowledge of that as that."

As is to be expected, truth in this sense is questioned by the Buddhists. Relational sentences, as a matter of fact any linguistic entity, cannot correspond to reality, for reality is the pure particular, the ineffable this-now. Since we do nevertheless empirically distinguish between true and false sentences, the distinction must lie, not in agreement with reality, but in "practical efficacy," in the ability of sentences regarded as true to lead to successful practice. Truth, as opposed to error, is then a pragmatic concept. It has been recently proposed that the single pre-theoretical concept that all the Indian theories seek to explicate further is "practical success," or rather "the ability to lead to practical success" (and not the "truth" of Western philosophy). While this may well be so, the Nyāya emphasized that practical success is only a test of truth, and not its nature; it is also not the only test of truth, for often truth is tested for by coherence (*samvāda*) with other cognition of the same or of other subjects. (Note that if practical success were the only test, the very distinction between a test and nature would appear to be pointless.) The Advaitin goes further and attacks the very idea of practical success. "Does not, within a dream, the (dream) water seen at a distance and leading a thirsty person towards it, eventually satisfy his (dream) thirst?" he asks.

In this rapid survey, two attempts at defining *prāmāṇya* may be discussed, each the result of a long process of maturation within a system. The first is a refinement of the original idea of "agreement" as expressed in Vātsyāyana's definition quoted above, and is formulated by Gaṅgeśa, the founder of the neo-Nyāya school. Truth, on Gaṅgeśa's view, is the property of a cognition to have a qualifier that belongs also to the object of that cognition. To know A as F is true if and only if F belongs to A. Subsequent neo-Nyāya logicians have further refined this definition to take care of various counterexamples, but we need not refer to those complexities in this essay. The other definition, reached by the Advaita epistemologists, again after a long search, is negative in form: a cognition is true in case it is not contradicted by another cognition and so not known to be false. While this negative definition, making use of the notion of falsity and seemingly collapsing the distinction between "being-true" and "taken-to-be-true," holds good, and is intended to hold good, of all empirical truths, trans-empirical truth (for example, of the identity sentences of the Upaniṣads) is defined as the property of not being negatable at all.

The Advaita epistemology thus focused on the concept of falsity and, for all logical purposes, accorded to it a primacy, the true being what is not false. The theory of falsity, however, became a preoccupation not of the Advaitin alone, but also of the other schools, which used their theories to refute the Advaita metaphysics. The questions that were raised concern, in the first place, the nature of a false cognition (Is it perceptual, or is it memory? Is it reducible to several true cognitions, not distinguished from one another?), and in the second, the object of a false cognition (What is its ontological status? Is the object that is cognized, when in error, itself a real object, or a subjective mental state projected onto the external world, or is it a sort of object, being neither real nor unreal, that we might call a *false* (*mithyā*) object?). It should be remembered that in this discussion the philosophers were chiefly concerned with perceptual error, including cases of hallucination, not purely intellectual error.

It should also be noted that "*apramā*" (not-valid) and "false" do not coincide. Doubt (*saṁśaya*) is neither true nor false, but is included within *apramā*, for it has one qualifier (in "is S p or not-p?") which does not belong to S. Memory, even when true, was regarded as *apramā* for various reasons, the chief of which is that it only *repeats* what is already known, and so does not deserve to be dignified with the appellation "true." It should have been realized that in memory alone the past is apprehended as past and so the entire content of memory is not repetition.

At this point, it may be appropriate to introduce a question which the Indian philosophers asked with regard to *prāmāṇya* (the property of being a valid cognition) and *aprāmāṇya* (the property of being an invalid cognition). Is *prāmāṇya* (and *aprāmāṇya*) apprehended *svataḥ* (intrinsically) or *parataḥ* (extrinsically)? What this amounts to is, when a cognition K is cognized, is it also *pari passu* cognized as valid? Or is its validity cognized at a later point in time? The same questions are asked with regard to invalidity. The possible answers are the following:

1 when K is cognized, it is also cognized as being valid, while later on its invalidity may be determined on the basis of unsuccessful practice (*svataḥprāmāṇya* and *parataḥaprāmāṇya*);
2 when K is cognized, it is cognized neither as valid nor as invalid. Both validity and invalidity, as the case may be, are determined later depending upon the success or failure of the practical response to K (*parataḥprāmāṇya* and *parataḥaprāmāṇya*);
3 when K is cognized, it is to be taken as invalid, unless later experience leads to successful practice, when it is judged valid (*svataḥaprāmāṇya* and *prataḥprāmāṇya*); and
4 for every K, both validity and invalidity are intrinsic – that is, it is in some respect valid, in some not so (*svataḥprāmāṇya* and *svataḥaprāmāṇya*).

(1) is the view of Mīmāṃsā in all its forms; (2) is the view of Nyāya. These are the two options that were fully developed. (3) is ascribed in doxographic literature to the Buddhists, (4) to the Sāṃkhya. Neither is proposed in a fully developed and defensible form.

Clearly, the proposals (1) and (2), in particular, make use of "cognition of K (which itself is a cognition)," and this latter itself is a highly controversial concept. Intertwined with the question, "How are validity and invalidity of a cognition determined?" is the question "How is a cognition itself cognized?" As a matter of fact, the latter is most probably an earlier controversy which was later taken into, and used by, the other controversy regarding validity and invalidity.

The answers to this question fall into the following patterns:

(a) a cognition is self-manifesting, self-revealing, self-intimating (*svaprakāśa*) in the sense that by its very occurrence it makes its own existence known, not unlike, in an important respect, the light of a lamp (*pradīpavat*);
(b) a cognition, by its occurrence, manifests its object – which is its function – but not itself. It itself is known only by being the object of a subsequent cognition, the latter being of the nature of an inner perception (*anuvyavasāya*); and
(c) a cognition is known only by a subsequent act of inference that seeks to account for the difference between the known object and the mere object by positing the act of knowing as what produces in its object the property of knownness (*jñātatā*).

Of these (a) – which in general is called *svaprakāśavāda* – is upheld by the Buddhists, the Advaita Vedānta, and Prabhākara Mīmāṁsā. Since each of these proposed a different version, we have three forms of the theory of *svaprakāśa*, which are:

(a1) each cognition, as it occurs, manifests itself;
(a2) each cognition manifests itself as a cognition, its subject as the knower and its object as the known, all in one act (known as three-fold perception or *triputipratyakṣa*); and
(a3) a cognition is manifested directly by the witness-consciousness (*sākṣīcaitanya*); the latter manifests itself. The qualifier "directly" is added, because while all objects (*viṣayāni*) are also manifested by the witness-

consciousness, they need the mediation of a cognitive state, but a cognition is manifested by the witness-consciousness without the mediation of another cognition. On this theory, then, to say that a cognition is self-revealing is to say that by its very occurrence it becomes *directly* manifested by the witness-consciousness (*kevala-sākṣī-vedya*). The witness-consciousness, however, is self-revealing in the strictest sense.

Of these three, (a1) is the view of the Buddhists; (a2) of Prabhākara Mīmāṃsā, and (a3) of the Advaita Vedānta. Another version of (a) was proposed by Rāmānuja (1017–1137 CE) in opposition to the Advaita:

(a4) a cognition manifests itself to its own subject or locus (*svāśrayam prati*), by its very existence (*sva-sattayā*), and only while it is manifesting its own object (*viṣaya-prakāśana-velāyām*). (These clauses take into account the fact that my cognition is not self-manifesting to you and that my past cognition is not self-manifesting to me now).

It should now be evident that if you take into account the diversity of views (a1), (a2), (a3), (a4), (b) and (c), and insert them into appropriate places in (1) through (4), you have an interesting range of theories of knowledge, the details of which may be worked out by interested readers for themselves.

Before I conclude the section on the theory of knowledge and pass on to metaphysics, one more large controversy needs to be mentioned, particularly because this controversy – together with the two earlier ones on *prāmāṇya* and on *prakāśa* – contribute to the overall metaphysical positions of the schools. This third major epistemological controversy concerns the question, "Does a cognition have a form or content (*ākāra*), or not?" Again, as in many other instances, the Buddhists created the initial stir. Since the Buddhists did not admit the existence of either enduring selves or enduring material objects, when I perceive a material object, or have the sense of "I," these objects (for example, the tree out there) can only be a form or content of a cognition. Cognitions must then be the sort of things that have their built-in contents. Dignāga, the Buddhist logician, clinched the issue thus: blue and sensation of blue are not different. Blue is always a content of a sensory consciousness; you do not experience the one without the other. This doctrine of *jñānasākāra* (that is, the theory that knowledge always has a form) came under severe criticism by the Hindu philosophers, led by Kumārila Bhatta in his *Ślokavārttika*, followed by the Naiyāyikas: a cognition, not being a substance, does not have real parts, and so it cannot have a form that consists in the arrangement of parts. The perceived "blue" is over there, far or near; such spatial features could not characterize an inner state such as a cognition. The Advaita epistemologists took up a position in which both extreme views were combined: consciousness in itself is formless and contentless (*nirākāra*), but the inner sense (*antaḥkaraṇa*), in the perceptual situation, assumes the form of an object; when this form is reflected in consciousness, consciousness appears to have a form, just as when the red color of a flower reflected in a clear crystal makes the crystal appear to be red.

Metaphysics

Realism–Idealism issue

All Hindu philosophers are, to say the least, empirical realists: the objects of empirical knowledge are admitted to exist independently of any knowledge. If, like the Nyāya, Vaiśeṣika and Pūrva Mīmāṃsā, they regard these empirical objects as ultimately real, their empirical realism also amounts to metaphysical realism. The Advaita Vedānta clearly regards the empirical world to be but a false appearance of a ubiquitous spirit, so that the system's empirical realism is but a part of a larger idealistic metaphysics, a preparation for a transcendental idealism, if you will. Idealism *par excellence*, which denies external objects and recognizes cognitions alone (*vijñānamātratā*) as real, is to be met with only in the Yogācāra school of Buddhism. Yogācāra Buddhism, which gave rise to logicians such as Dignāga and Dharmakīrti, not only spurred Hindu logic towards more sophistication, but also led the Naiyāyikas and Mīmāṁsākas, even the Vedāntins, to defend and safeguard their favored empirical realism. In the development of this defense of realism, several strategies became prominent:

First, if it can be established that cognitions could not have forms or contents, then any form or content that appears in a cognition (like blue in the sensation of blue, or the tree in the perception of the tree) must fall outside of that cognition.

Second, if, as the Nyāya insisted, a cognition is never self-illuminating and is known only in a subsequent introspective act, what is known in a cognition is its object (blue or the tree) and not the cognition itself, and when the cognition is known in introspection, the object is not thereby known leading to the position that a cognition and its object are known in different attitudes, and therefore are never known together. This refutes the Buddhist claim that since the two are always experienced together (*sahopalambhaniyamāt*), they must be identical.

Third, as some Advaitins emphasized, when a true cognition makes its object known, it also makes it known that the object had an unknown existence (*ajñātasattā*) prior to being known. All empirically real objects have unknown existence prior to being known. They cannot, therefore, be mere cognitions.

Finally, as Śaṃkara argued, if there are, as a matter of fact, no external objects, then an inner representation cannot appear *as if* it is external. Something appears *as if* it is a snake only because there are real snakes. The predicate "is external" cannot be, in *all* of its applications, a projection.

You may admit external reality, but still insist that the material things that we perceive are but composed of invisible atoms. The precise conceptual clarification of the relation between the whole (*avayavin*) and the part (*avayava*) becomes then a matter of great importance. Nāgārjuna's dialectical critique of this conceptual apparatus was directed as much against the Vaiśeṣika realist as against the early Buddhist theory of "elements" (*dharmāḥ*). The Buddhist preferred to keep the elements and deny a real whole. If all that we have are aggregates, we do not have a genuine whole. A heap of sand is nothing but those grains of sand. The epistemological consequence of this denial of a whole is that, since each element is not perceivable, an aggregate of them is no more perceivable. Ordinary perception of material objects must then be really inference foisted upon some non-conceptual apprehension of (some) elements. Empirical realism requires that its defenders establish two theses: one ontological and the other epistemological. The ontological thesis is that there are genuine wholes which are not mere aggregates; they are more than the sum of their parts. The epistemological thesis is that although in order to perceive a whole we need to perceive some of its parts, it is not necessary for that purpose to perceive all of the parts. These two theses support each other. Vātsyāyana and Kumārila established that there are genuine wholes. In terms of the Vaiśeṣika categories, the thesis is that the whole is a new entity that inheres in its parts in the relation of *samavāya*. While perceiving a part, then, one can perceive the whole inhering in it, provided suitable conditions exist. Vātsyāyana argued that the Buddhist inference cannot go through, for if the parts are unperceivable, you cannot infer them either, and if you never perceive a whole, you cannot also infer it. The inferred entity must be perceivable, the like of which must have been perceived on other occasions.

The Vaiśeṣika categorial structure

The Vaiśeṣika attempted to give a minimal number of types of entities, *padārthas*, such that everything whatsoever shall either belong to one of these types or can be analyzed into one or more of them. Kaṇāda, in his *Vaiśeṣikasūtras* (later than 300 BCE), and Praśastapāda, (500–560 CE) in his Commentary on it, recognize six positive categories – substance, quality, action, universal, particularity, and inherence. In the course of time, a seventh came to be added – absence (*abhāva*). Of these, the first three – substance, quality and action – are particulars, and exist in a pre-eminent sense; the other three belong to those three and to them alone. Inherence is the "ontological glue," as it were, which ties entities belonging to different types together. Without "inherence," they all would remain loose and disconnected. Without the seventh category or absence, pluralism cannot be saved. For difference (*bheda*) is a kind of absence, and pluralism requires that entities be different, both as types and as tokens – a stick from a stone, red from blue, and so on *ad infinitum*. Even with these seven, the story is not complete. Consider a perceived material object, that piece of red paper. It is a substance which inheres in its parts, in which the color red inheres; in that red inheres the universal redness. If the paper moves, action inheres in it. Each of its further indivisible parts possesses particularity by virtue of which this paper is a unique individual. But it is also not blue, not a piece of stone, a whole nexus of negations belong to it, its color, and all else. These negations belong to each appropriate entity by a special relation called the self-linking or *svarūpa* relation. Only then can we have a seamless unity of a thing in spite of all the differences that go into its structure.

The Nyāya began with a similar commitment to categorial types, but Gautama's interest was soteriological and the entities he lists – an odd list by any standard – are those the knowledge of which would lead to *apavarga*, the highest good, the cessation of all suffering. The theoretical interest in the structure of the world grew; the followers of Gautama appropriated the Vaiśeṣika list, pushing out some of the epistemological and affective concepts from Gautama's list to their rightful place within the appropriate Vaiśeṣika category. Thus accepting the Vaiśeṣika ontology, the Nyāya went on to develop its logical and epistemological theories.

In the course of its development, however, old Nyāya was replaced by the Navya-Nyāya, whose founder is generally acknowledged to be Gaṅgeśa Upādhyāya (ca. 1200 CE), but whose beginnings can be traced to Udayana (1050–1100 CE). Apart from the logical and epistemological sophistications introduced, and a technical logical language developed to articulate the analytical results, Navya-Nyāya also caused an expansion of the ontological horizon to a theory that the types of entities cannot be limited (to the classical list). Especially noteworthy is the introduction of many interesting abstract entities such as limitorhood (*avacchedakatā*), qualifierhood (*prakāratā*), relationhood (*samsargatā*). Some of these are purely epistemic elements. A drastic revision of the Nyāya-Vaiśeṣika ontology was proposed by the brilliant logician Raghunātha Śiromaṇi (1510 CE) whose list includes such new categories as "moment," "possessedness" (*svatva*), "causal power" (*śakti*), and "contentness" (*viṣyaytā*), and excludes space and time as separate entities by making them aspects of God. Some recent authors (Matilal, Mukhopadhyaya) have distinguished between an inner circle of genuinely ontological categories and an outer circle of epistemological posits.

We notice how the Nyāya and Vaiśeṣika philosophers wanted to preserve a common sense pluralism together with a unity *within* each thing as well as *of* the world, the latter by locating all things in one space and one time, everything being related to everything else by some temporal relation (*kālikasambandha*) or other. Unity of a thing was needed, as we saw, to preserve the validity of ordinary perception. Unity of the world was needed in order to prove the existence of God. The Buddhist challenged both. The Hindu philosophers, such as Udayana, met these challenges vehemently.

The problem of reconciling unity with plurality, identity with difference, is central to much of Indian metaphysics. The Nyāya-Vaiśeṣika preserved both with the help of the ontological glues – the relation of inherence and a self-linking relation – and clever use of the category of "absence" or "negation." Śaṁkara questioned the viability of this strategy. If you begin with radically separating entities by assigning to them radically different types, those categorial differences cannot simply be legislated into a unity by positing special relations which could effect the miracle. Instead, he proposes that at bottom, things have the "same self," that the most fundamental relation is identity (*tādātmya*), which underlies and makes possible differences. Ontologically, there is only one substance: qualities, actions and universals are only separated aspects, in reality having their being in the one substance. Identity is fundamental, difference is an appearance. Numerous philosophers belonging to Śaṃkara's school – more famously, Harṣa (twelfth century CE) and Madhusūdhana Saraswati (1320 CE) – dialectically refuted the category of "difference" by bringing out – in a manner reminiscent of F. H. Bradley –

incoherences, self-contradictions, and infinite regresses which vitiate this category.

Śaṃkara's critics, within the school of Vedānta, regarded him as having gone too far in the direction of pure, undifferentiated identity. Various fundamental relations were proposed: identity-in-difference by Rāmānuja (1017–1137 CE), identity-and-difference by Bhāskara (tenth century CE), inscrutable identity-and-difference by Nimbārka (eleventh century CE), and pure difference by Madhva (1197–1276 CE). It should be borne in mind that each of these proposals founded a specific interpretation (of the scriptures) bearing on the relation of human beings to God, individual souls to Brahman, world to God and on the nature of, and pathway to, salvation.

In this exposition, I have highlighted the mutual dependence of epistemology and ontology in various schools of Indian philosophy. This situation was used by Nāgārjuna to "deconstruct" both. If epistemology cannot begin without knowing what is there to know, and if ontology cannot begin without fixing the instruments of knowing, both the projects must be deeply flawed and so "overcome." Vātsyāyana has tried to meet this critique by arguing that there is no one-to-one correlation between the means of knowing and the objects of knowing. The relation is many–one and one–many. By one means of knowing many types of entities can be known, just as one and the same object can be known by many different instruments of knowing. It is the Buddhist who, insisting as he does on a one–one correlation, (perception ↔ pure particular; inference ↔ conceptual construct) is open to Nāgārjuna's critique.

The development of Indian philosophy presents a story that is greatly unlike the story of the development of Western philosophy. As said earlier, very early on Indian thought developed – certainly not from nowhere, but through a long process of largely unrecorded maturation – a spectrum of "points of view," "ways of seeing" or *darśanas*. The rest of the story is a process of the development of these *darśanas* through attempts to meet the challenges of others and also through attempts to make the ideas of each *darśana* more coherent, defensible, and logically sophisticated. A philosopher had to think from within a *darśana*, and not just from nowhere. But while belonging to a school, he could still do creative thinking, either by way of introducing a new interpretation of the basic texts, or by altogether new ideas within the broad framework of the system. It should not be thought, however, that a *darśana* is such a close-knit system that either you accept it as a whole or reject it as a whole. There have been changes of the *darśanas* from within. There have also been independent philosophers, such as Vācaspati Miśra and Vijñānabhikṣu, who wrote authoritative works in several different systems, and thereby earned the title of being "independent of all views" (*sarvatantrasvatantra*).

It has often been held that although Indians developed philosophy early on, they did not reflect on the nature of philosophy, and consequently did not come to have a name for this discipline. As regards the name, "*darśana*," it is a widely used term, occurring in the *Vaiśeṣikasūtra* IX.2.13, and is used also by Haribhadra (fifth century CE) in the sense of a system of philosophy. Another name for philosophy is "*ānvikṣiki*," defined by Kautilya as "examination of the objects with the help of means of knowing."

Three kinds of meta-philosophical views are to be found among Indian philosophers. Some, in the Vedic tradition, looked at all systems as mutually reconcilable and ultimately as leading up to Vedānta. The Jainas, consistently with their conception of reality as having infinite aspects, regarded each system as containing an element of truth. Nāgārjuna, consistently with his skeptical and "decontructionist" point of view, regarded all philosophical systems as "incoherent," "full of contradications," and so in need of being "overcome" and "transcended."

Practical philosophy

From the very beginning, philosophy, in India, had a practical orientation. Since it was generally held by the religions and philosophies that human existence is characterized by suffering, and that the goal of the reflective life was to be free from suffering, philosophical knowledge of whatever is real, especially of one's true self, was regarded as a means to that goal. If the Indian philosophies are divided into two groups – the spiritual (*ādhyātmika*) and the logical-analytical (*ānvikṣiki*) – the spiritual philosophies (Sāṃkhya, Yoga, Buddhism and Vedānta) were directly oriented towards a soteriological goal, while the logical philosophies also entertained such a goal and claimed that that goal was achievable by their sort of philosophical knowledge. While a practical orientation is thus markedly ubiquitous, it would be a mistake to say that there was no theoretical inquiry. On the contrary, pure theoretical thinking was cultivated, and it was this that was regarded by many as a means toward fulfilling the highest practical interest. In any case, the distinction between theory and practice assumes a different form in Indian thought than in classical Western thought.

Practical philosophy, or rather philosophy of practice, covers three kinds of action: ethical rules as well as virtues, yogic practice as a means of purifying and harmonizing the psycho-physical complex for a higher purpose, and religious practices and rituals with the ostensible purpose of pleasing the Godhead for whom they are intended. Of these three, the first, called *dharma*, becomes the specific subject matter of the Pūrvamīmāṃsā school of philosophy. The second comes under a specific school of philosophy, the Yoga system of Patañjali. The third is dealt with by the theistic schools of Vedānta, such as those of Rāmānuja, Nimbārka, and Madhva. Underlying all of these discussions is a large *karma* (action) theory with its belief in the "efficacy" of *karma*, efficacy which extends far beyond the time of the action into the afterlife and future rebirth. The idea of "fruits" (*phala*) of action becomes important. Actions come to be classified according to the nature of their "fruit," and since the ultimate goal is freedom from "bondage" (consequently, from the cycle of rebirth), the idea of doing actions in such a manner that their "fruits" do not "bind" becomes of paramount importance. Very early in the development of this concern, Bādari, an old Mīmāṃsā philosopher, proposed that when the scriptures recommended "one ought to do X," the emphasis was on "doing X" and not on the consequences of so doing. But classical Mīmāṃsā wanted a motivating cause for "doing X," and the thought of good, desirable and satisfying consequences was what was needed. With this general framework defined by the causal chain, knowledge → desire → will to do → motor effort → action, various theoretical explanations were given, in the different schools of philosophy, especially in Nyāya and Mīmāṁsā, as to how hearing an imperative sentence ("You ought to do X") could motivate a person to act appropriately. The Nyāya theory, consequentialist *par excellence*, required that the person believe that he can bring about the desired good by doing X, that he can do X ("ought implies can"), and that no greater harm will befall him for doing X. The Mīmāṃsākas, Prabhākara (seventh century CE) in particular, sought to simplify the causal mechanism by reducing it all to one factor: the power of the suffix-component of the verb in the imperative mood designating "should" or "ought to" (this latter distinction is not so clear in Sanskrit) to motivate a person to act, which means that the grammatical form of the imperative is adequate to motivate the prospective agent to act. The theory of Kumārila Bhatta, it may be noted, stands midway between the extreme consequentialist view of Nyāya and the extreme deontological view of Prabhākara. We can recognize the influence of Bādri on Prabhākara and eventually on Kṛṣṇa's celebrated teaching in the *Bhagavadgītā* that one ought to do one's duty without being concerned with the consequences – which were regarded, in accordance with the Indian mode of thinking, to be either happiness (*sukha*) or pain (*dukkha*).

Kṛṣṇa's discourse, in the *Bhagavadgītā*, must also be looked upon as being occasioned by a situation in which various components of *dharma* – the *dharma* of family (*kuladharma*), the *dharma* pertaining to one's "caste" (*varnāśramadharma*), and the *dharma* pertaining to humans in general (*sādhāraṇadharma*) – are in conflict. Kṛṣṇa attempts, with questionable success, to re-establish their harmony by assigning to each its sphere and legitimacy, all being geared towards the grand finale of "freedom" (*mokṣa*). In doing this, the text accomplishes what Vinoba Bhave has called a non-violent revolution in thinking by way of reinterpreting many of the traditional concepts. Thus, *varna* (caste) is said to be determined by attributes (*guṇa*) and actions (*karma*). Besides the duties attaching to caste etc., a new concept is introduced, namely, that of an individual's own *dharma* (*svadharma*). The ritualistic concept of "sacrifice" (*yajña*) is interpreted as symbolizing both a psychological-spiritual process and a cosmic process. In the *Gītā*, the idea of *yoga* is given a most interesting extension. It is made to include the *yoga* of action (*karmayoga*), the *yoga* of knowledge (*jñānayoga*), and the *yoga* of devotion (*bhaktiyoga*), and, in the long run the text establishes the mutual involvement of these "paths" to freedom. An attempt is made to harmonize a Kantian-like deontological thesis about "duty for duty's sake" with the idea of acting in the spirit of "offering the 'fruits' of action" to the Godhead as sacrifice.

In all this, *mokṣa* figures as the highest good – mightily above *artha* (wealth), *kāma* (sensuous pleasure), and *dharma* (morality). The concept of these four "human goods" (*puruṣārthas*) figures in the Sāṃkhya of Kapila, in the Yoga of Patañjali, as well as in the *Dharma* theory of Manu. The first three goods are correlated to the three *guṇas*: namely, *rajas*, *tamas*, and *sattva* respectively, and are concerned with enjoyment (*bhoga*), while in the fourth case, there is a turning away from enjoyment through the practice of a moral life.

Each school of philosophy, if it is committed to the Vedic tradition, has its own conception of *mokṣa* which reflects the metaphysical theory in experiential terms, which, in other words, assures that the theory under consideration can be "realized." Thus, for Śaṃkara's non-dualism, *mokṣa* is the experience of the identity of the individual self and the Universal Brahman arising out of the destruction of ignorance; for Rāmānuja's qualified non-dualism, *mokṣa* is the experience of absolute dependence of the individual upon God, to be realized through meditative contemplation. Whether the philosophy is a theoretical elaboration of the possibility of the experience, or the concept of *mokṣa* is a conception of what sort of experience will verify the theory, cannot be decided here. Both possibilities remain open – the latter a more plausible stance for philosophy, the former for the spiritual seeker.

Social theory and aesthetics

It would be a mistake, however, to suppose – as has not infrequently been held – that Indian thought was indifferent to the community (encouraging the individual to pursue his or her own spiritual destiny) and to communication. Within the brief compass of this introductory essay, I would like to draw attention to the place of social thinking in the Indian tradition, and to a theory of aesthetic experience and communication which arose from within that tradition.

A very early classification of disciplines is into *trayi* (the science of the Vedas), *vārtā* (the science of agriculture and animal husbandry), *dandanīti* (the science of punishment) and *ānvikṣiki* (philosophy). Kauṭilya says that of these four, the science of punishment, of law and order, is the basis of all other sciences; it makes them all possible. *The Mahābhārata* says that if there had been no punishment, men would oppress each other, and that in the absence of the king, no one can say, "This is mine." Śukra refers to the state of nature during which the strong prey upon the weak after the manner of larger fish devouring the smaller ones. This "logic of the fish" (*matsyanyāya*) is overcome by the institution of kingship. But all the lawbooks suggest that in ancient India the king's power was extremely limited. The king was not above the law; he could not violate *dharma* with impunity. *The Mahābhārata* even supports "regicide" under certain circumstances.

The same word "*dharma*" signified – besides its metaphysical meaning – moral law, political law, social conventions and practices. Like the German "*Recht*," it stood for both law and right, including the right of contract and property as well as the subjective morality of conscience and customary use in family, society, and state. Naturally, Hindu social thinking played on this ambiguity, and often surreptitiously justified unreasonable social laws in terms appropriate only for the highest moral principles. It is also important to recognize that law, for Hindus, was not the arbitrary legislation by the sovereign; nor does it derive merely from judicial decisions. Besides the Vedas, tradition, good custom, and "approval of conscience" (*ātamnaḥ priya*) were regarded as sources of law. Rules of interpretation developed in order to properly construe the texts, and matters of usage. The commentators and digest writers organized custom into "a juridical framework."

In general, as both Gandhi and Tagore have pointed out in our times, in Hindu social thinking, society or community enjoyed a primacy as against the state or the individual. Many of an individual's moral duties attached to his station in society – that is, to his position in the family and to his "caste." They concerned his duties to other men, to the Brahmins and to the king, and eventually, to the gods and to "nature," and to himself. These are brought together, in the *Gītā*, under the three concepts of *yajña* (sacrifice), *dāna* (charity), and *tapas* (austerity).

Hindu aesthetic thinking, concerned as it was with the aesthetic experience, occupied itself with the problem of the communication of the author's or actor's sentiments to the reader or spectator. There are two fields in which the Hindu thinkers applied themselves: first, with regard to literary works, and second, with regard to dramatic arts. So far as the first is concerned, Ānanda Vardhana (ninth century CE) gave a classic exposition of the theory of *dhvani* or literary meaning, as distinguished from the two kinds of literal meaning already recognized by epistemologists – namely, the primary ("cloud" means cloud) and the secondary ("cloud" means rain). The literary meaning is realized imaginatively and not understood logically. Literal meaning can be compared – as it is by Ānanda Vardhana – to various parts of the body, such as the eyes, the nose and the hands. Literary meaning, on the other hand, is like the beauty of a woman, which is experienced over and above these. Thus in experiencing the poetic meaning, various factors are involved: the speaker, the hearer, the tone of the voice, the expressed meaning, the presence or the absence of a third person, the context of utterance, the time and the place, etc. Out of the cooperation of these factors – especially of the hearer's and the speaker's imaginations, arises *dhvani*. But the final purpose of poetry – as also of dramatic performance – is to evoke in the audience *rasa*, variously translated as "taste," "flavor," "aesthetic sentiment" or "essence." The classical exposition of the theory of *rasa* has been given by Abhinava Gupta of the tenth century CE, although its earliest exponent is Bharata, the author of *Nāṭyaśāstra* (fourth to fifth century CE). Based upon a psychological theory about certain permanent emotional propensities, the theory goes on to say how a dramatic presentation arouses these propensities and brings to a state of pleasurable relish the emotions of love, laughter, sorrow, anger, vigor, fear, repugnance, and wonder – eventually leading to a state of peace (*śāntarasa*). The *rasa* which constitutes the essence of poetry or of a dramatic performance is not a mere psychologically subjective phenomenon. Personal experiences have to be transformed into public concepts. It is this "generalization" (*sādhāraṇikaraṇa*) that enables communication from the author or the actor to the audience. The theory struggles hard to overcome the opposite extremes of psychologism and intellectualism and achieves a new *via media* of "emotional ideality." Aesthetic experience is the act of "tasting" this *rasa*, but it is not a private incommunicable experience; it is rather sharing in what is already an impersonal essence. Thus, in aesthetic experience, the private ego transcends its spatio-temporal limitations, many minds meet, a common consciousness emerges, the aesthetic and the mystical coincide.

The twentieth century

Finally, before closing this essay, a brief reference only will be made to the way the classical philosophers of India have been dealt with by modern Indian writers. Writing, teaching, and studying have combined in the Sanskrit schools in Banaras, Calcutta, and other places, in the manner of several centuries ago. At present, that sort of scholarship is dwindling, although works in philosophy are still being written in Sanskrit. However, the main stream of philosophical work has, for almost a century, been pursued in the English language. Many of those who write on philosophy in English have acquired some competence in different schools of philosophy in Sanskrit. In the philosophy departments of the colleges and universities, Indian philosophy is studied along with Western philosophy. In this intellectual milieu, several types of works have emerged.

First, there are the histories of philosophy. To this group belong the works of S. Radhakrishnan, S. N. Dasgupta, and amongst Western scholars, E. Frauwallner. Of these, Frauwallner's work alone is strictly speaking historical in orientation.

Second, there is a large body of work by Indian writers devoted to what should be called comparative philosophy. Under this rubric fall works which institute comparisons of Śaṃkara with Kant and Hegel, of Rāmānuja with Hegel and the British personal Idealists, of Buddhism with Hume or Whitehead, to mention a few of the themes popular before the Second World War. In more recent times, comparisons have been instituted between Dignāga and the logical positivists as well as between neo-Nyāya logic and modern logic. Some scholars have focused on specific problems and have brought together philosophical theories from the Indian tradition and from the Western philosophical tradition in so far as they bear on such problems. Thus philosophers have focused upon epistemological problems such as the nature and criterion of truth or metaphysical concepts such as universals and substance. These works have served limited purposes, and have contributed neither to the development of Indian philosophy, nor to the growth of Western philosophy.

Third, many scholars have sought to reinterpret the Indian philosophical texts, using the tools of Western thinking. If contemporary Western thinking may be said to have produced two main philosophical methods: the logico-analytical and the phenomenological-hermeneutic, then one can find contemporary Indian thinkers using these methodologies, either separately or jointly, for the purpose of interpreting the Sanskrit material. In general, there is now a tendency – which may be read as a reaction against the trend that was predominant during the first half of the century – to highlight the secular-theoretical contents of traditional Indian thought as opposed to its spiritual-practical contents. This may be an overreaction, just as the earlier one was a hasty generalization. The truth perhaps lies in the middle.

Fourth, such interpretive attempts are carried out either with regard to the authority of the Indian tradition or with regard to specific schools, such as Buddhism, Nyāya, Vaiśeṣika or Vedānta. Some of these works, more "comparative" in spirit, fall under the second group. Others, more interpretive and textual-exegetical, stand apart.

A fifth group of philosophical work deserves to be recognized as original, creative advancement of Indian philosophy, in continuity with the tradition, but not constrained by it. To this group belong, on the one hand, a number of major literary figures and public thinkers such as Gandhi, Tagore, and Sri Aurobindo, and, on the other, a number of brilliant academic philosophers such as K. C. Bhattacharya, S. Radhakrishnan, Kalidas Bhattacharya, N. V. Banerjee, Rash Vihari Das, and T. R. V. Murti. A few remarks about the ideas of this group will follow.

The metaphysics of Advaita Vedānta looms large over the Indian mind, sometimes, as in the case of Gandhi and Tagore, tempered by the medieval-Indian *bhakti* (devotional-theistic) tradition. But the extreme illusionism of some earlier interpreters of Śaṁkara has been set aside in favor of a realistic reading, as by Radhakrishnan. Others, notably Sri Aurobindo, have rejected Śaṁkara's nondualism in favor of an integral monism that recognizes many aspects of Reality, including an evolutionary history promising to transcend the human mentality into a supramental consciousness. Śaṁkara himself asked if *mokṣa* was to be in a living body, and his school decided in favor of such a possibility, for otherwise the freed could not teach and those who taught would still be ignorant. The question of whether the highest form of freedom is that of an individual or of humankind (*sarvanmukti*) was also considered, and the Master seems to have favored the latter, making it obligatory, as in Mahāyāna Buddhism, for the wise to work for the redemption of all. In modern Indian thought, this aspect of the tradition has come to enjoy an importance – in Gandhi's idea of *Rāmarājya* ("the kingdom of Rāma") as an ideal social order, in Sri Aurobindo's idea of a "collective liberation" (or the ascent of mankind into a higher species), and in N. V. Banerjee's insistence that the source of "bondage" is insular individuality, while freedom consists in actualization of the "I with others."

Contemporary Indian philosophers are engaged in a two-fold conversation: conversation with their own tradition, which carries a high philosophical legacy, and conversation with the West, which is unavoidable given the history of the country during the last two centuries. These two conversations should be able to merge into one grand dialogue. It is not the case that the interpretive possibilities of the past have all been exhausted. Also, it is not true, to quote Kipling, that "East is East, and West is West, and never the twain shall meet." As a matter of fact, they not only shall meet, but they are meeting, not merely in technology, but in philosophy as well.

Bibliography

Note: Source material (in English translation).

Annambhaṭṭa 1976: *Tarkasaṁgraha* [Collection of Reasoning], tr. with explanations by Gopinath Bhattacharya (Calcutta: Progressive Publishers).

Madhavāchārya 1961: *Sarvadarśanasaṁgraha* [Collection of All Systems of Philosophy], tr. E. B. Cowell and A. E. Gough, 6th edn (Varanasi: Chowkhamba).

Radhakrishanan, S. and Moore, C. A. (eds) 1957: *A Sourcebook in Indian Philosophy* (Princeton: Princeton University Press).
Śaṁkarāchārya 1896: *Brahmasūtrabhāṣyam* [Commentary on the Vedānta Aphorisms], tr. G. Thibaut (Oxford: Clarendon Press).

References and material for further reading

Banerjee, N. V. 1972: *Glimpses of Indian Wisdom* (New Delhi: Munshiram Manoharlal).
Barua, B. M. 1921: *A History of Pre-Buddhistic Indian Philosophy* (Calcutta: Calcutta University Press).
Basham, A. L. 1951: *History and Doctrines of the Ajivikas* (London: Luzac).
Bhattacharya, K. D. 1956: *Studies in Philosophy*, 2 Vols (Calcutta: Progressive Publishers).
Dasgupta, S. N. 1922–54: *A History of Indian Philosophy*, 5 Vols (Cambridge: Cambridge University Press).
De, S. K. 1963: *Sanskrit Poetics as a Study of Aesthetics* (Berkeley: University of California Press).
Ghosh, Sri Aurobindo 1949: *The Life Divine* (New York: Sri Aurobindo Library).
Gnoli, R. 1968: *The Aesthetic Experience According to Abhinava Gupta*, 2nd edn (Varanasi: Chowkhamba).
Halbfass, W. 1991: *Tradition and Reflection. Explorations in Indian Thought* (Albany: State University of New York Press).
Ingalls, D. H. H. 1951: *Materials for the Study of Navya-Nyāya Logic* (Cambridge: Harvard University Press).
Kane, P. V. 1932–62: *History of Dharmaśāstra. Ancient and Medieval Religious Law*, 3 Vols (Poona: Bhandarkar Oriental Research Institute).
Kaviraj, Gopi Nath 1966: *Aspects of Indian Thought* (Burdwan: University of Burdwan).
Krishna, D. 1991: *Indian Philosophy: a Counter Perspective* (Delhi: Oxford University Press).
Krishna, D., Rege, M. P., Dwivedi, R. C., and Lath, M. (eds) 1991: *Samvāda: a Dialogue Between Two Philosophical Traditions* (Delhi: Motilal Banarasidass).
Lingat, Robert 1973: *The Classical Laws of India* (Berkeley: University of California Press).
Matilal, B. K. 1985: *Logic, Language and Reality* (Delhi: Motilal Banarsidass).
Mohanty, J. N. 1992: *Reason and Tradition in Indian Thought* (Oxford: Clarendon Press).
—— 1993: *Essays on Indian Philosophy, Traditional and Modern*, ed. P. Bilimaria (Delhi: Oxford University Press).
Murti, T. R. V. 1983: *Studies in Indian Thought* (Columbia, Mo.: South Asia Books).
Potter, Karl H. (ed.) 1977: *Indian Metaphysics and Epistemology* (Princeton: Princeton University Press).
Potter, Karl H. 1963: *Presuppositions of Indian Philosophies* (Englewood Cliff, NJ: Prentice Hall).
Raja, K. Kunjunni 1963: *Indian Theories of Meaning* (Madras: Adyar Library and Research Centre).
Sanghavi, P. S. 1961: *Advanced Studies in Indian Logic and Metaphysics* (Calcutta: Indian Studies Past and Present).
Sarkar, K. L. 1909: *The Mīmāṁsā Rules of Interpretation as applied to Hindu Law* (Calcutta: Thackerstink and Co.).
Sastri, G. N. 1959: *The Philosophy of Word and Meaning* (Calcutta: Sanskrit College).

3

Classical Polynesian thinking

JOHN CHARLOT

Polynesia is conventionally described as a triangle, with Hawaiʻi at the apex, Easter Island at the south-eastern corner, and New Zealand at the south-western. Sāmoa and Tonga are the main island groups of Western Polynesia; the Society Islands, the Tuamotus, and the Marquesas are the main groups of Central Polynesia. Polynesian outliers can be found in Melanesia and Micronesia to the west.

The first settlers reached Sāmoa and Tonga from Fiji around 2000 BCE and, living in comparative isolation, developed the earliest distinctively Polynesian languages and cultural forms. Around the turn of the first millennium CE, these early Polynesians began to settle the rest of the triangle, starting with Central Polynesia and branching out to the furthest inhabitable lands. The South Island of New Zealand was the last inhabitable area of the earth to be settled by human beings.

As a result of this history, Polynesian languages are cognate, and Polynesian cultures share major and minor elements. For instance, intellectual traditions share terms, symbols, concepts, personages, schemes, and questions. Samoan Tagaloa (pronounced Tangaloa and so written here) becomes the Māori Tangaroa, the Tahitian Ta'aroa, and the Hawaiian Kanaloa. Nonetheless, important differences remain. Polynesians are generally competitive and individualistic, which leads to a differentiation of practices and traditions at any one time and through history. Families and localities developed their distinctive specialties and styles, which were sources of pride and subjects of boasting. Students would perpetuate the achievements of their teachers, but would make their personal contributions to the ever-growing body of tradition. The intellectual quest was also more intense and elaborate in the larger groups than on a small outlier like Tikopia. As a result, Polynesian thought resists systematization, and all generalizations must be tentative.

Polynesian cultures are united, however, in the high prestige they accord to intellectual ability and achievements. Knowledge is praised with a wide variety of terms, sayings, stories, and chants; ignorance is scorned with a similar literary richness. Education starts with prenatal practices and does not end in death – through which the soul passes to new places and experiences. Life for the Hawaiian is *ka ʻimi loa* (the great search), an ever deepening appreciation of the universe into which one is born and of which one forms an integral part. As a result of this intellectual emphasis, a high degree of self-consciousness and reflexivity is characteristic of Polynesian thinking and communication.

This search inspires the vast Polynesian literature with its characteristic combination of intellectual challenge, emotional power, and poetic sensibility. Treasured and preserved through oral transmission, many precontact works were recorded on paper once Polynesians learned writing. For her doctoral thesis, Margaret Orbell, the foremost scholar of New Zealand Māori literature, studied more than ten thousand examples of *waiata*, a women's poetic genre. Samoans recorded their family traditions in chapbooks and have continued to pass them down as heirlooms. Hawaiians filled archives with manuscripts and published thousands of pages of books and newspapers containing old and modern compositions. Although much has been lost – or, in some locations, little collected for public use – the available Polynesian literature constitutes an unparalleled resource for the study of non-Western, non-Asian intellectual traditions.

The important place of knowledge and the need to transmit orally large quantities of information resulted in the development of formal systems of education. The best attested and certainly one of the most elaborate was that of the Hawaiians. Education started in the extended family, which was a complete cultural unit in itself. Families could also specialize in occupations such as medicine, dance, chant, canoe-making, religion, and political advising. Family experts could thus attract non-family members as students. Schools were established, based on the model of the family, with their own lineages of teachers, craft gods, literature, and ceremonies. Schools could grow to include a number of teachers, usually subordinate to a master teacher. An important chief would gather experts at his court, who would form a faculty both for young nobles and for selected commoners. The major temples became quasi-universities with a faculty of priestly experts in a wide variety of fields. Students trained in one institution would travel to others to complete their education and also to spread the knowledge they had learned. In fact, the whole community participated in the functions of education, attending the public graduation ceremonies and formal debates and contests of wits among experts. Knowledge circulated generally among all the sections of society. The stories, sayings, and songs of the commoners were adapted by the chiefs, and the new compositions of the court spread to the eager audience, the general population.

Hawaiian literature records in detail the ideals of education. Knowledge had to be effective, from the skills necessary to survival to the wisdom of knowing one's place in history and the universe. Knowledge was therefore power on every level of human activity – a power that could seem godly and magical to the ignorant. Because knowledge was powerful, it had to be used morally. The teacher of martial arts had to imbue his students with high ideals lest they turn into bullies and brigands. The prestige of knowledge had to be joined with that of usefulness to family and community.

An important ideal of Hawaiian culture was perfection of presentation. The student could practice as much as necessary, but the public display had to be faultless. Teachers from other schools were invited to criticize, and competition and controversy promoted excellence. Essential to perfection was completeness of knowledge. Fishermen had to know the names of all the fish; chanters the terms for all the styles and forms. Any detail left unlearned or forgotten would be lost to the oral tradition. So students and even experts were constantly tested. Completeness demanded also a continual effort to learn. An expert tried to master as many occupations as possible, and high priests were required to be polymaths.

Hawaiian literature discusses in detail the methods of education, many of which are perpetuated in the community today. Children and students were taught first to observe the activities of their elders and teachers, rather than to ask questions. Observation was a skill to be used throughout one's life, the basis of any advance in thinking. From observation, the student moved to imitation. The students of dance imitated the movements of plants in the wind; the chanters, the sounds of the winds and the waves.

The second basic skill to be learned was listening, clearly essential in an oral culture. Listening also was a life-long skill: the chief who ignored his counselors was derided as "unhearing." Students were taught first to grasp and then to memorize what they heard and finally to retrieve it when needed.

Although some physical devices were used, the main memory aid was verbal organization. The basis of this organization was the extraordinarily large and nuanced Hawaiian vocabulary. Well over a hundred words and expressions are recorded for the colors and states of the ocean. Occupations multiplied the terms they used in order to cover the finest details of their work. This drive towards terminological completeness was connected to the Hawaiian–Polynesian view of words as really connected to their referents rather than merely arbitrary. The study of words was therefore simultaneously a study of the things they referred to. Vocabulary was also a treasure created and transmitted by the ancestors – the product of generations of observation and cogitation.

This large vocabulary needed to be organized for memorization. This was done by creating lists with titles. A body of knowledge would be divided into categories by type. Items would be chosen that fit the type and inserted into the category. For instance, fish names would be organized as lists of shore fish, reef fish, deep-sea fish, and so on. Various literary forms were developed for such lists, with the introduction of the list designating the type or attribute of the items included. The ideal of completeness dictated that a body of knowledge be covered by its lists, even if lists of a single item had to be created to accommodate singular cases. Tests were devised for completeness of knowledge and quickness of recall. Children would play round-robins with rhyming words or list every placename on a trip around an island. Moreover, items could appear on several lists if they fit their attributes. *Pig* could appear on a list of animals, of food, of offerings, of gifts, and so on. Items needed to be reorganized quickly when a new attribute was introduced. For instance, *red fish* would require making a new list from the items of the more conventional lists mentioned above. This practice of categorizing items in lists by attribute reinforced the general Polynesian tendency to emphasize similarities over differences.

The proliferation of lists necessitated their heirarchical organization. The year was divided into hot and rainy seasons; these were divided into months, the months into days, and the days into periods. Descriptions of social organization followed the hierarchy of society from the chief at the top to the tramps and slaves at the bottom. As a result of this organization, Hawaiian discourse almost always moved from the general to the particular, from categories to included items. "The big knowledge and the small knowledge" that the student conventionally requested in prayer referred respectively to the categories and to the items that filled them.

At the highest level of organization, the earlier stages were organized as pairs of opposites – the most important of which were up/down, land/sea, male/female, and night/day. These pairs are used in this way throughout Polynesia, and in fact are found worldwide. Great amounts of information could be organized under these pairs, and each had its advantages. The first two pairs were particularly handy for physical items. Male/female had many ritual uses, and night/day provided a framework for passage through time. These pairs could also be used as completeness formulas. Up/down and land/sea described the framework of the universe: "The sky above, the earth below." All things could be divided into male and female, and the night/day pair encompassed all time from the beginning of the universe in the mating of the male sky and the female earth until its full development as we know it today. This organization by pairs supported the tendency of Hawaiian thinking towards balance; the members of a pair tended to be seen as equals rather than as forming a hierarchy. The statues of male gods on one side of an altar were balanced by those of goddesses on the other side. When one chanted the wind names of the easternmost islands, one needed to add those of the westernmost.

An item was therefore understood by being placed correctly in the universe or in history. One could take any given plant and move up the hierarchy of lists until it was placed as a land plant or sea plant; the totality of the lists with their associations placed and thus defined the plant. The so-called "cosmic thinking" of Hawaiians can therefore be defined precisely: an item or problem was not handled by a Cartesian exclusion of everything "extraneous"; rather its outermost parameters were probed through its many relations with other things until it was firmly placed in its ultimate universal or historical framework. Most often that placement was genetic, as will be seen below.

Hawaiians used their intellectual devices and organization with much confidence. That is, they did not feel that ambiguous items or those that seemed to cross conceptual boundaries rendered their categories insecure. Birds flew from down to up, but could still be categorized as land birds and sea birds. Fishes that spent some stages of their lives in fresh water and others in salt water were simply categorized according to the stage they happened to be in. Some ritual uses of such items are recorded, but not that they inspired doubts. The Hawaiian conceptual scheme proved its usefulness in the many practicalities of life.

The amount of material Hawaiians memorized greatly impressed the early visitors to the islands. But for Hawaiians, memorization was only the first step. To be useful, knowledge had to be retrievable and manipulable. Tests and contests of wits displayed one's quickness of recall and reorganization. Experts would participate in contests of wits that would ring the changes on this organization of data. Genuine education trained one to apply one's knowledge to new questions and situations, to innovate, to create new categories and frameworks. Creativity was the final mark of the true expert, the graduated student, the past master. The chanter performed the works he had learned and the ones he had himself composed. The advisor applied the many models of history to the novel problems of his day. All one learned had ultimately to be tested by one's own personal observation and experience. The master of knowledge had to be the master of living.

The Hawaiian character was largely formed by education. Early visitors describe their alertness, intellectual curiosity, quickness to learn, and tenacious memory. Hawaiian literature describes their pride in their accomplishments and their cultural confidence. Throughout the nineteenth century, despite all they learned from foreigners, despite all the areas of knowledge they revised and the elements of their culture they abandoned, Hawaiians retained a pride in the intellectual achievements of their ancestors, in the grand scheme of the universe they had constructed in such detail. The great intellectual Kepelino insists that knowledge of moon phases was not brought to Hawaiʻi by the Calvinist missionary teachers, but had been a part of native wisdom for a thousand years.

Intellectual pride is in fact characteristic of Polynesians and a mark of their appreciation of their traditions. In Samoan campaigns for the position of chief, a prime argument is the extent of a candidate's cultural knowledge. Even normal Samoan conversation requires education in the conventional use of sayings, symbols, allusions, and historical references. Literary forms were invented for the explanation of obscure sayings and chants. Indeed, no Polynesian tradition exists that depreciates education or intellectual ability.

The constructive tendency noted in Hawaiʻi is characteristic of Polynesian thinking in general. In literature, individual short stories are placed into a redactional framework to construct large narrative complexes. Various genealogical branches are connected, and the history of one area will be joined to that of another. The same accumulating method is used prominently to articulate one of the main subjects of Polynesian thought: the origin of the universe.

As in much ancient thinking, identifying the origin of a thing is considered a way of understanding its nature or principle of operation. The Hawaiian proverb enjoins, "*Nānā i ke kumu*" (Look to the origin or source). Stories are told of the origins of land features, peoples, customs, and so on. Great families define themselves through their extensive genealogies, memorized, discussed, and debated by the intellectuals of the society. Genealogies thus provided the model when those intellectuals asked about the origin of the universe. The present generation was traced back through its parents, grandparents, and earlier generations to the first human beings. Similarity of form was then used to trace the lineage further back through the animals, then the plants, and finally to the elements and the framework of the whole universe: the male sky and the female earth. In great chants and narratives, the universe was shown beginning with the elements and developing through the plants and animals and first human beings into its wondrous fullness. The general similarity of this picture to that of modern science is due to their both being based on the observation of the environment. Classical Polynesians enjoyed a continuity from their most practical experiences to their most mystical.

In this grand scheme of the origin and development of the universe, all things have a family relation and resemblance, and sexuality is the power that initiates and maintains the development of the universe through time. This scheme is the foundation of most Polynesian thinking, from the idea of the closeness of human beings to the environment, to the central importance of beauty, to the sexual emphasis of art, dance, and poetry. Lyrics describing weather changes in a fruitful landscape refer simultaneously to human emotions because the very same energies animate elements, plants, and animals. The study of the universe and the study of human beings are inseparable.

The genealogical scheme could be varied and developed in many different ways. A genealogy could be two-sourced, with a male and female element, or one-sourced, like the ancient Samoan genealogy of the rocks, in which one type of rock is born from another: broad rock bears flat rock, which bears spread out rock, etc. The New Zealand Māori formulated large organizational schemes in which each area of the environment was entrusted to a special god in the genealogy. The great chant, "The Kumulipo," uses the many devices of Hawaiian poetry to develop levels of meaning. The literal level of cosmic development is paralleled by one of human stages. Each human being reproduces on a small scale the progress of the universe to completion. Further levels include the history of culture and the yearly and daily cycle. Some Polynesians pushed their thinking past earth and sky to an origin in increasingly abstract antecedents, ultimately to *leai* in Samoan and *kore* in Māori – that is, to "nothing."

A radical innovation was the introduction of the idea of creationalism: the universe or parts of it are made by a god or gods. I see the first use of this idea in what is agreed to be the most historically important Samoan chant, "*ʻO le Solo o le Vā o le Foafoaga o le Lalolagi*" (The Chant of the Time of the Origin of All that is under the Sky). The god Tangaloa is flying around in the vast spaces under the firmament – the solid, blue, rock sky – feeling fear and vertigo at the sight of the waves of the vast ocean below. He soars over unimaginable distances without finding a place to rest. Then from the deep rise the islands of Manuʻa, the first and thus the most important land, the home of the chanter and his chief. Other privileged islands appear above the waves. But two islands hostile to Manuʻa are taunted with a less dignified origin. Tangaloa takes a little pebble from the firmament, molds it, and tosses it on the water. The sharp "*i*" sounds stress the smallness of those islands' origin (in modified orthography):

Tagi i lagi sina ʻiliʻili
ʻUpolu sina fatu laʻititi
Tutuila sina maʻa lângisingisi.

(He solicits some pebble from the firmament.
The island of ʻUpolu is some little particle.
Tutuila, some miserable rock.)

On the available evidence, the use of creationalism as a cosmogonic model seems to have started as a scornful joke. But the Samoan thinkers quickly saw that this new model provided a powerful device for articulating the power of the god: the more he made, the more powerful he was. They therefore combined the earlier genealogical model with the new one: the universe started and developed genealogically up to a certain point – then Tangaloa intervened with his creative powers. His creativity was extended ever further until in a late nineteenth-century text by Tauanuʻu, the principal Orator Chief of Manuʻa, Tangaloa begins by flying around in pure space, unbounded by sky and earth; then "in the place where he took his stand, there grew the rock." He strikes and commands the rock, and a variation of the classical genealogy of the rocks begins.

Creationalism evoked mixed responses from Polynesian thinkers. Tongans appear to have taken to it timidly; Society Islanders, enthusiastically. On the evidence of the available texts, Hawaiians seem to have rejected it with nearly complete unanimity. But most thinkers combined the two models in varying degrees to create their own teachings and traditions. The two models were used also in texts on the origin of human beings. In "The Kumulipo," humans are the late children of the whole development of the universe up to the point of their emergence. This explains their family resemblance to all their older cosmic relatives. In Samoan traditions, grubs arise by spontaneous generation from rotten wood. They are then carved into a human shape and given the special kinds of spirit or soul that enable them to be human. The origin of human beings is thus described as a construction, using the components into which human nature was analyzed. But this does not entail, as some have argued, that Polynesians had no sense of the integrity, selfhood, or personality of the human individual. (Westerners have certainly analyzed humans into components without being accused of lacking a sense of self!) Accounts of human origins could also provide the rationale for the social hierarchy. Tongans had commoners emerge from grubs, but chiefs descend from sky gods.

The mainstream constructive tendency of Polynesian thinking is related to the general confidence in and admiration for the order of the universe. Human beings are positively related to their environment, and their intelligence and accumulated knowledge enable them to live successfully within it. Similarly, society is ordered, and each person finds a place within it. Intelligence, morality, and demeanor are therefore closely connected. One knows one's place and acts accordingly, in harmony with society and the environment. Rules are multiplied often down to tiny details. In Samoan, *nofo* means to sit down; *nofoi* is to sit down with a little display of haste in order to show that one is aware that one should not have been standing. Discussions of etiquette and morality are frequent in Polynesia.

For all their appreciation of order, Polynesians do recognize discord, violence, and tragedy, and can find a place for them in their universal schemes. Samoans can substitute a war model for a genealogical one: each previous stage is conquered by the succeeding one. Whereas Hawaiians emphasize the continuous mating of universal elements to perpetuate the universe, the Māori emphasize the violence of the separation of earth and sky. Where Hawaiians emphasize the fertility along the shore, the Māori see the waves warring against the land. In "The Kumulipo," the whole first lineage of human beings is annihilated in a great tidal wave:

> Dead was the current flowing from the navel of the
> earth; they were war-leaders.

They rose up as many as leaves and vanished
vanished into the darkest night.

Polynesian thinkers can also challenge the very idea of order, both playfully and seriously. For instance, a host of trickster stories pit clever youngsters or outsiders against established authorities; they win by their wits. The trickster takes on a cosmic dimension with the pan-Polynesian god Māui, who challenges the conventionally higher gods, steals fire, fishes up islands, and dies trying to find immortality by returning up the birth canal. The Hawaiian pig-god Kamapuaʿa uses his physical, rather than his mental strength to defeat the authorities. He ruts out valleys and excretes hills at their mouths. He is *lelepā*, a fence-jumper, a crosser-of-lines, and burster-of-boundaries. Such roisterers offer a peculiarly satisfying relief within such a highly organized society and universe.

In Hawaiʿi, the constructive tendency was challenged by the followers of the volcano goddess Pele, whose destructiveness they relished. In their experience, the rain forest could without warning explode from the ground up. The most sacred temples could be overrun by molten lava. The grand cosmic constructions of the court intellectuals appeared pathetically flimsy when viewed from the volcano. If the rock stratum of the earth could liquefy, then the sky could crack and fall. The Pele worshippers saw beauty in her awful power, and they connected it to a particular type of womanly appeal. In one version, Pele tells her sister Hiʿiaka, "Death is by you, by the woman; there is no death by men." This emphasis on the power of women was as disruptive to Hawaiian society as the emphasis on disorder was to conventional cosmic speculation.

Pele's destructiveness divided her worshippers on the question of morality. If she overran someone's house with lava, was she acting morally, immorally, or amorally? Stories were told of people being punished for refusing hospitality to a disgusting old woman, who was in fact Pele. She was said to send her pet dog to warn her devotees of an eruption. But not all cases could be so explained, and for many Pele worshippers, "Pele stays wild," the one god the court priests could not handle and the Christian missionaries could not destroy. Her very disorderliness enabled her to survive the cultural chaos of the contact period, while the traditional order was shaken to its foundations and fell. But if Pele is not moral, then terrible things happen by chance or whim – a view most traditional Hawaiians find emotionally untenable.

Polynesians were clearly not united in their views, and their consciousness of that fact is an essential characteristic of their thinking. In the words of the Hawaiian proverb, "*ʿAʿole i pau ka ʿike i kāu hālau*" (All knowledge is not exhausted in your hall of learning). Dealing with the multiplicity of traditions was in fact a major problem for Polynesian intellectuals. Because of their training in verbal skills and rhetorical devices, their solutions appear at times surprisingly modern. For instance, David Malo wrote in the 1840s that Hawaiians had three opinions about the origin of land: it simply grew out of the sea, it was born from a goddess, or it was made by a god. Western scholars would require another forty years or more to recognize the use of these divergent models in Polynesian thinking.

Historical traditions were a prime example of diversity for Polynesians. Samoans and Hawaiians developed generally similar methods of dealing with the problem. First, the expert had to be knowledgeable in all the different traditions of a subject and display that knowledge in his presentation. He would begin, therefore, by describing or alluding to each of the traditions, which established his authority. He would then evaluate the traditions according to generally accepted criteria. For instance, Samoan intellectuals would use philological knowledge to test the authenticity of a chant offered as evidence. Were the vocabulary and diction appropriate for a chant of the antiquity claimed? Doubtful sources could be checked against accepted ones. Was the genealogy recited consonant with those acknowledged by the community of experts?

All of these discussions are based on the oral tradition, in which memorized works are used much as Western historians use written documents. Polynesian historical experts therefore devised a hierarchy of security. Most reliable were oral traditions that were both memorized and regularly contested. Genealogies and *māvaega*, in Samoan, or *kauoha*, in Hawaiian (last wills and testaments), were not only memorized in set literary forms, but were often questioned and contested until a consensus was established. That consensus could then be used as a basis for judging later disputes. Less secure were works that were memorized, but not normally contested, like chants. Least secure was prose narrative, which was not completely memorized, but was formulated to some degree by the teller. Polynesians also recognized works that were entirely fictional.

The Polynesian method of handling differing traditions was useful when confronting foreign teachings. They could simply be added to the list of "schools of thought." After listing the three models Hawaiians used to describe the origin of islands, Malo quotes the missionary schoolbooks to provide the foreign opinion on the subject. Polynesian methods of incorporating disparate traditions into complexes could be applied easily to new introductions. Tahitians and Hawaiians held long discussions on their genealogies. A twentieth-century Samoan incorporated monkeys into a genealogical description of the development of the universe. But as traditions accumulated, they became more difficult to accommodate.

This problem seems to have been felt most acutely by the intellectuals of the Society Islands, whose texts are combinations of an unusually large number of contradictory traditions. In fact, the authors begin to complain about how wearisome, indeed impossible, it is to unite all these accumulating materials into a convincing narrative. The thinkers have therefore been forced to create new, non-narrative means, an effort that resembles the movement of the Pre-Socratics away from myth. One redactor abstracts from the traditions a set of principles of operation that he sees at work through all the narrative variations: the nullity before the first generative and creative actions, the attraction of elements to each other, the lack of fixity of the uncompleted universe, the endurance of the cosmos, and so on. These principles are designated by words found in the traditions, but not so regularly that they could be considered recognized technical terms. A second redactor encapsulates a number of theological and narrative traditions into epithets, which he then applies to Taʿaroa, the Society Island cognate of Tangaloa. "Taʿaroa of the effective word" recalls narratives of his creating by his commands; "Taʿaroa who stood over the passage of the reef" evokes a story told elsewhere in full. In this way, the multitude of traditions is provided with a point of unity: the manifold person of the god.

These two solutions – impersonal and personal – indicate one of the most difficult problems in Polynesian thought. Secondary sources and some modern islanders often describe Polynesian thinking as entirely personalistic. But classical sources indicate that Polynesians recognized impersonal forces as well. Sky and earth could be personified, but Polynesians believed also that inanimate objects were sexual. The mating of sky and earth could therefore be considered the joining of impersonal, cosmic elements. Accordingly, Polynesian gods had distinct limits to their powers. They operated within an impersonal cosmic framework, although that framework was not articulated as explicitly as the *moira* of the classical Greeks. Other elements – such as winds, tides, rivers, and fire – could be treated as personal by some thinkers and impersonal by others. Each text must therefore be interpreted on its own terms. The problem of the relation of personality to impersonality arose in other areas as well. Words, prayers, and curses became impersonal forces once uttered, capable even of turning against the person who had spoken them. A law could be connected to a chief, but had its own power somehow independent of him. The difficulty involved in clarifying the relation between the personal and the impersonal is clear in secondary discussions of the word *mana*, generally defined as power. The word can be applied to persons and things, and the essential connection of *mana* to its holder is variously defined. No description has been generally accepted, and the subject needs to be studied on the basis of an adequate number of texts.

To understand the post-contact history of Polynesia, it is important to realize that Western culture and education were not introduced into a vacuum. Many of the mental characteristics visitors noted in Polynesians were the results of their classical culture. Indeed, their classical intellectual ideals led them actively to seek the new knowledge the foreigners were bringing with them. Polynesians had been interested in other islands within their own areas; now they could learn about continents they had never imagined. In traditional Polynesian fashion, they bombarded visitors with questions about their homelands. Great numbers of young men signed up as crew members in order to see the world. Polynesians could use their trained powers of observation and imitation to learn introduced manual skills, even when the foreigners wanted to monopolize them. Wherever and whenever regular schools were established, Polynesians flocked to them. When foreigners reduced their languages to writing, Polynesians used the new medium enthusiastically for their own purposes, recording the memorized works of the oral tradition, coordinating larger numbers of genealogies, and so on. Foreigners were astonished at how quickly and well Polynesians mastered elements of the introduced culture.

The new knowledge was, of course, vitally important for Polynesians – for its own intrinsic interest and for its practical value in their critical situation. Faced with the intrusive foreigners, Polynesians had to develop a new worldview and new political and economic skills. Polynesians were to follow a curve of response found in other non-Western developing nations. At first, Western culture elicited an enthusiastic response, especially from the brightest members of the younger generation. Foreign knowledge and ways were adopted, and traditional ones depreciated. However, as Polynesians became more familiar with Western culture, they criticized it more and became more appreciative of their old ways, even though they were now more distant from them. Modern navigation was accurate, but the first Polynesians had reached the islands without it. Written historical documents were valuable, but memorized ones had indeed perpetuated the names of the places visited before the migration voyage. Polynesian intellectuals began to use the new means at their disposal to research, record, and disseminate information about their own history and culture. They founded societies, corresponded, and published native-language books and newspapers. Their reflection on their history and contemporary situation was naturally a combination of traditional and introduced ideas and procedures.

This response to Western culture is illustrated by the careers of two of the most important nineteenth-century Hawaiian intellectuals. David Malo (1795–1853) received a thorough classical Hawaiian education and was employed as a court intellectual. As such, he was sent to the Christian missionaries in the early 1820s to obtain Western learning and to help them with their Bible translations and Hawaiian-language school books. He entered the first class at Lahainaluna high school in 1831 and became a teacher and, in 1841, Superintendent of Schools. Active in politics, he became increasingly anxious about the growing power of foreigners in government, and supported movements that offended his chiefly patrons. He devoted his writing increasingly to Hawaiian history and culture, presenting his information in the oral literary forms in which he had received it and arguing for the intrinsic value of native traditions. His works were used as a foundation by most of the later Hawaiian writers.

The most prolific of these was Samuel Mānaiakalani Kamakau (1815–1876), a schoolmate of Malo. Descended from priestly intellectuals who converted to Christianity, he added Western learning to his family traditions, pioneering in the development of a modern Hawaiian historiography. His career in government and politics was unsuccessful, and he converted to Roman Catholicism and concentrated on his research. In his writings, he continually contrasted Hawaiian culture favorably to Western and attempted to provide frameworks within which Hawaiians could understand their current situation. The different frameworks he proposed throughout his life varied in emphasis between religion and history.

In this quest, Kamakau was following classical Polynesian practice. He and other Polynesians were seeking to place themselves within the expanded view of the universe and history provided by the new knowledge. Most immediately, Polynesians could now investigate a subject for which their own historical traditions had prepared them: their relations to their Polynesian cousins. All through the early contact period, Polynesians were visiting each other, comparing traditions, and reporting home. They were quickly impressed – as Western academics were later – by their many similarities of language, literature, practices, and traditions. Hawaiian and Tahitian genealogists debated at the court of Kamehameha I. A small colony of Hawaiians living in Tahiti may have introduced the worship of the volcano goddess Pele. The results of this period of intra-Polynesian contact are now difficult to disentangle. But the intellectual and emotional impact is clear. Hawaiians felt their historical traditions were vindicated when Tahitians confirmed names and sequences of names in their genealogies and identified the places listed in ancient chants. Māori felt their legendary homeland, Hawaiki, had been rediscovered in Hawaiʻi. The nineteenth-century Māori intellectual, Wiremu Maihi Te Rangikaheke, was once introduced to a young Hawaiian sailor on shore leave in Auckland and bombarded him with questions. Were the Māori traditions correct about the first war in Hawaiki? Had he heard about this or that legendary figure? The sailor was embarrassed by his youthful ignorance, but promised Te Rangikaheke to refer any written questions to his grandfather in Hawaiʻi. Te Rangikaheke wrote through the night in great excitement. The next day the sailor appeared with the few presents he had managed to scrounge – a coin, a little tobacco. Deeply moved, the Māori wrote that Hawaiians shared not only the same traditions, but the same emotions as well.

Polynesians enlarged their focus also to the wider world and the foreign view of the universe. Teachers reported everywhere the popularity of geography. The islands appeared small on the new maps, but they had their place. Contemporary scientific and religious views of the origin of land and the universe were discussed avidly, and conclusions were drawn. Do you think all these foreigners descend from the god Wākea? polemicized David Malo. If not, he is no true god, and Hawaiians should turn to Jehovah.

Where then did the Polynesians come from? The question had intrigued foreigners as well, and a large number of theories were formulated through the nineteenth century. The basic question was how Polynesians were to be connected to world history: were they originally Chaldaeans, Egyptians, Indians, or a lost tribe of Israel?

For obvious reasons, most Polynesians, a number of Christian missionaries, and Mormons, preferred the last idea. Polynesian cultures could then be considered developments of Israelite culture, and Polynesian religions could be connected to the Bible. Comparisons were made between Biblical and Polynesian practices, which thus acquired legitimacy and could claim respect. Polynesian religions were reformulated to clarify their Biblical roots. The "four great gods of Polynesia" could be described as a quaternity or as a trinity if one were relegated to the role of devil. Biblical and Polynesian traditions could be viewed as separate but equal developments from an even older tradition. The Hawaiian Kumuhonua legends sought to reconstruct that tradition in newly composed narratives and chants. "Hawaiian religion may be a degeneration of Mormonism," one Hawaiian told me, "but on the other hand, we may have preserved some old traditions that regular Mormons have lost!" Reformulations of Polynesian traditions could rival Christian dogma in content and breadth. Some Māori intellectuals composed grandiose texts on the origin of the universe, in which a highly detailed organization was crowned with a supreme deity, the god Io, claimed to be the subject of a hitherto secret tradition.

Polynesian thinkers also contributed to the theology of the mainline Christian churches. Hawaiians recognized the Christian God as the creator of the universe and believed, as the Bible taught, that the universe proclaimed his Glory. Therefore, by studying the universe, they studied God, and all the long tradition of their love and appreciation of the environment could be brought into Christianity. The Hawaiian historian, Samuel M. Kamakau, used this insight in 1870 to justify Hawaiian medicine. He argued that God had given to all peoples what they needed for their well-being. So God made the earth and thus all the potential medicines in it. Correct knowledge of the earth and its elements enabled people to practice correct medicine. The correctness of Hawaiian medicine was proved by its results. Therefore, the medical knowledge of the Hawaiians was ultimately given by God.

In all of these efforts can be recognized the Polynesian tendency to accommodate the new without abandoning the old. The results can be simply syncretic: a Tongan child pictured Jesus and Tangaloa sitting together in heaven. Even nativistic thinkers were influenced, however unconsciously, by the new thought world. Nevertheless, the energy is remarkable with which the classical intellectual discussions were maintained. Masters of compartmentalization, Samoan intellectuals sermonized on Sundays and interpreted the ancient Tangaloa chants during the week.

Significantly, at no time and in few individuals if any, did the introduced culture gain complete dominance over the old. Polynesians have remained characteristically Polynesian in many aspects of their life and thinking – even if at times against their will. This endurance is a large part of the problem of identity that arose the moment the foreigners arrived and continues into the present day. Only too often, foreigners, prominently missionaries, depreciated the native cultures and thereby wounded the morale of the Polynesians. The movement to study and re-evaluate Polynesian culture has therefore been ultimately a movement to reformulate Polynesian identity.

This has been particularly true in island groups that have experienced much discontinuity since the contact period. Samoans and Tongans have generally been able to perpetuate their sense of identity almost as a matter of course along with much of their culture. Hawaiians and Māori have had to reflect much more intensely on their situation. In such places, the study of indigenous history and the perpetuation of native medicine, crafts, and the arts, have been, almost from the beginning, an affirmation of the intrinsic value of the native culture and thus the native character.

This affirmation has taken several other forms as well. Native cultures have been defended against the all too frequent foreign misunderstandings and misrepresentations. Native cultures have been compared favorably to foreign on such points as family solidarity, hospitality, and piety. Character defects have often been ascribed to the problems of post-contact adjustment and bad foreign influences. Nineteenth-century Polynesians were, however, too close to their classical culture to idealize it. Their own historical methods enjoined the use of negative as well as positive models.

Perhaps the greatest stylist among the nineteenth-century Hawaiian thinkers, Kepelino Kahoali'i Keauokalani (ca. 1830–1878) embodied the internal friction caused by his experience of the clash of cultures. Born into a family of priestly experts, he was educated by Roman Catholic missionaries to be a teacher, learning English, French, Latin, and Greek. Describing Hawaiian culture, he contrasts constantly the Hawaiians' admiration for their achievements with the foreigners' denigration of the same: what is beauty for the Hawaiians is sinfulness for the missionaries. Kepelino cannot stop loving the culture his new faith condemns, and he cannot resolve the tension. He can only articulate his pain with tragic intensity in lapidary affirmations of Hawaiian values and descriptions of Hawaiian character:

> *A 'o ka loina nui o na 'lii Hawaii nei, 'o ka ha'aha'a 'o ka oluolu, ke aloha a me ka lokomaika'i.*
> (The great law of the chiefs of our Hawaii was lowliness, amenity, welcoming affection, and inner goodness.)

These were the qualities with which Polynesians had welcomed foreigners to their shores, which had induced Polynesians to open their minds to new influences, and had readied them to solve the problems of culture contact and to create the new and beautiful cultures they perpetuate today.

Bibliography

Beckwith, Martha 1972: *The Kumulipo: A Hawaiian Creation Chant* (Honolulu: University of Hawaii Press).

Charlot, John 1983: *Chanting the Universe: Hawaiian Religious Culture* (Honolulu and Hong Kong: Emphasis International).

Henry, Teuira 1928: *Ancient Tahiti* (Honolulu: Bernice Pauahi Bishop Museum).

Krämer, Augustin 1994: *The Samoan Islands: An Outline of a Monograph with Particular Consideration of German Samoa*, Vol. 1: *Constitution, Pedigrees, and Traditions* (Honolulu: University of Hawaii Press).

Luomala, Katharine 1955: *Voices on the Wind: Polynesian Myths and Chants* (Honolulu: Bishop Museum Press).

Orbell, Margaret 1985: *Hawaiki: a New Approach to Maori Tradition* (Christchurch: University of Canterbury).

4

African philosophy: a historical overview

D. A. MASOLO

Introduction

African philosophy: the philosophy of Africa, the historical roots of which are purported by some scholars to be found in the pre-colonial indigenous cultures of African societies, which, according to this view, contained subtle philosophical elements within their respective worldviews. Because it claims that African philosophy is closely interwoven with the practical and verbalized cultural idioms through which it is expressed, this view of African philosophy, launched by the Belgian missionary Placide Tempels in 1944, has come to be designated as *ethnophilosophy*. Used critically and negatively, as in the earlier work of Paulin Hountondji, the term "ethnophilosophy" refers to the ethnographic and non-philosophical methods used by the ethnophilosophers, mainly disciples of Tempels, to recover from African cultural texts propositional beliefs and ideas that they purport to be philosophical. Used positively, however, ethnophilosophy could be understood as a branch of the more general ethnomethodology which is a phenomenological approach to interpreting everyday cultural expressions as a guide to philosophical research into, and interpretation of, socio-cultural contexts of participants' practices and speech.

According to another school, African philosophy consists of the work and thought of African philosophers in a more strictly academic context. In this sense, the practice of African philosophy is a much more recent development occasioned by a variety of factors. Its origin in the post-World War II period coincides with the beginning of access to university and college education by a greater number of African people. In a related way, its more visible and secularized occurrence in the post-independence period not only reaffirms the first factor; it also signals liberalization and diversification of education both for Africans, and generally in African institutions, in the post-colonial period. It is in this period that one observes the concurrence of the establishment of academic departments of philosophy in African universities, and the beginning of a distinctively critical phase in the practice of the discipline by the emergent, secularly trained African philosophers. In his now famous paper, "Four Trends in Current African Philosophy" (1981), the well known Kenyan philosopher Henry Odera Oruka (1944–1995) referred to this current in African philosophy as a "professional (critical) trend." He saw it as the antithesis of the "ethnophilosophy trend," and included within this current the works of St Augustine as well as the now widely discussed eighteenth-century works of Anton Wilhelm Amo and Jacobus Captein. His ordering of the African philosophy debate into trends resembles an earlier one by Alphonse J. Smet (1980), the well known Belgian historian of African philosophy at the Kinshasa school. The explanatory (historical and thematic) structures of both remain widely used today by scholars in their respective europhonic fields.

The other two "trends" identified by Oruka, and earlier by Smet, are the "nationalistic–ideological trend" and the "philosophic sagacity trend." The former consists of the political ideas and expressions, mostly of African leaders such as Kwame Nkrumah, Léopold Senghor, Julius Nyerere, or Kenneth Kaunda, aimed at defining and reorganizing African societies politically and economically in opposition to colonial and neo-colonial ideologies of modern imperialism. The latter trend, an original invention of Oruka himself, is a variant of ethnophilosophy but differs from its core in claiming that contrary to ethnophilosophers' collectivist view, "there exist in Africa critical and independent thinkers who guide their thoughts and judgments by the power of reason and inborn insight rather than by authority of communal consensus" (Bodunrin, 1981, p. 162).

Oruka's distinction between ordinary sages and philosophic sages redraws the divide between ethnophilosophy and what is variously referred to as critical or professional or academic philosophy. Ethnophilosophy can be said to be philosophical only in the generic sense in which people's beliefs and behaviour, individual or collective, are based on some more general and grounding premises or statements of opinion – such as "there are gender divisions of labor because the genders are created different." This, in Oruka's view, can be termed "culture philosophy" or the "philosophy of a specific culture," in which such a generally held belief can be seen as informative of how different gender-related issues are defined and handled at the cultural level. Ordinary sages are the cultural teachers of such basic cultural principles, which constitute the edifying "bricks" of every cultural *Weltanschauung*. In Oruka's view, there is no problem speaking about this kind of philosophy in everyday life so long as it is borne in mind that, as philosophy, it exists on the same level as, for example, "the business philosophy of AT&T," "the philosophy of the Japanese export industry," or "the philosophy or mission statement of a college."

He believed that philosophic sages, on the other hand, belong to the category of philosophy in the stricter sense, because their ideas, like most of what are recognized as philosophical works and ideas in this second (order) sense, are essentially critical, explicit and autocritical discourses on a variety of topics. Since his pioneer work in this direction, interviews and dialogues with sages have been increasingly employed as a promising way of engaging in philosophically critical analysis and commentary on indigenously produced knowledge. Hallen and Sodipo (1986) and Appiah (1992) are good examples. This is despite the controversy which Oruka's notion of philosophic sagacity provokes regarding the relation between literacy and philosophy as a practice of critical inquiry. While drawing on Socrates as a parallel, Oruka's defence of orality within a philosophical context adds a fresh perspective to the problem which takes a central place in Jack Goody's works (1968, 1977, and 1987).

The precursory schools

Given the above distinctions, the dating of African philosophy might depend on how the discipline and the identity of its practitioners are defined. The idea of ethnophilosophy in the first sense suggests that African philosophy is far older than its more recent and explicit discursive history. In other words, Africans' involvement with philosophy, particularly in the Western tradition, long predates the beginning of what is now recognized as the formally organized and sustained academic practice of philosophy in Africa and by Africans.

Related to this further regressive dating are two other but unconnected historical facts. First, that schools of philosophy have flourished in various parts of Africa at diverse times for several centuries, mainly in association with the spread of Christianity and Islam to the continent. The first of these is associated with the fourth-century Carthaginian school where St Augustine received his formal education. But because his philosophical and theological work has been closely associated with the doctrines of Western Christianity, few people remember or even notice that St Augustine was a native of Northern Africa. Hence both he and his work are generally treated as part of the history of mainstream Western thought. Today, much of Northern African cultural expression, including its intellectual traditions, is considered to be part of the wider Islamic world of the Middle East. Despite the existence of continent-wide philosophical associations, few texts, other than those seeking to make linkages with ancient African history, incorporate the work of philosophers from this northern region. Often, in the search for this linkage, focus is shifted to the Alexandrian school in Egypt, which is claimed to be not only the oldest school, but also a springboard of ancient Greek thought in philosophy and mathematics. This current finds its anchorage in the work of the Senegalese historian Cheikh Anta Diop (1954, 1960, 1967), and more recently in that of Martin Bernal (1987, 1991).

The next known schools, although considerably less well documented, are often associated with the southward spread of Islam across the Sahara, particularly at Timbuktu, Jenne, and Gao, all in the fifteenth-century empire of Songhai (today's Mali). The works of these schools were closely related to Islamic studies and were preserved in Arabic.

Another distinctive school flourished in seventeenth-century Abyssinia (today's Ethiopia) with texts which span the period between the mid-sixteenth century and the seventeenth century. These texts have been reorganized and reproduced, in a six-volume set of *Ethiopian Philosophy* with new editorial commentaries, by Claude Sumner, a Canadian Jesuit scholar working at the University of Addis Ababa. The volumes comprise *The Book of the Wise Philosophers* (Vol. I, 1974), *The Treatise of Zär'a Yaqob and of Wäldä Heywåt: Text and Authorship* (Vol. II, 1974), *The Treatise of Zär'a Yaqob and of Wäldä Heywåt: An Analysis* (Vol. III, 1978), *The Life and Maxims of Skendes* (Vol. IV, 1981), *The Fisalgwos* (Vol. V, 1982), *The Basic Texts* (Vol. VI, 1984), and several accompanying special analyses and commentaries. Of these, Volume IV is an Ethiopic version of the ancient (second century) text of Secundus of Athens. The *Hatata* (treatises) of the main protagonists of this school, Zär'a Yaqob and Wäldä Heywåt, have been preserved, translated, and relatively widely commented upon. Like most texts of their time, or of the Roman and Arabic traditions with which they became associated through encounters made possible by the cosmopolitanism of the ancient kingdom of Aksum, these texts focus strongly on moral teachings. In their endeavor to establish maxims of moral character, they often raise questions regarding the relationship between individual will and outward personal or collective character; or the relationship between private qualities and public social conduct.

Sumner has conclusively established that these texts are originally Ethiopian; that even the ones translated from their Arabic versions clearly indicate original adaptations to the local system. In this sense, the translated texts in this collection differ significantly from their Greek and Arabic counterparts. Sumner's efforts have helped to bring these older Ethiopian texts into the currency of contemporary African philosophical debate.

Finally, since Paulin Hountondji's *African Philosophy: Myth and Reality* (1983), much interest has been directed toward the work of Anton Wilhelm Amo, an eighteenth-century Ghanaian philosopher, taken in his youth from his native home (possibly by German missionaries) to Prussia, where he studied philosophy at the University of Jena. Later he taught and wrote philosophy at Halle, before returning to Ghana in his middle age. According to Hountondji, the works of Amo included such titles as *De Humana Mentis Apatheia* (1734) and *Tractatus de Arte Sobrie et Accurate Philosophandi* (1738).

Recent episodes: ethnophilosophy

Taken separately, each of the above-mentioned currents and schools contributes differently to one or another way of defining the historiography of African philosophy. The most recent history of African philosophy is, however, less contested and goes back about half a century. It depicts both the academic and the political reconstructions in the aftermath of colonialism and appears in stages: preoccupied at first with questions about its own possibility and methodology before moving in the last two decades or so toward more thematically oriented analyses.

Despite being the main target of varying critiques in this reconstructive undertaking, Western traditions and modes of thought, passed on through colonial and missionary-controlled education systems, have been particularly influential not just in shaping the content of this recent African philosophy, but also in determining its diverse approaches, thus reproducing in the landscape of African academic philosophy several of the diverse schools characterizing Western philosophical practice. In this sense, schools of African philosophy replicate the Anglo-American and continental dichotomies both academically and politically by following the same political boundaries drawn at the end of the nineteenth century by colonial powers. The analytic school confines itself rather visibly to the institutions of former British colonies, with the phenomenological/hermeneutic school(s) predominantly located in the academic institutions of countries formerly under continental European powers – that is, under either French, Belgian, or Italian colonial domination.

However, the missionary impact has been responsible for a certain imperfection in this distribution, by implanting the ecclesiastical framework across the colonial boundaries. The result has been the co-existence of diverse intellectual perspectives and approaches. Mudimbe and Appiah (1993) have attributed this co-existence, at least partly, to the accommodative attitude in African social order, for which diversity does not necessarily imply or lead to rupturous conflict.

As they put it, in traditional African societies, accommodating conflicting theoretical views is part of the general process of accommodation necessary for those who are bound to each other as neighbours for life. And this accommodating approach to daily interactions is part of the same range of attitudes that leads to theoretical accommodations. The universe is a complex of microcosmic systems which are themselves accommodated within larger cosmic orders in an ascending manner to the macrocosmic all-engulfing. In these senses, African philosophy, although cut along the inherited lines that divide the continental and Anglo-American traditions in Western philosophy, exhibits a fascinating mutual dialogical accommodation of its parts and groupings. As in real life situations as well as the cosmic order, the parts complement and depend upon each other. This, they argue, is something the rest of the world could learn from.

The strictly academic context of African philosophy started with the publication in 1945 of Placide Tempels's *La philosophie bantoue*, itself a translation from the Dutch original published the year before. The reception of Tempels's work and of its basic tenets is decisive for understanding the characteristics of academic African philosophy over the past half century. Considered a landmark within the context of the anthropological and missionary literature and attitudes in which it was produced, Tempels's work was first embraced by the early school of trained African philosophers and theologians as important for understanding the conceptual significance of Africans' worldviews and their application to the definitions and organizations of everyday experience.

According to Tempels, then, Bantu philosophy is based on very simple principles universal to basic human conditions. First, for the Bantu, as for all cultures, life and death determine human behavior. Second, if the Bantu are human beings, there is reason to seek the fundamentals of their beliefs and behavior or their basic philosophical system, since "All human behavior depends upon a system of principles." Despite the simplicity of these principles, Tempels considered his "discovery" of Bantu philosophy a milestone in African anthropology. It was the result of a complex intellectual transformation which he feared would seriously disconcert his European readers. "This 'discovery' of Bantu philosophy," he wrote, "is so disconcerting a revelation that we are tempted at first sight to believe that we are looking at a mirage. In fact, the universally accepted picture of primitive man, of the savage, of the proto-man living before the full blossoming of intelligence, vanishes beyond hope of recovery before this testimony" (1959, pp. 167–8).

In general, Tempels's text provided the occasion for the critique of the monolithic colonial framework and suggested its replacement with pluralism. His claim that African cultural perspectives were significantly different from Western perspectives precisely because they were logical derivations from (nonetheless *rationally* unacceptable) metaphysical, moral, and psychological tenets radically different from those defined through the long history of Western intellectual traditions was indeed for some a welcome pronouncement. In 1948 Marcel Griaule, a French ethnologist and philosopher, published the famous *Dieu d'Eau* (English translation *Conversations with Ogotemmêli*, 1965), a remarkable contribution to the field of ethnophilosophy opened by Tempels. According to Germaine Dieterlen, another prominent member of Griaule's ethnographic expedition team (in Griaule, 1965, pp. xiii–xiv),

> It became clear in the course of this work that African peoples had, like others, reflected on their own customs, that these customs stemmed from norms which were proper to themselves but which were nevertheless fundamental standards which it was indispensable for the ethnographer to understand. . . . Thus for example African techniques, so poor in appearance, like those of agriculture, weaving and smithing, have a rich, hidden content of significance. Religious gestures, whether spectacular or secret, and generally uncomprehended by outsiders, show themselves under analysis to be of an extreme subtlety in their implications. The smallest everyday object may reveal in its form or decoration a conscious reflection of a complex cosmogony.

Although this "philosophy" could be narrated by individual cultural experts, it was a collective property, most of the time unspoken, but nonetheless preserved by means of a meticulous oral system of signification.

While there is no evidence that Tempels's idea of a Bantu philosophy was in the second order sense described above, several of his early followers, who were mainly from the neophyte African Christian clergy, interpreted his work in that sense. In particular, they were concerned with providing, in a precise framework, the philosophy of a pagan culture ready for fusion with Christian theology. This catechetical approach provided both a critical response to Tempels' interpretation of Bantu philosophy and the metaphysical categories for the reinterpretation of African cultures and their integration with Christianity. Thus we have, for example, Kagame's *La philosophie bantu-rwandaise de l'être* (1956); Vincent Mulago's *L'Union vitale bantu chez les Bashi, les Banyarwanda, et les Barundi face à l'unité vitale ecclésiale* (1955), *Un visage africaine du christianisme* (1965), and *La religion traditionelle des bantu et leur vision du monde* (1973); A. Makarakiza's *La dialectique des Barundi* (1959); François-Marie Lufuluabo's *Vers une Théodicée Bantoue* (1962a), *La notion Luba-bantoue de l'être* (1962b), *Perspective théologique bantoue et théologie scholastique* (1966); Jean Calvin Bahoken's *Clairières métaphysiques africaines* (1967); Basil Fouda's *La philosophie africaine de l'existence* (1967); and John S. Mbiti's *African Religions and Philosophy* (1969) and *New Testament Eschatology in an African Background* (1971).

This literature revealed an excellent acquaintance with and use of Aristotelian metaphysics appropriated via its neo-Thomistic reinterpretations. Yet it also manifested at the same time the paradox of its general goal, which was to free the essence of Christian teaching of its European philosophical vestiges, claiming of it the fluidity which befits the saying that *quid quid recipitur, ad modum recipientis recipitur*. As Kagame put it, one of the aims of the literature was to demonstrate the relationship between the universality of content and the pluralism of form in philosophical discourse. The widespread post-World War II appeal of certain philosophical movements in Europe such as Marxism and existentialism made it possible for ethnophilosophers to find this form in the implicit tenets in myths, religious idioms, the structure of ordinary language, and social–moral order.

Recent episodes: discontent with ethnophilosophy

Others did not see Tempels's work in the same light. They saw it as just another colonial text that relegates African systems of thought to an inferior status compared to Western modes of thought generally, and to Western philosophy particularly. This political critique, spearheaded especially by the Martinican poet and writer Aimé Césaire, saw in Tempels's work and in the ethnophilosophical project generally a wider and Manichean political discourse, including that of Senghor's negritude, which viewed Western/non-Western differences as translatable into canonical/non-canonical oppositions. According to Césaire, Tempels deliberately presented African philosophy as built on non-genuine predicates which articulated lack of empirical knowledge. Other critics along these lines included Marcien Towa and Fabien Eboussi-Boulaga.

Another phase of the critique of ethnophilosophy, this time focusing on methodology, was launched by Franz Crahay's "Le Décollage conceptuel: conditions d'une philosophie bantoue" in 1965. This was followed, in 1970, by Hountondji's "Remarques sur la philosophie africaine contemporaine." In his famous article, Crahay criticizes Tempels of confusing the "lived" (*vécu*) experiences with "reflective" thought which privileges philosophy as a specific genre of discourse on and about experience. This discourse, he argued, has precise characteristics: it "is explicit, analytical, radically critical and autocritical, systematic at least in principle and nevertheless open, bearing on experience, its human conditions, meanings as well as the values that it reveals." Could one, so far, talk of the existence of a Bantu philosophy which satisfies these characteristics? Crahay answers this question in the negative. According to him, what Tempels called "Bantu philosophy" was only a sad misconstruance of the term "*philosophie*," and a gross confusion of its vulgar and strict senses.

> Negatively, we shall say that there is no implicit philosophy; that there is no irrational philosophy; that there is no naive nor [discursively] unmediated philosophy; that philosophical language is not the language of experience, but a language on experience or on the language of experience. We add [apparently referring to the existentialist positions of the time, which could have included a reference to the famous "*Témoignages*" of leading French and French-speaking intellectuals published by *Présence Africaine* in 1949] that the contemporary counterexamples are only apparent, [and] that they are not a case of rhapsodic philosophy constituted of unconnected pieces devoid of any internal [systematic] coherence. (Crahay, 1965, p. 64)

He then proceeded to define the "conditions" for the possible emergence of a true and thought-provoking Bantu philosophical thought. He lists them (1965, pp. 69–83) as: (1) the existence of a body of African philosophers living and working in an intellectually stimulating cultural milieu open to the world; (2) the practice of open discourse that allows the critical use of the tools of analysis, interpretation (*leviers*) and influences that build into "schools" of discipleships (*réflecteurs*); (3) an inventory of African values of knowledge such as attitudes, original linguistic resources, certain categories of thought and such symbols as will provoke thinking; (4) the existence and practice of a second-order discourse (*décollage conceptuel*) which is built on, yet different from, experience as it is lived, a transition to reflection through the dissociation of subject from his object of discourse; (5) the interrogation of even the kind of intellectual choices that seem so relevant and useful, as would promote an African contribution to a global discourse even while expressing the relevance of such theories to the specific African context.

Hountondji's *African Philosophy: Myth and Reality* (1983), a revised and abridged translation of the French original *Sur la "philosophie africaine": Critique de l'ethnophilosophie* (1977) is, as the French subtitle announces, perhaps the best known critique of the movement initiated by Tempels. Coming from the perspective of Althusserian neo-Marxism, Hountondji saw the ahistorical petrification of thought in ethnophilosophy as the negation of the historical subjectivity from which philosophy emerges as a form of free and creative engagement with socio-historical conditions. To Hountondji, philosophy is a discursive interpretation of texts which are themselves philosophical. Ethnophilosophy, on the contrary, is whimsical recovery, translation, and interpretation of assumed but non-existent cultural texts. Because it is based on non-existent texts, ethnophilosophy is only imaginary and as such cannot attain any truth as it treats of no positive subject matter. At the same time, ethnophilosophers also abdicate the responsibility and freedom that is both required and typical of proper philosophical thought by claiming to merely recover the fictitious *déjà là*.

Hountondji's critique was equally directed at both Crahay and the writers of the "*Témoignages*." Of the latter, he said it was regrettable that they chose to acclaim ethnophilosophy only because it was non-Western and even though it was evidently incongruent with the criteria of their own practice. Of Crahay, he critiqued the idea of a conceptual *décollage*, which was demanded by Crahay as a condition for a Bantu philosophy. To Hountondji, this demand was not useful as all civilizations are based on an already accomplished conceptual *décollage*. What was more useful, in his view, was the issue of destination or audience of ethnophilosophy. To create its own philosophical possibility and history, every discourse must develop a language that grounds itself in its own social environment – something that ethnophilosophy did not try to do as its target audience remained Western, thus disabling the emergence of a local philosophical discourse. Hountondji's view of philosophy, and particularly his description of the African philosopher as "a human being among human beings, an intellectual among his colleagues and a member of a given social class" (Hountondji, 1977, p. 70) has come under attack as élitist, an accusation he has strongly denied, contending that such criticisms are *ad hominem* (see Hountondji, 1989).

In Anglophone Africa, the predominantly analytic approach to philosophy is distinguished by a concentration on conceptual analyses. But even in these spheres of British political and intellectual influence, there continues to be some accommodation of the hermeneutic approaches, especially where the issue of discussion is related to ethnophilosophy's concern with the existence and discursive location of African philosophy. Theophilus Okere's (1971) is a good example of this hermeneutical approach.

The best examples of the analytic approach in African philosophy come from the Ghanaian school. The best known of these examples are the works of Kwasi Wiredu and Kwame Anthony Appiah, both British-trained Ghanaian philosophers currently teaching in the United States. But the tradition is equally and powerfully illustrated in the works of Kwame Gyekye, also from Ghana, Peter Bodunrin and J. O. Sodipo, both from Nigeria, Barry Hallen, an American teaching in Nigeria, and the late Odera Oruka from Kenya.

Wiredu's work is particularly distinguished for its high-quality analytic clarity, its articulateness, and the thoroughness of its reasoning. Several of his works have appeared in the form of articles in international philosophical journals as well as book chapters in distinguished collections since the early 1970s. A number of these essays were published in his famous collection, *Philosophy and an African Culture*, in 1980. While addressing the issue of African philosophy and its quest for a distinctively African form, Wiredu introduces the Popperian doctrine of fallibilism, which allows him to reject many ethnophilosophical expressions on the grounds of their essentialization of traditional knowledge in a manner that promotes authoritarianism, supernaturalism, and anachronism. Like Popper, he sees these three attitudes as hindrances to epistemological growth and argues that critical rationalism is the therapeutic means to the growth of knowledge and the improvement of living conditions in African societies. For Wiredu, propositional validity should depend on nothing other than either its analytic plausibility or the strength of its empirical grounding.

Taking analytic plausibility and empirical evidence as the sole and universal conditions of knowledge, Wiredu rejects most of the recent theories of rationality which smell of defending any sort of relativism. Without denying the presence of reflective activity by individuals in traditional societies, Wiredu nonetheless believes that philosophical orientation which employs the tools of analytic and empirical evidence is only now in the making through the fast-growing discourse amongst contemporary African philosophers. For him, the claim that traditional thought was philosophical in these senses is as unfair as comparing traditional thought with specialized Western science – as Robin Horton did in his widely critiqued paper, "African Traditional Religion and Western Science" (1967). Traditional thought, in Wiredu's view, is not devoid of reason (although, there as anywhere, some beliefs are less acceptable or less appealing than others), but is certainly neither aimed at nor based on the specialized, highly selective and often theoretically comparative analyses that professional philosophy and science depend upon. On the other hand, he believes that appropriate philosophical analysis and discussion of some of those beliefs can be a source of significant contribution, by offering fresh and alternative ideas and approaches, to the wider philosophical discourse on similar and related issues.

The avowedly universalist approach which these positions imply, as well as the rejection of the positions which approvingly set African modes of thought in opposition to Western thought, have earned Wiredu much criticism. In particular, his universalism has been criticized as camouflage for being uncompromisingly Western and for not taking seriously enough the full range of the social and historical grounding of the categories of thought (Gyekye, 1987). Other criticism and general debate generated by Wiredu's work is contained in Bedu-Addo's (1985) and Oruka's (1975 and 1988) reactions to the essay "Truth as Opinion."

As a way of continuing to engage in the wider recent philosophical debate, but also in response to some of the criticisms that his collection *Philosophy and an African Culture* has generated over the years, Wiredu's recent papers have focused on the meanings and epistemological implications of such things as "rationality," "translation," "commensurability," "conceptual frameworks," "cultural universals," and other issues in recent and current epistemological debate. Concern for these issues has been prompted in his case particularly by the resurgence of the debate on the nature of the rational assumptions underlying beliefs in, and accusations about, what europhone anthropology has referentially established as "magic" and "witchcraft."

A long-time attraction for Western anthropologists, the study of African magic and witchcraft became the object of intense international and interdisciplinary discussion following the publication of the British anthropologist Edward Evan Evans-Pritchard's famous book *Witchcraft, Oracles and Magic among the Azande* (1937). Since then, both the issue generally and Evans-Pritchard's work specifically, have become key references for those discussing the idea of epistemological similarities and differences between rival systems of knowing and defining the empirical world and its causal laws (see Masolo, 1994).

Robin Horton's paper "African Traditional Religion and Western Science" (1967), by rekindling this old debate (which goes back to Lévy-Bruhl's works of 1910, 1927, and 1931) contrasting the purportedly affective mentality of the so-called "primitive people" with the "scientific rationality" of the West, has influenced the writings of a number of philosophers of science and social science. These include Bryan Wilson, Paul Feyerabend, Martin Hollis, and Steven Lukes (1982), Peter Winch, John Skorupski, John Beattie, and Horton and Finnegan (1973). Other interesting texts in this regard include Barry Hallen and J. O. Sodipo's *Knowledge, Belief, and Witchcraft: Analytical Experiments in African Philosophy* (1986), and Michael Jackson's *Paths Toward a Clearing: Radical Empiricism and Ethnographic Inquiry* (1989), as well as Horton's responses to his critics. Selections from some of these works have been reprinted in a section of Albert G. Mosely's collection of essays, *African Philosophy: Selected Readings* (1995). Horton himself has published a single collection of his original papers and numerous reactions to critics in *Patterns of Thought in Africa and the West: Essays on Magic, Religion and Science* (1993).

The analytic school of African philosophy addresses a wide range of other issues as well. Metaphysical issues, such as the identity and nature of the self or personhood, as well as their ethical implications concerning moral agency have been widely discussed by African philosophers. Kwame Anthony Appiah's *In My Father's House* (1992), is an excellent and interesting collection of readings on a variety of issues related to the idea of identity. His analytically excellent refutation of the claims of scientific differences between races, and his refutation of the claim of a generalized African identity have generated much debate. Other works that discuss identity and its social, epistemological, and ethical implications in African conceptual schemes include Kwame Gyekye's *An Essay on African Philosophical Thought* (1987), Kwasi Wiredu and Kwame Gyekye's *Person and Community: Ghanaian Philosophical Studies 1* (1992), Michael Jackson and Ivan Karp's *Personhood and Agency: The Experience of Self and Other in African Cultures* (1990), and D. A. Masolo and Ivan Karp's *African Philosophy and Cultural Inquiry* (forthcoming 1997).

A critical study of the historical circumstances determining the production and characteristics of African knowledge is currently underway. This investigation owes much of its visibility to the work of Valentine Y. Mudimbe. Since the 1988 publication of his remarkably influential book, *The Invention of Africa: Gnosis, Philosophy, and the Order of Knowledge*, Mudimbe has been a major reference for the reconstruction of the Western epistemic fields and categories through which specific images of Africa and Africans have been invented, first by the fancies of travelers and later through the organized and self-fulfilling imaginations of missionaries and anthropologists. It is Mudimbe's view that the distorted images of Africa and Africans produced through these agencies were used to justify the colonization of Africa. These discourses have conditioned African responses, in ethnophilosophy and even in the critique of the latter. His project is, by "critically jump[ing] the '*bavardages*' of colonial discourses and its 'anthropological' applications, and center[ing] on the system of signification that allowed the 'colonial propositions' and their inferences," to reverse the order of knowledge from one in which Africans have no subjectivity to that, long proposed by Eboussi-Boulaga (1977), in which the historical reason and reasonable liberty of Muntu are based on a radical "*récit pour soi*."

Mudimbe's project may not be novel in its intent (see, for example, Tshibangu, 1973), but due to the recent influence of Michel Foucault's attack on the idea of "ideal rationality," to whom he is partly indebted, Mudimbe's work has enjoyed positive attention in its effort to unprivilege Western *epistēmē*. To the extent that his project, like Eboussi-Boulaga's idea of "*récit pour soi*" or Hountondji's notion of "local audience," aims at defining an epistemic field that is both independent and self-referencing, without compromising critical and analytic rigor or sacrificing cross-cultural dialogue, it can be said that a new order of knowledge, perhaps a new sense of *ethnophilosophy*, in a stricter sense defined by Hebga (1982), has been put in place at this point in the history of African philosophy.

Bibliography

Appiah, K. A. 1992: *In My Father's House: Africa in the Philosophy of Culture* (New York: Oxford University Press).

Bahoken, J. C. 1967: *Clairières Métaphysique africaines. Essai sur la philosophie et la religion chez les Bantu du sud-Cameroun* (Paris: Présence Africaine).
Bates, R. H., with V. Y. Mudimbe and J. O'Barr (eds) 1993: *Africa and the Disciplines* (Chicago: University of Chicago Press).
Bedu-Addo, J. T. 1985: "Wiredu on Truth as Opinion and the Akan Language," in *Philosophy in Africa: Trends and Perspectives*, ed. P. Bodunrin (Ile-Ife, Nigeria: University of Ife Press), pp. 68–90.
Bernal, M. 1987: *Black Athena*, Vol. 1: *The Fabrication of Ancient Greece 1785–1985* (New Brunswick: Rutgers University Press).
—— 1991: *Black Athena*, Vol. 2: *The Archeological and Documentary Evidence* (New Brunswick: Rutgers University Press).
Bodunrin, P. O. 1975: "Theoretical Identities and Scientific Explanation: the Horton-Skorupski Debate," *Second Order*, 4, 1, pp. 56–65.
—— 1981: "The Question of African Philosophy," *Philosophy: The Journal of the Royal Institute of Philosophy*, 56.
—— 1984: "The Question of African Philosophy," in *African Philosophy: an Introduction*, ed. R. A. Wright (Lanham: University Press of America), pp. 1–23.
Bodunrin, P. O. (ed.) 1985: *Philosophy in Africa: Trends and Perspectives* (Ile-Ife, Nigeria: University of Ife Press).
Césaire, A. 1950: *Discours sur le colonialisme* (Paris: Présence Africaine).
Crahay, F. 1965: "Le Décollage conceptuel: Conditions d'une philosophie bantoue," *Diogène*, 52, pp. 61–84.
Diop, C. A. 1954: *Nations nègres et culture* (Paris: Présence Africaine).
—— 1960: *L'unité culturelle de l'Afrique noire* (Paris: Présence Africaine).
—— 1967: *Anteriorité des civilisations nègres* (Paris: Présence Africaine. English tr., *The African Origin of Civilization: Myth or Reality*, 1974).
—— 1974: *The African Origin of Civilization: Myth or Reality* (Westport: Lawrence Hill & Co.).
Eboussi-Boulaga, F. 1968: "Le Bantou Problematique," *Présence Africaine*, 66, pp. 4–40.
—— 1977: *La Crise du Muntu, Authenticité africaine et philosophie* (Paris: Présence Africaine).
Evans-Pritchard, E. E. 1937: *Witchcraft, Oracles and Magic among the Azande* (London: Oxford University Press).
Fanon, F. 1967: *Black Skin, White Masks* (New York: Grove Press).
—— 1978: *The Wretched of the Earth* (London: Penguin Books).
Floistad, G. (ed.) 1987: *Contemporary Philosophy: a New Survey*, Vol. 5: *African Philosophy* (Dordrecht: Martinus Nijhoff Publishers).
Fouda, B. J. 1967: "La philosophie africaine de l'existence" (Doctoral dissertation, Université de Lille).
Goody, J. 1968: *Literacy in Traditional Societies* (Cambridge: Cambridge University Press).
—— 1977: *The Domestication of the Savage Mind* (London: Cambridge University Press).
Goody, J. 1987: *The Interface between the Written and the Oral* (New York: Cambridge University Press).
Griaule, M. 1965: *Conversations with Ogotemmêli* (London: Oxford University Press).
Gyekye, K. 1987: *An Essay on African Philosophical Thought: the Akan Conceptual Scheme* (London: Cambridge University Press; rev 2nd edn, Philadelphia: Temple University Press, 1995).
Hallen, B. and Sodipo, J. O. 1986: *Knowledge, Belief and Witchcraft: Analytic Experiments in African Philosophy* (London: Ethnographica).
Hebga, M. 1982: "Éloge de l'ethnophilosophie," *Présence Africaine*, 123, pp. 20–41.
Hollis, M. 1977: *Models of Man* (Cambridge: Cambridge University Press).

Hollis, M. and Lukes, S. (eds) 1982: *Rationality and Relativism* (Cambridge: MIT Press).
Horton, R. 1967: "African Traditional Religion and Western Science," *Africa*, 37, 1 and 2, pp. 50–71, 155–87. Reprinted as "African traditional thought and Western Science", in *Rationality*, ed. B. R. Wilson (New York: Harper & Row, 1970).
—— 1993: *Patterns of Thought in Africa and the West: Essays on Magic, Religion and Science* (Cambridge: Cambridge University Press).
Horton, R. and Finnegan, R. (eds) 1973: *Modes of Thought* (London: Faber & Faber).
Hountondji, P. J. 1970: "Remarques sur la philosophie africaine contemporaine," *Diogène*, 71, pp. 120–40.
—— 1971: "Le problème actuel de la philosophie africaine," in *La philosophie contemporaine*, t. iv, ed. R. Klibansky (Firenze: La Nuova Italia), pp. 613–21.
—— 1972: "Le mythe de la philosophie spontanée," *Cahiers Philosophiques Africains* (*African Philosophical Journal*), 1, pp. 107–42.
—— 1977: *Sur la "philosophie africaine. Critique de l'ethnophilosophie* (Paris: François Maspero).
—— 1983: *African Philosophy: Myth and Reality* (Bloomington: Indiana University Press).
—— 1989: "Occidentalism, Elitism: Answer to Two Critiques," *Quest*, 3, 2, pp. 3–30.
Jackson, M. 1989: *Paths Toward a Clearing: Radical Empiricism and Ethnographic Inquiry* (Bloomington: Indiana University Press).
Jackson, M. and Karp, I. (eds) 1990: *Personhood and Agency: the Experience of Self and Other in African Cultures* (Uppsala Studies in Cultural Anthropology, Uppsala: Acta Universitas Uppsaliensis).
Kagame, A. 1956: *La philosophie bantu-rwandaise de l'être* (Brussels: Académie royale des sciences coloniales).
—— 1976: *La philosophie bantu comparée* (Paris: Présence Africaine).
Laleye, I. P. 1970: *La Conception de la personne dans la pensée traditionelle Yoruba* (Berne: Lang).
—— 1975: *La philosophie? Pourquoi en Afrique? Une Phénomenologie de la question* (Berne: Lang).
—— 1981: "Philosophie et réalités africaines," in *Langage et philosophie* (Kinshasa: Faculté de théologie catholique), pp. 39–52.
—— 1982: "La Philosophie, l'Afrique et les philosophes africains: triple malentendu ou possibilité d'une collaboration féconde?," *Présence Africaine*, 123, pp. 42–62.
Lévy-Bruhl, L. 1910: *Les fonctions mentales dans les societés inférieures* (Paris: Alcan. English tr., *How Natives Think*, 1936).
—— 1927: *L'Âme primitive* (Paris: Alcan; new edn Presses Universitaires de France, 1963. English tr., *The Soul of the Primitive*, 1966).
—— 1931: *Le surnaturel et la nature dans la mentalité primitive* (Paris: Alcan. English tr., *Primitives and the Supernatural*, 1936).
—— 1978: *The Notebooks on Primitive Mentality* (New York: Harper & Row).
Lufuluabo, F. M. 1962: *Vers une théodicée bantoue* (Paris-Tournai: Casterman).
—— 1964: *La Notion luba bantoue de l'être* (Tournai: Casterman).
—— 1966: *Perspective théologique bantoue et théologie scholastique* (Malines).
Makarakiza, A. 1959: *La dialectique des Barundi* (Brussels: Académie royale des sciences coloniales).
Masolo, D. A. 1994: *African Philosophy in Search of Identity* (Bloomington: Indiana University Press).
Maurier, H. 1976: *Philosophie de l'Afrique noire* (Bonn: Verlag St Augustin; 2nd edn 1985).

Mbiti, J. S. 1969: *African Religions and Philosophy* (London: Heinemann Educational Books).
—— 1971: *New Testament Eschatology in an African Background* (Oxford: Oxford University Press).
Mosley, A. G. (ed.) 1995: *African Philosophy, Selected Readings* (Englewood Cliffs: Prentice Hall).
Mudimbe, V. Y. 1988: *The Invention of Africa* (Bloomington: Indiana University Press).
—— 1994: *The Idea of Africa* (Bloomington: Indiana University Press).
Mudimbe, V. Y. and Appiah, K. A. 1993: "The Impact of African Studies on Philosophy," in *Africa and the Disciplines*, ed. R. C. Bates, V. Y. Mudimbe, and J. O'Barr (Chicago: University of Chicago Press), pp. 113–38.
Mulago, V. 1955: "L'Union vitale bantu chez les Bashi, les Banyarwanda, et les Barundi face à l'unité vitale ecclésiale" (Unpublished dissertation, Rome).
—— 1965: *Un visage africaine du christianisme* (Paris: Présence Africaine).
—— 1973: *La religion traditionelle des bantu et leur vision du monde* (Kinshasa: Presses Universitaires du Zaire).
Nkrumah, K. 1970: *Consciencism, Philosophy and Ideology for Decolonization and Development with Particular Reference to the African Revolution* (London: Panaf Books).
Nyerere, J. K. 1968: *Ujamaa: the Basis of African Socialism* (Dar es Salaam: Oxford University Press).
Ocholla-Ayayo, A. B. C. 1976: *Traditional Ideology and Ethics among the Southern Luo* (Uppsala: Scandinavian Institute of African Studies).
Okere, T. 1971: "Can There Be an African Philosophy? A Hermeneutical Investigation with Special Reference to Igbo Culture" (Doctoral dissertation, Louvain University).
Olela, H. 1980: *An Introduction to the History of Philosophy: from Ancient Africa to Ancient Greece* (Atlanta: Select Publishing Co.).
Oruka, H. O. 1975: "Truth and Belief," *Universitas* (Ghana) 5, 1.
—— 1981: "Four Trends in Current African Philosophy," *Filosofiska Tidscrift*, 1, 2, pp. 31–7.
—— 1990: *Sage Philosophy* (Leiden: E. J. Brill).
Oruka, H. O. and Masolo, D. A. (eds) 1983: *Philosophy and Cultures* (Nairobi: Bookwise Publishers).
—— 1988: "For the Sake of Truth – a Response to Wiredu's Critique of 'Truth and Belief,'" *Quest*, 2, 2, pp. 3–22.
Serequeberhan, T. (ed.) 1991: *African Philosophy: Essential Readings* (New York: Paragon).
Serequeberhan, T. 1994: *The Hermeneutics of African Philosophy: Horizon and Discourse* (New York: Routledge).
Smet, A. J. 1972: *Philosophie africaine: Textes Choisis* (Kinshasa: Presses Universitaires du Zaire).
—— 1977: "Le Père Placide Tempels et son oeuvre publiée," *Revue africaine de théologie*, 1, 1.
—— 1980: *Histoire de la philosophie africaine contemporaine: courants et problèmes* (Kinshasa-Limete: Faculté de Théologie Catholique).
Sumner, C. 1974–84: *Ethiopian Philosophy*, 6 Vols (Addis Ababa: Central Printing Press).
—— 1980: *African Philosophy. Philosophie Africaine* (Addis Ababa: Chamber Printing House).
—— 1994: *Classical Ethiopian Philosophy* (Los Angeles: Adey Publishing Co.).
Témoignages 1949: "Témoignages sur 'la philosophie bantoue' du Père Tempels," *Présence Africaine*, 7, pp. 252–78.
Tempels, P. 1959: *Bantu Philosophy* (Paris: Présence Africaine). *La philosophie bantone* (Elizabethville: Lovania).

Towa, M. 1971a: *Essai sur la problématique philosophique dans l'Afrique actuelle* (Yaounde: Ed. Clé).
—— 1971b: *L'Idée d'une philosophie africaine* (Yaounde: Ed. Clé).
Tshibangu, T. 1963: "Métaphysique, cette philosophie qui nous vient d'ailleurs," *Cahiers Philosophiques Africaines* (*African Philosophical Journal*), 3 and 4, pp. 41–9, 133–5, 163–9.
Winch, P. 1964: "Understanding a Primitive Culture," *American Philosophical Quarterly*, 1, pp. 307–24.
Wiredu, J. E. (K.) 1972: "On an African Orientation in Philosophy," *Second Order*, 2.
—— 1973: "Mysticism, Philosophy and Rationality," *Universitas* (Ghana), 2, 3, pp. 97–106.
—— 1980: *Philosophy and an African Culture* (Cambridge: Cambridge University Press).
—— 1993: "Canons of Conceptualization," *The Monist*, 76, 4, pp. 450–76.
—— 1995: "Knowledge, Truth and Fallibility," in *The Concept of Knowledge*, ed. Ioanna Kucuradi and R. S. Cohen (The Hague: Kluwer Academic Publishers), pp. 127–48.
Wiredu, K. and Gyekye, K. (eds) 1992: *Person and Community: Ghanaian Philosophical Studies*, I (Washington: Council for Research in Values and Philosophy).
Wright, R. A. (ed.) 1984: *African Philosophy: an Introduction* (Lanham: University Press of America).

5

A survey of Buddhist thought

NINIAN SMART

Buddhist philosophy had its origins, there can be little doubt, in some seminal intuitions of Guatama, entitled the Buddha or enlightened one, who lived possibly from 563 to 483 BCE, but probably about a century later. His thought evolved from the sramanic milieu of his period in which various other movements, such as Jainism, were included; but conceptually it included motifs from the tradition of brahmins. The Buddha was critical of brahmin ideology, but made use of ideas which were prevalent in the society of the Gangetic plain, where most of his work was accomplished. We shall shortly outline some of the key notions of the initial phase of the Buddhist movement.

But it is useful to note some of its wider developments. First of all, geographically Buddhism came to be a vital, sometimes dominant, aspect of Indian religion, from its founding down to about the eleventh century, when it greatly faded from India save in parts of the North and in Nepal and beyond in Tibet and Mongolia, and in the island of Ceylon or Lanka. It spread into South-East Asia, from Thailand and Myanmar, into Cambodia, Laos, and Vietnam, so that by modern times Theravāda Buddhism became the dominant form (although not without the infusion of some Mahāyāna values and Hindu institutions). In the main millennium of Buddhist India the predominant form was Mahāyāna, which developed Buddhist philosophy in amazing directions. Much of this material, together with Tantric notions, were retained and elaborated in Tibet. Meanwhile, from the first century CE Buddhism had begun to move into China via the Silk Route (north of Tibet), and in due course some Chinese-flavored schools developed, notably Hua Yen and Chan. These had their influence in Korea and Japan, where Zen in particular evolved in a Japanese way. Some of the most vital modern philosophical developments occurred in Japan. Another vital school of modernism emerged in Sri Lanka. Other changes were registered in Europe and America. Differing parts of this article will be devoted to these varying forms of Buddhist philosophy. Despite the varieties, there are significant continuities: Chinese philosophical Buddhism is largely based on Indian sources, and some modern thinkers are consciously returning to traditional concepts.

The framework within which the Buddha thought contained three main ideas, but he gave a special spin to this worldview. One idea was that of rebirth or reincarnation. Generally, the sramanic movements accepted the thought that without special effort we are destined to continuous rebirth (and more gloomily, of course, redeath). The second idea was that, nevertheless, liberation is possible (such liberation was often called *mokṣa* or *mukti*, but other words also came to be used, such as *nirvāṇa* and *kevala*). The third idea was that of certain means, namely both austerity or *tapas* and yoga or meditation, as conducing ultimately to liberation from re-death. With these notions also went the conception of a soul of *jīva* or *puruṣa* who might continue into liberation. The Buddha's new spin was first to identify the problem of rebirth as having to do essentially with impermanence. The fabric of life is impermanent. But, second, this means that there can be no permanent soul or self: there is therefore no entity there in liberation. *Nirvāṇa* does not involve the persistence of the saint or the Buddha or Tathāgata. Or more strictly, since the Buddha's analysis of life reduces things to complexes of events, the very question as to whether the self exists after death is meaningless, like the query as to whether a flame goes north, south, east or west after it goes out. Though the means to liberation lies in yoga or contemplation, there are ethical prerequisites. The Buddha had an ethical interpretation of brahmanical rituals and ritual powers. The framework of his worldview was moral.

From an early time the Buddhist *sangha* created formulae. For instance, the four noble truths analysed the human predicament and its solution in the guise of a medical formula. The human condition of suffering (*duḥkha*) or illfare is caused by craving; there is a cure for suffering, and that is the eight-part path (the *aṭṭhangikamṭārga*, or *magga* in Pāli) which culminates in *samādhi*. This formula of four noble truths parallels the declaration that everything is conditioned – a view ultimately formulated in the doctrine of dependent origination, *paṭccasamuppāda* (Pāli) or *pratītyasamutpāda* (Sanskrit). The varieties of formulae are sometimes confusing. For instance, the last formula sees the chain of conditioning ending in ignorance. On the other hand, a common formula sees human problems as deriving from greed, hatred and delusion. This is akin to ignorance but slightly different. At any rate, the opposites of these "sins" (lack of grasping, benevolence, and insight) bring about liberation.

In some ways Buddhism came to resemble Sāṃkhya with its enumerations of categories. Certainly Buddhism proved to be highly analytic. It had a theory of the human individual, as consisting of events classified in four *skandhas* (Pāli, *khandhas*) or groups: bodily states, perceptions, feelings, dispositions, and conscious states. This gave concreteness to the doctrine of non-self (*anātmavāda, anattā*). The individual consists in a complex of events of differing groups adhering together, but she has no permanent self. The propensity towards lists occurs throughout the Theravādin or Pāli canon, and the final section of that three-part whole was the Abhidamma, or Analysis of the Dhamma (*dharma*) – that is, of the teaching or philosophical aspect of the doctrine.

The Theravādin tradition sees the Buddha as teaching a dualism between the world of *saṃsāra* or rebirth and the transcendent state of *nirvāṇa*. Nevertheless, this dualism was modified by the fourfold negation applied to certain questions, notably as to whether the Tathāgata (the Buddha and by implication a saint or *arhant*) survives death. Other questions deemed unanswerable are whether the soul or life-monad (*jīva*) is identical with the body, and whether the cosmos is infinite in space and infinite in time. About the things in question, it is averred that they neither are so, nor not so, nor both so and not so, nor neither so nor not so. Such questions are compared to the question of where a fire goes when it goes out. It seems that they are meaningless, at least within the framework of Buddhist metaphysics. Regarding *nirvāṇa*, since the individual is identified as the ongoing process of events, including bodily ones, at that person's decease, on attaining liberation, there is no individual to be referred to, and not accidentally, but in the nature of the case. The fourfold negation (*catuṣkoti*) makes it hard to assert the existence of the Buddha, and so the "dualism" between the samsaric world and the transcendent state of the Buddha does not strictly obtain, as if they were separate entities. It also of course implies that there can be no real transaction between the Buddha and one who reveres him: strictly, the system does not admit of worship, or any kind of reciprocity.

In the Abhidharma analysis of the Theravāda and other schools, realism obtains in this world. The analysis exhibits the real short-lived constituents (though questions arose about space, for instance) of the ongoing world. Still, the Theravādins shared with other Buddhists the theory that language is conventional and often misleading. For instance, we refer to the self even though there is not one, and objects are treated as solid when they really consist in swarms of events. Because of this almost Wittgensteinian view of language, Buddhism cannot be considered as naively realist. And in the Mahāyāna, doubt, to say the least, was cast on the realism of the Abhidharma analyses.

There were, however, paradoxes in early thought. It was they that helped to spur the evolution of Mahāyāna thought. Some were more strictly philosophical and others religious and ethical. It should, of course, be emphasized that Buddhist philosophy always had a spiritual significance, directly or indirectly. Moreover, Buddhist epistemology had its religious side. On the one hand, Buddhism was a *nāstika* tradition, that is, it rejected the brahmin appeal to *śruti* or revelation, as expressed in the Vedic hymns and later compositions. It is doubtful whether the Buddha himself was acquainted with the Upaniṣads, and evidence of the Pāli canon indicates knowledge of three Vedas (but not the *Atharva*). Still, the Brahmanist ideology was rejected in essence, although the Buddha seems to have used, but analogized, its principal concepts and practices. For instance, the true brahmin was one who restrained himself and acted morally, and this had nothing to do with lineage. In the *Tevijja-sutta* brahmins are criticized for speaking about gods they have never experienced. And so Buddhism did not appeal to revelation. Even the authority of the Buddha himself rests on his superior level of insightful experience. In terms of standard Indian types of sources of knowledge, Buddhism recognized perception and inference. Of course, perception was thought of in a stretched sense, as including paranormal and contemplative experience. Indeed, these sorts of perception were given a large role. For instance, the doctrine of rebirth rested on the memories of saints and buddhas. In general, Buddhism as described in the Pāli canon was an *ehipassiko* teaching – a "come-and-see-ish" doctrine. Because of the importance of the contemplative life, Buddhist philosophy has a spiritual heart to it. But other religious factors, such as developing devotion to the person of the Buddha, also need to be taken into account. Let us turn, then, to some ethical and religious paradoxes arising in the evolution of Buddhism in the first five centuries, up to the first century CE.

First, there was a dilemma involved in the pursuit of *nirvāṇa*. It was always true that the eightfold path contained a strong moral element, and the four *brahmavihāras* or holy states are a fine summation of Buddhist virtue: – that is, that a person should exhibit love, compassion, joy in another's joy, and equanimity. Yet the single-minded pursuit of *nirvāṇa* could appear to be selfish. This was a primary criticism of the so-called Lesser Vehicle by the Mahāyāna.

Second, already from his decease the Buddha was an object of veneration, for his relics were distributed to various centers. However, there evolved a more personalistic piety. Buddhist *bhakti* grew in parallel with similar proto-Hindu devotionalism. It was enhanced by the development of Buddhist art, partly under Mediterranean influence, following Alexander's incursion into the region. There was a paradox in the apparent worship of a (so to speak) non-existent Leader.

Third, on more philosophical grounds there was a problem with the theory of causation. Buddhists held to a version of what Hindu philosophy would categorize as *asatkāryavāda* or the non-identity theory. It involved the thesis that the effect and cause are different. This was in opposition to the *satkāryavāda* of Sāṃkhya and other schools. But because Buddhism held to impermanence, and therefore in effect abolished substances, the causal relation was between events. And questions arose about the extent of events: if they were instantaneous and were external to one another, there seemed to be a problem about an event disappearing before its effect. So there were metaphysical problems about causation, and these were exploited in early Mahāyāna. There was a subsidiary issue about *nirvāṇa* as being unconditioned: how then could it be brought about?

We shall see some of the consequences of these and other paradoxes shortly. Meanwhile, both Theravāda and other schools developed the Abhidhamma (Sanskrit, Abhidharma) as a separate "basket" or division of the Tipitaka (Tripitaka). Although both the Sutta and Vinaya had undergone considerable elaboration, the Abhidhamma was a very systematic creation which gave detailed structure to the teachings and their implications. It was a kind of scholasticism. The Theravāda became increasingly conservative in its doctrinal interpretations, and yet the structure of thought which emerged was remarkable. This in some ways reached its fullest development in the commentarial and systematic writings of Buddhaghosa (fifth century? CE), who worked in Sri Lanka, though possibly himself from India, and may have been a brahmin convert. His *Visuddhimagga* or Path of Purification is a masterly summary of contemplative practices. In general, Abhidharma literature seeks to define the varied elements or *dharmas* which constitute reality, such as the particles of earth, water, fire and air making up physical objects, the organic items and psychic inner states, such as the eye, ear, nose, tongue, body and visible object, audible object, and so on, together with the mind (roughly Aristotle's common sense), the mental object, consciousness, and the like. The meticulous cataloguing of features of the world and of our inner life was important to the specialists in Abhidhamma for the simple reason that right view was one of the conditions of attaining liberation. For right view it was necessary to have a detailed grasp of both the real world and of our inner states. So the Abhidhamma could be described as a catalogue of the items of the real world and of our psyches, which are part of that real world. There was a kind of technical and essentialist flavor to the Abhidharma writings which involved the thesis that the Buddha's critique of language issued from a distrust of ordinary and conventional language because it did not analyse events and things correctly. There are strange prefigurings of the ideas of Wittgensteinian analytic philosophers (prefigurings taken up by recent Sri Lankan philosophers).

The Theravāda achieved their definitive canon in the first century BCE, but prior to that there were some breakaway groups – notably the Sarvāstivādins (often called Realists in Western accounts). They believed in the pre-existence and subsequent existence of *dharmas*, so that an event is a manifestation of a continuous entity. In some ways, this seemed to undermine the belief in impermanence. The Realists tended to be keener on Abhidharma analysis than on the Sutta division.

Meanwhile Buddhist doctrine, in expounding the notion that everything is conditioned, made use of the doctrine of the *pratītyasamutpāda* or *paṭiccasamuppāda*. This "chain of dependent origination" involved the stipulation that old age and death are due to birth, which is itself due to the desire for living, which is itself due to clinging, which is itself due to craving, which is itself due to feeling, which is itself due to contact, which is itself due to the bases of perception, which are themselves consequent upon corporeality, which is itself due to consciousness, which is itself due to dispositions, which are themselves due to ignorance, the final cause.

But though later Buddhist schools accepted this formula (which is itself probably a combination of two), the deeper questions in later philosophy went beyond the technicalities of the Abhidharma. They affected both the issues of religion and philosophy. They affected the status of Buddhahood, and they affected the nature of reality. Together they changed the soteriology of Buddhism. And yet Theravāda survived well. It penetrated into South-East Asia, from Burma (Myanmar) to Vietnam, and it survived a depression in Ceylon prior to the British period (1815 onwards). Its modern revival has been spectacular. And it remains philosophically (and religiously) very different from the Mahāyāna, and indeed most other religious traditions. To these issues we shall come back. Suffice it to say that it is one of two significant religious traditions which denies a creator-God, and indeed tends to disprove a number of theories about the nature of religion. This, by the way, is not to say that Buddhism denies the gods. It looks as if the Buddha wanted to accept, in a limited capacity, the brahmins' and others' supernaturals, so as to offer an irenic and inclusive frontier to other religious cultures. The gods turn out to be forces within the samsaric world. People can become gods, by the way, through good deeds and giving, but that, though enjoyable, is not final liberation. They need to come back to gain *nirvāṇa*. So it is that Buddhist cosmology corresponds to deep ethical and spiritual distinctions.

The paradoxes to which I earlier referred were accompanied by a problem in canonical interpretation. The Buddha is reported to have referred to the one who bears or carries the *skandhas*. Does there then have to be a bearer behind the groups which make up the individual? If that is so, then there must be a *pudgala* or *puggala*

(Pāli), translated usually as "person." Those who argued this – known as pudgalavādins – drifted from mainstream Theravāda during the third century BCE, and were still a powerful force in Indian Buddhism in the seventh century CE, according to the Chinese pilgrim Hsüan Tsang. The *anattā* or *anātmavāda* doctrine of non-self was hard for many to grasp, though the idea of a *pudgala* was getting dangerously close to that of a permanent soul. There was no question, of course, of using the word *ātman*. Probably the Buddhist rejection of the self was, in terms of incipient Indian traditions of the period, closest to being a rejection of the Sāṃkhya concept of the *puruṣa*. At any rate, even the pudgalavādins did not assert a timeless or eternal self. In due course, the Mahāyāna made use of the idea of the Buddha-nature, which in its own way substituted for the soul. The general point to notice is that in the Theravāda the real substitute for the soul was the individual capacity to attain *nirvāṇa*. The Buddha-nature was likewise the capacity to attain Buddhahood.

The transition to the Mahāyāna took varied routes. We have mentioned some: the increased devotionalism towards the Buddha, backed by art; concern about egoism in the pursuit of *nirvāṇa*; and philosophical problems. Already in the schools which were proliferating in the first few centuries there was the movement known as the Lokottaravāda. This claimed that the Buddha was transcendental, or literally "beyond the cosmos or *loka*." The lokottaravādins were a branch of the Mahāsaṅghikas or those "who belonged to the great *sangha*." They illustrated something which was important in much of the history of Buddhism, namely that the *sangha* was the authority (it was the substitute for *śruti*), but it depended on inner, and therefore questionable, control. While the community exhibited amazing conservatism, it was also prone to schisms. Perhaps the Mahāsaṅghikas were the first schismatic movement. But they surely acquired, perhaps as early as the third century BCE, a devotional disposition towards the founder. Out of this there evolved a very "high" buddhology. Eventually, this tendency created the Three-Body Doctrine, of which more anon. But out of the womb of the Lokottaravāda there came into being a vigorous *bhakti* aspect of Buddhism. This imported a different logic into the tradition from that on which the early movement had been based. *Dhyāna* or contemplation was different both in logic and practice from the life of devotion. Apart from this, there were invasions of motifs from other cultures. The growing devotional emphasis was important because it helped to promote a kind of Absolutism in Buddhism. It helped to focus on a single Something, which could be manifested personally as the Buddha or a Buddha.

As for the question of the selfishness of the saint who achieves his own *nirvāṇa* (nuns had a slightly less favorable position), the solution was found for many Buddhists in the ideal of the Bodhisattva (or Being destined for enlightenment). This idea, present, of course, in the very story of the Buddha, and elaborated in the Theravāda through the *Jātaka* tales, offered a way of combining destiny and compassion. So it was that the ideal of a Bodhisattva could be mobilized in an emerging worldview. The concept was the Buddha-to-be who, already having earned the merit to leave the world and attain final liberation from the round of rebirth, compassionately turns away from his ultimate salvation in order to serve all living beings. He is a wonderful altruist who can help others. This Bodhisattva ideal also generated heavenly figures to whom devotion and worship could be addressed, thereby helping to combine the values of idealism and compassion.

The Bodhisattva ideal was ingeniously given a philosophical basis through the notion that *nirvāṇa* and *saṃsāra* (the life of rebirth in the world) were mysteriously identical. The reasoning was philosophical in that it arose from the notion that language was misleading, backed by arguments that key concepts in our understanding of the world are self-contradictory. From this it emerged that all theories are useless, so that our accounts of reality are empty: this emptiness is, so to speak, the true nature of the world. Such an apparently nihilistic doctrine was, as it happened, in accord with the character of the contemplative life which had always formed the substance of Buddhist praxis. Further, not only is the mystical state empty of concepts and images, it also has no subject–object structure. The person feels she merges as it were with the transcendental state in which she finds herself. This reinforces the mysterious doctrine that *nirvāṇa* and *saṃsāra* are identical. Consequently, philosophy and experience seem here to coincide.

One of the major arguments which came to be used in expounding this worldview was based on the apparent incoherence of the idea of causation. But before we move to consider the most systematic early philosophical representation of this point of view, that of Nāgārjuna (flourished about 100 CE), we must note that certain texts, called the *Prajñapāramitā* texts, or "Perfection of Insight" texts (often also called the "Perfection of Wisdom" texts), were important during the same period in putting forth a characteristically Mahāyāna point of view. While emptiness may be the absolute reality (or if you prefer unreality), the world as we encounter it is without self-nature or *svabhāva*. The world is depicted in a pithy verse as a mirage, a lamp, an illusion, a drop of water, a dream, a flash of lightning. In short, the world is illusory. This doctrine encourages withdrawal, from one point of view, yet immersion in the world is encouraged by the very idea of the identity of *nirvāṇa* and *saṃsāra*. The individual does not need to separate himself from worldly concerns and ethical activities, because, if he only knew, he is already in a sense liberated. He has to realize the true nature of his own life and that of the world.

The "Perfection of Insight" texts and others really mark a new beginning in the Buddhist worldview. For one thing, they are composed in Sanskrit – sometimes a blend of real Sanskrit and Indic languages, known as Buddhist Hybrid Sanskrit. This is far from the vernaculars in which the Buddha wished his teachings to be broadcast. It involves a convergence of brahmanic and Buddhist practices. Moreover, the logic of these new scriptures diverges somewhat from the epistemology of the early period. There the *suttas*, for instance, aim to record the words of Buddha in a relatively empirical manner. Moreover, as we have seen, they are not regarded strictly as scripture. While the new texts are traced to the Buddha, as if they were preached by him, it is often in a numinous and sacred manner. The people to whom he preached these thoughts were bodhisattvas, devas or gods, demons and disciples. These sermons were heavenly rather than earthly. Buddhism was moving away from its earlier, more empirical, ideals. That, of course, does not mean that in some sense the new Mahāyāna was not following the implications of the

Buddha's early teaching. Nevertheless, the move into Sanskrit and an ambience of worship and scriptural tradition does indicate a shift away from the mostly contemplative and psychological thrust of the early philosophy.

It is interesting that the core worldview is expressed in rather abstract terms. For instance, insight is seen as having three facets. In the first, it consists in realizing the emptiness of conditioned *dharmas*. Next, it involves the perception of the emptiness of the unconditioned elements of *nirvāṇa*. Finally, it consists in the gnosis that *nirvāṇa* and *saṃsāra* are without genuine distinction. Here there is a synthesis between contemplative realization and philosophical discernment. But despite the abstract character of *prajñā*, it was also personified as a goddess. This was in accord with the increasing importance of skill in means or *upāya* in Buddhist development – that is, the notion that the Buddha understands the cultural and psychological states of people, the better to adapt his teachings to their condition.

It is probable that the "Perfection of Insight" scriptures were composed in South India, possibly by lay disciples. It is interesting that we have here a cultural area in which Mahāyāna and Theravādin and other motifs flourished side by side. Despite the preservation of the core of early teachings through the authority of the *sangha*, there was room for disagreement between monastic establishments, and this gave Buddhism possibilities of leisurely creativity in the message. In addition to the *Insight* literature, other major scriptures emerged in this period of the formation of the Mahāyāna – notably the Lotus Sūtra or *Saddharmapuṇḍarīka*, the *Avataṃsaka* or the Ornaments of the Buddha Sūtra, and the *Sukhavatīvyūha* or Pure Land Description Sūtra. These emerged during the first and second centuries CE, though portions were almost certainly earlier.

The most important of the early Mahāyāna schools was undoubtedly the Mādhyamika or Madhyamaka. In effect, its founder Nāgārjuna gave systematic philosophical shape to some of the themes of the "Perfection of Insight" literature. The most important theme was that of emptiness. This in a sense arises from the *pratītyasamutpāda* or dependent origination. The fact that everything is conditioned means that its nature is relative. It has no "own-nature" or *svabhāva*. It is empty. But so is the ultimate, which lies allegedly "beyond" the empirical world. This also has no own-nature. Notable in all of his argumentation is Nāgārjuna's use of the tetralemma or fourfold negation. He universalizes that which the Buddha applied to certain questions about the Tathāgata, the self and the cosmos. Nāgārjuna's justification lay partly in the notion that the "beyond" and the empirical cannot be distinguished. This being the case, the fourfold negation which in essence applied to *nirvāṇa* (and because of that also to the other cases, having to do with the identity of the soul and the body, and the "ending" of the cosmos) could be applied to the whole of reality (or unreality). His use of the tetralemma highlighted the way in which he sought to destroy all *dṛṣṭis* or views or theories. This gave his system of reasoning a negative character. It was a system of *reductiones ad absurdum*, and a large number of his followers kept to this negative mode of *prasaṅga* (which, oddly enough, was not generally recognized in the Indian logic of the period as a valid form of reasoning). But it was, combined with the fourfold negation, an excellent vehicle for Nāgārjuna's attempt to refute all views. For instance, he could claim to have refuted all forms of causation theory, which divided into identity and non-identity accounts. And since the very fabric of our thought implies causal dependency, no theory at all could stand up to this intellectual assault.

In effect, Nāgārjuna was substituting a new kind of reflection for the more traditional attention to Abhidharma – that is, for intellectual discernment of the *dharmas* available to perception and meditation and so to empirical access. This traditional intellectual aspect of the process of self-advancement to liberation went with contemplative effort and ethical training. To these contemplative and ethical concerns Nāgārjuna was attentive. His mastery was due not just to his philosophical acumen, but to his pastoral influence and attentiveness.

Also important in Nāgārjuna's thinking was the distinction between higher and ordinary truth – namely, *paramārtha* and *samvṛti-satya*. This distinction was already implicit in the Buddhist conventionalist theory of language, which distinguished between ordinary discourse and correct analysis. But the important innovation of the sharper twofold distinction is that one truth is referred to spiritual and the other to empirical matters. The idea of levels of truth had deep effects not only on Buddhist religion, but also upon Advaita theory in the Hindu tradition. As regards Buddhism, it fitted in with later organizations of practice and thinking about levels of Buddhahood. To that we shall return shortly.

The notion that *saṃsāra* and *nirvāṇa* are identical implies that what we need to do to become liberated is simply to realize this: we shall realize liberation in the midst of our living. The change between being in *saṃsāra* and being liberated is not a substantive one, but rather a matter of deep attitudes. This chimes in positively with the aim of insight and negatively with the claim that our lack of liberation is ultimately due to *avidyā* or ignorance. Our trouble is that we take the cosmos as real. Rather, it is more like a mirage or illusion. From the worldly point of view, there is a higher truth to be attained, and though this is in a conventional sense true, the fact is that at the higher level the distinction between levels disappears.

At the practical level, the two-truth doctrine paved the way for a synthesis (which we may owe in its formulation to Yogācāra circles) of types of Buddhahood in the so-called *trikāya* or Three-Body or Three-Aspect teaching. This is the doctrine that the Buddha manifests at three levels. As the worldly Buddha who taught in North India, he is the Transformation Aspect, the *nirmāṇakāya*. At the celestial or heavenly level, he is the Bliss Aspect of *sambhogakāya*. It is, of course, a striking feature of the Mahāyāna that supreme Buddhas such as Amitābha and Kṣitigarbha are worshipped, as well as notable Bodhisattvas such as Avalokiteśvara (later Kanyin in China, having undergone a gender-change). This cult of many Buddhas coincides with a new view of the Buddha-nature, to which we shall come. In any event, the Buddhas are like Hindu gods, though less ritualized and magical. All this was a way of incorporating *bhakti* devotionalism into the tradition, and so in a way of beautifying it. This was *upāya* or skill in means, and was an extension of tendencies developing in the Hīnayāna or, as Hajjime Nakamura calls it, Conservative

Buddhism (to avoid the pejorative tone of Hīnayāna). The issue could be simplified as follows: Buddhism, in offering *nirvāṇa*, does not offer much. It offers serenity and insight in this life, and loss of individual personal existence in the beyond. It is like a kind of spiritual suicide. It exhorts us to give up, and to exert other-directed compassion. It eliminates both self and selfishness. From this perspective, it is unattractive. The glories of Buddhist art and the serenity of monks and nuns depict an ideal in attractive fashion which may skillfully seduce people into the path. In any event, the first two levels reflect an extension of the Buddhist piety. But there is a third level, which, so to speak, retains the integrity of the religion. The highest level is the *dharmakāya* of the Buddha – his abstractness as Suchness or Voidness (*tathatā* and *śūnyatā*). It is, as it were, the Buddha as ultimate truth, as *paramārtha*. For in the final state of enlightenment and inner mystical light there is no distinction between subject and object. There is no distinction between the Buddha and the Truth. So there is a radical difference between the highest Aspect and the others. Despite the apparatus of devotion, the ultimate aim is that white light in which all dissolves in emptiness and yet returns in ordinary life. The rest was a kind of apparatus to facilitate our training in the path.

All of this chimed in with a new view of the Buddha-nature. That notion grew from the perceptions of the Mahāyāna. It followed from the ideas just sketched that *nirvāṇa* and Buddhahood were identical – that is, that if the Buddha is in the last resort ultimate emptiness, then anyone who achieves that state is indistinguishable from the Buddha, is indeed a Buddha. That is why, as the saying went, Buddhas are as innumerable as the sands along the Ganges. Everyone is potentially a Buddha. By the same token, she or he is a Bodhisattva, a Buddha-to-be. By taking the vow, a person steps knowingly upon the path. Of course, a Bodhisattva in the Mahāyāna conception puts off his final liberation, or in other words Buddhahood, until other suffering beings have been liberated, and this is an extra twist to the myth. Still, in principle everyone can and will be a Buddha. So each contains the Buddha-nature within her or him. This is the final substitute for a soul. But it can be affirmed in the Mahāyāna context without sacrificing the essentials of the faith – impermanence, liberation, compassion. Indeed, the idea of the Bodhisattva-path is essentially a concrete restatement of the spirit of the *brahmavihāras* (with, however, a special emphasis on compassion).

In brief, the concepts of emptiness, non-dual awareness (*advaya*) and Buddhahood could combine in a fruitful way in this mixture of mythic creativity, philosophical sophistication and ethical concern. Into this framework Nāgārjuna fitted well. His Mādhyamika school became the most influential in the Mahāyāna, though it must be said that emphases changed somewhat in China, Korea and Japan with the migration of Buddhist thought and its alteration by translation and by coming into contact with Taoism and other forces in Eastern culture. Already it had been influenced in its north-western migrations into what is now Afghanistan and along the Silk Route. It had picked up new Buddhas, such as Amitāyus. In trying to bend local cultures in a Buddhistic direction, it inevitably was strongly affected by them in turn. Still, the Mahāyāna philosophy, such as Mādhyamika and the attendant ideas of skillful means and the Three-Aspect doctrine could make sense of its religious development. There were, however, further philosophical developments beyond the Mādhyamika, and to these I shall turn, before sketching some of the later changes in both "Lesser Vehicle" and Mādhyamika.

There were positive, rather than critical and negative, extensions of the central insight of Nāgārjuna. One was the Vijñānavāda or Yogācāra school, and the other the tradition which came to be known as Hua-yen in China – we shall come to that school when we consider the diversions and developments of Buddhist philosophy in China. As for Yogācāra, its chief progenitor was Maitreyanātha (ca. 270 to 350 CE). The various Yogācārin works, though attributed to him, seem actually to have issued from his various important disciples. The most notable of these were the brothers Asanga and Vasubandhu of the fourth century CE. The former codified Maitreyanātha's teachings in distinguishing between three kinds of phenomena: those which arise from *parikalpita* or illusory projections of the mind; those which are *paratantra* or dependent realities, which have merely provisional existence; and that which is *parinispanna*, or perfect suchness or *tathatā*. It is clear that the distinction between the last and the first two is crucial. However, more important in the structure of Idealist thinking (as it is sometimes called) is the thesis that events or *dharmas* are merely manifestations of so-called seeds or *bījas* which arise out of the so-called store-consciousness or *ālayavijñāna*, which occurs as a kind of collective consciousness accounting for the world as manifested. The doctrine implies that phenomenal existences are nothing other than "mere representations" or *vijnāptimātratā* and yet that there is some sense in which they are out there. The major treatment of the theory is attributed to Vasubandhu, Asanga's brother. His chief expository works were the *Viṃśatikā* or "Twenty Verses" and the *Triṃśikā* or "Thirty Verses." There is some debate as to whether he is the same Vasubandhu who wrote the magisterial "Realist" work the *Abhidharmakośa*. We shall treat this separately in due course: whether the author is the same Vasubandhu matters rather little, since the two sets of works are philosophically rather different in any case.

The Yogācārin doctrine is described as "representation only." Its most straightforward interpretation is to the effect that all experiences are subjective. The image of an object in consciousness does not tell us that there is an "object out there." The general view in the school is that the seeds contained in the stored consciousness generate images. In Asanga's work, the *Mahāyānasaṁgraha* or "Compendium of the Mahāyāna," it is argued that there are no "things-in-themselves" on the following grounds. First, differing states of existence generate differing consciousnesses. A stream of clean water is seen as a flaming burn by an inmate of purgatory, while a ghost would see it differently. (This is scarcely an empirical argument since ghosts and purgatory are not typically seen as parts of consciousness.) Then again, a yogin may perceive the future. Third, yogis and other meditators may acquire the ability to see something at will, and this does not imply the existence of such an object of consciousness. Finally, the higher mystic may perceive the transcendent, and there is no image of something "out there".

The bottom line of this idealism is that yoga-practice (and the Yogācārins are Yoga-practitioners literally) can transform life, in that once we realize that there are no external objects, then the consciousness has nothing to seize "out there." We see that we can transform our subjective life, eliminating the seeds which defile it. In due course, we can truly eliminate the effects of the store-consciousness and attain an undifferentiated unity of consciousness. This is liberation. The theory, of course, does give an account of why it is that we think that there is a real world out there. The seeds produce the various constituents of the individual, including the *manas* or mental organ, which, in synthesizing the deliverances of the senses, contrasts inner and outer realities. We can eliminate this sense of duality by the process of yogic training. It may be noted that the meditative consciousness is what helps to confirm the subjectivism of the school. In this we may note an epistemological slant. The true source of information is the consciousness of the yogin. It is his perception of the world, from within as it were, which determines the shape of the worldview. In short, though the school has its empirical basis, it is also partial in neglecting outer for inner perception. Nevertheless, it typically recognizes the subject-object structure of ordinary perception, though Sthiramati (sixth century CE) considered this structure to be merely imagined (*parikalpita*).

While Vasubandhu was the major thinker in the Vijñānavāda, he may have made an important contribution also to Sārvāstivādin thinking. (Whether or not he did depends, of course, on whether he was the author of the *Abhidharmakośa* as well as of the Yogācārin works.) This last work belongs to the Sautrāntika stream, which diverged from the Sarvāstivādins about four hundred years after the time of the Buddha. Their teachings were based more on the Sūtra texts than on theAbhidharma – hence their name. The Sautrāntikas held that there were real objects "out there," but by the time the impression emanated by them reached the consciousness they were already gone. They held to the *kṣanika* theory, according to which all events are momentary. Only the present really exists (since the past and the future, strictly speaking, do not exist), and it leaves behind it a trace of "perfume," which accounts for later effects. By contrast, the mainstream Sarvāstivādins held that *dharmas* exist all along, but manifest themselves only momentarily. Vasubandhu's magisterial work formed a main source for interpreting the conservative Buddhist tradition and was influential in China.

Meanwhile, somewhat in contrast to the Mādhyamika emphasis upon emptiness, and its "negative theology" in Buddhism, there emerged various Mahāyāna scriptures – most notably the *Lankāvatāra Sūtra* or Descent on Lanka Sūtra – which emphasized more positively the notion of the Buddhahood of individuals. This more "positive buddhology" is given to stressing the Buddha-nature in us all. But actually the contrast is not a strong one with the Voidism of the Mādhyamika. Its effects were fairly evident, however, in the Far East, where the *Lankāvatāra* was influential.

So far the Mahāyāna schools can be seen as philosophical, though always with outreach to the spiritual quest. There is little in Buddhist philosophy which is not genuinely related to pragmatics. Buddhism was a highly conceptual tradition, and this has revived in modern times. For Buddhism, philosophical doctrines are soteriologically vital. In the case of Pure Land Buddhism, which also emerged powerfully in the trend towards Mahāyāna and high Mahāyāna faith, the emphasis was heavily on the devotional; the philosophical dimension was much less evident. It arose as a religious movement based on the thought that as we get further and further away from the time of the Buddha Gautama himself there is less and less chance of attaining liberation, except that celestial Buddhas and Bodhisattvas may help us. The logic of worship is that we have nothing and God has much: it is through his or her grace that we raise ourselves. So too with celestial Buddhas, and above all Amitābha, who has created a Pure Land or Paradise, far to the West, whither the otherwise unfaithful may be transferred if they just call on the Buddha in faith. This parallel to Lutheranism is remarkable, and the faith caught hold in India, but even more strongly in East Asia, and especially in Japan.

Another trend in Mahāyāna philosophy had to do with logic. Perhaps the greatest of the Buddhist logicians was Dignāga (late fifth century CE), who simplified the existing (Nyāya) syllogism and gave new concision to Buddhist epistemology. The point was that logic itself was seen as a mode of acquiring knowledge, so that logic and epistemology were fused together. His successor, Dharmakīrti (about 600 to 650 CE), regarded the Buddha as a source of knowledge, in addition to perception and inference. This was logical in terms of the Mahāyāna, though it shifted Buddhism in the direction of Hindu thinking, which recognized testimony as a source of knowledge (including testimony through scriptures, or rather the oral brahmanical tradition).

As traditions moved on there were of course divisions. Thus the Mādhyamika school divided into those who considered Nāgārjuna's method to be *prasaṅgika* (the method of *reductio ad absurdum*) and those who saw it as *savtantrika* (the meaning of which we shall come back to). The most eminent interpreter advancing the Prasaṅgika view was Chandrakīrti (early seventh century CE). Before that there was Buddhapālita (470?–540?). He in turn was strongly criticized on logical grounds by Bhāvaviveka (late fifth, early sixth century CE). The dispute was an important one and was concerned more with metaphysics than with logic. On the one hand, the Prasaṅgikas argued that Nāgārjuna's dialectic was really negative. It argued for the destruction of all views, and thus even one's own view was empty. On the other hand, their opponents argued that there had to be some worldview being proposed. The debate was important, but it is difficult to see how a pure Prasaṅgika position can be maintained.

The dialectic between the negative and positive ways of treating the ultimate produced some vigorous notions of the latter type, notably the idea of the Buddha-essence or *Tathāgatagarbha*, which was already present in the earliest Mahāyāna texts, but which later received a more luminous exposition in the *Lankāvatāra Sūtra* and in works such as Maitreyanatha's *Ratnagotravibhāga* (fourth century CE). The Buddha-essence is thought of as dwelling in each living being, and has timeless significance. It substitutes spiritually for a soul or *ātman*. While its nature is considered to be emptiness, according to the two-level theory of truth, it has a transcendent nature: it is positively considered to be the ultimate.

Meanwhile, from the sixth to the twelfth centuries CE, when Buddhism was fading from India, partly under the impact of the Muslim invasions, a third form of religion and philosophy, the *Vajrayāna* or Diamond Vehicle, much identified with Tantric practices, was developing in India and came to be especially important in Tibet as Buddhism took root there. It also, of course, had influence further east and in South-East Asia too. From one point of view, Tantra could be seen as ritual in form. *Mantras* or ritual formulae and practices were absorbed into Buddhism, and brought it much closer to the Hindu tradition. The ritualizing of Buddhism meant the fusing of inner yogic practices, on the one hand, and external means of influencing *devas* and other supernatural forces. From another perspective, it involved the breaking of taboos in order to create higher states of self-control and spirituality. A number of vital texts can be mentioned. There was the *Mahāvairocanābhisambodhi* (seventh century CE or earlier), the *Hevajra Tantra*, a so-called mother tantra, and the *Gūhyasamāja*, a so-called father tantra. The former emphasizes the bliss of insight or *prajñā*, which was often portrayed as a goddess. The latter emphasizes mediation on the emptiness of *upāya* and the presence of the *dharma* aspect in the world. We shall return to an elaboration of tantric themes in treating of Tibetan Buddhism. The latter was important not only because it preserved and developed Tantric Buddhism, but also because it preserved a wealth of Sanskrit texts which represent important swathes of Indian philosophical and religious thought.

Meanwhile, from the first century CE, Buddhism was seeping into China via the Silk Route, and later into South-East China by sea. All forms of Buddhism came to be present in the Middle Kingdom. Philosophically, there were important developments arising from the interaction of Buddhism with various Chinese themes and schools, most notably Daoism (both philosophical and religious). The texts and monks, as they reached China, exhibited a bewildering diversity of schools emanating from India. The task of translation took several centuries, and it was chiefly in the Sui and Tang periods (589–906 CE) that new syntheses were achieved. As Buddhism became consolidated in a Chinese version it came to coexist reasonably amicably with the Daoist and Confucian traditions to form the so-called "Three Religions of China." It is true that in the second millennium it tended to be looked on as popular, rather than élite and intellectual, but in fact it was in this period that it had its greatest effect on Confucian philosophy, stimulating a more metaphysical and contemplative version.

The new synthesis achieved in the Sui and Tang periods was the product of two main impulses. One was the challenge of dealing with the splendid but difficult diversity. Could some sort of order be imposed on the heterogeneous texts and doctrines? The result was a kind of scholastic dispensationalism – a federalism of the Buddhist spirit, as it were, assigning patterns of development and growth. The other impulse was towards radical simplification. (See Erik Zürcher's fine article on this in the *Encyclopedia of Religion*). To some extent, this could be seen in Pure Land Buddhism, but it was most clearly evident in the formation of Chan.

Chan Buddhism helped to cut through the tangle of varied doctrines. It restored to Buddhism its main contemplative base. It is true that its style differed from, say, Theravāda, but it has strong affinities to early Theravāda, especially as seen in the *Theragāthā* and *Therīgāthā*. Another school that was important in the Chinese tradition and one which had a Chinese stamp, though it had its source in the *Avataṃsaka Sūtra*, was the Huayan school. We shall discuss this first, then the complex attempts at a dispensational synthesis, and finally Chan.

Huayan, based on the *Avataṃsaka* or "Flower Ornament" scripture, is important because it gave a highly positive interpretation of the *pratītyasamutpāda*. From a traditional Buddhist point of view, this was often interpreted as showing that, because of relativity, each event or entity in the world is empty – that is, lacking in its own substantial nature or *svabhāva*. But from the Huayan worldview, it means that everything in the cosmos is connected. It is true that there is much else in the miraculous text, with its wonderful depiction of the Bodhisattva's path. Nevertheless, the interdependency of all things in the world is the most important message. It is summed up in the metaphor of Indra's net, in which a jewel at each intersection of the web reflects every other jewel. This glittering metaphor for the universe has its echoes in some aspects of modern cosmology. Be that as it may, the picture conveyed a more positive view of the Buddha's message than typical interpretations. The Huayan tradition credits as its first patriarch Fashun (also known as Dushun, 557–640). The next important figure was Zhizheng (559–639). During subsequent developments, the influence of Huayan spread to Korea and Japan. Huayan produced a theory of other forms of Buddhism, and saw itself as the true and rounded doctrine. According to this account, the Theravāda and other kinds of Hīnayāna taught the emptiness of the self and of the things in the world, but they did not teach underlying insight. The early Mahāyāna radicalized the doctrine of emptiness, but became too idealistic. The tradition of the *Tathāgatagarbha* likewise ran the risk of a lack of realism about the events of the cosmos. The Chan school and some earlier texts underestimated the effectiveness of language and undervalued the importance of efforts at self-control. Only the Huayan, therefore, had a balanced and middle doctrine. It was the ultimate path, subsuming and surpassing the other forms of Buddhism.

In a way, it followed the idea of federalizing Buddhist schools. Other Chinese schools had other paths to this goal. The chief founder of the Tiantai school was Zhiyi (538–597). He inspired a schematism (finalized by later scholars) which saw the Buddha's teachings as being expressed in five periods: first the Huayan period (meaning the Buddha first taught this philosophy); second, the Agama or Deer-Park period, when the Buddha taught the Lesser Vehicle, because his audience was incapable of grasping the Huayan message; third, there was the first Mahāyāna phase, when the Buddha demolished the Hīnayāna, and praised greater perfection; fourth, he preached the Lotus Sūtra, the quintessence of his teaching; finally, though, as he was dying, he taught not only basic discipline, but the eternity of the Buddha. This schema was elaborated by subsequent Tiantai scholastics. Though it was a sort of dispensationalism, assigning diverse teachings to differing ages, it was projected back on the life of the Buddha without regard to real historicity. Still, it was a great achievement which seemed to make sense of the diversity of the texts and of Buddhist history. This was a main reason for its popularity in China and beyond. In addition, Zhiyi classified differing elements of teaching and differing styles of meditation, and in all of this aimed to create not only a historical synthesis, but a doctrinal and a pragmatic or pastoral one as well.

If Huayan and Tiantai represent two major achievements of Chinese Buddhist thinking, probably Chan is the most powerful in subsequent influence. According to the tradition, it was brought to China by Bodhidharma (died CE 520), a brahmin convert from South India. His historicity is open to question, but he plays a vital role in Chan narrative. The school he is supposed to have founded shows a strong Chinese flavor, partly because some of its principles are close to those of philosophical Daoism. While it is clearly Buddhist in its emphasis on meditation and loyalty to the figure of the Buddha, it has heterodox characteristics. This is summed up in a famous verse, dating from later in the tradition:

> A special tradition outside of the scriptures;
> No dependence on written words;
> Pointing directly at the human heart;
> Seeing into one's own nature and achieving Buddhahood.

It is true that Buddhism in theory does not depend on scriptures, but given the huge role they played in the transmission and development of the Buddha's message, the Chan announcement was alarming. Even Bodhidharma is supposed to have commended the *Lankāvatāra Sūtra*. In fact, Chan practitioners were often, like other Buddhist monks, keen scholars. Nevertheless, the directness of Chan methods led to a great simplification of Buddhist thinking. As the school developed, five branches emerged, of which the most important were the Linji (founded by Linji, who died in 866) and the Caodong (named after its two founders, both of the ninth century). The former was the dominant Chan school during the Song dynasty, and was associated with the notion of sudden enlightenment or illumination. It made use of paradoxical formulas and dialectical questioning, meant to jolt the conceptual activity of the adept. These *gongan* puzzles were proposed by a master to his pupil, and the latter, in struggling with their apparent absurdity, runs up against the boundaries of logic. Part of the idea has to do with language: while it is necessary for communication, it distorts reality, which is simply "there" (or if we are talking about the inner world, simply "here"). The discipline of Chan is itself perhaps paradoxical. It is supposed to give rise to spontaneous "conversion," but the method involves the master–pupil relationship. The master guides the pupil in his spiritual path and in his struggle to attain enlightenment. The Caodong school emphasized a gradualist approach in contrast to the sudden-enlightenment approach of the Linji. The school of Fayan (885–958) combined Huayan metaphysics with Chan meditation. Chan influenced Neo-Confucianism and later made a considerable mark in Korea and Japan. It was also of great artistic importance, its influence upon painting in China being considerable, as is seen in the several versions of the famous ox-herding pictures and in the genius of Liang Kai (early thirteenth century).

Mongolian rule in China between 1280 and 1368 had the effect of planting Mongolian and Tibetan Buddhist influence in China. The modern period saw the need for reform in China, especially after the 1911 Revolution, and indeed Buddhism attempted to purify itself, especially under the leadership of Taixu (1899–1947). However, the period was not a propitious one, with civil wars, World War II and the victory of Communism. It is only in recent years that

Buddhist religion in China is making a tentative recovery. Philosophical thinking was more vigorous in Japan.

Probably the most important contribution of Korean Buddhism lay in the thought of Chinul (1158–1210), who synthesized Sōn (Chan) Buddhism with Huayan. In this, he revivified scholastic Buddhism and the meditation tradition, which in his view had become somewhat degenerate during his time. Another vital Korean development was the founding of Won Buddhism, a kind of "perennial philosophy" Buddhism with Daoist, Confucian and other elements, by Pak Chung-bin (1891–1943) in 1916.

It was in the middle of the fifth century CE that Buddhism was first introduced to the Japanese court, but it was some time later that the regent Shotoku (574–622) systematically brought in important texts and traditions. Subsequently, in the Nara period (eighth century) three main philosophical schools were represented – namely, the Sanron (Mādhyamika), Hosso (Yogācāra), and Kegon (Huayan). There was also study of Lesser Vehicle texts, notably the *Abhidharmakośa* (or Kosha). Notable during the subsequent Heian period (794–1185) was the establishment of an ecumenical and pluralistic Tendai school (Tiantai), by Saicho (767–822), who had immersed himself in Hosso, Kegon, Sanron, and Zen forms of the faith. It was universalist in recognizing the Buddhahood of all of humankind, and indeed of sentient beings more generally, and he took a positive stance towards the world of phenomena. He was thus only partially idealistic, and not utterly nihilistic (as some members of the Sanron might have appeared). The Lotus Sūtra provided an embracing worldview. Tendai eventually won court approval and became profoundly influential in Japanese life, which characteristically often favored theories of harmony over those emphasizing division. Another school of influence during this period was Shingon, founded by Kūkai (also known as Kobo Daishi, 774–835). This esoteric movement combined yoga with ritual, both in the form of gestures of *mudras* and magical formulae (or perhaps we should say mantric utterances).

During the Kamakura period (1185–1333), there developed an intense sense of decline in Buddhism. It had long been thought that the further one gets from the time of the Buddha the further one finds oneself from the possibility of salvation. Hence during *mappō* (or the age of the decline of Buddhism), one needs to rely for liberation on the saving grace of Amida (Amitabha) Buddha, who conveniently has created a Pure Land far to the West whither all those who call on his name in faith will be conveyed. The Pure Land is paradise, but also a place where things are propitious for the rapid attainment of *nirvāṇa*. By means of this myth and maneuver, *nirvāṇa* is, as it were, translated from this world to the next. The second and strongest phase of Pure Land Buddhism was initiated by Shinran (1173–1262), who radically reshaped Buddhism in certain ways. As Shinran saw it, the vow to Amida Buddha became more important than taking refuge in the three jewels (*triratna*) of traditional Buddhism, since if a good person could be saved by Amida, how much more important would it be for a sinner to be saved in this way. This extreme doctrine of grace is strikingly similar to the teaching of Lutheranism and other forms of Protestantism – so much so that Francis Xavier on reaching Japan regretted the fact that Luther had been there before him! However, probably the most important development of Buddhist thinking in Japan was Zen, both in its Rinzai (Linji) form, founded by Eisai (1141–1215), and in its Sōtō (Caodong) form, founded by Dōgen (1200–1253). Eisai presented a radical view of language, but was more ecumenical in relation to other kinds of Buddhism. He tended to be nationalist in thinking of the role of Zen with respect to the state. While Eisai was keen on the use of the *kōan*, Dōgen was more traditional in his emphasis on sitting meditation or *zazen*. But both actually reflected central concerns of Buddhism, and in a way they were going back to the Theravāda, even though the latter was less optimistic about the attainment of enlightenment. In modern times, Zen came to have a considerable impact in the West.

Modern Japan, of course, underwent great changes during the Meiji period and after. Among the more important figures in Buddhist thinking in the modern period, there is Nishida Kitarō (1870–1945), no doubt modern Japan's foremost philosopher. He developed, against the background of Western Neo-Kantianism, a Buddhist philosophy of nothingness, sometimes using place as an analogy, according to which absolute nothingness or the mirror of Dharma presents itself in the individuals of the world. His student, Tanabe Hajjime (1885–1962), helped to form the famous Kyoto School. He was a philosopher of mathematics, but also developed a theory of ethnic species – in other words, nationalism. A not dissimilar philosophy was to be found in the works of Watsuji Tetsurō (1889–1960), who wrote *Ethics as Anthropology*, which saw morals as communitarian in origin and meaning.

Very influential after World War II was the writing of Suzuki Daisetsu Teitaro (1870–1966), otherwise known as D. T. Suzuki. His writings on Zen constantly stressed the importance of transcending the intellect. He had a philosophical side, not distant from Nishida's, to whom he was close. He saw religion as going beyond science, and in his later years critiqued the latter.

Meanwhile, though Buddhism influenced the Far East earlier than it did Tibet, it not only suffused that culture, but was developed there too, and in Mongolia. Probably the most important figures in Tibetan Buddhism were Atīśa (982–1054) from Bengal or Bihar, whose task in Tibet was to reform monastic discipline and spiritual life, and to introduce some important Indian ideas and texts, notably the *Prajñāpāramitā* texts, and Tson-kha-pa (1357–1382), whose scholastic *Lam rim chen mo* set out in some detail the stages of the meditative path. But Tibetan Buddhism is rich in documentation, so that part of its importance lies in its capacity to let us recover some of the more important Indian (and Chinese) ideas.

We may now look at modern developments in the various Buddhist countries of the world as well as in the West. It is obvious, of course, that the colonial period provided a profound cultural and intellectual shock to Buddhist cultures and countries. It tended to stimulate revivals in various nations, such as Sri Lanka, Thailand, China and elsewhere. In Sri Lanka it was to some degree an organizational reformation, as well as a spiritual one. But it was an intellectual one too. The foundation of the Pāli Text Society was important, in making the Pāli canon easily available to people in South-East Asia and in Sri Lanka. The translations of the texts opened Westerners' eyes to the sophistication of the Buddhist religion, while the *Sacred*

Books of the East (1879–1904), edited by F. Max Müller (1823–1900), the German Oxford professor helped to educate Westerners in Buddhist, Hindu and other writings. In Theravādin countries the revival of Buddhism was partly an early modernist movement in which Buddhist texts were seen in relation to science. A main mover in Thailand was the king, who was also a monk, Mongkut (1804–1868). He demythologized the older, more fabulous accounts of the cosmos. He had his foreign minister and friend publish a book, *Kitchanukt* (*Explaining Various Things*), issued in 1867, which used then modern astronomy, geology, and so on, to explain events without recourse to gods and other supernaturals. The intent was naturalistic. Heaven and hell were demythologized too, being presented as myths for the purpose of inculcating ethical behavior. He was also involved in reforming the *sangha*. Thus he and his son Chulalongkorn helped to radically modernize Thailand. Meanwhile, in Burma (Myanmar), Sri Lanka and elsewhere in the region, there were attempts to bring Buddhism to a stronger and purified state. It was, however, in Sri Lanka that a modern East–West synthesis took deepest philosophical root, especially through the work of philosophers such as G. P. Malalasekara and K. N. Jayatilleke. The former (1899–1973) was important in presenting a Buddhism which also cut through the differences between the Theravāda and the Mahāyāna. He was, in fact, the first President of the World Fellowship of Buddhists, founded in 1950, and was also editor of the important *Encyclopedia of Buddhism*. Malalasekara was perhaps more a philologist and a historian than a philosopher proper, but his contributions to Buddhist thinking were wide-ranging. He was a major creator of what may be called modernist Buddhism. (Others coined the less appropriate phrase, Protestant Buddhism.) He worked closely with Jayatilleke (1924–70), whose most vital book was *Early Buddhist Theory of Knowledge*. This presents a very plausible account of the Buddha's teachings from the Pāli canon, seeing them as "empiricism plus" – "plus" for two reasons: first, because paranormal experiences were subsumed under the head of empirical experience, and second, because of *nirvāṇa*, which is there (so to speak) ineffably beyond the empirical world, including the paranormal. In his posthumous *The Message of the Buddha*, Jayatilleke expressed a modernist Buddhism intelligible to the layperson. While other new movements in Sri Lanka have a more pragmatic and spiritual character, there is little doubt that Malalasekara and Jayatilleke presented a type of Buddhism well adapted to the thinking of the contemporary world, and aligned with scientific attitudes.

Finally, there is a Buddhist philosophy to consider in the West. Buddhism is a very philosophical religion, even if its philosophical thoughts are also pragmatic and contemplative. But even Bertrand Russell had his views on happiness. And so Buddhism has proved somewhat attractive to Western intellectuals and certainly in a modest way to thoughtful Westerners interested in spirituality. In Europe, Theravāda, being thought to be the more original and older Buddhism, was admired in part because, in dispensing with the idea of God, it could be seen as both agnostic and spiritual. It appealed to the disillusioned Victorian, and its ethics were noble and rational. However, it was philosophers who really first began to infuse Western intellectuality with Buddhist thoughts. Schopenhauer (1788–1860) was notable in affirming his solidarity with Buddhism, though in fact his ideas preceded his acquaintance with Eastern thought (including the Upaniṣads). Still there were overlaps with Buddhist ideas. His pessimism allegedly coincided with Buddhist gloom. In fact, Western apprehension in this regard was mistaken. It is true that there is in Buddhism the thought of *duḥkha* or illfare, but one of the great divine states or great ethical precepts is *mudita* or joy-in-others'-joy.

At a rather lower level of intellectual activity, but important all the same – in fact, most important in the renaissance of intellectual Buddhism in Ceylon – was the Theosophical movement of Blavatsky and Olcott. Olcott's trip to Ceylon and their design of the Buddhist flag were important for Theravāda Buddhists, and all of this helped to spark some of the intellectual renaissance we have alluded to in dealing with modern Ceylon. Meanwhile, parallel effects could be attributed to scholarly works on Buddhist texts. The work of Sir Edwin Arnold, namely *The Light of Asia*, a fine poem, had a great effect in late Victorian times.

Meanwhile Buddhism came to be perceived philosophically primarily through relatively popular works, such as Alan Watts's *The Way of Zen*, which became important in the United States in the 1960s, a period of scepticism, spirituality and revolt. Intellectuals could find it useful to espouse Zen, because of its view of language as purely human and distorting. It was an irrationalist position, for example, that Watts expressed, and irrationalism is useful to those who wish to adopt a spiritual position. Not dissimilar views, as we have seen, had been expressed earlier by Suzuki.

On the whole, Western philosophy has not paid much attention to non-Western thinking. It has therefore not paid much attention to Buddhist philosophy. The reasons are various, although chief among them must stand colonial arrogance. There is now, however, an increasing concern for Buddhist thinking. One reason for this is the greater interest in religions generally, dating in part from the turbulence of the 1960s. Another is the growth of Religious Studies departments in Anglophone universities. Another is the emergence of journals such as *Philosophy East and West*. Finally, there is a growing interest in cross-cultural issues, both in religion and in philosophy. New insights have been gleaned, for example, in comparative investigations into Buddhism and Wittgenstein, Buddhism and human rights, Buddhism and the environment. These inquiries may in the long run turn out to be very fruitful. There is in the meantime an immense amount of descriptive, rather than conceptual work being done in the field of Buddhist studies. It is reasonable to think that the divergence between the traditional Buddhist world and the so-called Western world has begun to fade. It is to be hoped that this will increasingly apply in the field of philosopy. In any event, the greater prevalence of Buddhist texts and of the books of Nishida and other important contemporary Buddhist philosophers will in the long run make a difference.

Bibliography

Ch'en, Kenneth 1964: *Buddhism in China* (Princeton: Princeton University Press).
Conze, Edward 1951: *Buddhism: Its Essence and Development* (Oxford: B. Cassier).

Dumoulin, Heinrich 1953: *The Development of Chinese Zen* (New York: First Zen Institute of America).
—— 1963: *A History of Zen Buddhism* (New York: Pantheon Books).
Eliot, Charles 1964: *Japanese Buddhism* (London: Routledge & Kegan Paul).
Fung, Yu-lan 1952–3: *A History of Chinese Philosophy*, 2 Vols. (Princeton: Princeton University Press).
Guenther, Herbert V. 1957: *Philosophy and Psychology in the Abhidharma* (Berkeley: Shambhala).
Jayatilleke, K. N. 1963: *Early Buddhist Theory of Knowledge* (London; Allen & Unwin).
Junjiro, Takakasu 1964: *The Essentials of Buddhist Philosophy* (Honolulu).
Murti, T. R. V. 1955: *The Central Philosophy of Buddhism* (London: Allen & Unwin).
Nakamura, Hajjime 1964: *Ways of Thinking of Eastern Peoples* (Tokyo: Print Bureau, Japanese Government).
—— 1980: *Indian Buddhism: a Survey with Bibliographical Notes.*
Robinson, Richard H. 1976: *Early Mādhyamika in India and China* (Madison: University of Wisconsin Press).
Smart, Ninian 1992: *Doctrine and Argument in Indian Philosophy* (Leiden: E. J. Brill).
Streng, Frederick J. 1967: *Emptiness: a Study in Religious Meaning* (Nashville: Abingdon Press).
Suzuki, D. T. 1961: *Essays in Zen Buddhism* (New York: Grove Press).
Thomas, Edward J. 1933: *The History of Buddhist Thought* (London: Kegan Paul, Trench, Trubner & Co.).
Tucci, Giuseppe 1980: *The Religions of Tibet* (Berkeley: University of California Press).
Walpola, Rahula 1967: *What the Buddha Taught* (Bedford: Gordon Fraser Gallery).
Warder, A. K. 1970: *Indian Buddhism.*
Zurcher, Erik 1959: *The Buddhist Conquest of China* (Leiden: E. J. Brill).

6

Islamic philosophy: an overview

TAMARA ALBERTINI

Islamic philosophy developed within a highly diversified doctrinal and religious tradition, and consequently represents a very complex phenomenon encompassing many different political, intellectual, dogmatic, and spiritual movements. Insight into the historical circumstances that shaped Islamic thought is necessary for an understanding of Arabic philosophical concerns in the early period of Islam and for subsequent Muslim intellectual interests. It also helps, of course, in approaching topics, themes and genres of Islamic philosophy that cannot be appreciated by applying only the standards set by occidental thought. Questions of philosophical significance relating to the Quran, the humanistic disciplines (particularly language and history), juridical theology or Shīʿite spirituality will therefore be treated in this paper with the same measure of consideration as the Western-originated concepts of the rationalist schools in Islam. Only in this way can we avoid the temptation to restrict our discussion to those few Muslim thinkers who, in constructing their philosophical systems, have stood on the shoulders of the ancient Greek philosophers, and whose books have therefore become known to the Latin West.

Historic survey

Considering the salient features of politics, theology, and education in the early Islamic empire, we notice three factors that have particularly contributed to the richness of Islamic intellectual life:

1 The influence of cultural sources foreign to the original Arabic cultural area and the intellectual competition among different religious and ethnic communities.
2 The division of Islam into Sunnism and Shīʿism, and subsequently into numerous religious schools with diverging (and occasionally contradictory) forms of spirituality.
3 The ideal of purity in language and religion and the struggle for religious orthodoxy in the dispute between Rationalists and Traditionalists within Sunni Islamic theology.

(1) The influence of cultural sources foreign to the original Arabic cultural area and the intellectual competition among different religious and ethnic communities. From the beginning, the Muslim world had to deal with various highly civilized nations

surrounding the Arabian Peninsula, the original territory from which Islam emerged. The Persian and the Byzantine empires, with their refined cultures and well established religions, presented particular challenges. When nations of the neighbouring empires converted to Islam and transferred their cultural achievements into a Muslim *Weltanschauung*, the early Islamic rulers faced serious difficulties in harmonizing the different traditional backgrounds of these nations, which had elaborated incompatible legal systems, produced their own forms of erudition, and learned to appreciate the highest standards of artistic expression in ways sometimes contrary to Islamic prescriptions. On the one hand, the religion of the Arab conquerors and their language (which they took to be the language in which God himself had chosen to manifest his will) contributed much to the creation of a religious and political union. As F. E. Peters puts it in his study, *Aristotle and the Arabs*:

> Islam . . . was not so much a State with an Established Religion as a Religion with an Established Language. The *Qur'ān* was in Arabic, and the prime miracle persuasive of the fact that it was indeed the Word of God was the perfection of its language. (Peters, 1968, p. 34)

On the other hand, however, problems arising from the new socio-economic conditions still had to be solved. The legal sphere in particular called for clear guidelines. Already the first ruling Islamic dynasty, the Umayyads (661–750), realized that neither the Quran nor examples taken from the Ḥadīth (the record of the actions and sayings of the Prophet and his companions) alone could help to decide all questions of socio-political life, not even all questions relating to religious and ethical matters. Sources and methods foreign to the Arabo-Islamic culture had to be explored and evaluated as to their applicability – and as to their compatibility with Islamic regulations. Besides, Islam considered itself to be a religion based on *knowledge*; the study of non-Islamic documents, therefore, did not represent *eo ipso* a threat to religious orthodoxy.

The lack of satisfactory theoretical principles in politics and ethics was, however, not the sole motive underlying the many translations commissioned by the Umayyads and their successors, the ʿAbbāsids. Thus one should not overlook the fact that the Islamic world of the seventh century represented a rising culture, anxious to measure its intellectual potential against the achievements of older cultures.

How deeply Islam felt its cultural backwardness can be seen from the way in which official positions were distributed in the early Muslim empire. While the higher offices in government and the army were entrusted to Arabs, the care of the arts and sciences fell to non-Arabs, in particular to Syrian Christians (who themselves spoke a Semitic language and had already appropriated much of Greek science into their own idiom and culture). Another indication of the new cultural orientation was the shifting of the capital of the Umayyad empire from Medina to Kufa (in Iraq) and finally to Damascus. The Arabic holy city continued to foster a knowledge of law and tradition, but it was the Syrian city that became the political and economic capital as well as the centre of the arts and letters. Kufa, on the other hand, remained a chief seat of intellectual life in which, as in Basra, Arabs, Persians, Muslims, Christians and Jews competed in knowledge and skills.

(2) The division of Islam into Sunnism and Shīʿism, and subsequently into numerous religious schools with diverging (and occasionally contradictory) forms of spirituality. Islam payed a high price for the rapid expansion of its empire in the first decades of its existence. While it could be proud of having conquered a territory reaching from the Indus to the Atlantic in just eighty years, it had to deplore the loss of its doctrinal union at a very early stage in its development. The political consequences of religious factionalism included numerous insurrections and long-lasting enmities within the Islamic world. At the same time, however, the doctrinal differences left their marks on the fields of politics, law and ethics, and thus clearly contributed to the enhancement of intellectual life.

The following discussion will concentrate on those movements that challenged the authority of the first Caliphs. (Information on the main schools of the Sunni tradition will be provided in the next section.) It will mainly concern their concepts of the Imāmate, since these had a major impact on the political theories of Islam.

The first to separate were the *Khārijites*, who in 657 protested against ʿAlī ibn Abī Ṭālib, the fourth Caliph (656–661), because he had submitted a theological dispute to arbitration and thus placed a human tribunal above the divine word. In the course of its dispute with ʿAlī the rigoristic Khārijite sect introduced a new criterion legitimating the power of the Imāmate. Qurayshi birth – that is, affiliation to the leading families of Medina – was no longer held to constitute a sufficient qualification; instead, every morally and religiously impeccable believer could be raised by the community to the dignity of the Imāmate. In connection to the formulation of this moral criterion, the sect developed a strict religious ethic, rejecting the doctrine of justification by faith alone. As a result, the commission of a mortal sin led to the loss of one's claim to the title of believer.

A few years after the Khārijite separation, which generated further subdivisions, the major schism in Islamic history occurred – one that still divides the Muslim world into two communities, a *Sunnite* and a *Shīʿite*. When Muʿāwiya, the former governor of Syria, defeated the fourth Imām and his sons in 661 and founded the Umayyad Caliphate, the party (*Shīʿa*) of ʿAlī split and gave birth to a new spiritual movement, that of the Shīʿite Muslims. The opposition, which at first appeared to be a merely political movement, soon developed its own doctrinal traditions including its own version of the Ḥadīth and, to some extent, of the Quran itself, since it accused the Sunnites of having purged the Quran of passages revealing the legitimacy of ʿAlī.

Despite the divergent versions of the two major sources of Islamic religion and even though Sunnites and Shīʿites follow their own respective schools of Law (the Twelver Shīʿites, for instance, are essentially *Jaʿfarites*, from Jaʿfar al-Ṣādiq, the sixth Shīʿite Imām, whom they considered a high authority in Islamic Law), their understanding and application of the *ʿibādāt* (laws regulating ritual and religious observances) and the *uṣūl al-fiqh* (methodology of Muslim jurisprudence) do not represent a serious basis of dispute. But the substantial doctrinal differences are related, as in the case of the Khārijites, to the notion of the Imāmate. While for Sunnites the Caliph is a political leader concerned with the care of religious matters without himself necessarily being a theologian, the Shīʿites made it an indispensable condition that the chief leader of the community be a descendant of ʿAlī, which, in their view, was essential to his office as the "Keeper of the Book." Other criteria to be considered included investiture (*naṣṣ*) and impeccability (*ʿiṣma*). Historically, the expectation that the Imām be capable of interpreting the Quran had to do with ʿAlī's own exegetic work. According to his testimony, the Prophet himself taught him the method to employ:

> Not a single verse of the Quran descended upon (was revealed to) the Messenger of God which he did not proceed to dictate to me and make me recite. I would write it with my own hand, and he would instruct me as to its *tafsīr* (literal explanation) and the *taʾwīl* (the spiritual exegesis), the *nāsikh* (the verse which abrogates) and the *mansūkh* (the abrogated verse), the *muḥkam* and the *mutashābih* (the fixed and the ambiguous), the particular and the general. (Corbin, 1993, p. 46)

We find here exegetic guidelines that came to be thoroughly explored and further developed in the later Shīʿite tradition – and which also determined some of the approaches to be used in works on grammar and lexicography.

The emphasis on the kinship with Muḥammad, however, is not to be understood as a mere sign of respect to the religious founder. It has rather to do with the Shīʿite, particularly Twelver Shīʿite, prophetology according to which there is an eternal Muḥammadan Reality (*ḥaqīqa muḥammadiyya*) – one could also say "Logos" – that is identical with the "true Adam," or the archetypal human Form. This prophetic Reality has a twofold nature, an exoteric and an esoteric one. While the exoteric nature had an earthly manifestation in the person of Muḥammad, the esoteric one manifestated itself in ʿAlī. By stating the existence of a spiritual relationship connecting the Prophet and the Imām prior to their earthly kinship, the Shīʿite doctrine clearly developed a concept of the Imāmate that is part of its prophetology. One problem, however, that this doctrine had to solve beforehand, had to do with the general Islamic belief according to which Muḥammad is the "Seal of the Prophets," the last of God's messengers. Shīʿism had therefore to explain the continuing manifestations of the esoteric dimension of the eternal Muḥammadan Reality. It dealt with this problem by stating that the closing of the cycle of prophecy coincides with the opening of another cycle, which is the cycle of spiritual initiation in which the Imām as the reader of the Quran's hidden message plays a preponderant role (Corbin, 1993, pp. 41–3). Even though not all Shīʿite sects accept all aspects of this belief in the Imām as the esoteric dimension of the eternal prophetic reality, a common ground among these sects can be found in the highly spiritual value that they place on the Imām's exegesis of the Quran.

Another common concept is the notion of the Imām's martyrdom (and more generally the concept of passion) that is historically founded in the assassination of ʿAlī and the violent death or mysterious disappearance of many Shīʿite Imāms. Some earlier Islamic sources distinguish three main branches of Shīʿism – the Zaydīs, the Imāmīs, and the Ghulāt – on the basis of how these interpreted the death of the Imām. Of these three branches, the Zaydīs came nearest to Sunnism (which eventually absorbed them) in that they conceived the martyrdom of the Imām to be of merely political significance. In addition, they expressed in purely rational terms their belief that God's manifestation in the chief religious leader was a matter merely of divine "right guidance." The Imāmīs, by contrast, believed in an influx of divine light into the descendants of ʿAlī, but still maintained the reality of the Imām's death. The Ghulāt (literally, the "excessive ones") is what the Zaydīs and Imāmīs called those Shīʿites for whom the epiphany is to be taken in an absolute sense. Zaydīs applied to this purpose the principle of *ḥulūl* (derived from the Aristotelian doctrine of hylomorphism) and believed that the death of the Imām was nothing but a withdrawal of the deified. The subdivisions of the Zaydīs include the Qarmaṭīs, Ismāʿīlīs, Druzes, Nuṣayrīs, and ʿAlī Ilāhīs, who differed from one another not only in some of the sources they used and commented upon, but also in the way in which they conceived society. The most extreme position was that adopted by the Qarmaṭīs (defunct already by the twelfth century) who pleaded for social reforms and equality as a base of justice. The common possession of property and, at times, of women – along lines similar to those advanced in Plato's *Republic* – were the most distinctive of the social features they advocated. Today, the main branches of Shīʿism are represented by Imāmīs and Ismāʿīlīs, who are also called Twelver Shīʿites and Sevener Shīʿites respectively, in accordance with the number of Imāms they recognize.

(3) The ideal of purity in language and religion and the struggle for religious orthodoxy in the dispute between Rationalists and Traditionalists within Sunni Islamic theology. The search for linguistic and doctrinal purity generated two prevalent intellectual movements in Islam: humanism and scholasticism. Since these are appellations that scholars in the history of ideas usually apply to periods of the Western tradition, some information needs to be provided in order to show the Muslim authorship of these movements – an authorship that does not imply that there were no other factors that helped to shape the later Western "equivalents" (Makdisi, 1990, pp. 329–31).

Humanism or *adab*, which is still in our day considered an ideal of learning and erudition in the Arabic world, arose in the first century of Islam in the context of a reaction to the plurality of languages in the Muslim empire, at a time when purity in language became for the Arabic élite part of the struggle for cultural identity. This is why the humanistic disciplines of Grammar, Literature, Rhetoric, Epistolary Art, History, and Ethics were also called the "Arab Sciences," as opposed to the non-Arab – or Greek – sciences of Philosophy (in the strict sense), Natural Science, and Medicine. (Later classification of the sciences, however, do not respect this division).

Adab had, with respect to its concern with philology, deep roots in the ancient Arabian emphasis on poetry and oratory. With the rise of Islam, the pre-existing preoccupation with language found, however, a new object in the study of the Quran, whose copious vocabulary, style, eloquence, recital, and interpretation required long years of study. This necessity eventually led to the development of a subtle methodology of learning and to the creation of a sophisticated educational system (Makdisi, 1990, pp. 202–27). The early denomination, "Arab Sciences," for the branches of *adab*, however, did not preclude foreign influence on their development. The introduction of the Stoic principle of analogy (*qiyās*) as a method of determining correct grammatical forms and derivatives reveals the influence of versions of Aristotle's *Peri hermeneias* that had been revised by the Stoics – who themselves applied that principle in their restoration of the original (and presumedly perfect) state of the Greek language.

On the other hand, the question arose as to whether the humanistic studies have a monopoly on all matters relating to language. The Sabean mathematician and astronomer Thābit ibn Qurra (836–901), who studied prosody extensively (Arabic versification uses 16 different meters), came to the conclusion that whereas languages as such are national achievements, the study of meters is common to all nations and must therefore be considered part of the natural sciences – and thus a branch of philosophy.

While parallels can easily be drawn between Islamic and Western humanism, Islamic scholasticism presents itself as a phenonemon with reversed premises if we compare it to its later Western counterpart. The theological education offered at Islamic schools had *law* as its subject matter, while the philosophical or rational theology (*kalām*), to which Western scholasticism is the actual equivalent, was excluded from the curriculum. The advancement of Quran- and Ḥadīth-based juridical theology in Muslim schools, and subsequently the rise of guilds of law, which were concerned with religious *and* civil life, came at the end of a long debate between "rationalist" circles that were open to the philosophical arguments and methods of Greek authors and "traditionalist" ones whose aim was, on the contrary, to purge the Islamic world of the influence of foreign thought. Both circles had their respective schools of law. The Rationalists were Ḥanafites, followers of Abū Ḥanīfa (d. 767) who was the first to introduce *qiyās* as a source of law. (He also defended personal opinion (*ra'y*) and the use of dialectic to decide disputed matters.) The anti-Rationalists were the Ḥanbalites, adherents of the school established by Ibn Ḥanbal (780–855). Between these two extremes, one found the Mālikites and the Shāfiʿites.

The struggle for supremacy among these opposing groups was fought over the question of whether the Quran was the uncreated, co-eternal world of God (a position that traditionalist authors strongly supported). While it appeared at first that the Rationalists (*Mutakallimūn*), whose doctrine had been adopted by three ʿAbbāsid Caliphs and who had the Inquisition (*Miḥna*) on their side from 833 until 848, would prevail, ultimately the Traditionalists won the battle. An important factor in that victory was the shift of the former Rationalist Abū al-Ḥasan al-Ashʿarī (872–935) to the Ḥanbalite position. Nevertheless, one finds in the later works of Traditionalists many topics developed by the adherents of *kalām*. George Makdisi lists in his book, *The Rise of Humanism in Classical Islam and the Christian West*, six problems that clearly reveal the impact of *kalām* on juridical theology:

1. the problem of the determination of good and evil;
2. the relation between reason and revelation;
3. the qualification of acts before the advent of revelation;
4. prohibition and permission;
5. the imposition of responsibility or obligation beyonds one's capacity; and
6. the imposition of legal obligation on the non-existent. (Makdisi, 1990, p. 4)

This selection of problems shows that even though Rationalism was defeated in the political arena, its intellectual value in shaping and solving religious and ethical matters was not rejected by Islamic scholasticism. The question of the Good could not be addressed without concepts and notions developed in Greek (and Christian) philosophy; the relation between reason and revelation itself, which was at the centre of the dispute between the Rationalists and the Traditionalists, had to be discussed in terms of arguments produced by the former; and finally, discussions of issues pertaining to moral conduct and religious obligations included concepts and judgments that had been generated in the tradition of *kalām*.

With the exception of inquiry into such things as the soul's nature and functions, which the law doctors Mālik and Shāfiʿī clearly prohibited with reference to the Quran (12,87), Islamic juridical theology continued to examine, transform, and assimilate arguments foreign to its tradition. But it also developed its own system of values and criteria. For instance, of the four "sources" of Islamic law – Quran, Ḥadīth, *qiyās* and consensus (*ijmāʿ*) – the fourth gradually became the prevalent one in deciding disputed cases. The general consensus of the "Congregation of the Faithful" also proved to be the most important means in establishing Muslim ethics. Only in this way could the traditional classification of moral acts that roughly distinguishes between (1) those that have to be put into practice, (2) those that are recommended, (3) those that are permitted, (4) those that are disapproved, and (5) those that are forbidden, be shaped into a truly ethical system of universal application within the Muslim world. There is no reason why the juridical theology of Islam should be denied its philosophical character; it has clearly constituted itself as a powerful *practical philosophy* combining law and ethics. On the other hand, Ashʿarism, the movement founded by al-Ashʿarī for the purpose of breaking the hold of reason upon cosmological, natural, epistemological, and ethical questions, generated some of the most challenging theories of Islamic philosophy, which were able to attract authors of the caliber of Imām al-Ḥaramayn al-Juwaynī (d. 1085), al-Ghazzālī (d. 1111), and Fakhr al-Dīn al-Rāzī (d. 1210).

Systematic survey

Philosophy in the Quran

The Quran is a book of revelation, not a work of philosophy. It does nevertheless contain statements applying to creation, humankind and God from which one can infer views of philosophical significance. Besides, an insight into Quranic cosmology, anthropology, and the Quranic conception of God will help us to understand the tensions that arose between Rationalists and Traditionalists in the second and early third century of Islam.

Cosmology

Before creation, heaven and earth "were of one piece (*ratq*)" (26,30), until God separated them. He shaped seven heavens, also called paths (*ṭarā'iqa*; 23,17), along which angels and spirits can ascend (70,4), and he fashioned the earth by providing it with hills and rivers. Every living thing has been created of water (21,31). Characteristic of the Quranic view is the idea that the entire universe – the sun, the moon, the stars, the hills, the trees, and the beasts (not merely humankind and the angels) – adores God (22,18), and thus it is a *good* creation. Nevertheless, by the end of the world, the divine work will be, as it were, reversed: the sun and the moon will combine, the stars will fall (81,1–2), and the earth will be flattened (79,30). This has to do with the Quranic *finalization* of the creation: the heaven has been lifted so that humankind should be protected; the sun has been created so that the earth has light; the stars have been placed in the sky so that they can guide men; the winds are fertilizing, and so on. Unlike humankind, whose only purpose is to worship God, all other beings have been created for specific ends – most of them of serve humankind.

Anthropology

Different passages in the Quran provide different versions of man's creation. Several verses mention that humankind was shaped from dust or the clay of black mud (6,2; 15,26; 15,28). Others inform us that the original substance was water (25,54) or a drop of thickened fluid (76,2; 86,6). Still other passages are more specific and help to solve the apparent contradiction:

> He began the creation of man from clay; Then He made his seed from a draught of despised fluid; Then He fashioned him and breathed into him of His Spirit (*rūḥ*). (32,7–9; cf. 15,28–9)

Elsewhere we read that God created humankind "from dust, then from a drop of seed, then from a clot, then from a little lump of flesh shapely and shapeless" (22,5; cf. 40,67). It seems that the origin of dust or clay indicates the actual creation, while the mention of a "drop of fluid" or "seed" is a reference to natural reproduction. The final shaping of man, however, requires God's bringing the human form forth from the "shapeless seed." It also implies that God breathes into him his Spirit and endows him with immortality. (Some exegetes, such as al-Ghazzālī, suggest that God has created all the human "seeds" (souls) in the pre-existence, and has caused them to "die" and to wait for the conception of their bodies in the maternal wombs before they are breathed into these. This is an intriguing interpretation in its suggestion that death is already an aspect of the pre-existence.)

The Quran is not very clear about the creation of the genders. The "Sura of the Women" suggests that both Adam and Eve were created from a single soul (4,1; cf. 6,98; 7,189). Unlike the Bible, the Quran does not make Eve (she is not even mentioned by name; her Arabic name, Ḥawwā, is recorded in the Ḥadīth) responsible for the fall. Either Adam alone is being seduced by the *devil* (*Iblīs*) (2,36; 20,120) or both are being tempted (7,22). It is noteworthy that the last passage is considered part of a later *sura*. Besides, Adam's and Ḥawwā's succumbing did not generate in Islam the notion of original sin. Thus, for example, men are not in charge of women because of their moral superiority, but because they excel by nature, and are their providers (4,34). The basic equality of the sexes is underlined by many passages in which the Quran addresses both genders: "men who believe and women who believe, and men who obey and women who obey" (33,35; 33,36; 33,58).

However, the medieval Muslim interpretation of the fall departed from the Quranic story. Ḥadīth statements (in conformity to biblical sources) establishing woman's weakness on the grounds of her dependent origin (from Adam's rib) and on her responsibility for the fall were accepted by scholarly consensus. This resulted in the denial that women possessed rationality and moral autonomy. Some exegetes, such as the Traditionalist al-Ṭabarī (d. 923) and the Ashʿarite Fakhr al-Dīn al-Rāzī, have expressed doubts concerning the legitimacy of the sources used. Still, it was only in the nineteenth century that the validity of the doctrine concerning woman's weakness came to be seriously questioned (Stowasser, 1994, pp. 28ff).

The Quran promotes an anthropocentric view similar to that expounded in the Bible. This could be inferred, of course, from some aspects of the finalization of creation discussed earlier. In addition, the second *sura* declares explicitly that God placed Adam on earth as a vicegerent (*khalīfa*) and endowed him with knowledge by teaching him all the names of things (2,30–1). Beyond this, God has given him power (7,10) by making night, day, the sun, the moon, the stars, the sea, the earth itself, and the animals to serve him (*Sura of the Bee*, 16,5–16, 65–9, 78–81). With respect to Islamic prophetology, it should also be mentioned that the Quran sees in Adam the beginning of prophethood (20,122; 3,33) – a privilege that one school of law has also conferred upon some women.

God: the search for the divine names

The Quranic God is an almighty, eternal, omniscient God who reveals himself in his creation and in the Islamic Scripture. The Quran invites believers to pray to God by using the most beautiful names (7,180). On the basis of this invitation, early authors searched in the Islamic scripture for these divine names, and the Ḥadīth claimed that they are 99 in number. From the point of view of faith, the topic is highly significant, for according to Quranic revelation God also manifests himself through his names. To the believer, then, the question "Which is the most beautiful name?" is tantamount to asking "Which is the name through which God expresses himself best?" – a question that raises a delicate issue, since Islam does not allow that any given passage of the Quran has any greater significance than other passages.

Theologians have responded to this question in various ways. They have stated either: (1) that there is no supreme name (*ism al-aʿẓam*) of God, that every divine name is adequate as long as the mind of the person praying is entirely turned towards his creator; or (2) that the supreme name exists, but is unknowable to humans; or, finally, (3) that the supreme name exists and is known to us. This last position has generated some highly complex suggestions concerning the identity of the supreme name, which one can find along with justifications and counter-arguments in a treatise by Fakhr al-Dīn al-Rāzī (Anawati, 1974, pp. 381–94).

Of the six suggestions offered there, three are of particular interest. One shows the influence of rational speculation, the second bears certain traces of cabalistic procedure, and the third involves elements of Shīʿite letter mysticism. According to the first, God's true name is *Huwa* (He). The focus in the following sentence is on self-identity: "O he, o who has no other he than he, o through whom is the 'he-ity' of every he." The personal pronoun also suggests the ideas of (necessary) "existence" and "absence" (of possibility); it indicates in that way the "uniqueness" (*al-fardāniyya*) of God's existence, whose true essence, being absent, necessarily escapes us. According to the second, the supreme name is *Allāh* (God), since Allāh is at the base of all names. Besides, if one decomposes "Allāh" one letter at a time, each removal of a letter leaves us with a divine name. (In order to understand this, one has to bear in mind that in Arabic only the consonants in a word are written.) Thus by removing the first letter, one obtains *lillāh* (to God); removing the second letter, one is left with *lahu* (to Him); and finally, erasing the third letter, one is left with *Hu(wa)*. Other arguments in favour of taking *Allāh* as the supreme name are that there is no etymology for that name, and that it designates the very essence of God since (unlike an attribute, such as "the Merciful") it cannot be detached from its object or be applied to any other being. And according to the third, God's name is to be found in the mysterious letters that precede the 29 *suras* of the Quran: ALM, ALMṢ, ALR, ALMR, KHYʿṢ, ṬH, ṬS, ṬSM, YS, Ṣ, ḤM, ḤM-ʿSQ, Q, N. The combination of some of these letters do match divine attributes; other letters, however, remain inexplicable.

Authoritative women in Islam

Among the early Islamic sources on women one finds Muḥammad ibn Saʿd's (ninth century) *Kitāb al-Ṭabaqāt al-Kabīr*, the eighth book of which is devoted to Muslim female figures, and al-Maʿāfirī's *Biographies of Famous Women* (1185).

Women from the Prophet's family

The wives of the Prophet (also called the "Mothers of the Believers") have played a major role as models of piety and also in the political events following the Prophet's death. Highly honoured is Khadīja (d. 619), the Prophet's first wife, to whom he remained faithful until her death. ʿĀʾisha (ca. 614–678), Muḥammad's most beloved wife is the only woman in whose presence the prophet received some of his revelations. She was a narrator of the Tradition and an expert in poetry. Her recollections of events and sayings of the Prophet became part of the Ḥadīth. ʿĀʾisha was also instrumental in the election of her father, Abū Bakr, as the first Imām. Fāṭima (ca. 606–632), the Prophet's youngest daughter by Khadīja, was married to ʿAlī ibn Abī Ṭālib, the fourth Imām, and the Shīʿite dynasty of the Fāṭimids is named after her. It is through her, moreover, that the Shīʿite Imāms claim direct descent from the prophet. In Shīʿite tradition, Fāṭima, as the "mistress of sorrow", bears many similarities to the figure of Mary as "*mater dolorosa.*"

Women mentioned in the Quran

Among the female models of righteousness in the Quran, one finds several biblical figures, identifiable as Sara, Hagar (ancestress of the Arabs), ʿĀsiya (the foster mother of Moses), and Bilqīs (the Queen of Sheba). The only woman whose name is explicitly mentioned is Mary (Maryam), the Mother of Jesus (ʿĪsā). The Quran refers to her more frequently than the New Testament and even names a *sura* after her. One of her sayings is often inscribed on the *miḥrāb* (the niche which shows the direction of prayer). The Ḥadīth, on the other hand, establishes an interesting equation that connects Mary with Adam and Jesus with Eve. Some Muslim theologians, particularly followers of the (short-lived) Ẓāhirite school have maintained that Mary (as well as Sara and ʿĀsiya) was a prophet. For that purpose, Ibn Ḥazm of Cordova distinguished between prophethood (*nubuwa*), in which women can participate, and messengerhood (*risāla*), which is reserved for men only. The doctors of law of the leading schools, however, rejected female prophethood.

Ṣūfī women

In his collection of texts on Ṣūfī women, Javad Nurbakhsh lists 130 female authors, of whom 76 are known by their full names (Nurbakhsh, 1990). Many of their works (primarily poems) have survived through the commentaries of male Ṣūfī authorities. Among the most productive Ṣūfī women, one has to mention Rābiʿa al-ʿAdawiyya, Tohfa, and Bibi Hayati Kermani. The first two authors were freed slaves, who eventually enjoyed more freedom than did free-born women who were under male guardianship. Bibi Hayati, born a thousand years later than the other two, underwent a formal Ṣūfī education.

Rābiʿa al-ʿAdawiyya (713/717–801) lived a life of extreme ascetism in Basra. She was noted for her mystic teaching concerning the main stages of the Ṣūfī path: Penitence, Patience, Gratitude, Hope, Holy Fear, voluntary Poverty, Asceticism, abnegation of personal will in the Will of God, complete Dependence upon God, Love, Intimacy with God, and Satisfaction. Her precepts on mystic love (*maḥabba*) and intimacy (*uns*) were particularly acknowledged during her lifetime and by all the leading Ṣūfī authorities down through the centuries. She was first mentioned by the Muʿtazilite author al-Jāḥiẓ (b. 781/82). Farīd al-Dīn ʿAṭṭār (d. 1230) wrote her biography, and Ibn Khallikān (d. 1282) considered her in his *Obituaries of the*

Eminents (*Wafayāt al-Aʿyān*). Abū Ṭālib commented on her writings in the *Memoirs of the Saints* (*Tadhkirāt al-Awliyāʾ*) and the great al-Ghazzālī refers to her as one of the supreme teachers of Sufism, especially in the 36th Book ("The Book of Love and of Passion") of his *Revival of the Religious Sciences*. Tohfa (d. 857) was a minstrel and a slave-girl until her master freed her because of the impressiveness of her mystical poetry. Al-Jāḥiẓ, who was a contemporary of hers, transmits much information on the education and professional qualities of women minstrels, which allows us to understand how the love sung about by slave-girls – consisting of the classical three steps, Love (*ḥubb*), Desire (*hawa*), and Longing (*ʿishq*) – could be transformed into a mystical language. ʿAbd al-Raḥmān Jāmī (d. 1492), himself a Ṣūfī from the order of the Naqshbandiyya wrote Tohfa's biography and quotes her verses in *Nafaḥāt al-Uns* ("The Breaths of Divine Intimacy").

Bibi Hayati Kermani (nineteenth century) was born into a Persian family with a long tradition of Sufism. She was initiated into the Niʿmatullāhī order and trained in the esoteric development (*sayr*) and exoteric ethics (*sulūk*) of the Ṣūfī path. Her Persian *Dīwān* is among the most remarkable of Muslim collections of mystical poems of the last century.

Philosophy in translations, language, and history

Baghdad was one of the most important centres of translation-work from Greek into Arabic, rivaled only by Jundishāpūr (in Persia) where Greek, Persian, and Indian sources were made available to Arabic readers. It is in the translator circles of Baghdad, however, that one can see best how closely philosophical research, reflection on language, and historic–encyclopaedic work were intertwined. These circles were well positioned to discover problems of a philosophical nature related to the unique resources of the Arabic language, and they were on excellent terms with some of the finest minds of their time – in particular, al-Kindī and al-Fārābī.

Translation

One distinguishes three periods in the translation activities in Baghdad. In the early period translations were literal: Greek terms for which no corresponding words were known were kept or substituted for by temporary Syriac equivalents. Figures from this period include Ibn Nāʿima and Eustathious (both of whom translated for al-Kindī), Thābit ibn Qurra and Yuḥanna ibn al-Biṭrīq (ninth century). The transitional period was marked by the school of the Christian Ḥunayn ibn Isḥāq (d. 876), which was less concerned with finding correspondences and opted for an *ad sensum* translation of the original text that eventually led to several variants. (Ibn Rushd, for instance, used some of these for his commentary on Aristotle's *De Anima*, which subsequently had a highly controversial reception in Western philosophy.) Finally, there was the late period, in which the earlier translations were revised by representatives of the philosophical circles of Baghdad. Among the important figures in this period, one finds Abū Bishr Mattā (d. 940), al-Fārābī, Abū Sulaymān al-Sijistānī (d. 985), and Abū al-Faraj ibn al-Ṭayyib (d. 1043).

If Arabs had not traditionally been inclined towards studying and meditating on their language, translators would still have drawn the philosophers' attention to Arabic as an object of reflection. They had to study the specific features of Arabic (whose abstract radicals allow, for example, the permutation of letters) in order to organize and generate urgently needed new lexemes. The Islamic tradition therefore owes the translators for some colossal grammatical and lexicographic works, and even for a phonetical alphabet for the transcription of foreign languages. On the other hand, a new type of "scientist," the philosopher-grammarian (*al-falāsifa al-naḥwiyyīn*) connected the "arts of language" (*ʿilm al-lisān*) with logic, a procedure that allowed, for instance, al-Fārābī to search beyond the limits of Arabic for laws that determine the structure of all languages and to work on what could thus be called an "international grammar."

Philosophy of language

Interestingly, the two major centres of grammar, Basra and Kufa, produced, despite similar tasks, radically opposed philosophies of language. One finds here the reflection of a more fundamental opposition – that is, the antagonism between a rationalistic attitude that sacrifices deviations and particular cases to general rules and an approach that (under the influence of Shīʿite philosophy) appreciates diversity and values the individual. Thus the school of Basra produced a rigid system aiming at the uniformity of forms, while the Kufa grammarians compiled a multitude of particular linguistic phenomena, and used the much discussed principle of analogy as a structuring, rather than an eliminative, device. Researchers have drawn parallels between these two schools and the Greek "analogists" and "anomalists." As Henry Corbin observes, however, the comparison is not entirely pertinent, since the decisions taken by Muslim grammarians did not simply preoccupy the intellectual élite but also had an impact on exegetic interpretations (Corbin, 1993, p. 144).

An example of Shīʿite-influenced reflection on language is to be found in the "Balance of letters", attributed to Jābir ibn Ḥayyān (Latin: Geber, eighth century). It is based on the permutation of letters – a science initiated, according to the Shīʿite tradition, by the Imām Jaʿfar. Its purpose is, as if it were an alchemical operation, to unveil the relationship between the visible and the hidden (*ẓāhir* and *bāṭin*), whereby letters are understood as the epiphanies of numbers in which the (Neo-Platonically conceived) world soul gives expression to her harmony. On this view, language cannot be explained by convention; it reflects the immediate acts of the *anima mundi*.

History

The Islamic humanistic tradition linked the study of history to the "arts of language" (*ʿilm al-lisān*) thereby defining it as a genre of prose literature. The historic literature in the first centuries of Islam is so abundant that one could easily fill an entire volume listing chronicles, histories of dynasties and political events, titles of chronological and alphabetical historic dictionaries, histories of prophets and saints, commentaries and classifications of books and sources, scientific biographies, and autobiographies. Some of these works are still indispensable sources for historic research – such as Ibn al-Nadīm's (d. 990) *Kitāb al-Fihrist*, which represents the first extended Arabic history of literature (with sections on the Quran, grammar, history, poetry, dogma, law, philosophy, prose literature, history of religion, and alchemy), and Ibn Abī Uṣaybiʿa's (d. 1270) *ʿUyūn al-Anbāʾ fī Ṭabaqāt al-Aṭibbāʾ*, which includes the lives and works of physicians and other scientists.

Of special interest are the many autobiographies, which implicitly challenge the claim that the discovery of individuality was a Western achievement. This genre too has been classified and commented upon – for instance, by Shams al-Dīn Muḥammad ibn Ṭūlūn (d. 1546), who lists in his own autobiography all prior autobiographies (and biographies), including those of scientists, political advisers, poets, theologians, and philosophers (Rosenthal, 1937). Scientists and philosophers typically used the narration of their lives as a means to clarify and defend positions that they had taken in their research – the subjective stand giving, as it were, more weight to their theories. The forms that these life descriptions took varied. Scientists, such as Ḥunayn ibn Isḥaq and Ibn al-Haytham (Alhazen; d. 1040), often followed Galenus' example of simply commenting on the contents of their own books. Many authors only gave a brief summary of their lives and works, while others chose more original modes of representation. ʿAbd al-Wahhāb al-Shaʿrānī's (d. 1565) voluminous autobiography (over six hundred printed pages), for instance, is written in the form of a Ṣūfī thanksgiving. Among the most prominent of philosophical autobiographies are Ibn Sīnā's, which was completed by his follower Abū ʿUbayd al-Juzajānī, Muḥammad ibn Zakariyyāʾ al-Rāzī's reply against the accusation of his not having followed a Socratic, which is to say, an austere life (*Kitāb fi Sīratī* or *al-Sīra al-Falsafiyya*), and al-Ghazzālī's confessional autobiography (*al-Munqidh min al-Dhalāl* or *The Deliverance from Error*), in which he takes his conversion from scepticism to faith as an occasion for theological reflection. A complete documentation of autobiographical material in Islamic sources, however, needs to take into consideration also works that are not explicitly labeled as autobiographical – such as Ibn Sīnā's "Mystical Recitals" or Ibn Ḥazm's book about love.

The case of the philosopher-historian ʿAbd al-Rahmān ibn Khaldūn (1332–1406) from Tunis, for whom autobiography and the study of history are intrinsically related, deserves special attention. Ibn Khaldun was a stranger to the metaphysical notion of active intelligence developed by the Muslim hellenizing philosophers. For the author of a universal history (*Kitāb al-ʿIbar*), "universal reason" is to be found in the specific concatenation of historic events. Thus the *Prolegomena* (*al-Muqaddima*) to Ibn Khaldūn's historic work – which represents, despite its encycopaedic structure, a synthesis of his reflection on history – asserts that the intelligibility of history is ensured not through causal linearity, but by the tracing back of historic events to the totality of a given social reality. Since Ibn Khaldūn thinks of history as dependent on social–political evolution, an evolution in which he, as an individual, takes part, one finds his autobiography (*Taʿrīf*) attached as an appendix to his universal history. History thus grounds the objectivity of individual life, and autobiography ensures the veracity of reflection on history.

The hellenizing authors

The following Sunni authors are rightly called the hellenizing philosophers, since they considered themselves the heirs of the ancient Greek thinkers. (Nor was this contradicted by their pursuit of typically Islamic philosophical interests.) Although the Andalusian thinkers (that is, authors from Arabic Spain) are "hellenizing" as well, in the sense that they too used Greek resources in the development of their philosophies, they are traditionally treated separately. Their geographical isolation, moreover, does not imply that they were intellectually isolated. Pilgrimages (and exiles) provided many opportunities for the exchange of ideas between the eastern and western ends of the Islamic empire. Thus the critique of Ibn Sīnā (and other hellenizing authors) by the Persian al-Ghazzālī, for instance, did not fail to arouse a reaction from Ibn Rushd in Andalusia.

Al-Kindī

Abū Yūsuf ibn Isḥāq al-Kindī (801–873) had a broad interest in philosophy and the sciences and also addressed questions relating to political matters. Of his 265 works, only a small number have survived. Four were translated into Latin and influenced Western medieval philosophy: the *Tractatus de erroribus philosophorum, De quinque essentiis* (matter, form, motion, space and time), *De somno et visione*, and *De intellectu*. Like most Muslim (and Christian) medieval philosophers, he accepted the traditional attribution of the *Theology* (a paraphrase of the last three books of Plotinus' *Enneads*) and the *Book on the Pure Good* (*Kitāb al-ʿIlal; Liber de causis*, an epitome of Proclus' *Elementatio theologica*) to Aristotle. Among the Greek authors who most deeply influenced his work, in addition to Plato and Aristotle, one has to list Alexandre of Aphrodisias and John Philoponus.

In the *Letter on the Intellect* (*Risāla fī al-ʿAql*), al-Kindī refines the Aristotelian conception of the cognitive powers (the possible and active intellects) of the soul by introducing the acquired (*intellectus adeptus*) and the demonstrative intellect (*intellectus demonstrativus*). The former designates the actualized intellect that has not made any use of its knowledge, while the latter represents the intellect which has not only attained its end but is also manifest to itself and to other intellects. (It is in this sense that it possesses "demonstrative" knowledge.) Al-Kindī's goal in introducing these additional intellects was to maintain the Aristotelian creed according to which actual knowledge has to precede the potentiality of the intellect. A purely empirical theory would not be capable of embracing intellectual processes accompanying the gaining of intellectual knowledge.

Al-Kindī's deep involvement with Greek epistemology did not incline him towards the movement of *kalām*. In his view, the Rationalists were only concerned with human (*ʿilm insānī*) knowledge, whereas he, al-Kindī, also considered divine knowledge (*ʿilm ilāhī*), so that themes pertaining to the realm of faith (the creation of the world *ex nihilo*, the resurrection of the body and prophecy) are part of the philosophical discourse.

Al-Fārābī

Abū Naṣr Muḥammad ibn Muḥammad ibn Ṭarkhān ibn Uzalagh al-Fārābī's (872–950) mother tongue was probably Turkish. He excelled in logic, music, mathematics, and the sciences, which earned him the title of *muʿallam al-thānī* (*magister secundus*), placing him second only to Aristotle as a recognized authority. His commentaries on Aristotelian texts (*Organon*, *Physics*, *Meteorology*, *Metaphysics*, *Nicomachean Ethics*) are lost. Among his most important works are the *Harmony between the Doctrines of the Two Sages: Plato and Aristotle* (*Kitāb fī al-Jamʿ bayn Raʾyay al-Ḥakīmayn, Aflāṭūn al-Ilāhī wa Arisṭūṭālīs*), which is based on the assumption that the *Theology* is an original work by the latter, the *Iḥṣāʾ al-ʿUlūm wa Tartībuhā* (*De scientiis*), which had an enormous influence on the classification of sciences in the Latin tradition, the treatise *Fī al-ʿAql wa al-Maʿqūl* (*De intellectu et intellecto*), which reworks al-Kindī's additions to Aristotle's concept of the intellect, a book on music (*Kitāb al-Mūsīqā al-Kabīr*), which is considered the major source of the theory of music in the Middle Ages, and works on political philosophy, such as the *Treatise on the Opinions of the Members of the Perfect City* (*Risāla fī Ārāʾ Ahl al-Madīna al-Fāḍila*), the *Book of the Government of the City* (*Kitāb fī Siyāsa al-Madaniyya*), and the *Book of the Attainment of Happiness* (*Kitāb Taḥṣīl al-Saʿāda*).

The heart of al-Fārābī's doctrine is to be found in his conception of the intellect, to which he dedicated two treatises – the *Maqāla fī Maʿānī al-ʿAql* and *Fī al-ʿAql wa al-Maʿqūl*. In the *Maqāla*, he differentiates in the best encyclopaedic manner six meanings of "intellect": in the common language, in the tradition of *kalām*, and in four Aristotelian works (*Analytica posteriora*, II, 15; *Ethica nicomachica*, VI, 4–6; *De anima*, III, 5; *Metaphysica*). In *Fī al-ʿAql wa al-Maʿqūl* al-Fārābī expounds his own theory of four distinct types of intellect (using somewhat different terms than did al-Kindī). He begins his account with a discussion of the possible intellect (*ʿaql bī al-quwwa*; *intellectus in potentia*), which is capable of abstracting knowledge from corporeal forms. Then he proceeds to explain the function of the intellect actualizing abstracted knowledge (*ʿaql bī al-fiʿl*; *intellectus in effectu*) – which is not to be confused with the *intellectus agens*. The third type, as in al-Kindī's scheme, is the acquired intellect (*ʿaql al-mustafad*; *intellectus adeptus*), which positions itself in respect to actualized knowledge as a subject to its object. Unlike Alexandre of Aphrodisias' third intellect – the *nous epīktetos*, which functions as an intermediary between the potential and the actual powers – the acquired intellect is the highest perceptual power of the soul, which truly enables it to reach the rank of intellect. The only intellect entirely independent of matter, however, is the active intellect (*ʿaql al-faʿʿāl*; *intellectus agens*). Unlike its counterpart in the original Aristotelian scheme, which only actualizes the potential knowledge of the soul, al-Fārābī's active intellect *is* actualized knowledge. It is the "giver of forms" (*wāhib al-ṣuwar*; *dator formarum*) which enlightens the possible intellects (of all human souls). As has been repeated ever since, in many variations, this intellect is "to the possible intellect of man what the sun is to the eye."

Al-Fārābī's doctrine of the intellect is central not only because it stresses the importance of epistemology in his work, but also because it connects within his philosophy the theory of cognizance with metaphysics and politics. On the one hand, the doctrine of intellect relates to al-Fārābī's system of ten intelligences which proceed – necessarily – out of God by emanation (*al-fayḍ*), the last of which is the active intellect, ruling over the sublunar world. On the other hand, it is essential for the understanding of his political theory, in which he harmonized Plato's notion of the philosopher-king with the Islamic ideal of the prophet-ruler. According to al-Fārābī, the political leader (we find here a reflection of Shī'ite prophetology) unites himself with the active intellect and paves the way for the happiness (*al-sa'āda*) of the entire community. The active intellect thus takes a substantial part in bringing about humanity's true destiny.

Ibn Sīnā (Avicenna)

Abū 'Alī al-Ḥusayn ibn Sīnā (980–1037) was born in the neighbourhood of Bukhara, Persia. The breadth of his studies, which included grammar, law, logic, mathematics, natural philosophy, medicine, and theology, is reflected in the list of his works, which includes no fewer than 242 titles. By the age of 17 he was already an accomplished physician, and his great work on medicine, *al-Qanūn fī al-Ṭibb* (*Canon medicinae*), was one of the key texts in the Western medical tradition for several centuries. Ibn Sīnā's philosophical summa, *The Book of Healing* (*Kitāb al-Shifā'*; *Sufficientia*), is often confused with the *Canon*, because of the medical connotation of its title, which is meant to suggest, however, only that philosophy constitutes an antidote against the "illness" of false opinions. *The Book of Healing* divides into sections on logic, mathematics, physics, and metaphysics, and ends with an abridgement of itself, *The Book of Salvation* (*Kitāb al-Najāt*). From the enormous encyclopaedia, *The Book of Impartial Judgement* (*Kitāb al-Inṣāf*), addressing twenty-eight thousand questions in the space of twenty volumes, only a few fragments remain. Ibn Sīnā is also famous for his trilogy of the Mystical Recitals, in particular for the *Recital of Ḥayy ibn Yaqẓān* (*Vivens filius Vigilanti*; *Alive, Son of the Awake*) which promotes the theme of a spiritual itinerary in the company of "the Angel who enlightens." It seems that it is a mistake to read the trilogy as a cycle of allegories. The sensible change of language reveals, according to Henry Corbin, Ibn Sīnā's deep dissatisfaction with the use (we might add, with the *sole* use) of the discursive form of philosophical exposition (Corbin, 1993, p. 177). This is supported by a further Avicennian work, the *Mantiq al-Mashriqiyyīn*, which, due to the lack of vocalization in Arabic, can be translated either as *Oriental Philosophy* or as *Philosophy of Illumination*. This book was intended for the "élite" (in contrast to the Aristotelian philosophy addressed to the "multitude"), and its remaining portions are still much appreciated in the Islamic world. Less well known are Ibn Sīnā's comments on single *suras* of the Quran, in which he offers mystical interpretations.

In his autobiography, Ibn Sīnā writes that he read Aristole's *Metaphysics* 40 times, wondering (as readers of that book still do today) whether it was dealing with "Being" or with the highest principles of knowledge, until al-Fārābī's *Intentions of Aristotle's Metaphysics* (*Fī Aghrāḍ Kitāb mā Baʿd al-Ṭabīʿa*) convinced him of the first hypothesis. Following al-Fārābī's lead, Ibn Sīnā developed a method (although somewhat more complex than his predecessor's) of investigating Being with respect to necessity. All that is, is either purely necessary (that is, God), or purely possible, or necessary through another (for example, angels, intelligences, planets). As a result, the order of the universe is defined by different degrees of necessity. The question to be addressed next, of course, is how from God's (unitary) Being the diversity of creation could be derived. Ibn Sīnā addresses this problem by adapting al-Fārābī's theories of intellect and emanation to his own purpose. The Avicennian language is rich in terms related to the notion of creation – such as *takwīn* (formation), *ibdāʿ* (providing with a beginning), *iḥdāth* (giving rise), and *khalq* (creation, particularly of composites). One must remember, however, that Ibn Sīnā is thinking of emanation (he uses primarily the term *fayḍ* or flow, but also *ṣudūr* or proceeding, and *inbijās* or emerging) when he explains the process of creation: God necessarily and eternally generates the first intelligence, which in its turn, creates through further emanations the other nine intelligences, and the heavenly bodies with their respective souls. The first intelligence is nothing other than the divine knowledge contemplating God and contemplating itself. This distinction between two objects of contemplation and the act of contemplation itself – in which the first intelligence, unlike God, does not coincide with the object of contemplation – constitutes the origin of multiplicity. The first intelligence thus becomes the indispensable link between God's unitary Being and the rest of creation. By contemplating itself as a necessary being, it generates the Soul of the outermost sphere; by contemplating itself as a possible being, the body of that same sphere is originated; and finally, by contemplating the pure necessary Being, the second intelligence proceeds forth. This process is repeated until the tenth intelligence, which is also the last, innermost animated heaven of the universe, is emanated. As in al-Fārābī's system, this last intelligence is identified with the active (and separate) intellect which, in its turn, creates the human intellects, souls, and bodies. The tenth intelligence, however, not only provides the human intellect with forms, but it is considered to be the "Angel of humanity", and the human capacity for prophecy is a matter of achieving reunion with it.

Epistemologically speaking, Ibn Sīnā's doctrine of emanation is a powerful theory that ensures a perfect correspondence between notions and objects of the mind. Since the human intellect and the visible world share the same source, cognizance is founded in the very origin that has given rise to the object of its intellectual perception.

Despite its theoretical appeal, many aspects of Avicennian philosophy have been criticized by Muslim (and Christian) theologians. It has been observed in this regard that Ibn Sīnā has restricted God's freedom and that the doctrine of emanation is contrary to the religious notion of creation *ex nihilo*, and finally that happiness in his philosophy is to be found in the union with an intelligence (itself a created being) instead of with God.

For Ibn Sīnā to speak of God's freedom implies a distinction between a divine choosing self and the action of choosing, which is contrary to the principle of God's unity. Therefore, divine freedom manifests itself in the diffusion of its goodness, which is why the universe cannot be conceived of as having been shaped, but only as having emanated from God. Rather than being a natural process, creation is due to an intellectual unfolding that has its origin in the divine knowledge. Ibn Sīnā's *intellectual concept of creation* fulfils two requirements: first, the preservation of God's transcendence as the only being in whom essence and existence coincide, and second, the elimination of chance in the universe, since every process is guided by necessity.

Ibn Sīnā's philosophy enjoyed a double reception – in the East and in the West – thus giving rise to an "Islamic" and a "Latin Avicennism." In the Islamic world, his philosophy generated a continuous tradition in Persia where his Peripatetic studies were interpreted as a preparation for illumination. Among the authors Ibn Sīnā influenced one finds al-Juzajānī, who translated and commented on the *Recital of Ḥayy ibn Yaqẓān* in Persian, and Ḥusayn ibn Zaylā al-Iṣfahānī (d. 1048), who wrote a commentary on the same *Recital* in Arabic. He had a major impact on the work of al-Suhrawardī (d. 1191), who, even though he was pursuing other philosophical tasks, felt called upon to complete Ibn Sīnā's project of an "Oriental Philosophy." A revival of Avicennian philosophy was initiated by Naṣīr al-Dīn al-Ṭūsī (d. 1274) and his circle. And one ought also to mention Sayyid Aḥmad al-ʿAlawī's (d. 1631) extensive *The Key to the Shifā'*, which develops themes found in *The Book of Healing*. In the West, Avicenna was probably first known to twelfth-century authors at Oxford and Paris. Roger Bacon, for example, thought of Ibn Sīnā as the second founder of philosophy (after Aristotle). Thomas Aquinas, although he came to criticize Avicenna in his later years, owes him his "third argument" for the proof of God's existence. Duns Scotus used Avicennian concepts in his attack on Thomist theology. And then, of course, there are those medieval philosophers who adopted what has come to be known since Etienne Gilson as an "Avicennizing Augustinism" – and which could be called a "Christian Avicennism." In modern times, Ibn Sīnā attained new fame in the context of political philosophy through Ernst Bloch's provocative book *Avicenna und die Aristotelische Linke* (*Avicenna and the Aristotelian Left*).

Al-Rāzī (Rhazes)

Abū Bakr Muḥammad ibn Zakariyyā' ibn Yaḥyā al-Rāzī (865–925) was born in Rayy, in the neighbourhood of Teheran. Early Muslim biographers report that an eye disease caused by alchemical experiments drew al-Rāzī to the study of medicine. He eventually excelled in that discipline and directed a hospital, first in Rayy and later in Baghdad. According to his own count, he produced 148 texts, commentaries and paraphrases on medicine, physics, logic, mathematics, astronomy, philosophy, and various other topics, but Muslim historians put the count at 250 books. In the Latin West his medical works were known: the voluminous encyclopaedia, the *Kitāb al-Hāwī* (or *al-Jāmiʿ*; *Liber de Continens*), and the *Kitāb al-Manṣūrī* (*Almansorius* or *Liber de Almansorem*), named after Abū Ṣāliḥ al-Manṣūrī, the Prince of Kirman and Khurasan, to whom it was dedicated. Those of his philosophical works that still exist include *The Spiritual Physick* (*al-Ṭibb al-Ruḥānī*), which was conceived as a companion to *al-Manṣūrī*, and in which he gives an interpretation of Plato's tripartite doctrine of the Soul as this is developed in the *Republic*, *The Philosophical Way* (*al-Sīra al-Falsafiyya*), and an autobiographical treatise on ethics. His major work, *The Divine Science* (*al-ʿIlm al-Ilāhī*), is lost and can only be reconstructed through the refutations of his opponents, while the *Metaphysica* (*Maqāla fī mā Baʿd al-Ṭabīʿa*) is of doubtful attribution.

Al-Rāzī waged many polemics: with Abū al-Qāsim al-Bakhtī, chief of the Muʿtazilites in Baghdad; with Shuhayd ibn al-Ḥusayn al-Bakhtī, over the problem of pleasure; with Abū Ḥātim al-Rāzī, an Ismāʿīlī missionary; and with ibn al-Tammār, over his theory of matter. Thanks to these authors, we have detailed information concerning al-Rāzī's rejection of Aristotelian physics, in which he declared the impossibility of the void and separated motion from the body. His critique becomes particularly evident in his doctrine of the five co-eternal principles: God–Soul–Matter–Space–Time, which shows the influence of Democritean and Platonic thought. God is conceived, as in Plato's *Timaeus*, as a divine craftsman (*al-Bāriʾ*; *demiurgus*). Consequently, God did not originate the other principles, nor did he create the world *ex nihilo* (as the scriptures contend) or by necessity (as al-Fārābī contends). Rather the world owes its existence to the Soul's attraction to Matter, which in turn, however, resisted the Soul's informing activity. The Demiurge then assisted the Soul by shaping Matter into a universe of forms. Intelligence, on the other hand, is a genuinely divine creation that God bestowed on the Soul so that it might remember its eternal nature. According to al-Rāzī, Matter is composed of atoms separated by the void (*al-khalāʾ*), which is located in Space (*al-makān*) and which attracts Matter. In opposition to Aristotelian physics, al-Rāzī detaches Space from the concept of the body occupying it, by distinguishing between a universal and a particular space. Analogously, Time also appears in two modes: there is the absolute time (*al-dahr*; *aeon*), which in other sources corresponds to the duration of the intelligible world, and there is limited time (*zamān maḥṣūr*). We find an echo here of Proclus' "separated" and "non-separated" time. Unlike Plato, al-Rāzī did, however, believe that the creation is subject to a limited duration and thus has an end. He asserted that all souls will be restored (the doctrine of metempsychosis) and that matter will then return to its original state and again become shapeless (Badawi, 1972, pp. 585–91).

Al-Rāzī, who strongly based his medicine on observation and experiments, was also in his philosophy an extreme rationalist. It seems that from all his theories only the statement on matter's return to shapelessness is in accordance with the Quranic doctrine. He writes in the beginning of the *The Spiritual Physick* that reason, being the most precious of God's gifts to humankind, should not be submitted to any judgment; it is itself a "governor," a "controller," and a "sovereign." The exaltation of rationalism in al-Rāzī's work is of such magnitude that there is no space for mysticism, nor for the cherished Islamic consideration for prophecy. Even the dogma of the insuperability (*iʿjāz*) of the Quran is refuted. For al-Rāzī, all humans have been given the same rational disposition. It is thus inconceivable that God should have endowed only a few men with the gift of prophecy. He consequently rejects prophetism and revelation in the name of egalitarianism, but also (as he expounded in a lost treatise on *The Tricks of the Prophets*) because he takes it for an imposture. Henry Corbin suggests, therefore, that al-Rāzī might have influenced the anonymous pamphlet "On the Three Impostors," which became so popular in Western rationalist circles (Corbin, 1993, p. 140).

Despite the clearly heretical character of his doctrines, al-Rāzī's ideas enjoyed a favourable reception – after his death and also outside of Persia. We know, for instance, through Ibn Ḥazm's critique of contemporary positions, that al-Rāzī's metaphysics was the predominant philosophy of Andalusian freethinkers.

The Brethren of Purity (Ikhwān al-Ṣafāʾ) of Basra

Even though their books were written in a spirit of anonymity and the names of the Brethren (ca. tenth century) were kept secret, some members of the confraternity have been identified – specifically, Abū Sulaymān al-Bustī, Abū al-Ḥasan al-Zanjānī, Abū Aḥmad al-Nahrajūrī, al-ʿAufī, and the famous Zayd ibn Rifāʿa. Their major work is an encyclopaedia comprising 51 (or 52) *Epistles* (*Rasāʾil*) and a compendium (*Risāla al-Jāmiʿa*). It is generally accepted that the Brethren of Purity, who recruited their members personally and confidentially, issued from an Ismāʿīlī tradition, into which they injected scientific and philosophic thought. Many different Greek influences can be identified in their encyclopaedia – Pythagorean, Platonic, Aristotelian, Plotinian, and Stoic, although the (Neo-)Pythagorean heritage is undoubtedly prevalent. This can be seen in the Brethren's emphasis on mathematics and numbers. The first epistle insists, for instance, that "the science of number is the root of the other sciences, the fount of wisdom, starting point of all knowledge, and the origin of all concepts" (Fakhry, 1983, p. 166). Genuinely Pythagorean is the importance given to the tetrad. It is thus no coincidence that the encyclopaedia divides into four parts; that among the Plotinian series of hypostases, the Brethren of Purity chose the fourfold series; that their confraternity includes four ranks – novitiate, leadership, kingship, and prophetic (or "angelic") rank; and that the "creed" containing the description of their politico-religious aims is located in Epistle 44. On the other hand, it appears that the number of Epistles contained in the encyclopaedia is related to a mystical understanding of Islamic origin (51 = 17 × 3). According to a Shīʿite belief, 17 people will be resurrected the day the (last) Imām returns, each of whom will be given one of the 17 letters constituting the supreme name of God (Corbin, 1993, p. 134).

The *Epistles* treat 4 branches of knowledge: (1) propaedeutics (mathematics and Aristotelian logic) in 14 epistles; (2) natural philosophy, including psychology (mineralogy, botany, generation, and corruption, the microcosm theme, the nature of pain and pleasure, transmigration and resurrection of the soul, the limitations of human cognizance, the diversity of languages) in 17 epistles; (3) epistemology and metaphysics in 10 epistles; and (4) law and theology (spiritual purification, the Brethren's Creed, prophecy, spiritual beings, providence, magic) in

10 (or 11) epistles. Central to the Brethren's system of knowledge is the Plotinian tetrad God–Reason–Soul–Matter. Unlike in many other Islamic philosophies, however, the focus lays on the World-Soul (*al-nafs al-kulliyya*) rather than on Reason. Since the human mind is unable to encompass the form of the world as a whole, the *Epistles* emphasize the primacy of self-knowledge over knowledge of the world. Applying the Stoic theme of man as a hierarchically organized microcosm, the Brethren's encyclopaedia then goes on to establish the relationship between humankind and the world.

The chief method in the encyclopaedia is derived from the Ismāʿīlī "principle of balance" (*mīzān*), a principle applied to language in the work attributed to Jābir, and which was now elevated to a metaphysical principle allowing determination of the exact equipoise between "manifesting" and "occulting" for each science examined. This equilibrium, which helps to define the epistemological value of a given science, is the only Key to knowledge, until the day of resurrection when the "supreme balance" will eventually be enacted. Some interpreters have maintained that the reconciliation between philosophy and religion is what best defines the Brethren's goal. It appears, however, that more important than the harmonization of Thought and Faith, was the establishing of different levels of "knowledge."

Despite the secret character of the confraternity of Basra, many manuscripts of the *Epistles* circulated and made the Brethren's views known to a broader public, until the Caliph al-Mustanjid ordered the burning of the encyclopaedia in 1160. Nevertheless, many copies survived and continued to exert a deep influence on the mystical Islamic circles. A copy, for instance, was brought to Spain either by al-Kirmānī (d. 1066) or by his teacher al-Majrītī (d. ca. 1008), to whom the famous *Aim of the Wise* (*Ghāyat al-Ḥakīm*; *Latin Picatrix*) has been attributed.

Al-Ghazzālī

Abū Ḥāmid Muḥammad ibn Muḥammad ibn Muḥammad generally known as al-Ghazzālī (1058–1111), was born into a Ṣūfī family at Tabaran, near Ṭūs in Persia. At the age of 20, he began studying theology and law at the Niẓāmiyya Academy of Nīshāpūr. There he studied under the dominant Ashʿarite theologian Imām al-Ḥaramayn and became a disciple of the Ṣūfī Abū ʿAlī al-Faḍl ibn Muḥammad ibn ʿAlī al-Fārmadhī al-Ṭūsī (d. 1084). Under the latter's guidance, al-Ghazzālī practised rigorous ascetic and Sufistic exercises without, however, attaining mystical heights. At the same time, his critical intelligence grew dissatisfied with scholastic theology, although he continued to study it assiduously. At the age of just 34 he was offered the prestigious Chair of Theology of the Niẓāmiyya of Baghdad, which established him as the highest authority of Ashʿarite theology in his time. Despite his academic success, al-Ghazzālī continued to be assailed by doubts, and he increasingly realized that theology could not be built upon reason alone. In 1095, he collapsed physically and mentally, and was unable to teach any longer. He renounced his career and wealth and opted for a life of pilgrimage, which took him to Damascus, Jerusalem, Medina, and Mecca. In 1105, after eleven years of wandering, he returned to his native town. He resumed teaching for a short time at the Niẓāmiyya in Nīshāpūr, until he retired and founded a school in which he taught theology and Ṣūfī doctrines until the end of his life.

The best introduction to al-Ghazzālī's philosophy is to be found in his autobiographical writing, *The Deliverance from Error*, considered the most impressive document of self-revelation in Islam. Al-Ghazzālī there tells the story of his tormented intellectual development. He scrutinized all sources, all sects, and all philosophers, but he found that he was unable to accept any of their creeds or doctrines. His method for reaching the certain knowledge that the philosophical and theological tradition could not offer him, is expressed in terms that remind modern readers of Descartes:

> The search after truth being the aim which I propose to myself, I ought in the first place to ascertain what are the bases of certitude. In the second place I ought to recognize that certitude is the clear and complete knowledge of things, such knowledge as leaves no room for doubt, nor any possiblity of error (Sharif, 1963, p. 588).

Al-Ghazzālī eventually determined that no part of the knowledge he had been trained in was able to satisfy his rigorous criteria, since neither sensational perception nor "necessary propositions" produced by reason are beyond doubt. It was only when he understood and experienced that there is a cognizance higher than mere rational apprehension, that he overcame scepticism. Still, he identified four classes of seekers and criticized them all equally: the theologians for not offering certitude; the philosophers for deluding themselves with allegedly certain propositions; the mystics for their excesses; and the "authoritarians" (that is, the Ismāʿīlīs) for following the teaching of their Imām only. Nonetheless, it was to the refutation of the second group of "seekers" that al-Ghazzālī devoted most of his critical works. He first thoroughly studied their works, which enabled him to produce a compendium on (Aristotelian) philosophy of such quality that Christian medieval authors believed it to be the work of a Peripatetic. This compendium, modestly called *The Intentions of the philosophers* (*Maqāṣid al-Falāsifa*; *Logica et Philosophia Algazelis Arabes*), was actually planned as the base for a major attack, the famous *Incoherence of the Philosophers* (*Tahāfut al-Falāsifa*), which can also be translated as the *Autodestruction* or *Collapse of the Philosophers*. Al-Ghazzālī's critique focuses mainly on three philosophers: Aristotle, and al-Fārābī and Ibn Sīnā as the main expositors of Peripatetic thought in Islam. Sixteen metaphysical and four physical propositions are examined, among which three are regarded as liable to religious sanctions: the eternity of the world, God's knowledge of universals only, and disbelief in the resurrection of the body. One of al-Ghazzālī's most brilliant refutations relates to the doctrine of causality which had already been attacked by earlier Ashʿarite theologians, who saw in the notion of "secondary causes" a threat to God's omnipotence. The author of the *Incoherence* contends that there is no necessary correlation between what Aristotelians call "cause" and "effect" since certain causal nexus can only be found in logic. It might appear that fire causes the burning of cotton, for example, but all that can be ascertained is that cotton burns with (*maʿa*) fire, not by (*bī*) fire. The occasionalist theory that al-Ghazzālī refers to in explaining the reaction accompanying the coming together of these two substances also does not allow God to be regarded as the cause of that reaction, since if God acted necessarily, he would cease to act voluntarily. Some of al-Ghazzālī's other criticisms apply to philosophical propositions, such as that of the immateriality of the soul, which are in conformity with the Quranic revelation but which cannot be asserted by reason.

Al-Ghazzālī's major critique was answered a few decades later in the Andalusian philosopher Ibn Rushd's powerful *Incoherence of the Incoherence* (*Tahāfut al-Tahāfut; Destructio destructionis*). The Andalusian's most effective reply consists in demonstrating that a reason incapable of attaining certitude is ill prepared to destroy philosophical certitude by means of rational dialectic. Ibn Rushd's defense of rational philosophy was little noticed by later medieval Muslim philosophers. Fakhr al-Dīn al-Rāzī, for instance, continued al-Ghazzālī's attack on Ibn Sīnā in his *Book of Directives and Remarks* (*Ishārāt wa al-Tanbīhāt*).

In the contemporay Islamic world, al-Ghazzālī is a highly respected theological authority whose main work, *The Revival of the Religious Sciences* (*Iḥyā' 'Ulūm al-Dīn*), is still considered for its ethical teaching. Among his numerous theological and Ṣūfī works, one ought to single out *The Precious Pearl* (*al-Durra al-Fākhira fī Kashf 'Ulūm al-Ākhira*), *The Niche of Lights* (*Mishkāt al-Anwār*), and the *The Ninety-Nine Beautiful Names of God* (*al-Maqṣad al-Asna fī Sharḥ Asmā' Allāh al-Ḥusna*).

The Andalusians

After the fall of the Umayyads in the East in 749, the only survivor of the dynasty, ʿAbd al-Rahmān ibn Muʿāwiya, escaped to the Iberian Peninsula where he shaped a new Muslim Emirate, Andalusia, with Cordova as its capital. Under his successors, Andalusia (which also incorporated western North Africa) was raised to the dignity of a Caliphate. The political rivalry with the Eastern Muslim empire was favourable to the growth of intellectual culture. As in early Islam, the Andalusian intellectuals were primarily interested in mathematics, natural science and medicine before they came to explore the philosophical works of the Greeks (and of their early Muslim commentators.) After 1031, the Andalusian Caliphate split up into a number of minor independent kingdoms, which facilitated the gradual recovery of Spain by Christian princes. Nevertheless, the eleventh century witnessed a new flourishing of arts and sciences, causing it to be called the Medicean age of Spain. By comparison with the East, however, far fewer individuals took a significant interest in philosophy, which possibly explains the strong emphasis in Andalusian works on the philosopher's solitary life. During the reign of Ferdinand V of Aragon and Isabella I of Castile, all of Arabic Spain passed under the dominion of the Spanish crown. The last Muslim city, Granada, fell in 1492, marking the end of Muslim culture on the Iberian peninsula.

Ibn Masarra

Muḥammad Ibn Masarra (883–931), born in Cordova, was not an Arab by race. After his teaching was denounced as atheistic, he deliberately went into exile to

Medina and Mecca. He returned, however, to the hermitage that he owned in the vicinity of Cordova, where he founded the first Muslim mystic society on Spanish ground. Ibn Masarra revived the philosophy of Empedocles, whom he regarded as a prophetic figure. (Muslim historians commonly offered the following line of affiliation: Empedocles–Pythagoras–Socrates–Plato–Aristotle.) Opinions are divided as to the historic derivation of his Neo-Empedoclism (or pseudo-Empedoclism). Asín Palacios sees it as a continuation of Priscillan's (fourth century) gnosis, while Henry Corbin clearly identifies Ismāʿīlī influences. The books that are indisputably attributable to Ibn Masarra include the *Book of Penetrating Explanation* (*Kitāb al-Tabṣira*) and the *Book of Letters* (*Kitāb al-Ḥurūf*), which presents a mystical algebra. Much of his philosophy can be reconstructed from quotations found in the work of another Andalusian, the famous Ibn al-ʿArabī (1165–1240) who left his native Spain for Persia.

Ibn Masarra is close to the hellenizing philosophers we discussed earlier in that he also developed a theory of hierarchical emanation. This theory develops the hypostatic chain: Primary Matter, Intelligence, Soul, Nature, and Secondary Matter. Unlike in Plotinus, from whom the basic scheme is derived, Primary Matter (or Intelligible Matter) takes the position of the "One." In the center of Ibn Masarra's philosophy are the two Empedoclean cosmic "energies": love and discord. The Arabic terms used show, however, a semantic shifting in the understanding of "discord." While *maḥabba* renders quite accurately the Greek *philía*, *qahr* (or *ghalaba*) is closer to the notion of "domination" (or "victory") than to Empedocles' *neikos* (especially since for Empedocles both principles are alternately "victorious" one over the other). Ibn Masarra's teaching influenced the school of Almería (Portugal) and the work of certain Jewish philosophers, particularly Solomon ben Gabīrol (Avencebrol; d. 1051/1070).

Ibn Ḥazm of Cordova

Another philosopher from Cordova is Abū Muḥammad ʿAlī ibn Ḥazm (994–1064). He was expelled twice from his city in connection with the political misfortunes of the Umayyad dynasty, to whom he remained faithful all his life. The first time, in 1013, he fled to Almería and then to Játiva, where he waited for the restoration of the dynasty. After the Umayyads failed to re-establish their rule over Cordova in 1023, Ibn Ḥazm resigned himself to a life dedicated to writing. He spent the years from 1040 until 1050 on Mallorca.

Ibn Ḥazm became famous for a philosophical, a theological–juridical, and a historic work. *The Dove's Necklace* (*Ṭauq al-Ḥamāma*), which he wrote in Játiva and in which he incorporated many autobiographical events, is considered the first treatise on Platonic love in Islam (and possibly a major source for troubadour poetry). It combines the doctrines of two Platonic dialogues, that of man's inner division and subsequent search for reunion as represented in the myth of the androgyne from the *Symposium*, and the philosophy of beauty presented in the *Phaedrus*. In company with *The Dove's Necklace*, one should read *The Book of Character and Behaviour* (*Kitāb al-Akhlāq wa al-Siyar*), in which many definitions of terms used in the former text can be found. The work that brought recognition to Ibn

Ḥazm in the field of juridical theology is the *Kitāb al-Ibtāl* whose critique of other schools is supported by the *Kitāb al-muḥallā*. Under the influence of Dāwād ibn Khalaf al-Iṣfahānī's (d. 883) Ẓāhirism (exotericism), Ibn Ḥazm promotes in that book a canonist position of strict literalism that rejects the determinants of juridical decisions: analogy, personal opinion, preference (*istiḥsān*), imitation (*taqlīd*), and causal interpretation (*ta'līl*). In the same way, he also refuted theological speculation and the rationalization of God's names and attributes. On the other hand, the institution of consensus is limited to the Companions of the Prophet and to his immediate successors. As can be inferred from his writing on Platonic love, Ibn Ḥazm's Ẓāhirism did not bar him from philosophical speculation, in which he could, on the contrary, even give proofs of "bāṭinism" (esotericism). It also did not represent an impediment to the study of other religions. His *Kitāb al-Fiṣal fī al-Milal wa al-Ahwā' wa al-Niḥal*, the first known treatise of the comparative history of religion, records the creeds and doctrines of Christians, Jews and other religious communities without any sign of prejudice, other than using the features of his own religion as a means of classification: atheists are divided into sceptics and materialists, believers into those who worship a personal or an abstract deity, believers in a personal deity into monotheists and polytheists, monotheists into communities who have a book and those who have no book (of revelation), and finally into monotheists who have preserved and those who have altered their book. The *Kitāb al-Fiṣal* is also a valuable source for Ibn Ḥazm's evaluation of other philosophical positions. He criticizes al-Rāzī, for example, for having adopted Zoroastrian doctrines, arguing that his co-eternal principles matter, space, and time correspond to the creations of Ahriman, the evil power of Zoroastrian religion.

Ibn Ḥazm's voice has also been heard by Christian philosophers. Raimundus Lullus owes him, for instance, the distinction between necessary (*burhān ḍarūrī*: Quran, Ḥadīth; immediate experience) and convincing proofs (*burhān ijnā'ī*), which he applied to Ibn Sīnā's classification of scientific premises, criticizing the Parisian theologians who knew only of the Aristotelian demonstration. Lullus' "*theologia positiva*" is also coined after one of Ibn Ḥazm's definitions.

Ibn al-Sīd of Badajoz

ʿAbd Allāh Ibn al-Sīd al-Baṭalyūsī (1052–1127) was born in Badajoz in Extremadura. He was a contemporary of Ibn Bājja, with whom he debated on questions of grammar and dialectic in Saragossa, and hence for a long time he was believed to be only a grammarian. He was forced to flee when his native town was conquered by the Christians in 1118. His main philosophical works are the *Book of Questions* (*Kitāb al-Masā'il*) and the *Book of Circles* (*Kitāb al-Hadā'iq*), which has been known mainly to Jewish philosophers through a Hebrew version provided by Moses Ibn Tibbon (d. 1283).

The *Book of Circles*, which combines (Avicennian) emanationist theory with arithmetical doctrine, betrays the strong influence of the neo-Pythagorean approach of the Brethren of Basra. It describes three "circles": one for the decad of pure Intelligences, a second for the decad of Souls (celestial spheres and active intelligence), and a third for the decad of material beings (form, bodily matter, elements, natural kingdoms, and humankind). As in the Brethren's encyclopaedia, man, representing a summary of the entire universe, is considered a microcosm. Human knowledge constitutes itself in a circular motion: the study of mathematics provides the foundation for physics; the study of bodies leads to the knowledge of the souls inhabiting them, from which the investigation proceeds to a discovery of the rational soul; the study of rationality renders possible the understanding of intellectual principles, through which metaphysical knowledge can be attained; and from there the exploration continues until it reaches the divine One. This ascending process is called "human speculation" as opposed to the "divine speculation" of the descending process. Its conceptual interest lies in the fact that the study of the material world is located between two intelligible realms of knowledge: mathematics and metaphysics.

Ibn Bājja of Saragossa (Avempace)

Abū Bakr Muḥammad ibn Yaḥyā ibn al-Ṣā'igh, better known as Ibn Bājja, was born in Saragossa at the end of the eleventh century, and lived there until 1116, shortly before the Christians took the city. He eventually moved to Sevilla where he worked as a physician and dedicated himself to teaching and writing. He died in Fez (Morocco) in 1138. According to the bibliography by Ibn Abī Uṣaybiʿa, Ibn Bājja wrote several commentaries on works of Aristotle and al-Fārābī, a summary of al-Rāzī's *al-Hāwī*, treatises on medicine and astronomy (in which he opposed Ptolemy's system), answers to Ibn al-Sīd's questions on mathematical matters, and several treatises on the soul and the importance of the active intellect. Among his chief philosophical works are the incomplete *Régime of the Solitary* (*Tadbīr al-Mutawaḥḥid*), the *Treatise on the Conjunction of the Intellect with Man* (*Ittiṣāl al-ʿAql bī-Insān*; *Continuatio* or *Copulatio intellectus cum homine*), and the *Letter of Farewell* (*Risāla al-Wadāʿ*; *Epistula expeditionis*) dedicated to his pupil Abū al-Ḥasan ʿAlī ibn ʿAbd al-ʿAzīz, in which he also addresses the problem of conjunction.

Ibn Bājja's notion of the "solitary" or the "stranger" (*al-gharīb*), a term that can be related to the title of a later work by al-Suhrawardī, the *Occidental Exile* (*al-Ghurba al-Gharbiyya*), was perhaps influenced by the figure of Plato as this was presented in certain Islamic documents. (Al-Fārābī's *Harmony between the Doctrines of the Two Sages*, for instance, depicts the Greek philosophical authority as fleeing social and political life). The solitary finds himself as the citizen of an ideal, but nevertheless terrestrial city. He abides exclusively by the laws of absolute reason which enables him to "con-join" – that is, to unite with the separate active intelligence. In order to clarify this "conjunction", Ibn Bājja distinguishes four "spiritual forms" (*al-ṣuwar al-rūḥaniyya*, the title of a treatise attributed to Alexandre of Aphrodisias): (1) the forms of the celestial spheres, which are immaterial and help to perfect the material forms; (2) the active and the acquired intellects that are both "in-formed" and "in-forming" powers; (3) the hylic intelligibles (*maʿqulāt hayūlāniyya*) abstracted from bodies, which exist in matter; and (4) the forms that are preserved in the powers of the soul (common sense, imagination, memory), which serve as intermediaries between the hylic and the universal forms. An understanding of these forms makes it possible to grasp why only solitaries, and not all humans, participate in the highest forms. As Ibn Bājja states in the *Treatise on the Conjunction*, human beings are divided into three ranks: the mass, the theorists, and the blissful ones. Most humans know the intelligible forms only insofar as these are related to the individual hylic forms; the theorists give priority to the intelligibles, and then look to the hylic forms and individual objects; the blissful ones, finally, are endowed with an intellectual "vision" in which intelligence, intellect and the intelligible are all one. Their intellects are not dependent on abstracting forms from bodies, but are provided by the separate active intelligence with pure intelligibles that have never been in matter. This is the divine gift of infused knowledge available to only a few humans – the prophets, the true believers, the martyrs, and the pious men who live in solitude.

As various interpreters have noted, Ibn Bājja's approach to philosophy is essentially Aristotelian, but (despite occasional attacks on the mystics) he nonetheless accepts the connection between the intellectual itinerary of the solitary and the Ṣūfī teaching of divine infusion. On the other hand, he remains committed to Aristotle's definition of humans as "political animals". Well aware that the solitary life is contradictory to the obligations of a social being, Ibn Bājja contends that solitude is not a good in itself, but rather a good *accidentaliter* – for those who are unable to find companions.

Ibn Ṭufayl of Cadiz (Abubacer)

Abū Bakr Muḥammad ibn ʿAbd al-Malik ibn Ṭufayl was born in Cadiz at the beginning of the twelfth century. He practiced medicine in Granada before he became a private physician to the Almohad Sultan Abū Yaʿqūb Yūsuf. In 1163 he advanced to the position of a vizir. In 1182 he resigned his office as the Sultan's physician, allowing Ibn Rushd to succeed him, and died at an advanced age in Morocco in 1185. Muslim historians report that he wrote works on medicine, astronomy, and philosophy. However, the only work of his that has survived is the *Ḥayy ibn Yaqẓān*, a philosophical novel that owes its name to one of Ibn Sīnā's recitals.

Ibn Ṭufayl tells the story of the intellectual and spiritual development of a child (Ḥayy ibn Yaqẓān) growing up in isolation from human society. (Unlike Ibn Sīnā, for whom the *Alive, Son of the Awake* stands for the active intelligence, Ibn Ṭufayl identifies Ḥayy with Ibn Bājja's figure of the "solitary.") As to the circumstances of the child's birth, the author offers two alternatives: Ḥayy is either the offspring of a secret marriage, who was placed in an ark and cast into the sea by his mother, acting out of fear that her liaison would be discovered, and who later landed on the shore of a lonely island where a doe who had lost her fawn took care of him, or he owes his bodily existence to the "spontaneous generation" of a fermented mass of clay located on that same island and infused by God's "spirit."

Most of the novel is dedicated to Ḥayy's intellectual growth, as L. E. Goodman observes:

> Ibn Ṭufayl postulates in Ḥayy natural capacities for brilliance, boldness, curiosity, and goodness. The very name . . . should indicate what Ḥayy stands for; he is wide-awake, ready to learn, unrivaled in sensitivity, receptivity, openness to experience. (Ibn Tufayl, 1972, p. 13)

Ḥayy's years of learning are divided into seven heptads each of which presents him with different lessons, and he reaches the age of (intellectual) maturity at 50 – a number that can be related to the 50 gates of knowledge in the Kabbala. In his childhood observations of his environment, the significance of "aversion" and "attraction" is explored. Ḥayy discovers in time how skilled his hands are in fabricating clothes and in defending him against other animals. His first painful experience, the loss of his doe-mother, spurs him to engage in anatomical studies until he understands at the age of 21 how death occurs through the spirit's leaving the body. Ḥayy's continued study of bodies and their parts leads him to such notions as extension, species, motion, nutrition, sensation, form, and (vegetative and animal) soul. Finally, he conceives of the entire universe as one body provided with different "organs", which leads him to questions concerning the origin and age of the world. Most remarkably, Ḥayy recognizes the implications of the two possible answers that he considers – that is, that the assumption of the world's eternity poses the problem of limitation, while the assumption that the universe comes into existence raises questions concerning the origin of time. By the age of 35, he comes to the conclusion that the world has been shaped by a perfect, good, and omniscient Craftsman.

A major spiritual breakthrough occurs when Ḥayy develops introspective abilities that allow him to recognize that he perceives the Author of the world through his own essence, and subsequently he reaches the stage in which his own essence vanishes, permitting him an undisturbed vision of the divine Craftsman himself. This mystical experience becomes increasingly frequent, until by the age of 50 Ḥayy masters the technique of initiating and ending his visions. In that year he meets for the first time another human being, A(b)sāl, who has come from the neighboring island to pursue a solitary life himself. A(b)sāl teaches Ḥayy how to speak, thus enabling him to share his mystical experience. In this way A(b)sāl discovers that the knowledge contained in the scripture is nothing other than the pictorial representation of a higher reality that can be accessed by human beings, and so he takes Ḥayy to his native island (which Ibn Ṭufayl may have intended to represent Andalusia, since in Arabic documents the Iberian peninsula is often referred to as an "island"), so that the society there can profit from Ḥayy's teaching. There they meet A(b)sāl's brother, Salāmān, who has become the ruler of the island, and who, like the rest of the population, is unable to grasp the "inward" truth of revelation. Like Ibn Bājja, Ibn Ṭufayl comes to the conclusion that only the solitary life, to which few people are disposed, can lead to a full harmony between reason and revelation.

Even though one may question the linear intellectual development described by Ibn Ṭufayl, a development which does not require language, as well as the assumption that faith in *one* God is the result of the natural growth of rational abilities, one must acknowledge the truth of some of his observations. The *Ḥayy ibn Yaqẓān* emphasizes, for instance, the discovery of the hand as a uniquely skillful organ which enables the solitary infant to detach himself from the animal world. Also it is noteworthy that the initial motivation underlying Ḥayy's scientific examination of bodies was the wish to overcome pain (represented by the death of the doe-mother). It appears that Ibn Ṭufayl wanted to think through human nature independently of biblical–Quranic sources. Ḥayy's Adamic position suggests that humanity's good nature can be restored if the individual is isolated from other human beings. Evil, in other words, is not connected with the desire for knowledge, but is rather due to corruption through society.

The Latin West knew Ibn Ṭufayl as Abubacer through Ibn Rushd's works on Aristotelian books – particularly through the commentary on *De Anima*, in which he criticizes him for making no distinction between the possible intellect and imagination. The *Ḥayy ibn Yaqẓān* was known to the Renaissance philosopher Giovanni Pico della Mirandola (d. 1494), possibly through the Hebrew commentary of Moses of Narbonne from the year 1349. A Latin translation was provided by Edward Pococke in 1671 which became a source for Leibniz' *Philosophus autodidactus*. Many more translations followed, making Ibn Ṭufayl's book the best known original Arabic philosophical work in the Western tradition.

Ibn Rushd (Averroës)

Abū al-Walīd Muḥammad ibn Aḥmad ibn Muḥammad Ibn Rushd (1126–1198) was born in Cordova into a family of famous jurists. He studied (mālikite) theology and law, poetry, medicine, mathematics, astronomy, and philosophy. In 1168 or 1169 Ibn Rushd was introduced to Abū Yaʿqūb Yūsuf through the good offices of Ibn Ṭufayl. As a result, he was nominated judge in Sevilla, then appointed as a physician to the Sultan in 1182 (a position from which Ibn Ṭufayl had resigned), and finally invested with the dignity of judge of Cordova. The meeting with Abū Yaʿqūb Yūsuf also had a decisive influence on the course of philosophy, particularly in the Latin West. Ibn Rushd responded to the Sultan's desire to see all the Aristotelian works commented upon and ensured himself through this gigantic task a lasting fame in the Western tradition as "The Commentator," eclipsing thereby for many centuries his other philosophical merits. After 1195, Ibn Rushd lost the favour of Abū Yaʿqūb Yūsuf's son, Sultan al-Manṣūr, who had his books burnt and sent him into exile, possibly hoping to appease in this way Ibn Rushd's many adversaries, who accused him of heresy. Al-Manṣūr had a change of heart, however, and soon recalled the philosopher to Morocco, where he died shortly thereafter.

Ibn Rushd is the only notable Muslim philosopher who has also written systematic juridical treatises. In the field of medicine he left a major work, the *Kitāb al-Kulliyyāt* (*Colliget*), a book on general medicine, as well as many single medical tracts and compendia of Galenic works. His commentaries on Aristotle are of three types: the large (*tafsīr* or *sharḥ*), the intermediate (*talkhīs*), and the short (*jāmiʿ*, pl. *jawāmiʿ*). The large address philological, historic, and doctrinal questions following a procedure similar to the method used in Quran commentaries. The intermediate offer continuous commentary on the original text; in these Aristotle's and Ibn Rushd's own thoughts are indiscriminately intertwined. The short commentaries, finally, do not follow the order of the text commented upon; here Ibn Rushd speaks in his own name. There are five large, eighteen intermediate, and four short commentaries on Aristotelian texts. All three types of commentaries were written for the *Physics*, the *Metaphysics*, *De anima*, *De caelo*, and *Analytica posteriora*. The only Platonic work that Ibn Rushd commented upon is the *Republic*, a text to which he dedicated *Jawāmiʿ* – in substitution for Aristotle's *Politics*, for which he found no Arabic translation. Recently, this commentary, in which the idea of gender equality is defended, has brought Ibn Rushd considerable recognition in feminist political philosophy. Other commentaries deal with works by Alexandre of Aphrodisias, Ibn Bājja, and al-Fārābī, which the philosopher of Cordova examined in his effort to distinguish the true Aristotelian doctrine from its later accretions. Among the "original" works, one finds, in addition to his greatest philosophico-theological text, *The Incoherence of the Incoherence*, addressed against al-Ghazzālī, titles on the compatibility of faith and reason, such as *The Decisive Treatise Determining the Nature of the Connection between Religion and Philosophy* (*Faṣl al-Maqāl fī mā Bayn Ashsharīʿa wa al-Hikma min al-Ittiṣāl*) and *The Exposition of the Methods of Proofs Concerning the Beliefs of the Community* (*al-Kashf ʿan Manāhij al-Adilla fī ʿAqāʾid al-Milla*), several works on celestial physics, among which the *Maqāla fī Jawhar al-Falak* (*De Substantia Orbis*) was particularly popular in the Christian and Jewish Middle Ages as well as in the Renaissance, writings on psychology, chief among them *The Treatise on the Union of the Intellect with Man* (*Maqāla fī Ittiṣāl al-ʿAql bi al-Insān*; *Epistola de connexione intellectus abstracti cum homine*), and finally a series of treatises on logical and grammatical questions.

Leaning on Abdurrahman Badawi's scheme in his *Histoire de la philosophie en Islam*, we will focus here on three aspects of Ibn Rushd's philosophy: (1) the relationship of faith and reason; (2) God – his creation and proofs of his existence; and (3) the doctrine of the unity of the intellect (Badawi, 1972, Vol. 2, p. 765). In his own lifetime, Ibn Rushd was already viewed as a rationalist, a semi-rationalist and, by contrast, as an orthodox philosopher. What speaks in favour of the rationalist attribution, is his theory of the eternity of the world and passages in his works asserting that religion cannot satisfy the philosopher's need to investigate the truth. On the other hand, he can be seen as semi-rationalist or even as orthodox on the grounds of his conviction that philosophy has to consider both reason and revelation; and that reason, being incapable of discovering all truths, needs to submit to religious dogma in case of conflict. What renders a final judgment particularly difficult is the contradiction between the different works dealing with the compatibility of reason and faith. Whereas *The Incoherence* and *The Exposition* offer a base for interpretation, *The Decisive Treatise* is clearly rationalistic. An explanation for the different ways in which it is possible to see Ibn Rushd may be given in terms of the different classes of people that he found himself addressing: the masses, who were open to imagery and rhetorical arguments only, theologians (*Mutakallimūn*), who understood dialectic discussions, and the philosophers, who could follow rational demonstrations. It is this distinction that is at the foundation of the "doctrine of double truth" (which should actually have been called the "doctrine of triple truth"). This doctrine was wrongly ascribed to Ibn Rushd by Christian medieval authors. Ibn Rushd's ideal consisted in harmonizing not different "truths," but different expressions of one and the same truth.

Unlike Ibn Sīnā, who used the Neo-Platonic concept of the One in describing God, Ibn Rushd worked with Aristotle's notion of divine mind thinking itself – a notion that he defended against al-Ghazzālī's attacks. In being his own object of thought, God also thinks the world with all its objects and events. He does that in a mode that cannot be expressed in terms of universals and particulars; his self-reflection does, however, generate providence. This is a doctrine that has been misunderstood by later interpreters, Christians and Muslims alike, who stated that there is no room for divine providence in Ibn Rushd's philosophy since God does not perceive the particular. The world that God thinks has an intermediary state; it is neither entirely co-eternal to God nor corruptible as a whole. While its shape has been created in time, its duration and its matter are uncreated. Rejecting the Avicennian principle "*Ex Uno non fit nisi Unum*," which he correctly traces back to Porphyry, Ibn Rushd thus dismisses the emanationist theory in which intermediary beings are acting as in-formers. God does not produce the world *ex nihilo*, but he is the Cause responsible for the union of form and matter. Proofs of God's existence from causality are, therefore, only valid if they operate with the notion of efficent cause. As for Ibn Sīnā's proof from the necessary and the contingent, Ibn Rushd replies that (since it defines the necessary by what has a cause and the contingent by what does not) it cannot prove the impossibility of the existence of infinite causes, and hence needs to be refuted. On the other hand, the proof from providence is only designed for the masses. For himself, however, Ibn Rushd clearly favors the proof from movement which is derived from the Aristotelian concept of "the first mover." This proof is supported by Averroës' principle, according to which physics establishes the existence of the subject matter of metaphysics.

An extensive discussion of Ibn Rushd's epistemology requires not only the study of his treatises on "conjunction" (*ittiṣāl*), but more especially a thorough examination of the intermediate and the long commentaries on *De anima*. As for Aristotle, knowledge begins, according to Ibn Rushd, with the perception of the particular. Once this is preserved in imagination and repeatedly perceived, the next step consists in recognizing (with the help of memory) the universal pertaining to that particular. For Ibn Rushd, cognizance of universals (*kulliyyāt*) is not just a philosophical goal, it represents the only means to reach supreme happiness (*al-saʿāda al-ʿuẓma*), a happiness that is reached, as al-Fārābī already argued, by the hylic (or possible) intellect "con-joining" with the active intellect. Only theoretical reflection helps the privileged few to "natural perfection," which is nothing other than an approximation of "divine perfection," while the masses at large only achieve moral excellence. (The élitist orientation of this theory is fairly obvious and rather problematic.) Part of the theory has become famous as "the doctrine of the unity of the intellect," which implies that as a consequence of the "conjunction," the hylic intellect, once actualized, becomes *one* to all humans. As a result, immortality is denied to individuals, leaving them only as so many perspectives participating in a universal perpetuity common to all of (thinking) humanity.

Ibn Rushd had little influence on the further development of Islamic philosophy. He was nevertheless highly regarded among Andalusian Jews, particularly by Moses Maimonides (d. 1204) and his pupil Joseph ben Juda, through whom many of Ibn Rushd's works have survived – in translations or in copies of the Arabic original using Hebrew characters. His impact on the Latin philosophical tradition is of such importance that Western thought between the thirteenth and sixteenth centuries is inexplicable without considering his conceptual contributions. Though seriously attacked for his doctrine of the unity of the intellect by Thomas Aquinas in *De unitate intellectus contra Averroistas*, he continued to be respectfully quoted as "the Commentator." He also inspired a Latin Averroism in authors such as Siger of Brabant (d. 1281/1284) and Boethius of Dacia (d. 1284), and more specifically, a political Averroism in the works of Jean de Jandun (d. 1328) and Marsilius of Padua (d. 1336/1343). Despite the Church's efforts to suppress Averroistic doctrines in the Middle Ages, Ibn Rushd's philosophy was revived in the Renaissance – hence H. A. Wolfson's well known phrase, "a twice-revealed Averroës." A series of philosophers at the University of Padua, which was considered an Averroistic stronghold in the fifteenth and sixteenth centuries, based their epistemological theories on Ibn Rushd's work, among them Nicoletto Vernia (d. 1499), Agostino Nifo (d. ca. 1538) and their disciples. As a result of the Averroistic debate, the (individual) immortality of the soul was declared a dogma at the Lateran Church Council in 1513.

In older surveys, the death of Ibn Rushd traditionally signalled the end of Muslim philosophy. But this is only justified for what has been called the "Arabic Peripateticism," although the philosopher of Cordova was not entirely forgotten in later centuries. Ibn Khaldūn, for instance, was a fervent reader of his works, the Turkish theologian Khwaja Zada (d. 1488) wrote a rejoinder to *The Incoherence of Incoherence*, and there is evidence that Ibn Rushd was discussed at the school of Iṣfahān (in Persia) in the seventeenth century. Philosophy as such, however, did not come to an end in the Muslim world, although it literally moved East. This is best illustrated by the life of Ibn al-ʿArabī, who was a contemporary of Ibn Rushd and left his native Andalusia for Persia. Ibn al-ʿArabī's journey has been interpreted by Henri Corbin as a metaphor for the return of Islamic mystical philosophy (which Ibn Masarra had taken to Andalusia centuries earlier) to its origin in the Eastern Muslim empire (Corbin, 1993, p. 292). An investigation of mystical philosophy would need to consider figures such as Athīr al-Dīn al-Abhārī (d. 1264), Dabīrān Kātibi (d. 1276), Quṭb al-Dīn al-Rāzī (1364), and of course, "the school of Iṣfahān," which was founded in the fifteenth century and the philosophical activities of which culminated with the works of Mullā Ṣadrā and his disciples. It appears that Iṣfahān again became a renowned center of philosophy in the eighteenth and nineteenth centuries after it recovered from the Afghan invasion.

Today Muslim intellectuals debate whether the rationalist tradition that Arab philosophers have nourished for so many centuries should be reintroduced into modern Islamic thought. Some Muslim researchers, such as Seyyed Hossein Nasr

(b. 1933), view the period of Arab interest in Aristotelian philosophy as a short interlude. They support the idea of purely Islamic arts, ethics, and sciences. Others, by contrast, deplore the fact that Islam abandoned the foundation of modern thought that it gave to the West, in particular through the rational philosophy of Ibn Rushd. Thus Mourad Wahba speaks of "The Paradox of Averroës," implying thereby that the absence of a Renaissance and Enlightenment in the Islamic tradition goes along with the absence of Averroism in the Muslim world. Nevertheless, the twentieth century has witnessed a gradual revival of Ibn Rushd's philosophy among Muslim intellectuals – admirers and critics, "traditionalists" and "modernists," religious and political authors. The promoters of the Andalusian's ideas do not, however, even think of accepting such typically Averroistic theses as the eternity of the world and the unity of the intellect. They focus rather on a rational and scientific mentality represented in Ibn Rushd's works, which could serve as a modern foundation for theoretical openness, political freedom, and religious tolerance in the Muslim world (von Kügelgen, 1994). Thus today, nearly eight hundred years after the death of the philosopher of Cordova, Ibn Rushd's philosophy, which gave rise to a Latin and a Jewish Averroism in the Middle Ages, re-enters the philosophical discourse in the shape of an "Arabic Averroism" (Wahba and Abousenna, 1996).

Bibliography

Primary sources

The Glorious Quran 1976: bilingual edition, English tr. by Marmaduke Pickthall (Albany: State University of New York Press).

Al-Ghazzali 1958: *Tahāfut al-Falāsifah. Incoherence of the Philosophers*, tr. A. S. Kamali (Lahore: Pakistan Philosophical Congress).

Al-Ghazzali 1910: *Iḥyā' 'Ulūm al-Dīn* [The Revival of the Religious Sciences] (Cairo: Maktaba al-Tijāriyya al-Kubra).

Ibn Khaldun 1967: *The Muqaddimah: an Introduction to History*, tr. by F. Rosenthal, 3 Vols. (Paris: Sindbad).

Ibn Rushd 1954: *Averroes' Tahāfut al-Tahāfut: Incoherence of the Incoherence*, tr. Simon Van den Bergh, 2 Vols (London: Luzac).

—— [1956] 1966: *Averroës' Commentary on the Republic*, ed. and tr. by E. I. Rosenthal, 1956 (Reprint, Cambridge: Cambridge University Press).

—— 1961: *Averroës. On the Harmony of Religion and Philosophy*, tr. G. F. Hourani (London: Luzac).

Ibn Sina 1985: *Al-Najāt* (Beirut: Manshurat Dar al-Afaq al-Jadīda).

Ibn Tufayl 1972: *Ibn Tufayl's Hayy Ibn Yaqzān. A Philosophic Tale*, tr. L. E. Goodman (New York: Twayne Publishers).

Nurbakhsh, Javad 1990: *Sufi Women*, tr. L. Lewisohn (2nd rev. edn, London and New York: K. Nimatullahi).

References and further reading

Anawati, Georges C. 1974: *Études de philosophie musulmane* (Paris: J. Vrin).

Badawi, Abdurrahman 1972: *Histoire de la philosophie en Islam*, 2 Vols (Paris: J. Vrin).

Corbin, Henry 1993: *History of Islamic Philosophy*, tr. Liadain Sherrard (London and New York: Kegan Paul International).

de Boer, T. J. 1970: *The History of Philosophy in Islam*, tr. E. R. Jones (London: Luzac).

Fakhry, Majid A. 1983: *History of Islamic Philosophy* (New York: Columbia University Press).

Goichon, Anne-Marie 1937: *La distinction de l'essence et de l'existence d'après Ibn Sina* (Paris: D. de Brouwer).

Kügelgen, Anke von 1994: *Averroës und die Arabische Moderne. Ansätze zu einer Neubegründung des Rationalismus im Islam* (Leiden: E. J. Brill).

Makdisi, George 1981: *The Rise of the Colleges: Institutions of Learning in Islam and the West* (Edinburgh: Edinburgh University Press).

—— 1990: *The Rise of Humanism in Classical Islam and the Christian West: with Special Reference to Scholasticism* (Edinburgh: Edinburgh University Press).

Ormsby, M. E. 1983: *Theodicy in Islamic Thought. The Dispute Over al-Ghazālī's Best of All Possible Worlds* (Princeton: Princeton University Press).

Palacios, M. A. 1978: *The Mystical Philosophy of Ibn Masarra and His Followers*, tr. E. H. Douglas and H. W. Yoder (Leiden: E. J. Brill).

Peters, F. E. 1968: *Aristotle and the Arabs. The Aristotelian Tradition in Islam* (New York: New York University Press).

Qadir, C. A. 1988: *Philosophy and Sciences in the Islamic World* (London and New York: Croom Helm).

Rosenthal, Franz 1937: "Die arabische Autobiographie," *Analecta Orientalia*, 14, pp. 1–40.

Schimmel, Annemarie 1975: *Mystical Dimensions of Islam* (Chapel Hill: University of North Carolina Press).

Sharif, M. M. (ed.) 1963: *A History of Muslim Philosophy*, 2 Vols (Wiesbaden: O. Harrassowitz).

Smith, Margaret 1974: *Rabi'a the Mystic and Her Fellow-Saints in Islam* (Amsterdam: Philo Press; originally 1928).

Stowasser, Barbara F. 1994: *Women in the Qur'an, Traditions, and Interpretations* (New York and Oxford: Oxford University Press).

Wahba, Mourad and Abousenna, Mona (eds) 1996: *Averroës and the Enlightenment. The First Humanist/Muslim Dialogue* (Amherst: Prometheus).

Wolfson, H. A. 1961–3: "The Twice-Revealed Averroës," *Speculum*, July 1961, pp. 373–93; Jan. 1963, pp. 88–104.

PART II

PHILOSOPHICAL TOPICS

THE CHINESE TRADITION

7

Ideas of the good in Chinese philosophy

SHUN KWONG-LOI

Ideas of the good are ideas of what is worthy of pursuit, and a thinker's conception of the worthy objects of pursuit may differ from that of the ordinary person. Suppose we call *ordinary self-interest* the objects of pursuit that relate to the ordinary person's own interests, including such things as health, possessions, power and honour. And suppose we call an *ethical ideal* a thinker's conception of how one should live – a conception of what, according to the thinker, should constitute the proper object of devotion for everyone. An attempt to understand ideas of the good in Chinese thought involves discussing the ways in which different philosophical movements view the ethical ideal and its relation to ordinary self-interest.

Chinese thought in the early period, from the sixth to the third century BC, emerged in a context of social and political disorder, involving war between different states and pervasive corruption in government. A major concern of both ordinary people and philosophical thinkers was the restoration of order and the well-being of the people. Suppose we call the *public good* the conditions of society and of the people that are worthy of being promoted. An attempt to understand ideas of the good in Chinese thought also involves discussing the ways in which philosophical movements view the relation between the ethical ideal and the public good.

In the following discussion, we will consider a number of philosophical movements in the early period, including Confucianism, Mohism, Yangism, and Daoism, and consider how they viewed the ethical ideal and its relation to both ordinary self-interest and the public good. Although some movements, such as Yangism, may seem to advocate an exclusive concern for one's own interests, this concern for oneself is nevertheless linked to a concern for the public. Conversely, although some movements, such as Mohism, may seem to advocate an exclusive devotion to the public, this devotion is nevertheless linked to a concern for one's own interests. Most philosophical movements in China regarded self-interest, or at least one's real interests, and the public good as converging rather than as standing in opposition to each other, and the ethical ideal as promoting both.

Let us begin with early Confucianism, whose representative thinkers include Confucius (sixth century BC), Mencius (fourth century BC) and Xunzi (third century BC). The Confucians believed that the way to bring about order is to restore and maintain certain traditional values and norms, which served as the basis for an orderly society in ancient times. These include various attributes within the family and state, such as affection for and being filial toward parents, a reverential attitude toward elders, loyalty to superiors, and kindness as well as a caring attitude toward those below oneself. They also include rules of behaviour governing the interaction between people in recurring social contexts, such as the way to conduct sacrifices, marriage ceremonies and funerals, the way for hosts and guests to interact, as well as various obligations one has toward another person in virtue of the different positions the two occupy within the family or state. The term "*li*," which refers to such rules, is often translated as "rites" because it originally referred to rites of sacrifice and, even when used more broadly to refer to various rules of conduct, it still emphasizes the ceremonial.

The Confucians did not adopt the traditional values and norms uncritically. They emphasized the importance of having the proper attitude in following the rules of *li*, an attitude akin to the reverential attitude involved in sacrifices. One should pay serious attention to those with whom one interacts, be cautious about one's demeanor and appearance, and yield to others in matters that bring good or honour. The traditional rules of *li* may be suspended in exigencies or adapted to cope with changing circumstances; the former is particularly emphasized by Mencius and the latter by Xunzi. Also, while emphasizing filial piety in the family and loyalty in the state, the Confucians also stressed that one should remonstrate with parents and superiors when they are in the wrong, and be prepared to leave government if one cannot help bring about desirable political changes. So underlying the advocacy of traditional values and norms is a sense of what is proper, or *yi*, which provides a basis for assessing and adapting such values and norms.

The Confucians advocated cultivating oneself to embody the attributes just described. Confucius used "*ren*", often translated as "humaneness" or "benevolence", to refer to the ethical ideal encompassing all these desirable attributes, but subsequently "*ren*" has often been used to emphasize the affective component of the ideal. Though one's affective concern is directed to all, it should involve a gradation in that one has special affection for and special obligations toward those standing in certain social relations to oneself, such as one's parents. Other aspects of the ideal include the observance of the rites (*li*) with reverence, a commitment to the propriety (*yi*) of conduct, and wisdom in the sense of an ability to assess what is proper in a way that is sensitive to circumstances and not rigidly bound by rules. In addition, one should cultivate a firm commitment to what is proper so that one is not swayed by the adverse circumstances of life, but will willingly accept such circumstances.

This conception of the ethical ideal links up directly with the public good. Someone who has approximated the ideal will have affection and reverence for others, and will seek actively to promote their well-being. This involves not just attending to their material needs, but also educating them and helping them cultivate themselves. If political opportunities are available, one will take part in government, whose purpose is to bring about social order and attend to the material needs and the education of the people. Self-cultivation is the ideal basis for government because the good character of those in office will have a transformative effect on the people; good character is also needed to institute policies serving the purposes of government and to properly carry out policies transmitted from the past.

The relation between the ethical ideal and ordinary self-interest is more complicated. On the one hand, the Confucians acknowledged a potential conflict between ethical pursuits and ordinary self-interest, and advocated subordinating the latter to the former. One should not be tempted by wealth and honour, or swayed by poverty and obscurity, to deviate from ethical pursuits. Instead, one should willingly accept the adverse circumstances of life, including even death, should these be unavoidable consequences of proper conduct. On the other hand, especially in the political context, they believed that self-cultivation will also bring about certain ordinary objects of pursuit; for example, one who has cultivated one's ability and character will likely be appreciated and employed by others, and as a result attain ranks in government. Sometimes what results from self-cultivation may be different from and yet bear an affinity to ordinary objects of pursuit. For example, Mencius believed that rulers who aspire to be invincible can attain their goal if they practice humane (*ren*) government. But they will be invincible not in the sense of superior military strength, but in the sense that, given the transformative and attractive power of their humaneness, they will confront no hostility or will easily overcome any minimal hostility that they encounter. Humane government is supposed to have all kinds of political advantages such as gaining the allegiance of the people, although the effect comes about only if one practices humaneness out of genuine concern for the people and not for the sake of gaining such advantages.

By comparison to Confucianism, Mohism, a school of thought originating with Mozi (fifth century BC), sees a more direct link between the ethical ideal and both ordinary self-interest and the public good. Coming from the lower stratum of society, Mozi focused primarily on the material well-being of the common people, and opposed many of the practices that the Confucians advocated, such as elaborate funerals and lengthy mourning of parents. According to him, such practices involve an unnecessary waste of resources, and the time and energy invested in them should be directed to more productive activities. He diagnosed the disorder of the times as having its source in discrimination – namely, one's having special concern for oneself and one's family and state, and seeking to benefit them at the expense of others. The remedy is to practice an indiscriminate concern for each, which involves one's seeking to benefit all without discrimination.

The ideal of indiscriminate concern may seem to show that Mozi advocated a concern for the public to the exclusion of one's own interests. However, in another context, Mozi also defended indiscriminate concern on the ground that the interests of oneself and of those to whom one stands in a special relation are best served by indiscriminate concern. According to him, if one desires to benefit oneself and one's parents, one should benefit others and their parents so that others will benefit oneself and one's parents in return.

There might appear to be a tension between the defence of indiscriminate concern on the ground that discrimination leads to disorder, and its defence on the ground that its practice promotes one's own interests. The former argument seems opposed to a concern for one's own interests, while such a concern provides a starting point for the second argument. However, there is no genuine conflict between them. What the first argument opposes is not a concern for one's own interests per se, but such a concern coupled with an indifference to others' interests. And what the second argument proposes is that it is only when one is also concerned for others that one's own interests can be served. Mozi's view is that ordinary self-interest and the public good converge, and by actively devoting oneself to the latter, one will at the same time promote the former.

One main difference between the Confucians and the Mohists concerns their conceptions of what is to be public interest. The Mohists were concerned primarily with order in society and the material well-being of the people. The Confucians, on the other hand, also stressed regulating and refining people's emotions and beautifying human interactions through the practices of *li*, and promoting such qualities as special affection for parents and fulfilling special obligations to them. The purposes of government include not just order and material well-being, but also transforming people's character through education and moral example. Another important difference concerns the content of the ethical ideal and how it can be attained. For the Mohists, the ethical ideal is primarily a devotion to the well-being of each without discrimination, and Mozi believed that it is easy to practice the ideal once one realizes that it is actually to one's own interest to do so. For the Confucians, the ethical ideal includes the various attributes described earlier, such as a graded affective concern and reverence for others. While believing that everyone can approximate the ideal, they also emphasized the need for persistence and devotion. Self-cultivation is a life-long process that often requires forgoing ordinary objects of pursuit, such as wealth and employment.

By contrast to Confucianism and Mohism, Yangism, a movement of thought of which Yang Zhu (fifth to fourth century BC) is a representative figure, might appear to be indifferent to the public good. We do not have detailed records of the earlier teachings associated with the movement, but certain materials have been identified as reporting its later developments. On the basis of such materials, we can infer that the Yangists advocated the nourishing of life, with an emphasis on health and longevity. Certain trends in the movement also advocated appropriate satisfaction of sensory desires, so long as sensory pursuits are not allowed to do harm to life. Likewise, external possessions are a means to nourishing life, and one should not let such possessions, even if it is possession of the empire, do harm to life.

Since political participation in those times could easily put one in danger, the Yangists idealized people who shunned offices or even declined the throne to avoid harm to their lives. On the assumption that it is often by taking office that one can contribute to the public good, critics such as Mencius regarded the Yangists as being selfishly concerned with themselves, to the neglect of public responsibility. While acknowledging that what Mencius ascribed to the Yangists was not a basic tenet of Yangism, some contemporary scholars nevertheless regard the neglect of public good as an implication of Yangist teachings.

However, at least for one trend of Yangist thought, the concern with oneself was probably viewed as instrumental to the public good. That the Yangists should urge each person to nourish his or her own life shows that they were concerned not just with nourishing their own lives, but with nourishing lives in general. Indeed, certain records of Yangist teachings describe the offices of government as serving the purpose of nourishing lives, and they contain a story about how a ruler of a state left his territories to save his subjects from being killed by invaders. The question remains, though, as to how this concern with the public can be reconciled with the strand in Yangist thought that advocates not letting external possessions, including offices in government or even the throne, do harm to one's life.

The answer lies with a certain diagnosis of the ills of the times. Certain records of Yangist teachings criticize rulers of the times for being preoccupied with power and possessions. As a result, they caused corruption in government and disorder in society. This is contrary to the purpose of government, which is to nourish the lives of the subjects, and the remedy is to discourage this concern with power and possessions. The Yangists' idealization of those who would not let power and possessions harm their lives stems from this diagnosis of the ills of the times rather than from an indifference to such problems. Given this diagnosis, it follows that it is those without concern for power and possessions who should ideally take office. And in the records of Yangist teachings, we do find several instances in which those who actively sought to avoid offices or even the throne are described as people who ideally should rule.

So, contrary to appearance, the Yangists were not indifferent to the public good. Like the Mohists, they regarded one's own interests and the public good as converging. But unlike the Mohists who believed that one's own interests are served by devoting oneself to the public good, they believed that the public good is served by everyone attending to his or her own interests. Yangism is regarded by some scholars as a precursor to Taoism, which shared this view of the relation between one's own interests and the public good, but which had a different conception of what is actually to one's interest. Two important early Daoist texts are the *Zhuangzi*, part of which reports the teachings of Zhuangzi of the fourth century BC, and the *Lao Tzu*, the date of composition of which is controversial but lies some time between the sixth and third century BC.

The *Zhuangzi* takes as its starting point the observation that there is no neutral ground for adjudicating between opposing judgments made from different perspectives, whether these are judgments about the desirability of ordinary objects of pursuit, such as power, wealth and longevity, or judgments about right and wrong, such as those of the Confucians and the Mohists. This realization, characterized in terms of a kind of illumination, leads to an altered perspective involving a relaxation of the importance one attaches to such judgments. As a result, the mind can respond spontaneously and appropriately to situations, in the way that a clear mirror or still water can reflect accurately what is brought up to it. The exact nature of this state of existence is subject to different interpretations – one strand seems to advocate distancing oneself from ordinary social life, while another seems to regard ordinary social life as unavoidable, but advocates a more relaxed attitude despite social engagement. Either way, when people attain this altered perspective, order will be restored because people will no longer compete with each other over worldly goods or combat each other over differing views about standards of conduct. It follows that those in power should not advocate standards of conduct or propagate moral doctrines, but should instead keep people free from the influence of such standards or doctrines.

The *Laozi* sees reversal as the way the natural order operates: everything that has gone far in one direction will move in the opposite direction, and to be in a low or weak position is to be in a state in which one will thrive. The analogous phenomenon in the human realm is that those who strive for wealth or power, though initially appearing rich or strong, will inevitably lose what they have and will also exhaust themselves in the process. Instead, by entertaining few desires and occupying an apparently low or weak position, one is rich and strong in the sense of not being subject to losses and exhaustion. Real strength is a matter of overcoming oneself rather than of overcoming others, and real wealth is a matter of contentment rather than of having plenty. Similarly, real longevity is a matter of not worrying about death rather than of not dying. Hence by having few desires and not striving after worldly goods, one accomplishes what ordinary people pursue, but in an altered sense. The task of government is to meet the basic needs of the people and to minimize their desires, thereby avoiding conflict and achieving order.

In their attitude toward the public good, the Daoists differed from the Confucians and the Mohists, who emphasized active social and political engagement. They were closer to the Yangists in thinking that order comes about when each person attends to himself or herself. However, unlike the Yangists, who emphasized biological life, the Daoists attended to the mind instead, and advocated freeing the mind from the restrictive influences of ordinary objects of pursuit, social norms and moral doctrines. In their attitude toward self-interest, they were unlike the Yangists and the Mohists, who viewed what is to one's interest in ordinary terms. They were closer to the Confucians in playing down the significance of ordinary objects of pursuit: if the ethical ideal is to one's own interest, it is only so in some altered sense. Just as Mencius believed that the practice of humaneness has consequences that are different from and yet bear an affinity to ordinary objects of pursuit, the *Laozi* regards the entertainment of few desires as also having such consequences. Another point of similarity is that, in both cases, the desirable consequences come about only if one is in the appropriate state of existence without directly aiming at such consequences.

As was already suggested, for most early Chinese philosophical movements, the public good and one's own interests were viewed as converging rather than as standing in opposition to each other, and the ethical ideal was regarded as promoting both. Since these movements were responses to the social and political disorder of the times, it is understandable that their proposed ethical ideals were also seen as ways of restoring order. On the other hand, given the fact that people are generally moved to pursue what is to their own interest, an ethical ideal has to link up with self-interest, even if only in some altered sense, to have a firm grip on people's motivations. For example, Mozi often faced the challenge that indiscriminate concern for each is impractical, because people are more concerned for their own interests and the interests of those to whom they stand in a special relation. By showing how indiscriminate concern can benefit oneself and those to whom one stands in a special relation, Mozi sought to address the challenge and to motivate his audience to actually practice indiscriminate concern.

So far, our discussion has followed the standard classification of early Chinese thought into schools, and we may conclude with three observations about this classification. First, the classification is retrospective and these schools might not have been clearly distinguished in the early period. For example, a chapter of the text *Guanzi* contains a trend of thought, probably datable to the late fourth or early third century BC, that combines both ideas associated with Daoism and those associated with Confucianism. On the one hand, like the *Zhuangzi*, it advocates not letting emotions or sensory objects disturb the mind so that one can respond freely and spontaneously to situations one confronts. On the other hand, such a state of mind is supposed to result from practices that the Confucians advocated, such as poetry, music and rites (*li*), and its responses are characterized in terms of humaneness (*ren*) and propriety (*yi*), the goals of Confucian self-cultivation.

Second, even after the classification into schools had become standard, the development of one school often involved drawing on ideas from another. Consider, for example, the commentary on the *Zhuangzi* by Guoxiang (d. 312), who is often classified as a "Neo-Daoist" thinker. Developing ideas in the *Zhuangzi*, Guoxiang advocated letting everything follow its own nature without intervention. However, according to him, different things have different natures, and different human beings may have different natures suited to fulfilling different roles in society. That is, some may have a nature appropriate to rulers, and some the nature appropriate to officials, just as a part of the body may have the nature of the head and other parts the nature of the feet. Hence, following one's nature involves fulfilling the social role to which one is suited. The traditional rules of *li* governing conduct between people in different social positions, as well as various governmental policies, are rooted in the different natures of human beings and should be followed. So, while emphasizing a kind of inner calm and contentment that is associated with Daoist thought, the way of life that Guoxiang advocated is nevertheless like the kind of social and political engagement that the Confucians upheld.

Conversely, thinkers often described as "Neo-Confucian," such as Zhuxi (1130–1200) and Wang Yangming (1472–1529), also appropriated Daoist (and sometimes Buddhist) ideas in their development of Confucian thought. While defending the Confucian way of life, they regarded the mind as originally pure, although subject to the influences of distortive desires and erroneous understanding. The task of self-cultivation is to restore the original state of the mind so that it can respond spontaneously and appropriately to situations, in the way that a clear mirror or still water accurately reflects whatever it confronts. While this depiction of the mind bears similarity to the one found in the *Zhuangzi*, the responses of the mind are supposed to have a Confucian content, involving the kind of values and norms that the Confucians upheld. Indeed, everyone is already a sage in the Confucian sense, since the original state of the mind encompasses such ethical attributes as humaneness (*ren*) and propriety (*yi*).

The third observation to be made about the classification into schools is that different branches of one school may significantly diverge, despite their sharing some key features. For example, Zhuxi and Wang Yangming differed in the way they understood the original state of the mind. For Zhu, it takes the form of a perfect knowledge, understood in terms of a kind of insight or clear perception, that guides human conduct in the way that the eyes guide the legs in walking. For Wang, it takes the form of a capacity to respond appropriately to any situation one confronts. Such responses involve one's being fully disposed to act in the appropriate manner and judging that this is the appropriate response, but the judgment merely accompanies without explaining one's action. This difference between Zhu and Wang leads to differences in emphasis in their views about self-cultivation, although both aimed at restoring the original state of the mind. Zhu emphasized learning, which includes the study of classics and history as well as examining daily affairs, to recover the insight that one originally has. By learning broadly and constantly practicing what one has learnt, one can regain this insight which in turn will guide one's behavior. Wang, on the other hand, de-emphasized learning because, according to him, the responses of the mind in its original state are not guided by the kind of insight that Zhu emphasized. Instead, he advocated attending directly to the mind and freeing it from the influence of distortive desires and erroneous understanding, so that the mind can again respond appropriately to situations free from such influences.

Bibliography

Writings

Wing-tsit Chan (tr.) 1963: *A Source Book in Chinese Philosophy* (Princeton: Princeton University Press).

Graham, A. C. (tr.) 1981: *Chuang Tzu: The Inner Chapters* (London: George Allen & Unwin).

Lau, D. C. (tr.) 1963: *Lao Tzu: Tao Te Ching* (London: Penguin Books).

—— (tr.) 1970: *Mencius* (London: Penguin Books).

—— (tr.) 1979: *Confucius: The Analects* (London: Penguin Books).

Watson, Burton (tr.) 1963a: *Hsün Tzu: Basic Writings* (New York: Columbia University Press).

—— (tr.) 1963b: *Mo Tzu: Basic Writings* (New York: Columbia University Press).

References and further reading

Creel, Herrlee G. 1953: *Chinese Thought from Confucius to Mao Tse-tung* (Chicago: University of Chicago Press).

—— 1970: *"What is Taoism?" and Other Studies in Chinese Cultural History* (Chicago: University of Chicago Press).

Fung Yu-lan 1952–3: *A History of Chinese Philosophy*, tr. Derk Bodde, 2 Vols (Princeton: Princeton University Press).

Graham, A. C. 1989: *Disputers of the Tao: Philosophical Argument in Ancient China* (La Salle: Open Court).

Hall, David L. and Ames, Roger T. 1987: *Thinking Through Confucius* (Albany: State University of New York Press).

Mair, Victor H. (ed.) 1983: *Experimental Essays on Chuang-tzu* (Honolulu: University of Hawaii Press).
Munro, Donald J. 1969: *The Concept of Man in Early China* (Stanford: Stanford University Press).
Nivison, David S. 1996: *The Ways of Confucianism: Investigations in Chinese Philosophy* (La Salle: Open Court Press).
Roetz, Heiner 1993: *Confucian Ethics of the Axial Age: a Reconstruction under the Aspect of the Breakthrough Toward Postconventional Thinking* (Albany: State University of New York Press).
Schwartz, Benjamin I. *The World of Thought in Ancient China* (Cambridge: Harvard University Press).
Shun Kwong-loi 1997: *Mencius and Early Chinese Thought* (Stanford: Stanford University Press).
Tu Wei-ming 1979: *Humanity and Self-Cultivation: Essays in Confucian Thought* (Berkeley: Asian Humanities Press).
—— 1985: *Confucian Thought: Selfhood as Creative Transformation* (Albany: State University of New York Press).

8

The Chinese conception of selfhood

ROGER T. AMES

The discrete and autonomous individual

Comparative philosophy, moving back and forth between two or more cultural sites, can ideally provide a window on alternative cultural narratives, and at the same time, enable us to excavate those presuppositions underlying our own tradition. But if, in the process, we fail to identify and set aside those cultural assumptions which illumine our own way of seeing the world, that same window will, in the glare of our own prejudices, serve as nothing more than a mirror with which to contemplate our own cultural reflection, concealing differences while redefining the alternative ways of living and thinking as deceptively familiar.

Within the broad sweep of the Western philosophical experience, there are few presuppositions that have become as firmly entrenched as those which have shaped and privileged the notion of discrete and autonomous human agency. Before we get to China, we must ask the question: Where did the autonomous individual of liberal Western thinking come from?

One dominant notion of self takes us back to classical Greece. In Plato's *Euthyphro*, we find Socrates in search of the essential definition of moral law. He implores of his would-be teacher, Euthyphro:

> Isn't it true that in every action piety is self-identical, and similarly impiety is in every instance the opposite of piety, but consistent with itself; in other words that everything that is to be regarded as impious has a single definite characteristic [Gk *eídos*] in respect of its impiety? . . . Then explain to me what this characteristic is in itself, so that by fixing my eyes upon it and using it as a pattern I may be able to describe any action, yours or anyone else's, as pious if it corresponds to the pattern and impious if it doesn't. (H. Tredennick tr., Penguin, 1954: 24–6)

It is a short move for Plato, having thus committed to natural kinds in respect of both natural and moral laws, to posit an essential defining condition for each "kind" of thing, including human beings. This notion of strict identity means that each thing is one of a "kind" by virtue of a single, self-identical characteristic: in the case of humankind, a *psyche* or soul.

What is true of the "kinds" that make up the world is also assumed to be true of the language that describes them. That is, as corollary to an essentialist definition of moral law and natural kinds, words – our repositories of cultural interests – are a currency which, upon investigation, are expected to yield up etymologies that not only reveal their particular historical careers, but more fundamentally, bring to light their ostensive root meanings – their essential and literal definitions.

The discrete individuality of the human being adumbrated with Plato's *psyche*, is reinforced by the teleology of Aristotle's formal cause and the notion of agency entailed by his efficient cause. And individuals become fully autonomous when, in Augustine, they are endowed with an independent volitional faculty: the individuated will. The volitional element affirms the dominance of efficient cause explanations that we associate with the actions of these individual agents. With the melding of the Hellenic and Hebrew sensibilities, human agency finds its analogy in the image of a creative and legislative Deity who both determines and disciplines a world independent of Himself.

An interesting irony in the Western philosophical dialectic is that it is precisely this classical commitment to *arche* – transcendent, originative principle – which makes human freedom, autonomy, creativity, and individuality problematic, and which has inclined philosophers to focus on these particular issues as priority philosophical concerns. Many of the best minds of the tradition have exercised themselves within a One/many, "chain of being" ontology, seeking to explain how truth, beauty, and goodness can be resident in some independent, objective, and determinative principle, while at the same time, allowing that human beings can be free and creative autonomous individuals.

As a tradition, we have, through the notion of strict identity, arrived at a definition of individuality that entails a strong commitment to human equality, evolving most recently into a liberal doctrine of human rights and entitlements, thereby subordinating human differences to secondary status. It is a conception of hyper-conscious, self-constructing, and self-choosing persons who hold sovereignty over their own private interiority. Autonomy and choice have become important values, while teleological assumptions encourage the pursuit of a life that aspires to be purposeful and noble. Each individual has irrevocable membership in humankind, where the rank of humanity on the chain of being guarantees the ultimate sanctity of each individual life. With this historical sketch in mind, we can now turn to the classical Chinese roots of a very different conception of person.

The paronomastic person

The concept of the natural human condition that has held sway in the Chinese tradition is radically different, and in many ways anathema, to such individualistic notions as have emerged and become dominant in much of Western thinking. The classical Chinese tradition begins from the assumption that the human being (or better, the human "becoming") is something that one *does* rather than what one *is*; it is *how* one behaves within the context of the human community rather than some essential endowment that resides within one as a potential to be actualized.

When the philosopher Confucius, like Plato, attempted to formulate a basis for human morality, he was far less ambitious than his Athenian counterpart. He did not posit the existence of some independent, foundational, universal, and objective standard beyond our empirical experience that can be appealed to for justification. On the contrary, he allowed that morality is invariably a function of those specific, and always fluid, circumstances that define any situation. "The exemplary person in making his way in the world, is neither bent on nor against anything; rather, he accords with what is appropriate" (*Analects*, 4:10). The classical Chinese term translated as "appropriate" (*yi*) has most often been translated into English as "right" or "righteous", suggesting compliance with some external standard. However, this classical Chinese notion viewed etymologically suggests that it is better rendered "appropriateness" – L. *proprius* → proper → property, "to make one's own" – combining as it does "me" or "us" (*wo*) and "felicitous circumstances" (*yang*). Morality, then, is the effort to get the most out of one's circumstances, where one's own interests and those of one's natural, social, and cultural environments must all be considered. *Yi*, resolutely situational and pragmatic, is frequently called upon to translate Western notions such as "rightness" and "justice" (*gongyi*), but in such cases requires a qualifying second term to provide it with the requisite sense of objectivity.

When we consult the Chinese dictionary which seeks to explain such a world, we discover that terms are not defined by appeal to essential, literal meanings, but rather are brought into focus paronomastically by semantic and phonetic associations. "Exemplary person" (*junzi*), for example, is defined by its cognate and the phonetically similar, "to gather" (*qun*), with the assumption that "people gather round and defer to exemplary persons". As it insists in the *Analects*, "Excellent persons do not live alone; they are sure to have neighbors" (4:24). "Mirror" (*jing*) is defined as "radiant" (*jing*): a mirror is a source of illumination. "Battle formation" (*zhen*) is defined as "to display" (*chen*).

What is remarkable about this sense of meaning is that a term is defined non-referentially by mining relevant and yet seemingly random associations implicated in the term itself. Further, erstwhile nominal expressions ("things") default to verbal expressions ("events"), underscoring the primacy of process over form as a grounding presupposition in this tradition. (See Article 39, CONTEMPORARY CHINESE PHILOSOPHY).

When we extrapolate from the understanding of words to the understanding of persons, as we did in discovering the essential soul in the *Euthyphro*, we find that instead of positing some intrinsically residing feature, some self-same identical characteristic that qualifies all human beings as members of a natural humankind, persons, like words, are to be understood by exploring relevant associations that constitute their specific patterns of meaningful relationships. Persons are not perceived as superordinated individuals – as agents who stand independent of their actions – but are rather ongoing "events" defined functionally by constitutive roles and relationships as they are performed within the context of their specific families and communities – by *li*.

As suggested above, the dominant philosophical preoccupations of cultures are often a function of assumptions made early in their narratives. As we saw, Greek metaphysical presuppositions melded with Judeo-Christian beliefs to produce the "God-model," where an independent and superordinate principle determines order and value in the world while remaining aloof from it, making human freedom, autonomy, creativity, and individuality at once problematic and of key philosophical interest. On the Chinese side, the commitment to the processional, transformative, and always provisional nature of experience renders the "ten thousand things" (*wanwu* or *wanyou*) which make up the world, including the human world, at once continuous one with another, and at the same time, unique. There is no "Being" behind the "beings"; only "beings" are. And the primary philosophical problem that emerges from these assumptions is *ars contextualis*: how do we correlate these unique particulars to achieve the most productive continuity? Ancestor-worship as the defining religious sensibility, family as the primary human unit, co-humanity (*ren*) and filiality (*xiao*) as primary human values, ritualized roles, relationships, and practices (*li*) as a communal discourse, are all strategies for achieving and sustaining communal harmony (*ho*). As it states in the *Analects*,

> The achievement of harmony is the most valuable function of propriety (*li*). In the ways of the Former Kings, this achievement of harmony through ritual was elegant, and was a guiding standard in all things large and small. But where there are situations which are not harmonious, to realize harmony just for the sake of harmony without regulating the situation on the basis of propriety, will not work. (1:12)

The Confucian person and right thinking

Given this emphasis on a ritually constituted community, what then is the value of the individual? A pertinent contrast can be developed between the Western liberal commitment to many voices (the right to think) and the traditional Chinese concern for a communitarian consensus as a social good (right thinking). It is this commitment to freedom of thought that underlies a Western sense of a healthy pluralism, our suspicions about rigid conservatism and orthodoxy, and our respect for a loyal opposition. It is the Chinese commitment to emergent harmony that underlies their sense of a centripetal center, evidenced in notions such as patriarchal hierarchy, institutional intellectuals, defining canonical texts, and the inviolable continuity of the Chinese tradition. At the same time, it is this same concern for communal solidarity that, on the Chinese side, encourages the perception of individual freedom as license, and individual choice as selfishness.

Following perhaps from this assumption about "right thinking," there is an equivocation that has plagued our understanding of person in the Chinese tradition. In much of the interpretive literature, there is the unfortunate assumption that community interest and self-interest are mutually exclusive, and hence, to be a viable member of community, one must become selfless. This attribution of "selflessness" to the Chinese tradition, both ancient and modern, seems to arise out of an unfortunate equivocation between "selfish" and "selfless." But to eschew selfish concerns does not necessarily lead to self-abnegation.

The classical Confucian position contends that, because self-realization is fundamentally a social undertaking, "selfish" concerns are to be rejected as an impediment to one's own growth and self-realization. A perennial issue in Chinese philosophy that has spanned the centuries has been the likelihood of conflict between the pursuit of selfish advantage (*li*) and negotiation of that which is appropriate and meaningful to all concerned (*yi*), including oneself. Concern for selfish personal advantage is associated with retarded personal development (*xiaoren*), while the pursuit of what is broadly "appropriate" – including, of course, one's own interests – is the mainstay of the self-realized and exemplary person (*junzi*).

In China, the traditional assumption has been that personal order and the order of society and the state entail each other, with the broader configuration always emerging out of the more immediate and concrete. When the country succumbs to disorder, the exemplary person returns to the more immediate and substantive precincts of home and community to begin again to shape an appropriate order.

On being asked by a rather unsympathetic second party why he did not have a formal position in government, Confucius replied that the achievement of order in the home is itself the basis on which any broader attainment of social and political order depends. The central doctrine of graduated love and ritually ordered community in which family plays such a vital role – in fact, where all roles are reduced to the familial – is predicated on the priority of participation in the immediate and concrete over determination by more general principles and ideals. Even when a higher order of social or political organization is deferred to, it is given definition and represented in the concrete embodiment of a particular person – a specific ruler or leader with whom one can assume a personal relationship.

It is certainly the case, then, that the Chinese tradition has been largely persuaded by a Confucian-based relational and hence social definition of person rather than by any notion of discrete individuality. It must be further allowed that there does not seem to be an adequate philosophical basis to justify self as a locus of interests independent of and prior to society. Under the sway of this relational understanding of human being, the mutuality and interdependence of personal, familial, societal, and political realization in the classical Chinese model can and has been generally conceded. But it certainly does not follow that the consequence of this interdependence is selflessness. Under scrutiny, the consequence of attributing "selflessness" as an ideal to the Chinese tradition is to sneak in both the public/private and the individual/society distinctions by the back door. To be "selfless" requires that an individual self first exist, and that it then be sacrificed for some higher public interest. And the suggestion that there are "higher interests" on the part of either person or society covertly establishes a boundary between them that justifies an adversarial relationship. The "selfless" interpretation of the Chinese person does not support the claim that the person is irreducibly social; ironically, it vitiates it.

The "selfless" ideal ultimately entails a contest between state and individual – the struggle between advocates of group interests over the priority of individual interests – that has in large measure separated collectivist thinkers from the liberal democratic in the Western experience, but which has little relevance for the Chinese tradition. While it is true that for the traditional Chinese model, self-realization does not require a high degree of individual autonomy, it does not follow that the alternative to autonomy is capitulation to the general will. Rather, becoming a Confucian person involves benefitting and being benefitted by membership in a world of reciprocal loyalties and obligations which surround and stimulate one, and which define one's own worth. The coterminous relationship between strong person and strong state presumed in the Chinese model contrasts with the liberal Western concern to limit state powers as a precondition for individual autonomy.

It is commonly noticed that in China, from ancient times to the present, conflicts are generally dealt with through informal mechanisms for mediation and conciliation as close to the dispute as possible. Society has largely been regulated through ritually defined relationships, and thus has required relatively minimal government. It is this same communal harmony that defines and dispenses order at the most immediate level that is also relied upon to define and express authoritative consensus without more obvious formal provisions for effecting popular sovereignty. Clearly, to the extent that the Confucian model is a project of cultivation directed at self-realization, the social and political order is derived from the participants themselves who cannot be fairly construed as self-abnegating.

The Confucian person and unique individuality

It can be argued that "self" does necessarily entail a notion of individuality. But exposed in the differences we have discovered between being "unselfish" and being "selfless," there is a further unnoticed conceptual equivocation on the term "individual." "Individual" can mean either one-of-a-*kind*, as in one human being as a member of the class of human beings, or *one*-of-a-kind, as in Turner's unique "Seastorm." That is, "individual" can refer to a single, separate and indivisible thing that, by virtue of some essential property or properties, qualifies as a member of a class. By virtue of its membership in a "kind," it is substitutable – "equal before the law," "entitled to equal opportunity," "a locus of inalienable rights," "one of God's children," and so on. It is this definition of "individual" that generates notions like autonomy, equality, liberty, freedom, will, and so on. By virtue of both its separability and its indivisibility, it relates to its world only extrinsically, and hence, where animate, has dominion over its own interiority.

"Individual" can alternatively also mean uniqueness: the character of a single and unsubstitutable particular, such as a work of art, where its own value is a function of its contextualizing associations – a particular *oeuvre*, genealogy, movement, period. Under this definition of "individual," equality can only mean parity – a comparable excellence.

In the model of the unique individual, determinacy, far from being individuation, lies in the achieved quality of a person's relationships. A person becomes "recognized," "distinguished" or "renowned" by virtue of his or her relations and their quality. Much of the effort in coming to an understanding of the traditional Confucian conception of self has to do with clarifying this distinction, and reinstating the unique individual in the Confucian picture. While the definition of self as "irreducibly social" certainly precludes autonomous individuality, it does not rule out the second, less familiar notion of unique individuality.

In understanding the Confucian person in this way, we resist the familiar move to separate *that which orders* (the self, rationality, volition) from *that which is ordered* (specific thoughts, desires, experiences). We abandon notions of a unitary self which makes our many experiences one, in favor of a more underdetermined range and locus of experiences expressed through specific roles and relationships.

Further, we really must go on to question the appropriateness of using "concept" rather than "narrative" language to discuss the Confucian self. Concept belongs to the "one/many" model according to which "self" can be understood as having some univocal and hence formal definition – it reifies or entifies self as an ego or an ideal. Concept is dependent upon formal abstraction. Given the dependency of the Confucian model on the particular image, then, we might have to allow that the Confucian self is precisely that particular and detailed portrait of Confucius found in the middle books of the *Analects*, in which each passage is a remembered detail contributed by one of the disciples who belonged to the conversation. And this portrait, as it attracts the deference of more adherents in the tradition, plays a role in shaping both their own unique self-images, and the shared communal life-forms.

It is this propensity for personal extension – Confucius as a corporate person – that is the basis for traditional religious practices in which the objects of religious veneration are the past makers of culture and value: one's ancestors and one's cultural heroes. These persons are precisely what "gods" mean within the Confucian world.

Bibliography

Ames, Roger T. 1991: "Reflections on the Confucian Self: a Response to Fingarette" in *Rules, Rituals, and Responsibility: Essays Dedicated to Herbert Fingarette*, ed. Mary I. Bockover (La Salle, Ill.: Open Court).

Ames, Roger T., Dissanayake, W., and Kasulis, T. (eds) 1994: *Self as Person in Asian Theory and Practice* (Albany: State University of New York Press).

Hall, David L. and Ames, Roger T. 1987: *Thinking Through Confucius* (Albany: State University of New York Press).

—— 1996: *Thinking From The Han: Self, Truth, and Transcendence in China and the West* (Albany: State University of New York Press).

Tu Weiming 1979: *Humanity and Self-Cultivation: Essays in Confucian Thought* (Berkeley: Asian Humanities Press).

—— 1985: *Confucian Thought: Selfhood as Creative Transformation* (Albany: State University of New York Press).

—— 1989: *Centrality and Commonality: an Essay on Confucian Religiousness* (Albany: State University of New York Press).

—— 1993: *Way, Learning, and Politics: Essays on the Confucian Intellectual* (Albany: State University of New York Press).

9

Human beings and nature in traditional Chinese thought

P. J. IVANHOE

This essay explores a variety of important Chinese conceptions of the actual and ideal relationship between human beings and the rest of the natural world. It presents views from the earliest period of historical China, the latter part of the Shang dynasty (ca. 1200–1050 BCE), and from representative thinkers of other periods, extending down to the last imperial era, the Qing dynasty (1644–1911 CE). There is a fairly clear line of development from the earliest period, when the Chinese saw the natural realm as chaotic, dangerous and largely inscrutable, to a later view of the world as well ordered, inclined toward human good and more open to understanding. This later view was first expressed during the "Eastern Zhou" (770–221 BCE), and reached a mature and systematic form in the following Han dynasty (206 BCE–220 CE). Subsequent periods saw remarkable variation in the specific features of this view but its general form – a belief in a well ordered and manageable world, inclined toward human good and open to human understanding – remained dominant throughout subsequent Chinese history.

Shang dynasty

Élite members of Shang civilization regarded the natural and spiritual realms with a combination of anxiety, uncertainty and fear. Important events such as bountiful harvests or success in battle were thought to be under the control of a capricious and powerful deity, Shang Di, who was not in any particular way predisposed to be concerned with human well-being. While the Shang could appeal to this god, they could not reliably influence him. The Shang king however could, through prognostication communicate, with and through prayer and sacrifice, influence his ancestors to intercede on his behalf with this distant high god. The most extensive written records we have of Shang culture are oracular inscriptions representing such efforts, incised on shell and bone.

The Shang were rather pessimistic about the fundamental relationship between human beings and the natural and spiritual realms. The latter were not in any discernible way inclined toward human good. And yet the Shang were at the same time extremely optimistic about the power of ritual as a way to both understand and order these potential sources of danger. Shang divination was from the start a means to understand and control the spiritual and by extension natural realms.

Over time, these divination practices became increasingly rational in the sense of becoming a more systematic and routinized method for controlling nature. (We see this general tit-for-tat conception of the relationship between human and spiritual forces retained in the later, Mohist school, which flourished in the succeeding Zhou dynasty.) But the Shang were not seeking to bend or reform an impassive nature to their will; they were attempting to mollify spirits and accommodate human activity to larger, unruly forces. Seen in this light, these early Shang beliefs and practices can be understood as setting the stage for, and providing many of the guiding themes of, subsequent Chinese views about the proper relationship between humans and nature.

Eastern Zhou dynasty human-nature analogues

Shang ancestral spirits provided a link with the largely inscrutable and powerful force of Shang Di. Their needs and ways of thought bore a close analogy and they had clear sympathy with the living descendants who sought their help. By the early part of the Eastern Zhou (roughly the "Spring and Autumn Period," 722–481 BCE), Shang Di and the royal ancestors had lost most of their already fading personal attributes and eventually dissolved into a rather indistinct set of *tian* "natural/heavenly" patterns, forces and processes.

We see a shift in the Eastern Zhou from an earlier faith in prognostication to a reliance upon people with the right kind of understanding as the most reliable guides for social, political and military activity. These two kinds of expertise – that of the priestly diviner and of the cultivated individual – are not wholly unrelated. Both possess a combination of technical expertise and personal sensitivity that allows them to understand events and predict what is to come. The Chinese conception of these capacities was, over time, increasingly naturalized.

In this period the spiritual realm blends with and infuses nature, lending it a moral curvature. The natural realm is believed to be disposed to cooperate and even to actively protect and support ethically good people (see, for example, *Analects*, 9:5). Nature is seen as the source of the goodness within human beings (see, for example, *Analects*, 7:23) and following one's nature is the way to both understand and fulfill heaven's plan (see, for example, *Mencius*, 7A1). Those who succeed in fulfilling their nature are part of a greater, though still loose and vaguely described, universal scheme: "Above or below they are in the stream of heaven and earth" (*Mencius*, 7A13). Given this much closer correspondence between the human and the natural, we find an increasing variety of analogies being drawn between nature and the ethically good person. For example, the ideal king is likened to the pole star – he remains in his proper place while his subordinates revolve around him with the stately order and regularity of the stars (*Analects*, 2:1). The wise, being active, flexible and wide-ranging, are thought to have a natural delight of water; the benevolent, being still, stable and unmovable, have a natural affinity to take delight in mountains (*Analects*, 6:23). Throughout the *Mencius* (for example, 2A6, 6A8–9) our nascent moral sense is described as a "sprout" – an active and observable tendency which naturally grows. In contrast, morally corrupt individuals are likened to a deforested mountain (*Mencius*, 6A8). This tendency to draw normative analogies between nature and human ideals is also evident in later texts like the *Daodejing*, which extols the many virtues of water (for example, chapters 8 and 78).

This tendency to draw analogies between natural phenomena and human ideals becomes a permanent part of the Chinese philosophical repertoire and re-emerges in later thinkers. But it also marks a change in the dominant conception of the relationship between humans and nature. In the Eastern Zhou, spiritual powers became an intricate and pervasive feature of the very fabric of nature. The correspondence between humans and nature became tighter, more widely observable and more easily accessible. This trend continues in subsequent periods.

Holistic conceptions of the Warring States Period

In the latter half of the Eastern Zhou, during a time known as the "Warring States Period" (403–221 BCE), a related but distinct conception of the relationship between human beings and nature arose. The clearest representative of this new view was the Daoist philosopher Zhuangzi (fl. 399–295 BCE). Earlier thinkers believed certain natural phenomena provided normative analogues for human activity. Zhuangzi too drew such analogues between the natural and human realms. Thus, for example, the sage's ability to respond to any situation was like the ceaseless and omni-directional movement of the star at the end of the handle of the Big Dipper, as it "swings" around the pole star. But he took things a step further and argued that human beings are part of, and inextricably woven into, nature.

Zhuangzi developed the idea that humans are part of a vast and all-embracing *natural order*. He believed that there is a deep structure to the cosmos which unites it together as a systematic whole. He was the first thinker to use the terms *li* ("pattern") and *tian li* ("heavenly/natural pattern") as central terms of art, expressing this ideal. This natural/heavenly pattern runs throughout and defines the proper structure and function of each and every thing in the universe. It is what the famous cook of chapter 3 follows in order to carve up the carcass of the ox without meeting the slightest resistance. Localized in a given thing, *li* describes its proper structure and spontaneous activity. Taken together, the *li* of the myriad things connect with one another to form a vast, interrelated network, the *dao* ("Way").

Human beings have a natural tendency to detect and follow this inherent pattern and doing so enables them to move through life – like the cook and other exemplary figures in the text – with extraordinary effectiveness and without the slightest contention or strife. This is because they avoid imposing artificial (that is, humanly derived) categories upon nature. By ridding themselves of their social preconceptions and avoiding an overly intellectualized approach to life, their minds attain a state of *xu* ("tenuousness") in which their natural, spontaneous tendencies begin to inform and direct their activity. Those who achieve this, like the divine Woodcarver Qing, "simply match up *tian* ('nature/heaven') with *tian*." They do not impose a personal will or human perspective upon the world. They merge into the patterns, processes and forces of nature – the *dao* – and let things take their spontaneous course. This deference to the deeper guiding pattern of nature results in a profound leveling of value among the things of the world. Human beings have no special status. From the perspective of the *dao* they are simply things among things: like the tiny figures in later landscape paintings.

While Zhuangzi believed that the properly cultivated person can "mirror" the world and respond to it appropriately, he did not propose any systematic scheme of mutual influence and response. Equally important, in his view there is no *direct* connection between human beings and the rest of nature. Humans are part of a larger natural system but not part of a single universal organism. As a result, human beings, while generally benign, do not have anything approaching universal concern, for the rest of nature or even for each other.

This new perspective had a profound effect on the Confucian thinker Xunzi (310–219 BCE), who incorporated much of Zhuangzi's vision into his own distinctive philosophy. Xunzi embraced Zhuangzi's idea that the *dao* defined a universal system of patterns, processes and forces. However, he rejected Zhuangzi's conclusion that such a view entails the equality of all things. Xunzi maintained a steadfastly anthropocentric point of view. According to him, the universe, in its original state, was disorderly, harsh and amoral. Human beings, by nature, reflected these characteristics which led them to be contentious, selfish and foolishly short-sighted. A series of particularly reflective and insightful individuals realized that this *state of nature* was wholly unsatisfactory and so began to fashion a set of social norms and practices designed to constrain, shape and transform human nature, in order to reorient it toward more productive and satisfying ends. They saw that human needs and desires were part of a larger, interconnected natural order and realized that they would have to understand and accommodate this greater natural pattern in order to bring human practices into synergistic harmony with nature. This they did by limiting and directing human activity in ways that protected the natural realm and brought it into accord with heaven's operations.

Xunzi believed the Confucian Way allowed human beings to live in mutual benefit, common peace and enhanced satisfaction by harmoniously locating them within a greater cosmos and tuning their activity to the deeper rhythms of nature. Through the Confucian form of life, human beings could "form a triad with heaven and earth." In the process not only human beings but nature itself was ordered and well-regulated. This vision of the proper relationship between human beings and nature is Xunzi's "happy symmetry" (Ivanhoe, 1991).

Human beings are clearly at the center of Xunzi's picture of the world. They command a dominant position and play a critical role, for they are the source of the good order not only among themselves but throughout the universe. In at least one sense, this is the mirror image of the Daoist view. For while Xunzi believed that nature itself must await the transforming influence of the sages before good order can obtain, Zhuangzi believed that nature became disordered whenever human beings think too much and go on to impose their artificial schemes upon an originally harmonious and benign natural order.

Correlative cosmology and Han syncretism

The idea that there is a correspondence between natural phenomena and human activity was not new to Warring States Period philosophy. But what had not yet been seen are comprehensive and systematic schema, "correlative cosmologies," relating natural phenomena and human activity. We know that such schema were used throughout the classical period by, "astronomers, diviners, music masters (and) physicians" (Graham, 1986, p. 8), but until around the middle of the third century BCE such thinking did not exert a major influence on philosophy. In the chapter "A Discussion of Music", Xunzi makes use of a pair of terms, *gan* ("influence") and *ying* ("response"), which were to play an important role in such thinking: "When *influenced* by depraved sounds, rebellious *qi* ('energy') will *respond* from within. When influenced by proper sounds, compliant energy will respond from within." It is worth noting that this first sign of the influence of correlative thinking on philosophy comes from the technical discipline of the "music masters."

Correlative cosmologies organize and interrelate human and natural phenomena according to basic conceptual templates. The earliest and simplest of these are the paired fundamental forces: *yin* and *yang*. Originally, these two were members of larger sets of different *qi* ("energies"), but they came to represent the most basic pair of forces in the cosmos. *Yin* was associated with earth, autumn, night, inaction, below, woman, and so on. Its complement, *yang*, was associated with heaven, spring, day, activity, above, man, and so on. The different phenomena within each set were thought to have particular affinities for one another: that is, there is mutual natural resonance between them, which facilitates "influence" and "response." These networks of natural resonances provided normative standards according to which one must organize and accommodate one's activity. To follow them meant to go with the natural flow of things; the result was enhanced ease and efficacy. Failing to accord with these patterns, processes and forces meant one's actions would cut against the grain and fight the running tide of nature, with corresponding negative results. Similar and at times overlapping correlative schemes developed around alternative conceptual templates, such as the "four seasons" and the "five notes." One of the most influential and enduring of these was the system of the *wu xing* ("five phases").

The *wu xing* originally were five elemental substances: soil, water, fire, metal, and wood, each of which had characteristic "powers" (for example, fire is hot, rises, burns and so on). These came to be associated with a "conquest scheme" largely due to the writings of a man named Zou Yan (ca. 305–240 BCE) who arranged the five in a "natural" sequence: soil dams water, which extinguishes fire, which melts metal, which cuts wood, which digs soil, and so on. By linking different historical dynasties to each of the five, he then was able to offer an "explanation" of dynastic succession.

The *yin yang* and *wu xing* schemes are prominent in texts like the *Lushi Chunqiu* (ca. 240 BCE) and exerted considerable influence on the thought and politics of the times. While it does not mention Zou Yan by name, this diverse and important text contains the earliest complete account of Chinese dynastic succession according to the "conquest scheme" which he devised. The first emperor of the Qin (259–210 BCE) believed in such a scheme and its corresponding correlations enough to choose black as the color of his dynasty. This showed that he ruled under the power of water and was thus the natural successor to the Zhou, which was associated with the power of fire and its corresponding color red. In more general practice, the five phases were correlated to a wide variety of phenomena: for example, the five directions (the fifth being "center").

Another text which prominently employs correlative cosmology is the *Yijing* (*Book of Changes*). Of particular interest are its attached appendices, the "ten wings." These traditionally are attributed to Confucius but were composed sometime around the third century BCE. The correlative cosmology of the *Yijing* is built upon the eight trigrams. These are composed of the different permutations of stacks of three solid/"strong"/*yang* or broken/"weak"/*yin* lines. The trigrams are joined in various combinations to produce 64 hexagrams which are correlated to a vast network of phenomena in the attached commentaries. For example, one of the attached appendices provides the following associations for the first hexagram: "*Qian* is heaven. It is round, the ruler, the father, jade, metal, cold, ice, deep red, a good horse, an old horse, a lean horse, a piebald horse, tree fruit" (Chan, 1969, p. 270). Accounts of the genesis of the 64 hexagrams stress that they were generated by the workings of natural processes. The hexagrams themselves were thought to be patterns which coalesced out of the play of fundamental natural forces.

These different streams converged in the thought of Dong Zhongshu (ca. 170–104 BCE). He proposed a correlative cosmology which provided its own "conquest cycle" and calendar of prescribed activities, and incorporated both the *yin yang* and *wu xing* schemes, the hexagrams described in the *Yijing* and a system of numerology. Most important of all, in his *Chunqiu fanlu*, he related these various cosmological schemes to the central ethical concerns of Confucianism in a systematic fashion. Perhaps this more than anything else is what enabled him to persuade Emperor Wu (148–87 BCE) of the Han to proclaim Confucianism the official state ideology, a position it was to hold until 1905.

In Dong's thought we see a vast and complex scheme correlating human activities, feelings, dispositions, thoughts and ideals with almost every conceivable natural phenomenon. Phenomena associated within the system of correspondences were thought to exert mutual "influence" and "response" upon one anther. As a result, human activities had to follow carefully prescribed temporal and structural patterns in order to keep the whole system balanced. Any instability or anomaly within this vast web was symptomatic of some imbalance and would be read as a sign of human failure and a portent of coming change. The correlative cosmology of the Han dynasty marked the height of indigenous Chinese views concerning the relationship of human beings and nature. The next major change was the result of foreign influence, that is, Buddhism, which arrived in China some time in the first century CE.

The identity of self and cosmos

The idea that *li* provided a normative pattern for the structure and function of each thing while also relating it to all other things, gave rise to the notion that *li* "unites" the myriad phenomena of the universe. This idea was developed in texts like the *Huainanzi* (ca. 140 BCE) and found its most developed expression in "Neo-Daoist" thinkers like Wang Bi (226–249 CE) and Guo Xiang (d. 312 CE). Wang talked of "ultimate *li*" as an object of religious veneration. Guo went on to insist that the universal "pattern" of the world arose spontaneously; it was not predetermined or self-consciously planned. It depended on "nothing," hence the ultimate nature of the universe was *wu* ("non-existence"). These beliefs gave rise to a concerted effort to achieve mystical identification of the self with the rest of the natural world. The thought was that the loss of a distinct sense of a separate and independently existing self, which would result from such an identification, would *realize* in a direct and personal manner the fundamental character of the universe: non-existence.

Chinese Buddhists adapted these Neo-Daoist views on the nature of *li* to express their own distinctive metaphysical beliefs. For example, Zhi Dun (314–366 CE) adopted the Neo-Daoist equation of *li* with *wu* ("non-existence") but understood the latter in terms of the Buddhist notion of "emptiness" – the lack of independent, individual nature. Hua Yan Buddhists further developed this line of thinking, taking the "emptiness" of reality to mean that all things in the universe are manifestations of a shared "Buddha-nature". Hua Yan works, such as the *Treatise on the Golden Lion*, argue that each and every "phenomenon" contains within it all the various *li*. This is a significant step beyond earlier claims concerning the "oneness" of human beings and nature. We now see *two* ways to be "one." Earlier Chinese thinkers had insisted that human beings were part of a single, grand natural scheme – rather like being members of the same team. Chinese Buddhists insisted on a fundamental *identity* of the self with all of reality – so that the individual looks more like a part of a single cosmic body.

This new understanding had a profound effect on the so-called Neo-Confucian thinkers of the Song (960–1279 CE) and Ming (1368–1644 CE) dynasties. Like the Hua Yan Buddhists, they believed that each and every thing in the universe contains within it all the *li*. But unlike the Buddhists, Neo-Confucians believed that because of different "physical endowments" individual things only manifest specific *li*. (This is what makes them the particular things they are.) Again like the Buddhists (and like Neo-Daoists as well), Neo-Confucians believed that the goal of the spiritual life lies in grasping this shared, unifying principle and living life in awareness of this, the true nature of reality.

One of the most moving and influential statements of this view is Zhang Zai's (1020–1077) *Western Inscription*,

> Heaven is my father, earth is my mother and even such a small creature as I finds an intimate place in their midst. And so, that which fills the universe I regard as my body and that which directs the universe I consider my nature. (Adapted from Chan, 1969, p. 497)

The use of the metaphor of "forming one body" with all the universe, or rather *realizing* that this is the way things really are, is the concrete statement of this *identification* of the self with all of nature. This provided a different foundation for Confucian ethical claims. One prominent Neo-Confucian, Cheng Hao (1032–1085) employed the "one body" metaphor and played upon the dual senses of the character *ren*. In Confucian ethics, this word often means something close to "benevolence" but in medical texts it meant "feeling" or "sensation." Cheng Hao explains,

> The *ren* ("benevolent") person regards all things in the universe as one body. There is nothing which is not a part of him. If he regards all things as parts of himself, where will his *ren* ("feelings") not extend? But if he does not see them as parts of himself, why would he feel any *ren* ("concern") for them? It would be like the case of a paralyzed arm or leg. (Adapted from Ivanhoe, 1990, p. 20).

In thinkers like Zhu Xi (1130–1200) we find a more developed expression of Zhang Zai's claim that human beings and all other things in the world share the same (basic) "nature." This belief did considerable philosophical work. For example, Zhu used it to explain the behavior of other creatures. Tigers and wolves express *ren* ("benevolence") and bees and ants display *yi* ("duty") because they share the same basic nature as human beings. Of course, their expression of these virtues is limited due to their less pure and limpid "physical endowments."

This general conception of the fundamental nature of reality entailed a profound and moving sense of the relationship between human beings and the rest of the universe. We are not only at home in nature, part of a greater harmonious family. We and nature are in some deep sense *coextensive*, forming a single universal body. This view of the world and its attendant concern for every thing finds clear voice in Wang Yangming (1472–1529). Wang insisted that the concern of the "great man" embraces, not only compassion for an innocent child in imminent danger and an inability to bear the suffering of an animal about to be slaughtered (both examples taken from Mencius); it includes a feeling of pity upon seeing plants broken and destroyed and regret upon seeing tiles and bricks shattered and crushed. It is nothing less than a universal identification of self and nature.

This conception of a fundamental identity between human beings and the rest of nature along with its belief in a shared nature came in for severe criticism in the succeeding Qing dynasty (1644–1911). Thinkers like Wang Fuzhi (1619–1692) and Dai Zhen (1723–1777) pointed out how foreign most of these ideas are to the earlier Confucian views their proponents purportedly defended. Both Wang and Dai argued that the true inspiration for many guiding Neo-Confucian ideas was a combination of Buddhism and Daoism. They rejected the idea that *li* provided some transpersonal, universal and unifying foundation for the world. They argued that *li* is simply the structure of the concrete things in the world and the relationships among them. In this regard, they were much closer to some of the earlier ideas we have examined.

Conclusion

The earliest Chinese did not see any fundamental harmony between human beings and the natural and spiritual world. In fact, they regarded the world as a largely chaotic, unpredictable, and dangerous place. But through divination, sacrifice and prayer to the spirits of royal ancestors, the Shang king could understand and influence the course of events. In time, such appeals became routinized and provided a rather straightforward way to protect human beings from natural and supernatural disasters and even to receive support for their endeavors. These beliefs established many of the central themes seen in the later tradition concerning the ability of human beings to understand nature, accommodate themselves to its power and even draw upon its strength.

These late Shang views gave rise to the Eastern Zhou tendency to draw normative analogies between nature and human ideals. This signaled an increasing domestication of the recalcitrant early god, Shang Di and a developing sense of a closer, more harmonious relationship between human beings and nature. Sacred forces became dispersed throughout the everyday world, leaving behind a conception of nature as disposed to support the work of ethically good people. Toward the very end of the Zhou period, Zhuangzi proposed his vision of a universe in which human beings are equal parts of a vast cosmic network. Influenced by and in response to this remarkable new view, Xunzi developed a Confucian version of this grand cosmic vision. Human beings were established as the most precious and important things in the world, for the enlightened among them were the source of all the world's order. By fashioning a perfect set of ideals and practices which satisfied, reformed and extended basic human needs and desires and matched these up in mutually beneficial and harmonious ways with nature's patterns, processes and forces, the sages brought forth a "happy symmetry" between humans and nature.

For both Zhuangzi and Xunzi, human beings and nature were inextricably bound together, parts of a universal web of interrelationships. But neither thinker provided a comprehensive or systematic scheme describing these complex interrelationships. This task fell to the correlative cosmologists, a group of philosophers inspired by the correlative schemes found in technical disciplines such as astronomy and music. These thinkers produced universal schemes of mutual "influence" and "response." In the succeeding Han dynasty, philosophers such as Dong Zhongshu produced cosmologies in which vast ranges of natural events and seasonal patterns were closely correlated with human actions and provided normative standards for human behavior.

The arrival of Buddhism and its subsequent influence on Neo-Confucianism marked one of the last great innovations in Chinese views concerning the relationship between human beings and nature. Buddhist metaphysics gave rise to a deep and comprehensive *identity* between humans and nature. According to such views, all things are part of a single cosmic body and share a common, basic nature. The ethical implications were dramatic, for the enlightened individual, one who sees the universe as coextensive with oneself, will have a comprehensive and profound concern for every aspect of reality. Here we find what can be understood as the culmination of a process begun in the late Shang, in which Chinese thinkers came to see themselves in an ever more intimate relationship with the rest of nature. What began with a belief in an ability to understand and influence nature grew into a greater sense of community, mutual resonance and intimacy and ended in the Buddhist and the Neo-Confucian belief in a fundamental identity. While these later views were challenged in the succeeding Qing period, they continue to exert a profound influence even into the present day.

Bibliography

Works

Dawson, Raymond (tr.) 1993: *Confucius: The Analects* (Oxford: Oxford University Press).

Graham, A. C. (tr.) 1981: *Chuang Tzu: The Inner Chapters* (London: George Allen & Unwin).

Knoblock, John (tr.) 1988–94: *Xunzi*, 3 Vol. (Stanford: Stanford University Press).

Lau, D. C. (tr.) 1963: *Lao Tzu: Tao Te Ching* (London: Penguin Books).

—— (tr.) 1970: *Mencius* (London: Penguin Books).

References and further reading

Wing-tsit Chan (tr.) 1969: *A Source Book in Chinese Philosophy* (Princeton: Princeton University Press).

Kwang-chih Chang 1980: *Shang Civilization* (New Haven: Yale University Press).

Cook, Francis 1977: *Hua Yen Buddhism* (University Park: Pennsylvania State University Press).

Graham, A. C. 1986: "*Yin-Yang* and the Nature of Correlative Thinking," *Occasional Paper and Monograph Series*, 6 (Singapore: Institute of East Asian Philosophies).

—— 1989: *Disputers of the Tao* (La Salle: Open Court Press).

Ivanhoe, Philip J. 1990: *Ethics in the Confucian Tradition: the Thought of Mencius and Wang Yangming* (Atlanta: Scholars Press).

—— 1991: "A Happy Symmetry: Xunzi's Ethical Thought," *Journal of the American Academy of Religion*, 59, 2, pp. 309–322.

Keightley, David N. 1976: "Late Shang Divination: the Magico-Religious Legacy," in *Explorations in Early Chinese Cosmology*, ed. Henry Rosemont, Jr, *Journal of the American Academy of Religion Studies*, Thematic Issue 50, 2 (Atlanta: Scholars Press), pp. 11–34.

—— 1978: "The Religious Commitment: Shang Theology and the Genesis of Chinese Political Culture," *History of Religions*, 17, 3–4, pp. 211–25.

Needham, Joseph 1985: *Science and Civilisation in China*, Vol. 2, reprint (Taipei: Caves Books).

Schwartz, Benjamin I. 1985: *The World of Thought in Ancient China* (Cambridge: Belknap Press).

10

Causation in Chinese philosophy

CARINE DEFOORT

A cause has traditionally been thought of as that which produces an effect, and in terms of which this effect can be explained or accounted for (Taylor, 1967, p. 56). However spontaneously we turn to the idea of a cause in daily life, and however inevitable in jurisprudence, in modern science it is generally considered a relic of the past, and in philosophy it remains a topic of inexhaustible controversy. For almost twenty-five centuries philosophers have been debating the nature of a cause, claiming that it is an object *producing* an effect by virtue of its power, or arguing that it is an explanation *accounting* for some effect. Which of all the conditions contributing to an event is to be selected as its cause? Do causes exist in reality or are they read into our experience with the force of our expectations, or produced by the *a priori* categories of our minds as they structure reality in causal relations? To widen the horizon of this discussion and trace the concept of causation in non-Western philosophical traditions – such as the ancient Chinese – might enrich this ongoing controversy and allow unfamiliar authors to contribute their views.

But attempts to translate ancient Greek, Latin or Chinese texts suggest that no such universal entity as "causation" is to be found under different labels in different languages. *Aitia, causa, cause* and *gu* (in classical Chinese) are terms that function similarly in their respective contexts. Their meaning is revealed through an analysis of their *coherence* with other terms in that context rather than through the identification of some thing with which they are all supposed to *correspond*. Aristotle's "four *aitia*," for instance, were quite different from what we would consider causes and perhaps ought not to be translated as such at all (Frede, 1987, p. 125). Thus the search for an exact equivalent of the contemporary English notion of "cause" or "causation" in ancient Chinese thought may lead to the collection, under this specific Western category, of various ideas that are unrelated to each other in their original context.

Because every survey of "causation" in Chinese thought consists of a specific combination of these two approaches – correspondence and coherence – the topic will be discussed from both angles and further restricted in various ways. One restriction is chronological: to pre-Han and Han texts. This comprises the first and foremost period of intellectual stimulation in Chinese history (Pre-Han: fifth century BCE–206 BCE), followed by four centuries of political unification and philosophical syncretism (Han: 206 BCE–219 CE). Buddhist thought, which only became firmly rooted in China after the Han, is not included despite its crucial importance in relation to the idea of causation. The second restriction is to those treatises that contain the most vivid discussions in the Chinese corpus: they were classified under "Masters" in the traditional bibliographies and labeled as "philosophy" around the beginning of this century – according to some scholars, another unfortunate equivocation of ancient Chinese and Western categories. A third restriction concerns the most vivid and explicit passages discussing the relation and hierarchy among things, often presented in definitions, dialogues or responses to what "some people say." However intriguing we may find the implicit connections or causal links made by the authors in arguing their case – stepping from one "therefore" (*gu*) to another – they will not be fully discussed in this survey.

The discovery of a corresponding notion in the Later Mohist canons

The search for ancient Chinese notions corresponding to the mechanical or "billiard-ball" view of causation commonly prevailing in the West has led scholars in opposite directions. While some have singled out a few classical Chinese authors who seem to express a similar notion of causation, others have marveled at the absence of a close equivalent in most of the Chinese corpus and at the alternative types of connection promoted in these texts.

According to Angus Graham, the only conception of "genuine" causation is to be found in the Later Mohist *Canons* (fourth century BCE), a collection of systematic treatises unrepresentative of early Chinese thought. Their discussion of causation is quite unique: unlike their peer texts, they select from all conditions constituting an event only the necessary ones as being its cause or reason (*gu*). The character *gu* was cognate with another *gu* meaning "ancient times," and referred to the origin of something, its original state, or its underlying reason. The authors distinguish between "minor *gu*" and "major *gu*," defining them as, respectively, a necessary condition and a condition that is both necessary and sufficient: "*Canons*: The cause of something is what it must get before it comes about. *Explanation*: 'Minor cause': having this, it will not necessarily be so; lacking this, it necessarily will not be so. . . . 'Major cause': having this, it will necessarily be so; lacking this, it necessarily will not be so" (*Mojing*, A1).

The Mohist interest in *gu* was no coincidence. The early followers of Master Mo (*Mozi*, fifth century BCE) were the first to seriously attack the tradition, giving reasons for their criticism and demanding the same from others. They asked the Confucians who followed their Master, Kongzi (sixth to fifth century BCE), in his defense of the tradition, what the *gu* was for playing music with its implied ritual extravagance. Unsatisfied with their answer, the Mohists illustrated their idea of an adequate *gu* with an example: "Suppose I ask 'For what *gu* does one make houses?' and you say 'To take shelter in them from cold in winter and heat in summer' . . . then you have told me the *gu* for making houses" (*Mozi*, 48). As this example indicates, the Mohists expected a "reason" or "purpose" for the traditional valuation of music rather than a "cause," except perhaps a "final cause" in Aristotle's sense.

A deeper source of the Mohists' interest in *gu* than its polemic use against traditional values lies in their practical attitude. The Mohists were lower class craftsmen and military engineers climbing the social ladder and trying to win over rulers with their efficient policies. Using a medical analogy, they argued that the only way to bring order to the empire is by knowing the source of political disorder: "It is like a doctor curing a patient's disease: he must know whence the disease comes and how he will be able to cure it. Otherwise, he will not be able to cure it. Why would bringing order to political chaos be any different?" (*Mo zi*, 14)

This untraditional and technological attitude reached a climax in the definitions of *gu* in the Later Mohist *Canons* and, more specifically, in their restriction of the notion of cause to necessary conditions. Because the Later Mohists realized that most fields of knowledge were characterized by the possibility of multiple causes, they pointed out one virtually unavoidable type of doubt in sciences, named "the coinciding." Their example was "the unknowability of whether a fighter's collapse is because of the wine he drank or the midday sun" (*Mojing*, B10). One can imagine that a similar problem would still puzzle Western philosophers trying to identify the exact nature of causation: even if one's opponent collapses immediately after receiving a firm blow, one can never be certain about the causal connection between the blow and the fall, due to our ultimate inability to definitely rule out other possible causes of his collapse, such as overconsumption of wine or sunstroke.

The Mohist insistence on necessity as a characteristic of causation may explain why they kept away from most contemporary sciences, such as medicine, in which one is unable to control multiple-causality, and thus, to eliminate doubt. The *Canons* totally bypass the more current *yin yang* type of explanation in terms of polar opposites, and they criticize the five-phase theory which explains situations by referring to the interactions between water, wood, fire, metal and earth. In the Mohist *Canons*, these connections are considered merely "appropriate," not "necessary" (*Mojing*, B43).

The absence of correspondence: a web without weaver

While Graham focuses on the Later Mohist type of causation as the closest possible equivalent to the Western concept, Joseph Needham calls attention to the absence of such a corresponding notion in the large majority of Chinese texts. The alternative, typically Chinese and, more specifically, Daoist type of connection which he discerns in pre-Buddhist texts, takes into consideration the current *yin yang* and five-phase explanations carefully avoided in the Mohist *Canons*. The Chinese type of causation (a phrase which Needham is somewhat reluctant to use, given the likelihood of its arousing misleadingly mechanistic associations for Western readers) sees things as *connected* or *paired* rather than *caused*. Their "own causality" was, according to Needham, "reticular and hierarchically fluctuating," rather than "singly catenarian and particulate." Events were not seen as caused by one powerful and preceding event, but as woven in a network of interdependent nodes, a colossal pattern in which things reacted upon each other by a kind of mysterious resonance rather than mechanical impulsion (Needham, 1956, pp. 281–91).

The fullest expression of such connections can be found in texts from the third century BCE onwards, when *yin yang* and five-phase types of thinking found their way into the philosophical corpus. The *Huainanzi*, a syncretist collection of treatises of the second century BCE, contains a long cosmogonic passage explaining the total order in nature – from the formation of heaven and earth to the behavior of birds, fish and oysters – as a gradual diffusion of primordial energy through the polar categories of *yin* and *yang*. "The furred and feathered are the kinds which fly and run, and *therefore* belong to *yang*; the shelled and the scaly are the kinds which hibernate and hide, and *therefore* belong to *yin*. The sun is ruler of *yang*, and *for this reason* in spring and summer the herd animals shed hair, and at the solstice the deer throw off their horns; the moon is bearer of *yin*, *which is why* when the moon wanes the brains of the fishes diminish, and when the moon dies full oysters shrink" (*Huainanzi*, 3).

Several passages in the *Huainanzi*, as well as in other works, mostly those classified as Daoist, insist that this whole order is itself uncaused – "so of itself." This is an important point for scholars like Needham, who insist on the absence of a transcendent Law-giver and His decreed "laws of nature" in Chinese thought. Because of this absence, China may have missed out on a scientific revolution such as that which occurred in the West, and yet ironically Chinese thought may have had closer affinities to present-day science, with its rejection of eternal laws in favor of waves, organisms, and networks (Needham, 1956, pp. 339–40).

Needham cites as the most explicit negation of an omnipotent efficient cause a passage from the *Jinizi*, a short treatise which he dates around the late fourth or early third century BCE. The Chinese alternative to a singly ordered universe presents reality as a "Web woven by no weaver," in which things and events are connected as nodes of a cosmic texture (Needham, 1956, p. 556). Jinizi explains to his king:

> We have *yin*, *yang* and the myriad things. Each of them takes part in the network. Sun, moon and constellations, and changes in their recession and accretion make up good and bad luck. Metal, wood, water, fire and earth conquer each other successively. The moon waxes and wanes alternatively. *Nothing rules their constancy*. Whoever follows it, gets power; whoever goes against it, meets with disaster. (*Jinizi, inner classic*)

The ideal of "*cognoscere causas*," which Needham mainly attributes to the Daoists, amounts to an insight into this orderly network in which "Nothing was un-caused, but nothing was caused mechanically" (Needham, 1956, p. 283).

As opposed to the Later Mohist technical identification and manipulation of selected causes in optics and mechanics, such speculations were able to account for the multiplicity of interacting factors in reality. Although one can hardly see them as germs of a technological or scientific attitude in the modern sense, the cosmologies emerging in the third and second centuries BCE provided man with an embracing and comprehensive universe, allowing him to make vague inferences, and occasionally even proving to have practical use. The fluctuating hierarchy, as Needham put it, and the absence of non-negotiable laws in the cosmic network ultimately allowed for the possibility of every node influencing another. Hence the belief of some authors that man could affect natural events through the manipulation of *yin* and *yang*. The chapter "Same categories move each other" from *The Luxuriant Gems of the Spring and Autumn Annals*, a compilation of the second century BCE, argues as follows:

> Heaven has *yin* and *yang*; man also has *yin* and *yang*. When the *yin* energy of heaven and earth is activated, man's *yin* energy in response also becomes activated. The fact that, when man's *yin* energy is activated, heaven's *yin* energy also becomes activated in response, is because they share one Way. Whoever is clear about this, when he wishes to bring rain, moves his *yin* and thereby activates *yin*; when he wishes to stop rain, moves his *yang* and thereby activates *yang*. (*Chunqiu fanlu*, 57).

However popular in Han times the belief was that man is able to cause such changes in nature, it did not remain unquestioned. For instance, Wang Chong, an author of the first century CE, installed a hierarchy in the network using the analogy of a tree. Because man depends on heaven as the twigs on the roots, he may be influenced by it through the workings of *yin* and *yang*, but he cannot possibly invert this relationship:

> One may say that cold and warm weather affect the ruler so that he activates an energy by which he rewards and punishes. But can we say that by rewarding and punishing, he affects August Heaven so that heaven makes cold and warm weather in response to the government? . . . One can say that, when the wind blows, it activates robbers and thieves in response to it. But it is not the case that the finest energy of men such as robbers and thieves could affect heaven so that it causes wind to blow. . . . Cold and warm energy is woven in heaven and earth, and knotted by *yin* and *yang*. How would human affairs and the state's government be able to affect them? (*Lunheng*, 43)

While preserving the network imagery, and without recourse to an omnipotent Weaver, the power of man is nevertheless restricted through the installation of hierarchy and priority.

Coherence in the Chinese context

An alternative approach to focusing on the presence or absence in the Chinese corpus of a notion corresponding to the modern Western idea of causation is to analyze the various contexts of terms translated in English as "cause," either as a verb or a noun. In the West as well as in China, awareness of causation seems to have originated in a human context, and only later was it applied to phenomena beyond the human realm. The terms *aitia* and *causa*, in ancient Greek and Latin respectively, emerged from a legal background. They refer to the juridical "explanations" of a contested case: the accusation of the injured party or the defensive self-justification of the accused. The search for a cause was thus immediately connected to the attribution of responsibility to someone followed by the meting out of retributive justice.

The verb which is most often translated as "to cause" in classical Chinese, *shi*, emerges from a political context, and primarily means "to send," "to commission" or "to dispatch." The term thus carries associations with political power and hierarchy rather than with juridical responsibility. Only the Later Mohists make an explicit distinction between two basic meanings of *shi*: "to tell" and "a cause" (*gu*).

> *Explanation*: To give orders is to "tell:" the thing does not necessarily come about. Dampness is a "cause." It is necessarily required that what it does comes about. (*Mojing*, A77)

For dampness to be the cause of illness, illness must have come about. Only this second sense of *shi*, dissociated from its political context, coincides with the English "cause" in the sense that *A* is only a cause of *B* if *B* has actually come about, not if it is merely intended or ordered, as in the first and more original sense of *shi*.

But again, except for the Later Mohists, ancient Chinese authors, unlike their Western counterparts, do not tend to strictly dissociate causation from its original, *in casu* political, context. The following passage from a third century BCE collection is a clear instance of the association of both meanings of the character *shi*:

> When spring energy arrives herbs and trees grow; when autumn energy arrives herbs and trees shed their leaves. Whether growing or shedding, there is something that causes [*shi*] them. It is not that they are so of themselves. Therefore, if what causes it arrives, no thing is not brought about; if what causes it does not arrive, no thing can be brought about. Men of ancient times were careful about the way they issued orders [*shi*]. Therefore, nobody remained unemployed. The handle of rewards and punishments, this is how superiors issued orders. (*Lüshi chunqiu*, 14.4)

As is the case in the following passage from the same collection, discussion of *shi* often entails the noun *gu*, "a cause," with its associations of historical antiquity and geographical origin.

> In general, for the way things are, there necessarily must be a cause [*gu*]. Not to know the cause, even if one happens to be right, is the same as not to be knowledgeable, and inevitably leads to trouble. The way in which former kings, famous knights and successful masters surpassed the masses, was by their knowledge. The fact that water leaves the mountains and runs to the sea is not because it dislikes the mountains and desires the sea, but height causes [*shi*] it to be so. . . . As for the endurance or fall of states, the worthiness or uselessness of persons, they also all have a reason to be so. Instead of examining endurance and fall, worthiness and uselessness, the sage examines the reason why. (*Lüshi chunqiu*, 9.4)

While Needham blames the Confucian authors of this passage for inhibiting with political morality the Daoist exploration of nature, it is difficult to find any discussion of causation in the classical corpus that is not directly related to political concerns. Even the quoted passage from the *Jinizi* concerning the "web without weaver" belongs to an argument in which Master Jini advises his king to rely on worthy ministers and respectfully accept their assistance. He lists five mythological rulers who were each assisted by a capable minister in governing one of the five areas (west, north, east, south and center) and ordering (*shi*) one of the five corresponding powers (metal, water, wood, fire and earth). "There were five directions side by side forming a network. Therefore, political assistance which switches between the territories is the constancy of things" (*Jinizi, inner classic*).

The controversies that surround the discussion of causation and constitute its larger context concern cultural, religious and ritual matters, such as the influence of spirits, the meaning of rites, the power of fate, or the impact of heaven on human affairs. For instance, Xunzi, a Confucian author of the third century BCE, argues against prayers for rain because he is convinced that spirits are not able to cause rain, nor is man able to influence them through prayers. "If you pray for rain and it rains, so what? I say there is no reason, just as when it would rain without your prayer." Although the author's claim that such events are caused by the interaction of *yin* and *yang* rather than by spirits may tempt one to declare him the first Chinese natural philosopher, Xunzi's real concern lies with ritual, not nature. His rejection of the power of spirits is not meant to promote a more efficient approach to nature, but to preserve the true value of prayers and ritual: "When heaven sends drought and we pray for rain, . . . this is not because we believe we will obtain what we seek, but to cultivate the occasion. Therefore, a gentleman considers it cultivation; while the majority considers it the work of spirits" (*Xunzi*, 17).

The Confucian author of *The Luxuriant Gems of the Spring and Autumn Annals*, who argued that man is able to cause rain by activating his own *yin* energy, also explicitly rejects the view that spirits would be able to influence nature. "Therefore, to bring rain is nothing spiritual. The fact that people suspect that spirits are at work is because the pattern is subtle and mysterious." The author's primary concern here, however, is not to draw our attention to a technical means of meteorological control, but rather to make a political point by means of analogy.

> It is not that only *yin* and *yang* energy can advance or retreat according to categories. Misfortune, calamity and fortune are likewise generated. It is always the case that things move according to categories in response to what one has first activated. Therefore, men of intelligence, sagacity and spirit introspect and listen to themselves so that their words become illumined and sagely. (*Chunqiu fanlu*, 57)

The focus of attention here is the ruler's responsibility: however subtly and mysteriously causation works at this level, his attitude and insight will ultimately determine the value of his assistants and the fate of his state. There is nobody else to blame, not even a spirit.

The same author also argues against the prevalent view, mainly expressed in Daoist texts, that things are uncaused. Because people fail to perceive the cause, he explains, they believe that everything is "so of itself." "In fact, it is not so of itself. There is something that causes [*shi*] them to be so. These things inherently have what actually causes them, although that which causes them has no form" (*Chunqiu fanlu*, 57). One may wonder about the relevance of identifying a cause which remains invisible and which, according to others, can be entirely dispensed with.

Why, then, is there this heated discussion concerning whether things are "so by causation" (*shiran*) or "so of themselves" (*ziran*)? The controversy clearly does not focus on different descriptions of reality, but rather on alternative explanations of it. Considering the political commitment of ancient Chinese philosophy and, more specifically, the political undertone of the verb *shi*, alternative explanations of reality can be seen to promote different political views and competing justifications of power. The insistence that things in nature are ultimately caused is scarcely separable from the promotion of a central government responsible for social order. The converse claim that nature is "so of itself" can be used to support a political stance opposed to governmental interference and central control. Although conclusions concerning the relation between discussion of causation in the classical Chinese corpus and the political controversies of those days may be premature, it is clear that the topic ought to be pursued further. Having neither emerged from a juridical background nor given rise to a scientific exploration of nature, the notion of causation in early Chinese texts lies imbedded in a context of political, cultural and ritual concerns. One's understanding, therefore, gains more from an acquaintance with these controversies than from a selection of exceptional statements pointing in the direction of a pseudo-scientific attitude.

Any serious discussion of causation in Chinese thought (and of many other topics, for that matter) seems to be caught in an unsettling movement between correspondence and coherence. While in the past discussion of the topic has been dominated by the former approach, there is now a growing tendency in favor of the latter. But the two need not to be considered mutually exclusive. Even someone who consciously opts for the coherence approach can scarcely deny that there is something transcultural about the idea that things are connected in such a way that one produces the other and accounts for it. This assumption not only underlies one's selection and translation of some terms in the Chinese texts as "the cause," "to cause," and even "because," "therefore" and "thus," but also allows one to examine where and how far they might overlap as nodes of two different networks of discourse. Although the attributed correspondence is inevitably colored by contemporary Western associations of the term "causation," it remains an indispensable though precarious bridge to the ancient Chinese world. Only a careful combination of both approaches might secure one a safe crossing.

Bibliography

Writings

Chunqiu fanlu 1973: [The Luxuriant Gems of the Spring and Autumn Annals], tr. of the quoted chapter in W. T. Chan, *Source Book in Chinese Philosophy*, 4th edn (Princeton: Princeton University Press), pp. 282–4.

Huainanzi 1993: [Writings of the Master of Huainan], tr. of the quoted chapter in J. Major, *Heaven and Earth in Early Han Thought* (Albany: State University of New York Press).

Jinizi 1919: [Writings of Master Ji ni] in the *Bai zi quan shu* (Shanghai: Saoye shanfang).

Lüshi chunqiu 1971: [Spring and Autumn Annals of Mister Lü], tr. R. Wilhelm, *Frühling und Herbst des Lü Bu We* (Köln: Diederichs Verlag).

Mojing 1978: [Mohist Canons], tr. A. C. Graham in *Later Mohist Logic, Ethics and Science* (Hong Kong: Chinese University Press).

Mozi 1976: [Writings of Master Mo], partial tr. Y. P. Mei, *The Works of Motze* (Taibei: Confucius Pub. Co.).

Wang Chong 1962: *Lunheng* [Discourses Weighed in the Balance], tr. A. Forke, *Lun-heng*: Part I, *Philosophical Essays of Wang Ch'ung* and Part II, *Miscellaneous Essays of Wang Ch'ung* (New York: Paragon Book Gallery).

Xunzi 1988–94: [Writings of Master Xun], tr. J. Knoblock, *Xunzi. A Translation and Study of the Complete Works*, 3 Vols (Stanford: Stanford University Press).

References and further reading

Frede, M. 1987: "The original notion of cause," in *Essays in Ancient Philosophy*, ed. M. Frede (Oxford: Clarendon Press), pp. 125–150.

Graham, A. C. 1989: *Disputers of the Tao: Philosophical Argument in Ancient China* (La Salle: Open Court).

Leslie, D. 1974: "Les théories de Wang Tch'ong sur la causalité," *Mélanges de Sinologie offerts à Monsieur Paul Demiéville, Bibliothèque de l'Institut des Hautes Études Chinoises*, 20, pp. 179–86.

Needham, J. 1956: *Science and Civilisation in China* (Cambridge: Cambridge University Press).

Peterson, W. J. 1990: "Some Connective Concepts in China in the Fourth to Second Centuries B.C.E," *Eranos 1988 Jahrbuch*, 57, pp. 201–34.

—— 1991: "What causes this?," in *Interpreting Culture through Translation. A Festschrift for D.C. Lau*, ed. R. T. Ames, S. W. Chan, and M. S. Ng (Hong Kong: Chinese University Press), pp. 185–205.

Taylor, R. 1967: "Causation," in *The Encyclopedia of Philosophy*, ed. P. Edwards (New York: Macmillan), pp. 56–66.

11

Chinese socio-political ideals

HENRY ROSEMONT, JR

1 Introduction

One of the basic ways of distinguishing the several "schools" of Chinese thought, especially during the classical period (sixth to third centuries BCE), is by their differing views of the ideal state or society. No formidable cultural barriers need to be breached in order to understand these several views, but they do not have close Western philosophical analogues. They are put forth within a conception of the universe that is uniquely Chinese, and both the grammar and the style(s) of discourse describing these views are similarly unique. Some preliminary comments are therefore in order.

The cosmos first. Although made most explicit by the Confucians, virtually all early Chinese socio-political thinkers presuppose a tripartite universe: a Way (*dao*) of the heavens; a Way of Earth; and a Way of Humankind. The first two of these ways are fairly constant, cyclical, and balanced. In the heavens the Chinese zodiac rose and fell like its counterpart in the West, the orbits of the planets were eccentric, but predictable, as were lunar eclipses. On Earth the days and nights succeeded each other, as did the seasons. Occasionally, it rained too much, or too little, and at times there were omens to be heard or seen, but in general the world was patterned, and the patterns known, or at least knowable.

Much less obvious was the proper Way of Humankind. Differing accounts of this third Way were proffered by a number of Chinese thinkers, and these accounts are what we have come to categorize as Chinese social and political theories. Again, the Ways of the Heavens and Earth are cyclically regular, in harmony, and such that there is a proper place for human beings, both as persons and as community members, within this cosmos. But what is that place? How is the Way of Humankind supposed to mesh with the ways of the heavens and earth? What is human nature? What conduct is appropriate for human beings? What is the meaning of it all?

In the West, such questions demarcate not only the field of political theory, but many other areas of philosophy as well: metaphysics, ethics, aesthetics, and the philosophy of religion at the least. But Chinese thinkers did not employ these Western categories, which brings us to a second problem in comprehending Chinese socio-political ideals: seldom are they stated and argued for in isolation. Rather, accounts of those ideals are interwoven with cosmological, historical, moral, aesthetic and spiritual descriptions, necessitating a different approach to Chinese philosophical writings on the part of readers accustomed to Western modes of philosophical discourse.

Relatedly, the ancient Chinese language in which these texts were written differs as much from both ancient Greek and modern English as each of the latter differs from the other. The logographic qualities of the Chinese script, when combined with syntactic constraints and historically favored narrative styles, permit the expression of a broad vision, or complex of attitudes and emotions, in brief compass, giving those expressions a force, beauty and scope that is more difficult to achieve in Indo-European modern languages. The cost of this narrative quality was a loss of precision; the percentage of ambiguous sentences in Chinese texts is high. While the language did not prevent precise statements, it does not seem to have encouraged them either, and the traditions of writing favored elegance, historical allusion, and brevity – appropriate for providing holistic views – over precision and the hypothetico-deductive style common in Western philosophical texts.

A final difficulty in coming to an understanding and appreciation of Chinese socio-political ideals concerns the vocabulary employed to describe the ideals. Contemporary Western political (and moral) philosophy has as central to its basic lexicon such terms as justice, rights, liberty, freedom, autonomy, individual, ethics, rationality, dilemma, choice, and ought. None of these terms has a close cognate in ancient Chinese. Thus while Chinese thinkers were greatly concerned to describe, analyze, and evaluate human conduct, it was not the conduct of purely rational, autonomous individuals freely choosing what they ought to do. Articulating Chinese ideals requires another, less technical, theoretical vocabulary.

But sharing an overall view of the cosmos, and writing in the same language with roughly similar vocabularies, does not entail that all Chinese philosophers thought alike. Far from it: the ways of humankind propounded by them are as varied as those advanced by their Western peers. We will begin with a brief description of three early, pre-philosophical texts which provide the best accounts of what Chinese socio-political life was like in the archaic period, texts which also influenced significantly all later thinkers: The *Yijing*, *Shujing*, and *Shijing*. Next we will consider the ways of humankind advocated by the Confucians (whose views eventually prevailed), their sharpest critics the Daoists, and then the third influential school of the time, the Legalists. Quick sketches of two less influential theories of the ideal state – Mohism and the "school of Farmers" – will then be given, and a brief overview of post-classical political thinking will conclude the essay.

2 The *Yijing*, or *Book of Changes*

The oldest strata of this text are divinatory in nature, and center on the concept of change, which occurs because of the complementary interaction of two basic principles, the *yin* and the *yang*. The former denotes (and connotes) receptivity, passivity, and descent, and its symbols are earth, a mare, darkness, water, valleys, and the mother. *Yang* is active and ascending, the heavens, a dragon, light, mountains and the father. The *yin* is represented by a broken line (- -), and the *yang* by a solid one (—). These twin "forces" – really metaphorical constructs – are fully relational.

Nothing is wholly *yin* or *yang* in itself, but only in relation to something else, at a particular time. Grandfather is *yang* to grandmother, but *yin* to his grandchildren.

By means of a formulaic counting out of yarrow (milfoil) stalks, a person consults the *Yijing*, obtaining at the end of the count either a *yin* or a *yang* line. The counting is repeated six times, concluding in a hexagram of six lines. Each of the 64 hexagrams in the *Yi* represent familial, social, and natural phenomena, and the hexagram obtained by the counter represents, in multiply symbolic form, the diviner's place in the universe at that moment.

The aim of consulting the *Yi* was not to learn how to alter the course of events in any significant way, but rather to learn more about the changes then occurring, so that the diviner could appropriately adjust his or her behavior to be in harmony with those changes. This harmony – being in tune with the rhythms of the universe – was taken to be the central goal of human life in the *Yijing*. It is less the "oneness" characteristic of the Western mystical tradition than it is the full realization of human life, which was an integral part of the universe, not isolated from it.

In guiding the diviner, a number of the hexagrams instruct him to more actively participate in socio-political affairs; they are more or less *yang* hexagrams. Other, *yin* hexagrams, instruct the diviner to withdraw from society, at least for a time, and consequently to interact more directly with the natural world. In this way the *Yijing* offers the first suggestion of what will later be articulated as two differing ways of humankind: achieving harmony with the patterns of the heavens and earth through society, or by confronting the natural world more directly, with much less social mediation.

3 The *Shujing*, *Book of History* or *Book of Documents*

This book, the earliest entries of which probably date from the eleventh century BCE, is made up a series of brief essays, memorials, and documents which record parts of the reigns of the legendary sage-kings Yao, Shun, and Yu (ca. the third millennium BCE), the reigns of several Xia Dynasty rulers (traditional dates 2205–1766 BCE), some Shang Dynasty rulers after them (1766–1050 BCE), and the early rulers of the successor Zhou Dynasty (1050–256 BCE), especially Kings Wen, Wu, and the Duke of Zhou.

The *Shujing* is not at all a complete chronicle of the most ancient Chinese past. It contains much that appears to be purely legendary, and all of it was written long after the events described therein were supposed to have occurred. It was nevertheless highly influential in the development of Chinese socio-political philosophy; virtually every classical text makes references to one or more of the sage-kings and their successors, and it is thus necessary to understand the qualities attributed to them in the *Shu*.

First, they were not supernaturally endowed; they lived to very ripe old ages, but all eventually died, and during their lifetimes they performed no tasks in violation of physical laws. Second, they were all highly intelligent, and put their wits to use in the service of the Chinese people by their inventions and discoveries. (The sage-kings are credited with, among much else, introducing agriculture, irrigation, writing, fishing and medicine to the populace.) Third, they governed with the assistance of a proto-bureaucracy, and appointed ministers thereto on the basis of moral and intellectual merit rather than birth or wealth. All of the sage-kings governed by suasion rather than force, and saw as their responsibilities, according to the *Shujing*: (1) securing the welfare of the common people; (2) maintaining the traditions of the ancestors; (3) being frugal; (4) seeing their position as a trust conferred by *tian* (usually translated as "Heaven," which was not so much a symbol of deity as it was of the natural order); and (5) keeping harmony within the social order, and between the social and natural order. In short, their task was to achieve and maintain a proper integration of the ways of the heavens, earth, and humankind.

4 The *Shijing*, or *Book of Poetry*, *Book of Songs*, *Book of Odes*

The 314 poems which comprise the *Shijing* collectively provide what is very probably the most accurate picture we have of the everyday and festival life of the Chinese people in the ninth century BCE. There are love poems and lamentations, poems celebrating the seasons and friendship, poems describing communal rituals and holiday gatherings, and more. We see a hierarchical society, which is supposed to reflect the hierarchy of nature, within which everyone is in a place, and there is a place for everyone. Religion permeates the social fabric, expressed in the regular performance of rituals great and small. Familial relationships are the foundation of the social order, and it is through the exemplification and realization of these relationships that the secular becomes sacred.

At the pinnacle of the hierarchy in all three of these early classics is the ruler, and he is simultaneously the center of the *politia*. All political theorizing in China assumes a monarch; to a significant degree, the several schools of Chinese political thought can be differentiated on the basis of the qualities the good ruler is thought to have, but for over two thousand years a monarch was always presumed, and he was supposed to be the living embodiment of the culture's socio-political ideals.

5 Confucianism

The doctrines which are gathered under the rubric of "classical Confucianism" were largely put forward in four texts written and edited roughly between the fifth and the third centuries BCE: *The Analects of Confucius*, the *Mencius*, the *Xunzi*, and the *Records of Ritual*, especially the two more metaphysical chapters of this last text – "The Great Learning" and "The Doctrine of the Mean." These works are not in agreement on all points (the *Mencius* and the *Xunzi*, for example, appear to present contradictory descriptions of human nature), but they do present a coherent picture of the good life for human beings. That life is an altogether social one. The Confucian Way of Humankind requires each of us to live properly the relational roles that define us as persons. Our first and most important role is as children, and filial piety is one of the most basic virtues of Confucianism. We owe unswerving loyalty to our parents, and our obligations to them do not cease at their death.

Concerning loyalty,

> The Master said, In serving his parents a man may gently remonstrate, but if he fails to change their thoughts, he should resume deference and not oppose them; he may feel disheartened, but not resentful. (*Analects* 4:18)

And concerning the constancy of our obligations,

> The Master said, If for the whole three years of mourning a son manages to carry on the household exactly as his father did, he is a good son indeed. (*Analects* 4:20)

From our beginnings as children, siblings, and pupils, we mature to become parents ourselves, and become as well spouses, neighbors, subjects, friends, and more. All of these roles are reciprocal relationships, best understood, perhaps, as holding between benefactors and beneficiaries. The roles are hierarchically structured, but each of us moves from benefactor to beneficiary, and back again, depending on the role, and the occasion. (For example, I am both son and father, benefactor of my friend when she seeks assistance, and beneficiary when I seek hers.) Collectively, the roles we live define us as persons and the way we live them give us our dignity, meaning, and satisfaction in life.

Both within the family, and in the larger society beyond it, custom, tradition, and ritual serve as the binding force of our relationships. The rituals described in the *Yijing*, *Shujing* and *Shijing* were based on archaic supernatural beliefs which were being challenged during the more rationalistic period of Confucius, and a part of the genius of the Master and his followers lies in their giving those practices a social, moral and spiritual foundation which was independent of their original inspiration. The importance of rituals for the early Confucians must be underscored. They did not believe that laws or regulations were the proper way to govern society:

> The Master said, Govern the people by regulations, keep order among them by chastisements, and they will flee from you, and lose all self-respect. Govern them by moral virtue [*te*], keep order among them by ritual and they will keep their self-respect and come to you of their own accord. (*Analects* 2:3)

At the same time, the Confucians did not believe that society should be governed by monarchical fiat; the ideal ruler was to reign.

> The Master said, He who rules by moral virtue [*te*] is like the pole-star, which remains in place while all the lesser stars pay homage to it. (*Analects* 2:1)

With respect to ritual, however,

> The Master said, If it is possible to govern by means of ritual and deference, what else is there to say? If it is not possible, of what use is ritual? (*Analects* 4:13)

The Confucian ruler is thus not a benevolent despot, but a living symbol of the Chinese cultural heritage, a person who manifests the highest Confucian virtue of *ren* (benevolence, human-heartedness), reverences ritual, and is at all times attentive to the needs of the common people. He will be assisted in his efforts by others who will hold office on the basis of their own exemplification of *ren*, reverence for ritual, and commitment to serving the people. Thus only moral exemplars are fit to rule, and when they do, the ruled will emulate their attitudes and behavior, guaranteeing a peaceful and harmonious society throughout "All under the heavens."

Moreover, these socio-political ideals extend beyond the social and political realms to the aesthetic, moral, and spiritual dimensions of human life. In fulfilling our manifold relational obligations, guided by ritual, we are simultaneously engaged in a process of self-cultivation that provides beauty, rightness, and meaning for our lives; our outer conduct can lead to inner fulfillment. Returning to the subject of filial piety,

> The Master said, In filial piety it is the proper attitude that is difficult to explain. It does not merely consist in young people laboring when things must be done, or serving the elders properly with wine and food. It is something much more than that. (*Analects* 2:8)

This "something much more" is not only evidenced in relation to parents – although it begins there – but is a sense of being a part of humanity, a sense that is the goal of self-cultivation. All of our interactive relations, with the dead as well as the living, are mediated by the customs, traditions and rituals we all come to share as our inextricably linked personal histories unfold, and it is by fulfilling the obligations defined by these relationships that we follow the Confucian Way of Humankind. In addition to the aesthetic and moral features attendant on meeting these obligations, to our elders and ancestors, on the one hand, and to our contemporaries and descendants, on the other, the Confucian ideal proffers an uncommon yet spiritually authentic sense of transcendence for us, a human capacity to rise above the concrete spatiotemporality of our existence, to form a union with those who have gone before, and those who will come later.

In sum, the early Confucian Way reflects not only socio-political ideals, but aesthetic, moral and religious ideals as well. The gulf that separates what is Caesar's from what is God's is not found in Confucianism, for the significance of human life can only be attained and understood in the context of social life. Confucian selves certainly have their individuality – there are many ways to be a good parent, spouse, friend, and so on – but the boundaries of those selves are not drawn as sharply as they have been drawn in the modern West, where our essence is thought to lie in our freedom, and autonomy.

The Confucian Way was never fully realized in China. Its history includes a sorry list of despotic rulers, uncaring parents, dull pedants, and worse. But China's political culture was more or less Confucian, and it is the world's most long lived. Tens of millions of people have lived and died in accordance with the Confucian vision, and for this reason alone the texts which describe that vision are deserving of our careful attention. Another reason for attentiveness is the fact that the great majority of the world's peoples continue to define themselves primarily in terms of kinship and community rather than as free and autonomous individuals, suggesting that Confucianism may, in part at least, transcend the culture of its birth.

6 Daoism

If Confucianism was the most socially and politically oriented of Chinese philosophies, Daoism was the least. Whereas the Confucians saw socio-political involvement as the only way to cure the human condition, Daoists saw it as the disease. We are creatures of nature according to the latter, and the artifices of society cause us to lose our sense of harmony with the natural order of things.

These views are most forcefully put forward in the two great classics of Daoism, the *Daodejing* and the *Zhuangzi*, and in many parts of the later eclectic works, the *Liezi* and the *Huainanzi*. The first of these works is, after the Bible, the most widely translated of all books; at last count there were over 90 translations of it in English alone. The work is made up of 81 brief and cryptic chapters composed largely in verse; it has been said, without much exaggeration, that to read it is an act of creation.

The penultimate chapter of the *Daodejing* succinctly describes the Daoist socio-political ideal – a small hamlet whose inhabitants lead lives of rustic simplicity, who can hear the cocks crow in the next village, but who are so unconcerned about social mores that they never venture to that village to see how its inhabitants live. At the extreme, the text urges us to abandon that most social of human attributes – language – and return to a system of communicating, when absolutely necessary, by means of knotted ropes (believed to have been an archaic form of communication).

Such socio-political ideals do not strike us as being of any relevance to a contemporary global village of more than five billion people, and they probably struck even most Chinese readers at the time of their promulgation in the same way. But Daoist ideals reflect an anarchic vision that is not politically chaotic, that returns us to a fuller appreciation of nature, that provides a vantage point from which to criticize social activities, and which surely must appeal to the "free spirit" in each of us. And in many respects Daoist reasoning is impeccable: the only guaranteed way of stopping law-breaking is to abolish the laws; if no one desires more than they need, there will almost surely be enough to go around; most of the emotions which bring us to grief – pride, greed, envy, jealousy – are products of socialization, not inherent in our nature; and the more we worry about tomorrow, the less we can celebrate today. Spontaneity, not planning (scheming), is the hallmark of the Daoist sage.

Confucianism is, in Chinese terms, largely a *yang* philosophy, and Daoism its *yin* counterpart:

> The spirit of the valley never dies
> This is called the mysterious female.
> The gateway of the mysterious female
> Is called the root of heaven and earth.
> Dimly visible, it seems as if it were there,
> Yet use will never drain it.
> (*Dao De Jing*, VI)

As a corollary, Daoists advocate *wuwei*, translated as non-action, or inaction, or spontaneous action. "The Way," according to the *Daodejing* again (XXXVII), "Never acts, yet nothing is left undone." If there is poverty, the cause is not natural disaster, but the social disaster of exacting burdensome taxes (LXXV). *Wuwei* has spiritual as well as socio-political consequences, for *Zhuangzi* says, "Cease striving; then there will be self-transformation."

In light of these views, it should be clear that while Daoists do not altogether deny that we are social beings, they do insist that we are equally natural beings, and that socialization can, and often does, cause us to become artifacts no less than the other products of social activity. When we are no longer able to answer the question "Are you hungry?" without checking our watches to see whether it is time for lunch, we are cut off not only from the natural world, but from ourselves as well. The good society, therefore, must be such that we can come to see the importance of the imperative to "Cease striving" and to learn to live more spontaneously, in close harmony with nature rather than in opposition to it.

7 Legalism

In a series of texts that span more than four centuries, a socio-political ideal was argued for that would initially strike modern readers as insensitive to the human condition at best, and at worst as totalitarian. These texts – the fragments of Shen Buhai, *The Book of Lord Shang*, the *Guanzi*, and most important, the *Hanfeizi* – differ in their details, but are in agreement on the necessity of establishing and maintaining an all-powerful state political apparatus to check and control the behavior of citizens.

Like the Confucians, Legalist authors believe that human beings are to be gathered socially, but they reject the idea that an inborn nature, and/or morality, and/or ritual observances, can serve to make the resultant society a functioning one. They likewise reject the ideal of the ruler as a moral paradigm and exemplar who reigns but does not rule, and they see custom and tradition as obstacles to efficient governmental administration.

Instead they insist, first, that the responsibility of the ruler is to establish and promulgate a series of laws absolutely binding on everyone under his jurisdiction. Rather like Hobbes, they conclude that the substance of those laws matters little; so long as they are not contradictory, if followed they will guarantee a peaceful society, because all violations of law are to be severely punished. Second, Legalists argue for a bureaucracy with rigidly prescribed duties. If the bureaucrats exceed or fall short of their duties, they are to be punished, and for the proper execution of those duties they are to be rewarded handsomely.

It is hard to put a kind face on the socio-political ideals of Legalism. Almost all that can be said of it is that it provided a series of checks on a capricious ruler, and provided incentives for everyone to behave in a manner that enhanced social cohesion. Having promulgated the laws, the ruler could no longer usurp them, for then they would no longer be a guide to behavior. The rewards and punishments for bureaucrats were equally not subject to whim: if they did their job, they were to be rewarded; and if not, then punished.

Perhaps human beings do indeed wish to live in a highly constrained social environment in which they are told what, and what not to do, and will behave well toward their fellows only under the threat of punishment for lapses. But otherwise the socio-political ideals of the Legalists do not have much to recommend them, except within a society in which cohesion has been lost, and life becomes a struggle of each against each, and all against all. (Which well describes the China of the time of Legalist influence: it has been known ever since as "The Period of the Warring States.")

8 Other schools

In the book that bears his name, Mozi (Mo Ti) argues for an ideal state that is more akin to the Confucian than to any of the others, yet which is different from it in crucial respects. About Mozi we know little except that he was a contemporary of Confucius, and was the first Chinese thinker to set down his views systematically and provide arguments for them.

His criterion for whether a political belief, practice, or institution was to be accepted, modified, or rejected was utility, or profit: did it bring benefits – usually material – to the people? If so, it was commended, and if not, condemned. The reach of this utility criterion was great in Mozi's writings, to the point that he has often been described as China's Jeremy Bentham.

Closely related to the utility criterion was an emphasis on frugality: the ruler, his ministers, the common people – all were to pinch pennies whenever possible. This spartan virtue has much to recommend it in a country whose soils must be cultivated intensively in order to produce a bounty sufficient to nourish the population, but Mozi's focus on it made him a sharp critic of the Confucian insistence on the importance of music and ritual in social and political life: the fruits of people's labor should not be dissipated in frivolous activities. This criticism was closely linked to Mozi's belief that religion was a personal matter between the individual and the "Will of Heaven," not the socially embedded spiritual cultivation insisted upon by the Confucians.

The most basic criticism of the Confucian way made by Mozi dealt with the "graded love" that must accompany a hierarchy of loyalties and obligations that are grounded in the family. Mozi saw a love that made distinctions as a major cause of social discord, and instead argued for a "universal love" of all, by all, and for all.

This spirit of egalitarianism was carried even further by the *Nong Jia*, or school of the tillers, which flourished briefly around 300 BCE. Their hero was the early sage-king Shen Nong (Divine Farmer), and they portrayed him as working in the fields along with everyone else, and consulting with everyone else when any decision had to be reached. The peasant utopianism that can be discerned in the few fragments of texts we have from this school reminds one of the peaceful hamlets earlier described in the *Daodejing*, and may well have served as the inspiration for the later brief novella *Peach Blossom Spring*.

The classical era of Chinese thought came to a close in 221 BCE, when Qin Shi Huang Di completed the conquest and unification of China. His Legalist-inspired dynasty lasted only sixteen years, and was succeeded by the Han, who ruled, with but one interregnum, for the next four centuries. Han rulers made Confucianism state orthodoxy, and established the civil service examination system, and for the next two thousand years the Chinese state was (more or less) a Confucian state.

With the coming of Buddhism to China, beginning in mid-Han times, the aesthetic, moral and religious elements of Confucianism began to be neglected, but it remained the theoretical foundation of government. The intellectual movement known as Neo-Confucianism had its origin during the Tang dynasty (618–906 CE), and was largely devoted to re-visioning Confucian ethics and religious practices to counter the Buddhist challenge. Much original philosophical work was done by the Neo-Confucians – especially during the Song (960–1279 CE) and Ming (1368–1644 CE) dynasties – but the socio-political ideal of government remained intact. The state system was not basically challenged: bad times were due to bad rulers and/or bad ministers; the early Confucian vision of rule by moral force and suasion continued throughout the course of Chinese intellectual history, and remains discernible today.

The socio-political, aesthetic, moral, and religious ideals of Confucianism won out over their competitors twenty-three hundred years ago, later withstood the challenges of Buddhism, and then Christianity, and are now recovering ground against Communist ideals. This historical perspective should lead us to think not that Confucianism must be irrelevant to the contemporary global village the world is becoming, nor that it should be put to rest. Rather might we think that there is much in that tradition which speaks not only to East Asians, but perhaps to everyone; not only in the past, but perhaps for all time.

Bibliography

Ames, Roger T. 1983: *The Art of Rulership* (Honolulu: University of Hawaii Press).

Creel, Herrlee G. 1970: *The Origins of Statecraft in China* (Chicago: University of Chicago Press).

Fung Yu-lan 1953: *History of Chinese Philosophy*, tr. Derk Bodde, 2 Vols (Princeton: Princeton University Press).

Graham, A. C. 1986: "The Nung-Chia 'School of the Tillers' and the Origins of Peasant Utopianism in China," in *Studies in Chinese Philosophy and Philosophical Literature* (Singapore: Institute of East Asian Philosophies).

Hsiao Kung-chuan 1979: *A History of Chinese Political Thought*, tr. F. W. Mote, Vol. 1 (Princeton: Princeton University Press).
Lau, D. C. (tr.) 1984: *Lao Tzu: Tao Te Ching* (Harmondsworth: Penguin).
Legge, James (tr.) 1959: *The Texts of Taoism* (New York: Julian Press).
—— (tr.) 1960: *The Chinese Classics*, 2nd edn, 5 Vols (Hong Kong: Hong Kong University Press).
Rosemont, Henry Jr. 1970–1: "State & Society in the *Hsun Tzu*," *Monumenta Serica*, 29.
Waley, Arthur (tr.) 1938: *The Analects of Confucius* (New York: Modern Library).

12

Reality and divinity in Chinese philosophy

CHUNG-YING CHENG

The Chinese approach to the theory of reality

In the *Xici Commentary* on the *Zhouyi*, we witness the emergence of the two basic concepts characterizing the ultimate reality of human experience. These two basic concepts are, respectively, that of the great ultimate (*taiji*) and that of the way (*dao*). Both concepts are derived from human experience of the formation and transformation of things in nature, which are referred to as "*bianyi*" or "*bianhua*" (change).

> Thus the change has its Great Ultimate from which Two Norms (*liangyi*) are generated. The Two Norms generates Four Forms (*sixiang*), [and] Four Forms generate Eight Trigrams (*bagua*). (*Xici-shang*, 11)

The 64 hexagrams of the *Book of Changes* are in turn generated from the combining of the eight trigrams. This process of generation is remarkable in establishing a cosmogonical picture of the rise and development of reality as a world of things, as well as in providing a cosmographical way of thinking symbolized in the systemic structures of trigrams and hexagrams. This process of generation we may also call the *dao*. The sustaining source of this process of generation is called the *taiji*. The *dao* is *taiji* in its process aspect, whereas *taiji* is the *dao* under its origination aspect. Together they refer to the same thing – namely, the whole of reality as creativity, change and transformation.

We may call this cosmogonic and cosmographical way of thinking and its description of reality the "ontocosmology of *taiji* and the *dao*," as the prefix "onto" suggests the meaning of *taiji*, and the root "cosmology" suggests the meaning of the *dao*. It is this theory of *taiji* and *dao* that represents the main stream of metaphysical thinking in the 3,200-year history of Chinese philosophy, and which thus should be regarded as the fundamental theory of reality in Chinese philosophy. (The *Book of Changes* or *Zhouyi* was formulated as early as the beginning of the Zhou dynasty in 1200 BCE, although it was believed that the notion of change (*yi*) and the method of divination (*bu*) based on the theory of change was developed much earlier, dating back to the very beginning of the Xia Era, circa 2000 BCE, as evidenced in the archaeological findings of oracle bone inscriptions.) Confucius, in his old age, studied and commented upon the *Book of Changes*. Ever since then it has been regarded as one of the Confucian classics, even as the leading one. There are no doubt elements of Confucian thought in the ontocosmology of the *Yizhuan* (commentaries on the *Zhouyi*, developed between the fifth and third centuries BCE), but these must be seen as basically implicit in the underlying philosophy or view of reality to be found in the original *Zhouyi* texts and symbolism. This means that the ontocosmology of *taiji* and the *dao* is not just Confucian but an articulation of the ancient way of thinking about reality in China. However, in order to distinguish this ancient view from the later Daoist approach to reality of Laozi (whose exact dates are uncertain, but who lived about the middle of the sixth century BCE) and Zhuangzi (circa 370–300 BCE), and their elaboration of the philosophy of the *dao*, we may refer to it as the "*Yizhuan* theory of reality", since the theory is suggested and implicitly formulated in the Commentaries on the *Zhouyi* known as *Yizhuan*, particularly in the *Duan* and *Xici* portions of the Commentaries.

In order to understand the *Yizhuan* theory of reality, we should take note of the following characterization of our experience of change:

(1) Reality as inexhaustible origination. We can trace the presentation and development of the world's reality to a root-source. This root-source, called "the great ultimate" (*taiji*), is the absolute beginning of all things, but it is also the sustaining base for all things in the present, because all changes in the world are based on it and contained in it. In this sense, the *taiji* is the primordial and inexhaustible source of creative and transformative energy, a fact conveyed by its designation as the "creativity of creativity" or "generation of generation" (*shengsheng*) in the *Xici*. In this sense, reality is not something static underneath a world of fleeting phenomena; nor is it a realm of forms or ideas reflected in a world of imitations. Neither is it something accessible only to abstractive human reasoning, or through divine revelation. Reality is concrete, vivid and holistic, not merely in the sense that all things are interrelated within a whole originally defined by the oneness of the *taiji*, but in the sense that changes and the non-changes underlying these changes are organically part and parcel of the same thing, and there cannot be any strict demarcation or bifurcation between appearance and reality. Changes and the constant and continuous regeneration of things are what reality consists of. Any scheme to divide or stratify reality can only serve a limited purpose. This means that all theories of reality share with reality itself the fact of change and are subject to the continuous challenges of an ongoing process of formation and transformation. Therefore, we may understand *taiji* as not just primary origination but constant and ceaseless origination. In a Whiteheadean spirit, we may say that the world is in-the-making, and is constantly and forever in-the-making.

(2) Reality as a polar-generative process. When the *taiji* gives rise to things in the world, it does so by introducing polarities: the positive and the negative, or the *yang* (the brightening/the moving/the firm) and the *yin* (the darkening/the restive/the soft). These polarities are subcontraries, which exist simultaneously and are conspicuous on one level. At the same time, they are also contraries which are hidden on the more concrete levels of things. In this latter sense, they are identifiable with the *taiji*, because the *taiji*, as the source of change, is always hidden beneath all

things. The generation of new things occurs on the basis of the coexistence and interaction of these polarities. Thus unlike Whitehead's postulation of the emergence of novelty from pure ideas, in this model novelties arise from the internal dynamics of a bifurcating of reality into *yin* and *yang* and the subsequent commingling of *yin* and *yang*. Thus the novelty of things is inherent in the very source of the world itself, and also in the creative potential of a thing, which requires the interaction of forces to bring it about.

(3) *Reality as a multi-interactive harmony*. An individual thing or an individual class of things always has two aspects: the *yin*, which pertains to its stationary state of existence (its given nature) and its receptivity to the outside world, and the *yang*, which pertains to its dynamic state in developing its propensities in interaction with the outside world. As the *yin yang* polarities are definitive of individual things or individual classes of things, that a thing must interact with the outside world is in the nature of the thing itself. It is in this process of interaction that a thing fulfills its potentialities and runs its course of bounded existence. It is with respect to a thing's maintaining itself as a given nature that we speak of the "centrality" of a thing, and with respect to its properly taking from and giving to other things that we speak of "harmony" between or among things. There could be non-centrality and disharmony in the formation and transformation of a thing, which would constitute a crisis for its identity and its survival in the world of reality as things. And thus we see the importance of the thing's natural abilities both to maintain itself and to enter into proper give-and-take relations with other things. In the case of human beings in particular these two aspects of existence must be cultivated in order to enhance and realize human potentiality.

It is said that "One *yin* and one *yang* is thus called the *dao*. To follow it is goodness and to complete it is nature" (*Xici-shang*, 5). How are we to understand this in reference to individual things? The *dao* is how things come into being and how they grow and develop over time, and the process of one *yin* and one *yang* consists of the alternation, conjunction and mutual interaction of the positive and negative forces and positive and negative activities of the individual things, which results in the formation and transformation of things.

(4) *Reality as virtual hierarchization*. The world is made of many levels, each of which exhibits the combination of the *yin* and *yang* forces or activities of things. For the *taiji* and *dao* model of cosmogony and cosmography (and hence ontocosmology), there are numerous general features of *yin* and *yang*, such as rest/motion, darkness/brightness, invisibility/visibility, softness/firmness, closedness/openness, and retrospective propensities/prospective propensities. Although these properties are basically described in phenomenal and experiential terms, there is no reason why they could not be described in a logical and scientific language of abstract and primary properties. One could, as many people have already done, for example, identify the *yin* and *yang* elements or processes in the genetic code and the theory of subatomic particles. Similarly, there is no reason why human values, emotions and intentions could not be described in the language of *yin* and *yang*. In this light, *yin*

and *yang* should be regarded as neutral and variant functors or operators, which interact to generate relationships and changes. The important point to remember is that, as there are levels of simplicity and complexity in the structures and activities of a scheme of things in being and becoming, so there are various levels of *yin* and *yang*. On the highest and most general level, there is the "Great Ultimate" (*taiji*). On the second level, there is *yin* and *yang* proper. On the third level, there are the four forms. On the fourth level, there are the eight trigrams. This can go on forever and without limit. But individual things must be understood as manifesting a complex hierarchy of levels of *yin* and *yang* background as well as a complex world of *yin* and *yang* interactions. This means that the individual thing or person can only be understood as acting within the context of a field or web of forces, and within this context it is still capable of having a creative impact and making a contribution to the formation and transformation of the world.

(5) Reality as recursive but limitless regenerativity. Although the Commentaries on the *Zhouyi* do not mention the recursive and regenerative nature of the *yi*, the presentation of nature in eight trigrams and of the world in 64 hexagrams in the original 1200 BCE symbolism, and the appended judgments of divination clearly suggest that nature is a process of both collective and distributive balance and that it functions as a process of return and reversion – as we see in the rotation of seasons and celestial cycles. The interesting thing to note is that once we are able to represent the world in a collectively inclusive and individually exclusive enumeration of stages or facets, these stages and facets will have to recur as patterns or forms of understanding or existential characterizations. We limit our understanding and characterization to a given level or particular domain initially, and then elaborate this in a definitive categorical system of description or projection. That is why one can use the 8 trigrams and 64 hexagrams at the same time: because they belong to different levels of relevance and meaningful description. What is implied in this description of reality is that it is both limited and limitless. It is limited on a specific level of description which serves a human purpose. On the other hand, it is limitless in that any specific level of description only serves a purpose in a limited way, and can be transcended or abandoned for a higher or more general level of description. We may say that there are virtually an unlimited number of levels of description, just as theoretically there could be an unlimited number of systems of scientific knowledge in the progression of scientific inquiry. On each level of description, there is the recursion of the finite categorized reality. This is the case because it is in the nature of change that reality has to be regeneratively represented. This may be called "regenerative recursion", and it is this which gives stability and structure to process.

In the *taiji* and *dao* model of reality what is shown in the symbolism of the *yi* is a regenerative recursion by reversion – which is to say, the *yin* stage has to revert to a *yang* stage and vice versa in order for creative change to be realized. It is in the nature of time that *yin* and *yang* interact through alternation. Because of this, one is entitled to expect that reaching the worst implies of necessity a return to a better condition. Although in practice, of course, it is difficult to know whether one has in fact reached the worst or how long the improvement will last, it is nevertheless possible to conceive of reality as an alternation between good and bad as a natural process of change.

(6) Reality as an organismic totality. From the above description, it should be clear that the world of reality on the model of the *taiji* and *dao* is totalistic in the sense that all things are included and there is nothing beyond it. It is said that, "*The Book of Changes* is extensive and all-comprehensive. It contains the way of heaven, the way of man and the way of earth" (*Xici-xia*, 10). For the early Chinese, the real world is confined to heaven, earth and the ten thousand things, among which humanity stands out as the most intelligent and the one capable of forming a tri-partnership with heaven and earth. Everything in this reality comes from the *taiji* and follows or embodies the *dao*. This implies, then, that there is no transcendent reality beyond this world. When we come to Laozi, we find that even when the notion of emptiness (*wu*) is introduced, what the term "*wu*" stands for is part and parcel of the universe of the *dao*. The *dao* in Laozi is simply enriched by something called the void or non-being (*wu*). Similarly, when Zhou Dunyi (1017–1073) speaks of the ultimateness (*wuji*) giving rise to the great ultimate, he is simply extending the *dao* to cover both void and non-void. There is no break between the void and the non-void and hence one does not have a transcendent nothingness or emptiness apart from reality. In this non-transcendence, we do not speak merely of immanence, but also of totality. Immanence refers to values and powers inherent in the things themselves, but totality refers to all of the interrelated parts of all things in the real world. The reason why things belong or hang together, is because in the ultimate reality things are not simply contained, but rather are interrelated or even interpenetrating. It is the organismic nature of the totality that not only can there not be any object "outside," but that all things exist together by way of mutual support and even mutual grounding. This is how the immanence of heaven in the nature of man leads to an interminable exchange between, as well as a unity of, man and heaven.

Although the *Yizhuan* developed the fundamental metaphysics of the *taiji* and *dao* in Chinese philosophy, which inspires or perhaps grounds the Confucian view on the moral propensity of man, it is in Laozi's *Daodejing* ("The Classic of Dao and De") that we find a better thematized theory of the *dao*. It might be said that a fuller and more distinctive theory of reality was formulated in the *Daodejing*. We may call it the Daoist theory of reality, and it has been frequently argued that it was the Daoist theory of reality of the fourth century BCE which influenced the *Yizhuan* theory of reality of the third century BCE. It is even suggested that the *Yizhuan* theory of reality is basically Daoistic. But this would seem not to be the case, given that there is a tight consistency and coherence of ideas in the *Yizhuan*'s notion of reality and creativity relating it to presuppositions that can easily be seen in the ancient texts of the *Zhouyi* and the even older practice of divination. It is in the way of thinking embodied in the *Zhouyi* symbolism and judgments that both the idea of the *taiji* as a root-source of creative change and the notion of the *dao* as a polar-generative process of totalization were developed.

A better suggestion would be that both the *Daodejing* and the *Yizhuan* share the influence of the *Zhouyi* and that they developed as a result of this influence and in an effort to understand the presupposed meaning of the *Zhouyi* symbolic texts. Hence there is no denying that there are shared grounds of ontocosmology (as formulated in the six points discussed above) between the two. But there should also be no denying that there are differences between the Daoist and Confucian approaches to reality, in spite of their shared debt to the *Zhouyi*, The strong consistency of the *Zhouyi* and *Yizhuan* theories of reality reflects a Confucian emphasis on the moral and social relevance and importance of our understanding of reality. Understanding reality is an essential requirement of genuine morality, for morality consists in practicing comprehensive care for life in society and politics, as this is derived from the way of heaven represented in the *Yizhuan* theory of reality. In so far as the *Zhouyi* is fused with the spirit of pragmatism and a concern for rectitude and an ethics of action, it is clear that the *Yizhuan* theory of reality is a continuation of the *Zhouyi* philosophy.

On the other hand, the *Daodejing* text, although to a great extent it exhibits the underlying spirit of the *Zhouyi*'s understanding of reality as a process of change and a process of reversion and return, has certain distinctive features which can perhaps be interpreted as a creative response to, and a serious-minded critique of, its own time. For this reason, the Daoist approach must be treated independently as a new development in the Chinese theory of reality.

There are four major features of the Daoist theory of reality which can be regarded as differentiating it from the *Yizhuan* theory of reality. In the first place, the *Daodejing* introduced a unique notion of the *dao* which cannot be conveyed by language. The first sentence of the *Daodejing* declares, "The *dao* can be spoken, but it is not the constant *dao*; The name can be named, but it is not the constant name." What then is the *dao*? It is apparently the power or force underlying all changes and transformations of things in the world. The key here is that even though each thing has its own manner of change, they all share a common moving or motivating force for change. They also share in being in a common time and a common space with one another. This oneness is further manifested in the interrelatedness of all things in the world. But this power of change and this oneness are not separate from each other; nor are they separate from the world or from each individual thing in the world. It is difficult to express this all-encompassing oneness, comprehensiveness and moving/motivating power. When we choose the word "*dao*" to indicate or refer to this power, we cannot identify it with any of the things in the world, because it is not any of the things that our language describes. It is rather like an inaccessible object, such as the moon, to which we may point with a finger. Hence the *dao* is to be experienced, reflected upon, intended in our speech, but it cannot be identified. But this is not to say that the *dao* is non-existent, although it is invisible, inaudible, and intangible. Nor is it to say that its existence is non-efficacious, although it is non-substantial. On the contrary, the *dao* is full of power and functions in all of the natural activities of things in the world. More specifically, one can say that the *dao* is a power giving rise to all things without owning them, sustaining all things without dominating them, enabling things to act on their own without claiming their work. (See *Daodejing*, chapters 10, 34, 51.) The *dao* (which we might call "the creative spirit of the world") therefore is real and profound and can be considered the absolute beginning and primordial source of all things. In this sense, the *dao* can be said to exist before heaven and earth, and is the forerunner of all things and the mother of all lives. It is also the naturally-of-its-accord spontaneity of things. Thus Laozi observes, "While man follows earth, earth follows heaven, heaven has to follow the *dao* and the *dao* would act of its own accord" (*Daodejing*, 25).

With all of this said, the important thing to keep in mind is that, although not the same as anything in the world, the *dao* is not separate from and does not transcend the world. Moreover, although it is the source of change and the ground of being for all things, it is not to be conceived of as God in any sense that a Western religion might understand this. It is rather the very nature of things when they are considered as an interrelated whole, as a unity of multiplicity, which exhibits its creativity and novelty through multifarious change and the abundance of life. One sees in the *dao* a dialectical unity of transcendence and immanence – which is to say, the transcendence of immanence and the immanence of transcendence in the relationship between nature and individual lives in nature. This understanding is intensified in the work of Zhuangzi, which stresses the idea of *dao* as the self-transformation (*zihua*) of things and the interpenetrating power of oneness (*daotong weiyi*).

We come now to the second point about the Daoist theory of reality. Because the *dao* is indescribable and non-substantial, it is conceived as void or empty (*chong*, *xu*). It is said that "*Dao* is void and its function is infinite" (*Daodejing*, 4). This voidness of the *dao* is also referred to as non-being (*wu*) by Laozi, when he says, "*Wu* names the beginning of heaven and earth, and *yu* [being] names the mother of ten thousand things" (*Daodejing*, 1). In fact, in order to appreciate how *wu* is a process of being's emergence from non-being, one might also see *wu* as a process of non-being's emergence from being. To become non-being is to void existence of all determinate characteristics and to go back to a state when all determinations of characteristics are in the offing. Things come into being, in other words, from a nebulous and indeterminate state of non-being, in which non-being could even be understood as indeterminacy of being. There are many passages offering this view. (See, for example, chapters 14 and 21.) In this sense, *wu* can be regarded as one aspect of the *dao*, the other aspect of which is simply *yu*. *Wu* is no-thing (*wuwu*), and *yu* is having-things (*yuwu*). As *dao* is a power creative of all things as well as the process of creative production, it has both the activity of *wu* and the activity of *yu*, just as all things have both the *yin* (emptying) and *yang* (substantiating) functions. It is through the interaction of these two functions and their conjunction that things become what they are and reach a state of harmony. It is said that, "All the ten thousand things shoulder *yin* and embrace *yang*, and in an intimate and strong mixing (*chong*) of the two vital forces (*qi*) a harmony results" (*Daodejing*, 42). It is also in this sense that Laozi speaks of the "mutual generation of *yu* and *wu*," by which he means that *yu* and *wu* are mutually defining and conditioning as well as mutually forming and producing. One sees here what the *Yizhuan* has described as the alternation of *yin* and *yang* in the *dao*.

One way to reach the state of *wu*, and hence the state of the natural functioning of the *dao*, is to have no desires (*wu-yu*) and no action (*wu-wei*) on the part of a person. This is important for the Daoist theory of reality because the theory is not simply a matter of abstract speculation, but of close personal embodiment of ontocosmological principles in one's life experience. In fact, without such an embodiment, Laozi (the Old One) would not have been able to describe so vividly the reality and creativity of the *dao*. From this, one may correctly conclude that, according to the Daoist, any human being can come to an intimate knowledge and understanding of the *dao* so long as he reduces his desires, knowledge and actions to a state of oneness. (See chapter 39.) This also means that, at a minimum, one should not let one's desires and knowledge block the open vision of the whole process of change and transformation in the *dao*. The idea that one's vision could be blocked by one's desires and knowledge is a result no doubt of a close observation of reality. Hence Laozi advises that one should keep oneself free from diversions of the senses, and the burdens of learning. For the *dao* reveals itself to those in a free state of mind or in an open state of the non-fixation of belief. This point is also strongly stressed in Zhuangzi.

We come to a third point in the Daoist theory of reality. Reality under the name "*dao*" is always a matter of return (*fu*) and reversion (*fan*). It is said that,

> To reach for the ultimate of emptiness and to abide by the utmost of tranquility, ten thousand things will agitate at the same time. I would therefore be able to observe the process of return. There are many things and each would return to its root. To return to the root is called "tranquility" and this is called "return to destiny" (*fuming*). (*Daodejing*, 16)

It is interesting to note that, whereas the *Yizhuan* approach to reality stresses the ceaselessness of productive creativity (*shengsheng buyi*), the Daoist approach to reality stresses the constancy of return. In this sense, then, the *Yizhuan* approach is dynamic and the Daoist approach is static. However, the Daoist stress on return as a distinctive feature of reality was already implicit in the *Zhouyi* symbolism of trigrams and hexagrams. One can see that the relationship between *yin* and *yang* in the Qian and Kun trigrams and hexagrams establishes such a return in that they refer to the temporal process of alternation of one *yin* and one *yang*. If the *dao* begins with *yin* and moves to a stage of *yang*, then the only place it can go from there is back to *yin*. Similarly, from *yin* it would return to *yang*. But if the root of being is non-being in the sense described above, one can see that the root is closer in nature to *yin* than to *yang*. This observation led the later Neo-Confucianist Zhou Dunyi to speak of a state of ultimateness (*wuji*) logically if not temporally prior to the state of the great ultimate (*taiji*) in his famous work *Taiji Tushuo* ("Discourse on the Diagram of the Great Ultimate"). In this work the idea of the return of things to their root is also articulated, for according to Zhou, not only has *wuji* given rise to *taiji*, which produces all things in the world, but the whole world is always the unity of the *taiji* and the *taiji* is no more than the beginning state of *wuji*. From an ontological point of view, one could regard *wuji* and *taiji* as two alternating states of the *dao* which exist at the same time and form a mutually defining unity. On this view, then, there need not be a temporal sense of return and we can speak of the reversion of the *dao* from one state to the other and vice versa. In fact, this is what is also observed by Laozi in the *Daodejing*.

It is said that "Reversion is the motion of the *dao*; weakness is the function of the *dao*" (*Daodejing*, 40). As return is a temporal reversion of the *dao*, reversion is a non-temporal return of the *dao*. They can be regarded as referring to the same action. On the other hand, it might be suggested that reversion is a more fundamental characteristic of the *dao*, as the *dao* always exists in opposites and reversion can be considered logically as the exercise of opposition within a unity. But then we would have to consider return as a different function of the *dao* as well – namely, the function of going back to the unity of the *dao*. This would make return and reversion two different functions, but although we can see *wu* and *yu* as two opposite and yet mutually related processes of the *dao*, there is no good reason to view reversion and return as dualistic rather than as one process described under two forms – a process which has its own true opposite in the process of ceaseless productive creativity described in the *Yizhuan*.

The fourth point is a brief one. Not only can man observe the *dao* both outside of himself and within his own person, and thus come to an understanding of it, he can also cultivate the *dao* (participating in it or imitating it) in order to achieve a desirable and ideal state of life. For the Daoists, just as for the Confucianists, there are ample grounds for speaking of the unity of man and heaven or the unity of the human person and the *dao*. This unity is important for both schools in so far as ethics, social action and political life are all dependent upon it.

We now have a composite picture of reality as it is understood in classical Chinese philosophy by way of the *Yizhuan* approach and the Daoist approach. Their different points of emphasis should not overshadow their common roots and common vision of reality as a world of interrelated things in a creative process of change and transformation. Later there arose the Neo-Daoist and Chinese Buddhist philosophies, in which reality was articulated either on the basis of the Daoist model or on the basis of a theory of false consciousness and the absence of wisdom or enlightenment. It was not until the rise of Neo-Confucianism in the Song Period that the *Yizhuan* model would become the standard and norm. Yet the distinctive features of the Daoist model of reality together with some features of the Chinese Buddhist model of reality have been absorbed into the Neo-Confucian system. This leads to a theory of reality presented not only in terms of the mutual production of *wu* and *yu*, but in terms of the new categories of *li* (principles) and *qi* (vital forces).

The Chinese approach to the theory of divinity

Any theory of divinity must be grounded on or presuppose a theory of reality. A notion of divinity might appear on the scene first, but in time it must disclose the theory of reality presupposed by it. It may happen, of course, that the theory of divinity in question could itself offer an account of reality, so that the notion of divinity is, as it were, logically prior to the notion of reality. It may also happen, however, that an early notion of divinity (and the notion of reality implicit in it) comes to be supplanted by a new, perhaps more sophisticated, theory of reality, which in turn makes possible a new and perhaps more sophisticated understanding of divinity. We can see the development of Christianity in the West as a classical example of the former case – of transition from a specific theory of God's nature to a theologically grounded theory of reality. On the other hand, we can see the development of Confucian and Daoist metaphysics as an example of the latter case – of transition from a theory of *tian* (heaven) or *di* (lord on high) to an ontocosmological theory of reality which traces the activity of the divine in the creative productiveness and transformativeness of things.

In the Christian case, the ontologization of God makes God the foundation of all reality in an "*Ontotheologik*" *à la* Heidegger. Hence this is always the leading theme of the theological interpretation of reality in the Western religious tradition. On the other hand, it is the "daoization" of the *tian* as God which resulted in the replacement of *tian* by the *dao*, and therefore a theory of reality has subsumed a potential theology or "tianology" in the Chinese philosophical tradition. This tradition is therefore one in which we see processes of the depersonalization, the naturalization, and the humanization of *tian*, without, however, any sacrifice of the spiritual meaningfulness of reality. Thus we have what may be said to be a notion of "divinity without theology". This "divinity without theology" is best expressed by a statement in *Xici* of the *Zhouyi* (*Book of Changes*): "Divinity has no form and change has no substance" (*shenwufang, yiwuti*).

As early as the beginning of the Xia Era in 2000 BCE, there were already references to the Lord on High (*di*) who would supervise and oversee human affairs and who controls human destiny from above. This notion of *di* could be regarded as a spiritual projection of a powerful and venerated ancestor who played the role of ruler and governor in his lifetime. The word "*di*" is also said to symbolize the bud of a flower, and hence the source of life. The Lord on High, then, as he is presented in the *Book of Documents* (*Shujing*) and the *Book of Poetry* (*Shijing*), is to be seen as a supreme being who combines the source of life and the source of power in one person, and who cares for the well-being of people (as his posterity) and the ordering of the state. He was thought of and worshipped as a personal god who could issue commands and mandates. In time, however, the idea of *di* fused with the notion of *tian* (heaven or sky, a term to be understood spatially rather than temporally). *Tian* too is to be conceived of as powerful and life-giving, although now the conception of infiniteness is added. (In the *Shijing* we read that "The great heaven has no limit.") It seems probable that a more sophisticated sense of reality made possible the transformation from a worship of *di* to a worship of *tian*, and that this took place as the Zhou conquered the Shang people (who were known for their faith in ghosts and spirits) around 1200 BCE.

This more sophisticated sense of reality diluted the personalistic character of *tian* as a supreme ruler on high and a supreme creator of life. As the Chinese sense of reality focused increasingly on the unity of man and heaven, understood in terms of a common bond of creative activity, *tian* eventually came to be regarded as the Way of Heaven (*tiandao*). We find this depersonization of *tian* already in Confucius, although Confucius still occasionally spoke of *tian* as if it were the Lord on High or a supreme moral being. The full naturalization and depersonalization of *tian* occurs in Daoism, where *tian* is seen as having been given rise to by the great *dao* (not the *dao* of any given thing, but the *dao* itself as a creative process and reality which generates things in the world and imparts to them the power of self-autonomy and self-transformation).

The transformation of *di* to *tian* and then to *dao* embodies a movement from a theory of personal divinity to a theory of depersonalized reality. Even though a personalistic notion of divinity is lost, which accounts for the fact that China, unlike the West, has not sustained a monotheistic religion, the sense of divinity is still present in the form of a profound understanding of reality itself as the process of creative change and as the inexhaustible source of novelty and life. This, again, is a kind of "divinity without theology."

What, then, is divinity in Chinese philosophy? The Chinese term "*shen*" is used to refer to all natural spirits, which may be conceived of as personalized entities vested with life and special powers. In fact, *shen* is the living presence of power which may be said to exist in all of those living things of nature that can exert their influence upon other things. More specifically, the term "*shen*" applies to human persons in their possession of this living presence of power to influence others. Thus a person who accomplishes great deeds and achieves exemplary virtues, and who is consequently respected and wields great influence during his life, leaves upon his death his *shen* (or influence, heretofore referred to as "spirit") to be worshipped or sought after. In this sense, the *shen* of a person is the natural extension of his life and the power of his influence projected into the present and the future even after the physical person is no longer present. When an unworthy person dies, however, his spirit is not sought after but rather avoided, and he is known not as a *shen*, but as a *gui* or ghost – something belonging (one hopes) only to the past. If *shen* is to be explained as the beneficial power of a person extending to the future from the present, *gui* is to be conceived of by contrast as the traces of a past human life. But even the *gui* of a person can affect the present, although a deceased person's coming back to the present would be a surprising and alarming event.

This conception of *shen* is well developed in both the classical Confucian and the classical Daoist philosophies of the constitution of the human person. (This basic theory is found in both the texts of Mencius, in the *Xici* of the *Zhouyi*, and the texts of the four chapters of the *Guanzi*, in Laozi and Zhuangzi. The theory is developed into a basis for alchemy and the search for immortality by the Neo-Daoists in the third century.) The human person is conceived of as formed of three or four levels of existence. On the first level, there is the physical reality which is his body (*shen*). On the second level, there is his essence of life (*jing*) or the essential elements of his life as an organism. On the third level, there is his energy and the circulating powers of life, which are referred to as vital breath (*qi*). Finally, there is the level of *shen*, which can be regarded as the quintessence of life and vital energy, or the *qi* of *qi*. It is the freest element of life, but an element which also survives physical life in a free manner in that it can be expressed in the arts and deeds, the work and the words of a person.

According to this conception, human existence is not a conjunction of mind and body, as Cartesian dualism would have it, but rather a holistic unity of interpenetrating life-elements, each of which is itself to be conceived holistically. The holistic conception of life differs from the atomistic conception in that there are no absolute simple elements postulated, but rather nebulous wholes, and these interactively support each other. Thus it is not simply that the higher levels depend on the lower levels, but the lower levels also depend on the higher levels. In this sense, any lower level of existence can be thought of as having a higher level which is its *shen*. Whether the *shen* stands out depends on the special influence or presence of power a thing has. Thus for the ancient Chinese, all major mountains and rivers have their *shen* or spirits which are worthy of worship and respect. On the other hand, the *shen* of a human being who achieved great power of influence would be more vividly entertained in the minds of the relevant people and would thus become more clearly an object of worship.

With respect to the last point, it is interesting to note that Confucius says in the *Analects* that we must "sacrifice to the spirits as if the spirits are present; if I am not engaging myself (*yu*) in the sacrifice, it is like not holding a sacrifice" (3:12). How does one feel that the spirits are present? To feel the presence of the person or the object involves using one's feelings and imaginative powers in a projection of the known person or object. In the case of an unknown person or object, it is to think of the person or object of worship. It is a total engagement of one's person in the projected construction of the object, and as a consequence the object becomes the subject, because it is infused with the best spirit and essence of life of the person engaged. A person who does not engage in sacrifice in this manner is not considered to have genuinely performed a sacrifice.

When we enlarge on and extend the notion of *shen* as explained above, we see that the whole universe has its *shen*, particularly when we reflect and observe the life-generating and life-preserving power of the universe conceived as an organic whole. The whole universe is then seen as a progenitor, maintainer and preserver of life. As we have seen, it is in this way that the idea of the "Way of Heaven" was developed, in which heaven is both a concretion and an abstraction of the whole of nature focused upon in its powers of life-generation and life-maintenance. *Tian* is conceived of as both the whole of nature and the whole process of life production, in which both birth and death are regarded as part and parcel of the life-maintaining and life-generating process. In this sense, death is absorbed into the larger process and circulation of life and must be faced by a person with equanimity and peace of mind, a point which Confucianism and Neo-Confucianism have specifically stressed.

When we speak of the *shen* of the whole of nature or the universe, we speak of the divine. The divine, in this sense, is an elevation of the spiritual, because in becoming the divine the spiritual is no longer confined to any projected or formerly existing person or thing, but pertains to the ever-present and ever-active life and vitality of the whole of nature. In essence it pertains to the ever-creative creativity of the source of life. Therefore, the power of influence becomes the power of the generation and transformation of life. We find this sense of divinity presented in the writings of Mencius and the *Doctrine of the Mean*. Mencius writes,

> What is desirable is goodness. One holding to oneself [in self-knowledge] is integrity. To fulfil one's potentiality is beauty. To have self-fulfillment and shining out [and being influential] is greatness. Being great and capable of transforming life is called sagely (*sheng*). When the sagely power is beyond the measure of knowledge, it is called the divine (*shen* – in the deeper sense of the spiritual or creative). (7B:25)

It should be noticed that the spiritual creative power which is the divine is to be built up from the basic desires of life whose fulfillment is a form of goodness, according to Mencius. Only when one attains goodness based on one's genuine desire for goodness, will one achieve integrity in the sense that the self is not just a physical event but a value of importance. This integrity would then be the starting point for the enlargement and extension of a transforming power that raises other beings and persons onto a higher level of existence. The key phrase here is "great and transforming", which is taken as the mark of the divine.

The divine is conveyed by the notion of sageliness (*sheng*), which culminates in the limitless influence and transformation it may entail. The combination of "sageliness" and "divinity" in the phrase "*shengshen*" (divine and sagely) can be said to capture the meaning of the sacred or holy in the best spirit of the Western religious tradition without assuming its concomitant theology. Thus there are two forms of "divinity without theology": the Confucian and the Daoist.

According to Mencius, the divine is rooted in human life and is continuous with human life and hence there is no transcendental state of the divine outside of life. For this reason, Mencius even suggests that "A 'genuine person' (*junzi*) is capable of transforming people and preserving his spirit in such a way that he is in the same vein with heaven and earth [with regard to its creative and transforming powers]" (7a:13). The reference to heaven and earth is meant to underline the analogy between the creative and transforming power of the divine over things in nature and the power of a ruler over his people.

The Confucian takes the political power of the ruler very seriously and sees in it the same creativity as in heaven and earth, because life and death and the transformation of people's lives are vested in such power. But this analogy is also literally a reflection of the underlying cosmology of the unity of heaven and earth and the human person which comes to the fore at about the time of Mencius – which is to say, in the Period of the Warring States, when Confucianism achieved a new stage of development based on the insights and experiences of the second and third generations of the Confucian School. This is how we come to the positions of the *Doctrine of the Mean* (*Zhongyong*) and the Commentaries of the *Zhouyi* (*Yizhuan*).

In the *Doctrine of the Mean*, it is said that

> A human person of utmost sincerity is capable of fulfilling his own nature; capable of fulfilling his own nature he is capable of fulfilling the natures of others; capable of fulfilling the natures of others he is capable of fulfilling the natures of things; capable

> of fulfilling the natures of things he is in a position to participate in the creative activities of heaven and earth. Being in a position to participate in the creative activities of heaven and earth, he is posed to form a tripartity with heaven and earth. (*Zhongyong*, 21)

This important passage is again a testimony to the inner and virtual divinity of the human person in the sense of participating in the creative activities of heaven and earth. If we understand this to mean that a human engaged in government could make decisions bearing on the life and well-being of people, it is quite clear how he could be creative and transformative, just as heaven and earth, which bring things forth, regulate and preserve them. This means there is a functional unity between man and heaven. But of course there is a deeper level of unity expressed in the *Doctrine of the Mean*, namely that man is endowed with his nature from heaven. This means that the creativity of man is derived from heaven and thus is capable of forming a unity with heaven and earth. Such is the vocation of man and such is the ideal state of human existence in a political community and family of heavenly mandated order. This is not to equate man with heaven, for man does not create things in nature as heaven does, but man can preserve them (just as modern ecologists would endorse), and in so doing man creates and preserves his own life and well-being as far as the human community is concerned.

What the *Zhongyong* stresses is that when a human person exhibits the utmost sincerity, he becomes creative and thus divine in the sense described above. But when the *Zhongyong* says that "the utmostly sincere is like the divine" (24), there is a special meaning attached to this use of "divine" – namely, the ability to foretell the future or to have foreknowledge (*xianzhi*). This may refer to the diviner's act of divination using tortoise bones. But there is definitely a sense of divinity that pertains to the power of knowing the future. One would know the future if one were able to grasp the totality of things and the direction of the whole process of change in addition to being able to participate in that change. This, then, defines the meaning of *zhicheng* (utmost sincerity). The utmost sincerity is utmostly real, and this means to know the real and participate in the real as fully as one can. This means, according to *Zhongyong*, to devise the great principles of governing the world, to establish the great ground of right action, to take part in the nourishing process of heaven and earth. In essence, it is to fulfil the heavenly virtue of creativity as a sage (32). In so far as this creativity is interpreted as profound love (*ren*), it is directed toward and based on the Confucian ideal of the self-cultivation of a human person. In this way, one sees as well how divinity in the sense described would result from the cultivation of a person in *ren*.

We need to elaborate on the key concept of sincerity (*cheng*) in order to understand the creative and transformative power of man. We read in the *Zhongyong*,

> Next, to fulfill the hidden and subtle [desires of a man], one must be sincere in one's desires. Being sincere, there will be form of action; action being formed, it will become conspicuous; being conspicuous, it will be illustrious. Being illustrious, it will move. Moving it will change; changing it will transform. It is the utmost sincerity of the world which can transform. (23)

I would identify "the hidden and the subtle" with the genuine desire for change in a person. It follows that if one really desires change, one is able to effect the change because one will act on one's sincere desires, which will provide a base for the change. This process of transformation is how an inner motive leads to an outer result.

Sincerity as motivating force is therefore a self-making and self-creating force. But *cheng* is not merely for self-making but also for the making of others, and is identified by the *Zhongyong* as the most fundamental force of origination and transformation in the world. In this sense, *cheng* is no more and no less than the root-source of all beings, and the human experience of sincerity is only a manifestation or sign of the creativity of reality itself.

The *Zhongyong* claims that when a person is able to achieve centrality and harmony there will be a proper positioning of heaven and earth and the nourishing of ten thousand things. This centrality (*zhong*) and harmony (*he*) are derived from the divinity of heaven and earth, which perfects a person, a community and the relationship between the community and the natural environment. We need to see the centrality and harmony operating on two levels: the human and the cosmic. On the human level, centrality is described as the state of human emotions not yet issued in response to things outside, because things outside have not yet called for any response. When and if such a response is called for, because there is an unbalanced situation in need of balancing, then the restoration of equilibrium would be the task of the emotions. The emotions lead to action and interaction between the subjective and the objective, which produces a new state of balance, and this is harmony. But this means, of course, that there is a primordial state of harmony and balance arising from the natures (or propensities) of things. In the primordial state everything follows its own nature, and thus this state can be described as the way of nature. Because not only the human being but all things have their natures, centrality is both the inner state of a thing and the totality of the natures of things, which leads us to the description of centrality on the cosmic level. Centrality is the state of nature in which the natures of things are not engaged in response to any outside situation. Cosmic harmony, on the other hand, is a matter of the actions and interactions among things and events being balanced so as to allow them to function naturally. Here we can see, then, how in centrality and harmony there will be a proper ordering of heaven and earth as well as the nourishing of all things therein. We might also suggest that centrality is a form of harmony, harmony in stasis, and harmony is a form of centrality, centrality in dynamism.

We may regard centrality and harmony as two aspects of the same thing along the lines of the ontocosmology of *yin* and *yang*. Thus we can speak of centrality as the nature (inward)-directed state of a thing while we speak of the harmony as the relation (outward)-directed state in which a thing is situated. A thing may at one and the same time exhibit two forces at work: it may centralize itself so that it maintains its given nature, and it may harmonize itself with other things in its development or growth. These two principles are opposite and yet interdependent and complementary with regard to both the development of the individual and the development of a larger system in which the individual is situated. But when we ask how this centralization and harmonization are possible, and how they are ontologically grounded, we have to return to the Commentaries on the *Zhouyi* for an answer. And in conjunction with this, we have to take into consideration the Daoist views of Laozi and Zhuangzi, which have been expounded in the first section of this article.

13

Reason and principle in Chinese philosophy: an interpretation of *li*

A. S. CUA

Perhaps the best approach to the Chinese conception of reason is to focus on the concept *li*, commonly translated as "principle," "pattern," or sometimes "reason." While these translations in context are perhaps the best, having an explication of the uses of *li* is desirable and instructive for understanding some main problems of Chinese philosophy. Because there is no literary English equivalent, one cannot assume that *li* has a single, easily comprehensible use in Chinese discourse. This assumption is especially problematic when it comes to appreciating the basic concerns of Confucian ethics. A closer examination of the uses of *li* and "principle" reveals a complexity that cannot be captured by a simple formula. Apart from the question whether *li* and "principle" are functionally equivalent, one may also ask whether *li* in Confucian ethics can be properly considered a context-independent notion in the way that "principle" can. For a contemporary Confucian moral philosopher, Confucian ethics is more plausibly viewed as a form of virtue ethics (Cua, 1992a). Absent an explanation of the uses of *li*, the translation of *li* as "principle" unavoidably leads to such misleading questions as: "What are the principles of Chinese or Confucian ethics?" "If such principles exist, do they serve as premises for the derivation of moral rules?" "Are Confucian principles universal or relative?" While these questions are fundamental in Western moral theory, their importance for Confucian ethics depends on a prior consideration of the status of principles in Confucian ethics (Cua, 1989b).

Difficulties also arise with the translation of *li* as "pattern". Again we need to have some clear answers to such questions as "What sort of pattern?" "Are these patterns natural or artificial – that is, products of human invention?" "If they are natural, how do we go about finding them?" More important, even if we regard "principle" or "pattern" as an acceptable rendering of *li*, we still need to explore its role in ethical argumentation (Cua, 1985). Such an inquiry presupposes that we have some understanding of the uses of *li* in Chinese ethical discourse. This essay is a tentative, highly selective treatment of *li*. It is an attempt at providing an ideal explication or constructive interpretation of *li* from the perspective of Confucian moral philosophy. Section I deals with the basic uses of *li* as a generic term. Section II discusses the function of *li*-binomials and the significance of principled interpretation of some basic notions of Confucianism.

I Basic uses of *li*

For pursuing the study of *li*, Tang Junyi's pioneering work is a most valuable guide, particularly for the place of *li* in the history of Chinese thought. Also instructive is Wing-tsit Chan's essay on the conceptual evolution of the Neo-Confucian notion of *li* (Chan, 1964). As a preliminary, following Xunzi (Li 1979, Book 22), let us distinguish *li* as a single term, that is, a single Chinese character or graph (*danming*), and *li* as a constituent element of a compound term (*jianming*), say, a binomial term, for example, *wenli*. For resolving problems of ambiguity and vagueness in single terms, it is a common practice of modern Chinese and Western Sinologists to appeal to relevant binomials. This method of interpretation is widely used by modern Chinese translators/annotators of classical Chinese texts. In section II, we will say more about this procedure.

Among pre-Qin classical Confucian texts, only in the *Xunzi* do we find extensive use of *li* as a single term or graph. In this text, we find about 85 occurrences of *li* with different uses. The descriptive use of *li* in the sense of pattern or orderly arrangement may be shown by using a *li*-binomial *wenli*, as Xunzi sometimes does. Since *wen* pertains to "(cultural) refinement," *wenli* can properly be rendered as "cultural pattern." Often, this descriptive use of *li*, has normative import – that is, *wenli* has not only *de facto*, but also *de jure* status. Chan points out that there are also uses of *li* in ancient literature in the sense of "to put in order or distinguish" (Chan, 1964, p. 125).

Since the descriptive use of *li* frequently has an explanatory function, its occurrence is sometimes associated with *gu*, which can be rendered as "reason" or "cause." While the explanatory use of *li* sometimes has normative import, the distinction between its descriptive cum explanatory and normative uses remains philosophically and practically significant. This distinction seems implicit in Zhu Xi's explanation of the meaning of *li*:

> Regarding things in the world, if they exist, then (*ze*) we may say that each must have a reason or cause (*gu*) that accounts for its being what it is (*suoyiran zhi gu*). Also, each must have a standard (*ze*) for [determining] what it ought to be (*dangran zhi ze*). This is what is meant by *li* (Chan 1964, p. 481, my translation).

The first remark suggests that *li* has an explanatory use and that the reason or cause of a thing's being what it is (*suoyiran zhi gu*), in some sense, is derived from observation or experience. This seems implicit in the first occurrence of *ze* as a conclusion-indicator. In the Neo-Confucianism of the Song and Ming Dynasties, however, we do not find any interest in natural causation akin to that of Western philosophy. Xunzi, perhaps the most "rationalistic" among Chinese philosophers, does acknowledge that participants in ethical argumentation must "exhaust the *gu* of things." The *gu* here pertains to reasons for supporting one's practical thesis, say, as a policy of action (Cua, 1985). Instead of a theoretical conception of causal explanation, we are more likely to find the notion of *ganying* (stimulus and response).

In the Song Confucian metaphysics, every entity consists of *li* and *qi* (ether, energy, material/vital force). *Li* and *qi* are inseparable. The former is static, the latter dynamic. Thus the preferred explanation of the interaction between things makes use of the notion of *ganying* or "stimulus and response". As A. C. Graham points out, these concepts of *gan* and *ying*

> occupy the same place in Sung [Song] philosophy as causation in the West. . . . If it is assumed that things consist of inert matter, it is natural to think in terms of "effect" which passively allow themselves to be pushed by "causes." But if inert matter is only the essentially active ether [*qi*] in an impure state, this kind of action will only be of minor importance; in the purer ether, when A acts on B, B will not only be moved by it, but will respond actively. (Graham, 1958, p. 38)

With the notion of *ganying* in mind, if we render *gu* in Zhu Xi's first remark as "cause," we must employ the notion of practical rather than theoretical causation (Collingwood, 1962). From the Confucian perspective, *ganying* conveys the idea of human sensitivity to natural things and events as having a decisive impact (*gan*) on human life. Humans must respond (*ying*) to these things and events by acting in a way that ultimately comports to the Confucian ethical vision or ideal of the unity and harmony of humanity and nature (*tianren heyi*). Differently put, things and events in nature are challenges to human ingenuity in coping with problems in their lives (Cua, 1975).

Zhu Xi's second remark that "each must have a standard (*ze*) for [determining] what it ought to be (*dangran zhi ze*)" stresses the normative sense of *li*. *Ze* can also be rendered as "rule" or "law." However, since we do not find any notion of "natural law" comparable to that of Western philosophy, *ze* is better construed as the standard that determines things as they *should* be (Chen Chun, 1979, pp. 144–5; Chan, 1986). Unlike compliance with rules, one can try to comport with standards according to one's conception of the best thing to do. There are, so to speak, degrees of perfection in individual efforts at attaining the ideal of the good human life.

While the *ze* of each thing is said to be inherent in it, it has ontological import. Nevertheless, if we are right that *ze* in Zhu Xi's first remark is a conclusion-indicator, understanding the *ze* of a thing is an outcome of study and reflection. For elucidation we may consider Zhu Xi's comment on the phrase "the extension of knowledge" in the *Great Learning* (*Daxue*):

> If we wish to extend our knowledge to the utmost, we must investigate exhaustively the *li* of things. . . . It is only because we have not exhausted the *li* of all things that our knowledge is still incomplete. In the education of the adult, the first step is to instruct the learner, about all things in the world, to proceed from what knowledge he has of *li* [of things], and investigate further until he reaches the limit. After exerting himself in this way for a long time, he will one day achieve a *wide and far-reaching penetration* [*guantong*]. Consequently, he can apprehend the qualities of things, whether internal or external, the refined or the coarse (Chan, 1963, p. 89, emended).

Guantong, rendered by Chan as "wide and far-reaching penetration," is an attainment of the comprehensive understanding of things through *qiongli* – the exhaustive investigation of the *li* of things. More important, as a metaphor, *guantong*, "the thread that runs through things," intimates the idea that understanding consists in having an insight into the interconnection of all things. This idea of *guantong* echoes Xunzi's notion of *liguan* or *li* as the thread that runs through things, events, and human affairs. Implicit in the idea of *guantong* is a holistic ideal or unifying perspective (Cua, 1993). Cheng Yi's famous apothegm *liyi er fenshu*, "*li* is one with diverse manifestations" – an idea he attributed to Zhang Zai's "Western Inscription" – is perhaps a good way of characterizing this Confucian ideal of the good human life (Chan, 1963, p. 550). As a component of *liyi er fenshu*, *li* is used as a generic term. On the other hand, the *li* in our citation from Zhu Xi is a specific term. This use of *li* as a specific term is clear in Zhu Xi's contrast between *dao* (the holistic, unifying ideal) and *li*, which is evident in a couple of terse sayings: (1) "*Dao* is a unifying term (*tongming*), *li* is [a term referring to its] detail items"; and (2) "*Dao* is a holistic word (*daozi hongda*), *li* is a word for details (*lizi jingmi*)" (*Zhuzi yulei*, Zhuan 6a). As a specific term, *li* has a plurality of uses that may be further specified in particular discursive context. Furthermore, Zhu Xi's remarks suggest that *li* is a generic term functionally equivalent to "reason," which can be contextually specified either as a descriptive/explanatory or normative term. This suggestion has a partial sanction in the modern Chinese notion of *liyu*, meaning "reason," "ground" or "rationale."

Before going further, a caveat is necessary. Because of their fundamental ethical orientation, for the most part Confucian thinkers, with Xunzi as a possible exception, do not clearly distinguish descriptive, explanatory, and normative uses of terms. Terms such as "father" and "son" are commonly used with implicit normative force. Differently put, factual statements made in ethical contexts are generally regarded as invested with moral import. Being a father or a son already implies certain obligations. In the classical Confucian language of the rectification of names, when a son does not live up to his obligations, the "name" (*ming*) of being a son requires ethical correction. Ideally, correction of misconduct will be accompanied by a transformation of the person's character. In this sense, rectifying names (*zhengming*) is a procedure for rectifying misconduct. This Confucian view finds a partial affinity with that of Arthur Murphy:

> The term "brother", in the statement of a ground of obligation, is not a practically non-committal term. To be a brother is not just to be a male sibling – it is a privilege, a burden and, whether we like it or not, a commitment. (Murphy, 1965, pp. 109–10)

While the doctrine of the exclusive disjunction of facts and values is questioned, the legitimacy of the distinction in appropriate contexts is still acknowledged. In cases where a reasonable Confucian agent is unhappy with the connection of facts and values, he or she may appeal to the distinction. Say that a father makes an unethical demand, the filial son, who is expected to obey his father's wishes, may quite properly disobey. The virtue of filiality does not require unconditional obedience. Xunzi points out that there are circumstances in which a son should follow *yi* (rightness), his sense of what is right, rather than his father's commands. For example, when obedience to parental wishes may harm or disgrace the family, or require bestial behavior. Accordingly, the Confucian may invoke the distinction between fact and value without adopting the doctrine of the dichotomy of facts and values. At issue is the problematic connection between fact and value. Doubt about the connection may result in divesting the factual content implied in one's moral attitude. The task of a Confucian moral philosopher is not to legislate on the connection between fact and value. The task is to provide an elucidation of the contexts in which questions about the connection may appositely arise for moral agents, and to map out possible answers that are consistent with an intelligent adherence to the Confucian ethical tradition.

If *li* is functionally equivalent to "reason," in relevant contexts, we may regard the common Confucian expression of the form "*x zhi li*," roughly "the *li* of *x*," as subject to specification in terms either of "reasons for belief" and "reasons for action." Zhu Xi's remarks on the two basic uses of *li* are amenable to this procedure of explication. "The reason that a thing is what it is (*suoyiran zhi gu*)" may be paraphrased as "the reason for believing that such and such a thing exists" and "the norm for what a thing ought to be (*dangran zhi ze*)" as "the reason for acting in accord with the norm or standard of action." In both cases, we are concerned with the *rationales* for accepting factual beliefs and norms for conduct, though, as stated earlier, we must not assume the exclusive disjunction of facts and values.

From the Confucian point of view, concern with facts is important because they have implications for conduct. *Dangran zhi ze* may thus be rendered as the rationales for accepting the norm or standard of action. Such rationales for norm-acceptance presuppose an understanding of the idea of Confucian tradition (*daotong*). This living ethical tradition, to borrow Josiah Royce's term, is "a community of interpretation" (Cua, 1992b). Members of the community of interpretation are united with a sense of common good or well-being, informed by knowledge of its cultural history and respect its relevance for dealing with problems of the present and the future. Moreover, like any ethical tradition today (for example, Daoist, Buddhist, Jewish, Christian, or Muslim), the tradition undergoes changes because of reasonable internal and external challenges (Cua, 1991).

Since the two basic uses of *li* represent the exercise of reason in the generic sense, that is, as a distinctive capacity of the human mind exemplified in such mental acts as thinking, deliberating, inferring, and judging, rendering *li* as a functional equivalent of "reason" is plausible. For a Confucian moral philosopher, the emphasis is placed on the practical and not the theoretical exercise of reason. However, this emphasis does not deprecate the importance of theoretical inquiry, especially in contexts where empirical knowledge is indispensable to ascertaining accurate grounds for ethical judgment. In the *Xunzi*, for example, "accord with evidence" (*fuyan*), along with conceptual clarity and consistency are important requirements for participants in ethical argumentation. An ideal of rational coherence (*tonglei*) is presupposed as the basis for ethical justification (Cua, 1985, pp. 61–5).

In one passage, Xunzi points out that the human mind can either fail (*shili*) or succeed (*zhongli*) in the exercise of reason (Li, 1979, Book 22, p. 527). The main obstacle lies in *bi* (obscuration or blindness of mind). A *bi* is any sort of factor that obstructs the mind's cognitive task. According to Xunzi, whenever we make distinctions among things, our minds are likely to be obscured or blinded (*bi*) by our tendency to attend to one thing rather than another. This tendency is a common human affliction. All distinctions owe their origin to comparison and analogy of different kinds of things. They are made according to our current purposes, and thus are relative to a particular context of thought and discourse. Distinctions, while useful, are not dichotomies. In *bi*, a person attends exclusively to the significance of one item and disregards that of another. Both common people and philosophers are prone to exaggerate the significance of their favored views of things. For examples of this among philosophers, consider how Mozi is beset by *bi* in his exclusive attention to utility, and his neglecting to consider the importance of culture (*wen*), and how Zhuangzi is beset by *bi* in his preoccupation with Heaven (*tian*), and his lack of regard for the importance of human beings and affairs. For Xunzi, the common sources of *bi* are desire and aversion (*yuwu*), distance and proximity (*yuanjin*), breadth and shallowness of knowledge (*bojian*), and past and present (*gujin*).

Since the state of *bi* is contrary to reason (*li*), it is unreasonable to attend to the significance of one thing at the expense of a careful consideration of another. Well aware of the distinction between desire and aversion, a person may pursue his current desire without thinking about its possible unwanted or harmful consequences. That person's mind may be said to be beset by *bi*. More generally, humans suffer because of their concern for the acquisition of benefits and the avoidance of harm. When they see something beneficial, they do not consider carefully whether it may lead to harmful consequences. Moreover, even if consequences are considered, they may fail to attend to distant consequences (*yuan*) and simply concentrate on immediate ones (*jin*), though well aware that distant consequences may have relevance for their lives. Conversely, a person may be preoccupied with distant consequences, without attending to immediate ones that could bring disaster to his or her life.

When the mind is in the state of *bi*, reason is not functioning properly. The opposite of *bi* is clarity of mind. Says Xunzi: "If a person guides his or her mind with *li* (reason), nourishes it with the view of attaining clarity (*ming*), and does not allow things to upset mental composure, then that person is adequately prepared to resolve perplexities concerning right and wrong" (Li, 1979, Book 21, p. 490; Cua, 1985, ch. 4).

II *Li*-binomials and principled interpretation

If the previous section provides a guide to understanding the generic sense of *li*, exploring its concrete significance in particular contexts of discourse is important. A useful line of inquiry is to ponder some uses of *li* as a component of *li*-binomials. Since this is largely an uncharted territory, our hypothesis concerning the function of *li*-binomials is proffered as a recommendation and not as an explanatory thesis.

Formally, our hypothesis may be stated by way of Xunzi's distinction between generic (*gongming*) and specific or differentiating terms (*bieming*) – namely, the *li*-binomials are specific terms for *li* as a single, generic term (Li, 1979, Book 22, pp. 515–16). A generic term is a formal, general, abstract term amenable to specification by other terms in different discursive contexts. These terms, used in practical or theoretical contexts, may be said to be specific terms in the sense that they specify the significance of the use of a generic term adapted to a current purpose of discourse.

Alternatively, a generic term may have various levels of abstraction differentiated by the use of specific terms. A specific term, in turn, may function as a generic term in a particular discursive context when the current purpose requires such further specification. In the language of concept and conceptions, a generic term designates a *concept* that can be used in developing various *conceptions* (Rawls, 1971, p. 5). To avoid misunderstanding, our hypothesis on *li*-binomials is not intended to cover all the specific terms for *li* as a generic term. For the generic sense of *li* can have many specific terms (*bieming*), say, as instantiations of the schema "*x zhi li*" (the *li* of *x*). For example, one can talk about the *li* of love (*ai zhi li*), the *li* of filiality (*xiao zhi li*), the *li* of rites (*li* zhi li*) or the *li* of tables or chairs. In all of these cases, we are talking about the rationales of our factual or normative beliefs about "*x*".

In his study of the history of the idea of *li* in Chinese thought, Tang Junyi employs six *li*-binomials. This brilliant study is intricate, and difficult to appreciate if one does not have Tang's encyclopedic knowledge of the texts – an ability rarely exemplified in the works of Sinologists today. For philosophical scholars who have some knowledge of Chinese thought, Tang's study of *li* should represent an exciting challenge. For those not so equipped, Liu Shu-hsien provides a valuable, succinct discussion of Tang's work on *li*.

Tang proposes the thesis that there are six different meanings of *li*, expressed in such *li*-binomials as *wenli*, *mingli*, *kongli*, *xingli*, *shili*, and *wuli*, exemplified in Chinese thought from the pre-Qin to Qing times. Roughly, these *li*-binomials, according to Tang, pertain to highly articulated conceptions of *li* in different periods of Chinese thought. *Wenli* focuses on the ethical significance of cultural patterns inclusive of social and political orders in the pre-Qin period; *mingli* on the use of "names" or language in quasi-theoretical speculations in the Wei-Jin period, often associated with "dark" or "profound" speculations (*xuanxue*); *kongli* on the Buddhistic notion of *śūnyatā* or emptiness; *xingli* on nature/human nature in the Song–Ming periods; and *shili* on human affairs in the Qing period.

Instead of stating his methodology, Tang stresses the pivotal role of *li* in Song–Ming and Qing Confucianism. Equally important is his reminder about the renewed attention to the significance of *li* after the introduction of Western philosophy and scientific thought in the late nineteenth and early twentieth centuries. He cites various examples of the use of *li* in the Chinese translation of various Western concepts. In each case, he uses a *li*-binomial. For instance, "reason" was translated as *lixing*, "axiom" as *gongli*, "theorem" as *dingli*, and notably, "principle" as *yuanli*. More examples are familiar to educated Chinese today. Given that *xue* is a familiar Chinese expression for an academic discipline, "physics" is translated as *wuli xue*, "psychology" as *xinli xue*, and "ethics" as *lunli xue*. Significantly, while "logic" used to be translated by some scholars as *lize xue*, this is now rejected by Chinese philosophers. The familiar Chinese term for "logic" today is a transliteration – *luoji*.

Since Tang gives no guide to the basis of his interpretative study of *li*, it is possible that his use of *li*-binomials is influenced by his knowledge of Western philosophy and modern science. The use of *li* in the translation of "physics" may be a native linguistic adaptation of *wuli* (the *li* of things), a familiar term in Neo-Confucianism (or Song and Ming Confucianism). Especially significant is Tang's example of *yuanli* as a translation of "principle". Among contemporary Chinese philosophers, the use of *lize* as "principle" is also quite common.

A Confucian philosopher would ask about the *li* or rationales for Tang's examples. What is the rationale for using *li* in such translation of English terms? If "principle" is translated as *yuanli*, what does *yuanli* mean for an educated Chinese who does not know that *yuanli* is originally a translation of "principle"? It is also worth noting that "principle" is also commonly translated as *yuanze*. Recall our earlier discussion of the use of *ze* as a conclusion-indicator or a standard for determining what a thing ought-to-be, in Zhu Xi's explanation of the meaning of *li* (section I). The translation of "principle" as *yuanze* is probably the result of the influence of Western preoccupation with "laws of nature," "natural law" or "rules for conduct." As a conjecture, these Chinese translations of key terms in Western philosophical discourse reflect the influence of Western philosophical education. One also wonders whether the acceptance of the translation of *li* as "principle" is an unconscious Western Sinologist's reading of *li* as *yuanli*, which is a standard Chinese translation of "principle."

Before we deal with the principled interpretation of *li*, in order to avoid misunderstanding, we must note that our hypothesis concerning *li*-binomials does not prejudge the issue of the proper reading of Chinese philosophical texts. Implicit in our hypothesis is the idea that these binomials express distinct notions, although they are specific terms (*bieming*) that differentiate the concrete significance of *li* as a generic term (*gongming*). An alternative hypothesis is to regard these *li*-binomials as simply conjunctions of single terms or graphs. Our hypothesis does not reject this alternative, especially as an approach to the study of ancient Chinese philosophical texts. Absent a punctuation system, the scholar has to use his or her linguistic intuitions in resolving queries on the reading of texts and arriving at a reasoned decision. In the *Xunzi*, this alternative approach is plausible in cases of the co-occurrence of *li** (rites) and *yi* (rightness). If one views the co-occurrence of *li** (rites) and *yi* (rightness) as a binomial, *liyi*, the punctuation problem is resolved by rendering passages of the co-occurrence of *li** (rites) and *yi* (rightness) as a compound term, expressing a single concept. This interpretative method of translation is sometimes used by Burton Watson, construing the co-occurrence of *li** (rites) and *yi* (rightness) as a binomial, thus "ritual principles" (Li, 1979, Book 23; Watson, 1963, p. 160). Arguably, a more plausible answer to the problem of the co-occurrence of *li** and *yi* in the *Xunzi* is to view the co-occurrence as a conjunction of single graphs (for example, Chan, 1963, p. 130). Many crucial passages are hardly intelligible if we read the co-occurrence of *li** and *yi* as a binomial *li*yi* (Cua, 1989a).

Perhaps the best way to deal with the plausibility of principled interpretation of *li* is to consider some common *li*-binomials in Song–Ming Confucianism. In Wang Yangming's case, we find four *li*-binomials: *tianli*, *daoli*, *yili*, and *tiaoli*. These *li*-binomials present a challenge to philosophical interpretation. As elaborated elsewhere, these *li*-binomials are unintelligible when construed as different sorts of principles (Cua, 1982, ch. 2). As compound terms (*jianming*), they function more like focal notions, expressing distinct ideas associated with *li* in different contexts of discourse. *Tianli* is often used to convey the Neo-Confucian notion of *ren*, the ideal of the universe as a moral community; *daoli*, the idea of the dynamic indeterminacy of the ideal *dao* (often used interchangeably with *tianli*); *yili*, the idea of the rightness or appropriateness of reason to an occurrent situation, which required independent judgment or discretion; and *tiaoli*, the idea of an occasional achievement of a temporal, practical order (Cua, 1982, ch. 2).

Suppose we adopt the translation of *tianli* as "principle of nature", and of *yili* and *daoli* as "moral principle" (Chan, 1963). Apart from the questions we raised at the beginning of this article, we may ask for a clear statement of the sort of principle implied, say, in *tianli*. *Tianli* is often used in Song-Ming Confucianism as something (an ethical ideal) obscured (*bi*) by human desires. We do not find any statement comparable to Kant's Principle of the Law of Nature. To Cheng Hao and Wang Yangming, as an ethical ideal, *tianli* is a matter of personal realization and not a principle to be used for deriving moral rules or standards. Similar remarks apply to the translation of *daoli* and *yili* as "moral principle", which suggests that the Confucians have a principle analogous to Kant's Principle of Humanity. The Confucians do have an ideal of dignity or respect for persons, but this ideal pertains to the recognition of meritorious performance rather than respect for a person qua person independently of actual conduct (Cua, 1978. ch. 7). The translation of *yili* as "moral principle" is especially questionable. In Wang Yangming's major works, this focal notion emphasizes reasoned judgment on an occurrent, problematic, exigent situation – that is, the situation that receives no guidance from established standards of conduct. In other words, in hard cases of the moral life, we must attend to the merits of particular situations independently of one's favored doctrines or beliefs about the proper application of established norms of conduct.

Ideally, disagreement and/or dispute concerning the current import of the Confucian tradition is subject to criticism. Thus the notion of *li* has a key role to play in ethical argumentation conceived as a cooperative enterprise in which the participants attempt to arrive at an agreeable solution to a problem of common concern. In such a discourse, *li* has both explanatory and justificatory uses in proffering and evaluating normative claims (Cua, 1985). Thus the translation of *li* as "reason" or "rationale," in the light of its argumentative functions, is more plausible and philosophically significant. Accordingly, we can ask questions amenable to reasoned answers, though these answers are matters of philosophical reconstruction. However, such scholarly efforts in reconstruction also contribute to the development of Confucianism. For example, with respect to *tianli*, we can now ask "What is the *li* or rationale for espousing the notion of *tianli*?" If *tianli* is alleged to be opposed to the pursuit of human desires as in Song-Ming Confucianism, then one must have some reasons for accepting their thesis. This was a momentous issue for Qing Confucianists.

Also, questions can be raised about the *li* of *yili*, or of *daoli*. Even if both *li*-binomials convey the idea of change and the indeterminacy of natural events and human affairs, one can still ask about the *li* or rationale for characterizing such matters in particular situations as falling outside the scope of the application of normal, established standards of human conduct. As to *tiaoli*, which clearly expresses the idea of pattern or order, questions about the translation of *li* as "pattern" may be asked, as was suggested at the beginning of this essay. Our questions, say, concerning the nature of pattern or order are best formulated as questions about the *li* or rationales for taking certain order as normative rather than as merely descriptive.

Although the translation of *li* as "principle" is misleading, the question concerning the role of principles in Confucian ethics or in Chinese philosophy is an important one. Presumably, it is the concern with this question that underlies the principled interpretation of *li*. Three different, yet complementary ways of exploring answers to this question must be considered. First, one may acknowledge that the occasional use of the concept of principle in contemporary Chinese philosophy or ethics is significant. "Principle" has a role in articulating preceptive principles – that is, "first-personal precepts adopted by particular persons and dependent for their authority entirely upon such persons' loyalty to them" (Aiken, 1969, p. 113). In this sense, principles represent the agent's understanding of the preceptive guidance of Confucian ethics. Second, as statements of belief and/or theses in argumentative discourse, principles can function as means for internal or external critiques of the established Confucian tradition. These principles are not mere instruments of criticism, but proposals for reconstituting the tradition. As argumentative topics, they are not fixed rules for ethical deliberation. Third, and perhaps most importantly, the use of the language of principle, in the light of wide intercultural contact today, is an attempt to reformulate the relevance of some basic Confucian concepts of virtue in order to set forth certain ground rules or procedures as preconditions for the adjudication of intercultural, ethical conflict. (This function of principle is perhaps the point behind translating "principle" as *yuanze*, since *ze* can be used as a Chinese translation of "rule" or "procedure" and *yuan* can be used to translate "fundamental" or "essential.") The presumption, though defeasible, is that external challenges to a particular tradition are reasonable only from the internal point of view of the tradition in question (Cua, 1991).

The preceding uses of the language of principle may be adopted in Confucian discourse and dialogue with other ethical traditions. Notably, the use of "principle" contextually implies that the claims at issue are in some sense fundamental, the *principia*, the originating sources of ethical discourse. (Perhaps this is the motivation for writers who adopt the translation of "principle" as *yuanli*, since *yuan* may be regarded as a functional equivalent of *principium*.) In other words, the professed claims formulated in the language of principles express convictions about the foundation or the core beliefs deemed to be inherent in the ethical tradition. Arguably tradition is an interpretative concept (Cua, 1992b). Principles, as claims about the *principia* of ethical discourse, are defeasible, however, and therefore cannot be considered final or absolute norms. As a focus on *principium*, one can appreciate the translation of "principle" as *yuanli*, for it suggests the idea that it is the ethical foundation of the tradition that provides the point of departure for intellectual discourse.

This essay presents some aspects of the Chinese conception of reason. As a single generic term, *li* is functionally equivalent to "reason" in the sense of our capacity for thinking, imagining or reasoning. Obviously, one may ask with respect to Confucianism the familiar philosophical questions concerning the relations of reason and experience, reason and passion, and reason and insight. An exploration of these questions will undoubtedly contribute to a further understanding and just evaluation of certain pivotal aspects of Chinese philosophy. In another sense, this essay deals with the Chinese, Confucian conception of rationality, provided that rationality is not so narrowly conceived as to be exclusive of reasonableness as an intelligent way to cope with exigent, rule-indeterminate situations of human life (Cua, 1982, ch. 4). It is hoped that this essay provides some useful guides for further study.

Bibliography

References

Aiken, Henry D. 1969: "On the Concept of a Moral Principle," *Isenberg Memorial Lecture Series, 1965–1966* (East Lansing: Michigan State University Press).

Chan, Wing-tsit (ed. and tr.) 1963: *A Source Book in Chinese Philosophy* (Princeton: Princeton University Press).

—— 1964: "The Evolution of the Neo-Confucian *Li* as Principle," *Tsing Hua Journal of Chinese Studies*, n.s. 4, pp. 123–49.

—— 1983: "*Li*," *Zhongkuo zhexue cidian daquan* [Comprehensive Dictionary of Chinese Philosophy], ed. Wei Zhengtong (Taibei: Shuiniu).

—— (tr.) 1986: *Neo-Confucian Terms Explained: [The Pei-hsi tzu-i] by Ch'en Ch'un, 1159–1223* (New York: Columbia University Press).

Chen, Chun (Ch'en Ch'un) 1979: *Beixi xiansheng ziyi xiangjiang* [Neo-Confucian Terms Explained] (Taibei: Guangwen).

Collingwood, R. G. 1962: *An Essay on Metaphysics* (Oxford: Clarendon Press).

Cua, A. S. 1975: "Practical Causation and Confucian Ethics," *Philosophy East and West*, 25, pp. 1–10.

—— 1978: *Dimensions of Moral Creativity: Paradigms, Principles, and Ideals* (University Park: Pennsylvania State University Press).

—— 1982: *The Unity of Knowledge and Action: a Study in Wang Yang-ming's Moral Psychology* (Honolulu: University of Hawaii Press).

—— 1985: *Ethical Argumentation: a Study in Hsün Tzu's [Xunzi's] Moral Epistemology* (Honolulu: University of Hawaii Press).

—— 1989a: "The Problem of Conceptual Unity in Hsún Tzu and Li Kou's Solution," *Philosophy East and West*, 39, pp. 115–34.

—— 1989b: "The Status of Principles in Confucian Ethics," *Journal of Chinese Philosophy*, 16, pp. 273–96.

—— 1991: "Reasonable Challenges and Preconditions of Adjudication," in *Culture and Modernity: East–West Philosophic Perspectives*, ed. Eliot Deutsch (Honolulu: University of Hawaii Press), pp. 279–98.

—— 1992a: "Confucian Ethics," *Encyclopedia of Ethics*, Vol. 1 (New York: Garland), pp. 194–202.

—— 1992b: "The Idea of Confucian Tradition," *Review of Metaphysics*, 45, pp. 803–40.

—— 1993: "The Possibility of Ethical Knowledge: Reflections on a Theme in the *Hsün Tzu*," in *Epistemological Issues in Classical Chinese Philosophy*, ed. Hans Lenk and Gregor Paul (Albany: State University of New York Press), pp. 159–80.

Graham, A. C. 1958: *Two Chinese Philosophers: Ch'eng Ming-tao and Ch'eng Yi-ch'uan* (London: Lund Humphries).

Li, Disheng 1979: *Xunzi jishi* [An annotated edition of *Xunzi*] (Taibei: Xuesheng).

Liu, Shu-hsien forthcoming: "*Li*," in *Encyclopedia of Chinese Philosophy*, ed. A. S. Cua (New York: Garland).

Murphy, Arthur Edward 1965: *The Theory of Practical Reason* (La Salle: Open Court).

Rawls, John 1971: *A Theory of Justice* (Cambridge: Harvard University Press).

Tang, Junyi 1978: *Zhongguo zhexue yuanlun, daolun pian* [Foundations of Chinese Philosophy: Introductory Volume] (Taibei: Xuesheng).

Watson, Burton (tr.) 1963: *Hsün Tzu [Xunzi]: Basic Writings* (New York: Columbia University Press).

Zhuxi 1962: *Zhuzi yulei* [Classified Conversation of Master Zhu], ed. Li Jingde (Taibei: Zhengzhong).

—— 1980: *Sishu jizhu* [Collected Commentaries on the Four Books] (Hong Kong: Taiping).

Further reading

Chan Wing-tsit (tr.) 1967: *Reflections on Things at Hand: the Neo-Confucian Anthology Compiled by Chu Hsi [Zhu Xi] and Lü Tsu-ch'ien* (New York: Columbia University Press).

Chu Hsi (Zhuxi) 1990: *Learning to be a Sage*, tr. Daniel K. Gardner (Berkeley: University of California Press).

Fu, Wei-hsun and Wing-tsit Chan 1978: *Guide to Chinese Philosophy* (Boston: G. K. Hall).

Fung, Yulan 1947: *The Spirit of Chinese Philosophy*, tr. E. R. Hughes (London: Routledge & Kegan Paul).

—— 1953: *History of Chinese Philosophy*, tr. Derk Bodde, 2 Vols (Princeton: Princeton University Press).

Graham, A. C. 1978: *Later Mohist Logic, Ethics, and Science* (Hong Kong: Chinese University of Hong Kong Press).

—— 1989: *Disputers of the Tao: Philosophical Argument in Ancient China* (La Salle: Open Court).

Knoblock, John 1988–94: *Xunzi: a Translation and Study of the Complete Works*, Vols 1–3 (Stanford: Stanford University Press).

Munro, Donald J. 1969: *The Concept of Man in Early China* (Stanford: Stanford University Press).

Wei, Zhengtong 1981: *Zhongguo zhexue cidian* (*Dictionary of Chinese Philosophy*) (Taibei: Dalin).

Wittenborn, Allen (tr.) 1991: *Further Reflections on Things at Hand: a Chu Hsi [Zhu Xi] Reader* (Lanham: University Press of America).

Zhang, Liwen 1994: *Li* (Taibei: Han-xing).

14

The way and the truth

DAVID L. HALL

Searching for the meaning of "truth" in the Chinese tradition would not immediately strike one as a controversial activity. The signal prominence of the quest for truth in shaping the sensibility of Anglo-European culture might easily suggest that the notion has had a similar import in China. But the fact of the matter is that scholars from China, Europe, and America continue to debate the question as to whether there is even anything like a concept of "truth" in China. On the surface, the claim that the Chinese have no concept of truth appears outrageous – surely the Chinese tell the truth as often as we, and lie as often. Even granting that this is the case, it turns out, nonetheless, that the issue is not as easily settled as one might think.

One thing is certain: we in the West are well-nigh obsessed with the notion of truth. The sibling values of "truth" and "rightness" have dominated the cultures of Western modernity. Other values, such as aesthetic *beauty*, or religious *holiness*, or philosophical *importance* have been clearly less significant. So much is this so that we are more likely to wonder whether it is *true* that *x* is beautiful than to consider the beauty of *x* in itself. And many of us will allow our interest in the *rightness* of something beautiful, construed in terms of its moral effects, to overrule any nascent aesthetic interest.

From Plato's discussion of the analogy of the Sun and the Good and Aristotle's privileging of the sense of sight as the ground of "wonder," to the medieval constructions of the *speculum mentis*, to the rationalisms and empiricisms of the modern period, the testimony has been that Western philosophy focuses its epistemological interests by an appeal to two sorts of "seeing" – one which entertains what appears to the senses, primarily the sense of sight; the other which "envisions" a reality lying behind appearances. Until recently, the assumption that knowing is a kind of "seeing" has guided epistemological reflections in the West. And from this understanding our principal meanings of truth have been derived.

One of the fundamental contrasts noted by both Chinese and Western scholars is that suggested by the Western quest for "truth" and the Chinese search for the "way" (see Graham, 1989, p. 3). This contrast very succinctly captures the problematics of Western and Chinese cultures with respect to the issue of how one might orient oneself within the natural and social worlds.

Indeed, a number of scholars in both cultures agree that the Chinese have no concept of truth. A. C. Graham argues in this fashion: In the West we have developed a concept of truth by extending the meanings of "fact" from instances involving the putatively accurate reporting of what is the case, to such issues as the truth of tautologies, the truth of narratives, and so on. Thus the semantic range of "true" and "truth" comes to extend far beyond first-order questions of a factual nature to logical, historical, and literary issues which are expressed in propositional form. What this means is that truth comes to be a second-order concern involving the comparison of propositions with states of affairs – or "facts."

To say that Chinese philosophers display a "lack of interest in questions of truth and falsity" amounts then to saying that like Western [philosophers], they are not primarily concerned with the factual, but unlike Western [philosophers], they do not use a word that assimilates other questions to the factual. That they would have no concept of Truth would be taken for granted, but is trivial (Graham, 1989, p. 396).

I agree with Graham that, as traditionally understood, there is no concept of "truth" among the classical Chinese. One might disagree, however, that this fact is trivial. Graham's claims about the Chinese sensibility are fundamentally linguistic and grammatical. And it is certainly true that, on purely grammatical grounds, the fact that the Chinese may not have shaped their language in the same manner as have we is in itself of little consequence. If, on the other hand, one is interested in the broadest of cultural evidences which shape the construction and expression of values and visions, the situation is quite different. On these grounds, the contrast of "Way" and "Truth" is significant for understanding the distinctiveness of the two cultures. For if it turns out that the Chinese are oriented by the "Way" (*dao*) rather than the "Truth," this means that we shall be hard put to find a word or word cluster that functions among the Chinese as the term "truth" functions in our own, and since a culture is constituted by an interactive, interdependent field of ideas, values, and beliefs, it will also be the case that most of the theoretical and practical correlates of the search for truth will themselves be absent, with the consequence that the shape of the Chinese cultural sensibility may be expected to be radically distinct from that of the West.

Primary understandings of truth in the West have been associated with the ideas of "correspondence" and "coherence." Either truth is realized through a correspondence of states of affairs as they "appear" and as they "truly are," or by virtue of the systematic coherence of one or more propositions with a broad-ranging system of such propositions. Both correspondence and coherence theories have ramified in any number of directions until today we are literally overstocked with contrasting theories of truth, almost all of which continue the spectatorial tradition of knowing patterned after a kind of "seeing."

Recently, Anglo-European understandings of "truth" have undergone a rather dramatic transformation. John Dewey's assault upon the "spectator" theory of knowledge, Heidegger's criticism of our tendency to "picture" the world, Wittgenstein's attack upon "sense data" theory which privatizes the act of knowing, Jacques Derrida's sardonic celebration of the dominance of the heliotropic metaphor and Richard Rorty's critique of the "mirroring mind," all carry the message that the attempt to understand knowledge, reason, and truth in *representational* terms is no longer thought to be a viable project.

As will be clear in the following discussion, it is what we call the "pragmatic" understanding of truth that best approximates the Chinese sensibility. This means that the contemporary movement from representational to non-representational understandings of knowledge and truth in the Anglo-European philosophy greatly increases the possibility of our appreciating Chinese approaches to "truth" which emphasize "way" metaphors rather than the sorts of "mirroring" metaphors associated with the spectator theory of knowledge.

It is not really that difficult, of course, to discover significant "Way" metaphors in our own tradition, both ancient and modern. The senses of truth encountered in the *Oxford English Dictionary* divide rather naturally into two categories. One class of meanings is associated with notions of rectitude, integrity, wholeness, lack of distortion, and the like: "the true course of an arrow," "following the true path," "having a true heart." A second class is concerned with the comparison of what appears to be the case and the reality itself: "conformity with fact," "real contrasted with imitation." The first class resonates well with the "Way" metaphors of the Chinese.

If we look to the Hebraic tradition at the time of the Major Prophets (eighth to sixth centuries), we find that the senses of truth (*æmeth*, *æmūnā*) are related to wholeness, integrity, the ability to maintain oneself as healthy and whole in all circumstances. Truth is a condition of a soul which has the strength to act in an integrated manner. The prophet is one whose words, being true, have *efficacy*. "A prophet must be true (*neæmān*) in order to be a prophet, to have the necessary strength of soul, that his words shall not fail to take effect" (Pedersen, 1959, p. 339).

The sense of truth as "the strength to maintain oneself" contrasts readily with the notion of truth as signalling a correspondence between appearance and reality. In the Western tradition, the latter sense was a gift of the post-Homeric Greeks. Subsequently, it is the Greek *alētheia* (αλεθεια) and the Latin *veritas*, read in terms of the affirmation of an appearance/reality distinction and the assumption of a single-ordered cosmos, which have shaped the dominant uses of the terms in Western philosophical discourse.

In modern Western philosophy, existentialist and pragmatic understandings of truth are concerned with the practical, consequential, nature of truth as associated with "ways" of thinking and acting. Existentialist perspectives often advertise an individualistic stance that does not resonate well with the Chinese sensibility. Nonetheless, the concern for "self-cultivation" in both Confucian and Daoist traditions is similar enough to the existentialist desire for personal "authenticity" to permit fruitful comparisons. But it is, most certainly, American pragmatism which provides the best resource for understanding Chinese approaches to the issue of "truth."

Of the three principal philosophical movements in classical China – Confucianism, Daoism, and Mohism – only Mohism contains speculations which seem to deal with issues of "truth" and "falsity" in terms familiar to a Westerner. But even here there is the absence of any underlying sense of a bifurcation between things as they essentially are, and as they appear – or between propositions and states of affairs.

The likeliest examples of the practice of logical argumentation in China is later Mohism. Mozi himself subordinated logical and rational argumentation to what we would term ethical considerations. He sought principles of ethical utility in a manner that would align him with certain rather broadly conceived forms of pragmatism. There is little by way of dispassionate "rationalism" to be found in the early Mohist doctrines. And whether we could speak of rationalism with respect to the later Mohist is also debatable.

> The Chinese opposition *ming/shi* (name/object) is very unlike the Saussurian "signifier/signified" which Derrida takes to be implicit in Western thought from the beginning. A name is used to "point out" (*zhi*) an object, and if appropriate to it, "fits" (*dang*). Nominalized *zhi* is sometimes conveniently translated by "meaning" [but] there is . . . no tendency (as I myself once thought) for the *zhi* of names to turn, like "meanings" or the "signified," into third entities on the same level as the objects and the sounds of names. In the hypostatizing terminology of Saussurian linguistics signifier and signified are two entities combined in the sign, specifically compared to the two sides of a sheet of paper, signifying has somehow disappeared, and for Derrida the object too has dissolved into the signified ("There is nothing outside the text"). For a Chinese thinker, on the other hand, there would be nothing, except the present or absent oxen to which the use of "ox" points, which could be credited with existence or reality in detachment from the phonic exterior of the sign. (Graham, 1989, pp. 227–8)

Graham is here noting a general fact about the Chinese language which qualifies the Mohist doctrines as well as any others concerned with the connections of "names" and "things." This fact is rooted in the contrasting senses of "being" in the Chinese and Western traditions. Since, in the Chinese language, the senses of "being" (*you*) do not have a copulative sense, there is no use of being which suggests *existence*. To say that something "is" or "is-not" is merely to indicate its presence or absence. Rather than the being of things being made present through the beings of the world, all we have are the beings of the world. This is the reason correspondence theories based upon a contrast of appearance and reality cannot easily be generated.

In any case, Mohism has never constituted a dominant strand of thought in China. It would be misleading to characterize Chinese notions of "truth" in terms of philosophical Mohism. Indeed, a principal reason for the decline and well-nigh disappearance of Mohism as a viable movement in China was that its more "objectivist" character contrasted so dramatically with that of the Daoists and Confucians which dominated classical China.

In an article entitled "A Chinese Philosopher's Theory of Language," Chang Tung-sun [Zhang Dongsun] contrasted the Chinese and Western approaches to knowledge in this very simple, but exceedingly apt, manner:

> In putting a question about anything, it is characteristic of Western mentality to ask "What is it?" and then later "How should one react to it?" The Chinese mentality does not emphasize the "what" but rather the "how." Western thought is

> characterized by the "what-priority attitude," Chinese by the "how-priority attitude." (Chang, 1959, p. 180)

The "how-priority" of the Chinese allows for no separation between phenomena and ontological ground. "Reality" is precisely that complex pattern of relationships which constitutes the myriad things of the world. Knowledge, then, is not abstractive, but concrete; not representational, but performative and participatory; not discursive, but a kind of "know-how." Knowledge, rather than entailing the discovery of originative principles, is presentational in the sense that knowing and what is known emerge together. "Truth" involves a trust in the quality of one's relationships. It is the capacity to foster productive patterns of relationship within one's natural, social, and cultural context, enabling one to enhance the possibilities of one's environing conditions in order to realize themselves fully, while at the same time maintaining one's own integrity as a unique and viable member of "the ten thousand things."

Chang Tung-sun notes the following corollary of the "how-priority":

> The Chinese are only interested in knowing the will of Heaven in order to seek good fortune and to avoid misfortune. As to the nature of Heaven, they are indifferent. This fact shows that the Chinese have not applied the category of substance to the idea of Heaven and have not taken Heaven as the ultimate stuff of the universe. (Chang, 1959, pp. 178–9)

"Knowing," in classical China is not grounded in a cosmological knowing-what as was the knowledge of the Ancient Greeks. The Greeks asked the question, "What kinds of things are there?" and responded by providing a sense of the *physis* of things – the "stuff" of which the world is made. For the Chinese the question was, and is, "How is life to be lived?" "How may I realize the Way (*dao*)?" Responding to this question provides knowledge of how to be adept in relationships, and how, in optimizing the possibilities that these relations provide us, to develop trust in their viability. The cluster of terms that define knowing are thus programmatic and exhortative, encouraging as they do the quality of the roles and associations that define us. The Chinese "knower" does not simply seek conformity between her perceptions and an antecedent reality, but participates actively in the "making real" or "realization" of the world through self-disclosure. Knowing for the Chinese is practical, and performative. "Truth" describes the appropriate accommodation one makes to one's environing community.

Truth, then, is not attached to propositions but to persons. And this truth cannot be a function of the adequation of appearance to reality in the sense that one's conduct may be said to realize an essential principle defining right conduct. It is rather a function of the efficacious integrity of the individual – efficacious because of the power of personal presence to evoke deferential response.

Rather than speak of truth and falsity, the Chinese concern themselves with questions of genuineness and hypocrisy – terms which apply to the presence or absence of acts of integrity rather than the adequacy of propositions.

The Confucian and Daoist traditions share the commitment to "self-cultivation," to deepening and refining those relationships that constitute one in one's environment. By examining the comparable goals of self-cultivation in the tradition embedded in the notion of a realized person it is possible to advance an understanding of "how" one becomes – the "way" one becomes – a realized human being. And it is this "way" that constitutes knowledge and truth in the classical Chinese tradition.

According to the Confucian book, the *Zhongyong*:

> Integrity (*cheng*) means self-accomplishing, and *dao* means self-articulating (or literally, self-*dao*-ing). To have integrity is a thing from its beginning to its end; to be lacking in integrity is to be nothing. For this reason, the exemplary person (*junzi*) prizes integrity. Integrity is not simply the means to accomplish oneself, but also the way to accomplish other things. To accomplish oneself is to distinguish oneself as a person (*ren*); to accomplish other things is comprehension (*zhi*). The potency (*de*) of one's natural proclivities (*xing*) is the way of bringing together what is inside and what is outside. Thus, integrity is appropriate anytime and anywhere. ("The Doctrine of the Mean" 25 – Roger Ames tr.)

Integrity (*cheng*) has the sense of both "becoming whole" and "making whole." Self-cultivation always involves "correcting the heart." Since the heart (*xin*) is in fact "heart-mind" – decision and judgment are harmonized and integrated along with the "emotions." Becoming whole involves the integration of one's person as defined through one's actions. This integration is demonstrated through acts of expression – right speaking. Thus the sense of speaking truly involves a recognition of the authenticity of the person whose words, intentions, and actions are perfectly integrated. The effort of becoming whole is a making whole of others who, recognizing integrity when they are confronted with it, are provoked to emulate it.

There is an important passage in the *Mencius* which speaks of the manner in which "trustworthiness" – "living up to one's word" (*xin*) – and "integrity" (*cheng*) act together to help create community:

> If serving in a subordinate office, a person is unable to gain the support of his superiors, he will not be able to win the people over to proper order. There is a way of gaining the support of one's superiors: one who does not live up to his word in dealing with his friends will not gain the support of his superiors. There is a way of a living up to one's word in dealing with one's friends: one who in serving his relatives does not bring them pleasure, will not live up to his word in dealing with his friends. There is a way of bringing one's relatives pleasure: one who on introspection finds that he lacks integrity will not bring pleasure to his relatives. There is a way of having integrity in one's person: one who is not clear on acting well will not have integrity in his person. It is for this reason that integrity is the way of nature, and to reflect on integrity is the way of being a person. There has never been a person of the utmost integrity who does not affect others, just as a person lacking in integrity has never been able to affect anyone. (*Mencius* 4a/13), Roger Ames tr.

This passage, in effect, describes the Confucian notion of the *junxi* – the realized person. For Confucius, *junzi* is a qualitative term denoting someone who has an ongoing commitment to personal growth as it is cultivated and expressed through leadership in his community. The *junzi* is not characterized in terms of specific skills or expertise, but rather by recourse to the quality of his interactions with others. Confucius repeatedly draws a contrast between the socially expansive and inclusive *junzi*, and the disintegrative and retarding characteristics of what he terms "the small person" (*xiaoren*). This "small person," is motivated by selfishness, and thus detracts from the effective coordination of community. Effective communication has a central role both as the medium through which one articulates oneself, and in attracting participation in the kind of order that the *junzi*'s articulation models for community. Language is performative – it shapes the world. It is the *junzi*'s speaking that brings the world into being.

If we move from the notion of the *junzi* to that of the Daoist *zhenren*, or "genuine" person, we will see that, though there are significant differences between the Confucian and Daoist understandings of a "realized person," these two traditions have much in common.

In the *Zhuangzi*, Confucius asks for the meaning of "genuineness" (*zhen*). His interlocutor gives the following account:

> Genuineness (*zhen*) is the highest degree of purity and integrity. Without purity and integrity, one cannot move others. Thus, the person who forces his tears, although pathetic, does not arouse grief; one who forces his anger, although severe, does not inspire awe; one who forces his affections, although cordial, does not effect harmony. Genuine pathos arouses grief even without tears; genuine anger inspires awe even without rising to the surface; genuine affection effects harmony even without cordiality. It is because the spirit of one who is genuine within moves those around him that genuineness is to be prized.
>
> When genuineness is applied to human relations, in the service of family, it is compassion and filiality; in the service of the state, it is loyalty and justice; in feasting and drinking, it is pleasure and enjoyment; in mourning, it is pathos and grief. Most important in loyalty and justice is effort, in feasting it is enjoyment, in mourning it is grief, and in service of the family it is accommodation. And there is certainly more than one path to follow to arrive at these. One serves the family to accommodate its members, and is not concerned with how this is done; one feasts to enjoy and is not concerned with the choice of dishes; one mourns to grieve and does not ask after the rituals. Rituals are laid down by convention; genuineness is received from nature. What is so-of-itself (*ziran*) cannot be supplanted. Thus, the sage emulates nature and prizes genuineness without being caught up in conventions. The fool is the opposite. Unable to emulate nature, he frets over what human beings have established, and not having the good sense to prize genuineness, he goes along altering himself to suit the world, never himself knowing contentment. It is indeed a pity that you were so early in being steeped in human devices and have come so late to hear the great way! (*Zhuangzi* 31 – tr. Roger Ames)

Genuineness is resourced in spontaneity and naturalness. Such naturalness expresses itself through the process of personalization in which the stamp of one's individuality is placed upon the structures of the world. *Zhen* is the natural means of experiencing the world – a process related to "how" rather than "what."

A person is always in the context constituted by the full complexity of existing things. Full disclosure of the individual in coordination with its environing particulars is the ground for optimum creativity. This creativity can be compromised, however, by attempting to express one's particularity in "dis-integrative" ways that cause "dis-ease" in the environment, and in so doing, by failing to accommodate the interdependence of things. This limitation on creativity can emerge either by interpreting one's environment reductionistically through one's own intentions and actions, thereby impoverishing context in service to self, or by allowing oneself to be shaped wholly by context without contributing one's own uniqueness, thereby impoverishing self in service to context. In order to be fully integrative, one must cultivate an optimum continuity with one's environs by contributing personally and creatively to the emerging order of things.

For both Confucian and Daoist alike, there is a primacy given the particular, where its realization is an end in itself. The insistent particularity of any person or thing is most fully disclosed under the conditions provided by integration. Energies are not diffused through attachment and contentiousness, but are fully focused in self-expression. The emergent pattern of existence returns to and is derived from the collaboration of harmoniously integrated particularity.

Discussions of truth in Chinese philosophy, which concern a search for the "way" rather than propositional truth, may seem to suggest an irrevocable division between China and the West. Perhaps, however, the distance is not that great. Consider the following. Toward the beginning of this essay I asserted the close connection of the Chinese understanding of knowledge and truth with American pragmatism. There are a number of aspects of contemporary pragmatism that prepare us to grasp the Chinese sense of the "way." First, the rejection of both realist and idealist ontologies (which is effectively an abandonment of the Western metaphysical tradition) allows for an appreciation of the more nominalist tendencies of Chinese philosophy. Second, the rejection of the "spectator" theory of knowledge (which is in effect an abandonment of the classical epistemological tradition in the West) resonates well with the Chinese reflections which have proceeded unburdened by an appearance/reality bifurcation. Third, the substitution of "language" for "mind" and "experience" as the central metaphor in terms of which to couch philosophical discussion allows resort to the far less controversial medium of linguistic expression rather than demanding some common view of human experience or mental operations.

Of equal significance with the above, a pragmatic "theory" of truth is not a theory in any significant sense. As William James said, pragmatism is "a method only." As a *methodos*, pragmatism is merely a *way*, a set of means or instruments which permit the accomplishment of certain practical actions involved in "getting on with it." Given the essentially non-theoretical character of classical China, the "informality" of the pragmatic vision is a real asset.

Further, the pragmatic understanding of truth is not easily conformable with either correspondence or coherence theories, and thus does not depend upon metaphysical assumptions foreign to the Chinese. According to James, "truth" is the expedient in the way of thinking. For the pragmatist a belief is a habit which guides action. If the belief brings the individual into productive harmony with his or her community, it functions expediently, and it is "true" *insofar as* it so serves.

Finally, one might go so far as to say that the pragmatic discussions of "the expedient in the way of thinking" hardly constitutes an understanding of "truth" in any standard sense. For the pragmatist surely shares with the Chinese thinker a lack of interest in the cultural requisites which underlie classical theories of truth. The Jamesian pragmatist denies an appearance/reality contrast, the notion of a single ordered world, and rejects any theory/practice dichotomy that would enable one to hold propositions apart from states of affairs, treats concepts not in terms of essences, but as tools for action, and accedes to the dominance of metaphor in language, thus denying the value of the quest for univocal language.

There are, of course, significant differences between the typical Western and Chinese forms of pragmatism. As normally understood, the Western pragmatist develops his understanding of knowledge and truth by appeal to the notion of "beliefs" as "habits of action." From the Chinese perspective, the human being is characterized in terms of ritual action (*li*). Realizing the path (*dao*) entails the fulfilment of ritual activities. Habits of action are realized through ritual activity. In this manner the Chinese "pragmatist" outdoes his American counterpart by dealing always with the actualization of patterns of action rather than ever being satisfied with beliefs as mere plans or dispositions to act.

A second contrast between the Chinese and Western forms of pragmatism lies in the forms of knowledge which are most preferred. Western pragmatism has come to be associated with instrumental knowledge warranted by a proximity to scientific activities. Charles Sanders Peirce and John Dewey, who deal with truth in terms of "consensus at the end of inquiry" and "warranted assertability," have provided this emphasis. The Chinese form of pragmatism is clearly better associated with the literary, Jamesian, strand of pragmatism. In this strand, the emphasis is upon images and metaphors as ensuring the efficacy of language. "It is pictures rather than propositions, metaphors rather than statements, which determine most of our philosophical convictions" (Rorty, 1979, p. 12).

Many interpreters of China have claimed that the Chinese search for the *dao* was a consequence of the breakdown of moral and political order at the very period in which reflective thinking began in China. The Chinese, in contrast to the more speculative Greeks, were forced to be overly concerned with social order and harmony rather than with a dispassionate search for Truth. This account is usually an implication of the *mythos* to *logos* narrative which we heirs of the Enlightenment like to employ as a means of accounting for our rational development. Such a narrative, when contrasted with the account of the Chinese sensibility, tends to suggest that the Chinese somehow have failed to make the great leap forward from *mythos* to *logos* and have so remained in the primitive past.

Contrary to this rather standard interpretation of the differences between Chinese and Western culture, there is every reason to believe that the Western search for Truth – for a reality beyond appearance, for a standard in accordance with which a plurality of distinctive beings might be measured – was itself a response to the problem of creating or discovering a social and natural order within which individuals might find a secure and harmonious existence.

The suggestion that the Chinese sought the Way because of their more practical and urgent political and social concerns, while in the West we went adventuring after Truth because we somehow had the luxury to be speculative, is on reflection, highly questionable. A more pragmatic interpretation seems equally plausible. The philosophical discourse shaped in large measure by the search for Truth itself had an ethical and political cast from the beginning.

In pluralistic, ethnically diverse societies, it is not so easy to chart a concrete and specific Way among the many ways suggested by diverse languages, myths, customs, and rituals. Harmony must be sought through ascent to abstract, and ultimately universalizable, principles and standards. The quest for capital "T" Truth serves the aims of social and political stability in both positive and negative manners. Positively, it promises, down the road, a standard of common assent which can ground common values and practices. Negatively, it suggests the necessity of a certain tolerant circumspection in the treatment of those who do not share our present truths.

By contrasting the search for the Way and the quest for Truth as goals of philosophical reflection, I certainly do not intend to perpetuate the clichéd interpretation of the West as theoretical and dispassionately reflective and Chinese thinking as vested in the need for social harmony. On the contrary, I would argue that the two cultures shared the only sensible goal for social beings: the realization of social harmony. The search for Truth in both China and the Western world was defined by this fundamentally pragmatic motivation.

Bibliography

Writings

Lau, D. C. (tr.) 1983: *Confucius: The Analects* (Hong Kong: Chinese University Press).
—— (tr.) 1984: *Mencius* (Hong Kong: Chinese University Press).
Watson, Burton (tr.) 1968: *The Complete Works of Chuang Tzu* (New York: Columbia University Press).

References and further reading

Chang Tung-sun 1959: "A Chinese Philosopher's Theory of Knowledge," in *Our Language and Our World*, ed. S. I. Hayakawa (New York: Harper), pp. 172–92.
The Doctrine of the Mean 1963: in *A Sourcebook in Chinese Philosophy*, ed. Wing-tsit Chan (Princeton: Princeton University Press).
Graham. A. C. 1978: *Later Mohist Logic, Ethics, and Science* (Hong Kong: Chinese University Press).
—— 1989: *Disputers of the Tao* (La Salle, Ill.: Open Court Press).
Hall, David L. and Ames, Roger T. 1987: *Thinking Through Confucius* (Albany, NY: State University of New York Press).
—— 1995: *Anticipating China: Thinking Through the Narratives of Chinese and Western Culture* (Albany, NY: State University of New York Press).

Hansen, Chad 1983: *Language and Logic in Ancient China* (Ann Arbor: University of Michigan Press).
Pedersen, Johs. 1958: *Israel: Its Life and Culture*, Vol. 2 (London: Oxford University Press).
Richards, I. A. 1932: *Mencius on the Mind* (New York: Harcourt, Brace & Co.).
Rorty, Richard 1979: *Philosophy and the Mirror of Nature* (Princeton: Princeton University Press).

15

Chinese aesthetics

STEPHEN J. GOLDBERG

In China creativity is construed as an ethico-aesthetic practice in which signifying acts of self-presentation (*yi*) are evaluated as to their efficacy in fostering harmonious relations of social exchange within specific historical occasions. To say this is to call attention to the performative dimension of aesthetic creativity; to recognize, beyond its constative meaning, the force of an expressive act to produce effects that profoundly affect its recipients.

Observe, for example, the following passage from the *Bizhen tu*, or "Diagram of the Battle Formation of the Brush," an early treatise on the art of calligraphy: "Anciently, the Ch'in [Qim] Prime Minister, (Li) Ssu [Si], saw the calligraphy of King Mu [r. 1001–946 BCE] of the Chou [Zhou] dynasty. For several days he sighed, grieving (only) at its lack of bone (structure)" (Barnhart, 1964, p. 15). Li Si's reaction to the inscription of an early ruler of the preceding Zhou dynasty is an expression of moral judgment, an affective reading of the qualities of the brushwork as visual indices of the character of its author.

Aesthetic judgments are thus not predicated on a set of universally applicable criteria for assessing the substantive formal properties of a work of art. Rather, they are evaluative discernments of the ethically normative force of a signifying act of aesthetic self-disclosure, within the concrete circumstances of a specific social context.

Tradition, preserved in the form of the material traces of self-signification of those who have gone before, serves as a repository for the creative appropriation and invocation of patriarchal precedents, the sanctioning past, which authorizes one's own self-presentation to others. Authorial identity is thus, in part, defined in terms of the "embodiment" of the meanings and values implicit in the artistic references to the significations of one's precursors, the "voice" of the Other, that is, tradition. Citations to the past are often made in deference to the particular recipient of one's self-signification. The intended recipient, therefore, may also serve as a significant determinant of one's self-signification. Authorship, in Chinese culture, is thus a profoundly relational identity, and never refers simply to the artist as an isolated individual self. As Tu Wei-ming has observed,

> The self as a center of relationships rather than as an isolable individual is such a fundamental premise in the *Analects* that man as "an ultimately autonomous being" is unthinkable, and the manifestation of the authentic self is impossible "except in matrices of human converse." (Tu, 1985, p. 83)

Chinese ethico-aesthetics has its genesis in the ancient ritual practices (*li*) of the Zhou dynasty (1122–221 BCE), a formative period in Chinese civilization, which "witnessed a transition from spirit-centered to human-centered ritual, from shaman-counsellor to sage-counsellor, from authority by virtue of one's position to authority of one's person" (Hall and Ames, 1987, p. 87). One of the ways of seeking moral perfection, of becoming an authoritative person (*ren*), is through the practice of art as a means of self-cultivation. *Xiushen* (self-cultivation; literally, cultivation of the body) speaks to the "importance of taking care of one's body as a necessary condition for learning to be human" (Tu, 1985, p. 60). The idea that art can serve as a means of self-cultivation finds its earliest expression in a passage on the meaning of music in *The Book of Rites* (*Liji*): "The perfection of virtue is primary, and the perfection of art follows afterward" (*Liji*, tr. Cahill, 1960, p. 122). An affirmation of the practice of art can also be found in the following statement by Confucius: "The Master said, Set your heart upon the Way, support yourself by its power, lean upon Goodness, seek delight in the arts" (*Lunyu*, tr. Ledderose, 1979, p. 29).

Calligraphy and music, two of the "Six Arts" (*liuyi*) in classical Confucian thought, emerge from this formative period of Chinese culture as ritual aesthetic practices for the upper class, as disciplines of the body (*ti*) and mind/heart (*xin*), which engage the gentleman-scholar in the cultivation of the self (*xiushen*). In this respect, it is interesting to note that, "[e]tymologically the character *i* [yi], which is commonly rendered as 'art,' signifies the activity of planting or cultivating fields" (Tu, 1983, p. 60). Noting the cognate relation between the characters for "ritual action" (*li*) and "body" (*ti*), David Hall and Roger Ames observe that "*li* actions are embodiments or formalizations of meaning and value that accumulate to constitute a cultural tradition" (Hall and Ames, 1987, p. 88).

The concept of the Six Arts did not survive the fall of the Han Dynasty. In the wake of the collapse of the Han Confucian order, Neo-Daoism and Buddhism began to exert an increasing influence on the intelligentsia in southern China. During the Six Dynasties period, a historical moment of political division and social instability, the perfection of selfhood came to be conceived, as a "dynamic process of spiritual development" the internal generative force of which was often said to be heavenly endowed in nature. Spiritual realization of this heavenly endowed humanity or selfhood could be accomplished through specific ritual acts of self-cultivation. It was during this time that members of China's cultured scholarly elite adopted the practice of calligraphy and the playing of the lute (van Gulick, 1969) as the specific means to pursue aesthetic self-expression and self-cultivation. As Tu Wei-ming has noted, "One learns to play the lute or to sing lyric songs in order to communicate with others and, more importantly perhaps, to experience the internal resonance one shares with nature" (Tu, 1983, p. 62).

The importance of cultural mediation for the project of spiritual realization can be seen in Tu Wei-ming's summary of the views of the Buddhist monk Hu Zhuren:

> although human nature in its original substance is completely identical with the ordering principle of the universe, the human mind has to be purified through learn-

> ing before it can fully realize the principle inherent in human nature. (Tu, 1979, p. 242)

The way of heaven (*tian*) is thus immanent to selfhood. "It is the root from which great cultural ideals and spiritual values grow" (Tu, 1979, p. 247).

In Neo-Daoist inspired calligraphy of the Eastern Jin dynasty (317–420 CE), for example, the metaphysical principle *ziran* (naturalness or self-so-ing), an impersonal creative potential, is cited as one of the most important aesthetic principles. The Northern Song calligrapher/connoisseur Mi Fu (1052–1107 CE) reserved the aesthetic ideal of *tianzhen* (natural perfection) to praise the calligraphy of the Eastern Jin master Wang Xianzhi (344–388 CE). Lothar Ledderose has observed that "plain tranquility [*pingdan*] and natural perfection [*tianzhen*] were not only stylistic and aesthetic concepts which could be used to describe and evaluate works of calligraphy, but these terms also described the ideal state of mind of the artist" (Ledderose, 1979, p. 58). According to Mi Fu, "the movement of the brush should come swiftly with a natural perfection and emerge unintentionally" (Ledderose, 1979, p. 64). An appeal to an egoistic source of creativity would simply be unthinkable.

One of the distinguishing features of early Chinese aesthetic discourse is a predominance of physiological and nature imagery. The following passage from the *Bizhen tu*, a text attributed variously to Wei Furen (272–349 CE) and to Wang Xizhi (321–379 CE), exemplifies the way in which the aesthetic discourse on Chinese calligraphy is framed in the terminology of human physiology:

> Calligraphy by those good in brush strength has much bone; that by those not good in brush strength has much flesh. Calligraphy that has much bone but slight flesh is called sinew-writing; that with much flesh but slight bone is called ink-pig. Calligraphy with much strength and rich in sinew is of sage-like quality; that with neither strength nor sinew is sick. Every writer proceeds in accordance with the manifestation of their digestion and respiration of energy, *hsiao-hsi* [*xiaoxi*]. (Hay, 1983, p. 85)

In another passage in the *Bizhen tu*, images from nature are used to characterize the ideal rendering of the seven strokes that represent the so-called "diagram of the battle formation of the brush":

> First stroke – Like a cloud formation stretching a thousand *li*; indistinct, but not without form.
> Second stroke – Like a stone falling from a high peak, bouncing and crashing, about to shatter.
> Third stroke – The tusk of an elephant or rhinoceros (thrust into and) broken by the ground.
> Fourth stroke – Fired from a three-thousand pound crossbow.
> Fifth stroke – A withered vine, ten thousand years old.
> Sixth stroke – Crashing waves or rolling thunder.
> Seventh stroke – The sinews and joints of a mighty bow.
> (Barnhart, 1964, p. 16)

The *Bizhen tu* appears in the earliest extant collection of texts on calligraphy, *Fashu Yaolu* (ca. 847 CE), by the ninth-century scholar Zhang Yanyuan. It was first translated into English by Lucy Driscoll and Kenji Toda (Driscoll and Toda, 1935, pp. 41–460). For a study of the authenticity of this text, see Barnhart, 1964, pp. 13–25.

The deployment of metaphorical imagery, referencing the human body and nature in Chinese aesthetic theory, is not simply a rhetorical semantic flourish but, in fact, serves a specific epistemological function. It constitutes an indigenous correlative rhetoric stemming from the Chinese view of spiritual development that sought within the ritual aesthetic acts of self-cultivation to embody patterns of behavior deemed consonant with the immanent patterns perceived within the natural order of things.

Early Chinese aesthetic theory is a representational practice that is based on the concepts of *lei* (kind or categorical correlations) and *ganlei* "responding according to categorical correlation." "Categorial correlation" is fundamental to the *Classic of Changes* (*Yijing*) and central to the ancient Chinese cosmological principle expressed in the statement by Dong Zhongshu (ca. 179–104 BCE) that "things that categorically correspond move each other' (Yu, 1987, p. 42). In Han and pre-Han dynasty texts, the concept of *ganlei* became the normative basis upon which human actions, particularly those of the ruler, were deemed to be linked in a chain of causality to the larger human order as well as the cosmic order of things. This is predicated on the existence of fundamental correlations between natural patterns or *wen* and human affairs.

The concept of *ganlei* plays a prominent role in Zong Bing's (375–443 CE) essay *Hua shanshui xu* ("A Preface to the Painting of Mountains and Rivers"), "the earliest extant philosophical treatise of painting ever written in China" (Kiyohiko Munakata, 1983, p. 105). This can be illustrated in the following passage:

> Now the Sage, with his spirit realizes the Way; thus the worthy can pass through it. Mountains and rivers (likewise), with their forms, relish the way; thus the virtuous can enjoy it. How *similar* they are to each other! (Munakata, 1983, p. 118)

The reference to "mountains and rivers" alludes to the Chinese term for landscape painting, *shanshui hua* (literally, "mountain-water painting"). Zong Bing's categorical correlation of the "Sage" and "mountains and rivers" brings to mind a passage from the Confucian *Analects* or *Lunyu*:

> The Master said, "The wise [*zhi*] find joy in water [*shui*]; the benevolent [*ren*] find joy in mountains. The wise are active [*dong*]; the benevolent are still [*jing*]. The wise are joyful [*li*]; the benevolent are long-lived [*shou*]." (Lau, 1992, p. 53)

The mountains and waters thus come to symbolize, respectively, the dimensions of constancy and change and, by metaphorical extension, tradition and its creative appropriation to the conditions of an ever-changing present.

These two citations offer a revealing insight concerning the implicit significance which the painting of landscapes has had for the Chinese artist. In the words of Hall and Ames,

> Tradition has it that the Sage-rulers of antiquity observed regularity and order implicit in the natural process and sought to devise formal rules of conduct that would enable human beings to make the same cosmological patterns explicit in their own lives. (Hall and Ames, 1987, pp. 88–9)

Although the correlative rhetoric of *ganlei* plays an important role in early Chinese aesthetic theory, it was soon eclipsed by such physiological concepts as *qi* (vital force or energy flow) or *qiyun* (resonance of vital force) and *xue* (blood) or *xuemo* (blood-pulse). *Qi* is variously translated as "breath," "spirit" or "energy" – the vital force that animates life. *Xue* or *xuemo*, when it appears in discussions on calligraphy, refers to the energy functioning through the rhythmic flow of the ink within and between the characters.

John Hay, in his seminal essay "The Human Body as a Microcosmic Source of Macrocosmic Values in Calligraphy," argues for the importance of interpreting these aesthetic terms in the perspective of contemporary medical treatises. Citing the studies of Chinese medicine by Manfred Porkert, Hay observes that *qi* and *xue* are the two most important states of energy within the body and that the vital function of the latter depends "on its particular intrinsic quality and its harmony with the other forms of energy, especially *ch'i* [*qi*]" (Hay, 1983, p. 86). Painting and calligraphy are thus conceived as configurations of energy, materializing through the brush into the traces of ink.

The quintessential use of *qi* as an aesthetic term appears in the *Liu Fa* or "Six Laws" of painting by the portrait-painter and theorist Xie He (active 500–535 CE). The "Six Laws" appears in the introductory chapter of Xie He's *Guhua Pinlu* or *Record of the Classification of Old Paintings*. (For a discussion and translation of this text, see Acker, 1954.)

The first, and thus most important of Xie He's laws, is "*Qiyun shengdong*," which can be translated as "Life-movement [is achieved through] spirit resonance (or resonance of vital force)." *Xue*, or the energy functioning through the rhythmic flow of the ink, is implied in the second of Xie He's laws of painting: "*Gufa yongbi*" or "Bone-method (that is, inner structure) when wielding the brush." This can be interpreted as indicating the precise way in which to achieve "spirit resonance."

The reference to Chinese medical theory suggests another important source for the deployment of metaphorical imagery referencing the human body and nature in Chinese aesthetic theory. Previously, we noted that ritual aesthetic acts of self-cultivation embody patterns of behavior deemed consonant with the immanent patterns perceived within the natural order of things. In traditional Chinese medical treatises, the body is conceived as a system or network of patterned energy flow and transformation, that is, as a *microcosmic correlative of the macrocosmic world of nature*. Painting and calligraphy, conceived as configurations of energy, materializing through movements of the brush into the traces of ink, thus came to be seen as ways of capturing the patterns of *shengdong* or "life movement" of the phenomenal world.

Jing Hao's *Bifaji* or "A Note on the Art of the Brush," one of the most important theories of landscape painting, is a reformulation of Xie He's "Six Laws" for the purpose of representing the landscape. Jing Hao was a Confucian scholar-painter (active ca. 900–950 CE) who, during the social and political turmoil of the Five Dynasties Period, retired to the Taihang mountains of Southern Shenxi. He wrote the *Bifaji* during a period that witnessed the emergence of true landscape painting in China.

The centerpiece of the *Bifaji* is the list of "Six Essentials" in painting a landscape, reported to have been conveyed to the author/narrator by a rustic old man whom he came upon while painting in the Stone-Drum Cave.

> *Spirit* (*ch'i*) [*qi*] is obtained when your mind moves along with the movement of the brush and does not hesitate in delineating images. *Resonance* (*yun*) is obtained when you establish forms while hiding [obvious] traces of the brush, and perfect them by observing the proprieties and avoiding vulgarity. *Thought* (*ssu*) [si] is obtained when you grasp essential forms eliminating unnecessary details [in your observation of nature], and let your ideas crystallize into forms to be represented. (Munakata, 1974, p. 12)

These first three essentials of landscape painting prescribe artistic norms and conventions for the use of brush and ink that are self-effacing, concealing all traces of the material or formal process of representation and thus, by implication, all traces of personal expression, in order to give transparent access to that which is represented.

Jing Hao's "Six Essentials of Painting" exhibits the influence of Neo-Confucian values when it emphasizes the disclosure and transmission, through the receptive mind and the responsive hand of the painter, of the immanent patterns of nature in terms of the rhythmic patterned relations of the painted landscape forms.

The re-establishment of national unity and order under the Song dynasty (960–1279 CE) ushered in social and political conditions that were conducive to the formulation of a new literati aesthetic. The feudal aristocracy of landed gentry, prominent during the Tang dynasty, gave way in the Song to an "aristocracy of merit" (Bush, 1971, p. 4), a "meritocracy," as civil service examinations provided truly talented scholars with access to high government office.

Toward the end of the Northern Song (960–1126 CE), a new and distinctive literati style of painting and calligraphy began to develop among a small circle of scholar-officials. A literati aesthetic theory was also formulated in an attempt to define the artistic and social identity of what the great Song poet and calligrapher Su Shi (1037–1101 CE) referred to as *shiren hua* (scholar's art), in contradistinction to that of the professional painter and calligrapher. Where professional artists were dependent upon and sought the patronage of others for their livelihood, the literatus engaged in the practice of painting and calligraphy as a means of self-cultivation, self-expression and social exchange with other, like-minded scholars.

A key tenet of literati aesthetics, the claim of equivalence between literati painting and poetry, appears in an inscription written by Su Shi on a painting by the great Tang poet Wang Wei.

> When one savors Mo-chieh's poems, there are paintings in them,
> When one looks at Mo-chieh's pictures, there are poems.
> (Bush, 1971, p. 25)

Song literati aesthetic theory discounted the mere technical skill of the professional painter to represent nature in favor of what would come to be termed *xieyi* (to sketch, or paint ideas). Terms such as *chu* (mood or flavor) and *pingdan* (plain-tranquility), figure prominently in the writings of Mi Fu (1052–1107 CE) and his son, Mi Yuren (1086–1165 CE). These aesthetic terms identify the emotionally nuanced *yi* (quality or idea) of a scene, which can only come to artistic expression through the cultivated sensibilities of the literatus. For example, in Mi Fu's opinion, "When Chu-jan was young, he made many [forms like] 'alum lumps'; when he was older, in his tranquility (*pingdan*) the flavor (*ch'u*) [Chu] was lofty" (Bush, 1971, p. 68). *Pingdan*, "a simplicity with underlying depth" (Bush, 1971, p. 72), was used by Mi Fu to describe both the artist and his work.

The literati style placed less emphasis on the descriptive depiction of nature, choosing rather to foreground the expressive potentialities of a more "calligraphic" handling of the brush. Landscape and architectural motifs are conceived in a rather schematic or ideographic manner, through the inscription of subtly articulated traces of brush and ink that make indexical reference back to the very gestural process of its execution.

To establish the special status of their artistic and social identity, literati such as Wen Tong, Huang Tingjian, Mi Fu and Mi Youren often referred to their own art and the art of other scholar-officials by the self-effacing term *moxi*, or "ink-play." It was, of course, a mock-humble way of asserting their amateur status as scholar-artists.

During the succeeding Mongol-Yuan dynasty (1260–1368 CE), literati theory consciously stressed the non-professional status of the scholar-painter and the expressive, non-representational style of literati painting. For Zhao Mengfu (1254–1322 CE), a brilliant painter and calligrapher, it was the intimate relationship between the two disciplines that marked the new literati style:

> Rocks like the "flying white" [brush stroke], trees like great seal script:
> To sketch bamboo also demands conversance with the "Eight Methods" [of calligraphy].
> If there should be one capable of this,
> He must know that calligraphy and painting have one origin.
> (Bush and Shih, 1985, pp. 278–9)

A traditionalist and high offical, Zhao Mengfu came to be associated with the concept *guyi*, or the "sense of antiquity":

> A sense of antiquity is essential in painting. If there is no sense of antiquity, then although a work is skillful, it is without value. Modern painters only know how to use the brush in a detailed manner and apply colors abundantly, and then think that they

> are competent artists. The fact is that if a sense of antiquity is lacking, all types of faults appear throughout a work, and why should one look at it? What I paint seems to be summary and rough, but connoisseurs realize that it is close to the ancients, and so consider it beautiful. (Bush, 1971, pp. 121–2)

A more individualist position is asserted by such reclusive scholar-painters as Wu Zhen and Ni Can (1301–1374 CE). Often, as in the following colophon by Ni Can (1301–1374 CE), dated 1368, there is a self-conscious affirmation of the status of literati painting as ink-play that takes great liberty in the rendering of motifs in the interest of expressing the artist's mood:

> Chang I-chung [?] [Zhang Yizhong] always likes my bamboo paintings. I do bamboo simply to express the untrammeled spirit (*i-ch'i*) in my breast. Then how can I judge whether it is like something or not; where its leaves are luxuriant or sparse, its branches slanting or straight? Often when I have daubed and rubbed awhile, others seeing this take it to be hemp or rushes. Since I cannot bring myself to argue that it is truly bamboo, then what of the onlookers? I simply do not know what sort of things I-chung is seeing. (Bush and Shih, 1985, p. 280)

In the Ming dynasty (1368–1644 CE), China was once again under native rule. Aesthetic theory as well as artistic practice came to take on an art historical dimension, as scholar-painters explicitly reasserted their social and artistic identities within a lineage of literati painters and calligraphers that is traced back through the Yuan and Song to the patriarchs of the tradition – Wang Wei, Tong Yuan, and Zhuran. Towards the end of the Ming, this tendency culminates in the formulation of the theory of the "Northern and Southern Schools" of painting (*nanbei pai*), variously attributed to the writings of Dong Qichang (1555–1636 CE), Mo Shilong (d. 1587 CE), and Chen Jiru (1558–1639 CE). The title makes reference to the Northern and Southern schools of Chan Buddhism, the schools of gradual and sudden enlightenment, respectively. This theory systematically establishes the canon of literati painting and calligraphy (the Southern School) as the orthodox tradition for future generations of scholar-painters.

Dong Qichang formulates an aesthetic theory and artistic practice that synthesizes the classicist and individualist tendencies of the preceding Yuan dynasty. This is examplified in Dong Qichang's "Hills on a Clear Autumn Day, After Huang Gongwang" in the Cleveland Museum of Art. An inscription on the painting by the artist informs us that it was based on a now-lost Huang Gongwang composition: "Huang Gongwang's 'Hills on a Clear Autumn Day' looks like this. It is too bad that the old master cannot see my work." James Cahill interprets this to mean that "the *shen-hui*, or 'communion of the spirit,' that ideally exists between a modern painter and the earlier artist he imitates should logically go both ways" (Cahill, 1982, p. 102).

For the Ming master, the proper approach to the canonical art of the past involves "creative imitation" (*fang*) and "transformation" (*bian*) within one's own personal style in a way that will allow one to speak with authority to the historical and art historical conditions of the present. As Dong Qichang writes,

> Chu-jan [Zhuran] followed [imitated] Tung [Tong] Yuan, Mi Fu followed Tung Yuan, Huang Kungwang and Ni Tsan both followed Tung Yuan. It was all the same Tung Yuan, but their several [versions of his style] did not resemble each other. If another kind of painter had done it, it would have been just like a copy. How could anything done that way be transmitted down through the ages? (Cahill, 1982, p. 123)

It is precisely through an interpretive re-inscription or "embodiment" of the "orthodox" tradition within his own body of artistic expression, that the scholar-painter, sanctioned by the past, comes to signify himself in the present. Dong Qichang's notions of *shenhui* (communion of the spirit), *fang* (creative imitation), and *bian* (transformation) established the basis for both the Orthodox and Individualist Schools of literati painting in the Qing dynasty (1645–1912 CE).

Bibliography

Writings

Acker, W. R. B. 1954: *Some Tang and Pre-Tang Texts on Chinese Painting* (Leiden: E. J. Brill).

Bush, S. 1971: *The Chinese Literati on Painting: Su Shih (1037–1101) to Tung Ch'i-ch'ang (1555–1636)* (Cambridge, Mass.: Harvard University Press).

Bush, S. and Murck, C. (eds) 1983: *Theories of the Arts in China* (Princeton: Princeton University Press).

Bush, S. and Shih, H. Y. (compilers and eds) 1985: *Early Chinese Texts on Painting*. Cambridge, Mass. and London, England: Harvard University Press.

Zhang, Y. Y. [1936] 1962: *Fashu Yaolu* (ca. 847), Ming edition of Mao Jin (1599–1659) (Reprinted in *Cong Shu Ji Cheng*, Shanghai, 1936, nos 1626–7; and the recent *Cong Shu, Yi Shu Cong pian*, Taipei, 1962, Vol. 1).

References and further reading

Barnhart, R. M. 1964: "Wei Fu-jen's *Pi Chen T'u* and the Early Texts on Calligraphy," *Archives of the Chinese Art Society of America*, 18, pp. 13–25.

Cahill, J. 1960: "Confucian Elements in the Theory of Painting," in *The Confucian Persuasion*, ed. A. Wright (Stanford: Stanford University Press), pp. 115–40.

—— 1982: *The Distant Mountains: Chinese Painting of the Late Ming Dynasty, 1570–1644* (New York and Tokyo: Weatherhill).

Driscoll, L. and Toda, K. 1935: *Chinese Calligraphy*. (Chicago: University of Chicago Press).

Hall, D. L. and Ames, R. T. 1987: *Thinking Through Confucius* (Albany: State University of New York Press).

Hay, J. 1983: "The Human Body as a Microcosmic Source of Macrocosmic Values in Calligraphy," in *Theories of the Arts in China*, ed. S. Bush and C. Murck (Princeton: Princeton University Press), pp. 74–102.

Lau, D. C. (tr.) 1992: *The Analects* (Hong Kong: Chinese University Press).

Ledderose, L. 1979: *Mi Fu and the Classical Tradition of Chinese Calligraphy* (Princeton, NJ: Princeton University Press).

Munakata, K. 1974: *Ching Hao's Pi-fa-chi: a Note on the Art of Brush* (Ascona: Artibus Asiae Publishers).

—— 1983: "Concepts of *Lei* and *Kan-lei* in Early Chinese Art Theory,' in *Theories of the Arts in China*, ed. S. Bush and C. Murck (Princeton: Princeton University Press), pp. 105–31.

Tu Weiming 1979: "Ultimate Self-Transformation as a Communal Act: Comments on Modes of Self-Cultivation in Traditional China," *Journal of Chinese Philosophy*, 6, pp. 237–46.

—— 1985: *Confucian Thought: Selfhood as Creative Transformation* (New York: State University of New York Press).

van Gulick, R. H. 1969: *The Love of the Chinese Lute*, 2nd revd edn (Tokyo: Tuttle).

Yu, P. 1987: *The Reading of Imagery in Chinese Poetic Tradition* (Princeton: Princeton University Press).

THE INDIAN TRADITION

16

Socio-political thought in classical India

DAYA KRISHNA

Indian classical thought about society and polity had to deal with a basic dilemma which was set for it by the fundamental premises of the culture in which it developed. This derived from the fact that both Buddhism and Jainism, which emerged as powerful forces on the Indian scene sometime in the sixth century BCE, regarded the social and political worlds not only as inferior realities in relation to the ultimate pursuit of man, but also as impeding that pursuit to a substantive extent. And this, strangely enough, occurred in spite of the fact that both of these religions spread with the active support of kings and wealthy merchants, as evidenced in the earliest stories pertaining to the times of the Buddha and the Mahāvīra (the founder of Jainism). Yet, as every thinker concerned with these realms well knows, they constitute the very basis and foundation of all the worthwhile pursuits of man, including the spiritual pursuits. Thinkers dealing with these subjects, therefore, had simultaneously to be true to the reality of the realm they were thinking about and also be on the right side of the values dominant in the culture in which they lived. In addition, they had to take into account the changes that occurred in their culture over time, for while both society and polity may have dimensions that are comparatively invariant, there are also those which are subject to important changes that inevitably occur with the passage of time. The latter feature is revealed more in the legal texts, which have to take note of the changes that occur in social customs and deal with them fairly directly, than in the theoretical and abstract issues relating to society and polity with which the social and political theorists are primarily concerned.

Any discussion of classical Indian thought about society and polity, has thus inevitably to take into account Indian thought about man, on the one hand, and law, on the other. The texts relating to these discussions are roughly known as the *Dharmaśāstras*, the *Vyavahāraśāstras*, and the *Rājanītiśāstras*. The term "*śāstra*" denotes a systematic body of knowledge, and the terms "*dharma*," "*vyavahāra*" and "*rājanīti*" denote what is generally conveyed in the English language by morality, law and polity. That society is primarily seen as belonging to the moral dimension of man speaks volumes for the way in which man himself was understood in the Indian tradition. Society was seen primarily as the realm in which an individual had obligations to others – obligations that were understood in terms of the roles that he or she occupied in the system. These obligations, however, had to be coordinated with the claims of the transcendent self as well as with the claims of all other beings – including the gods, close relatives who were dead, and other living beings in the world. The term "*dharma*" thus has a far wider connotation than is usually indicated by the term "morality" in the English language. The realm of *vyavahāra*, or law, was however far more concrete and related to the adjudication of disputes that were enforceable by the judicial and political authorities, and often, by quasi-judicial institutions whose authority, however, was formally recognized by the political system wherein rested the use of legitimate coercive power. The technical term for this was "*daṇḍa*," which primarily means both "punishment" and "instruments of punishment." The science of polity thus was also called *daṇḍanīti*. The realm of the political, however, was not confined wholly to the legitimate exercise of coercion in the service of the maintenance of *dharma* or the moral order, but had also to be seen in relation to other polities amidst which it was situated.

The relation of society, polity and law were complicated in classical Indian thought by a number of factors that are important to keep in mind. Thinking about society, as has been repeatedly stressed, was primarily undertaken in relation to the *varṇa* or class/caste scheme, in terms of which society has been thought to be integrally constituted. The well known scheme of four *varṇas* – that is, the *brāhmaṇa* (priest), the *kṣatriya* (warrior), the *vaiśya* (merchant) and the *śūdra* (worker) – is supposed to have been derived from the Vedas themselves, wherein it is allegedly said that the cosmic being divided itself into these four classes from different parts of its body. (The English equivalents of these terms, though fairly commonly used, are misleading, as is explained later in the article. The term "*brāhmaṇa*," for example, does not refer only to priests, but also to all those who maintain, transmit and develop systems of traditional knowledge in any field whatsoever. Similarly, the term "*vaiśya*" applies as much to those who cultivate land as to those who engage in trade or commerce. The term "*śūdra*" is a residual category and applies to the whole artisan class which is engaged in the manufacture of all sorts of things, including what are today called "handicrafts.") The body social, therefore, is supposed to represent, at the level of society, the cosmic being itself, from which it was supposed to have originated. However, the Vedic source of the theory of cosmic creation, or more correctly, of cosmic diremption, does not confine itself to the creation of these four *varṇas* alone, but rather is concerned with the coming into being of the whole manifest universe, with the important proviso that the cosmic being manifests itself in this universe with only one-fourth of its being, while three-fourths of it remains unmanifest. Moreover, if one looks at some of the original passages wherein the existence of the *varṇas* is first described, as in the *Śukla Yajurveda*, for instance, one finds that besides the basic four *varṇas*, others are mentioned that are specifically classified as *abrāhamaṇāḥ, aśūdrāḥ* (non-brahmins and non-śūdras) in the concluding line, so that it is difficult to see how the myth of there being *only* four *varṇas* in the body social ever arose. (It is obvious that these multifarious classes, professions, and so on, mentioned in the text could not be *kṣatriyas* or *vaiśyas* either). Not only this, there is sufficient evidence in Jaimini's *Mīmāṃsāsūtras* that if the Vedic injunctions were to be taken seriously, then at least two classes mentioned therein – that is, the *rathakāra* and the *niṣadapati* – could not be included in any of these *varṇas*. It should be noted that the former is an occupational class, that is, those who build chariots, while the latter perhaps designates a tribal chief. There are other places in the recognized portion of the "revealed" texts known as *śruti* that seem to question even the exclusion of the *śūdras* from access to the *śruti* and the performance of the *yajñas* or sacrifices prescribed therein. The most notable and radical example is found in the *Aitareya Brāhmaṇa*. However, these only show the ambivalence of the pronouncements in the texts which are by common consent included in what is known as the *śruti*.

In the Chāndogya Upaniṣad, the story of Satyakāma Jābāla is one of the internally subverting portions of the material included in the *śruti*. The ambivalence and the internal tension in the authoritative texts can perhaps be explained either in terms of the inner conflict in the tradition itself or by means of the hypothesis that those portions of the texts that seem to have questioned the orthodox positions might have appeared earlier or later, as the case may be. In fact, the explicit proclamation of Bharata in the *Nātya Śāstra* that it is *sārvavarṇika* – that is, open to all the *varṇas* – might be seen as a statement made in full self-consciousness against the claims of the Veda which, according to the orthodox view, was accessible only to the first three *varṇas*. Its self-description as the fifth Veda also seems to support this view, although there seems to have been a tendency for important works in the tradition to assume this title in order to claim for themselves an authority equivalent to that of the Veda or even superior to it. The Mahābhārata provides another well known example of this tendency.

The theory of *varṇa*, however, was only an ideal construct and seemed to have had only a formal classificatory validity, as what existed in fact was a very large number of *jātis* which, theoretically, were supposed to belong to one or the other of the four *varṇas*. However, whether seen as a formal classification or as an ideal construct, it should be understood as an articulation of the four primary functions that any human society will have to maintain, foster and develop in order to be a society. The functions may be regarded as relating to knowledge, power, wealth, and labour, and may be seen as associated respectively with the *varṇas* designated as *brāhmaṇa*, *kṣatriya*, *vaiśya*, and *śūdra* respectively. The contention, therefore, seems to have been that the body social is an organic unity of all these functions and those who primarily or predominantly perform these functions may be designated by these terms.

The first issue of debate among social theorists, therefore, was whether the terms designating the functions should be understood in terms of "ascription" or "achievement." Does a person belong to these categories by birth or by virtue of his acquired capacities or abilities to perform those functions? The well known statement that by birth everyone is a *śūdra* epitomizes this view, for presumably everyone can perform the labour function by virtue of the fact that one has a body. But such a view could never gain any large social sanction for the simple reason that society cannot wait for one's capacities to unfold before assigning one to a particular *varṇa*, even if only for ritual purposes. And, in any case, ascriptive determinations are always easier than those based on "achievement," which is hardly constant over time.

Yet though the classification by birth was overwhelmingly chosen, socio-political theorists still faced the difficult problem of establishing a method for determining who was qualified to be a king and perform the ruling function. In accordance with the *varṇa* theory, only a *kṣatriya* could perform this function, since to be a *kṣatriya* almost analytically entailed that one was fit to exercise this function. But obviously if one were to decide who was a *kṣatriya* by appeal to the criterion of birth, one might be landed with a ruler who was totally incompetent to rule. On the other hand, if one usurped the ruling function by force of arms or in any other way, then one became the *de facto* ruler and exercised power, and thus provided concrete evidence that one was a *kṣatriya*. Both horns of the dilemma are frequently encountered in the socio-political thought of India and, after long debate, the conclusion was reached that though it would be best if a ruler were born a *kṣatriya*, anyone who is capable of exercising the ruling function well should be the ruler and be reqarded as a *kṣatriya*. The history of India is replete with this *de facto* recognition of rulers as *kṣatriyas* – that is, as those who had the skill to become kings – without anyone caring whether they were born as *kṣatriyas* or not. The great empires known in India right from the Mauryan times onwards, were seldom founded by a person belonging to the *kṣatriya varṇa*, or to a *jāti* supposed to belong to this *varṇa*.

The socio-political theorists of India had, however, not only to face the question of who could exercise the ruling function, given the theory of *varṇa* that they had inherited from ancient times, but also the question of how exactly the ideal relations between the different *varṇas* were to be understood. Here, obviously, the problem related primarily to the three upper *varṇas*, as the *śūdras* did not enter the picture except in a residual or marginal manner. The conflict between power and knowledge and wealth is writ large in the history of all civilizations, but it took a peculiar turn in the history of thought about society and polity in India. In fact, the conflict between the *brāhmaṇas* and the *kṣatriyas* is well known from the most ancient times, recorded as it is in the earliest texts. However, the conflict that engaged the attention of the socio-political theorists most involved the "overseeing" by the brahmanical *varṇa* of those who exercised the ruling function, and of the former's attempts to ensure that the rulers observed the norms that were expected of them. This obviously was not palatable to the rulers, as they did not want any constraints placed on the exercise of their power. The realm of politics, like the realm of love, tends toward the violation of all norms whatsoever. In the Indian context, in which the general term for all norms is *dharma*, the conflict is thus centered around the observance of *dharma* by the king. The first move that was made to ensure the safety of the censors or the critics of those who ruled was to argue that they should be immune from any punishment, as it was feared that the king might implicate them with all sorts of false accusations and punish them for being outspoken in their criticism of what the ruling power did.

The technical name for this was *adaṇḍya* and many of the early legal texts laid down that the *brāhmaṇa* is *adaṇḍya*. But as this seemed to go against the principle of justice, later texts argued for a differential theory of punishment for the same offense, suggesting that the punishment should be correlated to what was expected from a particular *varṇa* and hence, while many offenses were lightly treated in the case of the *śūdras*, who were not supposed to live up to strict norms in certain areas of conduct, the *brāhmaṇa* was to be punished more severely, since more was expected of him. On the other hand, there were certain other types of offenses for which he was let off lightly. Ultimately, however, this also offended the sense of justice and it was argued that only capital punishment should never be given to a *brāhmaṇa*. But then the last of the important legal texts, the *Śukranīti*, argues for the abolition of capital punishment for all *varṇas* and seems to suggest that one ought not to make a distinction between the *brāhmaṇa* and the non-*brāhmaṇa* in this regard. The story of India's legal thought on this matter, moving gradually from the contention that *brāhmaṇas* should be *adaṇḍya* to the conclusion that they should be *avadhya* (that is, someone who cannot be killed), is fascinating, showing as it does the successive stages in the thinking of the legal theorists as they struggled to safeguard the brahmans' independence so that they might exercise their function fearlessly in the body politic of those times.

It has become fashionable these days to characterize classical Indian civilization as brahmanical in character, forgetting that all civilizations are inevitably brahmanical, since those who articulate, conceptualize, argue for and defend the deepest concerns of any civilization cannot but be those who are committed to intellectual pursuits and who are concerned preeminently with reflection on the norms by which individuals, societies and polities should be governed. The brahmanical class in India not only did this to a substantial degree, but also tried to ensure that the function they exercised was valued highly by the society itself. There can, of course, be differences among civilizations as to which social function they regard as the highest. Some may opt for power and others for wealth. But as far as the classical Indian tradition was concerned, the only rival to the claim made on behalf of knowledge as the highest pursuit of man was the claim advanced on behalf of the pursuit of transcendence or, to use the term coined by the tradition itself for this pursuit, *mokṣa*. The ascetic renouncer epitomized in the Buddhist *bhikṣu* and the Jain *muni* from the sixth century BCE onwards was regarded as pursuing something higher and nobler than what the *brāhmaṇa* pursued.

There were earlier precedents for this in the Upaniṣadic and even in the Vedic tradition, but there the life of the householder and the life of the renouncer were not separated in such a clear-cut manner or seen as radically antagonistic to each other. This ultimate superiority of the ascetic renouncer even to those who exercised the knowledge and the norm-establishing function in the Indian tradition introduced a new problematic for the socio-political thinkers of India. For while most societies and civilizations have known the conflict between knowledge and power, few have witnessed a comparable tension between those who have renounced the world (including not only family, society and polity, but also the pursuit of knowledge in the usual sense of the word) and those who have not. However, if one is a socio-political thinker, one has to accept the reality and validity of society and polity, and one cannot subordinate the claims of these realms that are the object of one's study to those which deny them altogether, at least in principle if not in practice. And yet an almost insoluble problem is set for such thinkers if the culture itself accords the highest value to the life of the renouncer. As everyone knows, this was the case in India, and consequently a large part of its socio-political thought was concerned with solving this insoluble dilemma. There are, of course, deep differences in this regard between the social theorists on the one hand and the political theorists on the other, particularly those among the latter who are exclusively concerned with the realm of the political.

The conflict between the *kṣatriya* and the *brāhmaṇa* is well known to students of Indian thought, as is the fact that they were mutually indispensable. Similarly, the conflict between the *brāhmaṇa* and the *śramaṇa* (the renouncer) is also well known, though not much emphasized in the socio-political thought of India. However, the relation between the *kṣatriya* – or to be more precise in this context, the *rājanya* or king – and the *śramaṇa* or renouncer has seldom been discussed. Yet right from the earliest Buddhist and Jain texts recounting the lives of the Buddha and the Mahāvīra, it was a point of special emphasis that the ruling kings in those times not only paid visits to these outstanding spiritual personalities of the time, but showed proper respect by getting down from their elephants and chariots and walking on foot to the abode of the master. Many of the Mughal paintings display continuity in this regard as they show Mughal emperors visiting the hermitages of saints, both Muslim and non-Muslim, in a respectful manner and generally on foot. In fact, in many of the stories in both the Buddhist and the Jain canons we hear of kings who got converted to these religions and sometimes even renounced their kingship to pursue the path of the renouncer. But normally the tension between the two roles seldom comes into the open. However, one does sometimes become aware of it indirectly, as in the stories in which the Buddha's own father requests him to make a rule that no young person will be allowed to join the *saṁgha*, or at least none who has not been permitted by his parents to do so. This obviously hints at the tension generated by the large-scale recruitment of the young to the life of the renouncers. But far more telling and explicit is the statement in the political texts of the tradition that any person desirous of *mokṣa* should not be appointed as minister by the king, and that the king himself should not think of leaving his responsibilities or retire to the forest.

The triangular relation between the seekers and wielders of power, and those who seek knowledge and to articulate norms for human behavior, and those who search for final liberation and transcendence from the world of space, time and causality would make an interesting theme for exploration, particularly in the context of the dilemmas that Indian civilization faced in its diverse pursuits. But it needs to be remembered that while many might be engaged in the pursuit of knowledge and some in the search for liberation, the ruler in any particular realm could only be a single person, and though the term "*rājanya*" generally stands for one who rules, it is flexible enough to be applied to anyone who exercises the ruling function over the smallest territory. By its very nature, the ruling function does not and cannot admit of plurality or multiplicity amongst those who exercise it in the political sense, that is, as wielders of legitimate coercive power. The term "*kṣatriya*," therefore, has an ambiguity about it that the term "*brāhmaṇa*" or the terms for the renouncers ("*bhikṣu*," "*muni*," or "*sannyāsī*") would not usually have. The term "*kṣatriya*" in the tradition applies both to one who rules in the political sense of the term and also to one who earns his living by means of carrying or wielding arms. The two functions are obviously related to each other, but they are also essentially different in that one who rules utilizes those whose profession consists in the skillful use of arms in the service of anyone who is prepared to employ them. The *brāhmaṇa*, on the other hand, is supposed to engage in the search for knowledge, especially of the Vedas, and in teaching this to others. It should be noted in this connection that the knowledge relating to the Vedas covered a very wide field and included even such sciences as astronomy, geometry, linguistics, grammar, and almost everything directly or indirectly related to the maintenance and preservation of the Vedic texts, on the one hand, and to the performance of the *yajña* or the sacrificial rituals enjoined in them, on the other.

The ambivalent relations between knowledge and power and of both to the renouncers have not gone unnoticed in the literature on the subject, but the same cannot be said about the relations between those who sought wealth, the *vaiśyas*, and those who wielded power and knowledge, on the one hand, and those who renounced the pursuit of all worldly ends, on the other. The texts on the subject also seem to show an awareness only of the problems concerning the relations of power and wealth, and not of those between wealth and knowledge, or between wealth and the pursuit of the radical renunciatory ideal. The discussion in the texts regarding the former is mainly confined to the question of how a king should try to get the maximum out of those who create wealth in his kingdom without making them feel that they are being excessively taxed, so that they may not be discouraged in the pursuit itself or leave the realm for other kingdoms. However, in times of emergency the king is both advised and permitted to extract as much as possible even at the risk of antagonizing those who create wealth in his kingdom. There are many amusing analogies given from other fields that suggest ways in which a ruler can collect taxes from the population, and the well known text of Kauṭilya on the subject offers detailed measures to check the loopholes in the taxation system. The ambivalent relations between the *brāhmaṇa* and the *vaiśya* are not discussed in the texts, since normally it is the ruler who is supposed to provide patronage and support to those who pursue knowledge in any form. The pursuit of wealth, however, was not rated very highly among the meaningful pursuits of man, at least as far as the texts are concerned. Yet the virtue of *dāna*, or the giving of gifts to brahmins is extolled very highly and, in fact, there are numerous ritual occasions, from birth to death, at which the brahmins are expected to be compensated for their ritual services. But one has to acquire wealth before one is in a position to give it as a gift to others. Yet the pursuit itself was considered inferior to the pursuit of knowledge or the renunciatory ideal whose practitioners had to depend on the merchant class for their sustenance. Such a dependence on those who sought wealth or power (two meanings of *artha* as a *puruṣārtha*, that is, as an ideal the pursuit of which conferred meaning on human life) was humiliating, for at least theoretically, what they themselves were pursuing was far, far superior to wealth or power. The dilemma and the ambivalence becomes even greater in the case of the renouncer, as he explicitly denies the realms of family, society, and polity altogether and the values that belong to those realms. And yet he has to depend, at least minimally, on society for his own survival and the pursuit of the trans-social and the transcendental value that he has chosen for himself. The dilemma becomes still more acute when, as in the case of the Buddhists and the Jains, their organization of themselves into a community is taken as an essential part of their spiritual pursuit. The Buddhists treat the *saṁgha* as almost coordinate in importance to the Buddha and the *dhamma*, and as for the Jains, though they do not seem to have anything as explicit as the Buddhist vow to take refuge in the *saṁgha* along with the Buddha and the *dhamma*, the actual reality is perhaps even more stringent in their case than in that of the Buddhists. The Buddhist *bhikṣu* or Jain *muni*, in other words, is not an individual wandering ascetic or a *sannyāsī*, who has left the world like the Buddha or the Mahāvīra in search of enlightenment or perfection. He is an integral member of a large community that dictates and determines the shape of his life and spiritual quest in the most detailed manner imaginable. This has far-reaching implications for the style of spiritual seeking itself, but what primarily concerns us here is that, right from the times of the Buddha and the Mahāvīra, the necessity of such forms of organization for the spiritual seeking that the *bhikṣu* and *muni* embodied in their individual lives created a new dimension of large-scale dependence on the ruler, on the one hand, and on the wealthy trading community, on the other. The large-scale support that such organizations required from the society and the polity must have meant that the society and the polity exerted at least some influence on the spiritual pursuit itself. There is some evidence, even in the Upaniṣads, of spiritual seekers depending upon kings – as is related in the stories of Yājñavalkya and Janaka – but there the encounter is primarily individual and involves a debate or discussion regarding certain kinds of knowledge. The Buddhist and the Jain texts talk almost from the very beginning of thousands of *bhikṣus* and *munis* being entertained by wealthy merchants eager to earn merit, which must obviously have meant a great deal given the expenditure incurred on such occasions. Somehow the Buddhist and the Jain forms of large-scale organizations became the dominant model to be revived later by Śaṃkara and followed by later masters and teachers (*ācāryas*) in the Indian tradition, even though the lonely, wandering individual ascetic never disappeared from the scene.

The profound effect of the formation of these "societies" or renouncers and the internal organization of discipline and hierarchies within them has hardly been the subject of study or reflection, particularly as these societies began to have both an economic and political aspect to them, mirroring almost all of the problems of the outside society and polity. The problems of seeking economic and political support and the tensions it generated for the pursuit of spiritual life are writ large not only on the histories of these institutions, but are also depicted on the walls of many of the places where such monasteries were supposed to have been located – as, for example, in Bagh or Ajanta. This, however, opens up a direction of thought that has not been dealt with by the classical thinkers of India.

The political thinkers of India had no such problems as those facing the social theorists, for while the latter had to consider almost all aspects of society and register the conflicting relationships between them, the former were concerned primarily with the realm of the political and treated everything else as a means to the maintenance and enhancement of political power. But as the political thinker was acutely aware, the polity was situated amongst other polities which were always potentially hostile to it. Thus the obligations of a ruler to his own people, even at the theoretical level, had to be balanced against the ever-present possibility of attack from the hostile neighboring kingdom. The political theorist, therefore, was concerned with a dimension that was absent in the work of those who theorized about society for, as far as I know, no one has placed the external relations of a society to other societies at the center of his thought about society. The Indian political theorist developed in this context, the well known theory of concentric circles of neighboring kingdoms, in accordance with which the relations of hostility and friendship were determined to a large extent by geo-political considerations. This is perhaps the first systematic attempt at geo-political thinking anywhere in the world and at seeing the realm of the political as primarily determined by relationships external to a polity, because of its intrinsic character as a polity among other polities and not an isolated unit in itself.

The situation was further complicated by the fact that, in traditional thinking everywhere, it was regarded as legitimate for a ruler to conquer other kingdoms and to extend and expand his area of control as far as possible. The great conquerors of the world have, in fact, been the heroes of history. And though today the ministries until recently designated as ministries of war have become ministries of defence, this change only camouflages the basic truth, which remains the same. Defensive preparedness inevitably includes offensive capability and the task of enlarging one's area of influence both by overt and covert means remains the legitimate exercise of nation-states today, even though each and every state swears by the authority of the United Nations, which it regards as superior to its own.

In the context of classical Indian political thought, however, the legitimation of conquest of neighboring kingdoms followed almost logically from the geo-political analysis of political structures, which entailed that a neighbouring kingdom was bound to be potentially hostile, not because of any perversity on its part, but because of the simple fact that it was situated as it was. As offense is supposed to be the best means of defense, the conquering of neighboring kingdoms was seen not only as the expansion of one's area of influence, but also as the elimination of a potential threat from the geo-politically conditioned hostility of one's neighbor. It was forgotten, however, that the problem of the "neighbor," just like the problem of the frontier, is always bound to be there, since even if a conquest is successful it merely moves the frontier forward, bringing one into contact with another neighbor with whom one will have to contend.

The Indian political theorist tried to come to terms with this inevitable reality imposed by the very structural situation of all polities in two ways. First, he tried to formulate the ideal of *cakravartin* or the ruler who had conquered all that could reasonably be regarded as "available" for conquest in his times. This was the notion of "globalization" in the political context and has continued to hold sway even in modern times in the notion of the superpower. With the elimination of the Soviet Union as the possible counter-contender for that role, the role of the universal *cakravartin* has been self-consciously assumed in our day by the United States, and this has been justified by its political theorists as legitimate in the contemporary context.

The second strategy was to concentrate not on the extent of the dominion over which the conquering function was exercised, but rather on the notion of "conquering" itself. The conquests were thus classified into *sāttvika*, *rājasika*, and *tāmasika*, terms which were borrowed from Sāṁkhya philosophy, but which were modified and used in distinguishing the virtuous from the vicious conqueror. It should be interesting in this regard to note that the motivation for conquest, the conduct of the war and the pacification after victory were all taken into account in this classification. The virtuous conqueror engaged in the exercise only to eliminate potential hostility and normally he was supposed to be satisfied with the acceptance of his suzerainty by the conquered king (or any of his close relatives, if he had been killed in the battle). In fact, the battle itself was supposed to be the last resort, for if one's suzerainty or overlordship was accepted in principle, one did not go to war for the sheer joy of conquest or loot, as conquerors belonging to the second and third category usually did.

The political theorist was also interested in theoretically countering the radically individualistic implications of the theory of *karma*, which almost led to a "moral monadism," implying as it did that no one could be held responsible for what happened to one and that, in turn, one could not really be responsible for what happened to anyone else, determined as each was by his or her own *karma* or what he or she had done in the past. The social theorist was also concerned with the issue, but while he developed a theory of debts and obligations to one's own parents, teachers and the gods, he did not develop a theory of collective responsibility in terms of which he could justify these claims. The political theorist, on the other hand, developed such a theory through the idea of the king's sharing in the merits and demerits earned by his subjects through the performance of good or bad deeds, for he was supposed to be directly or indirectly responsible for what they did. They thus developed a theory of the collective community of moral agents, in which there was a joint sharing in the fruits of action. Theoretical differences related only to the actual share of the king in the merits and demerits of his subjects. Some argued that it should be one-fourth, while the majority seem to have opted for one-sixth. But strangely, neither the political nor the social theorists moved forward to develop a full-fledged theory of *karma* in which collective responsibility could become the center of theoretical concern in reflection on human action. It is only the king who was supposed to share in the merit and demerits of his subjects, but as far as his subjects were concerned, there was no "sharing" in the fruits of the virtuous or vicious acts that they did.

The historical development of the socio-political thought of India has not been the subject of any detailed study. It has not even been paid much attention by those who have written on Indian philosophy. Nor have the interrelationships between the developments in different domains been the subject of serious investigation. Yet the very fact that such a large number of texts relating to *dharma, rājanīti* and *vyavahāra* (that is, society, polity and law) were written is itself evidence of such a development. There is, of course, a widespread impression that nothing new was said on the subject, but there can be little doubt that this is a superficial view of the matter. Laxman Sastri Joshi's *Dharma Kośa*, particularly in its *Rājanīti* and *Vyavahāra kāṇḍa*, is a monumental refutation of this facile impression. Also it should be remembered that it is the legal texts of a culture that respond more to the changing situation than the texts relating to society and polity, which can afford the luxury of remaining conservative in thought, if not in practice, over a longer period of time. In fact, even in the field of philosophy, in which radical developments are known to have occurred, the usual picture is of static systems that remained unchanged for millennia after the crystallization of their fundamental insights in the *sūtra* literature around the early centuries of the Christian era.

The vitality of this whole tradition of socio-political thought, even in recent times, may be seen from the fact that as late as the eighteenth century one of the ministers of the newly emergent Maratha successor state of the Mughal empire wrote a political text entitled *Ājñāpatra* in the older tradition and that, even in a place such as Thailand, political works were written in the earlier political tradition rooted in India. As for the legal literature, more than 150 works are supposed to have been written in the last two centuries alone.

However, all of this vast material needs to be critically examined and evaluated from a historically developmental point of view. The challenge is great, as it is in the social, political and legal thought of India that one may find a counter-picture to the still prevalent one that has been developed around the centrality of the renouncer tradition.

Bibliography

For a more detailed exposition of many of the points made in this article, see the author's (1996) book from Oxford University Press, entitled *Problematic and Conceptual Structure of Classical Indian Thought about Man, Society and Polity*.

17

Indian conceptions of reality and divinity

GERALD JAMES LARSON

Cultural and intellectual presuppositions

In any attempt to present an overview of the conceptions of reality and divinity in classical Indian (Hindu) civilization, it is helpful, first of all, to highlight some of the basic cultural and intellectual presuppositions that appear to be operative in classical Indian thought (which, for the purposes of this article, will be taken as consisting of the so-called six classical schools of Sāṃkhya, Yoga, Nyāya, Vaiśeṣika, Mīmāṃsā, and Advaita Vedānta during the classical period, from the first centuries of the Common Era up to the coming of Islamic traditions in the eleventh century). This can be accomplished in various ways, but perhaps the simplest way is to articulate some basic questions to which classical Indian thought provides some interesting, albeit unusual, answers. The questions can be framed as follows: (1) *What* truly is? (2) How does one *know* what truly is? (3) *Who* knows what truly is? (4) *With whom* does one know what truly is? And, finally: (5) What does *God* have to do with what truly is? The questions have to do, respectively, with (1) ontology, (2) epistemology, (3) psychology, (4) social anthropology, and (5) theology. Classical Indian thought, of course, provides a variety of answers to all of these questions, and there was much vigorous debate and polemic through the centuries about precisely how to form satisfactory answers. Generally speaking, however, it appears to be the case that the classical Indian philosophical schools tended to deal with these basic questions in a manner quite different from the way these questions have been dealt with in traditional or modern Western thought, and it is important to understand some of these differences if one wishes to appreciate the unique conceptual frameworks in classical Indian thought.

(1) *What* truly is? Regarding this first question, it is notable that the classical Indian philosophical schools did not for the most part make an ontological separation between mind and body or thought and extension, either in the traditional Platonic–Aristotelian sense of a realm of ideas or forms distinct from a realm of matter, or in the modern Cartesian sense of a distinction between thought and extension. S. Schayer has put the matter as follows:

> In this connection it must be strongly emphasized that the concept of a non-spatial Being, especially the hypostasis of a psychic, non-extended reality which has been

current in Occidental philosophy since Descartes, remained foreign to the Indian systems. (Larson, 1995, pp. 148–9)

E. H. Johnston comments:

> Early Indian thought, as exemplified for instance by Sāṃkhya, drew no clear line of demarcation between the material, mental and psychical phenomena of the individual. . . . All classes of phenomena are looked on as having a material basis, the difference resting merely on the degree of subtlety attributed to the basis. (Larson, 1995, p. 149)

In the systems of Sāṃkhya, Yoga and Vedānta, mind and body or thought and extension are dealt with solely in terms of the notion of "materiality" (*prakṛti*) or "phenomenal appearance" (*māyā*), and in the systems of Nyāya, Vaiśeṣika and Mīmāṃsā, mind, self, matter, and so forth, were all characterized simply as "subtances" (*dravya*). "What" truly is (*sat*) tended to be framed in terms of some entity that is, or some entities that are, eternal, indivisible, and ultimately unalterable. As far back as the ancient Upaniṣads (specifically *Chāndogya Upaniṣad* VI) it was generally accepted that something cannot come from nothing and that something cannot become nothing. For the Advaita Vedānta of Śaṃkara, *what* truly is the pure consciousness of Ātman or Brahman which cannot be negated by mutual negation or the negation of absence (Mohanty, 1974, pp. 329–30). For Sāṃkhya and Yoga, what truly is are the two primal entities of materiality (*prakṛti*) and pure consciousness (*puruṣa*). For Nyāya, Vaiśeṣika and Mīmāṃsā, what truly is are the nine ultimate "substances" (*dravya*), including the atomic substances (earth, water, fire, air and mind) and the all-pervasive substances of ether, time, space and selves. Ontological issues were never framed in terms of a mind–body problem, and most of the Indian schools (Sāṃkhya, Yoga, Nyāya, Vaiśeṣika and Mīmāṃsā) tended to deal with mind–body matters in a largely physicalist or reductive materialist fashion. The Advaita Vedānta of Śaṁkara dealt with mind–body matters in terms of its general treatment of all determinate formulations as phenomenal appearances that simply cannot be discussed in an ontologically intelligible manner (or, in other words, as "uncharacterizable" or *anirvacanīya*). What this means, then, is that the terms "idealism" or "realism" have very little meaning in an Indian philosophical environment, inasmuch as ontology was never dealt with in such terms. Another way of putting the matter is to say that Western notions of "idealism" and "realism" have no Sanskrit equivalents. One must hasten to add, however, that three of the schools, namely, Sāṃkhya, Yoga and Advaita Vedānta, do make an ontological distinction between a non-intentional "pure consciousness" (Ātman or *puruṣa*), on the one hand, and the mind–body realm of determinate manifestation (Māyā or *prakṛti*), on the other. "Pure consciousness" is without qualities (*nirguṇa*), contentless and/or non-intentional. For Śaṃkara, such "pure consciousness" is the only thing that truly is. All else, including the entire complex of mind–body awareness, has the questionable ontological status of being *anirvacanīya* or "uncharacterizable." For Sāṃkhya and Yoga, there is, in addition to "pure consciousness," the realm of materiality (*prakṛti*) to which "pure consciousness" is forever present as a witness (*sākṣitva*). The other classical systems, namely, Nyāya, Vaiśeṣika, and Mīmāṃsā, do not make an ontological distinction between "pure consciousness" and mind–body awareness, arguing that cognition as well as all ordinary awarenesses are simply attributes or qualities of the self (*ātman*) but not constitutive of the self. For these systems, then, when ignorance and suffering are overcome and the "self" attains "release" (*mokṣa*), there is no longer any experience or awareness. The self, in itself, is, finally, unconscious. Regarding "*what* truly is," then, the classical Indian systems are best characterized in terms of a polarity between those schools which accept the reality of a non-intentional consciousness (Sāṃkhya, Yoga and Vedānta) and those which do not (Nyāya, Vaiśeṣika, and Mīmāṃsā). The conventional ontological discussion of the Indian schools in terms of "idealism" or "realism" is, at best, misleading.

(2) How does one *know* what truly is? This question, of course, is closely related to the previous question, since the determination of what truly is cannot finally be separated from how one comes to know what truly is. Here again the classical Indian schools deal with the issue in a manner that is interestingly different from traditional or modern Western thought. J. N. Mohanty expresses the issue as follows:

> Let us note an important difference in locution, which, however, is not a mere matter of locution, but points to deep substantive issues. In the Western philosophical tradition, it was usual, until recent times, to ask: does knowledge arise from reason or from experience? The rationalists and empiricists differed in their answers. These answers, in their various formulations, determined the course of Western philosophy. In the Sanskrit philosophical vocabulary, the words "reason" and "experience" have no exact synonyms, and the epistemological issue was never formulated in such general terms. (Cited in Larson, 1995, p. 151)

There is no separate realm of reason, no pure rationalism, no pure realm of ideas, no pure possibilities and no transcendent "mind of God," Mohanty suggests. In the classical Indian systems there is no privileged realm of knowing of a purely rational kind or of a purely experiential kind that guarantees reliable knowledge. Even general inferential knowledge (*anumāna*) always has an empirical instantiation and is itself a material operation. Says Karl H. Potter:

> There is a general failure on the part of Indian philosophers to distinguish such opposites as *a priori* and *a posteriori*, analytic and synthetic, formal logic and empirical reasoning. No need seems to have been felt for any such distinctions. (Cited in Larson, 1995, p. 151)

Or as S. Chatterjee has commented: "In Indian logic an inference is a combined deductive–inductive reasoning. . . . All inferences . . . are at once formally and materially valid" (cited in Larson, 1995, p. 151). The classical Indian systems, rather than separating reason and experience, tend to deal with the epistemological issue in terms of what might be called cognitive frustration (*duḥkha, avidyā*). Epistemology has to do with the various means of knowing (*pramāṇa*), including perception, inference, reliable authority, comparison, and so forth. The various schools debated both the number and the nature of the *pramāṇas*.

Generalized notions of "reason" or "experience" are simply cognitive episodes within the unfolding flow of human awareness, and there is no privileged realm of knowing of a purely rational kind or of a purely experiential kind that guarantees reliable knowledge or certainty. The determinate realm is fraught with frustration (*duḥkha*) and uncertainty (*avidyā*). The determinate realm of mind–body or manifest reality is largely a realm of ignorance and non-discrimination (*avidyā, aviveka*). Some ordinary awarenesses, to be sure, are conducive to liberation in that they point to what truly is, namely, that indeterminate ultimacy which is pure unqualified and contentless consciousness or quiescence in Sāṃkhya, Yoga, and Vedānta or bare, unconscious selfhood in Mīmāṃsā, Nyāya, and Vaiśeṣika. The classical schools are deeply suspicious of the determinate realm, whether rational or experiential, and look, rather, for epistemological clues within the determinate that lead away from the determinate to an indeterminate realm that is apart from ignorance and suffering.

(3) *Who* knows what truly is? Even more so than in ontology and epistemology, the classical Indian systems construe the notion of personhood in dramatically different ways from traditional or modern Western thought. All of the systems accept the notions of karma and rebirth and, therefore, do not limit the notion of human being to a single lifetime. Nor do they limit the notion of embodiment to that of human being. It is quite possible over time to take part in various life-forms. The schools all accept what might be called a psychology of intrapersonal plurality or a diachronic ontogeny of more than one life. They accept, in other words, a greatly expanded notion of selfhood encompassing more than one life. The person is much more than the genetic heritage of father and mother. Father and mother contribute only the gross physical constituents of the person. The deeper identity is a transmigrating "subtle body" which enlivens the gross physical embryo at or shortly after the time of conception. The subtle body is "marked" by certain fundamental "predispositions" (*saṃskāras, vāsanās*) that have been accumulated as a result of the karmic residues from preceding rebirths. The quality of a given person's life is, thus, a composite of accumulated *karman* and the trajectories of previous rebirths (*punarjanman*). The various schools, of course, express the notions of karma and rebirth in different ways, but fundamental to all the interpretations is the basic belief that personal psychology involves intrapersonal plurality that stretches over many lives through myriads of unfolding cycles of time.

(4) *With whom* does one know what truly is? Closely parallel to the notion of a diachronic ontogeny of more than one life or a personal psychology of intrapersonal plurality is the related notion of an interpersonal plasticity or what McKim Marriott has called a profound "fluidarity" in terms of socio-anthropological notions of community. Important here, of course, is the notion of the caste system. McKim Marriott has expressed the essence of caste in terms of a basic "dividuality"

or "fluidarity" in interpersonal relations in contrast to traditional or modern Western notions of the discrete "individual." In the social reality of India there is a basic hierarchical network of ongoing transactions and ritual exchanges of things as well as bodily substances, or, to use the idiom of Louis Dumont, there are ongoing patterns of hierarchical interactions based on a twofold axis of purity–pollution and purity–power that determine the changing social identity of the person in community (Larson, 1995, pp. 154–8). As both Marriott and Dumont have stressed, Indian social reality is "dividual" and "hierarchical" in contrast to modern Western social reality that is "individual" and "egalitarian." The modern notion of the "individual" is almost completely absent except for the instance of the *sādhu* or ascetic or monk who rejects the "fluidarity" of caste life and enters upon the isolated life of a renunciant (*saṃnyāsa*). In this regard it must be remembered that many of the philosophers of the classical Indian schools were from the ranks of the ascetics and monks who had opted out of the conventional framework of *varṇāśrama-dharma* in order to seek the ultimate "release" (*mokṣa*) through renunciation.

(5) What does *God* have to do with what truly is? Here again the Indian schools differ markedly from traditional or modern Western thought. Many of the philosophical traditions do not accept a notion of God at all – for example, classical Sāṃkhya, Mīmāṃsā, early Vaiśeṣika, early Nyāya, and the early Buddhist and Jain traditions. In later centuries, the notion of God does enter the philosophical arena, but notions of God tend to be rather eccentric and frequently little more than add-ons for the sake of popular sentiment or stop-gaps, a sort of *deus ex machina*, to handle minor conceptual difficulties. The notion of God, of course, is much more important in the great theologies of the Vaiṣṇava, Śaiva and Śākta traditions. But even in the great theologies, God is not transcendent or wholly other as is the case in Jewish, Christian and Islamic theology. There is nothing like a *creatio ex nihilo* in the Indian philosophical and theological schools. Again, Mohanty has put the matter well:

> God's mind does not play that role of creating out of nothing in Indian thought. In the absence of *possibilia* and of abstract entities such as propositions, some standard concepts of necessary truth and its opposite contingent truth just cannot find any formulations in the Indian systems. Thus we have accounts of what the world does consist of, but not of what might have been or could not possibly be.
>
> If creation out of nothing, and so creation in the strict sense, has no place in Indian thought, that simply is not a marginal phenomenon for the *darśanas*, but – as I believe it can be shown – determines some very central features not only of the Indian cosmogonies, but also of the metaphysical notions of God, substance, time and negation. (Mohanty, 1988, pp. 252–3)

In the philosophical systems that do accept one or another kind of notion of God, God tends to exist alongside of other equally eternal entities. In Yoga, for example, God (*īśvara*) is one among the plurality of *puruṣas*. In later Nyāya and Vaiśeṣika, God (*īśvara*) is a self that provides the coordination and power necessary for the atoms to combine into more complex structures. In Advaita Vedānta, God (*īśvara*) is a lower form of the Absolute Brahman, a lower form as a projective Māyā that "creates" the phenomenal empirical realm of multiplicity. In the great Vaiṣṇava, Śaiva and Śākta theologies, theological reflection tends towards what might be called a cosmo-theology of polymorphic multiplicity which parallels in interesting ways the psychology of intrapersonal plurality and the social anthropology of interpersonal plasticity of "fluidarity" discussed earlier. For a divine being to become human (*avatāra* or "descending") is not at all an extraordinary occurrence. A Kṛṣṇa or Rāma is always a possibility. Any chosen Guru or spiritual teacher may embody the divine in this polymorphic sense, and believers take "*darśana,*" or, in other words, an actual visual contact with divinity by coming into perceptual contact with their Bhagavān or Lord. There are numerous devotional (*bhakti*) traditions that focus on the "grace" or "devotion" (*anugraha, praṇidhāna*) of Lord Viṣṇu, Lord Śiva, the Great Goddess (Devī, Kālī, and so forth), and many other forms of the divine including the *grāma-devatās* or "village goddesses" present in every village and hamlet, and in all of them, at least prior to contact with Islamic, Jewish and Christian traditions, there is an ease of access, a spontaneous emotional rapport, an absence of a separation in kind from the polymorphous divine that appears to be unique to the Indian context. Thus in philosophy as well as in theology, God is a most unusual player in the Indian scheme of things, but more on this in the sequel.

Concepts of reality

The six classical systems of Indian philosophy are usually discussed in terms of three basic pairs, namely, (1) the pair Sāṃkhya and Yoga, (2) the pair Nyāya and Vaiśeṣika, and (3) the pair Mīmāṃsā and Vedānta. The three pairs are referred to as "similar traditions" (*samāna-tantras*), and there is some heuristic justification for the pairing in the sense that each pair appears to have a distinctive use or application. The pair Sāṃkhya and Yoga clearly relate to traditions of meditation, with Sāṃkhya providing the theoretical framework and Yoga providing the patterns of practice. The pair Nyāya and Vaiśeṣika appear to relate to traditions of debate regarding the make-up of the physical world, with Vaiśeṣika providing the elementary physics and Nyāya providing canons for argumentation and successful debate. Finally, the pair Mīmāṃsā and Vedānta clearly relate to scriptural interpretation, with Mīmāṃsā providing the hermeneutical rules for interpreting the meaning of the sacrificial or action-portion of Vedic scripture and Vedānta providing the interpretations of the speculative portions of the Vedic scripture with special reference to the group of scriptural texts known as the Upaniṣads.

Regarding the issue of concepts of reality, however, the breakdown of the traditional systems into three pairs is not especially useful, or perhaps better, is somewhat misleading. With respect to concepts of reality, it is somewhat clearer to look at the six systems not in terms of three pairs but, rather, in terms of two distinct groupings. One grouping can be identified as looking at or conceptualizing reality from the perspective of the "whole," or, if you will, from the "top down." The other grouping can be identified as looking at or conceptualizing reality from the perspective of "parts," or, if you will, from the "bottom up."

The first grouping, that is, conceptualizing reality from the perspective of the "whole" or "top down," includes the Sāṃkhya, Yoga and Vedānta systems, with the key notions being (in the case of Sāṃkhya and Yoga) those of primordial materiality (*mūlaprakṛti*) made up of its three constituent "strands" or "constituent processes" of thinking (*sattva*), energizing (*rajas*) and objectifying (*tamas*), from which all determinate aspects of reality emerge, or (in the case of Vedānta) the creative projections of a cosmic Māyā, from which creative matrix all determinate manifestations show themselves. This first grouping also posits a non-intentional "pure consciousness" (*puruṣa* or *ātman*) that serves as a "witness" to the "whole," either in the sense that pure consciousness is totally separate from primordial materiality (in Sāṃkhya and Yoga) or in the sense that the creative manifestations of Māyā are finally dissolved in the extraordinary vision of the non-dual reality of Brahman (*ātman*). In other words, this first grouping in terms of the "whole" or "top down" encompasses a monist as well as a dualist conception of reality together with the claim that there is also an ultimate, contentless (*nirguṇa*) consciousness (*puruṣa* or *ātman* or Brahman) at the very heart of reality. This first grouping also usually interprets the emergence of determinate forms as emanations or evolutions (*pariṇāma* or *vivarta*) from a primordial creative source (*prakṛti* or Māyā), with such evolutes as intellect (*buddhi*), ego (*ahaṃkāra*), mind (*manas*), sense capacities, action capacities, subtle and gross elements all being made up of collocations of the constituent processes of thinking, energizing and objectifying. In the case of Vedānta, of course, the determinate forms have only a provisional, uncharacterizable (*anirvacanīya*) status as Māyā that is finally non-different from the pure consciousness of the Ātman that truly is! In the case of Sāṃkhya and Yoga, the realm of primordial materiality has its own characteristic integrity and status over against the pure consciousness which is *puruṣa*. Furthermore, in this first grouping there is the conceptual notion that all parts are encompassed by the whole or included in the whole such that all determinate effects pre-exist or are pre-supposed (*satkāryavāda* or its Vedāntin variant, *vivartavāda*) in the primordial matrix (*prakṛti* or Māyā). Finally, in this first grouping is the conceptual notion that there is a fundamental ignorance or non-discrimination (*aviveka* in Sāṃkhya and Yoga, *avidyā* in Vedānta) which cloaks or veils the reality of non-intentional pure consciousness (*puruṣa* or *ātman*), a cloak or veil that one can overcome through one or another kind of appropriate meditation, as has been revealed in the Vedic scriptures. Interestingly enough, it should be pointed out that this sort of philosophizing (with, of course, many variant conceptual formulations and without recourse to the authority of the Vedic corpus) is also characteristic of the Yogācāra or Vijñānavāda school of Mahāyāna Buddhist thought with its "consciousness-only" (*vijñapti-mātratā*) and its "store-house consciousness" (*ālaya-vijñāna*) serving as approximate equivalents to *prakṛti* and Māyā. The same is largely the case with the Mādhyamika school of Mahāyāna Buddhist thought, at least with its notions of "reality" (*tattva*) and an all-encompassing "voidness" or "emptiness" (*śūnyatā*).

This is not to say that all of these traditions of "whole" or "top down" philosophizing are the same. It is only to say that they all share "family resemblances" in terms of their conceptualizing about what is ultimately real.

The second grouping, that is, conceptualizing reality from the perspective of the "parts" or "bottom up," includes the Vaiśeṣika, Nyāya and Mīmāṃsā systems, with the key notions being the articulation of a set of explanatory categories (*padārthas*), a listing of discrete substances (*dravyas*) and an elementary theory of atomism (*paramāṇus*). Unlike the Aristotelian or Kantian notions of categories as types of predicates, "categories" (*padārthas*) in this second grouping represent actual aspects of reality made up of "substances" (*dravyas*), "qualities" (*guṇas*), "actions" (*karman*), "abstractions" (*sāmānyas*), "particulars" (*viśeṣas*) "inherence" (*samavāya*), and in some formulations, "absences" (*abhāvas*). "Substances" include atoms (*paramāṇus*) of earth, water, fire, air, and mind and the all-pervasive entities of ether, time, space and self. The world is built, as it were, from the "bottom up" from its constituent "parts." Imperceptible atoms, which are both quantitatively as well as qualitatively distinct, combine into dyads, and dyads combine in geometrical progression into triads, which are perceptible and which combine into more complex structures, and so forth, until one arrives at the fully fashioned world. Because reality is conceived largely in terms of discrete "parts" in this second grouping, it is generally the case that these schools see effects as being new and separate from their causal antecedents, or, in other words, they are largely adherents of *asatkāryavāda* or the theory that effects and causes are distinct. Some of the schools in this second grouping (especially some Mīmāṃsā traditions) maintain that the building up of the world occurs by the inherent nature of things (*svabhāva* or "own-being"), thereby not accepting the notion of God (*īśvara*). Others (the later Nyāya schools and especially the Nyāya thinker, Udayana) refer to God as the mechanism for getting things started. This second grouping also develops conceptions of an "unseen force" (*adṛṣṭa* or *apūrva*), a notion of delayed causal efficacy that explains why events may not have effects for long periods of time, together also with notions of "merit" (*dharma*) and "demerit" (*adharma*) by means of which the Karmic trajectories of beings come to be determined over time. For most schools in this second grouping, the self (*ātman*) is not constituted by "pure consciousness." There is only intentional awareness or consciousness, and such intentional consciousness is only a quality (*guṇa*) of the self, as are desire and effort. When ignorance and suffering are finally overcome, the self is no longer affected by any kind of experience and, therefore, is no longer conscious. "Release" (*mokṣa*) is, thus, only a negative realization, namely, the absence of ignorance and suffering, and indeed, the absence of experience of any kind. This second grouping also includes a rich tradition of philosophical argumentation and debate (especially in Nyāya and later Mīmāṃsā traditions) with detailed concern for logic and the correct formulation of inferences. In addition to the Vedic schools proper that fit into this second grouping, namely, the Vaiśeṣika, Nyāya, and Mīmāṃsā, conceptualizing reality from the perspective of "parts" or "bottom up" is also characteristic of the early Buddhist traditions (mainly Sarvāstivāda and Sautrāntika with their theories of point-instants or *dharmas*), and the Jain traditions (with their purely quantitative atomism). These latter traditions also put a great deal of emphasis on logic, argumentation and theories of predication and negation.

Regarding concepts of reality, therefore, it would appear that the Indian philosophical schools tend to fall into these two groupings, namely, what might be called a *prakṛti-pariṇāma-satkāryavāda(vivarta)* grouping, conceiving the "whole" from the "top down," and what might be called a *paramāṇu-dravya-asatkāryavāda(kṣaṇikavāda)* grouping, conceiving the "parts" from the "bottom up."

Concepts of divinity

What is rather striking to note with respect to the issue of concepts of divinity is that in early Indian philosophizing the notion or concept of divinity is frequently absent. As mentioned above, classical Sāṃkhya, Mīmāṃsā, early Vaiśeṣika, and Nyāya as well as early Buddhist and Jain traditions are all basically non-theistic. To be sure, there were popular religious cults flourishing in the early centuries of India's intellectual history, and there is some evidence for possible theistic traditions in certain pre-classical traditions of Sāṃkhya and possibly Vaiśeṣika traditions as well. There were also the early Vedic traditions involving the gods Varuṇa, Indra, and Agni, and such abstract formulations as Prajāpati (Lord of Creatures), Viśvakarman (the All-Maker), Skambha (the Support) and the cosmic Puruṣa (from whose sacrificed body the world and its social groupings were derived). The term "mighty one" (*īśāna*) appears already in the Ṛg Veda, and the term Īśvara ("God" or "Lord") appears first in the Atharva Veda. It is also used in the *Bṛhadāraṇyaka* Upaniṣad, but it is not until the later *Śvetāśvatara* and *Kaṭha* Upaniṣads that the notion of a personal, high god comes to the fore, and even in these contexts the notion of God is not especially clear. It is not really until the time of the *Bhagavadgītā* (final redaction in the first centuries of the Common Era) and the incorporation of the Bhāgavata cult, the Pāñcarātra tradition, the Vāsudeva-Kṛṣṇa cult, and the various Śaivite traditions (Pāśupatas, and so forth) into mainstream orthodox life that the notion of God or Īśvara becomes an important concept, and even then, as mentioned earlier in this essay, one has the impression that the concept of God in philosophical circles is either an accommodation to popular sentiment or some kind of stop-gap or *deus ex machina* formulation with little philosophical relevance. In later centuries, however, possibly due to the influence of Islamic traditions, the concept of God becomes much more important, and certainly in the great Vaiṣṇava, Śaiva and Śākta theologies the concept of God is central.

As was pointed out earlier, however, even in these later traditions when God becomes central, God is never conceived in these Hindu philosophical and theological contexts as a transcendent creator who creates *ex nihilo*. God is conceived as one among other eternal entities (atoms, selves, *mūlaprakṛti*, or whatever) or as a lower manifestation of the Absolute Brahman. And as was also pointed out earlier, in devotional contexts there is an intriguing polymorphous multiplicity in conceptions of divinity whereby "descents" (*avatāras*) become relatively commonplace, not only in terms of the mainstream cults surrounding Kṛṣṇa and Rāma but in traditions that grow up around certain holy Gurus – for example, Sathya Sai Baba, Paramahaṃsa Yogananda, Muktananda or Gurumayi.

Regarding this concept of divinity in terms of polymorphous multiplicity, it is interesting to note the various conceptual metaphors that have been devised through the centuries in both philosophical and theological contexts (and in popular religiosity as well). Seven conceptual metaphors in particular have been especially powerful in Indian thought.

(1) God as *feudal lord* or *governor*. This is the conceptual metaphor that is prevalent in the beloved *Bhagavadgītā*. Even though God need not act, he nevertheless comes to be in age after age to re-establish order (*dharma*). By doing obeisance to him as Lord and by giving over everything to him (*bhakti-yoga*), He will watch over his creatures and bring them to salvation.

(2) God as *stage actor*. This is a conceptual metaphor that is characteristic of Advaita Vedānta. Īśvara is "qualified" (*saguṇa*) Brahman who is the creative manifestation of Māyā, the mighty force that creates all of the determinate forms which represent the "play" (*līlā*) of Brahman. Īśvara conjures a world very much like an actor creates a scene on the stage, but finally the play shows itself as not being fully real, or perhaps better, as pointing to something beyond itself, namely, to Brahman as *nirguṇa*.

(3) God as *builder* or *contractor*. This is very much the metaphor to be found in Nyāya and Vaiśeṣika notions of God. God puts the atoms together, provides the inspiration to generate activity and motion, coordinates the "unseen force" so that the "merit" and "demerit" of the transmigrating souls are properly calibrated, and so that the world is maintained in age after age in an intelligible fashion.

(4) God as *exemplar*. This, of course, is the conceptual metaphor for God in classical Yoga philosophy. According to *Yogasūtra* I.24, God is a particular *puruṣa* among *puruṣas*, a *puruṣa* who has never been involved in transactions with the afflictions, Karmic destinies or Karmic residues. In other words, Īśvara does not act but stands as the perfect exemplar of the spiritual isolation (*kaivalya*) which all Yogins seek.

(5) God as *lover*. This is the conceptual metaphor for God in later medieval *bhakti* traditions, both Vaiṣṇava and Śaiva. The following passage from the *Gītagovinda* is typical, the devotee distraught at the loss of her lover:

> While her body lies sick
> From smoldering fever of love,
> Her heart suffers strange slow suffocation
> In mirages of sandalbalm, moonlight, lotus pools.
> When exhaustion forces her to meditate on you,
> On the cool body of her solitary lover,
> She feels secretly revived –
> For a moment the feeble girl breathes life.

She found your neglect in love unbearable before,
Despairing if you closed your eyes even for a moment.
How will she live through this long desertion,
Watching flowers on tips of mango branches?
(Embree, 1988, p. 262)

(6) God as *man* or *animal*. Here one thinks, of course, of the "descents" (*avatāras*) of God, not only as Kṛṣṇa and Rāma as found in the great epics, the *Mahābhārata* and *Rāmāyaṇa*, and the various *Purāṇas*, but also the "descents" of God as fish, boar, man-lion, monkey, and so forth. There is no better exemplification of the polymorphous multiplicity of divinity in India than the many lists of "descents" of God into human or animal form.

(7) God as *woman*. In many ways the most powerful conceptual metaphor for the divine in India is that of the Great Goddess. Devī, Lakṣmī, Chaṇḍī, Camuṇḍā, Durgā, Umā, Pārvatī, Mahāmāyā, and Kālī are but a few of her many names in Indian spirituality, not only in Śākta or Tantric contexts but widely in Vaiṣṇava and Śaiva contexts as well. But perhaps the *locus classicus* for the apotheosis of the feminine or femininity of the divine is in the great *Devīmāhātmya* ("The Majesty of the Goddess") in the *Mārkaṇḍeya Purāṇa* wherein the Great Goddess as Durgā stands forth as the great creative forces of Mahākālī, Mahālakṣmī, and Mahāsarasvatī (abundance and fertility, nurture and community, and wisdom and transcendence). She is at one and same time the fertile woman, the nurturing mother and the terrible destructive force of nature. The world emerges from her, is sustained by her and is finally destroyed by her. She is the power (*śakti*) within all things, consort, cosmic energy, primordial mother, and world-destroyer.

Bibliography

Dasgupta, S. N. 1963: *A History of Indian Philosophy*, Vol. 1 (Cambridge: Cambridge University Press).

Embree, Ainslee T. (ed.) 1988: *Sources of Indian Tradition*, 2nd edn (New York: Columbia University Press).

Larson, G. J. 1995: *India's Agony over Religion* (Albany: State University of New York Press).

Larson, G. J. and Bhattacharya, R. S. (eds) 1987: *Sāṃkhya: a Dualist Tradition in Indian Philosophy* (Princeton: Princeton University Press).

Larson, G. J. and Deutsch, E. (eds) 1988: *Interpreting across Boundaries: New Essays in Comparative Philosophy* (Princeton: Princeton University Press).

Mohanty, J. N. 1974: "Indian Philosophy," *Encyclopaedia Britannica*, Macropaedia, Vol. 9 (Chicago and London: Encyclopaedia Britannica, Inc.).

—— 1988: "A Fragment of the Indian Philosophical Tradition," *Philosophy East and West*, July, pp. 250–55.

Potter, Karl H. 1963: *Presuppositions of India's Philosophies* (Englewood Cliffs, NJ: Prentice Hall, 1963).

18

Rationality in Indian philosophy

ARINDAM CHAKRABARTI

Introductory remarks

You cannot say "thank you" in Sanskrit. It would be ridiculous to deduce from this (as William Ward, a British Orientalist, did in 1822) that gratefulness as a sentiment was unknown to the ancient Indian people. It is no less ridiculous to argue that *rationality* as a concept is absent from or marginal to the entire panoply of classical Indian philosophical traditions on the basis of the fact that there is no exact Sanskrit equivalent of that word.

For one thing, there *are* several words for the science or art of reasoning: for example, "*ānvikṣikī,*" "*tarkaśāstra,*" "*nyāya.*" (And one of these – namely, "*ānvikṣikī,*" and its role in the Indian metatheory of branches of learning or knowledge – will occupy us in a separate section of this article). There are also very ancient words for the institutions of rational debate and public problem-solving contests (for example, a "*brahmodya*"), like the famous one reported in the Bṛhadāraṇyaka Upaniṣad (third book) in which Yājñavalkya steals the show in the court of the philosopher-king Janaka. There are also words for the special form of reflecting by means of anticipated "pro" and "contra" arguments ("*ūhāpoha,*" "*manana,*" "*yukti-vicāra*"), which one is urged to cultivate as part of a contemplative culture.

Second, even if there were no such closely cognate words, that would hardly license the conjecture that the concept is foreign to the Vedic people. Of course, identity-criteria for concepts are hard to formulate. But, as the following discussion would demonstrate, articulated concepts of what makes a belief, an action, an interpretation, a preference, a choice of means or an end *reasonable* could be detected everywhere in classical Indian thought. Those concepts may not be easily recognizable as concepts of *rationality*, since unlike the standard Western concepts of rationality, the typically Indian notions of rationality are, on an average, non-hedonistic, non-individualistic, non-positivistic, and aim at surrendering the personal ego to an impersonal tradition or to some universal consciousness.

In this article, I shall first try to diagnose four major worries that can make even unprejudiced surveyors of Indian thought wonder whether the concept of rationality, with its positive value-overtone, is at all compatible with the general tenor of classical Indian philosophies. Although it is advisable to be suspicious of any talk of the "general tenor" of *all* Indian philosophies (except Buddhism, because I have avoided discussing it here), these deep worries are well grounded. By trying to face them, I think, we can get a better grip on the special contribution that Indian ways of thinking – in their inexhaustible variety of in-house disagreements and their passion for intra-traditional polemics – made to the multivalent concept of rationality.

After responding to these four major worries, I take up specific aspects of the Indian theoretical engagement with logical, epistemic, hermeneutic, ethical, aesthetic, and soteriological rationality. Besides demonstrating the diversity and enormity of this field, I hope my account will suggest the way in which the tensions between scriptural testimony and reason, mysticism and logic, poetry and analysis, action and theory were celebrated, partially resolved and partially allowed to remain unresolved by the ancient and medieval Indian thinkers, and how some contemporary Indian interpreters are coming to terms with these inner tensions within their own pluralistic cultural legacy.

How are humans special?

One important way in which the adjective "rational" has been understood in the West is as standing for the differentiating feature distinguishing human beings from other animals. It must have been part of popular thinking even in ancient India that cognitive and ratiocinative powers distinguish humans from beasts because a very important Hindu religious text (*Durgā Saptaśatī*, a part of *Mārkaṇḍeya Purāṇa*) warns *against* this idea and says in no uncertain terms: "True, humans are knowledgeable, but they are not the only ones; for even birds and beasts all have knowledge of some sort." Then it goes on to give examples of apparently self-sacrificing behavior on the part of bird-mothers feeding their young *knowing*, as it were, that they are totally dependent at that stage. Because of the continuity across species underlying the reincarnation theory (which enabled the wise, rational, morally sensitive Buddha to be born in many sub-human bodies or even Vishnu the god to assume the form of a fish or a pig), on the one hand, and the orthodox Vedic society positing caste divisions within human society as a natural given, on the other, the divide between humans and sub-humans was never such a major theme among the traditional Indians.

One can, however, point out three very striking ways in which the privilege of man has been thematized in the tradition. First, in the Aitareya Āraṇyaka (which is a part of the Vedic corpus) man (*puruṣa*, gender-neutral) is said to be privileged because in him the self (*ātman*) is more manifest; he alone discerns what he perceives and can liberate his understanding and speech from the immediate needs of hunger and thirst. Saying that beasts and birds are unable to foresee and plan, this text comments beautifully: "Man knows tomorrow . . . and by the mortal aspires after the immortal."

Second, Śabara in his commentary to the *Mīmāṃsā Sūtra* (VI, 1,5) remarks on this typically human capacity to wait and (as the *Ṛgveda* X.117 says, warning the short-sighted ungiving amasser of wealth) "look down the longer path." Rising above the proximate (*āsanna*) self-interest, a human being can perform "sacrifices" – both in the literal and the ritualistic sense – for the sake of "unseen" results in a remote future. A sacrifice (*yajña*) is therefore taken by the *Bhagavad Gītā* (4.28–33) as the human rational activity *par excellence*, so much so that even "trying to ascertain the meaning of Vedic sentences by logical arguments" is called "knowledge-sacrifice" (*nyāyena vedārtha niścayaḥ jñānayajnaḥ*). At the very end of *Nirukta*, Yāska (400 BCE) personifies Reasoning as a wise seer (*ṛṣi*), one "*tarka-ṛṣi*" who would guide the interpretation of obscure Vedic texts by humans.

Thus while both animals and humans are conscious pleasure-seekers, only humans are capable of *dharma* – considerations of piety and morality, right or wrong conduct. Hence the popular Sanskrit adage, found in some versions of the *Hitopadeśa*: "Without *dharma*, a man eating, sleeping, and engaging in sex is no different from a beast." The link between the ethico-ritualistic concept of *dharma* and rationality is very clear in texts like *Yogavāśiṣṭha Rāmāyaṇa*, which devotes an entire chapter (II, 14) to the nature and importance of *vicāra* (reflective analysis) without which human life is pointless. This is how the chapter starts: "With an intellect purified by understanding of the scriptures, the person who is aware of what causes what (*kāraṇa-jña*), must constantly examine and analyze himself." The chapter ends after 45 verses explaining the indispensability of reasoned reflection for moral, spiritual as well as worldly life with this echo of Socrates: "It is better to be born as a mud-frog or as a slime-worm or as a snake in a cave than to be an unreflective unexamining human being."

But all this praise for intellectual and moral superiority is qualified by a most interesting twist given by the *Mahābhārata* to its explanation of why "there is nothing nobler than humanity" in the story of a poor scholarly Brahmin (Mbh XII, 174). Knocked over by a rich man's carriage, he wants to die on the street out of utter frustration. Indra, the King of Gods takes the form of a jackal and tells him that he should make the best of his life as a human being because he is far better off than beasts who cannot even scratch themselves properly with their tails. For several verses this story goes on to explain why humans are great because they have a *pair of hands* with ten pliable fingers with which they can take out thorns, and make tools and shelters and clothing. Thus not so much as *homo sapiens* but as *homo faber* do humans rule over other creatures. What does this have to do with rationality?

Foreshadowing what I say, in the next paragraph, about rationality and the use of hand gestures to communicate (for example, in the Indian but not exclusively Indian ways of greeting with folded hands, giving reassurance, and so on), let us compare this "manual" view of man with the following remark by Kant:

> The characterization of man as a rational animal is already present in the form and organization of the human *hand*, partly by the structure and partly by the sensitive feeling of the *fingers* and *finger-tips*. (*Anthropology*, p. 323, italics Kant's)

The point that the *Mahābhārata* makes about the hands making humans "free" to clean or protect themselves or to dominate or torture others is exactly the point that Kant also makes in the remark: "By this, nature has made him fit for manipulating things not in one particular way but in any way whatsoever, and so for using reasons" (ibid.).

A dimension of these wonderful possibilities that the hands open up for us which Kant did not speak of (and perhaps would *not* have considered part of rationality) is the endlessly expressive and creative use of the hands, palms and fingers in dance and drama that Bharata, in the fourth chapter of his magnum opus *Nāṭya Śāstra*, lists as 140 different "poses" forming the basic postural alphabet (*karaṇas* and *angahāras*). That would be a typically Indian extension of the "reason of the hands."

It is by systematic reflection and debate about every aspect of life that the classical Indian learned traditions self-consciously tried to display the distinctiveness of human existence without making too much of a fuss about just the *cognitive* specialty of humans. An extreme example of the use of definition and dialectic in every sphere of rational thought – from etymology to erotica – can be given from the *Kāmasūtra* (VI, 2,27–8) where Vātsyāyana considers the view of those who "argue that massage is a form of embrace because it is a tactile contact." He observes that "there are three reasons why it is not so, because [in love-practice] they occur at different times, because they serve different purposes, and unlike an embrace which is ideally reciprocal a massage is non-mutual." The commentator adds a little reductio to the effect that "if any tactile contact were an embrace, then even a kiss would be so." When the zeal to theorize and support every theory with a reason was carried to this extreme in ancient Indian thought, one cannot but be surprised at the fact that "lack of theoretical orientation" is usually the first charge that is brought against the Indian mind.

Four worries dissipated

Of the four features of Indian thought that could be pointed out as reasons for skepticism about the very idea of an Indian conception of Rationality – the first that draws our attention is the alleged practical or goal-oriented character of Indian philosophy. Not only are pleasure (*kāma*), power/wealth (*artha*), piety/righteousness (*dharma*), and final liberation from suffering (*mokṣa*) distinguished as the four – and only four – alternative and actually pursued goals of life, but even branches of knowledge or subjects of study are divided accordingly.

Thus we have *kāmaśāstra*, *arthaśāstra*, *dharmaśāstra*, and a specially prestigious *mokṣaśāstra* dealing with these four goals respectively. Philosophy is often identified with the last of these, so that there remains no room for the pure theories of logic, mathematics, knowledge, reality, or morality, undertaken simply for the sake of intellectual satisfaction. Along with this ancient overarching theory of the fourfold "ends of man" (*puruṣārtha*), philosophical treatises followed the general pattern of opening with a statement of "purpose" or "use" (*prayojana*) – for "why should an intelligent person undertake a study or an action until he is told what purpose it serves?" (Kumārila Bhaṭṭa, *Śloka vārtika*, 1.1.12)

How can the out-and-out theoretical notion of reason and rational inquiry develop in an intellectual atmosphere so obsessed with practical concerns or with the goal of the end of suffering? There are several ways in which this worry can be allayed.

As early as the fourth century BCE, Kauṭilya, in his *Arthaśāstra*, divides disciplines (*vidyā*) into four: scripture (the three Vedas, *trayī*), agriculture and commerce (*vārtā*), politics and public administration (*daṇḍa-nīti*), and finally – "the light of all other disciplines, the methodology of all other practice, and the foundation of all moral virtues" – *ānvīkṣikī*, the investigative reflective science which examines beliefs acquired through observation and testimony by the means of correct knowledge (*pramāṇaih arthaparīkṣaṇam*). The very recognition of a metascience (*ānvīkṣikī*) which would examine what is moral and what is immoral in the Vedas (*dharmā dharmau trayyām*), what is efficient and what is inefficient in the sciences of material acquisition, and good and bad policies in the science of government – weighing their strength of evidence by arguments – and the identification of this metascience with philosophy (examples given by Kauṭilya include sāṃkaya, yoga, and the lokāyata materialistic philosophy) unquestionably proves that even the recognition of the purposefulness of rational inquiry or action was part of a *theoretical* orientation of these ancient Indian thinkers. The practical purpose of a study itself became a theoretical topic of discussion. Indeed, Jayanta (c. 950 CE) begins his book *Nyāyamanjarī* (*Logic Blossoms*) by constructing a paradox of inquiry (rather like the Platonic "Meno's Paradox") based on this requirement that one know the use of every study that one begins.

> If you insist on first knowing its use and then being interested in a subject, then you are involved in a circularity. After mastering the subject alone you know exactly what purpose it can really serve; but you are not even interested to start learning the subject unless you first know what its use is. So the required knowledge of use cannot be a thorough critical knowledge on pain of this circularity.

One of the reasons why the tension between theory and practice never became important in classical Indian thought is that practice, as it was laid out in the arts (of dancing, building, medicine and poetry), never was blind, and the theories themselves claimed to be somehow livable in practice. The distinction, however, between action (*karma*) and knowledge (*jñāna*) has been recognized since the Upaniṣadic times. A healthy competition between the ritualists, on the one hand, who took sacred descriptive speech to be subservient to Vedic injunctions concerning what is to be done, and the followers of the path of pure knowledge, on the other, who took prescriptions to be subservient to metaphysical parts of sacred speech, continued for at least a thousand years. Both the ritualists and the metaphysicians, nevertheless, had their own ā*nvīkṣikī*s or analytical methodologies. So, to quote J. N. Mohanty, "the Hindu mind was constantly engaged in theorizing about practice" and also committed to the idea that "a purely *theoretical* cognition will lead to the satisfaction of the highest *practical* interest" (Mohanty, 1995).

The scheme of the four ends of life (*puruṣārthas*) to which we alluded above is itself a rational theorization about what humans live for. Recent (that is, late twentieth-century) Indian philosophers have taken up this fourfold scheme for thorough critical examination. Daya Krishna, for instance, has provocatively asked, "What is the *puruṣārtha* of intellect (*buddhi*)," given that the intellect just wants to raise questions and get the answers right, not desiring sensual pleasure or political or economic power, not trying to be virtuous, and not always aiming at freedom from suffering? We should not be too far from the mainstream of Indian thought if we answer this question by positing knowledge of the self or understanding of texts to be the *puruṣārtha* of intellect. Alternatively, we could develop K. C. Bhattacharya's (*Studies in Philosophy*, p. 142) idea that rational reflection is primarily reflection on *pain* and is "a freeing process" – thus linking it up with liberation. The link between an intellectual discipline, such as *āvīkṣikī*, and self-knowledge or textual interpretation will become clear as we deal with the second and third "worries" concerning rationality in India.

The second major worry is this: how could autonomous rationality have developed in Indian thought given that most philosophizing was done with an allegiance to the unquestioned authority of the Vedas or some other root-text the truth of which was taken for granted? Where the forces of tradition and verbal testimony are so dominant, how could *reason* – in the Western sense of the term – flourish?

Three lines of response, of varying degrees of power, and by no means mutually exclusive, can be adopted in the face of this second worry. First, while it is correct that mere or "dry" reasoning (*śuṣka tarka*) has been belittled by great Indian thinkers like Śaṃkara because it is groundless, unstable and conflict-generating (*Brahmasūtrabhāṣya*, II.1.11), or because, as Bhartṛhari noted before him, "what expert reasoners have concluded with great logical acumen and effort is disproved by yet other more expert logicians," not *all* Indian thought is blindly supportive of scriptural authority. Having abused the authors of the three Vedas as impostors and cheats, the materialist-skeptical Cārvāka philosophers from very ancient times rejected all trust in religious texts as irrational. Of course, in their case, even inferences, and especially inductive generalizations, are epistemically unjustified, and insofar as testimony is reduced to a form of inference, our reliance on testimony too loses all rational respectability. Right from the Buddha's own sermons up to the sophistication of Buddhist epistemology in the Yogācāra-Sautrāntika school, the Buddhist mind shows opposition to unexamined "say so" as evidence. The Buddha urges his disciples not to believe his own words upon the basis of his personal authority, but to test them by reasoning and individual experience. Accordingly, only perception and inference are admitted as sources of knowledge in Buddhist epistemology, and testimony is either rejected or reduced away. Similarly, in what has been called the "Tradition of Rationalist Medicine" (Chattopadhyaya, 1980, pp. 85–115), appealing to religious or scriptural authorities in the context of clinical practice has been regarded by Caraka (from the very early Christian era) as committing the fallacy of irrelevance. We shall see, in a subsequent section on ancient Indian medical reasoning, how "medical integrity" was supposed to consist in reliance on empirical data, inductive probability, practical efficacy, and *not* on religious authority.

Within the mainstream orthodox schools, Sāṃkhya – in spite of its lip-service to the Vedas and the "word of the expert" as sources of knowledge – very clearly relied on its own variety of reflective reasoning as the sole means of attaining such knowledge as would lead to the pure and permanent cessation of suffering. In the two opening couplets of *Sāṃkhya Kārikā*, observed worldly means of removing pain and scripture-prescribed ritualistic means of removing pain are both rejected as unsatisfactory, because even the heavenly pleasures (after death) promised as rewards for the performance of Vedic rituals are exhaustible, mixed with pain and surpassable in degree. The only method of attaining an inexhaustible, unmixed and unsurpassable state of freedom from pain is rational reflection on the distinction between the manifest (effects), unmanifest (cause) and consciousness (which is neither effect nor cause). Sāṃkhya, therefore, is at heart an out-and-out reason-based system of thought with its own basic presuppositions, such as the three fundamental *guṇa*s and the doctrine of the pre-existence of effect in the material cause, defended by a series of internally coherent arguments.

Second, even Vedānta and Mīmāṃsā – the two pillars of Vedic orthodoxy – assign a crucial role to reasoning and critical argumentation in extracting the correct meaning from sacred sentences of the "heard" revelation (*śruti*). Far from being antagonistic, reason and scripture coexist peacefully together in coupling compounds strewn all over Vedānta literature (for example, *śruti-yukti, tarkāgama, śāstranyāya*). What is this assisting role that reason plays in Vedic hermeneutics? In the Upaniṣads – the philosophical cream of the Vedas – one finds statements like "you are that (*Brahman*)". In order to make sense of such identity claims, the reader must first "distill" the meaning of "you," which is coreferential with the reader's (ideally, listener's) use of "I." Causal links are established by what in Vedānta is called the method of presence in presence and absence in absence (*anvaya-vyatireka*). Now, signification or designation is taken as a special case of a causal link, because there is a lawlike connection between the utterance of a word and the consequent grasp, by the hearer, of a meaning. The Upaniṣads start from a proto-materialistic conception of the self (the referent of "I") as the food-constituted body. Śaṃkara the commentator uses this method of presence and absence to reject, one after another, these "object"-natured candidates for selfhood – the body, the life-breath, the inner sense, the intellect – because the self seems to be present even in the absence or non-functioning of these elements (in death, dreams, deep sleep, and so on). This method of elimination leaves only a pure non-individuated subjective consciousness as the possible meaning of "I." A similar isolation of relevant signification is performed on the word "that" (which directly stands for God and the totality of physical and mental entities of the universe). When the direct or primary referents of these two terms are seen to be in partial conflict, because the individual embodied "I" is not *prima facie* identical with "that" world or all that there is, the method of rational exegesis is employed. Secondary significance of words is generally derived from the literal sense by extension (for example, "crying over spilt milk" comes to include a whole lot of spilt other things) and elimination (for example, in "the opinion of the house," "house" does not signify house at all). Thus through "retaining a part and rejecting a part" of their literal sense, the words "I" and "that" are taken in their secondary significance. That part of their distinct literal meaning where they intersect: namely, pure subjective consciousness, is taken as the emerging oblique meaning of the scriptural identity statement. What can never be spoken of – the *Ātman-Brahman* – could thus be got at indirectly by its only testimony, the sentences of an authorless revelation. This is an oversimplified summary of the intricate interpretive technique through which reasoning is used to distill the indirect meaning of the "great sentences" of the Veda. Thus the text is trusted as the sole proof of the *Ātman-Brahman* (the Self which is All) but it is subjected first to a tradition-tested method of critical scrutiny. It is only relentless reasoning which can help us hold on to the distinction between the self (reality) and the not-self (appearance), and without such reasoned discrimination, no blind parroting of the scriptures would get us anywhere. As far as the role of testimony is concerned, even scripture is a ladder to be kicked away after the saving knowledge of non-duality dawns. Thus Śaṃkara's faith in the "truth" of Vedic text is also ontologically *provisional*. *Tarka* (reasoning) may be baseless by itself (*apratiṣṭha*), but even *śruti* (scripture) is, in the final analysis, ignorance that helps cure ignorance. While discussing the "instability" of autonomous reasoning, Śaṃkara, interestingly, considers and dismisses an objection which it is worthwhile to mention. "This alleged refutability and non-decisiveness of reason," the objection goes, "should be recognized as a good feature rather than a weakness, insofar as it keeps room for correction and improvement." After all, if you have conflicting Vedic texts, reasoning is your only basis for adjudication!

Third, we could question the very assumption that relying primarily on an impersonal unquestionable tradition is necessarily irrational. There are two ways in which not only the compatibility between reason and testimony but the essentiality of commitment to the tradition as a necessary condition for rationality can be brought out. The first way can be called the Nyāya–Dummett way and the second the Mīmāṃsā–Gadamer way.

By emphasizing the irreducible role of knowledge from words (*śabda pramāṇa*) in the acquisition and use of language, Nyāya epistemology exposes a fundamental error of Lockean individualistic epistemology. As Michael Dummett remarks,

> It is not a rule of etiquette, or a device for saving time, that we should accept what others tell us: It is fundamental to the entire institution of language. (*Motilal and Chakrabarti*, p. 266)

There is no rationality without social interaction, because as Wittgenstein showed us, no one can be a private rule-follower. But there is no social interaction without understanding of others' speech. And, as Dummett and Davidson, in spite of other major differences, both insist – there is no understanding of others' speech without a basic presumptive trust in their testimony. It follows, therefore, that there is no rationality without a basic trust in the veracity of competent speakers – "be that a sage, a lay Aryan or a *mleccha* foreigner" (to quote Vātsyāyana, the fifth-century Nyāya commentator) – unless there is reason to suspect ignorance or deceit or lack of commitment. While this way of putting testimony back into the heart of rationality proceeds through the inescapable *trustworthiness* of fellow-speakers of a language, the other way, adopted by Kumārila Bhaṭṭa and recently articulated by John Taber using insights from Gadamer, turns on an underlying *distrust* of individual speakers and treats a speaker-less body of received tradition to be the only possible source of moral knowledge. Perception or empirically grounded inference never gives us any knowledge of what ought to be done. The verdict of our conscience or moral emotions is highly unreliable. The only ineluctable source of knowledge of right and wrong action, under the Mīmāṃsā view, which is firmly rooted in the epistemological doctrine of the intrinsic validity of all knowledge, is the impersonal objective (beginningless) prescriptive sentences handed down by one's own cultural tradition. The only way meaningful speech could be unreliable is by being spoken by fallible individuals. If it is not spoken by anyone – as Mīmāṃsā takes the Vedas to be – then it is intrinsically knowledge-yielding. The knowledge it yields is also unique, because from no other source of knowledge can you have any rational insight into morality. To quote Gadamer, "The real force of morals . . . is based on tradition. They are freely taken over but by no means created by a free insight grounded on reasons." (*Truth and Method*, p. 281) Of course, neither Gadamer nor any modern person can swallow the orthodoxy of Kumārila that the Vedic tradition *alone* is the source of *all* moral knowledge. But it may be necessary to rectify the Enlightenment idea that a fully autonomous external critique of tradition is possible or desirable purely on the basis of personal rationality. A creative but sympathetic understanding of the traditionalist ethics of Mīmāṃsā may enable us to appreciate why it is perfectly rational for a Veda-rooted Indian to assert "I ought to feed the guest first because the Veda says so" and then claim, like Wittgenstein, that he has hit the rock-bottom of reason-giving and that is where his spade turns.

But by over-emphasizing discursive knowledge – whether derived from reasoning or from the word of the reliable authority – am I not falsifying the very spirit of Indian intellectual traditions, which eventually aspire after non-discursive, ineffable, direct mystical insight into a reality that transcends reason? How could *any* conception of rationality have developed in a philosophical milieu so deeply devoted to some kind of ecstatic vision where "the subject and the object are . . . eternally and absolutely lost in unity, and the din of phenomenal existence is forever hushed in the calm of sweet repose?" This is the third "worry" that I wish to address.

Mahamahopadhyaya Gopinath Kaviraj, whom I have just quoted, compiled, in his classic 1924 paper "The Doctrine of *Pratibhā* in Indian Philosophy," all the references to such supra-rational supra-sensuous intuitive awareness of "all things past, present and future in a simple flash" which was called "*pratibhā*." Even from that pro-mystical survey of Sanskrit sources, two things become clear: first, not all schools of philosophy believed in the possibility or centrality of such supramental experience; second, even the schools that relied heavily on *pratibhā*, like the Grammarians, did not understand by it anything which goes against or beyond reason.

Before discussing the anti-mystical position of Mīmāṃsā, let us take a quick look at the role of the so-called "immediate spiritual experience" (*aparokṣa anubhūti*) in Advaita Vedānta. Contrary to the claims of Neo-Hindu writers like Radhakrishnan, Śaṃkara nowhere claims that non-dualism is based on direct mystical experience. To quote Halbfass:

> that experience which the Veda itself teaches as a transcendent soteriological goal, the sheer undisguised presence of Brahman, should not be confused with "personal experiences". . . . Instead of being a documentation of subjective experience, the Veda is an objective structure which guides, controls and gives room to legitimate experience, as well as legitimate argumentation. . . . It is an objective, transpersonal epiphany, an authorless, yet didactically well-organized body of soteriological instruction. (Halbfass, 1988, p. 388)

Rāmānuja, the most prominent rival-Vedāntist, is even more unequivocal in asserting that no yogic trance can give knowledge of *Brahman*. Such Yogic visions, according to him, are, after all, results of intense imagination and vivid reproduction of previous sense-experiences. Such transient experiential states cannot be depended upon as a source of *knowledge*.

The most orthodox traditionalists are the harshest critics of mystical intuition or even divine omniscience. Kumārila ridicules the possibility that "all things could be *experienced* directly at once in a synoptic vision" as on a par with the possibility that we could "hear colors." Kaviraj, who is pained by this "bitter opposition," finds the following rationale behind it. As we have already noted above, the impersonal and exclusive authority of the Veda is the corner-stone of Mīmāṃsā. Personalities, however elevated or divine, even of an alleged Deity, are taken as sources of fallible and limited experiences. As Kaviraj insightfully remarks, "The very fact of being a subject involves the inevitable relativity of consciousness fatal to omniscience." So "omniscient person" is an oxymoron. Also, given the presence of the Vedic corpus as the ineluctable source of impersonal and hence intrinsically valid knowledge, any all-knowing person – divine or human – is strictly redundant.

Finally, if we look at the favorable accounts of intuitive knowledge in Patañjali's Yoga or Bhartṛhari's word-non-dualism (*śabdādvaita*), we come to realize that it is a deepened or sophisticated form of a reflective rationality which in Yoga takes the form of discrimination (*viveka-khyāti*), and in the hands of the Grammarian takes the form of innate or instinctive capacity for synoptic grasp – for example, of the sentence-meaning as a whole. Both of these contexts are, interestingly, deeply linguistic. A yoga-practitioner's *prajñā* (insight) becomes clearer and clearer, according to the *Yoga-sūtra* (1.42–43), first by reflecting upon the distinctness of a word, the concept, and the object, all three of which are confused inextricably in our ordinary consciousness. As one recognizes the conventional character of the word–object relation and the memory-mediated character of the concept associated with the word, the pure object in its individuality is supposed to shine more and more distinctly in isolation from its linguistic and cognitive cloaks. The last step of this stripping the pure object of words and imaginations through which the non-discursive "dropping out of the mind" is achieved is indeed hard to explain. But Kaviraj makes an excellent attempt:

> It sounds absurd to say that the object alone remains without the *citta* or *jñāna* to take cognizance of it, but what is meant seems to be that the *citta* through extreme purity, becomes at this stage so tenuous as to be in fact a luminous void; it does not exist.

Notice that this elimination of thought and language is achieved through a very careful rational reflection on the distinction between the sound "cow," the idea of a cow, and the particular animal cow in its uniqueness.

Although Bhartṛhari emphasizes the indescribability of *pratibhā*, he also finds its presence in birds and beasts and describes it as "testified to by the inner experience of every man." It is nothing esoteric. In a latent form it is innately present in every creature that can follow a rule. It is that instinctive flash of understanding through which, in practical situations, people come to decide what to do. *Pratibhā* is, indeed, a multifaceted concept. In its specially cultivated extra-ordinary forms, it can amount to clairvoyance or yogic powers of remembering one's own previous birth, and so on. But its central significance in Bhartṛhari's philosophy is more that of tacit knowledge of the total sentence-meaning which arises in a spontaneous way after individual word-meanings and their syntactical connections are separately grasped, so that the final flash of understanding remains inexplicable even to the understander. Such meaning-grasping tacit knowledge lies at the heart of all interpretive rationality, rather than going beyond or against it.

The fourth and final worry is of a different nature. Unlike the general anxiety regarding the alleged practical orientation, respect for authority and "mystical empiricism" of Indian philosophical systems, which were supposed to make the emergence of the idea of autonomous positivistic theoretical rationality unlikely, this has to do with a specific absence that India's intellectual traditions suffer from. The concept of deductive or logical necessity which is paradigmatically illustrated by proofs in mathematics and formal logic and the allied notion of *a priori* knowledge seem to be simply missing from the entire arena of Indian philosophical disciplines. Truths, even eternal truths, are recognized always as truths of fact, and never as truths of reason. Inferences have always been formulated as involving an inductive general premise (the *vyāpti* or rule of pervasion, about which more later) and never as demonstrative proofs. This absence of the notions of formal validity and logical necessity is linked at bottom with the failure to appreciate the idea of possible but non-actual worlds and, in a roundabout way, also with the tendency to define knowledge as "true presentative awareness" without any further "justification" clause! These are serious allegations which have bothered contemporary Indian logicians and epistemologists like B. K. Matilal, J. N. Mohanty, and Sibajiban Bhattacharya.

Broadly, two different sorts of response have been made to this crucial complaint. First, that in recognizing very clearly the law of non-contradiction *nyāya-vaiśeṣika* logicians do display adequate sensitivity to the concept of logical truths or necessity; and that in Buddhist logic deductive inferences find a place; and finally that the role of hypothetical reasoning (*tarka*) as buttressing evidence for universal generalizations shows that Indian logic has room for the modal notions of necessary connections between non-actualized possibilities. This is the line adopted by Matilal (1982) in "Necessity and Indian Logic" (chapter 7 of *Logical and Ethical Issues of Religious Belief*). Second, that Nyāya, at least, is not even trying to do logic in the Frege–Russell sense, but is doing a phenomenological–epistemic logic in which eidetic rules are discovered not concerning compatibility and incompatibility between *propositions* but concerning compatibility and incompatibility of episodes of awareness (*jñāna*) in virtue of their contents. This is the line taken by Mohanty (1992) in his "The Nature of Indian Logic" (chapter 4 of *Reason and Tradition in Indian Thought*). The second approach is more challenging and opens up newer notions of *logicality*, which of course are not all that new in Asia.

But let us discuss briefly Matilal's approach first. Formulations of the law of non-contradiction are very easy to find in ancient and medieval Sanskrit writings. Udayana famously formulates the law of excluded middle as his *a priori* justification for a dichotomous division producing the sevenfold taxonomy of the Vaiśeṣika categories. Just as a classificatory rationality is operative in the division of all things first into presences and absences, and then the presences into non-relations and relations, the non-relations into independent and dependent, and so forth, so too purely analytic inferences are accommodated when definitions are taken as inference-tickets, albeit for "inferences with merely differentiating marks" – for example, "Earth differs from all non-earth because it has odor," when having odor is taken as the defining mark of earth. Unlike other inferences, which require as supporting examples a series of cases where the mark (whatever property is mentioned in the "because"-clause displaying the sign, probans or ground) coexists with the property to be inferred, "in [these] inference[s] we do not need certification from a positive example. . . . Naiyāyikas . . . would insist that this inference (or its conclusion) is necessarily true, for the opposite situation would be impossible or a logical contradiction" (Matilal 1982, p. 142).

The Buddhist logicians talk about a universal concomitance which is not based on causal connection but issues simply from conceptually guaranteed class inclusions – for example, all elms are trees. From this they develop a theory of "inner connection" or "necessary pervasion" (*antarvyāpti*) which the fallibilist Nyāya school did not support. The most important evidence for an Indian sensitivity to logical necessity comes from their use of "*tarka,*" which has been translated as hypothetical or subjunctive reasoning. Ancient Indian atheists would strengthen their position by arguing:

> If God were the maker, then he would possess a body, make strenuous efforts etc; But God cannot have a body or make efforts to overcome obstacles. Hence God is not the maker.

For the inherent *modus tollens* to work, one must have a clear conception of connection between two false sentences or two unmaterialized possibilities. There is a vast literature on the role of *tarka* starting with Bagchi's (1953) pioneering *Inductive Reasoning* and proceeding to K. Chakrabarti's (1992) *Definition & Induction*. In spite of the acceptance of its probative value for generalizations, it remains puzzling why a sentence like "If *p* then *q*," in which both *p* and *q* are known to be false, is treated as expressing non-knowledge (*aprāmā*).

Notwithstanding extremely sophisticated distinctions made between self-contradictions (such as the liar-sentence) and pragmatic self-refutations (like "I am not aware of this"), the Naiyāyikas use "barren woman's son" and "horn of a rabbit" as empty terms without discrimination. Here is Matilal's explanatory conjecture:

> Suppose my car is red. This fact, a contingent fact, has already defeated (excluded) the possibility of its being non-red. Does this "excluded" possibility then join the group of impossibilities? No clear and explicit answers emerge from the Indian philosophers except in their discussion (Udayana) of citing a nonexistent entity as an example. In any case, consideration of the excluded possibilities have somehow been thought idle in the Indian context. (Matilal, 1982, pp. 150–1)

Mohanty, on the other hand, is not baffled by this apparent lack of interest in purely formal necessity/possibility on the part of the Indian logicians. Since Indian logic arose out of two different contexts – namely, as a science of adjudication of actually happening debates and disputations, and as part of a general epistemology in which inferential cognition as a form of veridical awareness had to be normatively thematized – it was natural that component sentences of a valid argument were usually confined to those which were materially true. Soundness was more important than mere validity. This epistemic and causal character of Indian logic becomes clear when we look at its definition of a fallacy or defect of a mark. (As a reminder, in the inference "*a* has *f*, because it has *g*," *g* is the mark.)

A defective mark or the defect of a mark is defined as "the object of such a true cognition as acts to prevent an inferential cognition." The idea is this: consider the fallacy of locuslessness (*āśrayāsiddhi*). "Sherlock Holmes must have been a psychopath because he took drugs." The veridical awareness that Sherlock Homes never existed would, according to Nyāya, *prevent* the serious inference that he actually was a psychopath, because the property of drug-addiction as a putative mark would find no real locus. We surely have a different conception of logic (Mohanty calls it "Logic 2") here, not only because the fallacy above would not count as a formal fallacy in Western logic but because the rejection or cancellation of a proposed inference that the discovery of the defect is supposed to lead to is conceptualized as "preventing." In later Neo-Nyāya schools, the relation of preventor-and-prevented cognitions became a hot topic of discussion. My perception that the sun has risen *prevents* any immediately succeeding inference that it is still night-time. But is this just a psychological generalization? Once we discover the fault in the mark, the inferential cognition is blocked or prevented. Is that just a causal law? Insofar as these rules are formulated in terms of the content-structures of the cognition and not in terms of any other mentalistic features of cognition, they must be structurally grounded. Logicians in the Indian context were partly evolving an ethics of belief and partly discovering naturalistic laws of compatible and incompatible cognitive acts (in the same subject) in virtue of their intentional content (*viṣayatā*) which is further broken down into the roles of qualificand (*viśeṣyatā*), qualifier (*prakāratā*), relation (*samsargatā*), and so on. The logic of awareness gets fascinatingly complex and the philosophical logic involved in trying to decide the ontological status of these cognition-conferred intentional roles of actual items which figure as objects, qualifiers and relational links becomes awfully subtle. But it is neither a formal logic that studies relations between sentence meanings or Fregean thoughts belonging to a non-mental non-material third realm, nor a psychologistic logic that studies merely how the mind functions with regard to cognitive acts. It is a logic of universal intentional structures interrelated in a normative way. Thus fallacies are called "apparent marks" (*hetu-ābhāsa*) a correct knowledge of which *prevents* inference because, Mohanty remarks, "as rational beings we cannot make a fallacious inference: we only appear to be doing so" (Mohanty, 1992, p. 113).

As far as the justification-clause in the definition of knowledge is concerned, Sibajiban Bhattacharya has made a virtue out of the common complaint that the Indian concept of *prāma* never developed beyond the second rejected definition of Plato's *Theaetetus* – namely, knowledge as true belief. By using simple principles of epistemic logic, he proves (see, "Epistemology of Testimony and Authority" in *Knowing from Words*) the following: "If knowledge is something more than mere true belief, then I should be able to know when I have knowledge and when I have mere true belief. Theorem 1 suggests, however, that no one is able to make that discrimination in his own case." This is a pretty strong stand to take, because Western epistemology starts from the distinction between knowledge and true belief – the space between the two being precisely the *space of reason*. Perhaps all that Bhattacharya has proved is that that distinction has no role to play in self-ascriptions or claims of knowledge. The rich skeptical literature in Sanskrit (see, Jayarāśi and Śrīharṣa) clearly demands a stricter notion of knowledge, because it is never tired of pointing out that accidentally slipping into a true belief by a route which could equally well have produced error is no knowledge (and that is all we can do!, hence the skeptical pessimism). But Bhattacharya's attempt cautions us against taking the usual Western account of knowledge as justified true belief plus something else (which the Gettier-industry has been hard at work on) as gospel truth. A more realistic rationality may require that we be happy with true beliefs achieved through epistemically virtuous means.

Axiomatic grammar

"To adhere to Indian thought," remarks L. Renou, "means first of all to think like a grammarian." The model of theoretical knowledge that appealed most to the Vedic mind was, as we find in the hymn to knowledge (Ṛg Veda X.71), that of "the seers fashioning speech by their mind, sifting as with sieves corn-flour is sifted." Patañjali, who quotes this at the beginning of his "great commentary" on Pāṇini's grammar, makes it clear that words are not "fashioned" by the grammarian like pots are made by the potter. Pāṇini was trying to come up with an adequate description of already existent ordinary and Vedic Sanskrit usage while remaining faithful to the criteria of simplicity and brevity. The method of this fourth century BCE grammarian has been compared to that of Euclid insofar as Pāṇini's rules or aphorisms (*sūtra*s) are divided into three kinds:

a) the defining *sūtras* which introduce technical terms,
b) the theorems which normatively describe linguistic facts while demonstrating their legitimacy through formation and transformation rules, and
c) the metatheorems (*paribhāṣā-sūtra*) explaining how rules have to be applied in particular cases (see, "Euclid and Pāṇini" in Staal 1988).

There are obvious differences between Euclid's subject matter, which demands a higher degree of generality and *a priori* validity of the axioms, and Pāṇini's subject-matter, namely, well formed words and sentences, to accommodate the contingent variety of which, rules have to be formed *ad hoc*. But Pāṇini's rigorous standards of consistency, completeness, and the avoidance of redundancy (amounting to independence) among his basic rules make the comparison illuminating. This grammatical model of generating all correct speech-units by sifting them through the parsimonious "sieve" of a set of systematically arranged *sūtras* (memorizable strings of words) became the paradigm for philosophers in the early Common Era in India. Thus we have the *Yoga-sūtras*, the *Mīmāṃsā-sūtras*, the *Vaiśeṣika-sūtras* and, from the point of view of the study of epistemic and dialogical rationality, the all-important *Nyāya-sūtras*.

Rationality in medical practice

Physicians in ancient India must have regularly held meetings for co-operative as well as combative debates in the presence of some expert judges. The Nyāya list of "tricks of reasoning" and "sophistical rejoinders" is thought to have emerged out of this older tradition of the science and art of diagnostic and therapeutic debates. The enormous medical text *Caraka Saṁhita*, which reports on this tradition, divides the entire practice of medicine into four factors: (1) the physician; (2) the substances (drugs and diet); (3) the nurse; and (4) the patient. The four essential qualifications of the physician are: (1a) a clear grasp of the science learnt; (1b) a wide range of experience; (1c) general skillfulness; and (1d) cleanliness. The four key factors concerning drugs and diet are: (2a) abundance of supply; (2b) applicability; (2c) their many imaginable uses or multifacetedness, which is now called the "broad-spectrum" nature; and (2d) richness. The four qualifications of the nurse are: (3a) a knowledge of attending techniques; (3b) skill; (3c) caring involvement with the patient; and (3d) cleanliness. The most interesting quartet of desiderata is that concerning the rational patient, who must have: (4a) a good memory (so as not to forget her own case-history!); (4b) obedience to the doctor's instructions; (4c) courage; and (4d) the verbal ability to describe the symptoms.

Interestingly enough, in spite of the presence of *karma*-theory in popular as well as theoretical consciousness, the text does not list "accumulated good *karma*" as a condition of the curable patient. As long as the patient is cooperative and courageous and articulate, his chances of getting well are good!

In the tenth chapter of *Caraka Saṁhita* we find the most fascinating argumentation about the efficacy of medical practice, where cases of cures without doctors, drugs or nursing as well as the death of a well attended and medically treated patient are discussed as counterexamples to the alleged necessity and sufficiency of medicine. We do not have space here to go into the details of this discussion. But what emerges out of this context is a clear sense of the need to defend the probabilistic workability/truth of a scientific practice/theory in the face of reasonable doubts arising from empirical data. (See Chattopadhyaya, 1980, pp. 107–13.)

Logical form and confirmation of universal concomitance

The center-piece of the Nyāya-theory of reasoning has been the problem of formulating and justifying the relation of invariable co-location or pervasion (*vyāpti*) between the mark (typically illustrated by smoke) and the property to be inferred (typically, fire). In this quick survey we shall first look at the way the universality of such a relation was captured, without resorting to extensional quantification theory, in terms of property, location and absence. Then we shall summarize the ways in which skeptical attacks against the possibility of the non-circular empirical confirmation of such universal concomitance were resisted.

Gaṅgeśa, the father of Neo-Nyāya (thirteenth century CE) discusses 29 different formulations of the definition of pervasion, rejecting 21 of them as flawed. Pervasion has been defined as "non-deviation," "natural connection," "relation of effect to its efficient cause," "accompaniment of all cases of one term with the other term," "unconditional relation," and as "not being located in any place where the property to be inferred is absent," to mention just a few of its definitions. The last of these – that is, pervasion's definition in terms of non-co-location with the absence of the major term (loosely identifiable with the property to be inferred, for example, fire) – has been rejected because it fails to cover cases where the major term is an unnegatable property which is located everywhere – for example, existence or nameability. Interestingly, "This cup is nameable because it is knowable" is regarded as a sound inference even though the mark and the property to be inferred are both unnegatable.

The final definition of pervasion, somewhat simplified, could be translated as follows: "Pervasion is the mark's property of being co-located with such an inferable property as is not the absentee of any absolute absence which is co-located with the mark." The subleties of these definitions are brought out by at least five centuries (that is, until the eighteenth century CE) of scholastic creativity, which continued to invent counterexamples, adding further qualifications to avoid undercoverage, overcoverage and inapplicability. A very small part of this literature is available in English now in F. Staal's (1988) *Universals* ("Means of Formalisation in Indian and Western Logic" and "Contraposition in Indian Logic"), in Matilal's (1985) *Logic, Language and Reality*, and in C. Goekoop's (1967) *The Logic of Invariable Concomitance*.

Coming to the issue of inductive justification of pervasion (*vyāpti-graha*), the Nyāya philosophers conceded Hume's point that there are no *a priori* necessities in nature. Against Sāṃkhya, which believes in inherent substantial identity between cause and effect, Nyāya believes that fire is one thing and smoke is another. But their account of contingent causal connection is realistic rather than psychologistic. Unlike Hume, Nyāya does not regard demonstrative *a priori* knowledge and irrational animal faith as the only options. Boldly affirming that it is perfectly rational to embrace fallible certitude after one has taken all possible empirical precautions to eliminate doubt (especially when asking for deductive necessity is irrational), Nyāya bases its knowledge claims of invariable concomitance on: (1) multiplication of instances; (2) subjunctive supporting arguments showing the material absurdity of the negation of the universal generalization to be established; (3) direct perceptual acquaintance with all cases of the inferable property through the experienced universal inherent in the observed cases (this is a controversial doctrine of seeing-all-through-seeing-the-class-character-in-one); and (4) showing how skeptical doubt concerning induction lands one in practical paralysis insofar as one cannot help believing that food will always nourish, fire will always burn, and words will often be understood. "Doubt reaches its limits in pragmatic self-refutation." (The clearest account of this is to be found in K. Chakrabarti's *Definition and Induction*.)

Dharma-rationality and self–other comparison

I have said earlier that Vedic orthodoxy regarded tradition as the sole spring of moral knowledge. Such rigidity was naturally called into question by the tradition itself, and in the *Mahābhārata* and the *Dharmaśāstras* we see an obsessive attempt to arrive at contextualized as well as universal criteria for determining the right way to live. Some parts of practical rationality were explained in terms of means–end adaptations, so that a command like "You must perform fire-rituals since you wish to attain heaven" would be understood in terms of three pieces of belief: (1) that such performance is do-able by the command-receiver; (2) that it would promote a desirable result, in this case, heaven; and (3) that it does not involve undesirable results which are counterbalancing – for example, the sin of killing animals. But there were other parts of practical reason which were deontological, and the *Mahābhārata* tries to come up with criteria for such universal *dharmas* (duties). The briefest statement of such a criterion is:

> Do not inflict upon others what is intolerable to yourself. This, in short, is *dharma* and it is other than what one naturally desires. (*Mbh.* XIII, 113, 8)

Probing deeper into the source of this morality, the next verse says,

> In refusals, generosity, pleasure, pain, approval, and disapproval a human being finds a decisive source of knowledge (*pramāṇa*) by comparison with oneself.

This coheres perfectly with the symbolic narrative of a just businessman who teaches *dharma* even to higher-caste brahmins because he has achieved "equal attitude towards all living beings." As he puts it, "My weighing scale remains balanced equally for everybody" (*Mbh.* XII, 262, 10).

But what does one do when there is a conflict of duties? The *Mahābhārata* is full of such moral dilemmas. Traditions and texts cannot solve them because they themselves are often in conflict with one another. That is why one needs intelligence (*buddhi*) and learning (*vidyā*), a special training in the *pramāṇas* (means of knowledge), to purify the moral knowledge derived from handed-down tradition. *Dharma* cannot afford to be intellectually blind or uncritical. Matilal quotes the following advice from Manu Saṃhita:

> What is to be done? If such a doubt arises with regard to a conflict of *dharmas* an assembly of not less than ten persons should deliberate and reach a decision – this assembly will be constituted by three Vedic scholars, one logician, one dialectician or debater, one expert in semantics, etymology, and three laymen from three different age-groups – a student, a householder, and a retired person. (Matilal in *Rationality in Question*, p. 203)

One sees the beginnings of a discourse-model of practical rationality quite clearly here!

Reason in emotions: the rasa theory of aesthetic relish

A similar process of universalization (*sādhāraṇikaraṇa*) or depersonalization, which has been called detached enjoyment through the "heart-universals," lies at the center of mainstream Indian aesthetic theory, which runs from Bharata's treatise on drama through Anandavardhana and Abhinavagupta up to K. C. Bhattacharya's early twentieth-century reflections on aesthetic rapture.

Bharata (first or second century CE) provides almost a functionalist logic of emotion in his classic sixth chapter, where he gives the cryptic formulation: "*rasa* (aesthetic rapture) comes from a combined functioning of the determinants (*vibhāva*) and the consequent expressions (*anubhāva*) and the passing states." The basic idea, somewhat shrouded by a millennium's worth of commentators' controversies, seems to be this: a certain depersonalized enjoyment (for example, at the representation of fury) is a function of the stable latent emotional disposition (for example, anger) and is achieved through the input of some determinants (for example, insult, vengefulnesss, threat, jealousy, assault) and the output of some consequent outer expressions (for example, red eyes, frowning, the biting of lips, the grabbing of one hand with another, and so on) via the passing sentiments (for example, energy, restlessness, obstinacy, perspiration, trembling, and so on).

Abhinava Gupta, who comes after a long tradition of commentators and thinkers on poetics and aesthetics, takes this obscure theory and develops an exceedingly complex epistemology of artistic enjoyment out of it. What is relevant for our purpose is to realize the importance of the process of the impersonalization of an emotional situation through which even the pain of actual or possible, real or imaginary others can become objects of aesthetic rapture by becoming, as it were, one's own. The same mechanism of self–other comparison, in two radically different ways, yields both moral imagination as well as aesthetic enjoyment. Without the viewer's loss of ego, emotional identification with a tragic hero should lead to pain rather than pleasure. K. C. Bhattacharya describes this beautifully in his 1930s essay "The Concept of *Rasa*." "When I imagine, with delight, an old man affectionately watching his grandchild play with a toy, my sympathy with the grandfather's sympathetic feeling for the child goes through the grandfather's heart-universal. The beauty of a child at play appears to me through a kind of knowledge-by-identification. My personality is as it were dissolved and yet I am not caught in the object like the child. I freely become impersonal." K. C. Bhattacharya's theory of aesthetic appreciation as "sympathy with sympathy" becomes rather obscure and contentious and he admits that this idea of the "heart-universal" is "semi-mythological." Yet there is a certain right-mindedness in his interpretation of the phenomenon of de-individuation through which even the humdrum or the ugly or the ludicrous become beautiful, and because of which, in spite of total empathy with the tortured heroine on the stage, one does not feel the need to go and attack the actor playing the villain, because while one enjoys "suffering" with the felt-heroine-in-general one cannot hit a villain-in-general.

Conclusion: the logical way to liberation

We started this survey of the ideas of rationality by mentioning the term "*ānvīkṣikī*," which is usually taken as synonymous with logic, Nyāya or the philosophical systems in general. What is profoundly interesting is that this metascience or logic of all other disciplines is said to be identical with the liberating science of the spirit (*ātmavidyā*). Through medicine and healthy diet, ethically correct behavior, intelligent and legally constrained utility-maximization and aesthetic enjoyment, we constantly engage in the most basic reasonable activity of all – that is, the avoidance of suffering. But as long as we are unclear about the nature of our selves, we continue to make errors which lead to recurring pains. Different philosophical systems, in consonance with, but not solely depending upon, one's own received tradition, try to give us knowledge of the self. This is as much a rational project as it is a practical, moral and spiritual one. As far as the major classical Indian philosophies such as Nyāya, Sāṃkhya, Vedānta, and the Kaśmir Śaiva schools are concerned, rationality is theoretically studied and practically used so that the thinking agent can ultimately lose her individual ego, the object-directed outward mind or intellect which pretends to be the self, the pleasure-seeking wish-generating cognitions which make one other-dependent, and hence unfree. The practice of *Dharma* which forces you to compare yourself to others, the performance of duties without desire for reward, the distillation of emotions through aesthetic universalization, a healthy dose of reasoned skepticism about reason's ability to yield stable knowledge – all of these lead to that saving self-knowledge which brings freedom from suffering. According to Akṣapāda Gautama (first century CE), in order to achieve such liberation you must have accurate knowledge of the means of knowledge, the objects of knowledge, doubt, purpose, example, tenet, the components of a syllogism, hypothetical reasoning, the determination of a conclusion, truth-finding discourse, defensive debate, polemics, fallacies, tricks, retorts, and the conditions of defeat. Thus in Indian thought spirituality and rationality merge into one discipline called *āvīkṣikī*.

Bibliography

Bagchi, Sitansusekhar 1953: *Inductive Reasoning: a Study of "Tarka" and its Role in Indian Logic* (Calcutta).

Bhattacharya, K. C. 1983: *Studies in Philosophy* (Delhi: Motilal Banarassidas).

Biderman, Shlomo and Scharfstein, Ben-Ami (eds) 1989: *Rationality in Question* (Leiden: E. J. Brill).

Chakrabarti, Kisor K. 1995: *Definition and Induction* (Honolulu: University of Hawaii Press).

Chattopadhyaya, Debiprasad 1980: "Tradition of Rationalist Medicine in Ancient India," in *Philosophy: Theory and Action* (Poona).

Goekoop, C. 1967: *The Logic of Invariable Concomitance* (Dordrecht: Kluwer).

Halbfass, Wilhelm 1988: *India and Europe* (Albany: State University of New York Press).

—— 1991: *Tradition and Reflection.* (Albany: State University of New York Press).

Kant, Immanuel 1974: *Anthropology from a Pragmatic Point of View*, trans. Mary J. Gregor (Holland: Mertinus Nijjoff).

Kaviraj, Gopinath 1990: *Selected Writings of M. M. Gopinath Kaviraj* (Varanasi: Centenary Celebration Committee).

Masson, J. L. and Patwardhan, M. V. 1970: *Aesthetic Rapture* (Poona: Deccan College).

Matilal, B. K. 1977: *Logical Illumination of Indian Mysticism* (Oxford: Oxford University Press).

—— 1982: *Logical and Ethical Issues of Religious Belief* (Calcutta: University of Calcutta).

—— 1985: *Logic, Language, and Reality* (Delhi: Motilal Banarssidas).

Matilal, B. K. and Chakrabarti, Arindam (eds) 1994: *Knowing from Words* (Dordrecht: Kluwer).

Mohanty, J. N. 1992: *Reason and Tradition in Indian Thought* (Oxford: Clarendon Press).

—— 1995: "Theory and Practice in Indian Philosophy," *Australasian Journal of Philosophy*, March.

Saha, Sukharanjan 1987: *Perspectives on Nyaya Logic and Epistemology* (Calcutta: K. P. Bagchi).

Solomon, Esther A. 1978: *Indian Dialectics*, Vols 1 and 2 (Ahmedabad).

Staal, Frits 1988: *Universals: Studies in Indian Logic and Linguistics* (Chicago: University of Chicago Press).

19

Humankind and nature in Indian philosophy

JOHN M. KOLLER

Overview

How does the Indian philosophical tradition view the relationship between human beings and nature? Is human existence an integral, though highly evolved, part of nature? Or is human existence radically different from natural existence? This question is fundamental and important, for its answer determines basic cultural values and life practices, including the primary aims of life (*puruṣārthas*) and the norms of life-stages and social classes (*varṇāśramadharma*). As might be expected, tradition does not provide us with a single, univocal answer to this question. Because the Indian tradition is made up of many sub-traditions, each with its own answer, and because these traditions are continuously changing, the answer varies across time, as well as across traditions. Nonetheless, allowing for necessary qualifications, these different answers share the view that both questions are to be answered in the affirmative. That is, the tradition's shared core of understanding across sub-traditions and time is that human existence is both an integral part of nature and that it is radically different. How is the apparent conflict between these two views resolved within the tradition? Is the attempted resolution successful? It is these two questions that form the problematic of this essay.

The view that human beings are an integral part of nature dates from the Vedic period, while the view that human beings, in their innermost being (*Ātman*), are radically different from nature is somewhat later, dating from the Upaniṣads. From Upaniṣadic times on the tradition strives to reconcile these two views, preserving the first while embracing the second. Thus our exploration of these two views and our analysis of the philosophical success of their reconciliation is situated within the context of the tradition's own central problematic.

Humans as an integral part of nature

First of all, the Indian tradition, from Vedic times to the present, views human beings as an integral part of the grand unity of organic existence that extends from the highest gods all the way to the lowliest plant life. Within this unity, embodied human existence is viewed as a natural living process that integrates a complex variety of mental and physical processes. Although they by no means speak with a single voice, *the Brāhmaṇa* and *Āraṇyaka* texts of the earlier Vedic period clearly view human existence as an integral part of nature, classifying human beings as domesticated animals. But they clearly regard humans as very special animals insofar as they engage in abstract reflective thought and intentional action, most notably in these texts, is their performance of ritual action. The most common word for humankind in these texts, *manuṣya*, is derived from the root *man*, meaning "to think," the same root from which *manas*, the word for mind is derived. Humanness (*manuṣyatva*) is marked especially by the intelligence that makes possible reflective thought and intentional action. Indeed, the *Śatapatha Brāhmaṇa* (7.5.2) tells us that Prajāpati created human beings out of intelligence (*man*), an eloquent way of saying that intelligence is the stuff humans are made of.

The Hymn to the Cosmic Person (Ṛg Veda 10.90), probably a late addition to the Ṛg Veda, summarizes a great deal of Vedic thought about the place of human beings in the world and the relation between humans and nature. This text, in describing a primordial world-creating ritual that creates the world out of the offering of a portion of the *Puruṣa*, the cosmic Person, affirms the underlying unity of the divine, cosmic and human realms of existence. Verses 8 through 14 describe how the cosmic Person, through the power of ritual offering (*yajña*), was transformed into gods, cosmos, humans and birds and animals. Indra and Agni, for example, originated from the *Puruṣa*'s mouth, the atmosphere from its navel, sky from its head, earth from its feet, and the four classes of human beings, *brāhmaṇa*, *kṣatriya*, *vaiśya* and *śūdra*, from its mouth, arms, legs and feet, respectively. Birds and animals came from the blessed offerings of milk and ghee. (See John M. Koller, *The Indian Way* (New York: Macmillan, 1982) pp. 42–6, for a discussion of this seminal text.)

The Hymn to the Cosmic Person makes four important points that are relevant to our investigation of the relation between nature and humankind. First, assigning the origin of the divine, human, and natural realms to the same source was the Vedic tradition's most powerful way of establishing their underlying unity. Second, by describing this source as a primordial person, the tradition declares that it regards human existence as the most basic and profound kind of existence. Third, by differentiating the four classes of humans in terms of their origination in different parts or functions of the cosmic person, this text emphasizes the species-like differences between them. Finally, in describing the creation of existence as the result of sacred ritual (*yajña*), the tradition affirms the fundamental and central value of ritual action. The ritual offering of the primordial Person is the prototype of the ritual action that humans must practice in order to re-create and maintain their existence. Ritual action is of fundamental value to human beings because it is how they open their existence to the deeper powers in which it is grounded. Through the fulfillment of ritual duty, humans establish communion with nature and the gods, and renew their life from moment to moment.

The continuing tradition enshrines the fundamental Vedic value of ritual and moral duty by making their fulfillment the first of the four fundamental human aims in life (*puruṣārthas*). Perhaps the single most important clue to the Indian tradition's view of the special place human beings have within the totality of existence is found in the concept of human aims. According to the theory of *puruṣārtha*, there are four fundamental values at which human beings should aim: namely, *dharma* (the fulfillment of ritual and moral duties), *artha* (success), *kāma* (enjoyment), and *mokṣa* (liberation). These aims represent the tradition's view of the most fundamental human values; their accomplishment represents the highest human perfection possible.

What sets humans apart from the rest of nature is their deliberate pursuit of the four basic human aims in life. Only humans engage in the performance of ritual and moral obligations, and in the liberating quest for self-transcendence. Furthermore, although other animals may be said to pursue success (*artha*) and enjoyment (*kāma*), it is not clear that they do so intentionally and with future orientation. Nor do they pursue success and enjoyment as circumscribed and determined by *dharma* or in preparation for *mokṣa*, as humans do. Thus although the tradition recognizes that other animals pursue success and enjoyment, because they lack the requisite reflective and intentional abilities to pursue them as aims in life, even the *puruṣārthas* of success and enjoyment are regarded as uniquely human. *Dharma* is regarded as the foundation of the other three *puruṣārthas*. *Artha* and *kāma* may only be pursued in accord with *dharma*. Furthermore, ultimately it is the fulfillment of moral and ritual duty that produces success and enjoyment, both in this world and the world beyond, according to Pūrvamīmāṃsā, the continuing tradition that embodies the enduring Vedic values and ideas. Even *mokṣa*, although it transcends *dharma*, *artha*, and *kāma*, cannot be achieved without the perfection of *dharma*.

While the first three *puruṣārthas* embody the Vedic vision of human beings as an integral part of nature, the fourth aim incorporates the Upaniṣadic vision of an inner self (*Ātman*) that is essentially independent of its human embodiment and therefore separate from nature. Consequently, when *mokṣa* became the primary aim of life in the late Upaniṣadic period, although the values of *dharma*, *artha* and *kāma* were preserved in the first three *puruṣārthas*, they ceased to be the primary effective means of perfection. Now it was knowledge that came to be regarded as the primary effective means, for only knowledge was seen as capable of effecting *mokṣa*. With this revolutionary change, what became of paramount value was liberation from nature, from society, and from embodied human existence itself, thereby devaluing efforts to attain perfection as a natural, social and human being.

Self as independent of its embodiment

Since the time of the Upaniṣads, Indian philosophy (particularly in the Vedāntic traditions) has been much more concerned with *Brahman* – the eternal, unchanging ground of being – than with the existence that embodies this ground, and much more concerned with immortal Self (*Ātman*) in human beings than with the human existence (*manuṣya*) that embodies this Self. Indeed, embodied human existence came to be seen as *saṁsāra*, bondage to repeated deaths, a condition from which liberation was sought. This is why *mokṣa*, the liberation of *Ātman* from its embodiment, became more important than *dharma*, *artha*, and *kāma*, the aims of perfecting human existence in its embodied condition.

Although it is true that for most of the Indian philosophical systems it is the pure Self that is of paramount value, embodied existence is of central importance in all of the orthodox systems. Precisely because of their emphasis on liberation of the pure Self from the saṁsāric bonds of embodied existence, these systems attach great importance to understanding embodied existence as one of the keys to liberation. Because the bonds to be loosened are those created by embodied existence and because the path to liberation is followed by the embodied self, full knowledge of embodied existence is seen as a necessary condition for liberation of the pure Self from its karmic bondage.

In particular, it is important to understand how bondage comes about: what are the processes that make and unmake bondage? The answer, in one word, is *karma*. One of the distinctive features of the Indian worldview is that embodied human existence is seen as a karmic process, a continuing process of the making and unmaking of personal existence that has no beginning and that is never completed. This karmic process of person-making is constituted by interaction with other processes in an ever-widening sphere that extends ultimately to the whole world, linking each person to every other person and to all other beings in a web of interconnections that extends to all times and places. Indeed, individual persons are viewed within the tradition as intersections within nature's network, analogous to the knots in a fishnet (*Yoga Sūtra Bhāṣya* II.13).

This karmic view of human existence integrates the human and natural spheres of existence, seeing them as constituting a single continuum, which is similar to the Vedic vision. Here, however, in contrast to the Vedic view, nature and human existence in all its karmic dimensions are no longer seen as ultimately real. Now they are transcended by *Brahman/Ātman*, the indwelling ground and Self of being. This is why the highest goal and ultimate value of the orthodox traditions is precisely the liberation (*mokṣa*) of the ultimate Self from its human condition – from the karmic self enmeshed in natural existence.

From the perspective of the *Ātman*, there is no fundamental differentiation between the human and the natural spheres; they continue to be seen as parts of an organic whole. Indeed, the workings of *karma* bind all living things together, allowing beings to be born and reborn in this great continuum innumerable times in a wide variety of forms, ranging from plants and animals to humans and gods. From the perspective of *Ātman*, however, the important boundary is not between nature and humanity, but between the karmic realm, which includes both nature and humanity, on the one hand, and the ultimate Self, which transcends both nature and humanity, on the other.

One of the classic formulations of the distinction between the ultimate Self and embodied human existence is found in chapter 13 of the *Bhagavadgītā*, where embodied human existence is viewed as a field on which the various physical and mental forces interact with and modify each other and where the ultimate Self is viewed as an independent "knower of the field." "Described briefly," says the *Gītā*, "this field, with its modifications, is constituted by the great elements (ether, air, fire, water, and earth), sense-of-self, intelligence, the unmanifested, the ten senses and the mind, the five sense realms, desire, aversion, happiness and suffering, the embodied whole, consciousness and steadfastness" (13.5). Rooted in Sāṃkyha metaphysics, this is a description of a person seen as a field of interacting energies of different kinds and intensities, a field which is simultaneously interacting with innumerable other fields, integrating the human and natural spheres. The individual person is a juncture or constellation of these interactions, born and reborn out of successively intersecting energy-fields.

From the perspective of the ultimate Self, however, this embodied human existence described as a field is merely the instrument of a Self that is essentially transcendent and independent of its embodied condition. The *Gītā* says of this ultimate Self, "the knower of the field": "This imperishable supreme Self, beginningless and without qualities, though abiding in embodied existence, Arjuna, neither acts nor is polluted" (13.31).

Like the rest of the orthodox traditions, the *Gītā* regards this Self as being held hostage by the karmically fashioned body-mind, and emphasizes strategies and techniques for its liberation. According to this view, the ultimate Self, essentially autonomous and independent of the mind-body complex, is held fast by the karmic bonds of passion and ignorance. This bondage, which constitutes the ground of suffering, can be terminated only by liberating the Self from embodied existence. This means that the Indian tradition draws an ontological line between embodied human existence, viewed in the *Gītā* as the field of body-mind, which has both physical and mental characteristics, and the Self, which transcends both the physical and the mental.

The ontological line drawn between the realm of embodied human and natural existence, which is only apparently but not ultimately real, on the one hand, and the ultimate reality of *Brahman/Ātman*, on the other, constitute a continuing problematic in Indian thought. The reason is that in order for *mokṣa*, the liberation of the Self from karmic existence, to be meaningful, the separation between these two realms must be absolute. At the same time, in order for karmically bound persons to effect their liberation from karmic bondage, these two ontological realms must be connected, because the power that removes karmic bondage cannot itself be part of karmic existence.

Reconciling ultimate and embodied existence

The Upaniṣads contain many interpretations of embodied existence and its relation to the ultimate Self (*Ātman/Brahman*). Most of these provide an organic, holistic account of existence. The *Muṇḍaka*, for example, suggests that even as a spider produces its web, as plants grow from the earth, and hair from a person's body, so does the universe arise from the ultimate (*Ātman/Brahman*) (I.1.7). Embodied human existence as well as nature arises from that ultimate Self: "From That are born life, mind, the sense-organs, and also ether, air, fire, water, and earth, all supported" (II.1.3).

The *Taittirīya* provides a holistic, evolutionary explanation, beginning with Brahman's manifestation as ether: "From this Self (*Brahman*) arose ether; from ether air; from air fire; from fire water; from water earth; from earth herbs; from herbs food; from food the person" (II.1). It then goes on to give a picture of individual human existence as an integral, organic layered process, where the physical processes envelop the life processes, which envelop the perceptual processes, which envelop the processes of understanding, which envelop joy, the innermost self, the *Ātman* which is the source and ground of the person (II.2–5).

The *Kaṭha* explains the Self and its relation to the embodied existence with the image of controller and controlled, using the analogy of a chariot driver and a chariot: "Self should be known as lord of the chariot, body as chariot, intelligence as chariot-driver, mind as reins, senses as horses, and sense objects the paths. The Self, associated with body, senses and mind, is the enjoyer" (I.3.3–4).

Aware of tension between the ultimate and the non-ultimate levels of reality, many Upaniṣadic thinkers make a concerted effort to describe the ultimate as fully present in all of its embodiments. For example, in the *Taittirīya* Upaniṣad (ch. 3), when Bhṛgu asks his father, Varuṇa, to explain *Brahman*, Varuṇa begins by explaining that matter, life, the senses, understanding, and speech are the basic elements of all existence. He then goes on to say, "Indeed, that from which these beings are born, by which they live, and into which they enter when dying, endeavor to know that as *Brahman*." Here Varuṇa, like most of the Upaniṣadic thinkers, is careful not to view *Brahman* as a separate existence. Instead, *Brahman* itself, as the ground and substance of all existence, is described as comprised of the levels of matter, life, lower awareness, higher consciousness, and finally, the deepest level, bliss. Then, lest this teaching of the highest level of reality as the bliss of *Brahman* be misunderstood to be a repudiation of the lower levels, Varuṇa immediately goes on to emphasize the importance of the lowest level of reality: "Do not speak ill of matter. That shall be the rule. Life, indeed, is matter. The body is the eater of material food and life is established in the body."

Varuṇa's explanation, while avoiding the risk of differentiating the ultimate and the non-ultimate into two completely separate kinds of reality, runs the opposite risk of not differentiating *Brahman* sufficiently from the ordinary existence of which it is claimed to be the ultimate ground and inner self. The Cārvākans, for example, rejecting the claimed differentiation of *Ātman* from its embodiment, are infamous for taking the embodied body-mind complex to be the ultimate self, denying the existence of any Self separate from this complex, thereby denying the very possibility of liberation. Because mind is inseparable from body, Cārvākans regard the death of the body as also the death of the mind, and thus, since there is no indwelling Self to be liberated, the final termination of a person's life. Although they were regarded as materialists by adherents of the other systems, they were not materialists in the typical Western sense of that term, for they viewed the body of a person as imbued with consciousness.

Because it is not possible to examine all of the Indian systems in the space available, in what follows I will provide two examples of how different traditions have dealt with the relation between the ultimate Self and its embodied existence in the world. Śaṃkara's Advaita Vedānta, continuing an important Upaniṣadic tradition, will be examined as an example of a system that insists that ultimately there is no duality, that *Brahman*/*Ātman* alone is real. Sāṃkyha-Yoga, on the other hand, will be examined as an example of a non-Upaniṣadic dualistic system that insists on complete differentiation of the ultimate and the non-ultimate, of the ultimate Self and its apparent embodiment in *prakṛti*.

Sāṃkyha

The Sāṃkyha account of human existence is explicitly dualistic, for it views a person as the conjunction of two fundamentally different and eternally opposed realities – *puruṣa* and *prakṛti*. *Puruṣa* is pure consciousness, eternal, unchanging, and self-illuminating. It is the true Self, the pure subject that can never become an object. The prakṛtic body-mind, on the other hand, is always of the nature of object, in itself unconscious, constantly changing, illuminated only by the light of *puruṣa*. Experience and knowledge are possible only because *prakṛti* is capable of reflecting the consciousness of *puruṣa*. That is, even though the prakṛtic body-mind is itself unconscious, it can become the instrument of a consciousness which shines through it because of its sattvic nature.

The metaphysics underwriting this corporeal view of embodied consciousness, though extremely subtle in its details, is simple in its outlines. *Prakṛti*, a unified whole, is seen as constituted by three interpenetrating kinds of energy or force-fields, which are revealed in the tendencies to manifestation found in the experienced world. *Rajas* is the vibrant energy that drives the entire manifestation process, which, if the sattvic energy level is high, appears as predominantly consciousness-like, and if the tamasic energy level predominates, as predominantly physical body or object-like. However, these constituent *guṇas* or force-fields are always present together in some proportion in every manifestation of *prakṛti* so that consciousness and physical existence are mutually dependent, always to be found together.

What is especially problematic in the Sāṃkyha explanation is that if *prakṛti* is by nature unconscious, and if consciousness as *puruṣa* is totally different from the prakṛtic objects it is said to illuminate, how can there be any interaction between the two? How can *puruṣa* illumine what is totally unconscious, and how can *prakṛti*, whose nature is to be unconscious, be illumined by consciousness, given that these two realities are regarded as ontologically exclusive of each other? The traditional answer is that one of the constituent strands of *prakṛti*, *sattva*, is transparent, capable of taking illumination from consciousness. But this is also problematic, for either *sattva* is *prakṛti*, and therefore unconscious, or else the strict dualism is given up. The other alternative, that the sattvic manifestations of *prakṛti* as embodied awareness (*buddhi*) is not absolutely different from the *puruṣa*, also destroys the dualism. Since *puruṣa* is unchanging and *prakṛti* is ever-changing, for *puruṣa* to take the form of *buddhi* means that it cannot be *puruṣa*.

Sāṃkyha philosophers have made many attempts to overcome the problems this rigid dualism presents, but they all appear to stumble at the critical juncture – the juncture where supposedly *puruṣa* and *prakṛti* meet. No matter how *buddhi* and *sattva* are construed, as long as they are admitted to be prakṛtic, they must be said to be essentially unconscious. This apparently serves the soteriological–

metaphysical interest of Sāṃkyha, for it supports the claim that *puruṣa* is never in fact in bondage to *prakṛti*, that the true Self, the *puruṣa*, is always free, and that liberation is simply the realization of this truth.

One of the fundamental reasons for holding this rigid dualism is to account for the fact that there is never experience unless there is an experiencing subject and an experienced object. This is, to account for the self-reflective character of experience in which a person not only experiences, but is aware that she is experiencing, it is thought necessary to posit a transcendent self, a self that remains always a subject totally different from the object experienced. But as we have seen, the very dualism that helps explain the self-reflective character of experience makes experience itself problematic, for experience requires a genuine meeting of subject and object, a meeting this dualism renders problematic.

What is especially interesting about the Sāṃkyha account of embodied existence is that despite the metaphysical problems presented by *puruṣa/prakṛti* dualism, *prakṛti*, including its embodied manifestation, is seen as the instrument of *puruṣa*, manifesting consciousness. Indeed, the very first manifestation or evolution of *prakṛti*, triggered by the presence of *puruṣa*, is *buddhi* (awareness), out of which self-awareness (*ahaṁkāra*), mind and the various capacities for sensation, perception and action evolve – and out of which eventually physical matter and bodies evolve. Clearly this *prakṛti*, as the ground of existence, is not merely material, at least not in the sense of inert or unconscious matter, for it is the ground from which embodied consciousness evolves. Accordingly, if *prakṛti* is taken to be a kind of materiality, it will have to taken as a conscious materiality. We might say it is a consciousness embodied within the very processes constitutive of existence, though from a Sāṃkyha point of view it would be more accurate to say that consciousness embodies materiality, for what are regarded as physical elements or bodies are declared to evolve out of *buddhi* or reflected consciousness, which is the first manifestation of *prakṛti*. On this view, the body and mind are both seen as conscious, and experience is interpreted in terms of the play between the various constituents of *prakṛti* – between the more and less conscious, rather than between the conscious subject and the unconscious object. Here we find no hard line between body and mind or between self and embodied existence. Rather, consciousness is seen as a pervasive and integral constituent of bodily existence. On this level human beings are an integral part of nature.

The Yoga system, which accepts much of Sāṃkyha's metaphysical anthropology and cosmology, focuses on the prakṛtic embodiment of consciousness as it constitutes the experiential life of a person. Drawing out the implications of the Sāṃkyha view of embodied existence as the continuing intersection of the energy fields constituting all persons and things, Yoga notes that human actions have the effect (*karmāśaya*) of changing both the surrounding world and the actor, disposing him or her in manifold ways. These dispositions (*saṁskāras*) condition subsequent experience and action, investing them with the traces (*vāsanās*) of previous acts. These traces or seeds (*bīja*) perpetuate the experimental stream, producing various afflictions, memories, and expectations. At death all the as yet unrealized karmic effects, collected in the subtle body of consciousness, move out of the physical body and enter an appropriate new body at its moment of conception. Thus whatever is born is already conditioned and disposed by prior actions, for embodied existence is a continuous creative process in which the effects of prior experience are transformed into present life, which, in turn, conditions future experience. The ultimate aim of yoga, of course, is to destroy the illusion that *Puruṣa*, the true Self, has anything whatever to do with the prakṛtic world of nature and embodied human existence.

Advaita Vedānta

As we have seen, the Sāṃkyha problem of the apparent irrelevance of theories of prakṛtic existence to a theory of the Self is connected to its main problem of explaining how genuine interaction between the dual realities of *puruṣa* and *prakṛti* can occur, a problem Advaita avoids with its non-dual stance. Śaṁkara's view, as expressed in the *Upadeśasāhasrī* (translation, Sengaku Mayeda), for example, is that the pure consciousness (*cidātman*) alone is ultimately real; everything else is only appearance. The Self (*Ātman*) that I truly am, he says, is "ever free, pure, transcendentally changeless, invariable, immortal, imperishable, and thus always bodiless" (I.13.3). Further, being bodiless means that the true self neither experiences nor acts. In Śaṃkara's words, "The false belief that *Ātman* is doer is due to the belief that the body is *Ātman*" (I.12.16). Thus when a student approached his teacher, a knower of *Brahman*, and asked how he could obtain release from the suffering of this transmigratory existence, the teacher advised him that he must overcome the ignorance through which he mistakenly thinks that he is an agent, an experiencer and a transmigrator, when in fact he is none of these, but the highest *Ātman*" (II.2.20).

From Śaṃkara's perspective, although I frequently identify my existence with my embodiment, this identification (*adhyāsa*) is a mistake, the result of ignorance, for the truth is that I am pure consciousness, *Ātman*, eternal and unchanging, having nothing to do with my embodiment. But how is this mistake to be explained? What is this ignorance wherein I identify with the body and regard myself as actor and experiencer? For the sake of showing that this identification is a mistake, that it results from ignorance, Śaṃkara needs to develop a philosophy of human existence that explains what embodied existence is and how it comes to be falsely imposed on *Ātman*. Thus he observes that if the student seeking the sacred knowledge which brings release from *saṁsāra* says, "I am eternal and different from the body. The bodies come and go like a person's garment," the teacher should say, "you are right," and then should explain how the body is different from the Self (II.1.12–13).

This advice is followed by a passage in which Śaṃkara explains what the body is and how it comes to be. Positing an unmanifest name-and-form (*avyakṛte nāmarūpa*), Śaṃkara declares that this unmanifest evolved into the world of name and form as we know it through an evolutionary process according to which it first became manifest as ether, air, fire, water, and earth, in that order. Each of these elements in turn became impregnated with the previous elements, until finally earth appeared as a combination of all five elements. He goes on to say, "And from earth, rice, barley, and other plants consisting of the five elements are produced. From them, when they are eaten, blood and sperm are produced, related respectively to the bodies of woman and men" (II.1.20). He then explains how this body is named at birth, how it gets its student name, its householder name, and also the name of the forest dweller and *saṅnyāsin*. Repeating that "the body is different from you (*Ātman*)," Śaṃkara says that the teacher should remind the student that the mind and the sense organs consist only of name-and-form, and quotes passages from the *Chāndogya* Upaniṣad (VI.5.4, VI.6.5 and VI.7.6) which declare that the mind consists of food (II.1.21).

Like the prakṛtic self of Sāṃkyha, this self of name-and-form is said to be unconscious ("like food"), but nonetheless constituted by an awareness enabling it to experience, act, and identify itself (mistakenly) as a transmigrating, experiencing, acting self. Thus, according to Advaita, a person consists of a physical body, made up of material substances; the senses (eye, ear, and so on); mind; agencies of speech, movement, sex, excretion, and grasping; sense-of-self (*ahaṁkāra*); as well as the internal embodied consciousness (*antaḥkaraṇa*), all of which are disposed and conditioned according to previous experiences.

The distinction between physical and subtle bodies (*sthūlaśārīra* and *sūkṣmaśārīra*) is very important, for it recognizes a distinction between mere physicality and humanly embodied physicality. It is a way of insisting on the bodily character of what we think of as mental functions, for the *sūkṣmaśārīra*, constituted by the five vital airs, the *buddhi* and *manas* through which the *antaḥkaraṇa* functions, as well as the ten organs (five cognitive-sensory; five conative-motor), is not only itself viewed as a body, but is itself further embodied in the *sthūlaśārīra*. Only for the embodied self are the knowledge and action needed for liberation possible (or necessary). The senses are seen as instruments of the mind, linking mind with the outside world, just as mind links senses with reflective consciousness, and reflective consciousness links up with Self. But senses, vital force, mind and reflective consciousness can function only when embodied; ultimately the inner organ (*antaḥkaraṇa*) cannot function except through the bodily self – through its *indriya* or senses.

To avoid the problems of dualism, Śaṃkara denies that human existence constituted by name-and-form is ultimately real or that it really embodies the Self. For him this account functions to explain only the *appearance* of experience and the world, the reality of which is never admitted. This view is deeply problematic, however, as Śaṃkara himself recognized, when he said not only that *avyakṛte nāmarūpa* evolved from *Ātman*, but also that it is different in essence from *Ātman*. How can it be both essentially different from and evolved from *Ātman* in a philosophy committed to *satkāryavāda*? *Satkāryavāda*, as a causal principle, insists that what is produced, the effect, cannot be a different kind of reality than its cause. Thus *Ātman* could produce only *Ātman*, never *nāmarūpa*, which is non-*Ātman*.

The analogy Śaṃkara introduces to explain this evolution of *nāmarūpa* from *Ātman* reveals the problem, for he says, "In this manner this element named 'ether' arose from the highest *Ātman* as dirty foam from clear water. Foam is neither water nor absolutely different from water, since it is not seen without water. But water is clear and different from foam, which is of the nature of dirt. Likewise, the highest *Ātman* is different from *nāmarūpa*, which corresponds to foam; *Ātman* is pure, clear, and different in essence from it" (II.1.19).

Clearly, this analogy breaks down, for foam combines two different things, clear water and dirt. Since Śaṃkara cannot admit such a duality, he denies the reality of *nāmarūpa*, relegating it to the level of *māyā* or appearance, as superimposition on *Ātman* through ignorance. Thus Advaita confronts a dilemma: though embodied existence must be assumed to account for experience, action and transmigration, to preserve the non-dualism that allows nothing other than *Ātman* to be real, its reality must be denied. As Sureśvara, one of Śaṃkara's followers, puts it: "Between worldly existence and the rock solid *Ātman* there is no connection at all except that of ignorance." And with this denial of any connection to the reality of *Ātman/Brahman*, embodied human existence, along with the natural and social worlds, is seriously devalued relative to *Ātman*.

In concluding, I should point out that while I have focused on what I perceive to be problems in the way in which Sāṃkyha and Advaita have tried to reconcile the discontinuity between embodied, worldly human existence and the ultimate reality of the pure Self, both of these traditions are of the opinion that they have successfully solved these problems. And indeed, if the radical discontinuity declared by Sureśvara and implicit in Sāṃkyha's *Puruṣa/Prakṛti* dualism can be overcome, then the value of human and natural existence is greatly enhanced, for then they are seen to embody, as their innermost being and self, the ultimate reality. However, if the discontinuity between the ultimate reality and worldly existence cannot be overcome, then it must be recognized that *mokṣa*, the supreme value, devalues human existence, for then it is not liberation *of* human beings, but liberation *from* being human. That is, then the value of *mokṣa* belongs to *Ātman*, not to embodied human existence, which ultimately is no more than the projection of ignorance.

20

The idea of the good in Indian thought

J. N. MOHANTY

If the good is what people desire or strive after, the Indian thinkers very early on developed a theory of hierarchy of goods: these are *artha* (material wealth), *kāma* (pleasure), *dharma* (righteousness), and *mokṣa* (spiritual freedom). Leaving aside the question about precisely how the first two in this list have to be ranked, one might suggest that the first two are what human beings do strive after, while the last two are what they ought to strive after. Such a distinction between what human beings in fact strive after and what they ought to strive after is indicated in a distinction between the *śreya* (morally good) and the *preya* (pleasant) found in the *Kaṭha* Upaniṣad, although it may have to be conceded that the is–ought distinction did not come to the forefront of Hindu moral thinking. One may as a matter of fact construct an argument to prove that even *mokṣa*, the supreme value, is not a mere ought-to-be. The argument would run as follows: we do want to get rid of pain and enjoy a state of happiness. This natural desire, by implication, may be extended to a complete freedom from pain and enjoyment of an uninterrupted state of bliss (even if no one ordinarily posits this as his or her goal). It is only on reflection, and after reaching the first two goals and finding oneself dissatisfied with them, that one self-consciously posits the last two goals – the third to begin with and, as a result of experiencing a similar dissatisfaction once it has been reached, subsequently the fourth and highest good, which is not a mere ought-to-be but an ideal state of being. If the English phrase "the highest good" translates into *niḥśreyasaḥ* in Sanskrit, then *mokṣa* is that state of excellence than which there is nothing greater and which leaves, upon attainment, nothing else to be desired.

While the Upaniṣads gave various descriptions of this state of being, the systems of philosophy developed their own accounts consistently with their philosophical positions. Let us look at some of the descriptions to be found in the Upaniṣads. The *Muṇḍaka* Upaniṣad says, one who knows Brahman becomes Brahman (II.ii.9). *Mokṣa* is described as a state of bliss not to be exceeded by any – a state of bliss which, in being reached, leaves nothing else to be desired. It is also described as a state in which all fear disappears, all sense of duality ("I" and the other, "I" and the world) vanishes. Yājñavalkya tells Janaka that one who knows Ātman becomes full of peace, self-controlled, patient and self-composed, that evil does not consume him while he consumes all evil (*Bṛhadāraṇyaka* Upaniṣad, IV.4.22–3).

Possibly, the most decisive text of antiquity on the topic of the highest good is Yājñavalkya's speech addressed to his wife Maitreyi. The text deserves to be quoted at length. When Yājñavalkya announced to his wife that he was about to renounce his life as a householder and assured her that he was going to divide his possessions between her and his other wife Kātyāyani, Maitreyi replied, "If now, Sir, this whole earth filled with wealth were mine, would I be immortal thereby?" When her husband said "No," Maitreyi asked, "What shall I do with that through which I may not be immortal? What you know, Sir, that indeed tell me." In reply, after saying of various things that are desired and that are dear – of such things as one's husband, wife, sons, wealth, gods and beings – that they are not dear for their own sake (that is, for the sake of loving them), but only for the sake of the Self (*Ātman*), Yājñavalkya concluded, "Lo, verily, it is the Self that should be seen, that should be hearkened to, that should be thought of, that should be pondered on, Oh! Maitreyi."

It is to this concept that we shall, in this essay, eventually attend. There is no doubt that this concept has loomed large before the Hindu mind, providing it with a practical end as well as a theoretical explanandum such that the various *āstika* (orthodox) philosophies may be regarded as providing theoretical justifications for the possibility (and desirability) of such an end. This, of course, does not imply either that there was agreement about the nature of the goal or that the theories that justified them were all alike. However, despite enormous internal differences and disputations, some large, indeed ultimate, goal attracted the Hindu mind, and this goal may be called "*mokṣa*." Before reflecting on this unity and the differences in understanding it, let me turn to more mundane striving.

I said "more mundane," for the four "ends of man" easily fall into two groups: the first three into a group which may be called ordinary and natural ends, the fourth being an extraordinary, supernatural goal. It is quite reasonable to surmise that the first three were identified earlier, and with the rise of reflective philosophy (and the discipline of Yoga) the fourth was added. Be that as it may, that distinction between ordinary and extraordinary goals does not coincide with the distinction between "is" and "ought." All four goals are pursued as a matter of fact, even if the third is pursued by fewer people than are the first two, and the fourth is pursued by very few indeed. It may be claimed, in one sense, as much of the first two goals as of the third, that they are striven after, and yet never reached with unsurpassable satisfaction. In other words, one can make a reasonable case for the claim that the first three goals can be reached only in degrees, "more or less," and never to an unsurpassable degree. Only the fourth, striven after by a few and reached by still fewer, when reached is reached with finality, without any scope for "more or less" or "degrees of attainment." The familiar is–ought distinction derived from Western moral thinking just does not seem to apply here.

Nevertheless, if we are to find a moral theory in Indian thinking on these matters, we must begin by focusing on theory of action. It may be, however, that what we have is a theory of value in a wider sense, which includes moral theory inasmuch as moral values are a subset of all values. In a specific sense, all ought pertains to actions and values which can be striven after through actions. In a larger sense, there are values making a claim on our being to be actualized – values which ought to *be*, without it being possible to find a correlative *duty*. The distinction between these two kinds of values – the values pertaining to duties and those pertaining to being, actional and ontological, and correlatively between two kinds of ought (the ought of duties and the ought of being) will, in spite of the breakdown of the is–ought distinction, help us to sort out things in the complex field of Indian ethics.

Theory of action

Theory of action forms the basis of practical philosophy, and this is true of Indian philosophy as well. Legal thought and ritualistic speculations, ethical and spiritual philosophies center around theory of action. Now a theory of action would inevitably cut across psychology, semantics and ontology. While all the philosophical systems had something to say about it, the common structure from which they all started may be represented as:

knowledge →	desire →	will to do →	motor effort →	the action
(*jñāna*)	(*cikirṣā*)	(*pravṛtti*)	(*ceṣtā*)	(*kārya*)

Within the general structure of this causal chain, there was, however, considerable difference in the theories that were developed. The differences concerned the precise nature of each member of the chain. Philosophers also differed in their interpretations of the verbal form of imperatives expressing moral duties. Leaving aside many niceties of discussion, we can distinguish between several different approaches. The philosophers of the Nyāya school held that the knowledge which brings about the desire (and then the will to do) is knowledge by the agent-to-be that the desired goal is achievable, that the performance of the action will bring about some good for the agent, this good involving an increase of *sukha* (happiness) and a reduction of *duḥkha* (pain). The members of the Bhātta school of Mīmāṃsā simplified the requirement considerably: an imperative sentence ("You ought to do ϕ") gives rise, in the auditor, to the cognition "The speaker wants me to do ϕ," which leads to the belief that a desired goal – one of the four ends of persons – can be reached by doing ϕ. This belief eventually leads the auditor to act. A much simpler theory is proposed by the Prābhākara school of Mīmāṃsā. According to them, conduciveness to future good is not a sufficient condition for desire and effort. Things past and things already present may be conducive to future good, but one does not act with regard to them. Neither is conduciveness to future good necessary for activity.

Only when an action requires a great deal of painful exertion does one need the assurance that the effort will result in happiness. The Prābhākara point is that even when an action is conducive to good, its being-something-to-be-done (*kāryatva*) and its being-conducive-to-the-production-of-good are different entities. All that is needed to act is the belief that it should be done. The imperative sentence's very grammatical form – when the sentence is a Vedic injunction – has the power to generate that belief (provided that you believe in the authority of the Vedas). Thus we have two different theories of action, especially of actions which follow upon imperatives: one which assigns a necessary mediating role to thought of the good that will come out of doing the action, the other which recognizes the resulting good but does not assign a mediating role to the thought of it. For the second theory, first espoused by Bādari, then revived by Prābhākara and given its classic popular statement by Kṛṣṇa in the *Bhagavadgītā*, the idea of duty is what mediates between hearing the imperative and performance of the course of action recommended.

Now one way of resolving this conflict between the opposed theories is to show that the teleological-cum-consequentialist theory holds good of the actions directed towards the first two goods (that is, towards *artha* and *kāma*), while the second, Kantian-type deontological theory holds good of actions inspired by the idea of *dharma*. Neither of the two theories, therefore, holds good for all actions. Actions which aim at acquisition of wealth and enjoyment of pleasure naturally must be preceded by the thought of the happiness that they would bring about, while it is plausible to hold that ethical actions, actions which follow upon moral imperatives (the scriptural injunctions, and so on), although they may sometimes be performed by agents who think of the happiness that would accrue to them as a result, do not necessarily presuppose any such thought. Since in the case of *dharma*-actions the result is regarded, generally in the Indian tradition, to be supernatural (that is, merits accruing to the soul) and to bear wholesome effects in the next life, thought about them, unlike thought about the empirical pleasure likely to arise from wealth and pleasurable objects, is emptily symbolic, lacks intuitive content, and so could not stimulate action unless the idea of duty intervenes. Both kinds of action can be brought under a consequentialist theory. In other words, it can be maintained that even in the case of causal *dharma*-actions the thought of happiness to result from those actions necessarily plays a role, only if *dharma*-actions, not unlike *artha*-directed and *kāma*-directed actions, are regarded as generating happiness here and now for the agent. This latter is indeed not an entirely implausible view – the view, namely, that leading a life in accordance with the scriptural recommendations brings about a certain kind of happiness, which, to be sure, is very different from the happiness which results from other two kinds of action. In that case, the thought of this happiness – which is neither the pleasure of wealth nor the pleasure of erotica, nor the supernatural well-being of the soul after death – may be an ingredient of the thought of duty which, on all accounts, must play a role in the causal chain leading from hearing an imperative to performance of the appropriate action. Now this Aristotelian theory, or rather Aristotelian way of combining happiness with virtue where happiness is conceived as an internal good of the practice of virtue rather than as an external good, can be ascribed to the theory of *dharma* only if we can give a suitable interpretation of the idea of *dharma*.

Nature of *dharma*

There are three stages in which I will develop the conception of *dharma*. It is well known that the word "*dharma*" stands for various things: sometimes for the harmonious order of the universe, sometimes for the essential function of things, sometimes for the ultimate elements of things, sometimes for moral duty, and sometimes for law in the legal sense. To look for a meaning common to all these usages would be a difficult project, and I will not attempt it here. For my present purpose, I will take *dharma* in the sense of ethical rules.

The first of the three stages of my exposition of "*dharma*" in this sense will involve the attempt to provide a formal definition. There are at least four such definitions in the literature. First, the Mīmāṁsā-sūtra of Jaimini defines *dharma* as *codanālakṣaṇo* – that is, as being of the nature of an injunction. One can construe that expression also as meaning "what is known by the imperative sentences which incite a person to act." The Vaiśeṣikā-sūtra of Kaṇāda defines *dharma* as "that from which prosperity and the highest good result." This definition clearly excludes those injunctions which may be against any moral sensibility. A third definition restricts the term to Vedic injunctions alone which also specify the high goal achievable by acting in accordance with them. A fourth gives up the attempt to define, and ends up by conceding that *dharma* is that which cultivated persons (*āryāḥ*) praise when it is done and *adharma*, the opposite of *dharma*, is that which they condemn when it is done.

The second stage of my explication of *dharma* consists of giving an account, however cursory, of the different kinds of *dharma*. The injunctions may be either obligatory (*nitya*) or occasional (*naimittika*) – that is, to be followed only on specific occasions. Still others are optional (*kāmya*) – that is, performed if so desired. All of these may pertain to one's own *varṇa* (usually, but misleadingly rendered as caste), or to one as a member of the family (*kula*), or to all humans irrespective of caste or family. Some may pertain to one's stage in life (as student, householder, forest-dweller and ascetic). These ethical rules may come into conflict. A famous case is that of Arjuna, portrayed in the epic Mahābhārata in the opening chapter of the *Bhagavadgītā*. Facing the "other side" on the battlefield and seeing his own family members lined up to fight against him, Arjuna realized that the *dharma* of his caste required him to fight for a righteous cause against the forces of evil, while the *dharma* of family forbid killing his own family members, and the common *dharma* forbid taking any life. The teachings of Kṛṣṇa set out to resolve this moral dilemma.

Lists of the most important *dharmas* are to be found in various treatises. Yājñavalkya lists nine such: non-injury, truthfulness, honesty, cleanliness, control of the senses, charity, self-restraint, love and forbearance. These are said to be meant for everyone. Manu mentions ten: fortitude, patience, restraint, abstention from wrongly appropriating another's property, culture, control over the senses, purity, correct discernment, truthfulness and sweet temper. The Mahābhārata adds, among others, modesty, forgiving disposition, serenity and meditative temper. Clearly we have here a theory of virtues as contrasted with a mere ethics of imperatives (that is, "do"s and "don't"s).

This leads me to the third stages of understanding the idea of *dharma*. The question at this point concerns the correct interpretation of this doctrine. Now in the secondary literature – not the Sanskrit commentarial literature, but the Western language interpretative literature – there appear to be several lines of interpretation. First, there is a metaphysical interpretation which connects the ethical with a metaphysical theory of *dharma* as the cosmic order of things. Suggestions for such a connection are to be found in texts such as the *Bhagavadgītā*, which describe the cosmic order as a system of sacrifices. But to think that the ethical can be deduced from the cosmic is just wrong. What rather takes place is, first, the development of ethical ideas, and then the analogous representation of the cosmos in terms of them. Second, there is a functional interpretation which looks upon one's *dharma* as deducible from one's place in the order of things. But no such deduction has been given or is possible. One refers to the well known four stages in the life of a person – the young student "practitioner of Brahman," the householder, the forest-dweller and the ascetic. Each of these has *dharmas* attached do it. But none of these stages is in any sense a reflection of man's place in the universe; at most it is the picture of an ideal journey through life on one's way towards *mokṣa* or freedom from *karma* and rebirth. As closely connected with the idea of *varṇa* or caste, the doctrine of *dharma* connects with an individual's place in society, and as connected with the *karma*–rebirth–*mokṣa* structure, it points beyond society in two directions: one determining the rationality of social ordering and of individual deserts, the other pointing beyond the social towards attainment of a place above the social – a free, spiritual individuality. A third interpretation is religious in the narrow sense, according to which the practice of *dharma* is intended to please the appropriate deities, so as to ensure one's entry to heaven or the higher worlds, while the practice of *adharma* leads one to hell or the nether worlds. Now this may be the way many practising Hindus today look at *dharma*. But Pūrvamīmāṃsā – as a traditional system of interpretation of Vedic ritualism – offers a minimal interpretation which makes no ontological commitment regarding the existence of deities, and rather considers deities as posits for making sense of appropriate practices. Practices are fundamental, ontological commitment is derivative.

The metaphysical interpretations are maximal interpretations. They want to "justify" practice by embedding it in a large metaphysical theory. A minimal interpretation, which I favor, concedes autonomy to practice, and looks for its own (that is, practical) rationality, rather than grounding it in a theoretical system. The maximal interpretation is to be found in the *purāṇas*, the minimal in the Mīmāṃsā and the *dharmaśāstra* tradition. For the interpretation that I am going to suggest, I want to make use of a concept which Hegel emphasizes, namely, the concept of *Sittlichkeit* or social ethos as contrasted with *Moralität* or individual, inner, morality. The *Sittlichkeit* of a people is the concrete ethical self, the actual norms, duties, virtues, and goods that a community prizes. It also includes the habitualities, customs, social practices and law, which Hegel regards as the medium for concrete freedom – as contradistinguished from the abstract morality, the purely subjective, inner freedom which one may pursue, in opposition to, or away from, concrete objective freedom. I hardly need to emphasize that I have no need for the Hegelian systematic concepts of spirit, history and dialectic. It is enough for my purpose to regard *dharma* as constituting the Hindu *Sittlichkeit*, the origins of which lie shrouded in an impenetrable past, and which is not a static, self-complete, unchangeable Identity, but which has continued to change, so as to permit new interpretations while still preserving a sense of identity.

Many contemporary writers have contended that the idea of moral rules needs for its grounding the idea of law-giver (that is, God), and that since that idea is not any more part of our moral thought, we need an ethics of virtues rather than an ethics of rules or laws. This, however, is not quite justified. Rules and laws need not be commands of a lawgiver, of a sovereign authority. Rules and laws may be components of a tradition, brought about by customary usage. This seems to be the case with *dharma* – whether understood as moral rules or as laws. Law, in Hindu legal theories, is not the command of a sovereign, but found in tradition and customary usage.

There is also a view, at one time widely held but fortunately less likely to be defended today, that ethics as a philosophical discipline needs to provide a community's ethical beliefs with a philosophical – metaphysical or epistemological – grounding. And consequently, since Hindu ethical writings abound in lists of virtues and duties, but do not provide theoretical grounding *à la* Kant or Mill, one should not speak of Hindu "ethics" in the context of Indian thought. Contemporary writers on moral philosophy have come to recognize that the project of a theoretical derivation of moral laws and principles must be abandoned. Given the enormous complexity of moral life, such projects are doomed to failure. Moral philosophy in the sense of a descriptive work with regard to the enormously variegated field of morality is possible, but not a "grounding" in the classical sense. In this sense, Aristotle's *Nicomachean Ethics*, rather than Kant's *Groundwork of the Metaphysics of Morals* should be the guide.

From this renewed perspective of phenomenological and "communitarian" virtue ethics, the *dharma* theory fares much better. No attempt need be made to ground the theory in a metaphysics. The different metaphysical systems from realistic pluralism to idealistic monism, notwithstanding their differences, accept the *dharma* as the handed down *Sittlichkeit*. The only legitimation that is offered is epistemological. The scriptures record that tradition, and the epistemological authority of the scriptures with regard to the codes of conduct and virtues to be praised, is defended by philosophers. The main point of the defence consists in arguing that a text's possible flaws are to be traced to possible defects in the author's competence and that the scriptures that record a tradition are not "authored" by a person; the tradition is beyond and more original than any authorship, and so is free from possible errors.

From *dharma* to *mokṣa*: the ethical theory of the Bhagavadgītā

The ideal of *mokṣa* transcends the claims of *dharma*. On the one hand, *dharma* is advanced as a means to *mokṣa*. On the other, *dharma*, with its elaborate hierarchical social–caste–family structure, is also recognized to be a hindrance to the attainment of *mokṣa*. The conflict between the two ideals pervades the history of Hindu thought just as much as do attempts to resolve the conflict. *Mokṣa* itself is construed differently in different systems of thought, but no matter what conception of it one takes into account, the conflict and the tension remain. In general, one can say, orthodoxy argued that *dharma*, as embodied in the words of the scriptures, had absolute validity even for the person who has attained *mokṣa*. Śaṃkara presented strong arguments to the effect that *mokṣa* and *dharma* are so radically different that the former cannot presuppose the latter. *Dharma* is a course of action the performance or non-performance of which depends upon the will of the agent. *Mokṣa* is a state of being consequent upon knowing the nature of things. One philosophical issue is: can knowledge be the subject matter of an imperative of the form "You ought to know"?

Liberalism holds that *dharma* is relative and changeable. The books of *dharma* are not *śruti*, the "heard texts," which are absolutely authoritative for the Hindus; they are rather *smṛti*, texts whose authority can be overridden, and whose doctrines conflict amongst themselves. You need some *dharma* or other for social cohesion, but there is no absolutely valid set of *dharmas*. The *dharma* regarding *varṇa* or caste has played out its role, and needs to be replaced by a more universalistic, non-hierarchical ethics.

What, then, is the connecting link between *dharma* and *mokṣa*? Indeed, is there a connecting link at all, or should one desirous of pursuing *mokṣa* make a Kierkegaardian leap?

I think it is undeniable that although one often speaks of *artha* as being a means to *kāma*, there is no necessary means–end relationship between them. One pursues *artha* for the sake, eventually, of the pleasure deriving from it, and not necessarily for the sake of erotic pleasure, which "*kāma*" signifies (unless one takes *kāma* in a much wider sense, as one often does in these discussions). Likewise, there is no necessary link between *kāma* and *dharma*. A person may devote his life to the pursuit of the two lower ends without being inspired to a life of virtues. But given the inspiration – derived either from the frustration experienced in the first two pursuits, or from study of the scriptures, or from the influence of a virtuous person – he can turn towards *dharma*, and the practice of *dharma* may eventually lead either to the abandonment of the first two pursuits, or to regulating them in accordance with the requirements of *dharma*. Likewise, a person may spend his life practising *dharma*, trying to lead a virtuous life, and yet never be led to a pursuit of *mokṣa*. As Śaṁkara said, the practice of *dharma* is not a prerequisite for asking the relevant questions, or for the desire to know the Brahman, which, on the Vedānta theory, leads to *mokṣa*. Again, there is no necessary link.

It is here that the teachings of Kṛṣṇa in the *Bhagavadgītā* become relevant. The *Gītā* is widely admired as a work on ethics and spirituality, and people of many different ethical persuasions have confessed to their indebtedness to this unique text. For my present purpose, I will look upon it as precisely focusing upon the link between *dharma* and *mokṣa*. Arjuna's "despondency," as the first chapter's title goes, may be understood as arising out of the internal conflict between different parts of the total *dharma*: the *varṇadharma* (that is, the *dharma* of caste) points in one direction, the *kuladharma* (that is, the *dharma* of family) in another, and the *sādhāraṇadharma* (the *dharma* common to all persons in all contexts) in still another. As a member of the caste of warriors, Arjuna knows he ought to fight a battle if the cause is righteous. As a member of a family, he ought not to kill his "grandfathers, uncles and cousins." In any case, he is subject to the universally binding rule of "non-injury." How is he to reconcile these conflicting demands?

Note that there are two similar situations portrayed in Western philosophical literature. One is to be found in Hegel's account, in the *Phenomenology of the Mind*, of how the Greek *ethos* broke down from within due to internal conflict (between what he calls the "human law" and the "divine law"), the other in Kierkegaard's account of how the ethical had to be suspended in view of the demand of the religious upon the will. Faced with this collapse of the system of *dharma*, Arjuna refuses to fight. Kṛṣṇa undertakes to bring him back to his senses and to fight for an undoubtedly just cause – that is, to do his duty. But how must he do his duty so that practice of *dharma* will be conducive to the attainment of *mokṣa*? Kṛṣṇa does not explicitly opt for one of the sides between which Arjuna is torn, although the situation requires that the *dharma* of the warrior has to override that of the family. Likewise, he does not say that the *sādhāraṇadharma*, or universal *dharma*, should override that of the caste, for then Arjuna should have been advised to practice non-injury (as Gandhi would have him, under his "symbolic" interpretation of the "battlefield"). Leaving that conflict untouched, Kṛṣṇa advises Arjuna against giving up his duties and the life of action, and insists that true freedom is achieved not by giving up all action (which, in any case, is not possible), but by giving up all attachment to the "fruits" of one's actions. Actions are ordinarily motivated by some desire. When performed, an action either satisfies or frustrates the desire in question, and so causes either happiness or pain. It is this causal chain that is the source of "attachment" to the mundane order. *Mokṣa* means minimally (for it may also mean more) freedom from this attachment. A necessary condition for it is desirelessness – which is the same as absence of attachment to the fruits of one's action. The concept of "fruit of an action" must be correctly understood. Not just any consequence of an action is called its fruit here. If a physician treats a patient, he is not asked to be disinterested in the consequence – that is, in the patient's well-being or lack of it. "Fruit" means the consequences of his actions in or for the agent: success or failure, pleasure or pain, reward or punishment. Kṛṣṇa urges the aspirer after *mokṣa* to do his duty without desire for pleasure, success, fame, reward, etc. He does allow "impersonal" motives, such as the "good of all" or the "preservation of mankind." If one performs *dharma* with this detachment and desirelessness, then one is truly free. Thus Kṛṣṇa attempts to save the *dharma* of *varṇa* as against Arjuna's temporary and occasional skepticism, and at the same time suggests a way beyond *dharma* towards quite another goal – that is, *mokṣa*, which is the highest good.

It is natural to ask at this point, how can anyone act without any desire? The bulk of Kṛṣṇa's discourse is devoted to show how this is possible, and for this purpose he makes use of metaphysical concepts deriving from Sāṃkhya and Vedānta. This is one place where a sort of metaphysical grounding is offered, not so much for the *dharmas* themselves as for the idea of desirelessness and non-attachment. If the former corresponds, as suggested earlier, to Hegel's *Sittlichkeit*, the latter corresponds to *Moralität*, the Kantian inner good will. The former provides the content, the latter the form and the spirit. The two together – *dharma* practiced with inner freedom – lead to *mokṣa*. The content needs and permits no grounding save in the idea of tradition. The form is grounded by Kṛṣṇa first in the Sāṃkhya distinction between the self and nature, then in the Vedāntic idea of the Ātman-Brahman, and finally in the theistic idea of the supreme self or the Lord of the universe. From the first, it follows that the three "qualities" (*sattva, rajas*, and *tamas*) which motivate and drive persons to action are parts of nature and do not touch the self, so that the true self of a person is not an agent, nor is it an "enjoyer" (*bhoktā*). From the second, it follows that the sense of otherness which underlies the ordinary life of action, giving rise to desires and other emotions, is false, all these being at bottom one, so that the wise man perceives all beings in himself and himself in all beings. From the third, it follows that acting in the true spirit (that is, with desirelessness and non-attachment) is also acting in the spirit of "offering the fruits of your actions" – instead of flowers, fruits and incense – to the highest deity (that is, Kṛṣṇa himself). The three Yogas – *karma* or action, *jñāna* or knowledge, and *bhakti* or devotion – join together, just as the three systems, Sāṁkhya, Vedānta and theistic religion, are grafted together. Among Kṛṣṇa's advice to Arjuna we find: "go beyond the three *guṇas*," "do your actions, while settled in Yoga," "take refuge in your intelligence," "be only an occasion," "Think of me, be my devotee." These instructions are calls to transcend moral distinctions (that is, the three *guṇas* or "qualities"), to do your duty with an inner freedom, to work with clear and enlightened intelligence and as if you are an instrument of God's purpose.

There are several tantalizing questions that inevitably arise. What does one mean by saying that the wise man transcends moral distinctions? Some statements by Kṛṣṇa seem to suggest that the wise man can do what he wants, not being bound by moral rules and obligations. But how are we to understand this "freedom" not only from evil but also from good – that is, freedom from both *pāpa* and *puṇya*, virtue and vice?

Louis Dumont has interpreted the difference of *mokṣa* from the first three "ends" (which he takes to be profit, pleasure, and religious duty respectively) to consist in the difference between the "individual-outside-the-world" and "man-in-the-world." By so understanding *mokṣa*, Dumont takes the world of caste as a world of relations in which the particular man has no substance, no reality, no Being (as he puts it), but only empirical existence. The person who attains *mokṣa* first becomes thereby a true individual who stands outside the relational structure of world and society and transcends morality, which is tied to that structure.

But the transcendence into *mokṣa* leaves the *dharma* unaffected, and we still wonder if the form of "non-attachment" is only prefixed to the already available *dharma*. Are there any contents (that is, any actions) that are just incompatible with the form of "non-attachment"? Many writers have sought to deduce some moral rules and virtues – such as love, non-killing and toleration – from the Vedāntic thesis of a fundamental identity amongst selves, and would argue that certain actions, which by their very nature entail egoistic and selfish desires and destructive emotions such as lust and anger, preclude non-attachment. While this may be an interesting project, it seems clear that the Hindu tradition did not critically examine the entire *dharma*-tradition in this manner in order to weed out many *dharma*-rules that are amoral or even immoral. As a result, a large part of that tradition remained untouched by critical reflection.

Let us nevertheless consider those *dharmas* that pass the critical test. What is the difference between practising non-killing on the part of a virtuous person who has not acheived *mokṣa*, and practising the same on the part of one who has? The former, we are told, is one in whose person the quality of *sattva* predominates: he is a *good* man. The latter is beyond the three *guṇas*, beyond good and evil, and yet he still abides by the moral rule. What difference, then, does his transcending morality make? A comparison with Kant is unavoidable: one begins with unconditionally obeying the moral law out of a sense of duty, and ends with the recognition that the moral law, being the law of "practical reason," has its source not in an external authority, however sublime and majestic, but in one's own rational nature. Thus one at the end acts without that sense of constraint which attends submitting to an external authority, but rather with a sense of freedom and spontaneity. Can we say that the person who attains *mokṣa* similarly follows the moral rule out of an inner freedom? But this Kantian-like answer, though perhaps partly true, fails us ultimately. The *dharmas* of tradition do not flow from my rational nature, as Kant would have it; they are the social *ethos* which it is better to abide by than to flout; they exert a hold on me only in so far as I belong to that tradition, and not in so far as I am a rational being. *Dharma* is ultimately relative and contingent, and only used as a means to a goal that transcends it.

The contingency of *dharma* is borne out by the fact that in Hindu ethics there is no categorical imperative, no unconditional moral principle. All moral laws have the form, "If you wish to attain such and such goal, then these rules and virtues are binding." To perform *dharma* with non-attachment is to aim at attaining *mokṣa*. If you are not geared to that goal, you can practice *dharma* with the purpose of going to heaven after death.

At the same time, the contingency of *dharma* and the fact that the *dharma* books do not have the authority of "heard" texts (*śruti*) but are only records of tradition (that is, *smṛti*), imply that philosophical thinking can subject the *dharmas* to criticism. One has only to take care that such criticism of the tradition must come from within, rather than from without. From within, there are at least two ways of criticizing the tradition: for one thing, the critic can argue that the existing *dharma*, or some component of it (for example, the caste hierarchy) is not consistent with some fundamental conceptions of the tradition (for example, of the Upaniṣads), and so needs rejection or revision (for after all, the *śruti* is "stronger" than the *smṛti*, according to that tradition). For another, one may criticize a received *dharma* by reinterpreting the texts. Such is, for example, Sri Aurobindo's critique of the traditional understanding of "*mokṣa*" and Gandhi's interpretation of the "*varṇa*" theory. Gandhi interpreted "*varṇa*" as meaning not the caste hierarchy, but a system of family-inherited-skills of production, so ordered as to avoid a competitive economic system.

It is to be regretted that with the philosophical thinking of the *darśanas* focused primarily upon *mokṣa*, the *dharma*-tradition was simply "passed over" as a means to that lofty goal, and yet life was more determined by *dharma*, which just escaped critical attention. It is only in the twentieth century that the demands of social and economic change have turned attention to the need for reexamining that tradition.

The highest good

It is generally held that in Indian thinking *mokṣa* is the highest good. While not wanting to challenge this claim, I want, in this essay, to raise several questions. In the first place, if the good is what is desired (*iṣta*), can it be said that *mokṣa* is a possible object of desire? If so, is it not the case that one is desiring desirelessness? Second, is not *mokṣa* simply an "experiential equivalent" of a system's metaphysical theory? For example, Advaita Vedānta holds that the finite individual and universal Spirit (that is, Brahman) are identical, and that all differences are false. In that case, *mokṣa* is an intuitive experience of that identity and this falsity. The same holds good of the other systems. One may then look upon a theory's concept of *mokṣa* as the practical consequence *par excellence* of the theory, or the theory, or the theory as the theoretical elaboration of the possibility of a certain understanding of *mokṣa*. There is indeed a logical correlation between a metaphysics and its concept of *mokṣa*. Third, it is not clear why it is to be called the highest good. The difference between it and the other three ends on any account, is not one of degree, but rather one of radical qualitative otherness. It simply lies on another dimension. It is not an "ought-to-do," at most it is an "ought-to-be," suggesting a radical transformation of one's mode of existence. Fourth, as is well known, on some conceptions of it, especially Śaṃkara's, the locution "my *mokṣa*" would be a contradiction in terms, for "my" ascribes an ego which appears to contradict the very idea of *mokṣa*.

Two other questions seem to have been discussed in connection with the nature of *mokṣa*. There was the question, whether the highest *mokṣa* could be achieved while alive in a bodily state, or whether it requires that one "gives up" the body (that is, dies). It is interesting to note that philosophical theories that regard the body and the world as unreal, as Śaṃkara's does, generally regard "liberation" to be possible in a living body, while those that regard body and the world to be real hold that the highest state of *mokṣa* requires cessation of bodily existence. Clearly only a state of "living liberation" can claim to be the highest good. The other question that was discussed is: is it possible for one person to achieve the highest state of *mokṣa*, or must the highest state of liberation involve the liberation of all? According to many scholars, Śaṃkara himself favored the second alternative. It is understandable that this idea of "liberation for all" – close to the Mahāyāna Buddhist view – should have found support from some contemporary Indian thinkers, such as Sri Aurobindo, who even speaks of collective *samādhi* or collective liberation, an ascent of the human race to a higher form of consciousness beyond the mental.

Back to ethics

Is "*dharma*" an ethical concept? Much of what has been said in this essay should have brought home the point that as long as one thinks along the lines of classical Western moral philosophy that it was the task of ethics to legitimize and ground our moral beliefs with the help of fundamental principles ("God as the lawgiver," the "categorical imperative," "universalizability," or the "Utilitarian Principle"), Hindu thinking on *dharma* does not provide an ethical theory, and the concept of *dharma*, like the German term "*Recht*," rather covers a large variety of different, even if loosely connected, phenomena. Today moral thinking has broken new ground, with a greater understanding of the Aristotelian theory of virtues, of various dimensions of human excellence, and of the impossibility of any set of principles legitimizing all ethical choices. From this new perspective, the *dharma* theory fares well. Part of it is a theory of ethical rules, part of it a theory of virtues and human excellence, another part communitarian, and added to all these there is a layer of Kantian-like theory of "duty for duty's sake" subserving a transcendent end of *mokṣa* (which itself is the "other side" of the ubiquitous belief in *karma* and rebirth).

A list of virtues, culled from the *Gītā* may help us to understand this ethical tradition well. For Brahmins, the virtues, or some of them, are serenity, self-control, austerity, purity, forbearance, uprightness, wisdom, and faith. For a warrior, they are heroism, vigor, resourcefulness, steadiness, generosity, and leadership. The universal virtues are friendliness, compassion, charity, forgivingness, and penance. There is something that Kṛṣṇa calls *svadharma*, which may mean either one's own caste-oriented duties and virtues, but which may also be interpreted as what uniquely suits one's spiritual nature.

For a contemporary understanding of *dharma*, the following quotation from Mahātmā Gāndhi may be helpful:

> One's respective *dharma* towards one's self, family, nation and the world cannot be divided into watertight compartments. . . . [W]e must sacrifice ourselves in the interest of the family, the family must do so for the nation and the nation for the world. But the sacrifice has to be pure. Therefore it all starts from self-purification.

Gandhi distinguishes *ācāra* or practice, which is the external mode of living, and can change from time to time. "The rules of inner living," he writes, "must remain the same." He adds, "All rules given in Sanskrit were not *śhāstra*. Even the book entitled *Mānavadharmaśhāstra* is not really speaking a *śāstra*. *Śāstra* is not anything written in a book. It should be a living thing."

Contemporary ideas

If Gandhi turned from the texts to "inward living," to conscience and inner conviction as the test of truth (from which his practice of "non-violence" was inseparable), he also turned outward to the social dimension of fairness and justice (as components of his conception of "non-violence"). The violence that he abjured was not merely killing or harming in speech, thought and action, but included as well – for him certainly, though presumably not for the Hindu tradition he was drawing upon – social inequity and injustice and economic exploitation. Gandhian ethics thus, although founded on some strains in the Hindu scriptures, also drew nourishment from the Jaina theory of *anekantavāda* (that truth has many aspects and no one doctrine has a monopoly on it) and the Jaina tradition of practicing non-injury (which also included trying to understand and appropriate the element of truth in the other's point of view).

If Gandhi's conception of the highest good was ethical ("God" = "Truth" = "Moral Law," subjectively lived within), the poet Tagore understood the moral point of view to consist in expanding the conception of our self, from the perspective of the selfish ego to the whole field of life, including the unrealized future – to realize in the long run one's life in the infinite. Through this progression, the human soul moves "from the law to love, from discipline to liberation, from the moral plane to the spiritual." "Bondage and liberation are not antagonistic in love. For love is most free and at the same time most bound" (*Sādhanā*, pp. 54, 106, 115).

Sri Aurobindo accommodates an element of Utilitarianism, and writes: "the highest good is also the highest utility. . . . Good, not utility, must be the principle and standard," and continues (in the spirit of G. E. Moore of Cambridge, where Aurobindo also studied), "There is only one safe rule for the ethical man, to stick to his principle of good, his instinct for good, his intuition of good, and to govern by that his conduct" (*The Human Cycle*, pp. 139, 183–4). But Aurobindo, unlike Gandhi, but much like Tagore, did not regard the ethical person to be the highest person. A perfect individual, for him, must make his entire life beautiful (ibid., p. 168). The spiritual man, in his estimation, integrates the ethical, the aesthetic and the cognitive in a harmonious unity.

21

Indian aesthetics: a philosophical survey

EDWIN GEROW

I Indian and comparative aesthetics

The term "aesthetics' is misleading when applied in the classical Indian philosophical context. Before the modern period, there is substantially no body of speculation on the pleasurable responses to created objects, as such, or on their formal capacities to induce such responses. What we do have, on the other hand, are: (1) several partly distinct traditions having to do with the elements out of which are constructed such objects – including literary "objects" – according to prevailing canons of symbology and use that have a ritual or religious basis; and (2) an intensely developed set of speculations on the narrower question of the observed power (often judged in emotive terms) of the dramatic work to transform us, its spectators. This second problematic, in time, comes to be seen as paradigmatic for all "art," including poetry, music, and the plastic arts. The first set of traditions focuses on what we might call the semantics of the work, contrasting it, in the case of the written work, with "ordinary" symbolical and ritual uses of language ("how does it mean what it means?"); the second set deals with the restorative or transformative capacity of dramatic and other "fictive" works, vis-à-vis those that immediately and practically provide, or presume to provide, a transcendent solution on human problems – most importantly, of course, the essentially religious problem of human suffering caused by the bondage of cyclic existence ("how does the work of art also accomplish human ends?").

Both these modes of inquiry focus on an *objet d'art* that is fundamentally utilitarian – an object that has a manifest power to communicate or transform; an object, furthermore, that is consonant with and even modeled on that of a devotional or ritual object – whose construction and even proportions also express a symbolism that is purposive. This "power," on the other hand, is neither immediately "useful" (namely, meaningful in some practical context) nor finally "salvific" (namely, accomplishing some ultimate condition of beatitude): between these extremes lies the ambiguity of beauty – anticipatory and transcendent at the same time – which belongs to the created object "in and of itself." The first mode discovers the "secular" powers of language; the second assures to artistic endeavor its serious place in the panoply of activities promoting human happiness – or, at least, human betterment.

Even though Indian "aesthetics," thus restricted, can be usefully compared to Western philosophical aesthetics, many of whose concerns are echoed in the Indian traditions, it would be a mistake to overlook the profound resonances between Indian "aesthetics" and its ritual and ethical context. This is perhaps only to say that it is, after all, "Indian."

The privilege that the written work, poetic or dramatic, enjoys in aesthetic speculation is a hallmark of the Indian tradition. As with Aristotle, the written work is both an icon to be judged in a way similar to other such constructions – flute-playing, the statues of Praxiteles, not to speak fo the carpenter's chair – and yet is also the most revealing and transparent such construction, being "made" (Gk ποιειν, "to make"; ποιητής, "maker, poet") of "stuff" that is already mediated – words and thoughts. In India too it is the powers of language, especially sacred language – the Veda – that have prompted the first speculations on poetics, and the poetics of language has become also the poetics of art itself.

What can we make of the contextual or situational peculiarity of Indian aesthetics? Rather than seek some timeless cultural "essence" that marks all things as "Indian," we will attempt to understand those factors that have given a characteristic "tilt" to the Indians' speculations – particularly on language – for it is the case that language lies at the heart of the Indian experience of the real. In this way, we may hope to avoid the twin pitfalls of a narrow historicism, that so emphasizes the uniqueness of the alien experience that it must, by definition, be unintelligible to anyone else, and an uncritical cosmopolitanism, too eager to reduce the obvious similarities in even the most divergent of traditions to commonplaces that express nothing more than the prevailing dogmas and shibboleths of the author's own time and place.

There have been, of course, attempts on the part of modern critics, both Indian and Western, to "appreciate" works of classical art in terms of some standard that is evidently extrinsic, albeit better suited to making those objects available to contemporary tastes, Indian or Western. This essay will differ, if at all, in its attempt to elicit a set of standards from the Indians' own speculations, fully realizing that there is nothing unusual about speculating on language.

II Recent scholarship

The first treatments of the Indian poetic and aesthetic tradition were philological essays whose aim was to decipher the texts in which this tradition was preserved. Sylvain Lévi's *Le Théâtre indien* could be taken as the best and still very useful effort of this kind. On the Indian side, the traditional polymath P. V. Kane, adopting Western text critical methods with a vengeance, produced a "history" of Indian poetics that, while recording verbatim many pronouncements extracted from the traditional literature, adds very little in the way of interpretation, but constructs around them an armature of facts – to the extent that any facts can be adduced – that arguably conditioned the writers themselves: their chronology, their vitae, and their "intertextuality" – borrowings and influence. Kane also grouped the writers into "schools" or subtraditions, on the basis of what he thought the subject matter of their works was, or their view of the "essence" of poetry. S. K. De attempted to go beyond this sere model, at least toward the end of his life, by adding to his impressive *History of Sanskrit Poetics* – similar to and roughly contemporary [1923] with Kane's work [1921] – interpretive essays that attempted to situate Indian poetics in the context of recent Western theories of aesthetics and literature. The Indian theories came out looking very inadequate in De's comparisons, for he, like many Indians of his generation, saw in the indigenous tradition little but the classificatory excesses of the ritual mind – lacking, in this case, a comprehensive aesthetic that would account for the work's uniqueness, its inimitable coming-to-be, its "inspiration," in short, a theory of authorial "genius," in the romantic style of Benedetto Croce. A. B. Keith, the Scottish polymath whose major work on Indian poetics is again approximately contemporaneous with De's and Kane's certainly shared this view that the attainments of the Indian learned tradition were inadequate and overly mechanical, but Keith went on to explore the interconnections between "poetics" and the other branches of traditional speculation, on the one hand, and between "poetics" and the literature it sought to account for, on the other. Some of the inadequacies of poetics could be explained in terms of larger inadequacies – in the śāstraic model itself, or in the overly academic character of Sanskritic belles-lettres. For all of these writers, it was the notion of *rasa* (emotional "tone") that represented both the culmination of Indian aesthetic thought, and its most characteristic statement. It is also where Indian aesthetics most closely approximates to our expectations of an "aesthetic."

In my own work, much of which has focused on the earlier, or "pre-*rasa*" period of poetic speculation, I tried to situate the achievements of these traditions in a more sympathetic context – that provided by the more formalistic theories of literature then in vogue; on the other hand, I sought a more exact appreciation of the critical dimension of these poetic traditions – that is to say, as explications of the kinds of works that were in fact written in classical India (where also notions of "authorship" were generally eschewed), rather than as immature collections of wooden formulae, intended to school would-be-poets. The *rasa* theory, in turn, was seen as a logical extension of the early theory, rather than a ground-breaking novelty, dimly responding to or anticipating Western or modern poetic expectations. I thus avoided measuring the Indian traditions against a standard they did not seek to emulate, and would have regarded as irrelevant.

Recently, following the lead of Eliot Deutsch, V. K. Chari, himself traditionally educated, but professing English literature in the West, has sought both to place the Indian aesthetic tradition more cogently in the context of modern Western poetic speculation, and to elevate the *rasa* aesthetic to the status of a "world-class" theory, valid not just for characterizing and judging Indian works, but itself a seminal theory of and for world literature. We have come thus full circle – from a notion of Indian aesthetics inadequate even for Indian literature, to a notion of Indian aesthetics as not relevantly Indian at all, but as valid for all literature.

III The Indian traditions

In this essay, rather than concern myself with the history of Indian poetics/aesthetics, I will attempt to define the various standpoints that have been taken up in that long history, disengage their postulates (both in relation to the objects they regard as relevant and to other theories that offer significant contrasts), and assess their claim to philosophical adequacy – in both the narrow sense of Indian theory (what kinds of explanations they offer) and the wider sense of theory per se (how they accommodate the claims of competing theories). This will not presume a traditional author-by-author account, but will disengage the various topics that are treated, sometimes without great overall consistency, within the treatises attributed to single authors. As is well known, the early treatises have the aura of compendia, and though this becomes less true as more and more integral theories are developed, it remains the case that certain topics recur with insistency, and themselves constitute the *loci communes* of the theoretical literature. It is undoubtedly a Western bias that seeks an organizing principle in the individual work or the individual author. When we speak of Indian "traditions" we do so with the stronger implication that these traditions, in fact, constitute the organizing principles of persistent discourse – organizing even that of individual authors into topoi and solutions.

I see five different perspectives in which "aesthetic" speculations have developed in traditional India. I will use these perspectives as the organizing principles of this essay, thus hoping to give it an immediately comparative, if not relevant, dimension – one that is ordinarily lacking if an exclusively historical framework be adopted (as it usually is). The five are:

1 The concern with "figures of speech" and other elemental devices of expression; the "structural" or "formal" mode.
2 The concern with "suggestion" within a general theory of semantics and the uses of language; the "functional" or "intentional" mode.
3 The concern with *rasa* within a general theory of psychology: awareness, consciousness; the contemplative mode – often aligned with Advaita in its various manifestations.
4 The concern with "play" – the aesthetics of *bhakti* as ritual transcendence; the mode of "acting" – aligned with devotionalism, though made explicit chiefly in Bengali Vaiṣṇavism.
5 The concern with "visualization" – the sensory presentation of the divine object (as idol, yantra, mental image); the "tantric" mode – and the only mode functioning primarily in the visual domain, as opposed to the linguistic. Although, with the *mantra*, the linguistic is also reduced to the mode of the visual.

Still, certain historical, or rather, "prehistorical" comments are in order, by way of introduction. For there is an inveterate tendency on the part of the Indian traditions to assign themselves an origin in the earliest period known to them, thus according themselves a quasi-divine status. It is not to a period, as such, that they see themselves thus adherent, but to a *literature*: the Veda, understood, in the strict sense, not only as original, but immemorial – coeval with creation, or uncreated. It is for this reason that the aesthetic theories, when they later develop, are largely concerned with literary problems; they arise out of attempts to situate, comprehend, rationalize, and defend this sacred source, which is, itself, also partly poetical, that is, composed of elaborately structured poems – the Ṛg Veda, the first "work" of the Indian canon, whose oldest parts are the earliest preserved works of any Indo-European literature (ca. 1500 BCE). Even though the poetic character of this early literature was soon submerged in an envelope of austere ritualism, it continued to be understood as the source of that ritual – in the still verbal form of *commands* that revealed the specific acts enjoined and that served, ipso facto, as the motivation or compulsion to accomplish them. Indian poetics begins as an adjunct to grammatical and lexical attempts to preserve, clarify, and understand the exact force of such authoritative utterance. (It could be said without exaggeration that the entire purport of the early scholastic tradition was thus exegetical, and thus, in a sense, a form of "literary criticism.") Poetics, in the narrow sense, shares this origin with grammar, lexicography, metrics, ritual codification – and even architecture and astronomy as "measurements" of the sacrificial enclosure and the calendar – all ultimately deriving from the project of understanding and defending the rationality and the givenness of the corpus of sacrificial texts. The discovery that language is not univalent was made in the context of such ritual concerns, by ritualists who distinguished command from statement (statements being ancillary to commands) and the literal from the figurative (the figurative being a defective usage that can be reduced to a literal sense to gain credence), in an effort to portray the ritual corpus as an organic, that is, a hierarchically organized, and therefore, seamless whole. The discovery that a group of texts, apparently randomly related, were possessed of a common structure independent of, and in part determining, their surface intentionality was itself a powerful impetus to – and also the result of – the development of formal theories of language. Nevertheless, there is no formal poetics in this early period. Vedic references to certain key aesthetic terms, such as *rasa*, are misleading or anachronistic, if taken in the sense of the later, developed aesthetic literature.

1 *Figures of speech, the elemental mode*

When a corpus of secular literature developed in the first centuries of the Christian era alongside the exclusively religious literature that had been the fief of the brahmin, similar questions were put to that literature and similar analytical methods applied to it – for its evidently different registers constituted a new problem. This "secular" literature appears thus as the requisite of a proper poetics – a literature which derived from the conscious exploitation of those aspects of language that had been regarded by the Vedic specialists as included and derivative: the declarative (or "non-injunctive") and the metaphorical. It is in this light that the first (and, arguably, oldest) of our strands of aesthetic speculation is to be seen – that focusing on figures of speech and other devices, seen as the mechanisms whereby this new kind of language both expressed a meaning, and was inherently different from Vedic, or religious, language. Characteristic early works in this vein are the *Kāvyālaṃkāra* of Bhāmaha (seventh century) and, especially, the *Kāvyādarśa* of Daṇḍin – arguably also the author of the *Ten Princes* (usually put in the eighth century, but if the identity of authorship be accepted, then, also, seventh). Although the stress of this strand was on the delineation of expressive devices, it should not be forgotten that an important part of the enterprise bore on larger questions of meaning – meaning understood both as the purpose of such secular composition (it was here that the notion of *camatkāra*), or pure delight, was posited as a legitimate end of language) and as the sense of the individual poetic utterance, for in this most rationalist of traditions, an utterance that was not precisely intelligible was, literally, unthinkable.

Different emphases are evident in this formalist critique, which, over time, fuse into a view that figures of speech, of which the characteristic instance is *simile* (comparison), constitute the decisive aspect of poetical usage: they are (in terms of the dichotomy of meaning) both inherently delightful and transparently intelligible – by principled interpretation. In the case of simile, the *tertium* or shared property, is a relation that rationalizes the mention of apparently irrelevant comparanda: "my Luv's like a red, red rose." But before this synthesis is reached, an interesting variety of features of non-literal language is examined – most of which are later incorporated into the synthesis, in ways reminiscent of the ritualists' tendency to hierarchize.

An example is provided by those apparently "meaningless" aspects of belletristic language that depend on the manipulation of its sound-system, rather than its vocabulary and syntax, but which are nevertheless "charming." Under this rubric are distinguished alliteration (of several sorts), types of full-syllable repetition (or rhyme), and metre, or the systematic exploitation of contrasts in syllabic quantity. All these sound-patterns constitute a differentia of poetic language to the extent that the regularities, even predictabilities, that they involve do not normally occur in non-poetic language, which is distinguished by a more random production of phonic characteristics. These features come to be considered, despite their apparent lack of intentionality – as "figures of sound" (*śabdālaṁkāra*), which are, ipso facto, assigned a derivative intentionality, in that some "suit" whereas others "hinder" the primary intentionality of the utterance. A line made up of harsh consonants, for instance, would not suit a comparison of my love's face to the silvery moon.

From such considerations emerged a theory of *style* (*rīti*, *mārga*, "course, path": the former term is Vāmana's (eighth century); the latter, Daṇḍin's) or overall consistency in the employment of expressive devices, which, as such, become "qualities" (*guṇa*) of the style. A corollary theory of *non-style*, that is, a theory of overall inconsistency, or defect (*doṣa*, "stain") between subsidiary devices and the reigning coherence of the utterance also arose. The treatment of the defects – which, like the qualities, are, in principle, relative to the overall style chosen – provides one of the rare glimpses into a classical type of practical literary criticism. Even the works of Kālidāsa are on occasion examined and his usages subjected to criticism – and not always vindicated, either!

The theory of style became quite complex when conjoined with observations of actual usage. It was evident that more than one standard of consistency was and had been employed by poets – or even by a single poet – and more than one kind of "charming" effect was possible. The effort to distinguish one style (in particular) from another led to the enumeration of stylistic differentia, which were thought to constitute the building blocks out of which a style was constructed (also, *guṇa*, "quality" – in both senses of the English term). Most such qualities are structural opposites, in a Lévi-Straussian sense. If basic is the dichotomy between the "transparent" and the "florid" (*vaidarbhī/gauḍī*) styles, then the use of long compounds and difficult-to-decipher words is a quality of the latter, but use of their opposites, a quality of the former. A standard list of ten such qualities and their opposites came to be accepted, sufficient, apparently, to distinguish the styles in use. In time, more styles than the basic two came to be recognized – for, of course, out of ten differentiae, many more than two can be realized. A third, excessive "softness" (*komala*), was early mentioned, distinguished by soft alliterations and easy diction – "clarity" taken to the extreme, it seems.

The theory of style seems to repose on several conflicting considerations – which perhaps accounts for its shadowy character and its eventual eclipse. Some of the dichotomies seem never to have defined alternate qualities, but rather a quality and a contrary defect, to be avoided in any style. And the various styles, no doubt in part descriptive of known regional variations (*vaidarbhī*, "from Vidarbha," modern Berar; *gauḍīya*, "from Gauḍa," modern Bengal), were never really devoid of normative implication: the theory seems in part aimed at privileging one style – usually the *vaidharbhī*, associated with Kālidāsa – vis-à-vis the others.

This more or less analytical approach to questions of style was quickly reduced to (or may well have been intended as) an adjunct of the theory of figuration. The "quality" that survives, most strikingly, in this altered context is *alliteration* – now understood as the "figure of sound" par excellence, and in its variations, the measure of stylistic variation. (This reduction is complete in Mammaṭa's canonical *Kāvyaprakāśa*, a late eleventh-century work that presumes also to incorporate the *dhvani* and *rasa* traditions.) Others, such as the use (or non-use) of long compounds, make a tentative entrance as the figure *ojas*, or "vigor." The general issue of stylistic coherence and its parameters survives in the later notion of "suitability" (*aucitya*), a much more flexible and less "measurable" idea, which seems to amount to little more than the prescription that the elements of a work should suit one another and not conflict with its principal theme. (Kṣemendra's *Aucityavicāracarcā* (eleventh century) is typical of the type.) As such, it may have been a reflex of the notion of "suggestion" (*dhvani*) which, in the ninth century, truly revolutionized Indian thinking on poetics, and which, in a sense, also put the older divagations on "style" on a firmer basis.

Another marginal concern of these writers was *genre*. Very brief, and to us, largely formulaic, accounts of known types of belletristic composition are found in the introductory matter to several treatises on the figures. Whereas the discussion of style seems to represent an effort to deal with the question of internal coherence, or the proper relation of parts to a whole (even if it is a single verse), that of genre appears as a vehicle for introducing questions of authorship and authorial choice – always a murky area in Indian antiquity. Traditional subject matters are contrasted with matters "imagined" by the author (*kathā, ākhyāyikā*); the length of the composition is considered relevant, as is to some extent the choice of a regulated or unregulated format, or a combination of the two (*gadya, padya, miśra*). It should be borne in mind that the unit of composition was not so much the total work (as for us moderns, at least before deconstruction set about its grisly work) as it was the individual assertion, sentence, verse – strings of which, like a chaplet, make up larger wholes. The poet revealed his "skill" – another preoccupation of the early theory – in such unitary and perfected "assertions," rather than in the construction of larger, more narratively conceived, wholes. Again, the Vedic model is patent. Only in time, and seemingly as an aside, does the Indian theory begin to deal with larger compositional frames of reference. Longer works – the epic poems of Kālidāsa, for example, taken as models – continue to be seen as accumulations of such well-honed minutiae. Sustained prose composition – for example, Daṇḍin's *Ten Princes* – was a very late addendum to the inventory of genres, and no need was felt, apparently, to develop a poetic suitable to it.

The major genres, drama (*nāṭya*) and strophic poetry (*kāvya*), were themselves, in the early literature, subjects of two distinct critical approaches, which do not therefore deal with the nature of the difference, but rather assume it as a given. Daṇḍin speaks of *dṛśya* and *śravya* types, which coincide with the genres mentioned, but immediately dismisses the former as proper to another discipline of study. It is in that discussion that the notion of *rasa* was elaborated – a notion that, in time, came to dominate the discussion of all types of written literature, and even music and the plastic arts. As for *kāvya*, it was evidently the figure of speech that was understood as its principle of composition and characteristic excellence – as was evidenced in the glorious similes of the great Sanskrit poets, Kālidāsa, Bhavabhūti, and so on. The otherwise nebulously defined *mahākāvya* or *sargabandha* constitutes the quintessence of the genre (*kāvya*) itself, but behind the loose and topical characterizations lies the reality of the figures of speech – the true definiens of the genre.

The presentation of the figures of speech by Rudraṭa (ninth century) is the clearest and most logical, though not the most extensive, that the tradition achieved. It may be taken as the implicit end toward which the various writers were working. They were, after all, "theorists of literature," not critics – more interested in the system of figures than in their concrete employment in literary works. Rudraṭa's treatment is noteworthy for its categorical approach. After distinguishing those figures whose effect depends on some phonological property of the language (*śabdālaṁkāra*, see above) from those whose effect depends on an idea, or a meaning conveyed by that language (*arthālaṁkāra*), Rudraṭa groups all the latter figures under four heads: comparison, hyperbole, "matter of fact," and pun. Taking simile as the basic figure, and the stock-in-trade of the poet, but not (as did Vāmana) seeking to reduce all figures to varieties of simile, Rudraṭa rather seems intent on integrating the theory of the figures into general philosophical and ritual discussions of the sentence, and of the kinds of relations that may obtain in predication.

Sādṛśya (similarity) is but one such relation, and the most indeterminate, according to the Mīmāṁsā, for the two terms at issue need have no circumstantial relation at all; it is to be radically distinguished from determinate, "factual" relations, such as "cause and effect," that involve the circumstantial presence of both terms. (The distinction parallels C. S. Peirce's "icon" and "index.") The first and third of Rudraṭa's categories are thus grounded. The second, hyperbole (*atiśaya*, "excess"), is again relational, but between a term and its property, rather than between two terms. Hyperbole plays on distortions of qualitative predication, just as simile plays on distortions of appositional predication. This distinction is more grammatical than logical, responding to the two basic nominal sentence types of Sanskrit and the Indo-European languages (Caesar is good; Caesar is king). The fourth type, not usually thought of as including "figures of sense," is, nevertheless, treatable as such, when the two meanings (the patent and the latent) apprehended via the pun in fact discover a relationship that highlights both – as when, for example, they are related as terms of a simile. As is well known, pun is a device thoroughly exploited in classical Sanskrit literature. Rudraṭa here accounts both for its serious side, and its place among the figures, for it increasingly occupies the place of simile as the figure par excellence, uniquely cumulating the effects of simile and hyperbole, inasmuch as the simultaneous apprehension of two meanings distorts the process of expression itself – for example, "Focus: where the sons raise meat" (the name of a cattle ranch in the south-west owned by three brothers).

Each of these four generic types of figure is, in the manuals, dissected into a seeming infinitude of varieties – 125 (including *śabdālaṁkāra*) in the late *Kuvalayānanda* of Appayadīkṣita (sixteenth century). Subsidiary structural and contextual factors can be multiplied at will. For example, in the case of simile, are the four structural factors (subject of comparison, object of comparison, shared property, and grammatical indicator of comparison – "like") all explicit, or are some implicit? Such distinctions have been taken by later writers as foreshadowing the theory of suggestion (*dhvani*): Is her face like the moon? Or is her face the moon? Or is her face gentle as the moon? Is the common property expressed as an adjective (as above), or as a verbal predicate? Does her face beam gently (as does the moon)? The mode of comparison may be subject to other affectations: Is this the moon or her face? (doubt); This must be the moon, it can't be a face (denial); The moon is like her face (reversal); and so on. As Ānandavardhana later says, "the varieties of speech are endless."

2 *Suggestion, semantic theory, the "intentional" mode*

This approach to the theory of literature developed out of the preceding, and incorporated it, to the extent that formal factors, figures, qualities, and so on, could be taken as devices serving, as expressive mechanisms, a higher (and essentially non-formal) end – the indirect sense, always implicit, that seemed to these theorists to constitute the true end of poetic composition, which never declares its real meaning in so many words. And, by a short step, the unstated could then be affirmed as the essence of poetry. Thus, Robert Burns's "red, red rose" is not poetic because of the simile, but because an essential element of the simile is unspoken – the suggestion that my love is as delicate, as odorous, (or as thorny) as a rose.

The line between the "elemental" and the "intentional" modes is, of course, quite blurry, and they seem to constitute different emphases along the same continuum. Formal interest in the devices of expression also recognized aims – the most interesting, it theoretically undeveloped, being the peculiar "charm" that derives from the clever exploitation of the figures of speech, which itself always involves speaking indirectly, for plain declarative utterance has no "figure" and no "charm": "the sun rises; the moon sets." By shifting the entire stress onto that aim, and away from the multiple means of realizing it, the *dhvani* theorists, and particularly Ānandavardhana (ninth century), provide a more universal and integral theory of poetic expression, and one that is even more formally grounded in the nature and functions of language.

The idea that poetic speech is by nature indirect has roots in the figurative tradition also in the sense that the figures and other devices were seen there to involve a necessary "deviation" (*vakratā*) from the standards of ordinary – ipso facto, literal – language. In the intentionalist tradition, this implication is drawn out by situating "suggestion" squarely in the context of the "powers" (*śakti*, or *vṛtti*) of language itself, that is, as part of a general theory of signification, or how language conveys meaning. Before the advent of the *dhvani* theorists, two such powers were widely discussed and accepted in the various schools of Indian thought: "denotation" (*abhidhā*) and "metonymy" (*lakṣaṇā*). The distinction was probably first made in the ritualist schools of Vedic interpretation, which were committed to the view that the Veda was ipso facto true and faultless; they were yet obliged to accommodate explicit Vedic statements, such as "the trees attend the sacrificial session" which are nonsensical if taken literally. Metaphor could now be decoded as covert literalism. (The statement serves to magnify the importance of the sacrificial session, and means that men too should attend the sacrifice.) The discovery of metonymy thus aided a project whose main thrust was defense of the literalism of the text.

As adopted by the writers on poetics, metonymy is understood in terms of a failure of the literal, and therefore a power inherent in language itself, for language is, in its essence, a communication. The Indian theorists recognized, in other words, what has come to be called the "symbol," and that the elements of language were, functionally, symbols. This failure of meaning is, however, always on a higher level than words, being found in some inconsistency or incoherence of the sentence (or assertion), of which the words are part. No word, by itself, conveys anything other than its literal meaning(s). Words are used, however, in syntactical combinations that often do not suit their literal meanings: "the grandstands are cheering." This lack of fit forces a re-evaluation of the meaning of the offending words. The alternative is assigning the assertion to the category of nonsense – not a valid option, given the Vedic roots of these speculations. By understanding "grandstands" relationally, that is, metonymically, as "men in the grandstands," the coherence of the assertion is salvaged.

Two points are in order. First, on this understanding, metonymy (and its clone, metaphor) have nothing inherently poetic about them; they are simply universal factors of language use. Secondly, it is not obvious whether this second "power" should be assigned to the words themselves, or to their syntax, their combination. As the explanation makes clear, metonymy never arises unless the words are joined in larger frames of reference. It might just as well be asserted that metonymy is a function of syntax, rather than an element of signification. This is, in fact, the position of at least one writer, Mahimabhaṭṭa (late eleventh century), author of the atypical *Vyaktiviveka*, but it is striking for its lack of general acceptance. Mahimabhaṭṭa accepts just one "power" – denotation – rejecting also the *dhvani*.

When the notion of "suggestion" was posited in the ninth century as the ground of poetic speech proper, it seemed natural enough to defend it as a third "power" of language, though it is even less directly related to the literal than is metonymy. In some respects, it is the inverse of the literal, being incapable, by definition, of direct utterance. The *dhvani* theory is thus founded on a paradox. And yet, there is likely a deeper linguistic significance to this attempt to ground poetry linguistically: when all is said and done, the postulated, self-evident, denotative level of signification is itself a scholarly construct, revealed rarely, if at all, in any real use of language. It is rather the suggestive, for all its poetic refinement, that characterizes ordinary language use, together with the metonymical. The *dhvani* theorists understood the paradox and turned it to their use.

The theory of suggestion also resolves another early problem of the figurationist model: a set of usages that did not employ any obvious figure of speech, or any exaggeration, the mark of hyperbole, but were nevertheless recognized as poetical – for example, a description of a moonlit night. The "charm" lies in the "facts" themselves, and their unspoken associations with trysts, reprieves from the day's heat, and so on. This "natural utterance" (*svabhāvokti*) was accorded an ambiguous place in the universe of figures. But it is, of course, the *dhvani* theory that really resolves the apparent paradox: the charm is indeed in the network of emotional associations that the description evokes. Although a figure, as we have seen, may also provoke a suggestion, suggestion arises often without any explicit device present. And this points also to the crucial difference between suggestion and metonymy: suggestion is compatible with, finds its best examples in, perfectly ordinary and fully functional language.

Suggestion is, itself, not a simplex, as this discussion already implies. To the extent that suggestion requires an expressive basis in language at all, its superadded "meaning" must coexist either with the denotative or the metonymical. In cases of irony, jokes, puns, and the like, the suggestion is nothing more mysterious than a thought or an idea that is hidden behind the language surface, but apart from its unexpectedness, perfectly capable of being formulated. Indeed, the explanation of an irony, for those who "don't get it," is nothing but the spelling out of that concealed idea. Those practicing deconstructive criticism will be familiar with at least this first kind of *dhvani*, discovered now not merely in belles-lettres but in all kinds of writing, such that the "plain" meaning is never the meaning to be "read."

Similarly, a figure of speech may be implied by the explicit utterance, though not spelled out. Many similes are thus understood, as when, for example, not mentioning his love per se, but only the comparandum, Abie sings of his "wild Irish rose." But the purest and most prized kind of suggestion is that which neither conveys an idea nor a covert figure, but an affective mood – a feeling, rather than a form. Affective suggestion is, for the canonical writers, the quintessence of all suggestion, in part because its meaning, an emotional tone, can never be evoked through the other functions of language: one may utter the word "love" a thousand times, and not once will the emotion named be communicated. But Burns's short poem evokes, with its first line, at least a simulacrum of the felt emotion. This simple observation doubtless accounts for the subsequent, and to us puzzling, postulation of *dhvani* as the third elemental function of language, along with denotation and metonymy. It is the status of this feeling, which seems both to escape the normal categories of expressive language, and yet calls for their re-evaluation and extension, that preoccupies the next aesthetic mode.

3 *The* rasa *tradition; aesthetic psychology*

Speculations on the emotional effect (or, properly, affect) of art have their origin in the other of the great genres of classical Sanskrit literature, the drama, whose vividness and presence appeared to require a poetic not entirely focused on the facilities of mediating language. Language, of course, occupies an important, though apparently subsidiary role, in the drama, which itself seems to arise out of a complex of other art forms – dance, music, an imagery grounded on religious icons, and so on – and to constitute some kind of integrative whole in respect of these "elements." That a search for the drama's integrative principle was a primary concern is evident in the oldest text of Indian aesthetics that has survived, the *Nāṭyaśāstra*, attributed to Bharata. The text, as received, is a congeries of traditional materials on every aspect of dramatics – from costuming, staging, even construction of the theater, to plot construction, techniques of acting, and dramatic language. The properly aesthetic portions of the treatise are thought to be among the latest matters added to the collection, perhaps in or by the sixth century CE. Two of its chapters (of perhaps 36) are devoted to an examination of *rasa* – the affective response to the drama on the part of its audience, said, in Bharata's laconic manner, to "arise" out of a combination of the other factors – scene, character, dialogue, and so on – that are presented to it. The "other factors" constitute, in effect, the entirety of the objective drama. Thus the *rasa*, or "taste"of the drama, appears here to be understood as the subjective organization of these factors – as the "result" of their peculiar combination, and as the "end" whose manifestation justifies that combination. Comparisons with Aristotle's notion of catharsis (of pity and fear, in the case of tragedy) are à propos. Thus the *rasa* also appears as a functional category, from the point of view of dramatic psychology.

But at no stage in the evolution of the *rasa* theory was much attention paid to the question of properly constructing this "effect." Instead, primary interest bore on three related issues, which had more to do with the status of the *rasa* as a mode of awareness: (1) how the *rasa* related to modes of emotional awareness that were not experienced in the context of dramatic or other art; (2) how the drama was to be understood in causal terms vis-à-vis the *rasa* that it awakened; and (3) what the limits of the *rasa* were – that is, how many kinds of dramatically induced experience there were, and how those kinds related to one another and to the notion of *rasa per se*.

It is clear, even in the *Nāṭyaśāstra*, that the *rasa* was not identified with any ordinary emotion or experiential state. The text distinguishes *rasa* from *bhāva*, and devotes separate chapters to each – the latter being, in all evidence, the psychologically real state on which the *rasa* is built, or which it dramatically reflects. Thus the love I feel for a certain woman (*bhāva* is always personal and situationally particular) is the basis of, but not the same emotion as, the "love" I experience (along with the entire audience) while attending upon Romeo's infatuation with Juliet. The *Nāṭyaśāstra* constructs a parallel terminology to reflect this difference, calling the *rasa* "*śṛṅgāra*," and the *bhāva* "*rati*," which latter term seems to translate "sexual passion, libido," thus marking its plain difference from the aesthetic *rasa*, which has elements of the contemplative, the platonic, and the vicarious. It is not only an emotional state that is fictive – generated in the make-believe context of the drama – but, more importantly, it is one that is inherently shared and universal; it is an emotion raised to the status of a communication, and therefore enjoyable.

How this transformation takes place, and what its precise ideational or psychological character is, are questions that become *pièces de resistance* of speculation on *rasa*. Abhinavagupta (eleventh century), in commenting on the obscure formula of the *Nāṭyaśāstra*, outlines three or four positions that were taken by his predecessors, before setting forth his own, which has become the standard view. Two of those positions are quite familiar to Western theory, though considered problematic in India. One is the straightforward view that the worldly emotions depicted in the play are causes of the aesthetic emotion's effect. This realistic and representational viewpoint obscures the real difference between the world and the theater, and can lead, *mutatis mutandis*, to the kinds of mistaken judgments that are a leitmotif of the daily press – that an art form directly causes certain kinds of behavior in its public. The second view uses language reminiscent of Aristotle: the play is an *imitation* (*anukaraṇa*) of the real, and it is its fictive character that allows the audience to participate in its action. This passive empathy is *rasa*. The second view has the advantage over the first of understanding the *rasa* as a quietistic state, rather than as part and parcel of the world's turbulence. But it fails to account for the remarkable sense of immediacy that the theater, in its best examples, conveys. (The last thing that I am aware of, as Hamlet sees his father's ghost, is that Olivier is imitating anyone.) These criticisms were first formulated by Abhinava's own teacher, Bhaṭṭa Tauta, and lead naturally to the third view, one very close to Abhinava's own, but which he attributes to one Bhaṭṭa Nārāyaṇa: the play is not so much an imitation of the real, as it is the essence of the real, and is thus *more* real than the real. The events, scenes, characters, dialogues, before us on the stage are understood as ideal representations, embodiments of types, if you like, already "generalized" (to use Nārāyaṇa's term), made into objects that can only be contemplated. The mundane real is related to the play as mere instance, if at all. The play celebrates the verities of emotional truth, love, hate, greed, loss, in such a way as to efface the gap between what is witnessed and the witness's own life, thus both drawing the audience into the play's consciousness and making the audience an object to itself, thus objectifying even terrifying emotions, and by that very distancing, providing a quintessential delight. Nārāyaṇa thus turns the play on its head. Its supramundane quality is not result, but cause. The play, in all its elements – moonrise, chance meeting, stolen glance – is such that it evokes all possible moonrises, or what is the same thing, the moonrise that each and every member of the audience has oftentimes experienced; the love that is displayed is, in part, the love that each in the audience has felt. This otherworldly (*alaukika*) capacity of the play Nārāyaṇa terms *bhogīkaraṇa*, thus attributing to dramatic art a novel, and quite philosophical, function, which is to evoke the tones that are latent in any particular experience and raise them to the status of a delectation quite independent of any particular experience.

This third view is essentially Abhinava's own, but with this novel function of "delectation" (which, perhaps modeled on the *dhvani*, as the linguistic function underlying poetry, was arguably a *petitio principii* anyway) replaced by a notion at once more psychologically based and more philosophically powerful – that of the joy (*ānanda*) that is implicit in the soul's experience of its own freedom. For Abhinava, the experience of *rasa* is a foretaste of the bliss of emancipation, promised by the great non-dual traditions of India. No special function need be imagined for this process, which presumes only the self-revelatory character of the eternal self, and no principle redolent of causality need be appealed to. The drama is thus a manifestation of that self, clothed, it is true, still in the vestiges of its emotional life – the *rasas*, which play here a role much like the persistent *skandhas* of the Buddhists that underlie the karmic process. With this bold stroke, Abhinava not only gives a defensible explanation of the dramatic experience but links aesthetic and religious concerns in a way again suitable to the times, for by the eleventh century all modes of life and letters were being brought under the great umbrella of *bhakti* or religious devotionalism. It is no accident that Abhinava was one of the great theologians of Kāśmīra Śaivism, professing a doctrine on the metaphysical level quite akin to his aesthetic theory – the self-manifesting character of the one, Śiva, as evidenced in and by the world of activity and purpose (*spanda*).

The question of the number of *rasas*, basic affective determinants of the soul's conscious life, is also illuminated by Abhinava's authoritative account. In Bharata's original formulation, apparently, eight such states were deemed serious and persistent enough to underlie an entire dramatic realization. Much of the Indian theory of plot construction, such as it is, depends on this observation, for it is the business of the plot to "demonstrate" a *rasa*. The *Nāṭyaśāstra* devotes one chapter to the construction of plots, seen, as in Aristotle, as mimicking actions that must be "complete." The intricate and quasi-ritualized analysis, developed around the notion of the five "junctures" (*saṁdhi*) of any voluntary action brought to fulfillment – motive, effort, obstacle, resolve, and success – is devoted to a display of that expected completeness. It is taken for granted that such completeness is a requisite of the drama's proper emotional effect. One *rasa* must thus be dominant; otherwise, the play would have no clarity and no form. The discrete elements of the play are judged hierarchically as they contribute to the evocation and development (often by contrast) of the dominant *rasa*. The complete drama is a mirror of life also in the sense, then, that the principal *rasa* can be developed only in the context of the others, made over into its appropriate subordinates. The affinity between Śiva (god of the cosmic dance), Advaita, and the arts has never been more cogently stated.

The eight are termed *śṛṅgāra, hāsya, vīrya, karuṇa, bhayānaka, bībhatsa, raudra, adbhuta* (roughly translated as: love, humor, courage, pity, fear, loathing, violence, and wonder). Even though these states, as principals, are very unevenly represented in the dramatic literature – which preponderantly illustrates *śṛṅgāra* and *hāsya*, with *vīrya* a poor third, and the others hardly in evidence, except as complementaries – no privilege is assigned any *rasa* on the theoretical level. (Bharata does suggest, enigmatically, a hierarchy of sorts, which appears to pair "as effects" *hāsya, karuṇa, adbunta,* and *bhayānaka* with their "sources", *śṛṅgāra, raudra, vīrya,* and *bībhatsa*. This is not well understood, and does not appear to be much developed in the later literature.) Abhinava's account of their arising, however, seems to point to a single principle active in all of them, the self-manifesting *ātman*, the unity implicit in the triple order of being, consciousness, and bliss – in the usual Advaita formula: *sat, cit, ānanda*. This "metaphysical" experience – precursor of final beatitude, as we have seen – though present in all the eight *rasas*, is also separable from them, which enables Abhinava to posit a ninth *rasa* – the *rasa* of *rasas*, or the "non-*rasa*" within the *rasa* – which he terms *śānta*, or "tranquillity," and which also allows him to incorporate within the domain of aesthetics the great body of epical and devotional literature that had grown up around the various medieval religious traditions. Most noteworthy is, of course, the problematic epic, *Mahābhārata*, whose themes of the ambiguity of *dharma* and the transcendence of *dharma* seemed to put it into another category of literature entirely. (The *Rāmāyaṇa* was never a problem for the aestheticians. Its unambiguous themes of love, devotion, and surpassing duty were only too easily accommodated. Even its *Uttarakāṇḍa* could be taken as a manifestation of *karuṇa*, or pathos: Bhavabhūti's *Uttararāmacarita*. A more typical play, illustrating the tension of love and heroism is the famous *Śakuntalā* (*Abhijñānaśākuntala*) of Kālidāsa. The *Mahābhārata*, it is observed, inculcates the *rasa śānta*, as its main theme – the peace that passeth all prideful striving for power and place.

4 *The aesthetics of "play,"* rasa *as theological principle*

Abhinava's influential commentary brings aesthetics into relation with theological speculation, but does so in the austere, monistic environment of the Śaiva Tantra. Others were evidently keen on working out this relationship in the warmer, and more emotional, environment of the devotional cults then forming around the other great personal god of Hinduism, Viṣṇu – especially, Kṛṣṇa, infatuating child and mischievous lover. It was inevitable, perhaps, that the older, de facto, preeminence of dramatic *śṛṅgāra rasa* would here be given a theological dress, separating *śṛṅgāra* (rather than the new-fangled *śānta*) out from the others and celebrating it as the supreme *rasa*. That much of the liturgy of Kṛṣṇa worship took the form of popular art forms – music, song, dance – was no doubt a contributory factor. Becoming increasingly explicit in this development is the notion that the *rasa* is not only a principle of dramatic literature, but lies behind the composition of other forms of written literature, notably strophic poetry and epic, and, since these are often sung, behind other art forms as well. The idea as such is not particularly novel, inasmuch as Bharata's drama incorporated all of these arts as subsidiaries, and hence saw them as ancillaries in the evocation of *rasa*. What does seem to be new here is the idea that any one of these arts, in and of itself, is a suitable vehicle for the expression of *rasa*, quite apart from a dramatic context. But of course, a dramatic context was not lacking in the liturgy of the devotional cults. Kṛṣṇa worship, in particular, was often framed as an imitation of Kṛṣṇa's exploits – chiefly, his *rasalīlā*, his amorous dalliances with the milkmaids – with the dramatic frame serving to evoke the presence of the god among those playing the roles of his attendants, and so on. The modern-day *kīrttana* and *bhajana* traditions of Bengal and south India continue this ritual model. The "aesthetic" also accounts for the "ritual," therefore.

This symbiosis of the arts in religious ritual was given a philosophical formulation in the writings of the sixteenth-century Vaiṣṇava theologians of Bengal, notably Rūpagosvāmin, followers of Caitanya and his ecstatic form of Kṛṣṇa worship. The key homology on which the synthesis of aesthetics and theology is here based is that *bhakti* – loving devotion to the god – is the supreme form of *śṛṅgāra rasa*, itself the *rasa* par excellence, or indeed, the only *rasa*. There were earlier attempts, notably Boja's encyclopedic *Śṛṅgāraprakāśa*, to single out *śṛṅgāra* among the *rasas*, but the Bengali theologians anchored their synthesis on a new form of cult practice, rather than on the dry logic of the academies, and it is their approach that we regard as defining this fourth mode of aesthetic speculation. The cultic aspects of this devotional movement have been widely discussed; we focus here only on its appropriation of the *rasa* aesthetic for cultic purposes – one of the rare examples, surely, of a theology formulating itself explicitly in aesthetic terms! This appropriation has implications for each of the aspects of the *rasa* aesthetic discussed above.

Abhinavagupta clearly distinguished between the emotion felt in the theater by an essentially contemplative and universal audience and the emotion felt in the world by individuals acting in their own particular interests. For that reason, he felt that the *rasa* was properly located in the audience, rather than, say, in the actor, or even in the author (not to speak of the characters). As the chief instrumentality of the play's realization, the actor is more a private individual than a passive spectator, concerned rather with the manifold details of his technique. Stanislavsky to the contrary notwithstanding, Abhinava holds that this prevents the actor from a full experience of the aesthetic effect. The Vaiṣṇava transformation has as its first and probably most far-reaching aesthetic consequence that the division between audience and actor is largely effaced. The devotees, by taking on the roles played by the companions of Kṛṣṇa in the eternal forest of Vṛndā, are at once witness to, but also participants in, the drama. It is obvious that the *rasa* is also theirs, but not in any contemplative capacity. It is by enacting the eternal play of the gods that *rasa* is experienced. The actor, in this sense, is the locus of *rasa*, and the boundary between the world and the theater becomes ambiguous.

The *rasa* can no longer be understood as a purely contemplative state, in and above all private emotions. It seems rather a condition of acute participation, involving as an essential element, the acting out of the divine story. The *rasa* may be nothing more than this transformation of character, wherein the worldling, for a moment at least, feels himself in the retinue of the god, and experiences a beatific and intimate affection. Although the ordinary world and the theater become ambiguous, it is still the case that the devotee, by his acting a role, makes the theater into his world – the only locus of his revalorized activity. While ordinary mortals may experience this bliss at times and for a moment, the saints of this tradition are those who have made that world of Kṛṣṇa their permanent abode. They are, as the saying goes, mad with the love of god. They have inverted the normal relation between action in the world and play in the theater.

As we have observed, the limits of the *rasa* also change. *Śṛṅgāra* not only comes to occupy the center of the stage (so to speak), for only in that mode can the human devotee find a relation with the delightful god; it is now the only *rasa*, the others being its permanent ancillaries. In part, this simply devolves from the plain fact that, of all the stories in the world, just one is deemed worthy of telling, and it is told repeatedly, *sub specie aeternitatis* – the tale of Kṛṣṇa and his milkmaid friends. One story, one *rasa*. But with this implosion of aesthetic effect comes a reevaluation of *śṛṅgāra* itself. It is no longer the rather straightforward "boy-meets-girl" imbroglio "that makes the world go round." Rather, it comes to incorporate within itself all the stages of the world's emotional consciousness. Five new *rasas* (at least) differently exemplify the one *rasa*, as five levels of devotion are recognized: duty (as expressed in the faithful performance of one's ritual obligations); service (as expressed in the unequal love of servant for master and, presumably, vice versa); parental love (as of a mother for her child – still unequal, but implying no permanent degradation of status); friendship (of equals, having overcome status differentiations); and, finally,"affection" (*prema*, or the all-consuming, ultimately sexual, mergence of two individuals in a common experience, impossible without their "difference"). The boundaries of *śṛṅgāra* are considerably enlarged by this attempt to include all aspects of dharmic behavior under its aegis, even the selfless performance of caste duties. But again, the pre-eminence of the fifth new *rasa* is only underscored by this evident hierarchization of devotions. So the net result is as moral as it is aesthetic, and allows the devotee to see his activity as the central informing act of a cosmos.

With this apotheosis of the aesthetic principle, we observe a corresponding magnification of the arts as ritually efficacious, and yet, this appears to be at the cost of sacrificing any concern for the ordinary work of art, the ordinary domain of aesthetics. Perhaps the universe of *bhakti* was so all-consuming that it left no place for secular art. More likely, the extreme devotionalism of the Bengali Vaiṣṇavas should be seen as a logical reference point, illustrating the convergence of sacred and secular, for those of us who continue to see utility in distinguishing them.

5 *The aesthetics of visualization,* rasa *in the non-literary domain*

Although it would be inviting to view the extension of the *rasa*-aesthetic from drama and literature to the non-literary arts (music, dance, and so on) as illustrating the rasa's seemingly inherent tendency to universalize itself at the expense of other modes of awareness, there are other factors that might be considered. We noted in the foregoing sections several modalities in which the arts were already grouped under a dominant principle – be it suggestion (the means to which need not be exclusively language-based), the drama (as mimicking the universe of human activity), or devotion (wherein the non-literary arts enjoyed a status at least equal to the written text in efficacy). It comes as no surprise, then, that the non-literary arts increasingly are conceived as expressive of that universalizing experience, *rasa*. The *rāgas* of classical Indian music, the folk-plays based on the old epic stories, the surviving stylized dance forms, all seem preoccupied, in their very conception, with freeing us from the petty selves that limit our experience in the everyday world. In this sense, the psychological theory underlying the *rasa* makes it almost inevitable that it be seized upon as the transformative product of those experiences – contemplative or not – that are sought after in a culture that values, in every domain, transcendence of the mundane as its highest goal. The survival of these aesthetic expectations in adapted Western-type media (movies, television) is proof of their persistence.

But there is another strain underlying the aesthetics of created objects, which may indeed intersect with the psychology of *rasa* in interesting ways, but which has another source: the visualizing techniques of the Tantra, both Buddhist and Hindu. It has long been remarked that the distinction between artist and artisan is very hard to draw in traditional India. The temple architect and the craftsman sculpting its gorgeous statuary labor within narrow limits set by traditional standards, in part ritually determined. They see their task as realizing a known ideal plan, not as giving free rein to their creative instincts within constraints set only by nature and human gullibility. To some extent, even the more imaginative media of the written word partake of this respect for ideal forms – witness the persistence of traditional stories and the prevailing critical emphasis on formal types – but it is in the plastic arts (otherwise so underrepresented in our aesthetic inventory) that "work to rule" seems to evolve into a true discipline, a *śāstra* – the *śilpaśāstra*. The model is adopted also in the domains of music and dance, also important ancillaries of Hindu temple worship.

In evaluating this notion of the created object, be it visual or aural, it is important to consider the role that certain meditative practices have played in Hindu (and Buddhist) ritual – wherein the meditator sees his task quite explicitly as the "creation" of objects in the mind's eye, and his absorption in them, quite as though they were the real objects of ritual. This, perhaps, is the Indian creative process par excellence, and its principles are bound to influence the creation of external objects – seen as mere simulacra of the corresponding mental images. Sound, as well, in the form of mantras and apparently meaningless syllables, is attributed the same quality as the visible object, for it too embodies and evokes the divine. It too has a power that the artisan seeks to capture. The prevailing religiosity of the Indian arts comes full circle here, as the artisan becomes a religious practitioner.

It would be hard to point to a non-religious exemplification of these aesthetic principles, in part because even the so-called secular domains – the needs of princes for self-display, and so on – are thoroughly integrated into the Hindu view of the cosmos. The rule of the king is an essential part of that cosmos (in fact, sustains the cosmos), and his activities can be separated only at great peril from that sacerdotal function. If I have conveyed some sense of the ways Indian aesthetics is part and parcel – and an increasingly essential part, over time – of religious and cosmological systems, then this article will have served its major purpose.

Bibliography

Byrski, M. C. 1979: *Methodology of the Analysis of Sanskrit Drama* (Warsaw: University of Warsaw).

Chari, V. K. 1990: *Sanskrit Criticism* (Honolulu: University of Hawaii Press).

De, S. K. 1960: *History of Sanskrit Poetics*, 2nd edn (Calcutta: Firma K. L. Mukhopadhyay).

Deutsch, Eliot 1981: "Reflections on Some Aspects of the Theory of Rasa," in *Sanskrit Drama in Performance*, ed. R. V. Baumer and J. R. Brandon (Honolulu: University of Hawaii Press).

Gerow, Edwin 1974: "The Sanskrit Lyric: a Genre Analysis", "Indian Poetics" and "The Persistence of Classical Esthetic Categories in Contemporary Indian Literature." All or parts of three chapters in *The Literatures of India: an Introduction* (Chicago: University of Chicago Press).

—— 1979: "Plot Structure and the Development of the Rasa in the Ūakuntalā," Pt I, *Journal of the American Oriental Society*, 99, pp. 559–72.

—— 1980: "Plot Structure and the Development of the Rasa in the Ūakuntalā," Pt II, *Journal of the American Oriental Society*, 100, pp. 267–82.

—— 1994: "Abhinavagupta's Aesthetics as a Speculative Paradigm," *Journal of the American Oriental Society*, 114, pp. 186–208.

Haberman, David 1985: *Acting as a Way of Salvation* (Bloomington: Indiana University Press).

Kane, P. V. 1961: *History of Sanskrit Poetics*, 3rd edn (Delhi: Motilal Banarsidass).

Keith, A. B. 1924: *The Sanskrit Drama: Its Origin, Development, Theory, and Practice* (Oxford: Oxford University Press).

Masson, J. L. and Patwardhan, M. V. 1969: *Śāntarasa and Abhinavagupta's Philosophy of Aesthetics* (Poona).

Sylvain Lévi 1963 [1890]: *Le Théâtre indien* (Paris, 1890; reprinted, Paris, 1963).

Wulff, Donna 1984: *Drama as a Mode of Religious Realization* (Chico, Cal.).

Indian works

Mentioned by translation, when known. Some recent Indian translations may have escaped my notice.

Appayadīkṣita 1907: *Kuvalayānanda*, tr. R. Schmidt (Berlin).
Ānandavardhana 1990: *Dhvanyāloka*, with the commentary *Locana* of Abhinavagupta, tr. D. H. H. Ingalls, J. M. Masson [=J. L. Masson], and M. V. Patwardhan (Cambridge, Mass.).
Bharata 1961 [1959]: *Nāṭyaśāstra*, tr. M. Ghosh (Calcutta, 1959, 1961); partial translations by many scholars: see De, *HSP*, 1, 44–5. Abhinavagupta's *Bhāratī* to the *rasanispattisūtra* tr. R. Gnoli, *Aesthetic Experience according to Abhinavagupta* (Rome, 1956); J. L. Masson and M. V. Patwardhan, *Aesthetic Rapture* (Poona, 1970); his commentary on śāntarasa tr. J. L. Masson and M. V. Patwardhan, *Śāntarasa* . . . (Poona, 1969), and by E. Gerow, *JAOS*, 114 (1994) [see above].
Bhavabhūti 1874: *Uttararāmacarita*, tr. C. H. Tawney (Calcutta).
Bhāmaha 1927: *Kāvyālaṁkāra*, tr. P. V. Naganatha Sastry (Tanjore).
Bhoja 1963: *Śṛṅgāraprakāśa*; see study by V. Raghavan, *Bhoja's Śṛṅgāra Prakāśa* (Madras) and subsequent editions.
Daṇḍin 1890: *Kāvyādarśa*, tr. O. Böhtlingk (Leipzig).
Daśakumāracarita 1927: tr. A. Ryder, *The Ten Princes* (Chicago).
Kālidāsa, *Abhijñānaśākuntala* 1984: tr. B. S. Miller, in *Theater of Memory: the Plays of Kālidāsa* (New York). Also contains translations of Kālidāsa's other two plays, by David Gitomer and Edwin Gerow, and three interpretive essays.
Kālidāsa, *Kumārasaṁbhava*, tr. Hank Heifetz.
Kṣmendra, *Aucityavicāracarcā*, not translated.
Mammaṭa 1918: *Kāvyaprakāśa*, tr. G. Jha (Benares).
Mahimabhaṭṭa, *Vyaktiviveka*, not translated.
Rudraṭa, *Kāvyālaṁkāra*, not translated, but see Gerow, *Glossary*, Introduction.
Rūpagosvāmin, *Ujjvalanīlamaṇi*, not translated: see Haberman, Wulff, above.
Vāmana n.d.: *Kāvyālaṁkārasūtrāṇi*, tr. G. Jha (Allahabad).

Other works mentioned

Ṛg Veda 1951–7: the best complete translation is still that by K. F. Geldner (in German), 4 Vols (Cambridge, Mass.).
Mahābhārata 1993: tr. K. M. Ganguly (alias P. C. Roy) (Calcutta, 1883–96); reprinted (Delhi, 1993); Bks I–V tr. J. A. B. van Buitenen (Chicago, 1973–8).
Rāmāyaṇa 1984–: translation in course by R. P. Goldman et al. (Princeton).

22

The self and person in Indian philosophy

STEPHEN H. PHILLIPS

1 Introduction

Classical Indian views of the self and person range from maximal to minimal conceptions, from a view of everyone's true self as the supreme being, infinite, immortal, self-existent, self-aware, and intrinsically blissful, to a view of the person as nothing more than the living human body that ceases to be at death. ("Consciousness is an adventitious attribute of the body, like the intoxicating power of fermented grain.") Every major school and subschool takes a stance on what a self is and how it is known; a rich diversity of opinion and argument marks this area of classical Indian thought.

Speculation about mystical possibilities are recorded in very old, pre-classical texts known as Upaniṣads ("secret doctrines"), from as early as 800 or even 900 BCE. The ancient Upaniṣads suggest that there lies in each of us, hidden, occult, a somehow spiritual self that enjoys ways of being and awareness superior to our everyday consciousness. The reality of this self would explain discoveries in meditation and the results of yogic or ascetic practices – such seems to be the implicit thesis. The classical schools of Vedānta, Sāṃkhya, and Yoga owe much to Upaniṣadic mysticism with respect to their views of a hidden, true or supreme self. But compared to the Upaniṣads, classical philosophies belong to a different literary epoch and genre, whose conventions are distinguished by an acute sensitivity to argument and systematic requirement. It is a literature that does not begin to emerge for several centuries after the early Upaniṣads, that is, not until around 100 BCE or later.

Here the first order of business will be to air Upaniṣadic conceptions along with the classical philosophies that are centered on a notion of a spiritual self – including, briefly, Buddhist philosophies which are similarly inspired. Buddhists, in contrast with other spiritually minded classical theorists, typically deny an enduring self; on our title topic, a distinctive polemics is theirs (see Tom P. Kasulis, Article 29, THE BUDDHIST CONCEPT OF SELF). We shall profit, nevertheless, from including certain Buddhist theses within a purview of philosophies that uphold a self that is mystically discoverable.

In the long period of classical argument and system-building (stretching approximately two thousand years), there are philosophers whose views about the individual person try to capture everyday regards and common sense and who are not much concerned with meditation and mysticism. Classical positions on what the self is and how it is known are usually tied in with stances taken on other issues, and we shall survey much at the heart of the outlook of Mīmāṃsā (Exegesis) and Nyāya (Logic), two realist philosophies. The one, Exegesis, is most concerned with principles of right conduct, while the other, Logic, is focused on questions concerning objects of common experience and desire (in Sanskrit, *vyavahārikārtha*). With regard to these two schools in particular, an individual self, which is viewed as an item in a complex universe, has to be understood in a larger context. With Exegesis, moral cosmology provides the most pertinent context, and with Logic, views in ontology and about the fundamental categories of things govern reflection about what a self is. A self, for example, is said to be a substance and a fundamentally different sort of thing from a quality, such as the color blue.

Now all classical philosophers, the spiritually as well as the worldly minded, admit a neutral touchstone or constraint on their theorizing, namely, common speech behavior (*vyavahāra*), which reflects, it is presumed, bits of everyday knowledge. With respect to the question of what a self is, usages employing the first-person pronoun (*aham* or "I", and so on) are taken to provide data for which any successful theory has to account. Thus those who propose an exalted spiritual self have special difficulties with such statements as "I am fat" or "I am tall" (since "being fat" and "being tall" are bodily attributes and the self is thought to transcend the body), whereas the extreme deflationists – known as Cārvākas – have to explain away expressions such as "My body" (implying that there is something, a self, that *has* a body, in opposition to the Cārvāka view that the body and the self are identical).

After surveying early mystical notions and views that are continuous with them, we shall scrutinize positions that have more of an eye to our everyday sense of what a self is. In the final section (out of four), positions on how the self or consciousness is known (that is, on self-awareness) will be reviewed. While in general these conform to views of what a self is, the nature of self-awareness is sharply disputed, as theorists appeal to the touchstones of linguistic practice and common experience and try to draw out untoward ramifications of an opponent's stance. Also in the final section, the issue that is key to the mystical philosophies will be aired, the issue, namely, of the epistemic value of meditation and yogic experience.

2 The spiritual self

The earliest Upaniṣads develop views of a spiritual self, *ātman*, with respect to questions about a supreme reality, its nature and relation to the world, and how it is known. Generally it is declared that through the self the supreme being, termed *brahman*, is to be found, and at places the self is proclaimed identical with Brahman. Dimensions or layers of self-experience are discovered: for example, a series of states of awareness in dream and sleep, and a series of bodies (*kośa*) ranging from a physical to a life and a mind "sheath" to one "supramental" and a final, most essential sheath said to be "made out of bliss."

A mystical awareness of Brahman, called *brahma-vidyā* ("knowledge of Brahman"), is said to be a person's supreme good. It is also called *ātma-vidyā* ("knowledge of the self"). The classical philosophies of Vedānta, Sāṃkhya, and Yoga develop varieties of this conception. All three systems are organized around the idea of a perceived mystical possibility, although a couple of qualifications should be kept in mind. First, only in Vedānta do we find mysticism expressed in terms of *brahman* and *brahma-vidyā*; Sāṃkhya and Yoga talk about multiple true "persons," *puruṣa*, and their native state of self-awareness and bliss. Second, there are theistic Vedānta subschools (opposed to a monistic and illusionist Advaita Vedānta) that while also upholding a mystical supreme good are centered more on a notion of God as the supreme being than on a notion of an "own true self." It is in the Advaita Vedānta subschool – along with Sāṃkhya and Yoga – that a true self is viewed as exclusively the locus of value and as that which is to be mystically sought.

Classical Vedānta derives its name from an epithet for the Upaniṣads. ("Vedānta" means literally the end of the Veda, and the Upaniṣads were appended to the Veda, an even older collection of verses or mantras viewed as sacred, as revealed "Knowledge.") Advaita Vedānta is the classical Vedānta subschool that upholds a non-duality (*advaita*) between the individual consciousness and the supreme Self, or Brahman, who is all-inclusive and "one without a second." Sáṃkara (ca. 700) is Advaita's most famous advocate. According to him and his numerous followers, including many moderns (Advaita remains a prominent philosophy today), the world of everyday experience is a dream or illusory projection (*māyā*) of this single self. Except for our self-awareness – which is itself non-dualistic, that is to say, direct and unmediated, not a matter of beholding ourselves in a mirror or apprehending ourselves in any way that external objects are apprehended – our sense of ourselves as embodied, as belonging to a family and having certain property and social position, is a false identification with aspects of a world that is a cosmic illusion, or at least it is so with respect to the mystical self-experience. Meditation is a way that our self-awareness can, so to say, return to its fuller self, although some Advaitins stress simply reading and studying the Upaniṣads as the means to true self-knowledge. The point seems to be that once we understand what we truly are through Upaniṣadic study, our immediate awareness of ourselves can awaken to its fuller reality. Finally, some classical Advaitins as well as modern philosophers influenced by Advaita point to the Advaitin understanding of a true self as the deep precondition for all our ordinary awareness. (This line of thought resonates with certain species of idealism in the West).

Sāṃkhya (the word means analysis) proposes careful understanding of nature, her organizing principles and her subtle presentations as thoughts and emotions, as the means for the true person or self to disidentify with the mind and body – mental occurrences, such as thought and emotion, being viewed as part of nature and external to the true person. In Western reflection about the self and person, philosophers concerned with criteria of personal identity make much of the facts that personality is developed or acquired and that an individual may have distinct or multiplc pcrsonalities during different stages of her or his life. According to

Sāṃkhya, all personality is a mask, to be analyzed as various personas which the true individual identifies with, thereby alienating himself (or herself or itself: the true person has no sex) from its native state of self-absorption and bliss. By understanding the nature of the masks that nature presents for us to assume – from reason and sense experience down to the body and its interpenetration with nature at large, in particular the subtle trick of ego-sense (*ahaṃkāra*) – we can more easily discover ourselves as the transcendent beings we are, whom nature serves but who in essence are from her labors free.

Yoga is a philosophy with much in common with Sāṃkhya; both view nature as real but as alien to the true individuals we are, and both describe true individuals similarly. But whereas Sāṃkhya advocates analysis of the components of natural bonds of personality and lays out the principles of nature in a rather comprehensive worldview, Yoga is the philosophy of the *Yoga-sūtra*, a text that is primarily a handbook on yogic practices and only secondarily a philosophical treatise. Apparently, through the practice of yoga (*yoga* in Sanskrit means "self-discipline"), one's true self is discovered – that is to say, it is discovered through the practice of certain psychophysical techniques centering on meditation and the ability to concentrate without distraction to the point of an entire mental silence. According to the *Yoga-sūtra*, what the true self is like, it bears repeating, is what Sāṃkhya philosophers hold it to be. But note that philosophers of other persuasions, Vedāntins and Buddhists, for example, advocate yogic practice while conceiving of a true self differently.

To be precise, Buddhists do not uphold any notion of a self, though they do uphold mystic discoveries. In fact, a doctrine of "no-self" (in Sanskrit, *an-ātman*) is promoted as key to the awakening or enlightenment that is the goal of Buddhist practice. (The word *buddha* in Sanskrit means "the awakened"; thus in Buddhism our ordinary experience with respect to enlightenment is compared implicitly to a dream.) As in Sāṃkhya, disidentification with elements we commonly take to be ourselves (the body, thought, desires, emotions) is viewed as essential to progress along the spiritual way, and apparently the no-self doctrine is considered to facilitate such disidentification. Furthermore, what is discovered in the supreme enlightenment should, Buddhists aver, by no means be compared to the self-regard that marks the everyday person. Enlightenment is *nirvāṇa*, an "extinguishing" of self-regarding desire, where something, or Nothing, indescribably wonderful is awakened and set free.

All told, there is little positive value found in the development of personality, according to the Indian spiritual philosophies that we have so far reviewed. However, in Mahāyāna Buddhism and in the twentieth-century mystic philosophy of Sri Aurobindo, certain forms of personality development are regarded in a very positive light. In Mahāyāna, one aims to become a Bodhisattva, who turns back from extinction of individuality in *nirvāṇa* to help every conscious being attain supreme felicity. If one strives for one's own personal salvation alone, if one has no career (*yāna*) of helping others to the supreme good, one would belong to the Hīnayāna, and would be "one with no career," a term used by Mahāyānists in deprecation of such a path. Mahāyānists, "those with wide and great careers," in contrast, seek not only their own personal salvation but "deliverance of every sentient being from suffering and ignorance." Individual personality is thus viewed as essential to a full religious life. A follower of the Mahāyāna path tries to develop in particular six moral, intellectual, and spiritual perfections (*pāramitā*), the most important of which is wisdom (*prajñā*). Thus he or she endeavors to become a Bodhisattva, a person who has one foot in the bliss of *nirvāṇa*, so to speak, but who develops a powerful individual personality to further the welfare of everyone.

Sri Aurobindo (1872–1950) combines the traditional emphasis on a mystical enlightenment and self-discovery with a world-affirming view to which individual development is key. According to Aurobindo, who lines up with Vedāntic theism among classical philosophies, the very reason that God, or Brahman, creates this world is to make possible a psychical evolution of individuals who are in part responsible for forging, over the course of innumerable lifetimes, their own personality – expressed bodily, emotionally, intellectually, and in other, occult ways. The universe has a purpose, mystical discovery of Brahman, Aurobindo claims; at least one side of it is that. The other is soul-making, the forging of a world-oriented self, a process for which God and the evolving individual soul share responsibility. In fact, Aurobindo views the mystic discovery as a factor in the development of spiritual individuality, and the development of strong personality a prerequisite for mystic discovery. Thus, in his philosophy, as in Mahāyāna Buddhism, mysticism and personality development are viewed as complementary.

3 The self in the world

Classical philosophy is in large part defined by views and disputes about what a self is, its distinguishing marks, and its role in those relations to external objects, such as perception and purposive action, that are crucial to human knowledge and accomplishment. Classical philosophic treatments of such issues are extensive, with so many considerations aired, and so many arguments, that here we must take only an overview. We shall focus mainly on schools and their stances, and put off most of our attention to arguments to the next section, on self-consciousness, where a few especially pertinent contentions will be reviewed. For other arguments – many having a life across schools – and indeed positions of schools not discussed here, see the references given below (Surendranath Dasgupta, *A History of Indian Philosophy*, Vol. 1, in particular).

The school of Mīmāṃsā, "Exegesis", is a major player in classical debates of all periods. Its most famous advocates were roughly contemporaries, separated by one generation – Kumārila (ca. 670) and his renegade pupil, Prabhākara (ca. 700). For philosophic positions, these two and numerous followers turn first to Vedic literature, but seem also to display a hard-headed common sense. Traditionally, questions of *dharma*, "duty" or "right practice," are what Exegetes are most interested in. This *dharma* they understand fundamentally as the performance of certain rituals, and by extension as one's entire conduct in life, with particular duties incurred according to a person's age, sex, and caste. Mīmāṃsakas see human actions and reactions as governed by laws that maintain cosmic order, and a person's *karma* (actions and dispositions to act) as reverberating within moral rhythms of the entire universe. Understanding *dharma*, the universe's backbone, enables a person to develop the very best *karma*, and thus to stand in right relation to the universe as a whole.

It is evident that a theory of *karma* is important background here, and though the theory is pan-Indian, not restricted to Exegete philosophy, let us look at it quickly. A psychological thesis (a) and one of moral cosmology (b) are central to the *karma* conception. Psychologically, (a) action undertaken creates a tendency – a habit, conceived as a real but unconscious force – to repeat that act. At any moment an agent may freely and creatively act in a novel way; moreover, any disposition formed by a previous act or sequence of acts, however firmly rooted, can be resisted psychologically, such that it does not become the motive or driving force of any future act. Nevertheless, much in life is considered determined by one's *karma* in the sense of the dispositions formed by previous acts. Virtue is its own reward, according to this side of the Indian theory. According to (b), the thesis of moral cosmology, actions have external consequences that invariably embrace a moral dimension: there is moral payback. You get what you deserve, if not in this, then in a future lifetime. Fortunately, by performing actions in accordance with duty, *dharma*, "the right way to live," thus making them in a deep sense rituals or sacrifices, all Veda-grounded, as explained by Exegetes, one develops the best sort of dispositions, and secures virtue and status in this lifetime and in lifetimes to come – here we return to Mīmāṃsā views and that school's version of the *karma* theory.

We cannot review in all its rich detail the reflection of Exegetes on the nature of a self. But we can now appreciate the task taken up by Kumārila, Prabhākara, and company, to spell out what a self is in the rather precise sense of a person who is able to perform sacrifices and follow *dharma*, who accrues karmic dispositions, and who will be reborn in a position and statues according to the moral law. The theory of a self that captures all this must also conform to everyday usages employing the pronoun "I" and so on. (The Exegetes are often ingenious at bringing linguistic evidence to bear on issues. I repeat that their supposedly Vedic positions make a strong appeal to common sense.) A self is in the Mīmāṃsā view as much a doer as a knower. Devadatta as a self is a lot more than an experiencer, indeed more than what an "experiencer" is according to the highest norms of a mystic askesis: Devadatta is the agent of important acts. Within this frame, Exegetes contribute much to classical discussions about what a self is and its place in the world.

Another major classical player taking up questions about the self and person is Nyāya, "Logic," or more precisely, Nyāya-Vaiśeṣika: Logic and Atomism (Vaiśeṣika) are sister schools in the earlier period of classical philosophy and a single school in the later (from about the eleventh century), referred to simply as Nyāya. The origins and early motivations of the two schools appear to be, first, in the case of Logic, principles of successful public debate (on practically any topic) and, second, in the case of Atomism, the science of grammar, how we can mean what we say, and the categories to things that words refer to (and that we experience everyday). The views of a self in these sister schools converge, and in conformity with the later practice, I shall speak only of Nyāya.

Against Buddhists in particular, Logic holds that a self is a substance that endures through qualitative change. As an earthen pot that is black before baking and red afterwards is, despite the change of colors, the same material thing, so one and the same self may be sad at one moment and joyful at another. Psychological qualities inhere in or qualify a self – states of awareness, desires, and so on – as physical qualities, such as color and shape, qualify a physical thing.

Two considerations put forward in support of this position are, first, the phenomenon of recognition, as expressed by the statement, "This is that Devadatta I saw yesterday." If the self did not endure through qualitative change, no sense could be made of such recognition, since there would be no continuity between the person who saw Devadatta yesterday and the person who recognizes him today. Second, the *Nyāya-sūtra*, Nyāya's foundational text (attributed to Gautama, ca. 200 CE), argues (at 3.1.1), "There is grasping of a single object through sight and touch. Therefore (the self is distinct from perceptions, and has distinct sense organs)." If there were no substantial self distinct from and enduring through different sense experiences, external objects would not be experienced as having distinct properties grasped through different sense media such as sight and touch. Thus whatever else a self is, it is something that endures, and the Buddhist view that there is no self apart from a stream of fleeting experiences is refuted.

Mīmāṃsā and Nyāyā are principally world-oriented philosophies, despite Mīmāṃsā's concern with *dharma*, religious rituals, and rebirth. Thus they contrast with the teachings focused on mystical discoveries. However, both Exegetes and philosophers of the Logic school do not actively oppose, generally speaking, the religious or spiritual teachings of other schools – except for (1) Buddhist teachings, which are usually not very well understood, and (2) Advaita Vedānta's doctrine of a single true self, a doctrine actively opposed in late Nyāya apparently as incompatible with late Nyāya's firmer commitment to theism. As I mentioned above in the introductory section, it is the Cārvāka materialist and sensationalist school that is the most vehemently opposed to any mystical, inflated notion of a self: the self is just the body. Cārvāka philosophers also make fun of the religious rituals championed by Mīmāṃsākas and beliefs in *karma* and rebirth. The linguistic evidence of such phrases as "my body" – implying that there is something, a spiritual self (others presume), that *has* a body – these materialists claim involve only a metaphorical usage.

4 How is the self known?

Although self-awareness is not all that a self amounts to according to the world-oriented views (such as Mīmāṃsā and Nyāya), the issue of self-awareness becomes a battleground for all schools: whether or not a self or person is more than self-awareness depends on the precise nature of self-awareness – such seems to be one idea that frames the dispute. In other words, classical Indian philosophers of all banners address the question of how we know ourselves by focusing on what is taken to be absolutely essential to a self by practically every party, namely, self-awareness. (This focus is probably due to the prominence of the spiritual views.) Thus the question is, how does awareness know itself?

Here we shall survey the debate between Nyāya (Logic) and Advaita Vedānta. Logician philosophers hold that an awareness is an episodic property of the self that is by nature intentional, that is, *of* something or other. The self can be the object of a cognition, but not of perceptual or immediate awareness, at least according to most Nyāya authors: the self is known by inference. How is an awareness known? An awareness is known in "apperception" (in Sanskrit, *anuvyavasāya*, an "after-cognition"), which is an awareness whose object is an immediately preceding awareness. A later awareness scopes a prior one, knowing its content as what the former awareness is of ("It seemed as though I was seeing a snake"), unlike a non-apperceptive awareness whose intentionality directs one to objects in the world ("I see a snake"). Even an apperception can be scoped, that is, can become an object of an immediately subsequent awareness, a second-order apperception ("I was noticing that it seemed as though I was seeing a snake"). But no awareness takes itself as object, according to Nyāya.

Advaita philosophers argue that the Nyāya view succumbs to an infinite regress, that there could be no self-awareness were a second awareness A_2 required to make an immediate awareness A_1 known. They also attack the Nyāya view by alleging that if a self *has* awareness, then there is a wedge between the self and awareness, an infinitely extensive wedge, moreover, since the wedge (the *having*) has to be related to awareness, on the one hand, and the self, on the other, by another relation in each case, and that further relation tied to its relata by still another, *ad infinitum*. Thus for these reasons – namely, (1) self-awareness (which is a reality) would be impossible on the Logic view because an infinite series of awarenesses would be required, and (2) the self, if separate from its awareness, could never be joined to it – the Advaita view of truly intrinsic self-awareness (which is also the view taught by scripture, that is, taught by the Upaniṣads) should be embraced instead. Furthermore, it is a plain fact that the self witnesses itself "by its own light" (*svayaṃ jyotiḥ*).

Nyāya responds by agreeing that awareness is essential to a self. Though awareness is episodic, changing all the time, there is never an instant when the self is bereft of awareness. The relationality here is much like the case of an individual cow, Bessie, and her cowhood, her "being a cow." Although cowhood, which is the class character shared by all individuals that are cows, is a property that Bessie has, such that there is a relation between the property and Bessie as property-possessor, Bessie is never bereft of cowhood. It is for her an essential property. No particular awareness is essential to a self; but a self, by nature, always has some awareness or other. Moreover, no infinitely extensive wedge occurs between a self and its awareness. Although the two are different types of things and although it is meaningful to talk about the relation between them, the relation is *self-linking*. A self and its awareness are hooked up by a self-linking relationality, requiring no additional term; similarly, a rope tying a goat to a tree does not require another rope to tie itself to them. Then concerning the contention that self-awareness would be impossible on the Nyāya view because an infinite series of awarenesses would be required, Logic philosophers say that it is a matter of plain experience that sometimes we notice that we are aware of something or other and sometimes we are absorbed in the worldly content of our awarenesses without noticing that we are aware. In principle, there is no limit to the orders of possible apperception. But normally we have little call to notice our own awarenesses, involved as we are in action and getting things done. In philosophy, we do have call to apperceive, and even to apperceive apperceptions. But it seems to be just a matter of what awareness *is* that it is invariably directed to something or other, and that this is sometimes a previous awareness. (Then it may be called, loosely, self-awareness.) This claim itself is based on apperception and inductive generalization ranging over a mental life.

Finally, there is the key issue for the spiritual philosophies of the epistemic value of meditation and yogic experience – value, or warrant, for spiritual claims, which would be transferred by way of mystics' testimony to us non-mystics, who would then have good reason to accept those claims. Advaita Vedāntins, for instance, insist that Logic philosophers, among others, do not appreciate the full range of possibilities of experience, that they ignore testimony about the opportunity to have a mystical realization of Brahman, who is one's true Self and the Absolute and the One. The reason one should accept Advaita views about all this is, simply, the general epistemic value of testimony, Advaitins claim. And similar positions seem to be at least implicit among spiritual philosophers of other camps. The testimony would derive its justificational force from first-person meditational and yogic experiences, just as my testimony to you that my dog Malone has long ears – testimony that gives you a good reason so to believe – is grounded in my thorough experiential acquaintance with Malone. A mystic empiricism is apparently operative in the Upaniṣads and in other works of Indian spirituality.

Is, then, mystical experience informative about reality? Classical discussions tend to assimilate this question to that of the epistemic value of sense experience – the assumption being that mystical experience is like sense experience in evidencing facts or objective states of affairs, although, with the mystical experience, these would be of a spiritual, not a physical, sort. But there is a lot of disagreement about just what claims would be justified. Can mystical or yogic experience provide grounds for belief that Brahman is real *and* for the reality of *nirvāṇa*, Sāṃkhya's *puruṣa*, and so on? This worry seems even more severe in a global context, where the diversity of claims supposedly mystically justified is greater still.

Bibliography

Chakrabarti, Arindam 1992: "I Touch What I Saw," *Philosophy and Phenomenological Research*, 52, 1, pp. 103–16.

Dasgupta, Surendranath 1922: *A History of Indian Philosophy*, Vol. 1 (Cambridge: Cambridge University Press).

Eliade, Mircea 1969: *Yoga: Immortality and Freedom*, tr. Willard R. Trask, 2nd edn (Princeton: Princeton University Press).

Koller, John M. 1982: *The Indian Way* (New York: Macmillan).

Mohanty, Jitendranath 1992: *Reason and Tradition in Indian Thought* (New York: Oxford University Press).
Oetke, Claus *"Ich" und das Ich: analytische Untersuchungen zur buddhistisch-brahmanischen Ātmankontroversie* (Stuttgart: Franz Steiner).
Organ, Troy W. 1964: *The Self in Indian Philosophy* (The Hague: Mouton).
Phillips, Stephen H. 1995: *Classical Indian Metaphysics* (La Salle, Ill.: Open Court).
Sinha, Jadunath 1958: *Indian Psychology*, Vol. 1 (Calcutta: Sinha Publishing House).
Smart, Ninian 1964: *Doctrine and Argument in Indian Philosophy* (New York: Humanities Press).

23

Truth in Indian philosophy

AMITA CHATTERJEE

I

If a quiz-master were to ask the question, "Is there anything common among the philosophies of the world?" the answer that should come from the participants with perfect aplomb is, "Yes, the concern for truth." The presumed unanimity of this response, however, does not imply that philosophers possess a uniform understanding of the notion of truth. There are, indeed, many similarities in the way great minds think on this topic, yet divergences among them are also too significant to be ignored. In this article, therefore, I propose to expound the various aspects of *truth* from a typically Indian perspective (although, of course, in the contemporary philosophical idiom) before making a comparative assessment of different philosophical theories of truth.

In Indian philosophical parlance three words – namely, "*satyam*," "*yāthārthyam*," and "*prāmāṇyam*" – have been commonly used to convey the idea of truth. While the first word is usually reserved for moral and metaphysical contexts, the remaining two have overwhelmingly logico-epistemic associations. Truth as the Ultimate Moral Value, as we find it, for example, in the motto of the Indian Republic, "Truth alone triumphs" (*satyameva jayate*), or as one of the essential moral duties (*sādhāraṇa dharma*) enjoined by the scriptures to be practiced across the barriers of castes and creeds, lies outside the purview of this article. The metaphysical notion of truth as the Ultimate Reality will be touched upon in course of the discussion of the Vedantic theory, for here the epistemic account remains incomplete without reference to the metaphysical. We shall concentrate mainly on the epistemic notions for a very good reason, which will soon be evident.

Any adequate theory of truth is expected to raise and answer the following questions:

1 What is it that can be said to be true? Or what kinds of entities can be truth-bearers?

2 What is the nature of truth, or how can truth be defined? The same question has often been reformulated as follows: What do we mean when we say that a proposition (or whatever) is true? In post-Tarskian Western philosophy (2) has yielded to:

2' Under what conditions is a proposition (or whatever) true?

3 What is the test of truth – that is, how can we ascertain whether a proposition (or whatever) is true?

Indian philosophers, in propounding their theories of truth, have not belied our expectations. Not all Indian philosophers, however, have kept (2) and (3) separate, even though tackling them as distinct questions has some definite advantages. (For example, most of the time it is easier to find a criterion of applicability than to define a concept. It is also possible to agree on a criterion in spite of having differences with respect to the nature of a particular concept. We shall return to this point later.)

There are some common presuppositions underlying Indian theories of truth, the foremost of which is related to the nature of the truth-bearer. Indian philosophers hold that what can be said to be true (or false) is neither a proposition, nor a statement, nor a sentence, nor a belief, but is a non-recollective awareness episodic and cognitive in nature. In different systems of Indian philosophy, in accordance with their diverse metaphysical commitments, this cognition or *jñāna* has been conceived differently. To the Nyāya-Vaiśeṣikas a cognition is a quality (*guṇa*) of the self (*ātman*), whereas to the Mīmāṃsakas it is an action (*kriyā*) of the self. To the philosophers belonging to the Sāṃkhya-Yoga or the Vedānta traditions, a cognition is a modification (*vṛtti*) of "the inner sense" (*antaḥkaraṇa*). These ontologically divergent entities are designated by the same name (*jñāna*), simply because these are all intentional occurrences about some object (*viṣaya*). In all of these systems, the form (*ākāra*) of a cognition is derived from its object, which is usually external. The only thesis to the contrary is that of some Buddhist Schools, in which a cognition is said to originate along with its own form.

A cognition that is capable of being either true or false is of the relational variety (*viśiṣṭajñāna*) and hence admits of logical analysis into its constituent elements. The logical structure of a cognition always extends beyond its linguistic structure. It is obvious, therefore, that a truth-bearer in Indian philosophy is not identical with a sentence. Nor can it be identified with a belief, which is generally taken to be dispositional in nature. Besides, Indian philosophers, excepting those of the Grammarian School, never felt the need for proposition-like abstract entities as the meanings of sentences. Even *bauddhārthas*, the meanings of words and sentences, to which the Grammarians are committed, are not, strictly speaking, abstract entities. *Bauddhārthas* undoubtedly form a third category over and above the linguistic items and their referents in the external world, but these entities do not inhabit any mysterious third realm.

Given that truth-bearers in Indian philosophy are cognitions, I shall now explain a few key Sanskrit terms. A true cognition is called *pramā*, and its means (*karaṇa*) is *pramāṇa*. "Truth" can be translated as *pramātva* or *prāmāṇya*, and a theory of truth as *prāmāṇyavāda*, though the term *prāmāṇya* may also mean the property of being a *pramāṇa* – that is, the causal condition which is immediately followed by a true cognition. Indian theories of truth or *prāmāṇya* have been broadly classified into two types: *svataḥ* (intrinsic) theories and *parataḥ* (extrinsic) theories. This *svataḥ–parataḥ* distinction follows naturally if truth is taken as a predicate of cognition and consequently is an important feature of Indian theories of truth. Indian philosophers introduced the notion of truth while developing a causal theory of knowledge. Naturally, they became interested in the question of whether the originating conditions of a cognition are adequate for producing its truth. Those who give an affirmative answer to this question are *svataḥ-prāmāṇyavādins* and those who give a negative answer are *parataḥ-prāmāṇyavādins* with respect to the genesis (*utpatti-taḥ*) of truth. The *svataḥ–parataḥ* debate has another dimension as well. It also revolves around the issue, how does one apprehend the truth of a cognition? The *svataḥ-prāmāṇyavādins* with respect to apprehension (*jñaptitaḥ*) hold that a cognition and its truth are apprehended together. By contrast, the *parataḥ-prāmāṇyavādins* maintain that the apprehension of a cognition does not involve the apprehension of its truth. It is only through a second cognition that one apprehends the truth of the first cognition.

There is thus a clear-cut division in Indian philosophy: the Mīmāṃsakas, the Vedāntins and the Sāṃkhya philosophers propound the *svataḥ* theories, while the Nyāya-Vaiśeṣikas and the Buddhists support the *parataḥ* theories. Only the Jaina philosophers cut across the divide. According to them, the truth of a cognition of a familiar object originates and is apprehended together with the cognition, but the truth of a cognition regarding an unfamiliar object requires the fulfillment of some additional conditions both for its origination and its apprehension. It is against this very special backdrop that I am going to discuss the different theories of truth on offer in the Indian philosophical tradition.

II

Let us begin this section with a résumé of the Mīmāṃsā views. All three Mīmāṃsā schools – viz., of Prābhākara, Bhāṭṭa and Miśra – agree on the following points.

1 Cognition is an action of the self.
2 The originating conditions of a cognition unaccompanied by any vitiating factor are the same as the originating conditions of its truth.
3 The conditions of apprehending a cognition are the same as those of its truth.

But these theories differ in their subtler details.

According to the Prābhākaras, the essence of a cognition lies in revealing its object as it is, and truth (*yāthārthya*) is nothing but the feature of a cognition's being non-discrepant with its object (*artha-avyabhicaritatva*). These two theses jointly imply that truth is intrinsic to cognition and that there can be no such thing as erroneous cognition. The Prābhākara account of the genesis and apprehension of cognition runs as follows. The genesis of a cognition depends on a number of conditions, including a series of contacts – for example, the sense–object–contact, the mind(*manas*)–sense–contact and the self–mind–contact. Since erroneous cognition is a misnomer, when the set of causal conditions are present, cognition is generated along with its truth. It is incontrovertible that as soon as a cognition is generated, it reveals its object. The Prābhākaras, however, maintain that at its moment of origination a cognition reveals three things at the same time – its object, its substratum (the self), and itself – for cognition is very intimately related with its substratum and is also self-revealing (*svaprakāśa*) by nature. But as a cognition is always true, its truth is also revealed at that very moment. So when, for example, there is visual contact with an object, say a pot, the resulting cognition has the form: "I have a true cognition of a pot." Thus in accordance with this theory, the same set of conditions is virtually responsible for generating a cognition, generating its truth, and apprehending the cognition as well as its truth.

The Bhāṭṭas define the truth of a cognition as "the property of being uncontradicted in its object" (*artha-avisaṁvāditvam*). A more elaborate definition of truth is extant in the literature, which is said to be accepted by both the Bhāṭṭas and the Vedāntins. I shall analyze that definition later in the course of my exposition of the Vedānta view. In consonance with their *svataḥ* theory, the Bhāṭṭas also maintain that the truth of a cognition is produced by its generating conditions. But they do not admit the self-revealing nature of cognition; cognition being an action, it is imperceptible like every other action and has to be inferred from its perceptible effects. Though a cognition cannot but reveal its object, revealing an object is not the same as cognizing. The former is an effect of the latter. Let me now explain the mechanism of cognition as this is depicted by the Bhāṭṭas with the help of the typical example of perceiving a pot. When there is a contact of the visual sense organ of a knower with a pot and other relevant causal conditions are also present, there arises a cognition of the form "This is a pot." Thereafter, there emerges out of this cognition a new property called "knownness" (*jñātatā*) in the object. This property of "knownness" is perceptible and serves as the mark (*hetu*) for the inference leading to the apprehension of the cognition of the pot. But this inference from "knownness" follows automatically if there is no counteracting condition.

To appreciate the Bhāṭṭa account of apprehending a cognition and its truth, a few other points need to be highlighted. First, *jñātatā* is the relation between the knower and the known, and hence attaches to the knower too. Second, though the property of *jñātatā* resides in the object, it is intentional in nature. Third, the relational structure of the corresponding cognition out of which it is produced is identical with the relational structure of *jñātatā*. It follows, therefore, that *jñātatā* resembles cognition in these respects.

We are now in a position to spell out how a cognition (say, of a pot) and its truth are actually apprehended with the help of an inference having *jñātatā* as the mark (*hetu*). Suppose I have a cognition of the form "This is a pot." Next there arises the property of *jñātatā* in the pot and I remember simultaneously the universal concomitance that holds between the structure of *jñātatā* and its corresponding cognition. Then I realize that this particular *jñātatā* has the structure "The pot characterized by potness," which could be produced only by a cognition having the same relational structure. Therefore, I infer that this *jñātatā* must have been produced by a cognition having the same relational structure.

We have seen that according to the Bhāṭṭas the truth of a cognition is nothing other than the property of being uncontradicted in its object. As *jñātatā* always preserves the relational structure of the corresponding cognition, whenever we apprehend a cognition through an inference depending on *jñātatā* the object of cognition is bound to remain uncontradicted – a fact which was evident in the previous example. In fact, when I know that I have the true cognition of a pot, what more do I need to know than that I have a cognition of the pot characterized by potness? Therefore, the inference based on *jñātatā* enables the knower to apprehend not only that she has a particular cognition, but also its truth. The third presupposition of a *svataḥ* theory thus fulfilled, the Bhāṭṭa commitment to *svataḥ-prāmāṇyavāda* remains intact.

The third Mīmāṁsā view is associated with Murari Miśra and his supporters. Miśra defines truth as "*tadvadviśeṣyakatve sati tatprakārakatvam*," which can be rendered in English as "the property of having *that* as its qualifer, while the qualificand possesses the that." This definition comes very close to the official Navya-Nyāya definition of truth. I shall, therefore, explain all the technical terms involved in the definition later. However, the crux of the definition, if informally rendered, turns out to be: truth is that property of a cognition which cognizes a thing as having a character when the thing actually has that character. Murari Miśra's view, once again, differs from the previous ones with respect to the question of apprehension. He maintains that truth is apprehended in the same after-perception (*anuvyavasāya*) that reveals the cognition. When all the originating conditions are present, I may have a cognition of the form, "This is a pot." Immediately after that, if there is no hindrance, I have an after-perception with the first cognition as its object. This after-percepton is of the form, "I know a pot." That is, the primary cognition of the pot is being apprehended in the after-perception. Now as the content of the primary cognition is embedded in the after-perception, the latter also contains the property of "having potness" as the qualifier which the qualificand pot really possesses. Thus the truth of the primary cognition also gets apprehended in the after-perception.

All of these *svataḥ* theories share one point in common: they need not admit any criterion of truth. The underlying reason for this is summed up by J. N. Mohanty, who remarks in *Gaṅgeśa's Theory of Truth* (1966), "Knowledge as such is true or is apprehended as true; the criteria, when applied, cannot any more prove its truth."

Let us now pass on to another *svataḥ* theory, the Advaita Vedānta theory of truth. This theory can be understood only in the light of the Advaita metaphysics and the Advaita conception of knowledge. It is well known that the Advaitins admit two levels of reality – the transcendental (*pāramarthika*) and the empirical (*vyāvahārika*) – and accordingly they admit two kinds of truth. There are four candidates for the position of truth-bearer in Advaita philosophy. Of these, the ultimate reality, which is the pure undifferentiated consciousness, is beyond the knower–known distinction. The witness self (*sākṣin*) is the knower *par excellence*, for it can never be the object of any knowledge. It is also consciousness and hence self-revealing. It even reveals ignorance and is not opposed to it. Of the witness self, therefore, truth or falsity cannot be ascribed, although its grasp of the object is characterized by immediacy. So knowledge of which truth can be predicated is, according to the Advaitins, the modification of the inner sense (*antaḥkaraṇa*). Whenever *antaḥkaraṇa* is modified (that is, a particular relation is established between an object on the one hand and *antaḥkaraṇa* on the other), the self gets reflected in it. The modification of *antaḥkaraṇa* may, therefore, be taken to be knowledge. But *antaḥkaraṇa* in the Vedānta ontology is material (*jaḍa*), hence non-conscious, and reveals itself only with the help of the witness self. So in the fitness of things consciousness delimited by a modification of the inner sense should be regarded as knowledge. Knowledge, when understood in either of the last two senses, is of the empirical variety. So it is evident that truth or falsity is ascribable only in the empirical realm.

The Advaita theory is *svataḥ-prāmāṇyavāda* with respect to the origination as well as the apprehension of truth because the Advaitins hold that: (1) the originating conditions of a cognition together with the absence of any vitiating factor are sufficient for generating its truth; and (2) the same witness self through which a cognition is apprehended also apprehends its truth.

The most familiar definition of truth accepted by both the Vedāntins and the Bhāṭṭas is: the feature of being an uncontradicted apprehension of some object not apprehended before. This definition of truth excludes recollective cognition (*smṛti*) from the range of truth-bearers. The uncontradictedness (*abādhitatva*) of the apprehension of which truth is a property serves to distinguish it from erroneous apprehension. So the term "*abādhitatva*" merits special attention and careful analysis.

"*Abādhitatva*" literally means "the character of not getting cancelled." We know that an erroneous cognition, for example, seeing a shell as a piece of silver, is cancelled by a subsequent cognition of the shell. So "*abādhitatva*" should mean not merely "uncontradicted at the time of knowing" but also "uncontradicted by any subsequent knowledge." But if, for that reason, "*abādhitatva*" is construed as "the character of never getting cancelled," then it would apply only to the knowledge of the ultimate reality or Brahman. As a result, no empirical knowledge would ever be true. For all empirical knowledge gets cancelled once one attains the knowledge of Brahman. So if truth is to be predicated of empirical knowledge at all, "*abādhitatva*" should be interpreted as "the character of not getting cancelled during worldly existence." Another word of caution. The complement of "*abādhitatva*" – that is, "*bādhitatva*" – should be construed as "the character of getting cancelled in the very locus where it appears." Otherwise, an Advaitin will not be able to distinguish between an illusory silver which is false (*mithyā*) and a sky-lotus which is totally non-existent (*alīka*). A sky-lotus stands eternally negated, but it is not false. For something can get cancelled only if it is presented first. A sky-lotus, being totally non-existent, cannot get cancelled in the same sense as an illusory silver, simply because it can never be presented anywhere.

It is obvious from the above discussion that in the Advaita context "false" can be used with respect to both a cognition and its object. As a matter of fact, an Advaitin declares a cognition to be false when its object is false. So falsity here is contrasted with truth as well as reality, and in the transcendental realm "*sat*" (existence) and "*satya*" (truth) become synonymous.

In the Sāṃkhya system too, cognition is regarded as the modification of the inner sense, and a true cognition is taken to be the certain, non-recollective apprehension of an object as it is (*aviparīta*). But the Sāṃkhya metaphysics is different from the Advaita, and Sāṃkhya philosophers establish their theory of truth with the help of their theory of causation, known as *satkāryavāda*. On this theory, a cause is not wholly different from its effect; an effect always resides in its material cause in a latent form prior to its coming into being. So an effect is a cause manifested and a cause is a non-manifest effect. In keeping with this view, the Sāṃkhya philosophers deny absolute difference between a thing (*dharmin*) and the character emerging out of it (*dharma*). So, truth and the cognition in which it is located not being wholly different, their originating conditions cannot be wholly different either. On the same ground, the modes of apprehending a cognition and its truth are taken to be non-different.

Having discussed the main *svataḥ* theories at length, let us proceed to a consideration of the *parataḥ* theories. We shall concentrate mainly on the Nyāya theory of truth, for the Naiyāyikas have made explicit all the intricate nuances of *parataḥ-prāmāṇyavāda*.

Jñāna, or cognition in the Nyāya-Vaiśeṣika system, is one of the 24 qualities (*guṇa*) which have embodied self as their substratum. It is an adventitious quality of the self produced by a series of causal conditions. *Jñāna* is the cause of all verbal behavior and must reveal its object. But no human cognition can reveal itself or its substratum. The Naiyāyika classifies cognitions into the non-relational (*nirvikalpaka*) and the relational (*savikalpaka*). As we have already seen, it is only to the relational cognition that truth or falsity can be ascribed. So, leaving aside the controversies centering around the nature and the status of non-relational cognitions, let us concentrate on the analysis of cognitions of the relational sort.

A relational cognition is the apprehension of a complex content (*viṣaya*) of the form "*a-(R-b)*" – that is, *a*-as-related-to-*b*-by-*R*. The components of this complex content are technically designated as "qualificand" (*viśeṣya*), "qualifier" (*viśeṣaṇa/prakāra*), and "qualifying relation" (*vaiśiṣṭya/saṁsarga*). In the symbolic representation of the content, *a* is the qualificand, *b* is the qualifier, and *R* is the qualifying relation. In the case of a relational cognition of a pot, the pot is the qualificand, potness is the qualifier, and inherence (*samavāya*) is the qualifying relation. These three constitute the complex content "pot-as-related-to-potness-by-the-relation-of-inherence."

The property of being the content of a cognition is called "*viṣayatā*," which, says the Navya Naiyāyika, attaches to the object. The correlate of *viṣayatā* in knowledge is called "*viṣayitā*," meaning "being the cognition of." In any cognition there is a one-to-one correspondence between *viṣayatā* and *viṣayitā*. Thus when the character of being the qualificand (*viśeṣyatā*) attaches to the pot, its counterpart, *viśeṣyitā*, attaches to the cognition of the pot. Cognition is nothing except this complex awareness-content.

To express such a complex cognition, the Naiyāyikas have developed a second-order language. To take an example, suppose I perceive a blue pot. The content of this cognition may be expressed loosely in ordinary language by "the pot is blue" or simply by "the blue pot." But if we want to make explicit the tacit structure of the cognition at hand, we have to make use of the second-order language. The perspicuous structure of the cognition of the blue pot will be: the cognition the qualifier of which is blue colour cognized under the mode of the feature of blueness, the qualificand of which is the pot cognized under the mode potness and the qualifying relation of which is the relation of inherence cognized simpliciter. Thus we arrive at the Nyāya Principle of the Analysis of Cognition: every cognition that is expressed in language has an unmentioned qualifier, which is either a universal (*jāti*) or an unanalyzable property apprehended directly. It thus becomes evident that, if we proceed from the side of the ordinary language expression of the content, we are sure to get a clue to the structure of the cognition, but the structure cannot be fully grasped through ordinary language.

Let us now consider the Nyāya conception of truth. The final definition of truth, as stated by the leading Navya Naiyāyika Gaṅgeśa, is: the property of having *that* as its qualifier which is delimited by the property of having a qualificand which possesses the that. In the case of a true cognition of a pot, the cognition has "potness" as the qualifier, which is delimited by the property of having a qualificand pot that possesses potness. "The qualifier, delimited by the right qualificand" emphasizes the unitary character of the notion of truth. Without this clause there is no difference between the Nyāya definition and Miśra's definition of truth. Though it has not been explicitly mentioned in the definition, a true cognition must reflect the actual relation by which the qualifier is related to the qualificand. So the cognition of a pot will not be true, unless the qualifier potness qualifies the qualificand pot in the relation of inherence, rather than in some other relation.

We have already mentioned that the Naiyāyikas are *parataḥ-prāmāṇyavādins* with respect to both the origination and the apprehension of truth. With respect to the genesis of truth, they are of the opinion that the originating conditions of a cognition are not sufficient to produce its truth. The truth is in need of some additional causal condition called "excellence" (*guṇa*) for its genesis. For example, in the case of perceptual cognition (*pratyakṣa*) the *guṇa* is the relation of a sense organ with the object which actually possesses the property that figures as the qualifier. There are numerous arguments and counter-arguments involving the *svataḥ*-theorists and the *parataḥ*-theorists regarding the issue of whether the admission of *guṇa* is warranted or not, into which we cannot enter here. The main argument that has been offered in support of the Nyāya thesis is that unless *guṇa* is admitted, the distinction between true cognition and false cognition cannot be maintained. The conditions that give rise to cognition qua cognition remain present even at the time of the origination of false cognition.

With respect to the apprehension of truth, the Naiyāyikas point out that while a cognition is apprehended in after-perception (*anuvyavasāya*), its truth is apprehended by a subsequent inference following either from volition leading to successful activity, or from the mark (*hetu*) "*tajjatiyatva*" ("belonging-to-that-type"). If at the time of apprehending a cognition one could apprehend its truth, then it would not be possible to have any doubt regarding the truth of that cognition afterward. But we do have such doubts. For example, a person who has previously seen a mirage often asks, "Am I seeing water?" on seeing water from a distance in an arid region. This shows that though the person is aware of seeing water, she is not sure of the truth of this perception. How, then, are we to ascertain the truth of the cognition in cases like this? The Nyāya answer is: with the help of an inference ensuing from successful volition. Suppose that a thirsty person, after seeing water, wants to drink it. She secures a glass of the liquid, drinks it and quenches her thirst. Thus she becomes sure that she did really see water. Assurance about her previous cognition takes the form of the following inference: My previous cognition is true, for it has resulted in a successful volition (*saphalapravṛttijanakatvāt*).

Though this type of inference from successful volition is necessary for ascertaining the truth of cognitions of unfamiliar objects, when the object of cognition is a familiar one, the assuring inference is usually of the form: This cognition (say, of water) is true because it belongs to a type of cognition previously established as true. In this case, one need not wait for a successful volition.

The Naiyāyikas are hardcore fallibilists. They do not think that inferences warranting the truth of a cognition can yield rock-bottom certainty. But whenever a doubt is raised regarding the truth of a cognition, inferences of either of the above types may be resorted to, depending on the familiarity or unfamiliarity of the cognition in question.

III

A close look at the rival theories of cognition and truth reveals that there is more of philosophical significance in the theories than simply meets the eye. Apparently, the entire discussion of truth in Indian philosophy has been pursued in an epistemic setting. But that is simply not true. Like every other issue of philosophical importance, the *svataḥ–parataḥ* debate regarding truth is also intimately connected with the question of the attainment of liberation (*mokṣa*), the ultimate end of human life. It has been unanimously admitted in the tradition that the performance of duties (*dharma*) enjoined by the Scriptures leads to liberation or at least prepares the ground for it. The question that a philosopher needs to address at this point is: from where do these scriptural imperatives derive their moral obligatoriness? The question is bound to be a source of embarrassment for those who believe in the *sui generis* nature of the scriptures. For, on the one hand, they are unable to resort to any divine sanction and, on the other hand, they fail to provide any criterion of truth for scriptural imperatives, since most of these are *adṛṣṭa-phalaka* – that is, such that the results that one is supposed to attain by performing these duties cannot be realized in the worldly life. So they fall back on the only answer available to them. They assert that scriptural imperatives are morally obligatory because these are eternally true and are apprehended as true. Hence inquiries concerning the source and legitimacy of such truths are uncalled for. As opposed to these thinkers, those who believe that the scriptures are authored attempt to explain the moral obligatoriness of scriptural imperatives by relying on their divine origin. Probably this is how the question of the genesis of truth came to the forefront. But in the course of time, once the debate was no longer restricted to scriptural knowledge, but was extended to all types of knowledge, the original question was lost sight of and got integrated into the scheme of a causal explanation of knowledge.

Another important question that can no longer be forestalled is whether or not the participants in the *svataḥ–parataḥ* debate have used "cognition" and "truth" in the same sense. Mohanty is of the opinion that "*jñāna*" and "*prāmāṇya*" have different meanings for the rival theorists. In the *svataḥ* theories "knowledge" has been used in a strict sense, whereas in the *parataḥ* theories "knowledge" has been used in a rather weaker sense, including within its scope both true and false knowledge. Regarding truth, Mohanty says that at least three different notions can be found in different versions of the *svataḥ* theory – namely, the psychological, the epistemological, and the analytical. The Nyāya concept of truth is again different from all the three types acknowledged by their rivals. But if this analysis is correct, then it seems there cannot be a genuine debate between the two contending groups. For apparently they are arguing at cross-purposes and their conceptions of truth are not commensurable. Is there any way out of this impasse? Karl Potter, in his article "Does Indian Epistemology Concern Justified True Belief?" attempts to solve this problem by suggesting that "*prāmāṇya* does not translate truth (i.e., correspondence with reality) . . . but rather connotes a more pragmatic criterion of being capable of producing or helping to produce satisfaction in action."

Potter's is a commendable effort to unify the apparently conflicting theories of truth, including those of the Buddhists belonging to the heterodox tradition. But I do think that this conclusion on Potter's part is hasty. The common thread unifying the different Indian theories regarding the nature of truth is not pragmatism, though undoubtedly all of them subscribe to the pragmatic criterion of truth without hesitation. The *svataḥ* theorists, who are not in need of any criterion of truth at all, are also ready to take successful practice as an "authorizing" criterion of truth. And the Naiyāyikas, as we have seen, mention explicity "*saphala-pravṛtti-janakatva*" as the test of truth. The pragmatists in the West have been criticized for not drawing a sharp line between the nature and the criterion of truth. In Indian philosophy too, the Buddhists, being pragmatists, are found to adopt the same stance.

I wholeheartedly agree with Mohanty's observations on "knowledge," and I do not intend to deny that the different definitions of truth so far offered exhibit differences in overtone. But in spite of that, I think that there is a minimal sense of truth to which all of the different systems assent. Let us recall the definitions already mentioned. The Prābhākara definition of truth in terms of "*artha-avyabhicaritatva*," the Bhāṭṭa definition in terms of "*artha-avisaṁvāditva*," the definition of Miśra in terms of "*tadvadviśeṣyakatve sati tatprakārakatva*," the Sāṁkhya definition in terms of "*aviparītatva*," the Vedānta definition in terms of "*abādhitatva*," and the Nyāya definition in terms of "*tadvadviśeṣyakatvāvacchinnatatprakārakatva*," all highlight the feature of a cognition's being non-discrepant with its object. So, I think, Gaṅgeśa was correct in his insight that even the *svataḥ* theorists have to grant this minimal notion of truth. Śaṃkara's characterization of false cognition, knowing *x* as *y*, also lends support to this thesis. It is only to emphasize the ontological priority of the ultimately real and to accommodate the multiple tiers of falsity that the Advaitins have offered the alternative definitions of truth. That the Buddhists are also committed to the minimal sense of truth becomes obvious from Dharmottara's definition of right cognition (*samyag-jñāna*). Right cognition, says Dharmottara, is the property of being non-discrepant (*avisaṁvādaka*) with something. It is true that this *something* is that which causes us to attain a previously identified purpose. But the Buddhist will not consider awareness of such a purpose a right cognition unless it leads to the coveted object and enables us to grasp the object *as it is*.

Accepting the minimal sense of truth does not blur the demarcation between the *svataḥ* and the *parataḥ* theories regarding the nature of knowledge. Rather, it will enhance the depth of our understanding of the *svataḥ* thesis "to know is to know the truth." This minimal sense of truth is to be expressed by uncontroversial instances of the equivalence schema:

It is true *that p* iff *p*

where *that p* stands for the relational content of cognition and *p* for its reference. One may wonder why I have gone in for this deflationary schema of the minimalist conception of truth, instead of the straightforward correspondence schema. The reason is that in the Indian context it is controversial what corresponds to what. We have mentioned previously that Indian philosophers do not admit propositions. Nor do they subscribe to the ontology of facts over and above things-in-relation (*viśiṣṭa-padārthas*). Besides, Frege has taught us that any definition of truth in terms of correspondence is bound to involve a vicious infinite regress. Moreover, the Naiyāyikas have denied any relation of correspondence in the sense of a picturing relation between the content of cognition and the thing-in-relation. They propound a theory of truth very similar to the theory of the early Russell in *The Problems of Philosophy*, which Mohanty describes in his *Reason and Tradition in Indian Thought* (1992), à la Sibajiban Bhattacharyya, as follows:

> What is lacking in the case of an erroneous cognition but is present in the case of a true cognition is a total unitary, not further analyzable content (*vilakṣaṇa viṣayatā*) – in addition to the component contents – such as "the-this-as-qualified-by-silverness."

This means that the relational content of a true cognition would be identical to the thing-in-relation. This view can best be represented by the deflationary schema as:

$\langle p \rangle$ is a thing-in-relation $\leftrightarrow$ $\langle p \rangle$ is true $\leftrightarrow$ p

(in which the relational content of a cognition is symbolized by "$\langle p \rangle$" and iff by "$\leftrightarrow$"). Taking the minimalist conception as the core of Indian theories of truth, if we go on adding the relevant metaphysical and epistemological theses of the respective systems to it, we shall arrive at the specific definitions of truth upheld in different philosophical systems. Even the relativistic notion of truth propounded by the Jainas can be easily represented by the deflationary schema by restricting it in accordance with the Jaina "doctrine of may be" (*syādvāda*). The different Indian theories of truth are, therefore, perfectly compatible, the essential insight of which is reflected in the dictum:

To *know* of what something is that it is, or of what something is not that it is not, is true.

Bibliography

Annambhatta 1976: *Tarkasaṁgraha with Dīpikā*, trans. and elucidated by Gopinath Bhattacharya following *Nilakanthi* (Calcutta: Progressive Publishers).

Bhattacharyya, Sibajiban 1987 [1976–7]: "Some Principles and Concepts of Navya Nyāya Logic and Ontology," in *Our Heritage* (Calcutta: Sanskrit College, 1976–7). Reprinted in *Doubt, Belief and Knowledge* (New Delhi: Indian Council of Philosophical Research in association with Allied Publishers, 1987).

—— 1990: *Gadādhara's Theory of Objectivity (Viṣayatāvāda)*, Pts I and II (Delhi: Indian Council of Philosophical Research in association with Motilal Banarasidass).

Dharmarājadhvarīndra 1970: *Vedānta-paribhāṣā*, ed. and explained by Pancanana Sastri (Calcutta: Sanskrit Pustak Bhandar).

Kumārila Bhāṭṭa 1985 [1908]: *Mīmāṁsā-ślokavārtika*, trans. Ganganath Jha (Calcutta: Asiatic Society).

Matilal, B. K. 1986: *Perception* (Oxford: Clarendon Press).

Mohanty, J. N. 1966: *Gaṇgeśa's Theory of Truth* (Santiniketan: Visva-Bharati).

—— 1992: *Reason and Tradition in Indian Thought* (Oxford: Clarendon Press).

Potter, Karl H. 1991: "Does Indian Epistemology Concern Justified True Belief?" in *The Philosophy of J. N. Mohanty*, ed. Daya Krishna and K. L. Sharma (New Delhi: Indian Council of Philosophical Research in association with Munshiram Monoharlal Publishers), pp. 121–142.

Saha, Sukharanjan 1991: *Meaning, Truth and Predication* (Calcutta: Jadavpur University in collaboration with K. P. Bagchi & Company).

Sen, Pranab Kumar 1991: "Truths without Facts," in *Reference and Truth* (New Delhi: Indian Council of Philosophical Research in association with Allied Publishers).

THE BUDDHIST TRADITION

24

Ideas of the good in Buddhist philosophy

P. D. PREMASIRI

One of the problems usually encountered in comparative studies on systems of thought belonging to cultures far removed in space and time is the difference in the manner in which they conceptualize their experience. This difference in conceptualization is reflected in the difference in the words and other linguistic forms adopted in articulating their experience. Studying the thought of a specific social group involves studying the concepts special and peculiar to that group through the language that mirrors their mode of thinking, their peculiar conceptual categories and forms of life. These facts have to be borne in mind in any attempt to search for the ideas of the good in Buddhism from the perspective of comparative philosophy.

In common English usage, it is meaningful and philosophically significant to ask the question "What is good?" Indeed, Western philosophy has traditionally been understood as an inquiry into the nature of truth, goodness and beauty. But one runs into difficulties if one raises this question in the same way in relation to Buddhist philosophy, because it does not seem to have used a term which corresponds exactly to the English term "good." This does not mean, however, that there is no place for the concept of goodness in Buddhism. Buddhism has other ways of expressing its concerns about the nature of the good.

Buddhism raises the question "What is *kusala*?" or "What is *puñña*?" and the range of application of the terms "*kusala*" and "*puñña*" is narrower than that of the term "good" in English. For one could, in Buddhist usage, speak of a *kusala* or a *puñña* deed, but not of a *kusala* or a *puñña* knife, whereas in English one can speak of both a good deed and a good knife. What is evident is that Buddhism also has used numerous terms for both moral and non-moral evaluation. The two most important terms used in Buddhism to commend human behavior are *kusala* and *puñña*. Both are sometimes translated into English as "good." Although it can be admitted that there is a commendatory sense built into the meaning of both terms, the concept of *kusala* and the concept of *puñña* are distinct. If they are interpreted as having the same meaning, some statements made about the role of *kusala* will turn out to be incompatible with those made about the role of *puñña* in Buddhism. Buddhism does not seem to have raised the question "What is good?" at the level of abstraction that could lead to an answer in terms of a Platonic Form of the Good. Nor has Buddhism shown an interest in discussing the logic of the term "good." For

Buddhist thought is concerned less with the abstract and the general and more with the specific and the concrete, the experientially real and the practically relevant.

The Buddha says in his discourse on the noble search, the *Ariyapariyesana Sutta*, that as a young man he renounced all the pleasures of life in search of what is *kusala* (*kiṃkusalagavesī*) (*Majjhimanikāya*, Vol. 1, p. 163). The Buddhist search for *kusala* can be seen as a search for what is good for man. Therefore, an examination of the concept of *kusala* in Buddhism is likely to clarify the Buddhist idea of the nature of the good.

The term *kusala* is used in Buddhism to qualify human performances. Whatever action a person performs, if it is performed skilfully the person who performs it is described as one who is skilled (*kusalo*) in that kind of act. In this wide sense of the term "*kusala*," it is applied mostly in non-moral contexts. In this sense one could speak of a skilled (*kusalo*) horse trainer, a skilled archer, and so on. *Kusala* is also used in the general sense of the good of mankind, and in the sense of the merit of actions that human beings perform. The more significant and frequent use of the term "*kusala*" in Buddhism is in the sense of "good" qualifying human action. Buddhism classifies all phenomena in terms of what is *kusala* (good), *akusala* (bad), and *avyākata* (undetermined). According to this classification, thoughts, actions and character traits or any voluntary attainment of a human being could be *kusala* or *akusala*, but material things and processes could not. Thus although the term "*kusala*" in Buddhism does not have the same connotations as the English term "good," it is used to cover a wide area of activity to which the term "good" may meaningfully be applied.

Kusala is used in the sense of what is worthy of being pursued by human beings as an intrinsic good or as an end in itself. Buddhism has the notion of a supreme good (*paramakusala*) which all human beings ought to aim at attaining. It is believed to be the end *(niṭṭhā)* to be attained by all right conduct specified in the Noble Eightfold Way of Buddhism (*ariyaṭṭhaṅgikamagga*). An examination of what this ultimate end or good is, and why it is considered as the ultimate end or good in Buddhism can throw much light on the Buddhist idea of the good.

The highest *kusala* or the *summum bonum* according to Buddhism is *nibbāna*. It is not a good to be attained after death, but a good to be attained in this life itself (*diṭṭheva dhamme*). Among all things that are *kusala*, it is said that the personal realization through one's own supercognition of the undefiled state of emancipation of mind and emancipation through wisdom, an attainment which is free from any future tendency to defilement, is the highest (*Dīghanikāya*, Vol. 3, p. 102). The ultimate goal of living the good life (*brahmacariya*) under the Buddha was considered to be the attainment of *parinibbāna*, with no further latent tendency to attachment, grasping or clinging (*Majjhimanikāya*, Vol. 1, p. 148). All other states to *kusala* are said to lead to this final goal and to serve as a means to it. *Nibbāna* is defined as the destruction of lust, hatred and delusion (*Saṃyuttanikāya*, Vol. 4, p. 251; Vol. 5, p. 8). The implication of this Buddhist position is that the highest good involves the transformation of the psychological constitution of personality. It is a twofold transformation involving the elimination of certain emotional traits of personality and a transformation involving one's understanding of the nature of reality.

The entire system of values in Buddhism can be seen to be structured on the basis of the above assertion that the highest good of man is the attainment of *nibbāna*. In the Buddhist evaluation of persons, those who have attained the goal of *nibbāna* are considered to be the most praiseworthy persons. Such persons are to be commended as those who are fully endowed with *kusala* (*Majjhimanikāya*, Vol. 2, p. 29). A person who has attained *nibbāna* is referred to as a worthy one (*arahanta*). A disciple of the Buddha who follows his instructions with a view to attaining this goal is referred to as a noble disciple (*ariyasāvaka*). Among men and gods it is the person endowed with understanding and good conduct who deserves to be called the most excellent (*Dīghanikāya*, Vol. 1, p. 99). It is said that as far as the abodes of living beings extend, as far as the end of the realm of becoming, those who have realized the goal of *nibbāna*, the *arahanta*, are the highest and the most supreme beings (*Saṃyuttanikāya*, Vol. 3, p. 83). The Buddha is sometimes referred to as the highest being to be born in the world because he was the founder of the supreme goal of *nibbāna* and the person most competent to guide others in their attempt to attain this noble end (*Saṃyuttanikāya*, Vol. 5, p. 66).

The life that conduces to the attainment of *nibbāna* is called *brahmacariya* (the good life). The truths, the understanding and realization of which ensure this attainment, are called *ariyasaccāni* (noble truths). The path to its attainment is called *ariyamagga* (the noble path). Each item of the path is qualified as *sammā* (right).

The reason for taking *nibbāna* as the highest good or the supreme goal that all rational beings ought to attain is, according to Buddhism, that it is the ending of all unhappiness and misery and the attainment of the highest happiness. One might consider the implication of this position to be that Buddhism holds a hedonistic theory regarding the nature of the good. The first Noble Truth of Buddhism is the truth of unsatisfactoriness (*dukkha*). All unenlightened beings are, according to Buddhism, destined to suffer the cyclic process of repeated births and deaths, involving an immense quantity of disappointment, frustration, and misery. The very existence of a personality consisting of five aggregates to which one clings with a notion of self-identity is said to lead to the continuance of this cyclic process of *dukkha*. *Nibbāna* is the antithesis of *dukkha*, for its attainment amounts to the ending of all *dukkha*. It follows that it is also the highest happiness. If *nibbāna* is the highest good, or what is good in itself, and if it is the highest happiness (*paramaṃ sukhaṃ*), it is reasonable to conclude that happiness is what is good in itself. One may even attribute to Buddhism the view that happiness alone is what is good in itself.

There are three terms which usually occur together in Buddhist usage. They are "*attha*," "*hita*" and "*sukha*." These terms seem to merge logically into each other. The terms "*attha*" and "*hita*" correspond more closely to the English terms "welfare" and "well-being," whereas "*sukha*" corresponds more closely to the term "happiness." In spite of the importance of these concepts, it would be misleading to consider Buddhism as a system that subscribes to a hedonistic theory of the nature of the good without qualification. Buddhism clearly acknowledges that the good of man consists in being free from both physical and mental pain. This is clear from the statement of the Four Noble Truths in Buddhism. The Buddhist concession to a hedonistic thesis about the nature of the good applies only to this negative aspect of recognizing the desirability of attaining freedom from physical and mental pain. But Buddhism does not conceive of its ultimate goal as the maximization of pleasure. The ultimate attainment does not consist of the experience of pleasure (*vedayita sukha*), but rather a state of well-being, tranquility and equanimity, free from defiling desires and impulses, from clinging to the notion of selfhood and thirst for sensuous gratification. *Nibbāna* is therefore described by the apparently self-contradictory expression *avedayita sukha* (happiness which does not involve sensing).

Buddhism uses the term "*sukha*" to refer to ordinary sense pleasures as well as more refined experiences of a sense of well-being which are usually the consequence of transcending the ordinary experience of sense pleasures. Ordinary sense pleasures are described as *kāmasukha. Kāmasukha* is considered to be the lowest form of happiness that a human being can experience. Buddhism seems to recognize qualitative distinctions between different kinds of *sukha*. The Buddha says for instance,

> There are these five strands of sensuous desire. . . . There are material shapes cognizable by the eye, delightful, agreeable, pleasant, lovely, associated with sensuous desire and alluring, sounds cognizable by the ear . . . smells cognizable by the nose . . . tastes cognizable by the tongue . . . touches cognizable by the body. . . . These are the five strands of sensuous desire. Whatever pleasure, happiness arises due to these five strands of sensuous desire, this is called the happiness of sensuous desires (*kāmasukhaṃ*). But with regard to those who may say thus: "This is the highest pleasure, the highest happiness that living beings experience," I do not agree with that view of theirs. What is the reason for this? . . . For there is a happiness which is more delightful and more pleasant than this. (Saṃyuttanikāya, Vol. 4, pp. 225ff)

In this context the more delightful and pleasant forms of happiness are explained by the Buddha as resulting from the withdrawal of the mind from sense pleasures and the attaining of higher levels of mental composure (*samādhi*). In these higher levels of meditative consciousness, the happiness experienced at each level of the mind's progression is said to be more delightful and pleasant than that experienced at the preceding level. Pleasures that do not involve harmful consequences are considered to be intrinsically good. However, the Buddhist position is that sense pleasures involve more harm than good because of their tendency to enslave the person by their enchanting nature. The Buddha's reasons for assigning a low status to sense pleasures are given in the Māgandhiyasutta of the Majjhimanikāya. Here the Buddha says:

> Māgandhiya, when I was formerly a householder, I lived endowed with and provided with the five strands of sensuous desire, with material shapes cognizable by the eye agreeable, pleasant. . . . But later having known as it really is, the origin, the cessa-

> tion, the enjoyment, the harmful consequence of and the emancipation from sensuous desires themselves, I abandoned the thirst for sensuous pleasures, got rid of the affliction from sensuous desires, and having become devoid of thirst I live with a mind inwardly calmed. I see other beings who are not free from passion for sensuous enjoyment being consumed by the affliction of sense desires, excited by sense desires. I do not envy them, I do not delight therein. And why is that so? Māgandhiya, this delight which is free from sensuous desires, and free from *akusala* states, stays even surpassing the divine *sukha*. Delighting in this delight I do not envy the lower, nor do I delight therein. (*Majjhimanikāya*, Vol. 1, p. 506)

According to the Buddha, the true good of man does not consist in indulgence in sense pleasures (*kāmasukhallikānuyoga*). It is condemned as one extreme life-style which an intelligent person ought to avoid. Although there is some aspect of pleasure (*sukha*) in the gratification of sense desires, in terms of a wider perspective it conduces to more harm than good. It results in enslavement to passions giving rise to frustration, anxiety, dissatisfaction, mental confusion, and instability. A thorough comprehension (*pariññā*) of the nature of sense pleasures and the realization of a happiness which transcends the meager happiness found in sensuous delight leads the Buddha to view them as evil rather than good. The Buddha declares as a universal fact, true in the past, present, and future, that indulgence in sensuous desires eventually gives rise to unpleasant experience.

> In the past sense desires gave rise to unpleasant sensation, they were immensely afflicting, immensely painful; in the present they are . . . and in the future they will be. . . . These beings, not free from their passions for sensuous things being consumed by the thirst for sensuous things, being afflicted by the affliction of sensuous things with their sense-organs adversely affected, take a perverted notion of sensuous things whose contact is painful by taking them as pleasurable. Māgandhiya, it is like a leper, a man with his limbs all ravaged and festering, and who, being eaten by vermin, tearing his open sores with his nails, heats his body over a charcoal pit. . . . But the more those open sores of his become septic, foul smelling, and putrefying, . . . there is only a meager relief and satisfaction to be had from scratching the open sores. (*Majjhimanikāya*, Vol. 1, p. 507)

The Buddha makes the claim that the happiness and well-being that a person who has eliminated greed, hatred and delusion experiences is stable. A person who has experienced such a state of well-being will under no circumstance fall back on the transient pleasures of ordinary life. Speaking of his own experience of other pleasures that life could afford, the Buddha says that, viewed from the standpoint of the experience of *nibbāna*, the enjoyment of the pleasures of a sensuous kind is comparable to an infant's play with his own excrement.

> "Just as Upāli, an infant, feeble and lying on his back, plays with his own excrement, what do you think Upāli, is this not fully and entirely a childish sport?"
>
> "It is, Sir."
>
> "Well then, Upāli, that boy, on another occasion, when he has grown

older, with the maturity of the sense faculties, plays with whatever may be the playthings of such children. . . . Now what do you think, Upāli? Does not this sport come to be finer and more valued than the former?"

"It does, Sir." (*Aṅguttaranikāya*, Vol. 5, p. 203)

Having made these remarks, the Buddha describes the spiritual attainments of the person who leads the holy life, as it was laid down by him, and assures Upāli that in each of the higher stages of spiritual attainment there is a more refined form of happiness and sense of well-being.

The Buddha, like Mill, who attempted to explain the good in terms of happiness, appears to have made qualitative distinctions between different forms of happiness. The Buddha also made moral distinctions, dividing happiness itself into noble happiness (*ariyasukha*) and ignoble happiness (*anariyasukha*). This shows that Buddhism, on the one hand, determines *kusala* and *akusala* on the basis of *sukha* and *dukkha*. On the other hand, *sukha* and *dukkha* are themselves evaluated as *kusala* and *akusala*. This problem is raised in the *Milindapañha* where Milinda asks Nāgasena whether *sukha* is *kusala*, *akusala*, or *avyākata*. Nāgasena's reply is that it could be characterized as any one of the three. Milinda put this question perhaps because he was aware of the fact that the Buddha used *sukha* and *dukkha* as grounds for determining *kusala* and *akusala*. He therefore observes: "If *kusala* is not *dukkha*, and *dukkha* is not *kusala*, then there cannot be *kusala* which is *dukkha*."

Nāgasena's explanation here does not seem to answer satisfactorily the question raised by Milinda. What Buddhism seems to recognize is that some conditions under which *sukha* is experienced can be productive of much greater *dukkha* when considered from the point of view of their long-range consequences. The pleasures of a sensuous nature may give immediate and momentary satisfaction. But a prudent person abandons the momentary pleasures which are associated with harmful long-term consequences and performs certain deeds which conduce to one's well-being and happiness in the long run of events. Such conduct, although it may involve displeasure for the moment, is called *kusala* in Buddhism.

Buddhism sees a close relationship between the reality of change or transience (*anicca*) and the absence of happiness or the reality of *dukkha*. Anything that changes from being an object of satisfaction to an object of pain and anxiety cannot be conducive to the good of man. For this reason, Buddhism does not attach ultimate value to any of the objects of grasping, including even one's own personality. Whatever is subject to change gives rise to unhappiness (*yadaniccaṃ taṃ dukkhaṃ*). Our own individual personality is believed in Buddhism to consist of five transient aggregates. Thus the Buddha says that the typical case of unsatisfactoriness is to be found in the very personality which we grasp with attachment (*saṅkhittena pañcupādānakkhandhā dukkhā*). The ultimate good to be achieved by man, therefore, does not consist in anything connected with transient objects of desire. The peace of mind attained by the very removal of the thirst and desire, the destruction of the notions of "I" and "mine" is considered in Buddhism to be the highest good.

The Buddhist value system appears to take a monistic approach with regard to the nature of what is good as an end. Buddhism seems to value no other human achievement as a good end other than *nibbāna*. There are many things that the Buddha considered to be good as means to the attainment of the goal of *nibbāna* – for example, knowledge, learning, beliefs, and some forms of ritual. But none of these are considered as ultimate goods. In fact, Buddhism warns that some things which are good as means may sometimes become a hindrance to the realization of the ultimate good, if one develops a clinging to them and the progression towards the full destruction of the cankers of mind is impeded. It will become clear later that the Buddha also insisted on the transcendence of *puñña* for the same reason.

The epistemology of value has been one of the principal philosophical issues in the West. Some philosophers, such as Plato and more recently G. E. Moore and H. A. Prichard, have held a non-naturalist or idealist theory of the nature of the good. According to such a theory, "good" and related words are names of objects or properties that have a real existence. However, they are not sensible properties, and hence are non-natural objects or properties that can only be apprehended by means of intuition. Naturalism maintains that "good" refers to scientifically determinable relations between things. According to naturalism, the concept of the good can be analyzed in terms of some empirically ascertainable property or set of properties. Naturalism also attempts to explain the good in terms of human needs. According to teleological naturalism, all things in nature are endowed with inner tendencies toward an ideal state and "good" signifies whatever is conducive to the attainment of that ideal state. Hedonistic utilitarianism identifies the good with pleasure and maintains that anything is good to the extent that it produces a greater balance of pleasure over pain. According to evolutionary naturalism, "good" stands for all traits that help to realize the process of evolution. The epistemological position common to all naturalistic theories is that questions regarding what is good could be settled like all other scientifically significant issues – by means of empirical observation. Naturalism and intuitive non-naturalism are committed to cognitivist theories about the nature of the good. Two major non-cognitivist theories about the nature of the good are emotivism and prescriptivism. According to emotivism, "good" and other related terms do not state facts. Their function is not description, but evincing and redirecting of emotion. The primary meaning of "good" is thus not descriptive, but emotive. According to prescriptivism, the term "good" performs the function of prescribing ultimate principles of choice. Such prescriptions in moral contexts are distinguished by the criterion of universalizability.

Although Buddhism does not discuss issues concerning the epistemology of the good with the rigor characteristic of Western Philosophy, it is possible to identify the basic Buddhist position with regard to such issues. The true good is, according to Buddhism, identical with happiness and the ending of unhappiness. The goodness of the volitional activity of human beings is determined in Buddhism in relation to this true goodness. Since we have so far concentrated on the Buddhist notion of *kusala* in attempting to elucidate the Buddhist theory of the nature of the good, it will be appropriate at this point to examine the epistemology of *kusala*. According to the Buddha, those who lack knowledge of what is *kusala* and *akusala* suffer from a deficiency. For knowledge of the distinction between *kusala* and *akusala* was considered by the Buddha as an essential component of the knowledge of an enlightened person. That abstention from actions such as stealing and killing or causing injury to living beings is *kusala* is part of the knowledge that is essential in the ethical life of the individual. A person is said to be ignorant and deluded if he or she does not know the distinction between *kusala* and *akusala*. (The cognitivist stand of Buddhism with regard to the nature of the good is substantiated by the ideas expressed in the following passages: *Saṃyuttanikāya*, Vol. 5, p. 106; *Majjhimanikāya*, Vol. 1, pp. 47, 310; *Aṅguttaranikāya*, Vol. 3, p. 165.) In speaking of knowledge of *kusala*, Buddhism uses forms of the verbal root *jñā*, which means "to know" (mostly *pajānāti* and *jānāti*). This too shows that Buddhism holds a cognitivist view about the nature of *kusala*. Buddhism does not seem to have made a distinction between fact and value. The Buddhist term "*pajānāti*" is used to refer to knowledge of matters of fact as well as knowledge of value. The distinction which is emphasized in modern Western thought between fact and value raises an important logical problem for the moral philosopher. The emphasis on this distinction has led recent Western moral philosophers to hold that knowledge and truth are confined to descriptive scientific statements or to logical or mathematical statements, but are inapplicable in the realm of ethical evaluation. How could Buddhism overcome the objection that a contemporary analytical moral philosopher might raise regarding the impossibility of deriving a value judgement from descriptive premises?

In the *Kālāmasutta* the Buddha rejects an authoritarian basis for moral beliefs, and affirms that "personal knowledge" of *kusala* and *akusala* is possible (*Aṅguttaranikāya*, Vol. 1, p. 189). It is clear that in the context of the *Kālāmasutta* the Buddha is speaking of knowing what is *kusala* and *akusala* and hence speaking of ethical knowledge. But how is such knowledge to be explained in such a way that it could escape the objection raised by those who draw a distinction between fact and value?

Can it be maintained that Buddhism admitted a realm of ethical facts which can be objectively known? The Buddha sometimes maintains that there are things which are *kusala* and *akusala* (*atthi bhikkhave kusalākusalā dhammā*). Mrs Rhys Davids, in *Buddhist Psychology*, suggests that Buddhism, as opposed to Western philosophy, recognized a realm of ethical qualities. But the analysis of the means of knowledge admitted in Buddhism does not reveal that early Buddhism ever acknowledged the existence of an objective realm of ethical qualities which can be directly known by means of any sensory, extrasensory or intuitive faculty. Even Rhys Davids is not attributing to Buddhism a theory about directly intuitable moral qualities. She interprets the Buddhist view as a naturalistic one. For she says that according to Buddhism, "A good moral or meritorious act means that a desirable result will follow such an act sooner or later, inevitably." By a desirable result, she means a happy result or a result associated with happiness rather than suffering.

Unlike in the cognitivist and objectivist doctrine of Plato, Buddhism does not seem to accept the metaphysical notion of a transcendental realm of Ideas in which the Ideal Form of the Good is to be discovered. One might mistakenly think that the Buddhist recognition of paranormal perceptions puts Buddhism on the same epistemological footing as Platonism. But there is clearly a difference between what the Buddha claims to know by means of paranormal vision and what Plato claims to know by means of rational intuition. Buddhism does not reject the validity of sense experience in preference to a higher order of knowledge to be gained by means of rational intuition. The data of paranormal experience in Buddhism are not different in kind from the data of normal sense experience. Paranormal experience only enables a person to transcend the limitations of normal sense experience. The data of paranormal experience cannot be anything other than forms (*rūpa*), sounds (*sadda*), and so on. Therefore, one cannot maintain that Buddhism directly recognizes a kind of metaphysical order of values which could be known by means of paranormal experience (*abhiññā*).

Instances dealing with the epistemology of *kusala* in Buddhism show that some aspects of naturalist theories of the good are implicit in the Buddhist theory. For Buddhism seems to move with facility from statements about *kusala* to statements about what is beneficial, advantageous and what is conducive to a person's well-being and happiness. We have already observed that the terms *attha*, *hita*, and *sukha* usually occur together in Buddhist usage. In the Kālāmasutta where the Buddha explains how one could personally know the distinction between *kusala* and *akusala*, the following dialogue between the Kālāmas and the Buddha occurs:

> "Now what do you think, Kālāmas, when greed arises within a man, does it arise to his benefit or harm?"
>
> "To his harm, Sir."
>
> "Now, Kālāmas, this man, thus become greedy, overcome by greed, with his mind completely filled with greed, does he not kill a living creature, take what is not given, commit adultery, tell lies and induce others too to commit deeds as those which would conduce to disadvantage and unhappiness for a long time?"
>
> "He does, Sir." (*Aṅguttaranikāya*, Vol. 1, p. 189)

A similar movement from evaluation of behavior as *kusala* to observation of behaviour as not productive of harm to oneself, harm to others and harm to both oneself and others and as productive of happiness and well-being is to be found in the *Bāhitikasutta* and the *Ambalaṭṭhikā-Rāhulovādasutta* of the *Majjhimanikāya* (Vol. 2, p. 114; Vol. 1, p. 415).

The Buddhist view implicit in all judgments regarding what is *kusala* and *akusala* is that considerations of human happiness and well-being are logically relevant to such judgments. One cannot describe an action as good unless it is in some way connected with human happiness. One cannot logically produce any arbitrary reason for maintaining that some course of action is good. A possible objection to this view is that what constitutes human happiness itself is an evaluative question and that it cannot be determined in the way an empirical fact is determined. Buddhism, however, appears to take questions regarding what constitutes human happiness and unhappiness as questions to be determined objectively by the examination of all the relevant facts. Buddhism admits that one may be mistaken about what constitutes happiness due to perversion of perception, belief and thinking (*saññāvipallāsa, diṭṭhivipallāsa, cittavipallāsa*) (*Aṅguttaranikāya*, Vol. 2, p. 52). It is due to the possibility of such mistaken notions about happiness that the Buddha admits that what is called *sukha* by others (that is, by ordinary people) is called *dukkha* by the noble ones (that is, by those who have attained enlightenment), while what is conceived as *dukkha* by the former is conceived as *sukha* by the latter (*Saṃyuttanikāya*, Vol. 4, p. 127). Buddhism clearly commits itself to the view that what is good from the point of view of one's own self is the eradication of all unhappiness along with all future prospect of its recurrence, and the attainment of mental stability, tranquility and calm by the destruction of all psychological cankers (*āsava*). It is the good to be sought by each and every one. From the Buddhist point of view, a person who says that the good of man consists in suffering the extremities of physical and mental pain for its own sake is misusing the term "good."

Regarding such a notion of the good, one might point out that it is concerned with self-interest and that it promotes an egoistic attitude. One might maintain that it is open to serious moral objections. It may be argued that such a conception accords with a prudential morality, but not with true morality as such. True morality demands concern for the interests of other people more than for one's own interest. Hence one may argue that the ultimate good which the Buddhist seeks to attain has nothing to do with morality. However, Buddhism does not take this as a serious objection against its conception of the ultimate good. For according to Buddhism, the self-transformation which leads to the ending of all unhappiness is conducive to the promotion of the happiness of others as well. Such enlightened beings, free from all inner and outer conflicts and bonds, have reached a state of moral perfection that enables them to express their true humanness in their relationships with other people. The very existence of such human beings in society promotes the happiness and well-being of many others (*bahuno janassa atthāya hitāya sukhāya saṃvattati*). Buddhism conceives of man's effort to get rid of all moral evil rooted in greed, hatred and delusion as the most commendable kind of social commitment. Those who devote themselves to this task are referred to as the doers of the greatest action (*kammaseṭṭhassa kārakā*). This explains the great veneration shown in Buddhist communities to those individuals who supposedly devote themselves entirely to the attainment of the Buddhist goal of *nibbāna*.

As we noted earlier in this discussion, Buddhism also uses the terms "*puñña*" and "*pāpa*" to signify particularly the goodness or badness of human conduct. We also noted that although these terms have an evaluative function, they cannot, without qualification, be translated as "good" and "evil." The term "*puñña*" is used in Buddhism to signify the good in terms of the happy consequences to be determined under the law of *kamma*. *Puñña* has the tendency to produce the repeated cycle of births and deaths and thereby is opposed to the attainment of passionless *nibbāna*. Therefore, although *puñña* may be conceived as the good for those who remain in the life of *saṃsāra*, because it is productive of desirable consequences, such as rebirth in heavenly spheres of existence where there is a preponderance of pleasure over pain, for full freedom from the sufferings of *saṃsāra* even *puñña* has to be transcended. The real good consists not in the maximization of *puñña*, but in its final abandonment and the perfection of *kusala*. Some scholars have mistakenly attributed to the Buddha the view that the final goal of Buddhism is beyond both good and evil on the ground that the Buddha recommends the giving up of both *puñña* and *pāpa* (a view which I have critically examined in "Interpretation of Two Principal Ethical Terms in Early Buddhism," *Sri Lanka Journal of the Humanities*, Vol. 7, nos 1 and 2, pp. 62–81).

In the foregoing discussion, we have attempted to examine the ideas of the good in Buddhist philosophy on the basis of an examination of the Buddhist value system. The main focus of attention was on the Buddhist notion of *kusala*, which is the primary ethical notion of Buddhism. It was noted that Buddhism takes a cognitivist position with regard to the idea of the good expressed in terms of the notion of *kusala*. Buddhist cognitivism is based on an affirmation of a logical relation between the idea of the good and the concept of happiness. The happiness which Buddhism speaks about in this connection is not identical with sensous pleasure. It is the happiness consisting of the calming of all passions resulting from the attainment of emancipating wisdom. The highest good of man is liberation or emancipation from *saṃsāric* suffering. The Buddhist position may be compared in its form, though not in its content, with the Aristotelian notion of the human good as *eudaemonia*. To this extent it may also be concluded that Buddhism takes a teleological position regarding the idea of the good rather than a deontological position.

25

Reflections on social and political ideals in Buddhist philosophy

JOHN ROSS CARTER

I

The Buddhist cumulative tradition is enormously complex and variegated, having been a part of the human record for over two thousand years, and having contributed massively to the shaping of a variety of cultures in South, South-East, and East Asia. More recently many in Europe and the Americas are responding to the teachings offered by one or another of the continuing strands of this cumulative tradition. Attempting both to communicate and to interpret in any degree of detail the positions this great tradition has developed about what constitutes the ideal in human relationships and polity, in an ever changing process over these many centuries and in the remarkable variety of these many contexts, would border on the bewildering. But the attempt might be instructive, since it could creatively place in juxtaposition an awareness that we human beings begin at different starting points in constructing our views of ourselves and the contexts in which we live out our lives.

Where might one begin in a consideration of "Social and Political Ideals in Buddhist Philosophy" that would comprehend both the dynamics of historical process and the variety of cultural contexts? One might choose from a number of current analytical categories: "canonical," "traditional," or "modern Buddhism," "apotropaic," "nibbanic," or "kammatic Buddhism," or "Buddhism" as a "civilizational form" or "cultural religion." Or one could utilize a distinction between "text and context," between the Buddhist teachings, on the one hand, and the actual religious behavior of men and women who understand themselves to be Buddhists, on the other. We not only meet dynamic historical vicissitudes over centuries, numerous cultural complexes in Asia, and several ways proposed by scholars of conceptualizing the historical process that is the cumulative Buddhist tradition: we, in the West, also confront patterns of speculative thought, of the Theravāda Buddhist tradition and Indian culture in general, which do not arise from customary Western assumptions.

Then how are we to proceed in our attempts to understand Buddhists who share concerns and presuppositions in some cases radically different from Western philosophy? It is possible, by integrating commonsense anthropological theory, to understand others, whether they live next door or in other cultural contexts – not completely, certainly, but not negligibly either. Is it helpful, then, to utilize notions like "Buddhist Philosophy" in our efforts to understand the social and political ideals of Buddhists? Asian thinkers frequently comment that misunderstanding might quickly arise in investigations like this were one to take "philosophy" to be somehow something other than, and even in opposition to, "religion": two concepts peculiar to the development of the Western intellectual heritage.

Within the Buddhist cumulative tradition there has been sustained reflection, even meditation, on aligning human existence with the soteriological efficacy which is at the heart of the cosmos. This alignment, ideally, involves orientation of one's life, consistency in one's thought and coherence in one's life and thought. The English term "philosophy" might be used here to refer to this kind of sustained reflection and its related articulation of a worldview involving both an interpretation of one's life and a way to liberation. One is not cut adrift, isolated, as it were, in this kind of integrative consideration in which human life is not only understood but ennobled. Rather, one, in so far as one has become a Buddhist, has a foundation from which to regain the insights of the past, a support on which to build for the future.

Eliot Deutsch has provided an insightful way of catching this sense of "philosophy" in India. In short, he sees "this idea of philosophy as 'recovery' rather than 'discovery'" and argues that it "is central to the traditional Indian understanding of a philosophical text." For Deutsch, "what constitutes the text in Indian thought [note well] is precisely the *sūtra . . . and/or* [my emphasis] other authoritative sources, together with the ongoing exegetical work" (Deutsch, 1988, p. 169). We are dealing with a human process, a form of what Deutsch calls a text, whereby one recovers truth and thereby rediscovers it for oneself. As Deutsch puts it, the philosopher,

> is not so much remarking on an already finished text as he is himself contributing to that text through his appropriation of its content. The key term here is "appropriation." If knowledge is something that is basically recovered rather than discovered, then it is incumbent upon the philosopher to be committed to the truth of his "school," to be entirely open to its teachings as he makes it his own. (Deutsch, 1988, pp. 171–2)

We acknowledge, therefore, that persons who have lived within the Buddhist heritage have drawn from a cumulative tradition ideas and norms that have sprung from different assumptions and, at the same time, we celebrate a mode of understanding that is distinctively human – a critical self-consciousness of ourselves as persons seeking to understand persons.

Although it is difficult to explain precisely how the multifaceted dimensions of a cumulative religious tradition contribute to the shaping of a culture, an historical human process of sharing comprehensive cognitive processes and behavioral codes and the consequent articulation of relationships in society – and the interdependent dynamic between the two – on a most general level of interpretation, such tradition provides a foundation for a coherence in an individual life-context with personhood in community that enables one to discern a supportive ground over against a chasm of chaos, both personally and collectively, and it enables one to perceive an integrative worldview of human life-time and transcendence.

II

Much confusion continues to fragment our view of the cumulative process of a religious tradition through history, keeping us from discerning the *sine qua non* of such a tradition: the engaged participation of persons in different contexts in different centuries. Analyses that do not allow scope for the authenticity of human creativity and both the importance and validity of tradition-altering human responses over the centuries tend to dismantle a historical process that has continued precisely because it has been cumulative. A focus on the Buddha as "the founder" of a religious tradition tends to lead one to infer that the original intent of the entire enterprise was an ascetic orientation designed to bring about "a flight from the world" involving, of course, a break with all ties forming ordinary society. Yet Buddhists living today remind us of the positive social ramifications of a religious life.

There is an enormous difference between "flight from" and "going forth" (Pāli: *abhinikkhamana*; Sanskrit: *abhiniṣkramaṇa*) as heuristic means for interpreting the religious quest as Buddhists have perceived it. And further, which interpretation of "the world" is one to hold? If "the world" is being used loosely to mean something like "society," then what notion of "society" does one have in mind? For Buddhists, "society," in the broadest sense as pertaining to a realm for moral behavior, refers to all sentient beings. In such a view, the cultivation of benevolence has as its chief social function the alleviation of misery (Pali: *dukkha*; Sanskrit: *duḥkha*) for all sentient beings.

It is not difficult to discern moral foundations for Buddhist social philosophy by inference, keeping in mind Deutsch's notions of "recovery" and "appropriation," when we reflect upon the emphasis given to the person in the Buddha's teachings and infer that the praiseworthy moral evaluations attributable to an individual's life cannot long endure in human history if those moral evaluations are not applicable to the social context in which that individual life is lived. What is morally praiseworthy in a person's life is not held by Buddhists to be morally detrimental for persons forming a community; what is repugnant in a person's life is not morally ennobling in the lives of the majority of persons living in that context or tradition. The soteriological process, although focused on the person, *is* socially relevant.

When we press this further, we find that part of the thrust of the Buddha's message was the interiorization of ethics, of moral living, the purification of one's intentions. Of primary importance is mental disposition, awareness, intention, and attitude. Related to this is an affirmation that a sense of "separateness," on the part of a person, is, at first blush paradoxically, at the heart of personal disintegration and individual dislocation within society. A sense of separateness involves a sense of "mine-ness," from which follows so much in practical orientations involving possessiveness, competitiveness, defensiveness, even distrust and divisiveness. To counter this, Buddhists have long averred that there is no substantial self beyond activities and relationships.

Frank Reynolds and Robert Campany begin their consideration of Buddhist ethics by noting four general characteristics, the first of which is the importance of a sense of insubstantiality combined with an emphasis on wholesome actions, "the central Buddhist insight into reality as 'selfless' (*anattā/anātman*) or 'empty' (*suñña/śūnya*), on the one hand, and authentic moral activity on the other." Second is the quality of intention: action (*kamma/karma*) sprung from wholesome intentions will yield beneficial consequences for an agent and others; the reverse holds true, too. We do well to keep in mind that this notion is undergirded by a deeper discernment: the universe of human experience is grounded in a moral order. Third, a set of guidelines is provided for one to follow, and fourth, an expectation that there will be a correspondence between one's ethical living and one's soteriological realization, or, as the case may be, one's status as a monk (Pali: *bhikkhu*; Sanskrit: *bhikṣu*) or layperson. Throughout their presentation, these authors make the point that although there are textual references regarding aspiring for one's own well-being and the well-being of others, and that from time to time, a tension might be sensed between these two emphases, "for the mainstream of the tradition the dichotomy does not exist" (Reynolds and Campany, 1987, pp. 498–500).

If there is one key orientation that would enable one to see through to the point of the Buddhist contribution to our understanding of what might constitute human social and political ideals, it would be an orientation that simultaneously frees one and connects one, cuts one adrift from the moorings of individuality and a sense of substantial separateness and at the same time allows one to "be at home" in the ever-changing, causal-interpenetratedness of all that can be known. One becomes free genuinely to receive the given and authentically to give what one has received without the slightest calculation of self-interest.

III

The early Buddhist texts that have continued to be held as scriptures provide evidence that the early Buddhist movement in India did not fail in providing guidelines for living life well for those in the monastic order, of course, and also for the laity and for political leaders. Stories drawn from this scriptural source, even in the nearly two millennia since they were written, were heard, for the most part, rather than read, and insofar as laypersons became engaged with those stories about establishing social order, whether through consensus building in a republican context, or leadership by a righteous king (Pali: *dhammarājā*; Sanskrit: *dharmarājā*) or an ideal monarch (Pali: *cakkavattin*; Sanskrit: *cakravartin*), say, those laypersons would also appropriate from those stories whatever might be personally ennobling. This early sense of a religious heritage, one's appropriation of that heritage in one's life-context, and the structures for social order involving kingship have continued in the cumulative development of the Theravāda tradition even into modern times. Stanley Tambiah draws our attention to three dimensions that comprise the "totality of Buddhist Polity": (1) the religious institution that is the Buddhist cumulative tradition (*sāsana*), comprised of the multilevel and comprehensive notions of Buddha, Dharma/Dhamma, and Sangha; (2) notions of kingship, found in a complex of considerations pertaining to a righteous ruler (*dhammarājā/dharmarājā*), a being whose purpose is the achievement of enlightenment (*bodhisatta/bodhisattva*), and a wheel-turning, world-ruling monarch (*cakkavattin/cakravartin*); and (3) an awareness of being "a people" shaped by this cumulative heritage and commissioned, as it were, to assure its continuity (Tambiah, 1976, pp. 111–12).

Along with the foundations for ethical living that we find in the canonical texts, one can note also an ongoing process of recovering the heritage that has itself become a part of the cumulative tradition. In that process, the memory of one figure has been recovered and has played a large role: Aśoka, third in a line of Mauryan rulers, who established an impressive empire over much of India and who ruled from around 270–232 BCE. This great figure, having secured an empire through military conquest, experienced remorse and, reorienting his life with a new set of priorities, sought to establish his rule on that which is humanely fitting (*dharma*). In later centuries within the Theravāda cumulative tradition, the remembered image of Aśoka became a paradigm for appropriate lay life and a model for Buddhist kings.

Although there is little doubt that the ideal of Aśoka contributed enormously to the formation of a social ethic for Theravāda Buddhists in South and South-East Asia, with the possible exception of Burma, how one is to interpret the role of that ideal could vary. The question is whether there is a kind of interacting parallelism that exists between the ideal of the Buddha on one side, and that of Aśoka, on the other, or whether there is a kind of opposition. A more workable interpretive model is one that is hierarchical and inclusive rather than parallel and contrastive. The ideal of Aśoka has been inherited within a more comprehensive notion of abiding *dharma* – as cosmic norm, as supportive teaching, as salvific truth. This tends to provide a rationale for the presence of the righteous ruler, following the Aśokan paradigm. But the continuity of such a ruler depends directly on a supportive engagement with the Buddhist institutions in the realm. This is the zone of pragmatic interaction. Political order and the stable well-being of society contribute massively to the continuity of the monastic order (*saṅgha*), and support of the *saṅgha* enhances a supporter's sense of personal fulfillment, what is often spoken of as "merit" (*puñña*). Further, this relationship, being symbiotic, benefits also the *saṅgha*.

The monastic order (*saṅgha*) has also contributed enormously to the shaping of Buddhist society. Often one might see the monastic order as representing an institution established and set over and against the ordinary activities of day-to-day living. To a degree this is so. There has been in the heritage of the *saṅgha* an ancient strand of solitary questing within community represented by forest-dwelling monks. But one should note well that for as long as the *saṅgha* has been known to exist, it has demonstrated a missionary impetus and a pastoral nurturing nature, both evangelistic and didactic. A symbiotic relationship has also developed between the *saṅgha* and the Buddhist laity: the *saṅgha* depends upon those who depend upon it. The *saṅgha* depends upon material support from those to whom it extends the supportive guidance of the gift of *dhamma*. So the *saṅgha*, without established political power, was dependent upon the laity and especially upon the king.

Although there is a clear-cut institutional differentiation between the monastic order and lay life, there is considerable overlap in religious dispositions to be cultivated by both monks and laity. And further, the mere presence of monks enables a layperson to reflect on the definition of life – that is, that it is more than a mere biological process, that human relationships, although foundational, are not in themselves ultimate. The relationship between the *saṅgha* and the king and people has been a basic feature in the evolving of social and political ideals in Sri Lanka, Thailand, and Burma.

IV

The idea of a *bodhisattva*, a being having as its purpose in living the attainment of enlightenment, although known in the early tradition and popular in the Theravāda heritage, became featured and celebrated as an ideal in the Mahāyāna movement. The *bodhisattva*, an embodiment of compassionate involvement in life in the world in the here and now, became a paradigm for virtuous living. Occasionally interpreters have said that the Mahāyāna movement emphasized compassionate behavior more strongly than was the case in the earlier period or in the Theravāda tradition, that the Mahāyāna was more involved with life in the here-and-now. Although compassion is replete in all strands of the Buddhist tradition, there is reason for this interpretation. Whereas the older tradition held that the four noble truths and dependent origination (Pali: *patītyasamuppāda*; Sanskrit: *pratītyasamutpāda*) were middle-way articulations of the Buddha's salvific realization, between sensual indulgence and rigorous asceticism in the first case and eternalism and annihilationism in the second, the Mahāyāna tended to extrapolate the full implications of the latter, of dependent origination. Whereas the older tradition worked primarily with the description of dependent origination as a sequential process over lifetimes giving rise to this whole mass of misery or unsatisfactoriness (*dukkha/duḥkha*), the early Mahāyāna thinkers clustering around a school known as the Mādhyamika, the "middlers," tended to focus primarily on the principle of dependent origination: briefly, "when that is, this arises, with the cessation of that, this ceases." Everything – you name it (and this wording is intentional) – arises in dependence upon something else and also ceases, also in dependence. There can be no substantiality in this frame of reference, nothing self-existing.

Nāgārjuna, a great second century contemplative, recovered from the older heritage and emphasized greatly the liberatory quality of "emptiness" (*suññatā/ śūnyatā*) that is at the heart of dependent origination. If *saṃsāra* is empty of an inherent, abiding own-nature (Pali: *sabhāva*; Sanskrit: *svabhāva*) and if *nirvāṇa* is also empty of an inherent, abiding own-nature, both *saṃsāra* and *nirvāṇa* are identical in this absence, identical in emptiness. If, indeed, emptiness is the end-all, what might the new *bodhisattva* career project as the objective of the religious quest? Not the attainment of *nirvāṇa*, as other Buddhists had held. There is no *other* place or objective to which one might aspire, other than to live freely in the emptiness realization in the here-and-now. Without dwelling on the notion of emptiness, one can readily discern in the idea of dependent origination the interdependency of all that becomes or arises, and its corollary of sociological relevance.

There is a deeper dialectic involved in this grand notion of dependent origination, one that was recovered by Nāgārjuna and the Mādhyamika school, and recovered anew by the Yogācāra school in India, and appropriated afresh as the Buddhist tradition continued to develop in China and Japan. The emptiness that is realized in this dialectic is an emptiness that is trans-ontic and also trans-deontic – both beyond and at the same time subsuming being-and-non-being. The given world/world-as-it-really-is, in which one lives and dies – the world of animals, insects, birds, and so on – is the natural, neutral, given world/world-as-it-really-is. The unawakened mind places this given world/world-as-it-really-is into a superimposed complex by projecting imaginary frames of interpretation upon it. The awakened ones are the ones who by discipline and constant awareness are enabled to see this given, neutral world/world-as-it-really-is in its consummated naturalness.

There is no "world rejection" going on here. The other-dependency embedded in the notion of dependent origination simultaneously dislodges the hold of isolated individuality, both of persons and of things, and loosens attachments to both rejection and non-rejection, allowing the natural world to arise in one's awakened perception as the consummated, perfected world that it is in reality, a world entirely suited for and completely open to the twin expressions of a *bodhisattva*'s life: compassion and wisdom.

When the Buddhist tradition entered China, the features we have already noted, of *saṅgha* and cumulative thought, spun a variegated web of ideals social and political that is cumulative, complex and at the same time demonstrates a pattern that is distinctively Chinese. Although the old monastic disciplines were continued in the *saṅgha* in China, the *saṅgha* of China underwent numerous significant changes responding to and incorporating long-established Chinese customs, such as filial piety, while adjusting to a practice of following clearly articulated hierarchical structures providing centralized political authority. But neither the *saṅgha* nor China was, nor have they been, monolithic. In the fourth through sixth centuries CE, in the south of China, Buddhists, who were not immediately involved with central Asian influences, appropriated some key notions of Chinese religiousness, while in the north of China, the non-Chinese rulers appear to have been impressed by some of the great monks who brought with them from central Asia a disposition to use rites and incantations to bring about protection from natural calamities and assurance of success in human affairs. One can trace other patterns of development of social ideals in China by noting how practices among rural Buddhist temples tended to blend with older Chinese religious practices, while the temples in urban settings became directly dependent upon the state. During the Tang (618–906 CE) and Sung (960–1279 CE) dynasties, land ownership by the monasteries led them to assume roles akin to those of aristocratic land-holding families, and a developing dependence upon the state gave rise to an interpretation of religious ceremonies at a Buddhist temple as a means of assuring the welfare of the state. In time, the monks became subordinated to the civil bureaucracy. This development was not witnessed in India, Sri Lanka or Southeast Asia. There has been recurring tension between the centralized authority and the *saṅgha* through the centuries in China. We can see this recurring recently – pressure has been brought upon Chinese Buddhists by the Chinese Communist government. It is reported that cadres were planted within monasteries to persuade monks and nuns to renounce their non-productive, parasitic status.

When we turn to Japan and consider the development of social and political ideals in the Buddhist tradition there, we soon realize that it is difficult to determine clearly whether one should speak of Japanese Buddhist or Buddhist Japanese ideals, so much happened within the movement as it became rooted in Japanese culture. From the beginning, the tradition was received and subsequently transmitted by the aristocratic class who arranged for persons to become monks so as to perform rites and ceremonies in the interest of the ruling class.

Whereas in China there was considerable emphasis given to structuring the Buddhist heritage, as it was being transmitted sporadically in texts, into some kind of comprehensive system – a classification of the tradition (*p'an chiao*) – in Japan, to a much greater extent, particular texts not only colored but significantly shaped the social and political ideals of Buddhists in light of the creative responses given to those texts. One would want to note particularly the monumental role of the *Lotus Sūtra* (Sanskrit: *Saddharmapuṇḍarīka-sūtra*) among Japanese Buddhists in general and particularly with Nichiren and his followers (*Nichiren-shū*) and three great texts of the Pure Land tradition (*Jōdo-shū* and *Jōdo-shinshū*), the *Larger Sukhāvatī-vyūha Sūtra* (*Daimuryōjukyō*), *Amitābha Sūtra* (*Amidakyō*), and the *Meditation Sūtra* (*Kanmuryōjukyō*). The process is fully akin to Deutsch's interpretation of the mode of philosophy in India. Persons were recovering and appropriating the heritage that was theirs as recorded in these major texts.

With Shinran, for example, the focal figure of the true teaching of the Pure Land (*Jōdo-shinshū*) movement, which became by far the most popular expression of Buddhist piety in Japan, self-power was found to be entirely inadequate. Hence Shinran put aside his monastic endeavors and, while still a religious leader, married, noting that he was neither a monk nor a layman. It is noteworthy that among some branches within the *Jōdo-shinshū* tradition, blood succession in temple leadership developed and has been maintained. Followers of *Jōdo-shinshū* chose to organize themselves into local congregations, which immediately produced a creative tension with the aristocratically linked and government-controlled temples. Furthermore, much of the life of Nichiren and the broad wake that his life created in the development of the Buddhist tradition in Japan has focused on bringing the nation to righteousness, that it might become an ideal Buddha land, in response to the teachings of the *Lotus Sūtra*. So central was faith in the *Lotus Sūtra* that gender distinctions were loosened in determining leadership roles. Indeed, among Nichiren's direct followers there were more women than men. Although there was considerable warring between the followers of Nichiren and other Buddhist groups in Kamakura Japan (1192–1338 CE), today a lay movement,

Rissho-Kōsei-kai, that is greatly indebted to the vision of Nichiren is active throughout Japan and more recently in the world at large providing economic relief for the poor in seeking international understanding, inter-religious colloquia and peace.

There has continued to be a running dialectic between Buddhist thought and Japanese culture. We can spot this, somewhat ironically, in Zen where, for example, there is a central metaphor inherited from China found in "Lin-chi's True Man of No Rank," communicating subtly a profound Zen Buddhist awareness of spontaneous presence. At the same time, there arose in Japan a ranking system of Zen temples (*gozan*): temples of the first rank, of the second rank, of the third rank, and so on.

We see in the development of the Buddhist tradition in Japan features that were not a distinctive part of the Indian record: a proclivity toward nationalism, an emphasis on magic, prominence of ceremonies for the dead, a tendency to have a compromising spirit, and a kind of formalism. These characteristics were a result of Buddhist reflection, but primarily they arose as a result of that reflection among Buddhists who were Japanese.

Another feature one might note with regard to this dialectic between Buddhist thought and Japanese culture was referred to as "the submerged tradition of transcendence in the history of Japanese values" (Bellah, 1970, p. 118). Whereas, from the start, there was an association of the received Buddhist heritage with the aristocracy in Japan and this led to the performance of rites for the good of the ruler and the people, expressive of clan loyalties and giving rise to association with nationalism, the complex and remarkable emperor Shōtoku Taishi (574–622 CE) found in his response to his Buddhist heritage a quality of transcendence sufficient to provide perspective for social change. Robert Bellah notes that this sense of transcendence became submerged, but arose again with force during the Kamakura period; in its Buddhist mode, however, it has tended to remain submerged since.

One can see flashes of it reappearing, however. In the social consciousness among some *Nichiren-shū* and *Jōdo-shinshū* lay-oriented movements, there remains this "distance" between the sanctity of the *Lotus Sūtra*, in the former case, and the sanctifying reality of Amida Buddha, in the latter, that gives to a reflective Buddhist seeking to recover and appropriate his or her heritage a prophetic distance, as it were, from which a person committed to social reform can see clearly, analyze with discernment, and act responsibly for the welfare of others.

Bibliography

References

Bellah, Robert N. 1970: *Beyond Belief: Essays on Religion in a Post-Traditional World* (New York: Harper & Row).

Deutsch, Eliot 1988: "Knowledge and the Tradition Text in Indian Philosophy," in *Interpreting across Boundaries: New Essays in Comparative Philosophy*, ed. Gerald James Larson and Eliot Deutsch (Princeton: Princeton University Press).

Reynolds, Frank E. and Campany, Robert 1987: Entry on "Buddhist Ethics," in *The Encyclopedia of Religion*, editor in chief Mircea Eliade, Vol. 2 (New York: Macmillan), pp. 495–504.

Tambiah, Stanley 1976: *World Conqueror and World Renouncer: a Study of Buddhism and Polity in Thailand against a Historical Background* (Cambridge: Cambridge University Press).

Further reading

Adikari, A. (ed.) 1991: *Sambhasha: Mahabodhi Centenary Commemorative Volume*, Vol. 1, No. 2 (Nugegoda, Sri Lanka: Ministry of Education).

Bechert, Heinz 1987: Entry on "*Saṃgha*," in *The Encyclopedia of Religion*, editor in chief Mircea Eliade, Vol. 13 (New York: Macmillan), pp. 36–40.

Bellah, Robert N. 1965: *Religion and Progress in Modern Asia* (New York: Free Press).

Carter, John Ross 1993: *On Understanding Buddhists: Essays on the Theravāda Tradition in Sri Lanka* (Albany: State University of New York Press).

Ch'en, Kenneth K. S. 1964: *Buddhism in China: a Historical Survey* (Princeton: Princeton University Press).

Gombrich, Richard 1971: *Precept and Practice: Traditional Buddhism in the Rural Highlands of Ceylon* (Oxford: Clarendon Press).

Jayasuriya, M. H. F. (ed.) 1994: *Buddhist and Vedic Studies: a Miscellany by O.H. De A. Wijesekera* (Delhi: Motilal Banarsidass).

Malalgoda, Kitsiri 1976: *Buddhism in Sinhalese Society 1750–1900: a Study of Religious Revival and Change* (Berkeley: University of California Press).

Matsunaga, Daigan and Matsunaga, Alicia 1976: *Foundation of Japanese Buddhism*, Vol. 2 (Los Angeles: Buddhist Books International).

Nagao, Gadjin M. 1991: *Mādhyamika and Yogācāra: a Study of Mahāyāna Philosophies*, Collected Papers of G. M. Nagao, ed., collated, and tr. by L. S. Kawamura in collaboration with G. M. Nagao (Albany: State University of New York Press).

Seneviratne, H. L. 1987: "*Saṃgha* and Society," *The Encyclopedia of Religion*, editor in chief Mircea Eliade, Vol. 13 (New York: Macmillan), pp. 40–6.

Smith, Bardwell L. (ed.) 1972: *The Two Wheels of Dhamma: Essays on the Theravada Tradition in India and Ceylon* (Chambersburg: American Academy of Religion).

—— (ed.) 1978a: *Religion and Legitimation of Power in Sri Lanka* (Chambersburg: Anima Books).

—— 1978b: *Religion and Legitimation of Power in Thailand, Laos, and Burma* (Chambersburg: Anima Books).

Spiro, Melford E. 1982: *Buddhism and Society: a Great Tradition and its Burmese Vicissitudes*, 2nd edn (Berkeley: University of California Press).

Swearer, Donald 1995: *The Buddhist World of Southeast Asia* (Albany: State University of New York Press).

Takeuchi Yoshinori and Keenan, John P. 1987: Entry on "Buddhist Philosophy," in *The Encyclopedia of Religion*, editor in chief Mircea Eliade, Vol. 2 (New York: Macmillan), pp. 540–7.

Watanabe, Shoko 1968: *Japanese Buddhism: a Critical Appraisal* (Tokyo: Kokusai Bunka Shinkokai [Japan Cultural Society]).

Wright, Arthur F. 1990: *Studies in Chinese Buddhism*, ed. Robert M. Somers (New Haven: Yale University Press).

26

Causality in Buddhist philosophy

G. C. PANDE

The Buddhist philosophy of causality is primarily a theory (*naya*) of the human world. Its methodology, however, is objective and critical. It rejects the weight of mere authority or tradition, relies upon experience and reason, and emphasizes the critical examination and verification of all opinions. Although the Buddhist conception of knowledge and truth has a strong empirical and pragmatic bias (cf. *Nyāya-bindu* 1.1), its conception of experience does not exclude introspection, rational intuition or mystical intuition (cf. *Nyāya-bindu* 1.7–11). Although its conception of reason creates a logical gulf between reason and experience, the gulf is bridged by a transcendental illusion (*avidyā*). Its employment of reason is highly analytical and it seeks to discover the ultimate elements constituting the structures of objects and experience. The constituent elements as the locus of causation are regarded as more real than their composite structures – *dharma*, *dhātu* or *kṣaṇa* as contrasted with *saṅghāta* or *santāna*. At the same time, it raises dialectical questions and seriously considers the possibility of the empirical world being merely a working illusion. It discounts the apparent stability of objects, stressing their transience, finally defined as momentariness (see, for example, Ratnakīrti's *Kṣaṇa-bhaṅga-siddhi*). It rejects the category of substance for that of process. Causality is thus regarded not as a dynamic interaction between substances, but as a functional, many–one relationship of order characterized by invariance and uniformity within any given type of process.

The first phase of this theory of causation is the one to be found in the original formulation of Buddha. Here it is called the "Principle of Dependent Origination" (*pratītyasamutpāda*). The second phase is represented by the analysis of analytical (Abhidharmic) philosophers who elaborated the theory of causes and conditions (*hetu* and *pratyaya*). The third phase is represented by the work of logicians who analysed the concept of causality, its relationship to reality and the source of its valid knowledge. The fourth phase belongs to the dialecticians who denied the reality of causation. As a result of this development, the Buddhist theory of causality is three-tiered. At the empirical-pragmatic level (*saṁvṛti*) causality characterizes processes of change, at the analytical or "elementary" level, causality is the invariant order of point-instants (*kṣaṇas*), at the dialectical–intuitional level causality is illusory.

The history of speculation about causality may be traced to two distinct sources. On the one hand, various types of cosmological reflection have sought to discover the First Cause of the universe – a tendency exemplified by pre-Buddhistic Vedic thought. On the other, radical empirical sceptics have questioned the validity of the notion of universal laws of causality – a tendency exemplified by the Lokāyata contemporaries of Buddha. Between these two extremes, common sense and science have never ceased to investigate particular causes of events and to use this knowledge for successful practical activity. The successful application of knowledge in practice was, in fact, generally regarded as the hallmark of intellectual or scientific truth in the Indian, including the Buddhist, tradition.

From the beginning, Buddhist philosophy was averse to cosmological speculation. Vedic seers had conceived the First Cause as the Spirit and its will. Buddha sedulously avoided assuming the reality of any spiritual substance, whether soul or God. Nor did he think of the causal operation as a species of volition, though volition was a prime species of causation for him. In his estimation, causation was primarily impersonal and adynamic (see, for example, *Āryaśālistamba-sūtra*), coextensive with empirical phenomena (*dhammā*), physical and mental. His interest in causality lay primarily in the explanation of human suffering.

Buddha has been credited with having been the first thinker to formulate the abstract and universal law of causality and to apply it to human psychic events and experiences. He took the decisive step away from the theological, animistic and magical ways of understanding the world to its scientific understanding in terms of definite causal laws which could be rationally discovered and practically used. Buddha's theory of causality is well known as the "Theory of Dependent Origination." It asserts that any object of experience depends for its existence or occurrence on the necessary and sufficient presence of its cause. Several different propositions are implied here: (1) that all phenomena have an origin; (2) that their existence depends on causes; (3) that causes do not operate singly but in networks; (4) that causality stands for a necessary and sufficient relationship between cause and effect; (5) that causes operate inevitably, uniformly, and spontaneously by their own nature. That all objects of experience have an origin is a thesis which the Buddha supported in opposition to many of his contemporary philosophers who were described as eternalists or semi-eternalists. They held in different ways that all reality endures perpetually, without any origin, change or end. The Vedāntins held reality to be an undifferentiated spiritual being and the changing world of "name and form" to be merely virtual. They asked, "How can being pass into non-being and non-being into being?" And concluded, "What a thing really is, it must be unalterably." The Sāṁkhya held reality to consist of eternal consciousness witnessing the ceaseless transformations of natural forces. These exemplify *satkāryavāda* or transformationism, which makes the effect essentially identical with the cause and hence in some sense pre-existent. The Vaiśeṣikas held reality to be divisible into distinct categories, including elementary substances characterized by distinctive qualities and actions. Impermanent substances, qualities and actions are subject to origination and destruction depending on the functioning of different types of causes. The effect is totally different from the cause and does not exist prior to its causation. This is *asatkāryavāda* or *ārambhavāda*. Materialists upheld the changing reality of matter but denied the reality of any spiritual being and were hence dubbed Nihilists. Being ultra-empiricists, they rejected the possibility of any definite knowledge in the form of universal judgments, or inference, and hence of necessary causation. Practical life depends on probabilistic knowledge. Events happen by chance (*adhītyasamutpāda*) and their perceived connections may be accidental. All explanations have ultimately to appeal to the nature of things, which cannot be questioned (*svabhāvavāda*). In between lay various types of commonsense views. Thus Nigganṭha Nātaputta, the founder of Jainism and Buddha's contemporary, defined reality as "that which originates, endures and ceases."

Buddha's doctrine of the nature of reality as characterized by origination has to be understood as the denial of the rival eternalist and annihilationist views. Hence Buddha's view was described as the Middle Way, the way between absolute being and absolute non-being. What it meant, in effect, was that human beings are not to be regarded as eternal spirits, nor as mere transient material states. What is characteristic of human reality is its psychic or experiential process, which is constituted by a ceaseless succession of impermanent states originating from causal conditions and passing away. Physical objects are to be understood analogously as impermanent functions dependent on causes but without any endurance or substance and ceasing to be by nature (cf. *Āryaśālistambasūtra*).

Buddha denied accidentality as much as he denied eternalism or nihilism. Causation embodies the principle of necessary and sufficient reason. The nature of things is fully understood by way of understanding their causation. The most famous Buddhist formula runs, "Of all the phenomena derived from causes, the Lord has given the explanation. He has also explained their cessation." ("*Ye dharmā hetuprabhavāḥ* . . .")

The Principle of Dependent Origination is believed to have been discovered by Buddha intuitively as an aspect of his supreme experience of Enlightenment. He dichotomized the Truth (*dhammā*) that he discovered into two parts – Dependent Origination (*paṭiccasamuppāda*) and Quiescence (*nibbāna*). Since the second of these was regarded as the final principle or experience, the former may be described as the principle of non-ultimate being or experience – "In short, as the principle of phenomenality, of the nature of things transcended in *Nibbāna*" (G. C. Pande, 1995, p. 407ff).

This exposition would appear to assimilate the position of the Buddha to that of the Upaniṣadic seers who declared that the "face of Truth is covered by a Golden Chalice." So some modern interpreters for whom Buddha was not a Buddhist have likened *nibbāna* to *Brahman* and *paṭiccasamuppāda* to *māyā* or *nāma-rūpa* (name and form). Traditional Buddhist philosophers, however, make a sharp distinction between the position of Buddha and the Upaniṣads. They explain the distinction of the "two principles" realized by Buddha as a distinction between reality, which is wholly empirical, and its negation. Dependent Origination thus elucidates the nature of reality, while Quiescence (*nibbāna*) is only a non-ens, the absence of empirical reality, the realization of which leads to the cessation of the stream of consciousness. Some absolutized causality as the principle of reality or the essence of phenomena (*dharmadhātu, dharmānāṁ dharmatā*). The starting point of the diverse schools, however, remained the original formulation of the Buddha, which runs thus, "That being given, this comes to be; from the birth of that, this is born.

That not being given, this does not come to be; from the cessation of that this ceases." This formulation negates the independence or self-subsistence of finite objects, in particular of the empirical "self," which is really equivalent to causally conditioned psychophysical states. Common sense is apt to regard its world as a virtual anarchy of substances, wherein each individual person and thing enjoys the independence of its nature. But in its scientific mood, it also posits an invisible order that not only somehow contains this anarchy, but also derives the "powers" of each constituent from its own overarching constitution. Buddha's formulation of the causal principle denies that finite things have any sovereign right of existence. They derive it as a brief tenure from their dependence on others. "As parts of an ordered world of relations, they possess only a conditioned reality."

The celebrated philosopher Buddhaghosa pointed out that the emphasis in the Buddhist formula is "not on origination (*uppāda*) but on conditions and relations." "Dependent Origination is to be understood as the totality of conditions and relations." Similarly, another famous philosopher, Vasubandhu, identified Dependent Origination with the totality of conditioned phenomena (*saṁskṛtadharmas*).

The Principle of Dependent Origination thus seeks to define the fundamental relatedness of things. Stcherbatsky has suggested that this relatedness is intelligible more in terms of mathematical "functional dependence" than in terms of the conventional idea of causality (1962, Vol. I, pp. 119–24). However, the Principle of Dependent Origination is more specific than the general notion of functional relation as such, since the latter "contains nothing more than the notion of determinate correspondence in its abstract form" (Hobson, *Theory of the Functions of a Real Variable*, Vol. I, p. 257). A functional relation between x and y can be specified by saying simply that "to some values of x at any rate correspond values of y." Dependent Origination, on the other hand, "asserts, in effect, that if x assumes any of the two values "*e*, *Ne*," y also assumes the same, and that "*e*, *Ne*" must be interpreted as "existent, non-existent." Thus Dependent Origination refers not only to "what is but a special type of Function, it also lays down an ontological interpretation of the domain of the function." The idea of Dependent Origination, then, "though less general than the idea of Function, is yet more general than the idea of cause, which is usually associated with such ideas as those of 'action,' 'force,' production out of something."

This Middle way between original Being and original Non-being is sometimes understood as the resolution of both into the flux of becoming. Within this flux nothing can be or be understood except in terms of a necessary and sufficient causal assemblage, which is neither the same nor different from the effect. Neither the effect, nor the cause can be regarded as an isolated unitary event. Thus all things are only processes, not entities. Identities are nothing but analyzable sequences, and independence an illusion. Thus the human person is only an insubstantial psychophysical continuum of instantaneous functions or responses to objective stimulations. The notion of an identical self is only an illusory projection. What holds together the psychic continuum (*vijñāna-santāna*) is its immanent causal determination. There is no agent or experiencer apart from momentary actions and experiences. Nevertheless, there is an invariant order in the succession of types of psychic events. These sequences move up or down like escalators and constitute the objects of choice guided by wisdom.

The original and prime focus of this causal theory was the explanation of human suffering, not principally as a social fact, but as an existential feature of human life. Philosophical theories oriented towards moral and spiritual therapy patterned themselves formally on the theory of causation as developed by the medical science of the age. The medical theory first determined the observable symptoms of affliction and then went on to trace the morbid process which, beginning with some abnormality in the natural constitution, produces a series of changes that culminate in the overt symptoms of disease. It then went on to indicate the curative process as a complex causal process in which the medicine or other curative measures led to changes eliminating the disease as the deep cause of the symptoms. Finally, it ascertained the cure to be effected and health established. Thus the medical investigation of causes had four stages: symptomatology, etiology, therapy, and cure. The basis of the investigation was the observation of present data, inferential hypothesis drawn from generalization on past observations and its testing to establish a differential diagnosis, formulation of therapeutic processes through the inductive methods of agreement and difference, and the definition of health on the basis of certain primary assumptions about the natural constitution and functioning of the human organism.

Buddha also regarded the human condition as one of illness and sought to deal with it on the analogy of medical science. In this process, he accepted the validity of the methods of observation, inference and intuitive supposition subject to empirical testing. Observation included not merely the systematic sense-perception of external data, but also the introspection of mental states, and the rational intuition of universal and essential principles that cannot be directly perceived but function as the basis of logical deduction and the ultimate definitions of essences underlying all typal identifications and characterizations. While Buddha followed the formal and procedural four-fold of the medical theory of causation (namely, symptom, diagnosis, therapy, and cure), he departed radically from the philosophical presuppositions of the medical theory which was based on the Sāṁkhya system.

Buddha rejected all three current philosophical alternatives on the subject of causation. Causation is not the continuation of being with transformation, nor an emergent creation out of nothing. Nor is extreme empiricist scepticism about causality well grounded. Transformationism and creationism are both defective because they seek to determine the relation of cause and effect exclusively in terms of identity or difference between them. Similarly, to seek to determine the existence or non-existence of the effect prior to its origination would be to step beyond the normal application of these terms. Buddha rejected the notion of absolute being or non-being, since neither could be perceived or validly inferred. Buddha also rejected, on the basis of an empiricist and nominalistic employment of Occam's Razor, the notion of reality as the underlying ground of the phenomenal flux, a ground constituted by independent individual substances with characteristic or accidental forms or modes which alone could be perceived. Nor can perception be regarded as the sole valid source of knowledge, since even if it were granted that the extreme particular is amenable to perception, such extreme particulars could not become the content of verbal, conceptual and pragmatically verifiable knowledge.

Buddha's theory of Dependent Origination is thus not a theory that accepts the commonsense picture of the world and then seeks to explain it within the conceptual parameters of such a view. It rejects the concept of individual substances and treats the concepts of identity and difference, being and non-being, duration and action in a dialectical manner. It resolves objects into sequences of transient phenomena with an invariant order, and the world into a flux. The human individual is resolved into a succession of psychic functions where each moment depends on the preceding one. The transience of the experiential states is the fundamental illness which affects them. While the specific character and content of psychic states depend on specific causes, the whole "flow of Illness" depends on pervasive and immanent causes such as Ignorance, Egoism, Desire and the force of past actions.

Thus the Principle of Dependent Origination refers not only to the general theory of causation, which is intimately bound up with the dialectical negation of the metaphysics of substance, but also to its application to the chain of human suffering ultimately grounded in the illusion of substance – especially the illusion of the ego-substance. Believing in its own individual and enduring reality, the ego invests the objects of experience with a similar reality and thus engages in action out of desire and aversion for what is unreal.

As applied to the origin of suffering, the Principle of Dependent Origination indicated various causal factors, often serial. Ultimately, all of these factors were combined by traditional analysts into a causal chain with twelve links. This chain constitutes the most popular form of Dependent Origination. In its classical form, the chain runs thus: Ignorance, Predispositions, Consciousness (= Conscious Organism), Name and Form (= Mind and Body), Spheres of Experience (sensory and mental), Contact (of the Cognitive organs and their objects), Feeling, Craving, Grasping, Transmigration, Birth, Old Age, and Death. Although ancient Buddhist theologians and philosophers have spent much energy in trying to give this causal chain some logical order, such attempts cannot be said to have been very successful. The most plausible explanation states that the first two links belong to the past life of the individual, the next seven belong to this life and analyze the process of experience into its basic factors, the tenth link connects the present with future life, and the last two indicate the future life. The individual is conceived as a stream of experience running through different lives or bodily incarnations. The present incarnation begins with the heritage of the past, the predispositions acquired through a course of experiences ultimately rooted in the illusion of a separate, independent, and permanent ego-substance. In this life experience results from the contact of subjective and objective factors. The former are constituted by the psychophysical organism endowed with cognitive faculties. The latter consists of five types of sense data, immediate introspective data, and the various kinds of ideal data accessible to the intellect. The feeling resulting from this contact already presupposes the radical factor of ignorance. As a result, it is characterized by a distinct hedonic tone, pleasant, unpleasant, or indifferent. Owing to this hedonic tone, a sense of craving and consequent attachment to the objects of experience is generated. This attachment is the inner component of action which reconstitutes the ego or the stream of experience, leading ultimately to its transmigration and reincarnation. The core of this causally deterministic empirical process is constituted by Ignorance, Desire and Action. Ignorance is the mistaken identification of the self with the psychophysical organism and its consequent egoistic appropriation, desire is immanent in the felt experience of objects, and action is will and willed motion. In so far as volition is motivated by desire, it determines suffering.

However, it remains a fact that in its classical form as a Chain of Twelve Causes, the formula of Dependent Origination is not a series with homogeneous terms which may all be ordered in the same manner. It remains a "hyper-series" produced by the conflation of several different kinds of sequences. One such sequence is the sequence of incarnations. Another traces action to desire and feeling. Still another emphasizes the role of Ignorance as an immanent and persistent cause. There is also the causal relation of action and consequent experience. Of these three, the first is psychological, the second metaphysical, the third ethical. One may sum up by saying that while the constitutive cause of suffering has to be seen in the psychic process, its occasioning cause is regulated by the moral law of Action and Retribution, and its ultimate ground is an illusion about the nature of the self.

The interpretation of Dependent Origination in early Buddhist philosophical schools followed several different lines. According to Theravāda, one of the principal schools out of the traditional 18, the formula of *pratītyasamutpāda* (PS) is an extended statement of the fundamental principle that the active process (*kamma-bhava*) of one life determines the experiential process (*upapatti-bhava*) of another. Although the original formula is held to have described the life process of *karman* and suffering of the individual highlighting its principal successive stages, its Abhidharmic interpretation understands it from the standpoint of the metaphysical *dharma* theory. From this standpoint, there is ceaseless transformation of elementary complexes in which the substratum elements are regrouped, although they are separate particulars and never repeated.

Four different aspects were underlined for understanding the formula: instantaneous, sequential, relational, and modal. The first shows that all the twelve causal factors are realized in any act within the process of suffering. Conation arising from ignorance produces a cognitive state with various concomitant factors. Dependent Origination thus is an immanent factor within the life of suffering (*kleśa*). The sequential aspect emphasizes the necessary order and succession in the elements, while the relational brings out the more obvious cause–effect relationship in them. The modal aspect emphasizes the succession of the states of the Five Skandhas. It was sometimes stated that it was this aspect that Buddha had most in mind.

Buddha's Theory of Dependent Origination had logical, metaphysical, psychological, and ethical implications, but it was formulated briefly and with much contextual variation so that a conflated and not too coherent formula gained currency, since it seemed to put together several different aspects. Logically, the theory explained causality as a special functional relation in which the presence and absence of the cause imply the presence and absence respectively of the effect. Metaphysically, it denied the substantiality of cause and effect, affirming that they are no more than sequentially ordered functional composita (*santāna* and *saṁghāta*). Psychologically, it replaced the notion of a permanent individual soul-substance with that of a stream of consciousness determined by immanent causality rooted in the concatenation of conative factors culminating in volition. Ethically, it affirmed that the moral quality of volition and voluntary action determines the hedonic quality of subsequent experience. To be happy one must act morally. To be free one must be detached from the ego-complex.

In its logical, metaphysical and psychological aspects this theory has many points of contact with modern theories. Its ethical aspect, however, makes it totally different. The kind of distinction that is now made between fact and value is totally foreign to it. Nor does it accept the notion of moral law as simply ideal. According to the Buddha, the moral law is a causal law that operates autonomously, without requiring any divine or human agency for its effectuation. It does not keep psychology and ethics separate, but unites them in a single psychological ethics. As to the plausibility of this assumption, it needs to be remembered that all religions take the moral law to be inexorable, although they generally attribute its effectiveness to God. God's will is thus moral, and causally effective at the same time. Buddhism simply eliminates God, along with the soul, as gratuitously assumed substances that are unnecessary, given the existence of certain immanently determined and ordered functions. Besides, Buddha claimed to be able to directly intuit the working of the law of *karman* determining human destiny.

Abhidharma seeks to clarify the metaphysical aspect of causation as simply an invariant series of *dharmas* or elementary functions. Characterized by the innate features of temporality called *saṃsktra-lakṣaṇas*, they are like flashes of energy, insubstantial and non-recurrent, without duration or motion. Their being, appearing and functioning are identical. The term "*dharmas*" has been translated as "phenomena" or "element." As an appearance, shining as the content of experience, it is a "phenomenon" without, however, this implying that there is a noumenon behind it. Similarly, it is an element in the sense that when the analysis of experiential content is taken to its limit, we seem to reach just recognizable distinct types or marks. These typal characters are not substances or real universals or any kind of permanent objects. Nor is there any real underlying identity between the different type-instances. Each instance is unique and non-recurrent, but the sense of similarity arising from their cooperative participation in the origination of similar or practically indiscernible effects (*bhedāgraha*) leads to the construction of pragmatically recognizable identities. The analysis of sensation and ideation gives the irreducible types and marks of what may be recognized in experience. These are the *dharmas*, or the ultimate components of experience, each with its recognizable mark or character (*lakṣaṇa*) which constitutes its own being (*sva-bhāva*). *Dharma* or the experiential component is so called because it holds or maintains a recognizable identity or character (*sva-lakṣaṇa*) or own being (*sva-bhāva*). All objects are transient, structured compounds of these components which function, not in isolation, but in groups. Nothing produces anything singly, without combining. "An element is non-substantial, it is evanescent, it is in a beginningless state of commotion, and its final suppression is the only calm" (Stcherbatsky, 1962).

Philosophical exegesis produced a new classification of causes and conditions within the general theory of *dharmas*. The Abhidharmic theory of causation rests on the three concepts of cause (*hetu*), condition (*pratyaya*), and effect (*phala*). "Cause" and "condition" are distinguished only by their context. It seems that originally *hetu* or cause referred to the rationale of explanatory factors generally, while *pratyaya* or condition referred to specific antecedent factors and circumstances. It has been suggested that the *Pratyaya*-system was earlier than the *Hetu*-system.

The causes (*hetus*) were divided into six types, the conditions (*pratyayas*) into four and the effects (*phala*) into five. This classification arose as a result of the detailed analysis of different "causal" processes principally within the "stream of consciousness." It was an alternative to classifications based on substance-metaphysics.

The four conditions (*pratyayas*) are: *Hetu-pratyaya* or cooperating condition, such as the seed for the plant or light for visual sensation; *samanantara-pratyaya* or the immediate antecedent and homogeneous condition, such as attention preceding perception; *ālambana-pratyaya* or objective condition, such as form and colour for visual sensation; *adhipati-pratyaya* or ruling condition, such as the eye for vision. Of these, the *Hetu-pratyaya* corresponds to five types of causes or *hetus*, while the *adhipati* corresponds to *kāraṇa-hetu* or the general cause. The five types of causes are: simultaneous cause (*sahabhū-hetu*), such as material elements and qualities (*bhūta* and *bhautika*); conjoint cause (*samprayuktaka*), such as cognition and conative factors; homogeneous cause (*sabhāga*), such as a benevolent disposition and the accumulation of virtue in a psychic stream; pervasive cause (*sarvatraga*), such as the *anuśayas* or passions; retributive causes (*vipāka*), which are good dispositions afflicted by passions. *Kāraṇa* or the general cause comprises all those factors that facilitate the effect by not hindering it.

Puruṣakāra-phala or the "anthropomorphic" result arises from the simultaneous (*sahabhū*) and conjoint (*samprayuktaka*) causes and is so called because it appears to issue from their energy or will, as it were. *Niṣyanda-phala* or the "automatic" result issues from homogeneous (*sabhāga*) and pervasive (*sarvatraga*) cause. *Vipāka* or the retributive effect is caused by *vipāka-hetu* or moral causes not free from passion. *Adhipati-phala* or the dominant effect corresponds to the ruling condition or general causes, such as the visual sensation to the eye.

The precise nature, interrelationship and location of these causes and conditions were subject to many debates. For example, the question was raised whether cause and effect can be simultaneous like the lamp and its light, the object and its shadow, or the three legs balancing a tripod. Whether the antecedent homogeneous condition (*samanantara-pratyaya*) applies to physical processes was disputed. The notion of general cause (*kāraṇa-hetu)* appears to link together the whole process of being into one directly or indirectly. But the major focus of the discussion of causality still remains on the moral and spiritual life of man, on the process of human bondage and suffering.

The school of Logicians concentrated on two aspects of causality: the ontological and the epistemological. Empirical and real objects had already been distinguished. The former are composites (*saṁghāta*) and sequences (*santāna*), like the flame or sound; the latter are point-instants (*kṣaṇas*). At the former level, causation appears to be the relationship of dynamic entities, which appear to remain identical while changing. The reality of such entities, however, can be nothing except the reality of the point-instants that compose them. Since identity and change are contradictory, the sense of identity must arise from the failure to notice the differences between similar successive moments cumulatively contributing to the same effect. Now a real object differs from an unreal one by virtue of its causal efficiency. What is real can make a difference to behavior; it can cause a sensation, though the resultant cognitive judgment may be erroneous. Thus the reality of empirical objects appears to be their activity of producing practically observable effects, but this implies the impossible simultaneity of identity and change. However, such an appearance of empirical objects is not wholly illusory, being a regular appearance pragmatically confirmable but grounded in the succession of atomic moments or point-instants. But in the case of an atomic momentary real, origination, being, activity and cessation can only be identical. In such a real there can be no motion or change, but only a regular succession of instantaneous functions. "Whatever is, is causally efficient and hence momentary." This was elaborated as an analytical deduction called *svabhāvānumāna* or inference based on essential identity. The validity of the first part of the argument, "whatever is, is causally efficient," is shown by the absurdity of its contradiction. If there is something that has no causal efficiency, it would be indistinguishable from a "sky-flower." The second part, "whatever is causally efficient, is momentary," is shown by the fact that its contradiction leads to the absurdity of the inefficient second moment or of the partly efficient moment.

When two objects are different, as they must be if real, a universal or "non-deviant" (*niyata, avyabhicarita*) connection between them can only be based on causality and such a relation can be discovered by a series of positive and negative observations (*Pratyakṣānupalambha*) called *Pañcakāraṇī* or Five Steps, which has been interpreted as a Joint Method of Difference. (See, for example, *Jñānaśrīmitra-nibandhāvalī*, pp. 160–82; *Tattva-saṅgraha*, Vol. I, pp. 211ff) The scepticism of Lokāyata about the knowledge of "universal relations" (*Pratibandha, Vyāpti*) was answered in Buddhist logic by distinguishing phenomena from noumena and perceptions from judgements presupposing innate constructs (*anādi vikalpa*). A transcendental illusion superimposes the universalizing concepts (*sāmānya-lakṣaṇa*) on the sensible particulars (*sva-lakṣaṇa*) to generate the phenomenal objects (*saṁvṛti*). The knowledge of causality as a relation arises from mental construction but is valid for phenomena (*avisaṁvāda*).

The dialectical implications of causality were taken up by the Mādhyamikas, who rejected the notion of causation as contradictory. How can the non-existent or what already exists be produced? How can something be produced out of itself or out of another? The cause cannot produce without activity, alteration or cessation, but if it ceases, how can it produce anything? When the cause is there, the effect has not yet come; when the effect is there, the cause is gone. How can there be any relation of dependence between them?

The dialecticians concluded that the phenomena have a pragmatic reality, but are devoid of any real or intelligible nature (*svabhāva*). The Law of Dependent Origination was thus interpreted as the relativity of concepts and the insubstantiality of empirical objects presupposing them. What is finite is unreal, what is infinite is ineffable. Starting by regarding causation as the hallmark of reality, Buddhist analysis ends up by denying it.

Bibliography

Murti, T. R. V. 1960: *The Central Philosophy of Buddhism* (London: George Allen & Unwin).

Pande, G. C. 1993: *Studies in Mahayana* (Sarnath: Motilal Banarsidass).

—— 1995: *Studies in the Origins of Buddhism*, 4th edn (Delhi: Motilal Banarsidass).

Seal, Brajendranath 1985: *Positive Sciences of the Ancient Hindus* (Delhi: Motilal Banarsidass).

Stcherbatsky, Th. 1962: *Buddhist Logic* (New York: Dover).

27

Humankind and nature in Buddhism

KNUT A. JACOBSEN

Buddhism teaches that the diversity of living beings in the world is caused and upheld by intentional acts performed in this and previous lives by karmic trajectories, beings whose continuity through rebirths is not dependent on a transcendent substratum such as a self (*ātman*), and that the order of beings in the world exactly correlates with the consequences of acts (*karman*) operative for their present life. The central Buddhist doctrine of dependent co-arising (*pratītya-samutpāda*) shows how these karmic trajectories are sustained by twelve conditions, the primary of which is ignorance. The goal of Buddhists is ultimately to transcend rebirth and attain *nirvāṇa*. This is possible because the world is both a rebirth realm and a realm in which awakening from ignorance can be attained. The natural world of living beings is a moral order and this moral order functions in a physical setting. The physical setting of the rebirth system is the cosmos as the abode of beings, and the beings participating in the rebirth system constitute the world of living beings. These together constitute the world of rebirth (*saṃsāra*). By "nature" in this article is understood that part of the cosmos that constitutes the physical setting of humans and the world of non-human beings also living there – that is, animals and plants. This is, one should note, only a very small part of the Buddhist cosmos, which consists of a huge number of world systems, and which is immense in time and space and eternally manifests and dissolves.

Karmic trajectories live in five rebirth realms (*gati*-s). These are the realm of hell (*naraka*), the realm of animals (*tiryagyoni*), the realm of the departed (*preta*), the realm of humans (*manuṣya*), and the realm of divinities (*deva*). Sometimes a species of divine beings called *asura* is considered a sixth rebirth realm. Their existence is not denied by those who accept only five rebirth realms, but the need to distinguish them as a separate realm is. No other form of rebirth is possible. Another classification divides the cosmos into three realms (*dhātu*-s), the realm of the formless (*ārūpyadhātu*), the realms of form (*rūpadhātu*) and the realm of desire (*kāmadhātu*). Human and animal realms belong to the realm of desire. Only some of the realms of the divinities belong to the realm of desire, while the rest of the divinities belongs to the formless and the form realms, and they correlate with states of meditation and Buddhist doctrines. The realms of the formless and of form seem to be attained not by means of ethical acts alone but by meditational skills. However, rebirth in these meditation realms was deprecated as the duration of life there was so long that progression towards *nirvāna* was seriously delayed. The human species, as part of *saṃsāra*, is on the same footing as the animals in being driven by ignorance and craving and in undergoing rebirth in accordance with karma. The most important distinction is between all beings bound in *saṃsāra* and a Buddha. This is because Buddhahood is different from all forms of existence known to humans. All other beings are constituted by the five groups (*skandha*-s) of material shape (*rūpa*), feeling (*vedanā*), perception (*saṃjñā*), programmed tendencies (*saṃskāra*), and consciousness (*vijñāna*), and the faults (*āsrava*) of sense-desire, desire for existence, views and spiritual ignorance, but the Buddhas are not.

The five rebirth realms differ in the degrees of happiness (*sukha*) and suffering (*duḥkha*) experienced in each. In hell, the animal realm and the realms of the departed, there is more suffering than happiness. In the human realm these two are in a balance, while the realm of divinities is dominated by happiness. However, since every experience of happiness will disappear, even happiness is ultimately suffering. Nevertheless, an important division of the five rebirth realms (*gati*-s) is that between humans and divinities, who live in relatively good rebirth realms (*sugati*), and the departed, animals and hell-beings, who live in relatively bad rebirth realms (*durgati*). That the realm of the departed is considered less painful than the animal realm might be because the *preta* realm is seen as a prolongation of the human realm, since they are departed humans. The distinction between humans and animals correlates with the distinction between the happy and unhappy realms. Animals are therefore absent from the exclusively happy places, such as the pure land of Sukhāvatī. Rebirth as an animal is caused mainly by acts conditioned by confusion and delusion, although imitation of an animal species by a human might also be the cause of rebirth in that species (*Majjhima Nikāya*, Vol. 2, p. 55). The animal experience, although less painful than the experience in hell, is compared to when one, feeling exhausted, overcome by the heat of the hot season, falls into a cesspool and experiences feelings that are painful, sharp and severe. Human life, by contrast, is compared to when someone, after having been overpowered by the heat of the hot season, and having become exhausted and thirsty, arrives at a tree with dense leaves and foliage giving thick shade, and experiences pleasant feelings while sitting or lying down on the even ground under that tree (*Majjhima Nikāya*, Vol. 1, p. 100). Nature can provide both pain and pleasure, but the world is constantly decaying because beings are most often reborn in a realm worse than their previous life. This is one of the aspects of suffering and a reason for realizing the four noble truths.

A classification by the Buddha of animals into five classes is found in the *Majjhima Nikāya*. These are: first, the grass-eaters, such as horses, cattle, asses, sheep, and deer; second, the dung-eaters, such as cocks, swine, dogs, and jackals; third, beings that are born in the dark, grow old in the dark and die in the dark, such as beetles, maggots, and earth-worms; fourth, beings that are born in water, grow old in water and die in water, such as fishes, turtles, and crocodiles; and fifth, beings who are born in filth, grow old in filth and die in filth, such as beings living in rotting fish, in rotting carcasses, in rotting rice or dirty pools. This classification of animals may seem incomplete and somewhat arbitrary, but the more common classification of beings in ancient India into four classes according to the immediate cause of birth was also accepted by the Buddhist. Birth as any of the animals is caused by deeds conditioned by confusion, and the anguishes of the animals are many. In general, these beings do not do good acts but devour one another and feed on the weak (*Majjhima Nikāya*, Vol. 3, pp. 213–15). This classification follows a description of hells and is meant as a warning about the terrible destiny of humans who do evil deeds and shows the overriding role of ethics and the quest for liberation in the Buddhist understanding of nature. Nature is here understood and classified as a punishment realm for evil-doers. Absent from this strange classification are such wild animals as tigers, and the Indian royal animals, such as elephants and snakes. The point of the classification is to show the disgusting aspect of nature, and as a result, tigers and elephants did not quite fit into this classificatory system. Buddhaghosa seems to upgrade the animal experience by calling rebirth in the animal realm a state of loss, but denying that it is an unhappy rebirth realm (*Visuddhimagga*, 13.93, p. 469). The reason he gives is that the Royal *nāga*-s (snakes) belong to the animal realm and they are greatly honored. The existence of animals worshipped as gods seems to have caused some insecurity about the correctness of classifying the realm of animals as an unhappy rebirth realm.

One of the most important human transactions with nature is the consumption of animals and plants as food. The Buddhist ascetics aimed at eliminating or minimizing their participation in the production, storage, preparation and consumption of food, because food was an important source of craving and greed. Thus the practice of non-attachment to food was part of the project of overcoming craving and attaining total withdrawal from the rebirth realm. In order to help minimize this particular human–nature interaction, the repulsive aspect of nature as food was emphasized. Buddhaghosa describes in great detail a meditation on the repulsiveness of food, starting with the repulsiveness of walking to the village, the repulsiveness of collecting the food, the repulsiveness of having to swallow food mashed up in the mouth, food which, after it is chewed, but before it is swallowed, is said to be similar to a dog's vomit, the repulsiveness of digestion, which can be like the rotting of carcasses in the sun, and the repulsiveness of urine and excrement (*Visuddhimagga*, 11.1–27, pp. 372–80). Food should be eaten only as a medicine for staying alive so that the cessation of rebirth can be attained, and food should not be a source of the enjoyment of nature.

In the poems *Theragāthā* and *Therīgāthā*, an aspect of nature other than its status as the painful rebirth realm is emphasized:

> In a cave and on a mountain crest, frequented and plunged into by wild boars and antelopes or on a naturally pleasant space, or in a grove sprinkled with fresh water by rain, having gone to your cave-house you will rejoice there.
> Birds with beautiful blue necks, with beautiful crests, with beautiful tail feathers, with beautiful wings of variegated feathers, greeting the beautiful-sounding thunder, will delight you as you meditate in the wood.

> When the sky (*-deva*) has rained, when the grass is four-fingers high, when the grove is in full flower, like a cloud, I shall lie among the mountains like a tree.
> It will be soft for me, like cotton.
>
> (*Theragāthā*, 1135–7, p. 104)

Here the beauty of nature and its ability to delight the renunciant is celebrated.

There is a continuous flow of life through the rebirth system of the five rebirth realms which goes round and round, says Buddhaghosa, like an ox harnessed to a machine (*Visuddhimagga*, 8.34, p. 255). There is in this flow of life no hiatus between humans and animals, as all humans have already lived many lives as animals and animals have also previously had human rebirths. There is, therefore, no crucial difference between animals and humans. The concepts of karma and rebirth situate one's humanity as provisional, as only a sign of previous good karma, and not as a permanent identity. It should be appreciated as a good rebirth, but it also indicates that one is not really a human being, nor an animal, but a configuration of parts in a process of flux causing rebirth in different realms according to volition and acts. The rebirth system also implies a kinship with nature. Animals are ourselves in different rebirths; they experience pain and we should show them compassion. There are no absolute borders between species. This view is biocentric rather than anthropocentric.

That it is possible to attain liberation from *saṃsāra* only from a human birth, however, is an element of anthropocentrism common to many Indian systems of thought. A human birth is difficult to attain, and when one happens on a human birth one is given an opportunity to improve one's karma and perhaps realize *nirvāṇa*. But the anthropocentrism involved here is not a matter of the world's existing only for the sake of the salvation drama of humans, as most versions of the Judeo-Christian-Islamic traditions contend, since according to Buddhism, all living beings, including animals and divinities, are participants in the soteriological drama.

Although in general living beings in non-human realms are not producing new karma and are just enduring the consequences of acts performed in previous lives as humans, the activities of some beings in the animal realm do have karmic effects (see McDermott, 1989). This is perhaps because some animals are able to restrain themselves, as is shown in their ability to be tamed. The fact that animals produce karma seems to explain how the taming of them is possible. The emphasis on the taming and restraining of humans seems to have produced in Buddhism an admiration for restrained animals. Even among the wild animal species, such as monkeys, some are perceived as consciously restraining their behavior. In many *Jātaka* tales the theme of loving kindness (*maitrī*) is illustrated by animals restraining themselves and showing living kindness to others. In one tale a young hare (a rebirth of the Bodhisattva) gave himself as food for a Brahmin. Because he did not want to break the moral law by taking animal life, before he entered the fire he "thrice shook himself that if there were any insects within his coat, they might escape death" (*Jātaka*, Vol. 3, p. 35). When the Bodhisattva was an elephant he was pierced by a poisonous shaft, but "he allowed no hate towards the hunter who had wounded him" (*Visuddhimagga*, 9.30, p. 329). When the elephant heard he was being hunted for his tusk, he broke it off and gave it to the hunter. Buddhaghosa mentions that the Buddha, in previous rebirths as a snake, undertook the disciplinary precepts of a monk (*Visuddhimagga*, 9.32–3, pp. 329–30). Thus some animals were considered able to follow these precepts. According to a *Jātaka* tale, a hare, a monkey, a jackal and an otter "dwelt happily and harmoniously together, fulfilling the moral law and observing holy days, till they departed to fare according to their deeds" (Vol. 3, p. 37). These animals are good Buddhists, it seems. But the ethical behavior of animals is not worked out systematically, and a prevailing view is that animals are not capable of growth in the teaching and the discipline (*vinaya*), and the ordination of animals into the order is seen as an invalid practice (McDermott, 1989, p. 270).

According to Buddhism, the human–animal relationship is a moral issue. The first and most important of the ethical rules relating to that part of the eightfold path called "right action" is non-injury (*ahiṃsā*). The doctrine of non-injury was based on the belief that violence to any living being belonging to the wheel of rebirth had karmic consequences. The Buddhist denial of the existence of a permanent self (*ātman*) did not have negative consequences for the status of violence towards animals. But compared to the other great Śramaṇa movement, the Jains, Buddhism seems to have undergone a process of limiting greatly the types of beings which were considered part of the wheel of rebirth. For the Buddhists *ahiṃsā* meant that one should not kill or injure any humans or animals, such as mammals, birds, fishes or insects – that is, beings born in the human and animal rebirth realms. These beings are, with respect to *ahiṃsā*, ordered hierarchically because it is generally considered a greater fault to kill a mammal than a fish or an insect, and killing a human is considered a much worse crime than killing an animal. According to the *Vinaya*, killing a human is a *pārājika* offense requiring expulsion from the order, while killing an animal is a *pācittiya*, requiring only expiation. Even if killing animals was considered a fault, the Theravāda monks were not strict vegetarians. One reason for this is the Buddhist identification of will or intention (*cetanā*) as the karmic cause. The Buddha therefore permitted eating of meat by the monks when they did not know that the animal was killed specifically for them. Other reasons might have been the wish not to deny the gaining of merit from giving food to monks by meat-eating laypersons, and to make sure the monks did not get attached to certain kinds of food. In general, since animals and humans are in most respects non-different, their relationship should be governed by the same spirit as that of monastic life in general – that is, loving kindness (*maitrī*), compassion (*karuṇā*), sympathetic joy (*muditā*), and equanimity (*upekṣā*) which apply to all beings (McDermott, 1989, p. 277). The general attitude should be one of universalizing love, since there is no living being who has not once been one's own mother, father, brother, son or daughter.

Buddhism does not consider plants as constituting a rebirth realm (*gati*). These beings are not part of the wheel of rebirth. While the line between happy and unhappy rebirth realms is drawn between humans and animals, the line between beings consisting of the five groups (*skandha*-s), producing karma and undergoing rebirth due to ignorance and craving and beings not consisting of the five groups, not producing karma and not undergoing rebirth, is drawn between animals and plants. In the Buddhist scheme of four immediate causes of birth (*yoni*-s) – that is, egg, womb, moisture, and life that rises spontaneously – plants are not included. In this scheme, beings born from moisture are beings produced from rotten fish or in rotting corpses or in a dirty pole – that is, worms and insects. Beings that arise spontaneously are the divinities and the hell-beings (*Majjhima-Nikāya*, Vol. 1, 73). According to Hinduism, the fourth class is beings born from seeds – that is, plants. The *Vinaya* describes rules of the non-destruction of plants, but the justification is often not that violence against plants has karmic consequences, but that it is bad for the reputation of the Buddhist community. The rule of the *Vinaya* (*Pācittiya*, 11) that concerns the destruction of plants shows that the beliefs of non-Buddhists were taken into consideration, because the monks did not themselves believe in the sentience of plants, but they recognized that other people would look down upon them if they cut down trees (*Vinaya-Piṭaka*, Vol. 2, p. 226). Similarly, a rule prohibiting the monks from wandering around in the rainy season is justified by referring to the people's disapproval of the monks crushing green grasses, injuring living beings with one sense-faculty, and killing many tiny animals. And a rule against plucking mangoes for eating is justified with the suggestion that the act might give other ascetics the impression that the Buddhist monks lack compassion. The prohibition against digging up the earth was justified by the widespread belief that by digging one performed an act of injury against the earth. The Buddhist monks did not share this belief, and the prohibition probably existed because the monks did not want to contravene society's expectation of how an ascetic was to behave.

There is no dogmatic denial of the existence of sentience in plants in earliest Buddhism. It is clear, however, that plants were not considered part of the karmic rebirth system. One reason for this may have to do with the Buddhist denial of the self (*ātman*). While both the Jains and the Hindus believed that plants possess selves (*jīva*/*ātman*), according to Buddhism, living beings are constituted by the five groups (*skandha*-s) without a transcendent substratum. The five groups, moreover, are bound up with human experience, given the emphasis on intention and volition (*cetanā*) which presupposes a degree of freedom and the possibility of restraint. It is perhaps difficult to imagine plants being constituted by *skandha*-s, since they show no aggressiveness or craving and their development is so thoroughly determined by such external factors as the seasons, and the access of water and heat. Plants, in other words, are perhaps too different from humans to be anthropomorphized.

Living beings, when further analyzed, are divisible into *dharma*-s, or elements of existence that come to be and pass away lasting only a moment, and the conception of living beings as wholes is an illusion. Only passing physical and psychical elements exist. From the ultimate point of view, living beings are non-existent and are merely a concept (*Visuddhimagga*, 9.123, p. 352). The *dharma*-s that constitute the matter of bodies and the natural environment are the four elements (*mahābhūta*-s) believed to be the irreducible factors that make up the physical world. In contrast to many other Indian systems of thought, according to Buddhism, the *mahābhūta*-s are the ultimate data of matter and are not reducible to any other principle, such as the ultimate material principle (*prakṛti*) of Sāṃkhya. Any given material thing, in the outer material world or in the body, is analyzable into these ultimate factors, and apart from them no matter is recognized. The four elements are *pṛthivī* (solidity and extension), *āpas* (fluidity and cohesion), *tejas* (coldness and heat), and *vāyu* (motion). The *mahābhūta*-s are without sound, touch, sight, taste and smell, but these are produced by the *mahābhūta*-s and exist separately from them. That which speaks of selves, persons, animals, plants and so on is only conventional truth (*saṃvṛti*), and that which speaks in terms of the analytical categories, such as the elements of existence (*dharma*), is ultimate truth (*paramārtha*). This Theravādin and Sarvāstivādin idea that reality is constituted ultimately by a number of *dharma*-s was rejected by the Mahāyāna. According to the Mahāyāna, even the ultimacy of *dharma*-s is an illusion; there is only emptiness (*śūnyatā*). From the point of view of conventional truth, the world exists, but since it escapes every attempt at rational analysis, it is empty from the ultimate point of view. But that emptiness is the truth about phenomena means that the world is really empty and therefore non-different from *nirvāṇa*. This identification of *saṃsāra* with *nirvāṇa* entails a re-evaluation of the rebirth realm. The world, it follows, does not need to be transcended, but the perception of it has to be changed. Thus the emphasis shifted from the goal of liberation from *saṃsāra* to a concern with the enlightenment experience in itself.

The growth of Mahāyāna Buddhism and the spread of Buddhism beyond South Asia contributed to these changes in the Buddhist conception of the natural world. An idea of great importance in East Asian Buddhism but of Indian origin was the Buddha-nature (*tathāgathagarbha*) doctrine. The *tathāgathagarbha* doctrine claimed that all sentient beings are or have Buddha-essence or Buddha-nature, a spiritual element which is naturally pure. They all in reality possess the innate potential of Buddhahood, regardless of their current existence in different rebirth realms. A dramatic consequence of the *tathāgathagarbha* doctrine was that vegetarianism became an established doctrine in Buddhism. Even that meat which one had been allowed to eat according to the *Vinaya*, such as meat not knowingly killed for one's own benefit, was now prohibited.

The idea of emptiness for the Chinese Hua-Yen school meant that all things exist in a web of interdependence and interpenetrate each other like a jeweled net in which each jewel reflects every other jewel in the net. In each small part the ultimate is present. The transcendental realm was understood to interpenetrate the world of separate phenomena and the concept of emptiness caused a positive appreciation of the living beings of nature, which were understood to constitute an organic unity.

The emphasis on interdependence and the lack of self-being favored monism and universalism. Given this universalistic nature of Mahāyāna, the question of the limits of the concept of sentient beings was raised, and in East Asia a discussion arose concerning whether plants could attain Buddhahood. The T'ien-t'ai thinker

Chan-jan (711–782) concluded from the premise of universalism that non-sentient beings also had to possess Buddha-nature. The affirmation of their Buddhahood was especially strong in Japan, because Buddhism there had to adapt itself to the high religious value given to certain aspects of the natural world. The Japanese thinker Kūkai (774–835) asserted that, since the world was ontologically one with the Absolute, the *dharma*-body, plants also had to be capable of possessing Buddha-nature. But how do plants attain the realization of their possessing Buddhahood? According to Ryōgen (912–985), the life-cycle of plants corresponds to the process of enlightenment: sprouting out corresponds to aspiration for the goal, residing corresponds to undergoing discipline, changing corresponds to reaching enlightenment, and dying corresponds to entering into extinction. In observing the life of plants, we are therefore witness to sentient beings (Buddhist yogis) performing Buddhist discipline and realizing *nirvāṇa*! The natural process is here presented as being in actuality a religious process and an enlightenment process. Another vision of the enlightenment of plants was presented by Chūjin, who saw plants and trees as a already possessing Buddhahood because they possess the marks of Buddha – for example, roots and stems, which correspond to the 32 marks of the Buddha. The 32 marks of the Buddha are limited to Buddhas in human shape, while Buddhas in plant shape possess other marks. Here a higher degree of realization is in fact attributed to nature than to humans. Plants, which according to Indian Buddhism are not even part of the salvation system because they are not part of the rebirth wheel, are now believed to be Buddhas. Since they are sentient, but not part of the rebirth system, they are already enlightened.

According to the poet-saint Saigyō, the material forms of nature are identical with the Tathāgatha. Nature is enlightened because it accepts impermanence, while humans still need to abandon that illusion. Contact with nature means contact with the Tathāgatha and nature, like the Buddha, is a teacher and the source of human salvation (see LaFleur, 1973). Dōgen (1200–1253) thought that to accept the belief in Buddha-nature as something that all beings possess but might not actualize implies a dualism between an eternal unchanging essence and the changing phenomena. Buddha-nature for him, therefore, is no longer a seed or potential in beings but the concrete phenomena, something all beings are. This means that "in the entire universe there is not even a single object alien from Buddha-nature, nor is there any second existence other than this universe here and now" (Abe, 1971, p. 117). Since there is nothing permanent unchanging anywhere in the universe, Buddha-nature could be nothing else than the impermanence in grass, trees and forests. Nature also teaches Buddhism but it teaches in a different way than humans do. Echoes teach us the truth of emptiness and the dependent co-arising of all phenomena; raindrops teach us the truth of impermanence, and so on (see Abe, 1971; Shaw, 1985). The beauty of nature, it seems, is also an experience of *nirvāṇa* here and now. The difference between this view of nature and the Early Indian Buddhist view is indeed great. Perceiving this difference, several Japanese Buddhist scholars have argued that the idea of the inherent enlightenment is antithetical to such

Buddhist ideas as non-self (*anātman*) (see Swanson, 1993; Schmithausen, 1991a, 53–62).

Buddhists too are aware that, in the light of recent large-scale transformations in the natural environment caused by human activities, it is necessary to reconsider the human–nature relationship, and they have participated in a reinterpretation of their religion to address contemporary environmental issues. Aspects of Buddhist teaching found relevant for this reinterpretation include the idea of the interdependency of everything (the idea that things exist only in relation to everything else), which is thought to coincide with the ecological paradigm of interdependency and biocentrism, the idea that the flow of life that is religiously significant is not restricted to humans, the idea that everything contains Buddha-nature, the idea that false egocentrism and greed drive modern human beings in their exploitation of nature, and the idea of the necessity of controlling greed and craving, of changing our pattern of consumption and being satisfied with less. Finally, the emphasis on *ahiṃsā* in human-animal relations is understood to apply to the attempt to control the human destruction of ecosystems. Buddhism seems to tell us that since greed and thirst are fundamental characteristics of human beings and decay and impermanence are characteristics of the nature of things, humans, because they are in search of permanent happiness, when they are ignorant, will find their desires continually unfulfilled, and greed, unless consciously restrained, will know no limits.

The environmental concern for world maintenance in contemporary Buddhism might seem paradoxical when viewed against Buddhism's origin as a Śramaṇa renunciant movement. The renunciant movement in India established dichotomy between the ultimate goal of the liberation of individuals from the world of rebirth (*saṃsāra*) and the maintenance of the world. The ascetics were to realize liberation, while world maintenance was the task of householders and lay persons occupied with production and reproduction. The lay persons were to maintain the life of the monks by providing the food necessary for their survival, and thereby improve their own karma. The problem of maintaining the natural world, from the perspective of the monk in search of *nirvāṇa*, was irrelevant. His aim was to destroy attachment to the world. But since injuring living beings was understood to be wrong, even if the natural world had no ultimate status, the living beings of nature would have to be treated with ethical restraint and friendliness. Thus the fact that the monks ultimately aimed to transcend the natural world did not cause them to mistreat the living beings of nature. In fact, quite the opposite was the case. Showing compassion and friendliness to animals as well was taken as a necessary condition for progressing on the path towards *nirvāṇa*. The tension between liberation and world maintenance was reduced with the advent of the Mahāyāna emphasis on the identity of *nirvāṇa* and *saṃsāra*, and the implication that it is not necessary for the Bodhisattva to seek escape from *saṃsāra* in order to attain *nirvāṇa*. Here the maintenance of the world and the attainment of *nirvāṇa* are thought, to a greater degree, to coincide.

Buddhist ethics emphasizes will and intentions. Only acts that are intended by an agent are ethically significant, and therefore the real act is the volitional act. Much of the damage done to the natural world has been an unintended consequence of ignorance. As humans become increasingly conscious of the consequences of our acts for the natural environment, those consequences can no longer be described as unintended. Thus the acquisition of knowledge changes our situation. As knowledge replaces ignorance, the karmic consequences of our destruction of nature become more serious.

Bibliography

Writings

Jātaka 1895–1907: *Stories of the Buddha's Former Births*, tr. by various scholars, ed. E. B. Cowell, 6 Vols (London: Pali Text Society).

Majjhima-Nikāya 1954–9: *The Collection of The Middle Length Sayings*, tr. I. B. Horner, 3 Vols (London: Pali Text Society).

Theragāthā 1969: *The Elders' Verses*, tr. with introduction and notes by K. R. Norman, Vol. 1 (London: Pali Text Society).

Vinaya-Piṭaka 1938–66: *The Book of Discipline*, tr. I. B. Horner, 6 Vols (London: Pali Text Society).

Visuddhimagga 1976: *Buddhaghosa: the Path of Purification*, tr. Bhikkhu Ñyāṇamoli, 2 Vols (Berkeley: Shambhala).

References and further reading

Abe, Masao 1971: "Dōgen on Buddha Nature," *The Eastern Buddhist*, n.s., 4, pp. 28–71.

Badiner, Allan Hunt (ed.) 1990: *Dharma Gaia: a Harvest of Essays in Buddhism and Ecology* (Berkeley: Parallax Press).

Callicott, J. Baird and Ames, Roger T. (eds) 1989: *Nature in Asian Traditions of Thought: Essays in Environmental Philosophy* (Albany: State University of New York Press).

Cook, Francis H. 1977: *Hua-yen Buddhism: the Jewel Net of Indra* (University Park: Pennsylvania State University Press).

Harris, Ian 1991: "How Environmentalist is Buddhism," *Religion*, 21, pp. 101–14.

Hopkins, E. Washburn 1907: "The Buddhist Rule Against Eating Meat," *Journal of the American Oriental Society*, 27, pp. 455–64.

Karunadasa, Y. 1967: *Buddhist Analysis of Matter* (Colombo: Department of Cultural Affairs).

LaFleur, William R. 1973: "Saigyō and the Buddhist Value of Nature," *History of Religions*, 13, pp. 93–128, 227–48.

LaVallee Poussin, Louis de, "Cosmogony and Cosmology," in *Encyclopedia of Religion and Ethics*, ed. J. Hastings, Vol. 4, pp. 129–38.

McDermott, James P. 1989: "Animals and Humans in Early Buddhism," *Indo-Iranian Journal*, 32, pp. 269–80.

McGovern, William Montgomery 1923: *A Manual of Buddhist Philosophy* (London: Kegan Paul, Trench, Trubner).

Schmithausen, Lambert 1991a: *Buddhism and Nature*, Studia Philologica Buddhica Occasional Paper Series VII (Tokyo: International Institute for Buddhist Studies).

—— 1991b: *The Problem of the Sentience of Plants in Earliest Buddhism*, Studia Philologica Buddhica Occasional Paper Series VI (Tokyo: International Institute for Buddhist Studies).

Seyfort Ruegg, D. 1980: "*Ahiṃsā* and Vegetarianism in the History of Buddhism," in *Buddhist Studies in Honour of Walpola Rahula*, ed. Balasooriya, et al. (London: Gordon Fraser), pp. 234–41.

Shaw, Miranda 1985: "Nature in Dōgen's Philosophy and Poetry," *The Journal of the International Association of Buddhist Studies*, 8, pp. 111–32.

Swanson, Paul L. 1993: " 'Zen is not Buddhism': Recent Japanese Critiques of Buddha-Nature," *Numen*, 40, pp. 115–49.

28

Buddhist reality and divinity

KENNETH K. INADA

In the quest for Buddhist reality, the inevitable comparison is made between it and the Brahmanic concept of supreme reality. In some quarters, it is alleged that both systems point at an identical nature of reality and maintain a similar method in arriving at it. After all, the historical Buddha was a Brahmin oriented in the Upaniṣadic tradition. He also engaged himself in the prevailing disciplinary practice of yoga to overcome the ill-nature of the ordinary self (*ātman*) and like other fellow Brahmins, he consummated his goal by immersing himself in the Supreme Self (*Ātman/Brahman*). Proponents go even further to identify this Supreme Self with the contents of Buddhist *nirvāṇa* and conclude rather facilely that Buddhism is nothing but an extension of Brahmanic thought.

We must attempt to understand the philosophic difference between Buddhism and Brahmanism because the appearance of the Buddha represents an important break, an auspicious beginning to a uniquely novel way of life. The task is initially complex, because both systems use similar terms – such as, *duḥkha* (suffering), *karma* (action), *jīva* (soul), *pudgala* (personal self), *ātman*, *vijñāna* (consciousness), *śīla* (moral conduct), *samādhi* (yogic concentration), *prajñā* (insightful wisdom), *pratītya-samutpāda* (conditioned or relational origination), *madhyamā-pratipad* (middle way), *śūnyatā* (emptiness), *skandha* (aggregates of being), *saṃsāra* (ill-nature of the wheel of life), and *nirvāṇa*. Some of these terms are similarly used, but with some – for example, *duḥkha*, *karma*, *pratītya-samutpāda*, *madhyamā-pratipad*, *śūnyatā*, and *nirvāṇa* – Buddhism forged ahead to give new meanings to the Buddha's insight.

One of the key differences is the approach to metaphysics. Brahmanism readily engaged in metaphysics in defining and analyzing the ordinary nature of the self and the ultimate path to the Supreme Being. Empirical and rational elements were kept in place, always framed within and subsumed under the absolute realm of being, although the opening was always there for an identification with the Supreme Being through the awakening of the pure spiritual nature (*puruṣa*) nascent in all beings.

By contrast, Buddhism from the outset refrained from any form of metaphysical thinking. In the famous *Çūlamālunkya-sutta* (Shorter Discourse to Mālunkyaputta), the Buddha kept his silence on such metaphysical questions as whether the world is eternal or not, whether the world is finite or not, whether the soul and body are the same or different, and whether the Tathāgata (the Buddha) does or does not exist after death. He considered answers to these questions to be merely speculative and to have no merit in terms of conducing one to the proper life and proceeding on the path toward enlightenment. Indeed, this denial of metaphysics and metaphysical thinking can be looked upon as the first great breakaway by the Buddha from his Brahmanic moorings.

Although the systems were opposed in their attitudes towards metaphysics, they nonetheless started out with the same ontological conception regarding the nature of the ordinary self (*ātman*). This might seem to suggest that even the Buddha could not completely relinquish the metaphysical framework. This is not true, however, because the self or *ātman* situation was merely the starting point for him. As both systems proceeded in their respective quests, they took different paths, one retaining the metaphysical house and the other relinquishing it and concentrating on the newly discovered ontological/existential scheme of things. In other words, Brahmanism began with the ordinary ontological self, but in the end this had to immerse itself within the Supreme Being, thereby losing its individuality and independence. In the case of Buddhism, the ontological/existential self was not blotted out completely, but instead opened up and revealed new dimensions as the process progressed – signifying, for example, such traits as purity, clarity, penetration and expansiveness. For instance, the ontological nature improved itself by extending its sphere of existence and absorbing everything in its wake. It should be cautioned here that the expansive ontological nature is not another instance of a metaphysical element or object. It has a character of its own which we must now clarify as we set out to explore the Buddhist concepts of reality and divinity.

Buddhist reality begins and ends in the Buddha's enlightenment regarding the truth (true grounds) of existence – namely, *nirvāṇa*. He realized *nirvāṇa* through long vigorous yogic discipline and divulged its content only after repeated entreaties by his erstwhile fellow truth-seekers. In all candidness, though, the content of *nirvāṇa* is an open question, entangled in myths, metaphors and symbolic representations, such that even today, its nature and function have yet to be delineated in any satisfying manner. We must, however, persevere in our search for it and be guided by the basic doctrines and principles that are proper to Buddhism.

What, then, did the historical Buddha realize? Since Buddhist literature does not relate or hint at any sequential development of ideas or doctrines, we are compelled to speculate on them based on their repetitive occurrences and importance in the total historical and literary context. In the earliest literature, however, there is a valuable foundational text unanimously acclaimed and accepted by scholars as being a capsule, a crystallization, of the basic philosophy (teachings) of the Buddha. It is the aptly titled, *Dhammacakkappavattana-sutta* (The Sutra that Turns the Wheel of the *Dharma*). The *dharma* refers to the truth of existence, the essence or content of nirvanic experience. Since the term "*dharma*" is also used by other Indian systems, notably Jaina and Brahmanism, the Buddhists distinguish their use by the conjunctive term, "*Buddha-Dharma*" (The *dharma* realized by the historical Buddha).

In the sutra, the Buddha expounds on the famous Four Noble Truths:

1 the universal nature of suffering (*dukkha* in Pali);
2 the rise ("cause") of suffering (*samudaya*);
3 the cessation of suffering (*nirodha*);
4 the way to the cessation of suffering (*magga*).

As suffering is the common denominator of the truths – that is, describing different facets or aspects – it might be well to change the pluralistic designation of "Four Noble Truths" to a singularistic "Fourfold Noble Truth." In this way, the basic focus in placed on the inception of suffering and its resolution.

The Buddha, for example, delineates the nature of suffering by boldly asserting that just to be born is suffering. This assertion seems simple enough and yet it is one of the principal causes of much misinformation and misinterpretation. The irony is that its sheer simplicity distracts us in the sense that we regard it with levity and indifference and do not care to probe further into its deeper meaning. In brief, "just to be born is suffering" does not refer merely to the birth process, nor does it merely limit suffering to physical pains or to emotional, psychological or rational stresses and strains. It is much more profound than all of this. Rather than the mother in labor, the focus is on the newly born child whose desire to live already manifests the makings of suffering. That is to say, the child, from its very first exposure to the world (nowadays we may even think of the life in the womb), starts to grasp at things -- air, food, warmth, security, and so on – and thus begins the conditioning or habit-forming life. In general, we would be quick to say that there is nothing improper about the child grasping at things, since this is an essential biological process. True, there is little to debate on this point. However, what the Buddha realized in virtue of his yogic discipline and eventual nirvanic experience is that the grasping has a subtle aspect heretofore unknown but which constantly takes its toll without the organism being conscious of it. This unknown factor is the phenomenon of attachment (*upādāna*), which is the inception of suffering. Thus to grasp at something entails concurrently the phenomenon of attachment, which may not show up immediately but which will in time – as we notice, for example, in any form of addiction, mild or severe, whether of eating, drinking, smoking, the taking of drugs, or gambling.

The inception of suffering, then, occurs at the very birth of the child, given these earliest stings of passion or desire with their built-in condition of attachment. This is a universal trait that continues into adulthood and covers every phase and function of all living beings. It is perpetual in the sense that living beings are obsessed with what Buddhists refer to as the three basic ills – namely, greed (*rāga* or *lobha* in Pali), hatred (*doṣa*) and delusion (*moha*) – all of which seem to indicate egoistic drives. Greed has a positive grasping nature, hatred a negative nature and delusion an indecisive nature.

At this point, we must carry our discussion of the phenomenon of suffering a step further. For this, we introduce the three famous characteristics ("signs") of the Buddhist way – namely, the impermanent nature of things (*anicca* in Pali), the doctrine of non-self (*anattā*), and universal suffering (*dukkha*). On the third characteristic we need not elaborate here, except to indicate at the outset that these three characteristics not only define Buddhist thought as distinguished from other systems of thought, but they also mutually support and define each other. In other words, they are conceptual poles that support each other and must be taken together or not at all.

The phenomenon of suffering based on desire-attachment (*taṇhā-upādāna*) must now be considered within the context of impermanence. In a truly organic sense, suffering is not static or permanent because nothing persists or is at a standstill, even for a moment. Within the context of momentariness, the nature of the desire-attachment framework too is dynamic, in that both desire and attachment are ephemeral. To think otherwise would be like chasing after rainbows, disregarding the importance of dynamically changing conditions. Thus within the dynamics, neither the desire nor the attachment are possible, but failure to understand this dynamic nature of things would, of course, lead to and perpetuate suffering.

Within the dynamic context, then, a self that desires is nowhere to be found. In consequence, the Buddhist proffers a most astounding doctrine of non-self (*anātman*), a concept that goes against the grain of ordinary logic. Indeed, our ordinary understanding of the self is, for the Buddhist, a mere figment of the imagination, a designation for the dynamic aggregation of the five elements of being (*skandha*). Because of its dynamic character, we can only give a post mortem analysis of an experiencing self, but this in no way gives us license to postulate a self as an independent entity, nor as a point of empirical and epistemic departure.

Finally, we are able to understand the function of the three characteristics in tandem. There is suffering because our conventional understanding of things constantly reaches out for the nature of permanence, for static entities, forms, qualities, and so on, but paradoxically, nothing permanent exists, nor is there to be manipulation of anything to serve the conditional self within the dynamic context. To manipulate the impermanent nature of things into something permanent is like trying to establish identical natures in experience. It would be a step backward, so to speak, for biologically or organically such experiences are non sequiturs. And finally, it is often said that to know the nature of suffering is really to know Buddhism itself. That remains an open and fundamental challenge.

The Buddha showed the way and in the process further revealed the inner content of his nirvanic experience. Yet this content is difficult to grasp because it is (1) couched in terms of the dynamicity of things and (2) viewed and uttered from the lofty heights of his insight. His instructions were simply to engage oneself in the middle way. By instructing thus, the Buddha was careful to keep intact the basic existential character of the truth-seeker. According to the *Dhammacakkappavattana-sutta*, he admonished those who embraced either of the two extremes: sensual indulgence, which is the natural disposition of all beings, or self-denial and self-mortification, for example in the excessively disciplinary techniques of certain approaches to yoga. By avoiding the extremes, he left the "middle" open for the ultimate fulfillment of nirvanic content. He goes on to say that the middle way consists in the Eightfold Noble Path -- namely, right view, right thought, right speech, right action, right livelihood, right effort, right mindfulness, and right concentration.

It is crucial to note that the noble path begins with right view and right thought, for should one proceed without the proper attitude and understanding – for example, without accepting and comprehending the nature of suffering and the middle way – no amount of time spent practicing right speech, right action, right livelihood, and so on will be fruitful. The phases of the path are serial and presuppose the accomplishment of prior phases, especially when the final three yogic phases of right effort, right mindfulness and right concentration are in question.

When the Buddha succeeded in realizing *nirvāṇa*, he made a startling remark: "This is the last birth, there are no more rebirths." This is an insightful philosophic assertion which should not be taken literally. What is involved, in brief, is the Buddha's insight into the nature of becomingness. He means to say that the phenomenon of suffering has been dissolved of any attachment or taint and, as a consequence, the dynamic of "birth" is no longer present or meaningful, and that the strained or forced nature of repeated "rebirth" no longer happens, and finally, that the natural or pristine state of becomingness remains as it is.

We pause to recapitulate. The starting point is human suffering, which is the locus of reality, an experiential reality, focused on the dynamics of suffering and on the coolness of *nirvāṇa*. Suffering is a dynamic phenomenon based on false attachment to the elements of desires. It can be removed by involvement in the middle way, by avoiding the extremes of grasping for something (the form of substantialism) and of denying everything (the form of annihilationism). (Even the latter is a form of attachment.) But this middle is not calculable, physically and mentally, because it involves the total detached experiential process. It is open, full, untainted and dynamic.

To afford a closer look at the experiential process, the Buddha introduced the concept of conditioned or relational origination. This concept is normally seen as depicting the wheel of life – that is, how the wheel, starting with ignorance (*avijjā* in Pali), turns and keeps on turning until old age and death (*jarā-maraṇa*). The continued turning, due to false attachments in the presence of unwholesome *karma*, is known as *saṃsāra*, a wave-like ill-condition of life and the very antithesis of *nirvāṇa*. But relational origination, like the phenomenon of suffering, has the unwholesome aspect, which can be corrected and transformed into the pure, untainted process which is analogous to the nature of the middle way. Thus developing wholesome karmic conditions by following the Eightfold Noble Path is a desideratum.

We have now laid out the fundamentals of Buddhist reality. After the demise of the Buddha, the Buddhist tradition spread through the appearance of different schools of thought roughly divided along conservative and liberal lines, but all of which affirmed and perpetuated the basic doctrines.

We will now discuss a few momentous developments in the quest for *nirvāṇa*. The Abhidharma school, for example, presented a neat systematic treatment of the factors of experience (75 *dharmas*) and came up with the novel idea that the factors can be divided into karmically unwholesome *dharmas* (72 *saṃskṛta-dharmas*) and wholesome *dharmas* (3 *asaṃskṛta-dharmas*). The wholesome *dharmas*, as expected, are the opening to *nirvāṇa* and are comprised of non-manipulable space, the extinction or cessation of unwholesome *karma* by yogic effort, and extinction or cessation by the removal of any causal (karmic) elements. This school spanned both the Theravāda (Southern) and Mahāyāna (Northern) traditions and contributed extensively to the development of Buddhist psychology of experience.

In the early founding of the Mahāyāna tradition, a high point was reached with the appearance of the Prajñāpāramitā Sutras, by authors unknown or unrecorded. Their great contribution consists in the discovery and exposition of the novel concept of emptiness (*śūnyatā*) as a vital component in the experiential process. This discovery became the single greatest force behind the further development and dissemination of Mahāyāna thought beyond the borders of India. The experiential nature of emptiness does not have any negative or destructive feature. Instead, its real feature is to reveal the empty-of-attachment-nature within the experiential process of relational origination. The nature is at once open and full, absorbing everything in its wake. Thus the momentary relational origination is an open dynamic functioning as a full component at all times in the process because of emptiness. In this sense, the enlightened experiential process is nothing but a depiction of the fullness of existence.

One of the abbreviated Prajñāpāramitā Sutras, the *Vajracchedikā Sutra* (Diamond Cutter or Thunderbolt Sutra) exhibits graphically that the *prajñā* (supreme insight) developed as a result of taking up the six or ten *pāramitās* (moral excellences) has the swiftness and cutting edge of a diamond or thunderbolt and lays waste the tangled attachments that our five aggregates of being generate. The sutra concludes by enunciating the famous equation – form (*rūpa*) is emptiness, emptiness is form – to reveal the fully perfected nature of existence in which things are as they really are from the beginning and in which nothing is added or subtracted.

The greatest Mahāyāna thinker is Nāgārjuna (ca. 150–250). His genius was to crystallize the prevailing Mahāyāna doctrines into a coherent system of thought, especially in his monumental work, *Mūlamadhyamakakārikā* (Verses on the Fundamental Middle Doctrine). He drew attention to the fact that we speak on two levels: the lower conventional (relative) level of empirical and rational thought, and the higher non-conventional (absolute) level of non-discursive thought. However, while the former cannot relate to the latter, the latter can indeed relate to and absorb the former. So in our world of discourse, the understanding of conventional truth is prior to the understanding of absolute truth. The realm of the latter is always open to the "mechanics" of the former and becomes the transforming grounds for the experiential process. Nāgārjuna concludes with a remarkable equation to tie things up:

> relational origination is emptiness and emptiness is a provisional designation for the locus and grounds in which there is mutual penetration of all elements; indeed, it is the middle way. (Inada, 1993, p. 148)

A brief discussion of Vijñānavāda (the Consciousness-only School) is now in order. This school introduced the famous Eight Vijñāna Theory – the eight consisting of the five sense organs (as consciousnesses), plus the sense-center consciousness (*mano-vijñāna*), the deliberative consciousness (*manas*), and the all-containing consciousness (*ālaya-vijñāna*). This philosophy asserts that so long as the eight consciousnesses are in turbulence due to unwholesome karmic forces (*pravṛtti*), suffering will continue. But suffering can subside when, by yogic effort, there is a complete "revulsion" (*parāvṛtti*) of the eight consciousnesses into a pure state of existence. This school carried the emptiness theory to new heights, especially in the psychological realm, and contributed immensely to the development of schools in countries such as Tibet, China, Korea, and Japan.

Having arrived at Buddhist reality with the function of *prajñā*, we are now able to draw certain inferences regarding the nature of Buddhist divinity. It should be clear by now that Buddhist divinity has nothing to do with the nature of a Supreme Being, and that it is not to be found outside the realm of human experience. It is always related to and seen within the dynamic context of pure existentiality or the open experiential process.

In the *Visuddhimagga* (Path of Purification), for example, the four *brahma-vihāra* (sublime or divine abodes) are analyzed in conjunction with the final stages of meditative discipline. They are also called the four boundless states (*appamañña*) – namely, loving-kindness (*mettā* in Pali) compassion (*karuṇā*), altruistic or sympathetic joy (*muditā*), and equanimity (*upekkhā*). The significance lies in their inception and sustenance of the boundless or illimitable dynamic nature of things. Each is marked by openness, borderlessness, extensiveness, and reflexiveness. Loving-kindness is the beginning, a personal trait that causes one to open up and involve another in one's own realm of existence. The same thing can be said of compassion, except that here all beings, including non-sentients, are involved. Altruistic or sympathetic joy is quite novel but it depicts another dimension of the human relationship – that is, the reflexiveness, mutuality and blissful state in a group setting. And finally, equanimity indicates the firmness and stability of all three previous states and the envisionment of all things under the aegis of sameness or equality.

Needless to say, the four boundless states are beyond manipulation and deliberation, for they are in the nature of so-called "soft relationship," and are firmed up in solid meditative discipline. They are the stuff that makes and sustains our social life on the highest level. Soft relationship is here contrasted with hard relationship, which deals with the function and use of set empirical and rational elements.

In the Mahāyāna tradition, divinity or divine acts are seen in the conduct of the *bodhisattva* (*bodhisattvacaryā*). The *bodhisattva* is a would-be Buddha, one who delays entrance to the nirvanic realm, but who already exhibits traits of *nirvāṇa* or Buddhahood. Numerous stories and anecdotes in the texts relate how human beings as well as non-human creatures are pitied and saved through self-sacrificial acts. In the human realm, the *bodhisattva* exemplifies both *prajñā* and *karuṇā* (supreme penetrative insight and extensive compassion) which are two facets of the selfsame becomingness. Both are mutually reflective as well as mutually defining of each other. A mother, for example, who loves all children, inclusive of her own brood, manifests at once wisdom and compassion – that is, the highest form of intelligence and the deepest concern for all beings.

The highest point in bodhisattvahood as an expression of divinity was reached in the Pure Land (*sukhāvatī*) School in China and Japan. This school even today commands the greatest following in both countries, but its external religious activities and practice shroud much of the true nature of reality and divinity. Mythical figures, such as Amida Buddha and Dharmākara, are invoked to promote the pure realm of existence, but they must be interpreted in their proper roles.

As with all other schools, Pure Land Buddhism too is grounded in the basic doctrines of Buddhism and geared to the quest for *nirvāṇa*. The only differentiating characteristic is that in the final stages of the quest, the adherent must acknowledge the unbounded infinite realm in which he resides. In addition, his or her finiteness must be admitted and oriented within the unbounded nature. Indeed, the power to make that admission and to seek that orientation, in the final analysis, comes from the unbounded realm itself, thus exemplifying in the grandest way the principle of mutual penetration and identification of existential matters.

Bibliography

Buddhist Wisdom Books 1975: (containing *The Diamond Sutra* and *The Heart Sutra*), tr. and commentaries by Edward Conze (London: George Allen & Unwin Ltd).

Dhammacakkappavattana-sutta 1956: [The Sutra that Turns the Wheel of the *Dharma*], tr. by F. L. Woodward in the *Samyutta-nikāya* [The Book of the Kindred Sayings of the Buddha], Pt V, Book XII (London: Luzac & Co. Ltd).

Majjhima-nikāya 1995: [The Middle Length Discourses of the Buddha], tr. Bhikkhu Ñāṇamoli and Bhikkhu Bodhi (Boston: Wisdom Publications).

Mūlamadhyamakakārikā 1993: [Verses on the Fundamental Middle Doctrine], tr. by Kenneth K. Inada in *Nāgārjuna: a Translation of his Mūlamadhyamakakārikā with an Introductory Essay* (Delhi: Sri Satguru Publications).

The Path of Purification 1956: [Visuddhimagga], tr. Bhikkhu Ñāṇamoli (Colombo, Ceylon: R. Semage).

29

The Buddhist concept of self

THOMAS P. KASULIS

Buddhism did not begin twenty-five centuries ago as a philosophical system. Yet, insofar as its founder Gautama Siddartha made claims about the nature of self and reality, the seeds of philosophical reflection, analysis, and argument were already planted. The Buddha himself may not have been a philosopher in the strictest sense of the term: the earliest texts give us less of a philosophical system than a set of practical sermons, intriguing metaphors, and provocative parables. At around the time of the Buddha, however, a tradition of Indian thought that can be loosely identified as "Hindu" was already well underway, as can be seen in sections of some later Vedas and especially the early Upaniṣads. As the Hindu philosophers sharpened their own skills and became more systematic in their rationales, the Buddha's followers found themselves in philosophical competition with not only a set of indigenous beliefs, but increasingly also with sophisticated analyses supporting those beliefs.

The issue of personhood and its nature turned out to be a key point of contention. No idea in Hinduism was more central and had more philosophical luster than *ātman*, which could mean simply "self" but in Hindu thought typically added the connotations of "true self" or "soul." In fact, some early Hindu texts identified the true self with the oneness of reality, *brahman*. Buddhism, on the other hand, explicitly took the position of denying the reality of such a self. The Buddha himself made *anātman*, the negation of *ātman*, an emblem of his break from the Hindu tradition around him.

The intra-Indian philosophical controversies are complex enough, but Buddhism became a transcultural Asian religion spreading to Tibet, China, South-East Asia, Korea, and Japan. The Buddhist terminology of personhood not only had to be translated into a variety of often unrelated languages, but the concept itself had to find a new home vis-à-vis the indigenous ideas and philosophical systems of Buddhism's new cultural homes. It is instructive, therefore, to discuss the Buddhist concept of personhood as this was developed in at least two cultural spheres: South Asia and East Asia.

Ātman vs. anātman in the Indian philosophical context

In developing an understanding of Buddhist philosophical views in relation to personhood, it is useful to bear in mind two general principles behind Buddhist thought. First, Buddhist philosophy arises out of Buddhist praxis. Of course, one could claim that there is always a connection between theory and praxis on some level, but there are important distinctions in how the two may interrelate. For example, sometimes a theory of reality precedes the development of a certain praxis that is then used as a means of verification within the theory. In the case of controlled laboratory experimentation, for instance, the scientist's practical procedures developed out of a theory that events follow a specific kind of reproducible pattern ("causes") that can be observed and measured by strictly empirical means. It is not always true, however, that theory precedes praxis in this way. For example, the praxis of learning and using language preceded the subsequent development of linguistic theory about language acquisition. In such cases, the praxis (of acquiring and using speech) was not acquired to confirm or disconfirm a theory, but rather the theory of reality (including the linguistics and cognitive science of how the mind and body work) was a metapractical reflection on the praxis in order to explain how and why the praxis works. In an analogous fashion, as we shall see, Buddhist philosophies about the self tend to arise out of metapractical reflection rather than prior theoretical systematization.

This point about the priority of praxis has clear philosophical implications. For example, Buddhism generally shies away from speculative metaphysics and argumentation about cosmic realities. It is typically less interested in analyzing reality to increase our understanding of it and more interested in probing and eliminating our resistance to accepting realities that, at least on some level, we already recognize. For example, what we ordinarily experience is impermanent and not eternal. Buddhism's inclination is to examine our flight from accepting that apparent fact and our quest to try to access some other reality transcendent to our ordinary sensory experience. To put this in terms more familiar to the contemporary West, Buddhism is more interested in the psychological than in the metaphysical aspects of philosophical reflection.

Of course, no philosophical position can be totally devoid of all assumptions about reality. Any philosophical position ultimately makes some initial assumptions within which it then develops its case. There is one premise that Buddhism does take as an unprovable starting point – namely, that there is a real presence besides the workings of the mind, and that the presence does not disguise itself to our ordinary ways of knowing. Again, using a Western terminology that offers only a rough fit, we can say that Buddhism is foundationally *realist* rather than, say, idealist or even constructivist.

In discussing phenomenal appearance, it is important to add one further point about the general Indian context. In Buddhism, as in most other Indian philosophical systems, the "ordinary sensory experience" to which we have referred are products of six, not five, senses. Besides the five outwardly directed senses usually recognized in the West, Buddhism includes also the sense of inner awareness or introspection. From the Buddhist standpoint, that I feel hungry or embarrassed, for example, are as "empirical" and "objective" as that I see the color red or hear a thud. Introspection is not considered a different order of knowing from extrospection. The acceptance of the reality and objective accessibility of psychological states is important to Buddhist praxis as the foundation for its understanding of self.

According to tradition, the Buddha developed his distinctive forms of praxis in response to a pervasive sense of anguish, anxiety, or unsatisfactoriness (*duḥkha*). Through a series of meditations that allowed him to cease making conceptual constructions, he introspectively focused on the stream of immediately available psychophysical events. He concluded that what we directly experience is what actually is and that anguish arises from our refusal to accept what exists for what it is. Ordinarily, he claimed, we project onto the immediately accessible phenomena a desire for things to be otherwise: to be "mine" rather than simply "to be"; to be enduring instead of transient; to be substantial – to be independently existing entities – instead of interdependent processes. Through the meditative praxis, the Buddha was purportedly able to disengage those projections. In so doing, he was able to gain the insight that allowed him not to form the fixations or attachments that lead to our ordinary sense of ego, substantiality, permanence, and self-dependency. In other words, the fruits of the praxis carried over into his ordinary life by liberating him from the tendency to structure his experiences around those categories. Freed of their effects, he was said to be able to accept things for what they are. The anguish disappeared.

The story of the Buddha's awakening ("*buddha*" means "awakened one") is peppered with various accounts of his achieving supernormal or paranormal powers (the ability to remember previous lifetimes, for example). It is significant, however, that none of those powers were considered necessary for underpinning his account of reality and of the self. To duplicate the Buddha's insight, one need not add something to what one ordinarily experiences. On the contrary, the Buddhist praxis is aimed at disengaging the conditioned responses that lead one to think things are other than they are. The praxis is a therapy that eliminates delusional, anxiety-provoking behaviors or constructions of reality. In this context philosophical analysis, with its propensity to build systems around fixed categories, could be a liability rather than a positive tool. The early Buddhist texts relate the Buddha's own hesitation to enter into analyses not conducive to breaking the patterns leading to delusion. For better or worse, however, Buddhism developed in India at a time when Hindu philosophical reflection, speculation, and analysis were beginning to blossom. The Buddhists found themselves being asked philosophical questions that could not be avoided. To understand Indian Buddhist philosophy, especially its analysis of the self as *anātman*, we need to appreciate that larger intellectual context of the time.

In the Buddha's era there was already an Indian trend toward distrusting the ordinary senses. It is significant, therefore, that Buddhist praxis worked against that tendency. The Hindu texts often referred to *māyā*, the idea that reality takes on an illusory mask that must be understood if its true nature is to be fathomed. According to this common Hindu view, reality does not appear to us the way it essentially is. What we see as multiplicity, evanescence, and distinctions may be, in fact, only the superficial appearance of a deeper, transcendent reality of oneness and changelessness (*brahman*). Therefore, with the proper knowledge, we may still see the illusion, but also see through it to the reality beyond. This allows a detached (sometimes even playful) engagement with the world analogous to how we might find ourselves caught up in the illusion of a magic show or cinema. While enjoying the show, we also *know* that the distinctions with which we are engaged are illusions.

Buddhism disagrees fundamentally with the Hindu viewpoint. In Buddhism, the issue to be addressed is not illusion, but delusion. According to Buddhism, we experience the unreal not because the real presents a false appearance, but because we project our own desires onto what is presented. In that projection we delude ourselves. The goal of Buddhism, therefore, is not to see through the appearances, but instead to accept them without the distortion of egocentric projections. The phenomenal world is not illusion (*māyā*), but "suchness" or "thusness" (*tathatā*). This difference had a fundamental impact on the *ātman/anātman* debate between Hindu and Buddhist philosophies of self.

The general position developed in many Hindu Upaniṣads was that behind the sensory functions, there must be a faculty or agency possessing the function. If there is seeing or hearing, for example, there must be that which sees or hears. Yet whatever the seer or hearer is, it itself must be unseen or unheard, or there would be an infinite regress: we could endlessly ask, if the seer is itself seen, then what sees that seer? Therefore, argued this group of Hindu philosophers, there must be something that is the subject, but never the object, of human sensory experience (including introspection). It is the unseen, unheard, untasted, untouched, unsmelled, and unintrospected self behind a person's various experiences. It itself is unchanging and inaccessible to ordinary sensory knowing, yet it defines what one is: it is the *ātman*, the "true self."

The gist of this Hindu argument already existed in the early Upaniṣads current at the time of the Buddha and the details were further developed by subsequent philosophical analysis in the ensuing few centuries. It is important to point out, however, that the acceptance of *ātman* was not just the result of abstract reasoning. There was an experiential or practical component to the belief as well.

For understanding the Hindu position, the central point is what we mean by "direct experiential knowledge." If we limit such knowledge to what is accessible to the six senses, then *ātman*'s very definition excludes its verification. We need not limit "direct experiential knowledge" in that way, however. Yogic disciplines for controlling the mind and body were already highly developed in ancient India, and adepts were said to be capable of achieving a state of complete quiet in which sensory experience (including inner awareness) disappeared altogether. This "experience" (if that Western term can be stretched to apply to such an event) was said to have no subject–object distinction and to be simply a state of oneness. The "I" would be doing nothing other than being "I" – a state of pure *ātman* awareness without discrimination or distinctions.

One might question the possibility of such an event. For example, what continuity would there be between the trance state and the return to normal consciousness? With no distinctions, what or who would emerge from such a state and how would that be connected to the person who existed before the trance event? To such questions, a common reply was to refer to the everyday event of dreamless sleep. It lacks content, the subject–object distinction, and even inner awareness. Yet, when we awake every morning, we remember who we are and have been. To the proponents of the *ātman* theory this was further evidence that personal identity resides in a level of reality not accessible to ordinary sensory experience and which is beyond distinctions. This justified, in their view, the identification of the true self (*ātman*) with monistic reality (*brahman*).

At least in general form, it is that type of theory of *ātman* that the Buddha rejected in his position of *anātman*. Even in its earliest texts, Buddhism rejected both parts of the Hindu theory of *ātman* – namely, (1) the logical argument that action requires an independently existing agent (for there to be seeing, there must be a seer that is not itself seen); and (2) the metapractical argument that the possibility of having events of sensory cessation implies there is a "true self" behind the experience. Let us consider Buddhism's critique of each of these issues.

As we have seen in our discussion of Buddhist praxis, the Buddha maintained that what we experience through the senses (and, therefore, what really is) is a nexus of interconnected processes, not unchanging things (such as *ātman*). Buddhism insists that a process does not require an agent that has or undergoes the change. Ordinary language can be misleading. We say "the river flows in its channel," but this does not mean that the river is something other than the continuing process of water's flowing in the channel. Similarly, nature does not "cause" or "undergo" the change of seasons; the changing of the seasons is one of the processes that constitutes "nature." The analogy to an idea of self is clear: "I" am not what "has" or "undergoes" the processes of psychophysical change. Rather, those processes themselves constitute what is called "I."

According to traditional Buddhist thought, there are five interrelated processes constituting the self: the physical bodily form, sensations or feelings, sense perceptions, habitual mental formations or volitional tendencies, and consciousness. The self is, therefore, the name for the continuities and interactions among those five processes and not something in addition to them. An implication of this theory is that the self is an activity, not a thing, and that its nature is to be the locus where the five processes intersect. Not only is there no "soul" or "true self" behind that locus of events, but there is also no tendency to identify the "real self" with consciousness alone. For Buddhism, there are no sharp lines demarcating the boundaries of the self. In everyday circumstances it may often be convenient to think of a person's existence as strictly bounded, but that is no different from thinking of the boundaries of a river as clearly defined. If we try to be too precise, however, the sharp distinctions disappear. As the river is interdependent with its riverbank – splashing up against its sides, eroding chunks to settle into its own riverbed – so too is the self conditioned by surrounding factors separated from the self by fuzzy boundaries.

With this process image of the self, the various schools of Buddhist philosophy addressed in slightly different ways the issue of continuity. Common to all of them was the idea that the self is an ongoing interaction with other processes. Persons have an identity not because they contain some unchanging core, but precisely because they do change. The self is a pattern of the linked changes, each changing condition leading to reconfigurations that help set the conditions for the next phase. The continuity of the self is in the continuity of those patterned, conditioned changes.

This Buddhist critique undercuts the Hindu argument for *ātman* as the "true self" or the "unseen seer." If seeing, for example, is a psychophysical process, there does not have to be some self or seer behind the process. The interrelated psychophysical processes themselves are what we call "I." A Buddhist philosopher can be as sophisticated in the analysis of these constituent processes as a scientist might be in analyzing a river in terms of the geology of the riverbed and the water's erosion patterns, the rainfall cycles, the seepage of minerals or artificial toxins into the water, the biosystem of river life, and so forth. Yet, just as the scientist does not find, nor feel any need to look for, the "river" as something other than those processes, so too does the Buddhist rest content with a characterization of the self as the name for a set of interrelated psychophysical processes.

With this logical critique behind us, let us turn to Buddhism's metapractical ground for rejecting the Hindu assertion of *ātman*: the reflection on the nature and meaning of the trance state of sensory cessation. Significantly, the Buddha did not deny the possibility of such an experience. In fact, a famous account of his death reports that while giving his last sermon to his assembled disciples, he interrupted his talk because of stomach pain to enter a trance. Re-energized, he then continued his lecture. The disagreement with Hinduism, then, is not whether such a state of sensory-cessation is possible, but the metapractical issue of the meaning of that state. For at least some Hindus, that state suggests what the true self may be. For Buddhists, on the other hand, it means only that under the right conditions the flow of sensory experience can be temporarily frozen. There is for them no reason to jump to the conclusion that such a frozen state is more fundamental or truer than other states. For the Buddhist, it is noteworthy that such trance states and dreamless sleep are temporary events. Those purported experiences of eternity are themselves transient and temporary. Even in dreamless sleep or trance states, there is a continuity of some processes defining the self – the physical processes of the body, for example.

In summation, by rejecting the contemporaneous notion of *ātman*, the early Indian Buddhist philosophers were not denying the existence of the self, but only insisting that there were logical, empirical, and metapractical reasons for denying the self as a substantial, permanent, transcendent entity. The Buddhists certainly maintain that the self exists, but only as a name, like "river" or "nature," for a set of interrelated processes.

The self in East Asian Buddhist philosophy

As we have seen, the Indian Buddhist philosophy of the self developed in opposition to the indigenous Indian notion of *ātman*. When Buddhism made its way into China in the first century CE, however, it entered a radically new cultural context. In the East Asian countries of China, Korea, and Japan, there was no indigenous equivalent to a theory of *ātman*. The East Asian cultural traditions (Confucianism, Daoism, and shamanism – including early Japanese Shintō) sometimes entertained the notion of immortality. Yet the nature of that immortal existence, whether in this life or in some afterlife, was generally conceived to be continuous with what we know as everyday existence. The Confucian heaven was imagined to be much like an ideal Chinese bureaucracy in which individuals who died continued to have clearly defined hierarchical offices and functions. The Daoist immortals were conceived to be much like the rest of us except for the addition of specially acquired supernormal powers, including immortality. The shamanistic traditions recognized ghosts, spirits, and gods that lived in a separate realm from us but who could, through the medium, enter into conversations with people in this realm. Their needs, wishes, and concerns were much like those of this world.

In short, in East Asia there was generally neither skepticism about the reality of phenomenal experience nor the notion that there was an eternal true self behind, or transcendent to, the flux of ordinary experience. The cultural assumption was that we are what we appear to be. In that respect, the Buddhist view of the self was quite congenial with its new East Asian cultural surroundings and its history there is more one of assimilation that of confrontation. As is often the case, of course, the assimilation worked in both directions. For example, with its sophisticated analysis of psychological states and practical techniques for controlling habitual attitudes and behavioral tendencies, Buddhism brought a new dimension to the understanding of the self in East Asia. For our purposes, however, the issue is how the East Asian context affected the Buddhist view of the self.

One aspect was the impact of Confucian ideals on the social and communal aspects of self. As Buddhism took hold in China, its centers assumed an increasingly Chinese character. For example, although both major branches of Buddhism – Abhidharma (Hīnayāna) and Mahāyāna – were introduced into East Asia, only the latter took root. A reason may have been that the former emphasized the individual achievement of awakening, whereas the latter emphasized a collective context in which one achieves awakening for and with others. In this respect, when *anātman* was translated into Chinese as "non-I," it was generally understood to mean something close to "without ego," or "unselfishness." Another subtle indication of this Sinification process was that, as new schools of Buddhism developed in China, they often took the name of their geographical location (for example, names of mountains) or the particular leader around whom the community coalesced. More common in India was the custom of naming schools by what was distinctive in their doctrinal system. In other words, in India it seems what was distinctive about a school of Buddhism is what they believed, whereas in China it was with whom they practiced.

Of course, in India as well there were Buddhist communities, and many rules for that monastic life were brought to China and accepted there. So although the influence of Confucianism on the Buddhist view of the self was discernible, it was rather muted. The impact of Daoism was more striking.

Almost as soon as it entered China, Buddhism closely interacted with Daoist ideas. For example, in rendering the Sanskrit technical vocabulary of Buddhism into Chinese, the translation often drew on Daoist terminology. Probably the most important Daoist influence on the Buddhist view of the person was its theory of spontaneous creativity. The Daoist position was that deliberation leads to artifice and the alienation from what we naturally are. Instead, Daoism argued for patterning human behavior in harmony with the natural cycles and rhythms of nature. With Buddhism's emphasis on the dangers of rationalistic thought and its blurring of the line separating self from world, the Chinese originally thought of the two traditions as natural allies. Aimed at simply being aware of the flow of phenomena, Buddhist meditative techniques were considered complementary to the meditative techniques that Daoists had developed for overcoming needless conceptualization, merging with the processes of nature, and acting without artifice.

Furthermore, in articulating its theory of creativity, traditional Daoist thought conceived of non-being as the source of being. In the Chinese rendering for the term "*anātman*", the character used for the negative prefix "*an-*" was also the character for the Daoist term for nonbeing (*wu*). This suggested to Chinese steeped in the Daoist tradition that the Buddhist self could also be a source of creative action. The idea arose within Chinese Buddhism that awakening had to be not only personally experienced, but also expressed or enacted in some creative or spontaneous manner. The notion was that if one overcame attachments, one would become fully responsive to surrounding circumstances and one's self-expression would be naturally creative or spontaneous.

It might seem that the Confucian emphasis on the analysis of social relations and the Daoist emphasis on naturalness might pull Buddhism in opposite directions. After all, in China Daoism and Confucianism were often explicit rivals. How could they both coherently influence Buddhism's view of the person? The development of Chinese Chan (Korean Sōn; Japanese Zen) Buddhism is an excellent example of how the assimilation worked itself out.

According to tradition, Chan Buddhism began when the Indian Buddhist, Bodhidharma, made his way to China in the early sixth century, residing at the Shaolin Temple. He stayed there for nine years facing a blank wall in meditation. Consistent with this behavior, the early Chan tradition often used terminology for describing awakening as, for example, the "purification of mind." Bodhidharma expressed his antisocial tendencies by consistently refusing disciples, until at last Hui-ko convinced him of his earnestness by cutting off his own arm. Obviously, the specific tradition Bodhidharma had brought with him from India thought of the monastic community as no more than a means for physical support. The meditative praxis was for him a solitary affair and the verification of enlightenment was within himself. The Hui-ko story suggests that matters might change as Chan developed in its Chinese context. They in fact did.

If we look at the Chan tradition just a few centuries after Bodhidharma, at the time of Lin-chi (ninth century) for example, the effects of Chan's Sinification are visible. By that point, Chan praxis centered around monastic communities with charismatic leaders. The central focus of the praxis was no longer solitary but dyadic: the student's praxis was formulated around the guidance and even aggressive intervention of the master. The master challenged the students to express or show their enlightenment through their creative self expression. Lin-chi shouted logically irresolvable conundrums at his students, requiring an immediate, unpremeditated response. Other masters called for poems or paintings that would reveal the egoless core of the student's self-expression. As the Japanese Zen master Dōgen (1200–1253) put it, the master "entangles" the student so that "student and master practice together." Then, according to Dōgen, the entanglement becomes an "intertwining" of the two Zen Buddhists.

In short, in the development of the Chan tradition within East Asia, we can identify both the influence of the Confucian emphasis on social interaction and the Daoist emphasis on spontaneity or creativity. Throughout this assimilation, Buddhism was able to maintain its central core teachings about the self: non-attachment, the acceptance of impermanence, the distrust of empty conceptualization, and the immersion in what is phenomenally present in the here and now.

In the twentieth century, the East Asian context for the Buddhist philosophy of the self has begun another process of assimilation. With the influx of Western philosophy, an academic form of Buddhist philosophizing has begun to emerge. The most famous tradition in this trend is the so-called Kyoto School of Japan, founded by Nishida Kitarō and succeeded by such philosophers as Tanabe Hajime and Nishitani Keiji. These philosophers were excellent students of Western thought, especially of the German tradition, and brought new issues to the Buddhist's philosophical table. Each developed rich philosophical systems of his own that cannot be readily summarized here (but see Michiko Yusa's entry, Article 44, CONTEMPORARY BUDDHIST PHILOSOPHY). In their books, they took up the Western ideas of soul, the transcendental ego, nihilism, scientific empiricism, and individualism, giving them a distinctively Buddhist critique. As their works have become available in Western languages, they have helped initiate a broad-based Western–Buddhist philosophical dialogue about the nature of self.

Bibliography

Writings

Dōgen (thirteenth century) 1985: *Moon in a Dewdrop: Writings of Zen Master Dōgen*, ed. Kazuaki Tanahashi, tr. Kazuaki Tanahashi et al. (San Francisco: North Point Press).

Lin-chi (ninth century) 1975: *The Recorded Sayings of Ch'an Master Lin-chi Hui-chao of Chen Prefecture*, tr. Ruth Fuller Sasaki (Kyoto: Institute for Zen Studies).

Warren, Henry Clarke (ed. and tr.) 1896: *Buddhism in Translation* (Cambridge: Harvard University Press).

References and further reading

Collins, Steven 1982: *Selfless Persons: Imagery and Thought in Theravada Buddhism* (New York: Cambridge University Press).

Dissanayake, Wimal 1993: "Self and Body in Theravada Buddhism: a Topological Analysis of the 'Dhammapada,'" in *Self as Body in Asian Theory and Practice*, ed. Thomas P. Kasulis with Roger T. Ames and Wimal Dissanayake (Albany: State University of New York Press), pp. 123–45.

Giles, James 1993: "The No-self Theory: Hume, Buddhism, and Personal Identity," *Philosophy East and West*, 43, pp. 175–200.

Griffiths, Paul J. 1986: *On Being Mindless: Buddhist Meditation and the Mind-Body Problem* (La Salle: Open Court Publishing Company).

Heisig, James W. 1990: "The 'Self That Is Not a Self': Tanabe's Dialectic of Self-awareness," in *The Religious Philosophy of Tanabe Hajime*, ed. Taitetsu Unno and James W. Heisig (Berkeley: Asian Humanities Press), pp. 277–90.

Hershock, Peter 1994: "Person as Narration: the Dissolution of 'Self' and 'Other' in Ch'an Buddhism," *Philosophy East and West*, 44, pp. 685–710.

Kasulis, T. P. 1981: *Zen Action/Zen Person* (Honolulu: University of Hawaii Press).

Kimura, Kiyotaka 1991: "The Self in Medieval Japanese Buddhism: Focusing on Dōgen," *Philosophy East and West*, 41, pp. 327–40.

King, Sallie B. 1991: *Buddha Nature* (Albany: State University of New York Press).

Nishida, Kitarō 1990 [1911]: *An Inquiry into the Good*, tr. Masao Abe and Christopher Ives (New Haven: Yale University Press).

Nishitani, Keiji 1982 [1961]: *Religion and Nothingness*, tr. Jan Van Bragt (Berkeley: University of California Press).

Rahula, Walpola 1959: *What the Buddha Taught* (New York: Grove Press).

Tanabe, Hajime 1986 [1946]: *Philosophy as Metanoetics*, tr. Yoshinori Takeuchi (Berkeley: University of California Press).

30

Rationality in Buddhist thought

DAVID BASTOW

I

I shall first describe what I take to be the parameters of the task set by my title and state certain assumptions that I shall make in what follows.

(1) "Buddhist thought" will be taken for the purposes of this essay to refer to thought within the Buddhist religion; so the rationality to be investigated is that of a religious tradition (MacIntyre, 1988, chapter 1). Certain things follow from the notion of "a tradition" – in particular, unity and historicity. The unity which justifies talk of *a* tradition is complex. In an extensive tradition like Buddhism, there will be discontinuities as well as continuities, disagreements and divergences within the tradition, distinct phases or chapters within the narrative story.

The present account will deal with what, from a philosophical point of view, are the three determining chapters in the story (see for example Conze, 1962). First, what may be called Early and Nikāyan Buddhism (ENB) – that is, the Buddhism set out in the early texts (for example, the Pali Vinaya and Sutta Piṭakas), and in the developments of doctrine in the various "Hīnayāna" school (*nikāyas*), of which the modern Theravāda is the notable survival. Second and third, the two great Mahāyāna developments of Buddhism: the Mādhyamika movement, which found its religious expression in the Perfection of Wisdom Sūtras and its philosophical development in the work of Nāgārjuna and his successors; and the Yogācāra, articulated philosophically by Vasubandhu and Asaṅga. Is there an overall unity here? Are the chapters really part of the same story? Is there an "essence" of Buddhism, such that all developments within the tradition can be shown to be derived from this one central deliverance or insight? In what follows the unfashionable idea of a religion's essence will be taken seriously, though its application to Buddhism must be sophisticated and complex. Within the tradition, both unity and historical diversity were recognized, and explained in the theory of Three Turnings of the Wheel (Williams, 1989, p. 79). According to this theory, the whole of Buddhism derives from the teachings of the Buddha ("*sūtra*" is the term for the verbal expression of these teachings), the Buddha teaches in ways that are appropriate to his audience, and the three systems of thought referred to above are therefore different because addressed to different audiences. But the Buddha's aim, and in a fundamental sense the content of his teaching, are always the same: salvation and the means to achieve it.

(2) "Rationality", in its application to the Buddhist religious tradition, is a concept that operates at two levels. "Tradition-rationality" refers to rationally defensible interrelations, dependences and derivations, within the tradition as a whole. We may use here the concept of "worldview," and the idea that typically worldviews, religious or non-religious, have three interdependent dimensions: experience, a way of experiencing or perceiving reality; belief, a set of beliefs about the true nature of the world and our place in it; and action, a morality, a way of living and behaving. The rationality of the Buddhist tradition concerns the precise interrelationships between these three dimensions: the ways in which beliefs may derive from experience, the relative logical priority of belief and action, and of theoretical and practical rationality. "Belief-rationality," though, has a narrower application, to developments within the systems of Buddhist belief. It covers the verbal articulation of doctrines, their systematisation, their development into something like metaphysical theories, the marshalling of arguments for doctrines and theories, and the working out of their near and remote implications for belief and practice.

(3) Theoretical and practical rationality, or the relationship between the type of thinking that works out what is true, what one should believe, and the type of thinking that works out what should be done. Here the primary consideration is that Buddhism is a religion of salvation. It has "one flavour, the flavour of liberation." So the overriding task is practical, to provide an answer to the question "what should I do to be saved?" But in (almost) all developments of Buddhism, the answer to this practical question has reintroduced the theoretical/practical dichotomy. That is, part of the answer is always cognitive – the overcoming of ignorance, misapprehension, confusion. But it is never enough to have the right beliefs; there must also be a radical change in motivation, a move from self-centeredness to selflessness, the overcoming of desire or craving, the development of the perfection of compassion. Furthermore, the standard Buddhist position is that these two aspects of the goal – theoretical and practical – are necessarily related. Ignorance and desire prop each other up and must be overcome together.

II

So much for generalities. My main concern will be to investigate the rationality (in the first sense described above) of the Buddhist tradition as a whole – that is, to ask whether the three "chapters" are, from the point of view of rational relationships, part of the same story. I shall use for this purpose the idea of a founding insight or discovery made by the Buddha. For many Buddhists this discovery would be a historical event which took place in the life of a remarkable man who lived some 2,500 years ago. But historicity is not necessary to the idea of a founding insight; the Buddha's existence and his knowledge may be thought of as timeless (Williams, 1989, pp. 29–33). In any case, I shall take it that the Buddhist tradition has been a long and complex attempt to come to terms with, to understand and articulate, to put into practice, this founding insight.

What was or is this insight, this discovery? The answer will determine the mode of rationality by which the founding insight gives rise to and justifies the tradition. I shall speak of an experience [A], which gives rise to doctrines [B], but also acts as a dynamic force or a progressive method of analysis or questioning [C], which challenges and undermines particular formulations of doctrine.

These three facets or elements of the founding discovery will be explored in turn. But first I shall comment on the implications of this notion of "founding discovery" for the relationship between rationality and authority (Jayatilleke, 1963, chs 4, 5, 8). The important idea is that the Buddha's knowledge is saving knowledge, and that *this same knowledge* must be acquired by the Buddha's followers for liberation from suffering to be achieved. This knowledge involves both experience and belief, or rather the belief must be experiential as well as intellectual. In fact, it must permeate one's whole experience, and so become a way of life. The early texts say many times that what the Buddha teaches is a "come and see thing," and that a purely intellectual adoption of the doctrines does not constitute wisdom or insight. In principle the saving vision is accessible to everyone, but in practice its achievement depends on purity of vision. This requires the overcoming of the obstacles, described, for example, as the three defilements of greed, hatred and confusion, or the contaminations or pollutions of sense-desire, desire for (personal) existence, and ignorance. To achieve the complete cessation of these obstacles is precisely to become a perfected being, an *arahant* or a Buddha; so pure vision is not within the immediate reach of someone starting on the path. Such a person must therefore take the Buddha as an authority, but only provisionally so. Faith is a Buddhist virtue, but it means not blind acceptance of revelations which are uncheckable because of their transcendent source, but provisional trust in a being who as far as one can tell is worthy of this trust, and whose claims about experience and doctrine may be progressively checked.

Now to a characterization of the founding experience [A] itself. This first description will be general and external, more abstract than the various doctrinal systems of the tradition. The Buddha, on the night of his enlightenment, had a "vision" – not a glimpse of some unearthly realm, but a radically new way of seeing what is nearest to us all, our own experience – that is, our normal experiences of seeing, hearing or touching something, of reacting to it affectively, and of desiring and acting to get hold of it or to get rid of it. The "vision" seems to have been of the experience-in-itself, abstracting as one might say from the object of the experience, the external reality which may be thought to be revealed by the experience, but also from any supposed subject, any person who "has" the experience or does the action. This "bare" experience has some analogies with Husserl's phenomenological *epoché*. It focuses on what is found, rather than seeing through it to a transcendent reality, either subjective or objective. It is a detached, pure, impersonal vision. It reveals a "world" that is permeated by interrelationships, by a kind of causality. But these relations are internal, structural, in the nature of things, rather than the external contingencies discovered inductively by empirical psychology. The vision is, and is seen to be, a saving knowledge. It is not just a possible way of looking, but reveals itself as the true way, exposing our ordinary way of taking our experiences as false, artificially constructed, and the source of all our suffering. It constitutes a release from the obsessions of selfhood.

The doctrines [B] of ENB are naturally taken as a description of and reflection on the "reality" so revealed, though it must be immediately noted that this reality is of a "middle" nature – neither object nor subject of experience, but experience itself. In fact, the term "experience" has already moved away from its ordinary sense in which subject and object are implied. These doctrines, accepted in one way or another by most schools of Buddhist thought, take the form of lists of types of experience and of their interrelationships, general reflections on their nature, and a statement of the soteriological implications of this knowledge.

(1) Lists of types of *dharma* (Nyanaponika, 1965). "*Dharma*" is perhaps best taken as a concept devoid of theoretical implications, something like "phenomenon" in the sense of whatever is revealed by the pure vision. It has been the focus of many of the crucial philosophical debates within the tradition. Stcherbatsky's term "thing-event" gives an idea of the problematic nature of the concept (Stcherbatsky, 1979). An early typology gave five basic types: sense-organs and their objects, feelings, perceptions, motivations and consciousness. Later systems were much more complex, mainly in that many subdivisions were made in the "motivations" class.

(2) Lists of causal or structural relationships between types of *dharma*. The conditions under which *dharmas* arise are said to be "seen," rather than discovered by inductive searches for constant conjunctions. It is as if a *dharma* is actually constituted by its conditionality, its causal relationships, which are taken as part of its very nature. So these relationships lie open to the view of a pure perceiver who can see things as they are. Examples of these structural interdependences are the "*karma*" relationships (that volitions corrupted by desire and ignorance result in suffering) and the complex but necessary assemblage of types of element which go to make up the perception→craving→action sequence. These were put together in the systematic and in a sense comprehensive account of the causality of *saṃsāra* called conditioned-co-arising (*pratītyasamutpāda*). Of course, this was not a deterministic causal system. There is always the possibility of branching off on the path of freedom.

(3) General reflections on or conclusions about the nature of experience, as seen in terms of *dharmas*. The central observation is that nothing is to be seen, in this clear-sighted way of looking, except *dharmas*. The objects and most importantly the subjects with which the commonsense world is peopled are not to be found. All that is to be found is a complex stream of constantly changing yet multiple interdependent phenomena. "From the summit of the world downwards [the Buddha] could detect no self anywhere" (Conze, 1959, p. 50). The no-self doctrine is the most revolutionary and disturbing of the Buddha's insights – especially challenging to a Western individualism which at its extreme regards the personal self as a self-standing and self-sufficient entity, possessor of absolute rights and the source of all

value. As anyone who has tried to come to terms with it will testify, "no-self" operates in the mode of [C], as a disturber of all settled views, breaking through every attempt to systematize its implications, to work out a living accommodation with it. Experience is then unstable, constantly changing, devoid of subject and object, but it is by no means chaotic or meaningless. Interrelationships between *dharmas* are rule-governed, in principle predictable. Therefore, the normal course of events, the wheel of *saṃsāra*, can be understood and changed. If suffering results from, and is conditioned by, ignorance and desire, then the cessation of ignorance and desire must lead to the cessation of suffering. Understanding brings hope.

A specific example of the samsaric causality which is open to pure vision is that which leads to belief in the existence of persons – in particular, in "one's own" existence, as a long-lasting though changing entity, but also as a focus of value. Motivated by desire concerning a projected future, there is a synthetic construction of a being that endures from the present to the future and so can benefit from the satisfaction of desires. This pseudo-entity is constructed out of the short-lived, ever-changing *dharmas*. (Of course, the activity of construction has itself a merely dharmic reality.) Its origins in conditionality are then forgotten and it is seen as self-subsisting, the object of hopes and fears for the future.

(4) As I have pointed out, the overriding mode of rationality for a religious tradition is practical: "What must I do to be saved?" In the Four Noble Truths the rationality of seeing and understanding the causality of *saṃsāra*, of suffering, is put in this practical context. There is a way in which this causality can be brought to an end; there is a path to the end of suffering.

In the early texts, there is no doubt that these doctrines [B], described in (1) to (4) above, are represented as deriving from the Buddha's vision, his new way of experiencing. But once formulated, such a body of doctrines tends to acquire a life of its own, and there are certainly tasks of reformulation and systematization which may proceed independently of reference to the founding experience [A] – tasks not unlike those which may arise within an academic Western philosophical context. These would also include the formulation of philosophical arguments supporting the basic doctrines. In the early texts there are, for example, several arguments for the no-self doctrine – arguments that operate in different ways for different hearers (Collins, 1982, section 3.2). To non-Buddhists (with whom the Buddha often debated) the everyday concept of experience is used, in arguing (in a Humean way) that all of the experiences that we know of, all of our memories, can be classified as feelings, perceptions, consciousnesses, and so on, and nowhere is there the experience of a self. Of course, for the person on the path this is not so much an argument as a pointing to what is, in the very nature of the "vision," between subject and object. For such a person, the terms "feeling," "perception," and so on have shifted in meaning, no longer bearing their everyday implications of the existence of someone who feels, perceives, and is conscious. Other arguments test out the hearer's sense of what a self should be – if there were one. Surely a true self would be stable and unchanging; surely whatever is truly me should be completely under my control. But that which we ordinary people think of as ourselves changes from moment to moment. It is wildly out of our control, continually imposing upon us sickness and suffering – whatever we least desire. For the believer, this argument is a reminder of the true causality of suffering and of the fact that in the end, if "self" notions are given up, suffering can indeed be controlled.

III

As I said, doctrines [B] tend to acquire a life of their own. Within a few hundred years of the time of the Buddha, questions began to arise, even amongst the schools (*nikāyas*) themselves, about whether the detailed description of the *dharma*-world had become an enterprise detached from its true origins in [A]. In the terms of my introductory remarks, there was a danger of belief-rationality becoming dominant at the expense of tradition-rationality.

It was partly as a result of this disquiet, and also because of unease about possible misinterpretations of the Buddha's practical or moral teachings, that there came about a profound shift of doctrine. The Mahāyāna developments (Williams, 1989) constitute in some ways a complete change of scenery. Yet it seems to me that the claim that the tradition has a rational unity may be defended, if we see the new formulations as arising primarily from a new awareness of how the ENB ways of expressing the Buddha's founding discovery laid themselves open to misinterpretation. In the Prajñāpāramitā Sūtras, and in the Mādhyamika philosophical school founded by Nāgārjuna, radically new ways were found of expressing and articulating the founding discovery. Much of this may seem to be polemic against the concepts, doctrines and values of ENB, but it may also be seen instead as addressed to potential dangers and misinterpretations into which the ENB modes of expression might lead the shallow and unwary.

ENB *dharma*-theory was produced as a way of representing the "new world" revealed by the saving vision. It provided an alternative to the common sense metaphysics of a world of people liable to, and in fact immersed in, suffering. And in its new account of reality, closer to bare experience, it provided a justification for the abandonment of that common sense metaphysics. The shift was, in philosophical terms, a kind of reductivism: people are "nothing but" streams of interrelated *dharmas*. But for Mahāyāna thinkers, *dharma*-theory could be justified, if at all, not as an account of a brave new world, but as a means to the realization of no-self. The real import of the shift of thought was negative, the dissolution of self-belief. The danger of *dharma*-theory was that the "middleness" of the vision would be missed, and the subject–object duality, with *dharmas* as the object-world, reinstated. So the process [C] of dissolution of entities has to continue, to be applied to *dharmas* themselves. "No-self" has to be generalized, to become no self-being (*svabhāva*) – taken to mean no self-standing entities, no substantiality. Everything that might be thought of as an object is empty, empty of self-nature. Emptiness (*śūnyatā*) became a central characterization of this new way of thinking. It is not that emptiness is to be asserted as a new mysterious and ineffable reality, but rather the absence of *svabhāva* is to be extended without limit. There are no ultimate entities. Of course, the point of this relentless opposition to substantiality – which brought with it a reassessment, a new understanding, of all the traditional doctrines, even the Four Noble Truths – was not an ideal of intellectual purity. The corresponding soteriological path is a progressive and shocking deconstruction of any shelter in which one can look after oneself:

> In form, in feeling, will, perception and awareness
> Nowhere in them they find a place to rest on.
> Without a home they wander, *dharmas* never hold them
> Nor do they grasp at them.
> (quoted by Conze, 1973, pp. 9–10)

This iconoclasm is paralleled by Nāgārjuna in the terms of [B], the conceptual, doctrinal, philosophical. Here it takes the form of demonstrating the incoherence of the concepts that were fundamental to the ENB statements of doctrine (Kalupahana, 1986). For example, the Buddha's move away from ontology (he asserts neither existence nor non-existence) is standardly followed by a "teaching by the middle," conditionality – for example, that of the twelve links of conditioned co-arising. But how is conditionality to be understood in the absence of own-being? The normal assumption must be that it is a relation between things which can be identified independently of the relation. But the absence of own-being implies the absence of related things.

Similarly with *nirvāṇa*, the culminating concept of Buddhism, if it is beyond all the distinctions of the samsaric world, how may it still be related to that world? How may it be reached by a path, a causal process beginning in that world? In fact, if neither existence nor non-existence can be asserted of *nirvāṇa*, any more than of the samsaric world, if neither of them has any substantial reality, even their essential difference cannot be asserted.

What can we make of these moves? Do they indicate the abandonment of all rationality, the embracing of a sceptical nihilism, an anti-Buddhism? Rather they are a new attempt to convey the founding and saving vision, and to bring people to it by the middle way. *Nirvāṇa* is not distinct from the world as might be the loftiest of all heavens, a retreat to be striven for, in which the individual will himself be free of the suffering inherent in samsaric existence. To think thus is to have completely misunderstood the Buddha's teachings.

> It is because of his non-attainmentness that a Bodhisattva, through having relied on the perfection of wisdom, dwells without thought-coverings. In the absence of thought-coverings he has not been made to tremble, he has overcome what can upset, and in the end he attains to Nirvāṇa. (Conze, 1958, p. 93).

"Absence of thought-coverings": it is often said that Mādhyamika sees reality from an ultimate point of view, in which all distinctions collapse and therefore all concepts and words are idle. But of course the texts we have been considering do use words, do require precise and careful thought for their analysis and understanding, do need to be understood for them to have any saving effect. What they aim at is not the abandonment of thought, of doctrine, of the belief in the soteriological structure set out in the Four Noble Truths. Rather a new attitude to words is necessary, in which their usefulness, their necessity is acknowledged, but only so that one can see through them to what gives rise to them, but always surpasses and moves beyond them.

The Mahāyāna Yogācāra sub-tradition (Nagao, 1991) may, from the point of view of the rational unity of the Buddhist tradition as a whole, be seen as a synthesis of the two sub-traditions discussed so far. It takes seriously the developed *dharma*-theory of ENB, but also the Mādhyamika criticism of its dangers. Yogācāra attempts to obviate these dangers by giving a clear and positive account of the status of *dharmas*. The *dharma*-world is not a world of self-subsistent entities, but it does have a kind of reality. It is in a sense mental. Vasubandhu said (Anacker, 1984, p. 161) "In the Mahāyāna the three realms of existence [that is, the whole realm of *saṃsāra*] are determined as being perception-only (*vijñapti-mātra*)." These perceptions ("representation" is a more appropriate translation) are not mental events in the context of a mind/body duality. They are not representations *of* something existing externally and independently. The system is idealist, explaining experiences – mental events – as the causal consequences of other mental events, the desire-provoked motivations which alone have karmic potency. Samsaric experiences have a dual internal structure: being conscious, they are intentional, but their only objects are internal. So there is, as it were, a relational structure within representations, but the normally postulated relata, the substantial subject and the external object, are illusory.

The Yogācāra sub-tradition also takes seriously the Mādhyamika insights with respect to the relation between *saṃsāra* and *nirvāṇa*. Again a detailed positive account is presented, which wards off the accusation of nihilism, which might be made by the bewildered believer who sees all distinctions and seemingly all doctrines collapse into emptiness. (If *saṃsāra* is equivalent to *nirvāṇa*, what could possibly be the point of the practice of Buddhism?) This positive account is a three-fold ontological/epistemological analysis. What exists is *paratantra-svabhāva*, dependent nature. Here "dependent" means "conditioned", and refers to the flow of conditioned but insubstantial phenomena – what we may identify as the founding vision. Of course, this phenomenal reality is subject to false construction to produce the appearance of a world with external objects and perceiving subjects. This illusory world is implicitly believed in by the ordinary "person," who invests in it his hopes and fears, and whose life in it is one of deep-rooted suffering. This illusion of a dual world is the "constructed nature" (*parikalpita-svabhāva*). The third "nature" is *pariniṣpanna*, perfected. This is defined as the non-existence of the constructed nature. It may be thought of as the correct epistemological perspective on dependent nature. So *saṃsāra* and *nirvāṇa* are ontologically identical. They are both perspectives on an existing substratum – that "seen" in the vision. At the same time, of course, they are epistemologically distinct. It is this epistemological difference that gives point to the Buddhist path. However, the symmetry – the two views, samsaric and nirvanic, of the same reality – is not complete. First, the perfected "person's" *dharmas* are undefiled and so different in many ways from those which are constructed to form the ignorant person. Second, the notion of a perspective suggests a duality – of the viewer and what he views – which is quite inappropriate here. As can be seen, this is a sophisticated contribution to "the Buddhist tradition." It refers back to the founding discoveries and expresses them in a "middle" way that is designed to obviate the extremes of substantialism and of nihilism.

These systematic Yogācāra developments have as their point the effective teaching of the Buddha's message. That is, they aim to be "tradition-rational." But to serve this purpose, they must in themselves be coherent and well argued. That is, they must be "belief-rational."

IV

Finally, I shall comment on a problem of practical rationality that is common to several religious worldviews concerned with salvation: what is the relation between salvation and the demands of morality? "What must I do to be saved?" "(Amongst other things) be good." "But can this be real goodness, if it has an ulterior motive – that is. to achieve salvation for myself?" It must be a degradation of the idea of salvation, the culmination of all religious practice, to have it as a personal goal to which morality is only a means – thus making altruism serve the ends of egoism. In the Buddhist case (Katz, 1989), much of the new energy of Mahāyāna thought was directed against this degradation, this misinterpretation, of the Buddha's message. The polemic sometimes seems to focus on the ENB concept of the perfected person, the *arahant*, but its real concern is those who pervert this concept in a shallow and self-seeking way.

The question is really about the practical implications of the realization of no-self. In the early texts "*arahant*" was the term for those of the Buddha's followers who followed his path to its end, and acquired his saving knowledge. But the Buddha himself was often said to be an *arahant*, and there was little real distinction between "*arahant*" and "*buddha*." The Buddha in his life and death offered a two-part model of no-self. For several decades after his enlightenment he went about doing good, teaching people of his insights, giving them the opportunity to transcend suffering. Then his life came to an end; he was not reborn, but passed into a state about which he himself would say nothing, but which certainly was not in active contact with the world. The temptation for his followers was then to downgrade the "noble person" and the moral acting out of selflessness – to see this as a means, perhaps not even a necessary means, to the absolute cessation of samsaric existence.

As Theravāda commentators point out, to interpret the notion of *arahant* in this way is in no way true to the ENB understanding of the Buddha's message. But in any case, the Mahāyāna tradition was more explicit about the danger of a self-seeking attitude to the religious goal, and formulated a positive doctrine to avoid it. This was a new, or at least newly delineated, model of the perfected being, the *bodhisattva*, the enlightenment being. Compassion, suffering with and helping others is at the centre of this ideal.

The place of the *bodhisattva* ideal within the rational unity of the Buddhist tradition may be established from the following considerations. First, the fundamental teaching of conditionality shows the interdependence of all beings, including "people," who are falsely claimed to be independent, self-subsistent. Second, the Four Noble Truths focused the practice of the religion on one aim, that of the overcoming of suffering. These two claims together imply that what might appear to the beginner on the path to be his goal, the overcoming of his own suffering, must, when seen from the standpoint of wisdom, be generalized to the overcoming of the suffering of all beings capable of suffering. Only to the extent that this has been achieved is the path at its end.

Bibliography

Anacker, S. 1984: *Seven Works of Vasubandhu* (Delhi: Motilal Banarsidass).
Collins, Steven 1982: *Selfless Persons* (Cambridge: Cambridge University Press).
Conze, E. 1958: *Buddhist Wisdom Books* (London: George Allen & Unwin).
—— 1959: *Buddhist Scriptures* (Harmondsworth: Penguin).
—— 1962: *Buddhist Thought in India* (London: George Allen & Unwin).
Conze, E. (tr.) 1973: *The Perfection of Wisdom in 8,000 Lines and Its Verse Summary*. Bolinas: Four Seasons Foundation.
Jayatilleke, K. N. 1963: *Early Buddhist Theory of Knowledge* (London: George Allen & Unwin).
Kalupahana, D. J. 1986: *Nāgārjuna: the Philosophy of the Middle Way* (New York: State University of New York Press).
Katz, N. 1989: *Buddhist Images of Human Perfection* (Delhi: Motilal Banarsidass).
MacIntyre, Alasdair 1988: *Whose Justice? Which Rationality?* (London: Duckworth).
Nagao, G. 1991: *Mādhyamika and Yogācāra. A Study of Mahāyāna Philosophies* (New York: State University of New York Press).
Nyanaponika Thera 1965: *Abhidhamma Studies* (Kandy: Buddhist Publication Society).
Stcherbatsky, T. 1979: *The Central Conception of Buddhism and the Meaning of the Word "Dharma"* (Delhi: Motilal Banarsidass).
Williams, Paul 1989: *Mahāyāna Buddhism* (London and New York: Routledge).

31

Buddhist perspectives on ontological truth

MATTHEW KAPSTEIN

Propositional truth and ontological truth

The Sanskrit term most frequently rendered in English as "truth" is *satya*, which is derived from a form of the verb "to be" (*as*). This can be traced etymologically back to the ancient Indo-European copula, which is preserved also in Greek *eimi*, Latin *esse*, English *is*, and German *Sein*. The relationship between truth and being in Sanskrit is not just a discovery of modern linguistic science: Sanskrit grammarians, though not engaged in Indo-European historical linguistics, were always sensitive to the derivational principles of their own language, and they explain the term "*satya*" as being formed by the application of the suffix *ya* to *sat*, the present participle of the verb "to be." *Satya*, given a strong interpretation of the semantical influence of the derivational suffix, is therefore literally "what stands in relation to, has affinity with, being." Read more weakly, it is simply "what has being."

From the earliest times, Indian thinkers regarded speech as one of the things that, in some instances at least, could be characterized as *satya*, "related to being." The use of the epithet *satyavādī* – truth-speaker, one who "tells is like it is" (compare Kahn, 1978) – suggests that true speech was regarded as speech that discloses being through a correspondence thereto, a conception that was later given systematic expression in Hindu philosophical literature. That very early Indian thinkers sometimes did regard language as capable of standing in a relationship of correspondence or adequation to being is confirmed by even so ancient a work as the *Bṛhadāraṇyaka Upaniṣad* (ca. eighth century BCE), where the apparent impossibility of designating some objects – here *brahman* or *ātman* – in this manner had already become a topic of discussion. This emerges, for instance, in a particularly striking selection from that text:

> Uṣasta Cākrāyaṇa said: "This has been explained by you just as one might say, 'This is a cow, this is a horse.' Now explain to me the *brahman* that is immediately present and directly perceived, that is the self within all."
>
> "This is your self that is within all."
>
> "Which is within all, Yājñavalkya?"
>
> "You cannot see the seer of sight, you cannot hear the hearer of what's heard, you cannot think the thinker of the thought, you cannot know the knower of knowledge. He is your self which is within all. Everything else is wretched." (III.iv.2)

It is of considerable interest here, in a passage belonging to the germinal age in the history of Indian linguistics, that Uṣasta adopts a linguistic model to indicate what he considers to be an unsatisfactory explanation of *brahman*. He says not, "You have explained this as you explain cows," but rather, "... as one might say, 'This is a cow.' " The question thus is not merely one of seeking the "what," whereby the self may be identified, but equally of seeking the "how," the means in virtue of which the very identification itself becomes a possibility. How can language refer at all to that which has no determinate defining marks? It was with such questions, suggesting that the truths we may claim to know cannot all *be* of the same kind and in the same way, that the seed was planted for the eventual emergence of the theory of "two truths" (*satyadvaya*) that became prominent in much later Buddhist and Vedantic scholasticism, and to whose Buddhist versions we shall return below.

We may distinguish tentatively, then, between two differing ways of framing the question of truth, one of which, in a manner resembling the traditional Western conception of adequation, concerns the relationship between a propositional entity (for instance, a knowledge-claim, a thought or a statement) and something, of whatever type, that obtains in the world. This we term "propositional truth." Beyond this, however, one may inquire into the relationship between that which so obtains and the modalities of being itself. This involves what we call "ontological truth." These two conceptions permit us to make sense of many philosophical assertions – particularly in Indian and ancient philosophy – that otherwise sometimes seem paradoxical, and to see that they are in fact relatively straightforward. We may say, for instance, that it is true that there is a mirage in the desert but that the mirage is false – meaning, of course, that the person who reports a mirage when one in fact appears reports truly, though the mirage is nevertheless a deceptive appearance. Modern Western philosophy has tended to attempt to reduce confusion here by separating the two conceptions, so that the second is no longer generally discussed in terms of "truth" at all, but rather in terms of "being" or "reality." For this reason, in some contexts contemporary scholars of Indian and Buddhist thought have preferred to translate *satya* as "reality." This is not usually objectionable, though one loses in this way an explicit reminder of the rich continuities linking – for much of classical Indian thought, as for many aspects of classical Western thought – the realms of what we are calling the propositional and the ontological. Therefore we maintain here the use of the world "truth," leaving context alone in most cases to clarify the intended usage sufficiently.

The truth(s) of Indian Buddhism

Throughout the history of Buddhism in India the paradigmatic notion of "truth" was revealed in the teaching of the "Four Noble Truths" (*catvāri āryasatyāni*). Even so late a philosopher as Mokṣākaragupta (twelfth century), separated from the age of the Buddha by no less a span of time than was Luther from Jesus, in his exposition of the peculiar mode of perception or knowledge possessed uniquely by the insightful sage, refers to the Four Noble Truths as the "genuine objective," contemplation of which is productive of the knowledge in question (Singh, 1988, p. 24). When we inquire into what "truth" meant to Indian Buddhists, therefore, we would do well to begin by asking, what sort of "truth" is intended when one speaks of "Four Noble Truths"?

The discourse in which the Buddha first reveals his teaching of the Four Truths is reported universally to have been his first sermon. In the *Sutta on the Turning of the Wheel of the Doctrine* (*Dhammacakkappavattanasutta*) of the Pali canon, for instance, the crucial passage with which we are here concerned reads as follows:

> Now this, o monks, is suffering, a noble truth: birth is suffering; aging is suffering; illness is suffering; death is suffering; coming in contact with what is unpleasant is suffering; separation from what is pleasant is suffering; not getting what one desires is suffering; in short, the five acquisitive aggregates are suffering. Now this, o monks, is the origination of suffering, a noble truth: it is this thirst, causing further birth, accompanied by delight and desire, taking pleasure here and there, namely, erotic thirst, thirst for being, thirst for annihilation. Now this, o monks, is the cessation of suffering, a noble truth: it is that thirst's cessation due to dispassion without remainder, its abandonment, releasement, liberation, removal. Now this, o monks, is the path conducing to the cessation of suffering, a noble truth: it is this eight-limbed path, namely, correct view, correct intention, correct speech, correct limits on action, correct livelihood, correct effort, correct presence of mind, correct meditation. (Anderson, 1917, pp. 66–7)

It seems uncertain that the term "truth" is used univocally in these passages. The manner in which the first truth, that of suffering, is expressed, suggests above all a propositional conception of truth: the truth of suffering is articulated in propositions of the form *X* is suffering, *Y* is suffering, and so on. But in the case of the second truth, that of the origination of suffering, it is a particular property, "thirst," that is identified with the truth in question; and in the third the cessation of that property. Finally, the fourth truth embodies a recommended course of action. "Truth," therefore, would appear to be what is really the case, or a fact about the world, or an appropriate course of human action, or else it is a proposition or assertion corresponding to such a reality or fact or action. "Noble truths" are those truths, contemplation of which culminates in the attainment of the status of a "noble" in the classical Buddhist sense, that is, one whose final liberation is secure.

In the scholastic literature of early Buddhism a distinction is sometimes made between those terms or statements which are of "ultimate significance" (*paramattha*) and those which are matters only of "conventional usage" (*sammuti*). Thus, for instance, the *Questions of Milinda* (*Milindapañha*, second century BCE) paraphrasing here earlier scholastic writings: "In an ultimate sense, no person is apprehended . . . 'there is a being' is conventional usage" (*Milindapañha*, p. 21). It is this distinction that, refined and further developed, becomes a distinction of "two truths." Nāgārjuna (second century CE) introduces it thus:

> Relying on two truths is the Dharma-instruction of the Buddhas:
> The truth of the world's conventional usage, and the truth in an ultimate sense.
>
> (*Mūlamadhyamakakārika*, 24.8)

Though I do not accept the general thesis of those who seek to disassociate Nāgārjuna from the Mahāyāna schools of Buddhism (see, for example, Warder, 1973, pp. 78–88), I can see no reason not to take the technical terms in this verse as meaning just what they do in the tradition represented by the *Questions of Milinda*. It is true that Pali *sammuti* is here represented by Sanskrit *saṃvṛti*, but, as will become apparent below, that should not in itself convince us that any semantic shift has yet taken place.

The context of Nāgārjuna's verse also requires some comment. In occurs in the middle of his discussion of the Four Noble Truths, and is clearly introduced here, as it had been in the *Questions of Milinda*, to provide a metalinguistic device through which to interpret differing, apparently incompatible, assertions of doctrine, in this case the teaching of emptiness and that of the Four Truths. The two truths can plausibly be regarded as originally hermeneutical categories, and not as a metaphysical theory at all, much less a theory about the general concept of "truth." Nonetheless, it would appear that during the first centuries of the common era, Buddhist scholiasts came inceasingly to regard the two truths as a scheme parallelling, or supplementing, that of the Four Noble Truths. Vasubandhu (fifth century) writes:

> Four truths were uttered by the Lord, and also two truths: the truth of conventional usage and the truth of ultimate significance. What is the defining characteristic of those two? [The response is given in a verse:]
>
> With reference to some thing, upon there being a breaking up or
> mental reduction [of it] to other [constituent elements],
> should no perception of that [thing then remain],
> It is truth of conventional usage; otherwise, truth of ultimate
> significance.
>
> (*Abhidharmakośam*, pp. 889–90)

In the commentary which follows, Vasubandhu makes clear, however, that he conceives of truth primarily according to a linguistic paradigm: *satyam evāhur na mṛṣā*, "they speak truth, indeed, not lies." And Yaśomitra, in his subcommentary (which quotes in full the verse of Nāgārjuna that we have already cited above), glosses *saṃvṛti* with the expression *saṃvyavahāreṇa*, "according to common usage."

If Nāgārjuna's explicit doctrine of the two truths can thus be plausibly understood as a variant on early Buddhist scholastic usage, it seems nevertheless possible to hold that his teaching as a whole necessitated a transformation in the understanding of that doctrine (see Nagao, 1989). Indeed, the later history of Mahāyāna thought, above all within the Mādhyamika tradition stemming from Nāgārjuna, reveals a deepening and ever-widening preoccupation with the problem of the two truths. The history is long and complex, but due to recent progress in the study of the history of Indian Mādhyamika philosophy, many significant details have now come into view (see Williams, 1989, ch. 3). It will not be possible to survey this material at all within the limits of the present essay; so to adduce the great changes that were to take place, we shall leap ahead to the final phase in the history of Indian Mādhyamika, and consider briefly some of the remarks on the two truths found in Prajñākaramati's (tenth or eleventh century) commentary on Śāntideva's (seventh century) *Introduction to Enlightened Conduct* (*Bodhicāryāvatāra*). In most respects, this follows the tradition of Nāgārjuna's great commentator Candrakīrti (ca. 600 CE). Śāntideva's evocative verses, the comments on which will concern us here, are these:

> Convention and ultimate significance – this is thought to be the pair of truths.
> Reality belongs not to the field of intellect; for intellect is said to be conventional usage. 9.2.
> In this case the world is twofold: there are the adepts and the commoners.
> Here the common world is defeated by the adept's world. 9.3.
> Defeated, too, according to distinction of thought, are the adepts in ascending succession. 9.4ab.
>
> (*Bodhicāryāvatāraḥ*, pp. 170–8)

A superficial resemblance with Plato's parable of the Cave (*Republic*, VII, 514) will be noticed immediately. As the condition of the prisoners is separated from that of the realizer of the "Idea of the Good" by an intervening realm in which one has turned painfully away from the shadows flickering on the wall, so here the commoner who knows only convention is separated from the realizer of the truth of ultimate significance by a hierarchically ordered realm of adepts, who, though free from the constraints of the commoner, have not yet realized that reality that is the truth of ultimate significance. Thus, the apparent bivalence of the two truths notwithstanding, the scheme, as presented here, can be made out to comport rather well with the Platonic progression from that which merely appears to be "true" or "unhidden" – Plato's *alethes*, Śāntideva's *saṃvṛtisatya* – through that which is "more true" – *alethestera, yogīsaṃvṛti* – to that which is "most true" – *to alethestaton, paramārthasatya*. Let us turn now to Prajñākaramati's discussions of the essential concept of the two truths.

Prajñākaramati opens his comments on verse 9.2 by explaining the term *saṃvṛti*, so far translated as "conventional usage." He writes:

> *Saṃvṛti* is so-called because by it the comprehension of what is as it is is concealed, or occluded, by reason of the occlusion of essential being, and by reason of occluded

> disclosure. Ignorance, stupefaction and error are synonyms [for *saṃvṛti*]. For ignorance, being the imputation of the forms of non-existing things, and of the nature of occlusion of the vision of inherent being, is *saṃvṛti*. (*Bodhicāryāvatāraḥ*, p. 170)

Thus "concealment" has displaced "convention" as the primary signification of *saṃvṛti*. This late Mādhyamika interpretation of *saṃvṛti*, it should be emphasized, is etymologically correct: the root-form from which it is derived, *saṃ-vṛ*, means essentially "to cover over, to close." Hence, "closing of the throat, articulation" (and thus "convention"), but also "concealment." That Mādhyamika thinkers came in time to emphasize the latter signification was a historical decision, linguistically correct to be sure, but not delivered to them by the language even prior to their reflection upon it (see Nagao, 1991, ch. 2).

Prajñākaramati's discussion of *paramārtha* reveals a subtle intermingling of two themes that had been associated with this term from antiquity. On the one hand, following a tradition established in the analytical aspects of Abhidharma thought (that is, early Buddhist scholasticism), as represented above primarily in the selection from Vasubandhu, it is that which is ultimately real, that which is not destroyed through a reductive analytical procedure. For Vasubandhu this meant that it was paradigmatically two sorts of things: physical atoms and phenomenal atoms or *dharmas*. For Prajñākaramati, as a Mādhyamika thinker, analysis can find no such points of termination; it must be pursued until it reveals the radical contingency of all conditioned phenomena, their ultimate emptiness:

> The ultimate, highest, significance, is . . . the uncontrived form of things owing to the comprehension of which there is the abandonment of affliction that is bound up with all dispositions [involving] obscuration. It is the absence of the inherent being of all *dharmas*, [their] emptiness, just-so-ness, genuine limit, the sphere of the highest principle – these are among its synonyms. (*Bodhicāryāvatāraḥ*, p. 171)

Analytical ultimacy here is closely associated with soteriological ultimacy – at the limit of analysis there is an "abandonment of affliction". While the Buddhist tradition seems to have always associated the two, the later Mādhyamika tradition accentuates this in a manner that is in certain respects to be distinguished from the earlier tradition. For *paramārtha* can mean not just "ultimate significance" in an analytic sense, but equally it can stand for *paramapuruṣārtha* – that is, the highest end of man, *mokṣa*, liberation. In the tradition represented by Prajñākaramati, there is an apparently perfect convergence between these notions. One result is that the two truths scheme is no longer essentially a hermeneutical device used to interpret Four Truths discourse. Nor is it merely an alternative classificatory scheme. Rather, the two truths embrace and include the Four Noble Truths themselves:

> Four Noble Truths have been explained in the Abhidharma by the Lord, whose defining characteristics are suffering, origination, cessation and the path. How, therefore, can there be just two truths? . . . [I]t is because of their being included in the two. In

> this manner the truths of suffering, origination, and the path, being essentially concealment, are included in the truth of concealment, and the truth of cessation in the truth of ultimate significance. Thus there is no contradiction [between the two schemes]. (*Bodhicāryāvatāraḥ*, p. 175)

The doctrine of two truths, having assumed an all-embracing character, begins to look increasingly like a general doctrine of truth. But we have not yet said how truth, *satya*, is here to be understood. In particular, if *saṃvṛti* is concealment, occlusion, then in what sense is it *satya*, truth, at all?

> *Saṃvṛti* is one truth, inerrant, and *paramārtha* is the other truth. "And" conjoins them as being equivalent insomuch as they are just truth. Here, the truth of concealment is the non-inadequate form of [that is, adhered to by] the common world. The truth of ultimate significance is the incorrigible reality of [that is, realized by] the nobles. (*Bodhicāryāvatāraḥ*, p. 174)

The world of common experience, including its linguistic and cognitive experiences, is thus true just insofar as it is not actually falsified. Its "truth" is not a question of adequation, but rather of non-inadequation: whether my concept of a vase involves a relationship of adequation to that vase, in the Aristotelian-Scholastic sense, can never be established, but the Mādhyamika's notion of non-inadequation (*avitatha*, lit, "non-not-thus") is no mere double negation of the Western scholastic concept. So long as my concept of the vase is not defeated in experience, it is not inadequate. In quotidian life that is generally all the truth we need. Prajñākaramati adds:

> It may be [objected], how is it that *saṃvṛti*, being of the nature of what is revealed in ignorance, and which is devastated by hundreds of investigations, because it is of the nature of imputations of what is not, is truth? This too *is* truth. It is spoken of as the "truth of concealment" in that it is a determination of the common world. For it is the world that is here the truth of concealment. In conformity with it, the Lord too has just so spoken [in terms of] that truth of concealment, without reference to those seeking reality. Hence, the qualification "and the truth of the world's conventional usage" has been asserted by the venerable teacher [Nāgārjuna]. But, in reality, ultimate significance is the only truth. (*Bodhicāryāvatāraḥ*, p. 175)

Conventional truth, in short, is pragmatically justified and so valued. Like Newtonian mechanics, which though false may be regarded as "true" for the purposes of investigating relatively small parts of the physical universe, conventional truth is true whenever it suffices for the purposes at hand. (Although unlike the example from physics, this is not a matter of approximation.) Thus so long as the ultimate has not been realized, the dialectic of the two truths must be posited. In the final analysis, however, for the sage who has realized the ultimate, the truth can only be one. The theory of the two truths, therefore, belongs to the very domain of the conventional that ultimately it undermines.

The two truths beyond India

The spread of the Buddha's teaching throughout much of Asia in late antiquity and the early medieval period brought with it a great proliferation of new philosophical approaches, reflecting in part the efforts of thinkers to assimilate the doctrine to the requirements of diverse communities and cultures. The richness of these developments as they bear upon the conception of the two truths cannot be adequately reflected here, but to exemplify them in part we shall briefly consider some salient innovations articulated by philosophers of the Mahāyāna in China, Japan and Tibet.

We may begin by observing that, despite the many pronounced differences between the East Asian Buddhist traditions (including those of China and Japan), that relied upon the Buddhist scriptures and philosophical treatises as they had been translated into classical Chinese, and the Tibetan Buddhist schools, that followed distinctive scriptural canons in literary Tibetan, both were united in their puzzlement concerning *the relationship between the two truths*. We have seen already that Indian sources provided no simple solution to this problem, and so it is not surprising that it would generate considerable interest when the difficulties to which it gave rise were compounded by issues of translation and transmission across linguistic and cultural boundaries.

One of the most daring solutions to the problem was proposed by the Chinese monk and scholar Chih-i (538–597), whose teachings formed the basis for the T'ien-t'ai (in Japanese, Tendai) school of Buddhism. What Chih-i proposed was to resolve the dialectical tension of the two truths by positing a third truth. In its essential structure, then, Chih-i's theory very roughly reminds us of the Hegelian conception of the *synthesis*, that arises from the dialectical opposition of *thesis* and *antithesis*. It is a theory with its own distinctive twist, however, as is made clear by Neal Donner, a contemporary scholar of Buddhism:

> [T]he third truth is generated from the other two by regarding them as extremes, dialectically reconciled in the middle truth. That things *are* is the first truth (provisional); that they are *not* is the second (ultimate); and that they *both* are and are not, as well as *neither* are nor are not, is the third truth, considered necessary by Chih-i in order to avoid the extreme of negation into which he perceived many of those falling who clung to the doctrine of emptiness as an ultimate. . . . The third or middle truth, expressible as above in two equivalent ways ("both" and "neither") is not truly a compromise, a "middle way" between extremes as we might think, but instead emphasizes that paradoxical nature of reality: that the truth cannot be reduced to a single formulation. (Donner, 1987, p. 205)

Chih-i's three truth theory, however, did not meet a favorable reception in all quarters. It invited, among others, the objections that by identifying the ultimate with the "not," Chih-i had misunderstood the second truth, and that by propounding a third truth he had failed to grasp the significance of complete freedom from conceptual alternatives. Thus, for instance, Kūkai (or Kōbō daishi, 774–835), the founder of the Shingon school of esoteric Buddhism in Japan, clearly suggested that

Chih-i, though deriving his teaching partly from that of Nāgārjuna, had not really comprehended the depths of the latter's insights (Kūkai, 1972, p. 210). Kūkai's own view of the two truths was, by contrast, elaborated primarily on the basis of the esoteric teachings he championed. Though it will not be possible to introduce his complicated system here in a satisfactory manner, we must note that, in esoteric Buddhist practice, in contrast to other approaches to Buddhist meditation, there is a powerful emphasis on ritual performance and positive symbolism (including visual imagery, incantation and gesture). In this approach, emptiness suffuses the brilliance of divine and sacred forms, and these, in turn, are identified with the manifest nature of living beings. Expressing this in relation to the doctrine of two truths, Kūkai paraphrases a passage from Nāgārjuna:

> In Buddhism there are two standards of truth, that is the conventional truth and the ultimate truth. For the conventional truth it is explained that there are sentient beings. For the ultimate truth it is explained that there are no sentient beings at all. But here again there are two standards. For those who do not know the characteristics of expression and esoteric symbols, it is explained that from the points of view of the ultimate truth there are no sentient beings; and for those who know the characteristics of expression and esoteric symbols, it is explained that from the point of view of the ultimate truth there are sentient beings. (Kūkai, 1972, p. 260)

Kūkai's conception here is similar to that of some of the esoteric traditions of Tibetan Buddhism, which speak in this context of a "coalescence of appearance and emptiness" (*snang-stong zung-'jug*). A recent doctrinal manual of the Nyingmapa (Rnying-ma-pa) tradition, for example, states:

> The body of reality according to the vehicle of dialectics has fallen into the extreme of emptiness, whereas the body of reality according to the mantras [that is, esoteric Buddhism] does not fall into extremes of eternalism and nihilism since there is no dichotomy between appearance and emptiness. (Dudjom Rinpoche, 1991, Vol. 1, p. 144)

Passages such as these, however, are deliberately framed to reflect the polemic of certain proponents of the esoteric traditions against the dialecticians (in Kūkai's words "those who do not know characteristics of expression and esoteric symbols"), and so to some extent stereotype the viewpoint of the latter. But, by contrast, the dialectical traditions of Tibetan Buddhism, basing themselves upon the close study of the writings of the Indian philosophical masters, arrived at a whole range of differing interpretations of the two truths, while seeking to avoid those perspectives characterized as "extreme." Among these interpretations the most controversial, certainly, was propounded by Dol-po-pa (Shes-rab-rgyal-mtshan, 1292–1361), who was famous for his peculiar doctrine of the "extrinsic emptiness" (*gzhan-stong*) of the absolute, that is to say, its emptiness with respect to all relative or conventional phenomena, that are thus extrinsic to its proper nature (see Ruegg, 1963). Entailed by this doctrine is a radical division between the two truths: the nature of the absolute is such that relative reality is in some sense wholly other. The following comments are drawn from Dol-po-pa's remarkable essay on the two truths:

> The defining characteristic of relative truth is that it is an object of consciousness that in its fundamental nature is itself essentially empty of veridical being, while the defining characteristic of absolute truth is that it is an object of authentic, sublime gnosis that in its fundamental nature is itself essentially not empty of veridical being. . . .
>
> Because the relative does not exist in fact, it is intrinsically empty, and appears to consciousness but not to gnosis. Because the absolute exists in fact, it is not intrinsically empty, but is extrinsically empty, and appears to gnosis but never at all to consciousness. . . .
>
> Thus, to those who are childish, according to their own dispositions, only inauthentic characteristics appear, but not the authentic suchness, and in the same way, to the bodhisattvas, according to their own dispositions, only the authentic appears, but not what is inauthentic. (Dol-po-pa, 1992–3, pp. 812–15)

Dol-po-pa's views were hotly contested by those who thought they amounted to a form of radical dualism. His most vociferous opponents even charged that he was a covert adherent of the Hindu Sāṃkhya philosophy! Among those who articulated opposing interpretations of the teaching of two truths, the renowned Tsong-kha-pa (Blo-bzang-grags-pa, 1357–1419), founder of the Gelukpa (Dge-lugs-pa) school that would later dominate Tibetan Buddhism, sought to re-emphasize an essentially dialectical conception of their relation (see Tauscher, 1995). A successor to his teaching, the Mongolian cleric Ngak-wang-bel-den (Ngag-dbang-dpal-ldan, b. 1779), summarizes the reasons for regarding the radical separation of the two truths as unacceptable:

> If the two truths were different entities, then (1) the mind realizing the emptiness of true existence would not overcome the conception of true existence; (2) the emptiness of true existence of a form would not be the mode of abiding of that form; (3) the non-affirming negative that is the mere excluder . . . of the true existence of a form would not be the real nature of that form; and (4) Buddha[s] . . . would see forms as truly existent and would see emptiness as truly existent separately. (Newland, 1992, p. 65)

The supposition here is that the extreme bifurcation proposed by Dol-po-pa effectively establishes the metaphysical equivalence of the two truths. Thus, for instance, to conceive that something exists veridically and to realize its emptiness ((1) above) are no longer contradictories, one negating the other, but are now independent intentions directed upon disparate objects (the veridical existence of *x* and the emptiness of the veridical existence of *x*). Such a theory of the two truths, far from revealing to us a soteriologically valuable dialectic, leaves us with the unedifying vision of two mutually exclusive, but somehow compresent, orders of being, in which our discovery of a higher truth does nothing to overturn our previous unknowing. The central ontological and epistemological dimensions of the two truths theory, as understood in Tsong-kha-pa's tradition, have been well-summarized by Jeffrey Hopkins:

> [T]he division of the two truths is not an ontological division. Both exist only conventionally . . . with *saṃvṛti* here referring to a valid dualistic cognizer; both truths exist for valid dualistic cognizers and not in ultimate analysis. The division of the two truths emphasizes two types of objects of consciousness, truths and falsities. Both, however, are falsely existent or falsely established because neither is independent; each depends on its imputing consciousness and on the other. . . .
>
> The division into two truths on epistemological grounds is a call to eradicate ignorance and to attain the highest wisdom. It is a call to recognition that a conventional cognizer, even if valid with respect to the existence or non-existence of objects, is not valid with respect to their suchness. It is a call to a new mode of perception, to a cognition of a reality that has been ever-present, (Hopkins, 1983, pp. 418–19)

As Hopkins's reference to "a cognition of a reality" makes clear, however, there are some strong ontological commitments at work here, despite the refusal to countenance an ultimate ontological basis for the distinction between the two truths themselves. Perhaps we may say that, on this account, the dialectic of the two truths discloses ontological truth, which involves nothing to be posited over and against the dual aspect of its disclosure.

Concluding reflections

Realists, as the late B. K. Matilal remarked in a critique of Mādhyamika thought, tend to be "rather suspicious of such bifurcation of truths into two levels." He continued to argue, however, that "such criticism misses the mark if we do not take into account the soteriological significance of the doctrine" (Matilal, 1973. p. 57). The theory of the two truths thus provides a means to interpret the apparent contradictions that obtain between the Buddha's conventional and practical teachings, on the one hand, and the insights that are only to be realized by the most accomplished and perceptive of disciples, on the other. Moreover, by accepting that convention had the status of a sort of truth, and was not to be regarded as sheer falsehood, a bridge was effectively established along which those receptive to the teaching might be guided until they themselves arrived at the highest realization.

As an approach to the role of the two truths theory in Buddhist discourse, such a view of the matter is not without merit, but it sidesteps, I believe, a crucial question: besides its utility for the soteriologies of particular religious traditions, is there any good reason for us to countenance the theory *philosophically*? For, as we are all aware, there are many specific religious doctrines (that of the virgin birth among Christians, or of the sanctity of the Sabbath among Jews, for instance) that we regard as certainly significant in their proper contexts, but that seldom command sustained philosophical discussion outside of those contexts. If all we can say for the theory of two truths is that it was useful for the soteriologies of Buddhism, Vedānta and some similar traditions, then we may be implicitly *removing* it from the sphere of philosophy after all.

Now, it seems often to be the case that philosophically valued questions are those that neither yield a precise solution, nor permit themselves to be easily dismissed (for example, by recognizing the supposed problem to have been based only on the misuse of language). To redeploy a metaphor of W. V. O. Quine, philosophical problems are like recurring itches, that will not go away when left alone, and are at best only momentarily relieved by scratching. Recalling now the Platonic theory of knowledge (as in the famous example of the divided line), Kant's conception of phenomena and noumena, the appearance–reality distinction in Hegelians like Bradley and Royce, or the abyss dividing commonsense realism from contemporary physical theory, it seems plausible to regard our problem as one connected with some of our most persistent philosophical itches. For in these and many other instances we find ourselves confronted with the apparent dichotomy between the truth as we think we know it, and the possibility of discovering that that cannot be the truth in fact. For this reason, it seems that often we must entertain something like a two truths theory, even if in the end, like soap, we have to rinse it away with the soil it was intended to cleanse. To put the point in somewhat different terms, every science can be said to have its own soteriology.

Gadjin Nagao rightly expresses caution regarding the application of the concept of "ontology" to Mādhyamika thought, but concludes, "[I]f an ontology of a Buddhist kind is to be considered seriously, then it would have to be based, not on an ontology of 'being' – that is, not in an ontic sense, but on transcending both existence and non-existence – that is, in the movement towards *śūnyatā*. In other words, ontology in a Buddhism [sic] context is not an ontology of 'being,' but that of *śūnyatā*" (Nagao, 1991, p. 187). With this in mind, the puzzling aspect of the two truths theory is underscored when we return to the notions of propositional and ontological truth introduced earlier. For the two truths theory appears, in its form, to be a theory of ontological truth, that is, a theory about how things are, but at the same time, in order to discuss it at all, we must entertain it propositionally. In such a framework, however, the theory must result in paradox, because propositional truth operates wholly within the sphere of the conventional. That is to say, assuming the two truths theory to be true, then any statement of the form "thus-and-such theory of truth is true" can be true only conventionally, never ultimately. But supposing the theory to be false, we must countenance the probability that much of what we think we know is not in any sense "true," but false *simpliciter*.

Such an approach to two truths discourse is perhaps descriptive of a type of dialectic in which thought frequently finds itself – a dialectic that involves the criticism of assumed truths in an effort to refine knowledge to a higher degree. Though this, in its generalities at least, is not deeply objectionable, we may still wish to hold that, *per impossibile*, were we perfect cognizers, our thought would never need be involved in such a dialectic at all. From the perspective of a perfect cognizer, it will be urged, the truth of things must be one. As we have seen above, some Buddhist thinkers – Prajñākaramati and Tsong-kha-pa were examples – arrived at just this conclusion. And it is a conclusion that, within the domain of conventional truth, appears to be entirely reasonable.

Note

The present paper is in part based upon my earlier article "The Trouble with Truth: Heidegger on *Alētheia*, Buddhist Thinkers on *Satya*," *Journal of the Indian Council of Philosophical Research*, 9, 2 (1992), pp. 69–85, in which some of the topics raised here are examined from an explicitly comparative perspective. I wish to thank Professor Daya Krishna (Jaipur) and Professor David Seyfort Ruegg (London) for their comments to me about it, contributing to the discussion offered here.

Bibliography

Anderson, Dines 1917: *A Pāli Reader*, Pt I (Copenhagen).

Dol-po-pa 1992–3: *Bden gnyis gsal ba'i nyi ma* [The Sun Illuminating the Two Truths] in *The 'Dzamthang Edition of the Collected Works of Kun-mkhyen Dol-po-pa Shes-rab-rgyal-mtshan*, collected and presented by Matthew Kapstein, Vol. 5 (series Vol. vii) (New Delhi: Shedrup Books and Sherab Drimey).

Donner, Neal 1987: "Sudden and Gradual Intimately Conjoined: Chih-i's Tien-t'ai View,' in *Sudden and Gradual: Approaches to Enlightenment in Chinese Thought*, Studies in East Asian Buddhism 5, ed. Peter N. Gregory (Honolulu: University of Hawaii Press).

Dudjom Rinpoche and Jikdrel Yeshe Dorje 1991: *The Nyingma School of Tibetan Buddhism: Its Fundamentals and History*, tr. Gyurme Dorje and Matthew Kapstein, 2 Vols (London: Wisdom Publications).

Dvārikādāsaśāstrī, Svāmī (ed.) 1972: *Abhidharmakośam*, Bauddha Bharati Series 7, Vol. 3 (Varanasi).

—— 1979: *Milindapañho*, Bauddha Bharati Series 13 (Varanasi).

Hopkins, Jeffrey 1983: *Meditation on Emptiness* (London: Wisdom Publications).

Kahn, Charles H. 1978: "Linguistic Relativism and the Greek Project of Ontology," in *The Question of Being*, ed. Mervyn Sprung (University Park: Pennsylvania State University Press, 1978), pp. 31–44.

Kapstein, Matthew 1992: "The Trouble with Truth : Heidegger on *Alētheia*, Buddhist Thinkers on *Satya*," *Journal of the Indian Council of Philosophical Research*, 9, 2, pp. 69–85.

Kūkai 1972: "The Precious Key to the Secret Treasury" and "The Meanings of the Word *Hūṃ*," in *Kūkai: Major Works*, ed. Yoshito S. Hakeda (New York: Columbia University Press).

Matilal, Bimal Krishna 1973: "A Critique of the Mādhyamika Position," in *The Problem of Two Truths in Buddhism and Vedānta*, ed. Mervyn Sprung (Dordrecht: D. Reidel).

Nagao, Gadjin M. 1989: *The Foundational Standpoint of Mādhyamika Philosophy*, tr. John P. Keenan (Albany: State University of New York Press).

—— 1991: *Mādhyamika and Yogācāra*, tr, Leslie S. Kawamura (Albany: State University of New York Press).

Newland, Guy 1992: *The Two Truths* (Ithaca: Snow Lion Publications).

Ruegg, David Seyfort 1963: "The Jo naṅ pas: a School of Buddhist Ontologists according to the Grub mtha' śel gyi me loṅ," *Journal of the American Oriental Society*, 83, pp. 73–91.

Singh, B. N. (ed.) 1988: *Tarkabhāṣā: a Manual of Buddhist Logic* (Varanasi: Asha Prakashan).

Tauscher, Helmut 1995: *Die Lehre von den Zwei Wirklichkeiten in Tsoṅ kha pas Madhyamaka-Werken*, Wiener Studien zur Tibetologie und Buddhismiskunde 36 (Vienna: Arbeitskreis für Tibetische und Buddhistische Studien Universität Wien).

Vaidya, P. L. (ed.) 1960a: *Bodhicāryāvatāraḥ*, also containing commentary by Prajñākaramati, Buddhist Sanskrit Texts 12 (Darbhanga: Mithila Institute).

—— 1960b: *Madhyamakaśāstram*, containing *Mūlamadhyamakakārikā*, Buddhist Sanskrit Texts 18 (Darbhanga: Mithila Institute).

Warder, A. K. 1973: "Is Nāgārjuna a Mahāyānist?," in *The Problem of Two Truths in Buddhism and Vedānta*, ed. Mervyn Sprung (Dordrecht: D. Reidel).

Williams, Paul 1989: *Mahāyāna Buddhism: the Doctrinal Foundations* (London: Routledge).

THE ISLAMIC TRADITION

32

Truth and Islamic thought

ANDREY SMIRNOV

The problem of truth was raised in medieval Islamic philosophy within the framework of discussions starting from the question of whether our knowledge corresponds to the "actuality of affairs." The notion of validity thus elaborated was comprehended as a quality of knowledge established through a comparison with "matters of fact." What was intended is not coincidence with what *is* and *has existence*. Existence (*wujūd*) was generally understood in Islamic thought as one of the attributes (*ṣifa*) that a thing might or might not possess while still being "a thing" (*shayʾ*), and since our knowledge embraces things independently of their accidental attributes, the question about truth was placed on a wider footing. Validity, from that point of view, testifies that our knowledge conforms with reality in the immediate meaning of the term – *thing-ness*. This notion of reality (*shayʾiyya*) does not necessarily exclude Divinity, for God in Islamic sciences is often comprehended as The Thing, although different in every respect (except that of *thing-ness*) from all other things. The concept of "thing" serves to introduce something into the current of intellectual discourse rather than to state anything definite about it; to be a thing – that is, fixed and established – means to enter the field of discussion.

Validity as affirmation of conformity with reality was referred to as *ṣidq* (veracity, truth) or *taṣdīq* (certification of truth). The "actuality of affairs" to which our knowledge conforms was comprehended also as a sort of "authenticity," and the corresponding term *ḥaqīqa* may be rendered into English as "truth" as well. Thus verification is carried out by comparing our knowledge to the "truth of things," and if the result is positive, knowledge is "true (*ṣādiq*); if not, it is "false" (*kādhib*). Knowledge is valid by virtue of its coincidence with the truth of things, while the truth of the latter needs no verification. It follows from the fact of their "being affirmed": they just "are there" as "fixed" and "true." The ideas of truth, fixity and thing are closely linked in Arabic. The term "thing" (*shayʾ*) is usually explained as "something that is established" (*thābit*), and the root *ḥ-q-q*, from which "truth" (*ḥaqīqa*) is derived, renders the same meaning. (For example, *ḥaqq* means both "true" and "unshakable.")

The problem of truth was raised rather early in Islamic thought, and already the al-Rawāfiḍ discussed it. As al-Ashʿarī informs us, most of them maintained that all human knowledge is "necessitated" (*iḍṭirār*). From their point of view, a person is not free to acquire true knowledge or to reject the false; moreover, knowledge about the falsity or validity of our knowledge also cannot be obtained at our will. This argument proceeded from the general assumption that all human deeds are "forced" (*iḍṭirār*). At the same time, some of the al-Rawāfiḍ considered the human mind able to receive true knowledge independently, for example, to learn of God's unity (*tawḥīd*) before the prophets inform people of it. Knowledge gained independently, they argued, is obtained with the help of *qiyās* (literally "co-measuring"). The term designates rational epistemological procedures that produce new knowledge "by measure" of the old one and was used not only in Kalām, but in other sciences as well, denoting analogous judgment in *fiqh* (Islamic jurisprudence) and the syllogism in logic. However, al-Rawāfiḍ who affirmed the independent ability of reason to gain new knowledge were in the minority (al-Ashʿarī, 1980, pp. 51–3).

The discussion of truth was deepened by the Muʿtazila. First, they were concerned with determining the types of propositions that can be true or false. These are statements containing "denial and affirmation" (*al-nafy wa al-ithbāt*), "praise and reprobation" (*al-madḥ wa al-dhimm*) as well as "wonder" (*taʿajjub*), while "question" (*istifhām*), "order and interdiction" (*al-ʾamr wa al-nahy*), "regret" (*ʾasaf*), "hope" (*tamannī*) and "request" (*masʾala*) are neither true nor false (al-Ashʿarī, 1980, p. 444). The Muʿtazila seem to have been little occupied with *how* true knowledge is reached, and this is perhaps due to the fact that they discussed truth in connection with the reliability of prophetic sayings – which is not an art to be taught. The Muʿtazila had different opinions as to whether a proposition can be called true or false if its author was ignorant of the "actuality of affairs." (The question here is whether unintended deception can be called a lie, or whether a statement that incidentally happened to be exact can be called truth). When the relevant "actuality of affairs" does not exist (for example, if the event has not yet occurred) or is unknown to a person, the verification procedure that compares a proposition to the "truth of things" cannot be executed – for objective and subjective reasons respectively – and such a proposition is to be regarded as neither true nor false. This argument, however, was not generally accepted by the Muʿtazila.

As for Aristotelian logic, it took root in medieval Islamic thought above all due to peripatetism. This school gave much more sophistication to what the Mutakallimūn said about truth and the possible ways of acquiring it. Many elements of Aristotelian logic introduced by the Islamic peripatetics became indisputable patterns of reasoning for Islamic thinkers, and no school of medieval philosophy seriously challenged the syllogism as a paradigm for the preservation of truth in argumentation. What *was* disputed was the *sphere* in which the syllogistic method is relevant. This method appears to have gained less favor among Islamic thinkers than it did among ancient or medieval Western thinkers, and in philosophy *per se* we find even among the peripatetics great reservations in this respect.

Elements of Aristotelian logic were rather well known to Islamic scholars from translations of Aristotle's works as well as from writings of his great commentators, among which must be mentioned in particular Porphyry's *Eisagoge*. There also existed quite a number of logical treatises of educational and propadeutical character composed in Arabic, many of which belong, or are ascribed to, al-Farābī.

According to the peripatetics, the purpose of logic is to gain true knowledge. Such knowledge is twofold, consisting of "notions" *(taṣawwur)* and "certifications of truth" (*taṣdīq*), which are both accessible only on the basis of some *a priori* knowledge. As for "notions" (that is, understanding *what* the thing is), this knowledge in the final analysis is based on the units of meaning that definitions, later used in arguments, are composed of. In "certifications of truth" this primary knowledge is represented by "principles of intellect" (*awāʾil al-ʿaql*), that very intellect with the help of which, as al-Farābī interprets Aristotle, we perceive the "certainty (*yaqīn*) of necessary and true general presuppositions" (al-Farābī, 1890, p. 40) with no prior investigation or argument.

This is how Ibn Sīnā expresses the point in his concise *Book of Remarks and Admonitions*:

> The purpose of logic is to provide a canonical tool (*āla qānūniyya*) that prevents aberration of thought. By "thought" (*fikr*) I mean here what takes place when a person, having pulled himself up, passes from what is present in his mind, what he has a notion of or what he is certain of . . . to what is not [present] there. This transition has a certain order and figure that might be correct and might happen to be incorrect. The incorrect often looks correct or makes you believe that it is correct. So logic is a science that studies ways of transition from what is present in the human mind to what it acquires, . . . the correct modes of ordering this transition and its figures, as well as the kinds of incorrect ones. (Ibn Sīnā, 1960, Pt 1, pp. 167–78)

Atomic "individual meanings" (*maʿānī mufrada*), from which complex logical structures are produced by "ordering" (*tartīb*) and "composing" (*taʾlīf*), constitute the basis for all logical operations (Ibn Sīnā, 1960, Pt 1, pp. 179–80). These meanings entirely correspond to the things in question. The correspondence is based on what is established by the language-giver who assigns certain "meanings" (*maʿānī*) to certain "sounds" (*alfāẓ*); this correspondence is therefore called "established" (*bi al-waḍʿ*). For example, the sound "human" corresponds to the meaning "animal endowed with speech." The sound and its meaning are the two elements that make up a "word" (*kalima*); the relation of "denotation" (*dalāla*) exists between the first and the second. What is denoted by the "sound" is that very "meaning" that constitutes the "truth" (*haqīqa*) of things. Thus logic, dealing with sounds and their meanings, deals in fact with things – as long as the denotation originally established in language is preserved.

In order to acquire the correct notion of a thing, one must arrive at a "clarifying saying" (*qawl shāriḥ*) about it. This can be achieved, first, in a "definition" (*ḥadd*) of the thing. The construction of definitions is described in every detail as a procedure of answering the question *what is it?* by providing its genus (*jins*) and specific difference (*faṣl*) to produce a definition of the species (*nawʿ*) that informs us of the quiddity (*māhiya*) of the thing in question. Besides a definition, a "description" (*rasm*) can also be given to clarify the notion of a thing, although this does not deal with thing's quiddity. A description has to be given to those tools that serve us in setting out definitions – that is, notions of genus, species and specific difference – as well as to the highest genera that have no genus above them (and, consequently, for which no definition can be given). Second, a description may be given to the things that have quiddity; for example, "animal endowed with laughter" serves as a description for "human."

As for arguments, they are composed in the form of syllogisms. Aristotelian syllogistic doctrine was exposed in Islamic peripatetism in every detail, accompanied by the examination of possible errors, mistakes and sophisms. The validity of conclusions reached through syllogisms is based on the accuracy with which we establish true meanings in definitions.

A great project of the unification and hierarchization of sciences was advanced in Islamic peripatetism. The hierarchization was to be based on differences in the degrees of generality of the various sciences' subjects. What is proved in the more general sciences may serve as non-provable principles for the more particular ones. From that point of view, sciences form a pyramid of axiomatically subordinated branches of knowledge. Al-Fārābī, in *Kitāb al-milla*, al-Kindī, in *Kitāb al-falsafa al-ʾūla*, Ibn Sīnā, in *al-Burhān* (part of *Kitāb al-shifāʾ*) (to give only examples, and not an exhaustive list) speak about such subordination of the more particular to the more general sciences. This structure of knowledge is conceived as corresponding to the universe, which is ordered along the same lines of generality-particularity.

Logic is an important instrument of cognition. This does not mean, however, that the peripatetics tend to exaggerate its significance. Besides knowledge acquired by means of logic, direct, intuitive (*ḥadasiyy*) knowledge is possible. This is granted as immediate manifestation, in which the thing unconditionally and completely expresses itself *as such*.

Knowledge of our ego serves as a paradigm of intuitive cognition. Ibn Sīnā introduces this thesis in his famous fragment about the "flying person" in his *Book of Remarks and Admonitions*:

> Look at your soul and answer: when you are in sound health, or even not, but correctly perceive things, did it ever happen that you were ignorant of your self (*dhāt*) or didn't ascertain your soul? . . . Imagine that your self has just been created; assume that it is in its right mind and figure, sees none of its parts and its members don't feel each other, but it is spread and suspended at some moment in pure air. Then you will find that it notices nothing; however it observes fixity of its *egoness* (*anāʾiyya*). (Ibn Sīnā, 1957, Pt 2, pp. 319–20)

The ego is always manifest to itself, and this manifestation is the primary fact of our consciousness. It depends on nothing and, furthermore, no sophisticated proof is needed to understand it: it suffices to imagine the situation described above for the fact of the ego's manifestation to itself to become clear.

Immediate manifestation can be considered a sort of completion for the logical form of cognition. This concluding step, however, already transcends the path that it completes and opens fundamentally new horizons. According to Ibn Sīnā, Ibn Ṭufayl and other authors, a person acquires complete and true knowledge through union with Active Intellect – the last of the Cosmic Intellects, repository of all forms and governor of the sublunar world. This full contact with the source of forms that are the subject of logical inquiry no longer presupposes any necessity of *transition* from the already-present to the yet-unknown, and thus places one outside the framework of logical reasoning. Certainly, not everyone is able to achieve this union; only if the soul is pure, Ibn Sīnā argues, can it be inflamed by Active Intellect and directly imprinted with the forms of all possible knowledge. It is the same intention of achieving immediately manifest self-evidence that speaks for itself in these cases, as also when these authors abandon philosophical jargon and talk about directly witnessing the Divine world. It is also obvious that the patency of our ego for itself guarantees its ability to reach absolutely complete and true knowledge by witnessing the Divinity, for the two kinds of evidential witnessing differ with respect to their subject, rather than in their essence.

The exposition of the peripatetic doctrine of truth is in no way complete before Ibn Rushd's work *Kitāb faṣl al-maqāl wa taqrīr ma bayna al-sharīʿa wa al-ḥikma min al-ittiṣāl* (or "Decisive Saying Establishing the Connection between Law and Wisdom") is mentioned. Despite its title, the chief idea of this little treatise is that the spheres of "wisdom" (that is, philosophy) and "Law" (the theoretical postulates followed in religious life as well as its practical prescriptions) may be separated. The work attempts to fix independent rights of reason for obtaining the truth that – within the limits defined for it – no one can violate. It is noteworthy that Ibn Rushd had predecessors among the Mutakallimūn in the differentiation of what falls under the Law, which is established and can be revised under no circumstances, and what reason is permitted to discuss and decide. "What is known by reason and what is known only through Law," a chapter in *Uṣūl al-dīn* (or *Principles of Religion*), a book by an Ashʿarite author, Abū Manṣūr al-Baghdādī, bears a resemblance to Averroës's treatise not only by its title. Al-Baghdādī definitely states that only Divine prescriptions, either direct or transmitted through prophets, constitute the domain of Law, whereas problems of the world's origin and similar questions involve theories that human reason elaborates.

Ismāʿīlism may to a certain degree be regarded as a successor of peripatetism with respect to the theory of knowledge and truth. Ismāʿīli theoreticians, on the one hand, have no doubt concerning reason's capability of knowing the truth; moreover, cognition of the truth is, in their view, indispensable for the person who wants to reach salvation. On the other hand, they give up the syllogistic method as the principal means of cognition. The Universe, in their estimation, is not a unified structure arranged in the hierarchical (generality–particularity) order that the peripatetics described. It is rather a *system* of structures that stand with respect to each other in relations of similarity, isomorphism and correspondence. This ontology presupposes a special method of cognition.

This is how Ḥamīd al-Dīn al-Kirmānī, the most prominent Ismāʿīli theoretician, expresses these theses. Any science, he argues, has its own "laws" (*qawānīn*) – that is to say, criteria by which knowledge is tested in order to determine whether it really corresponds to the "true order" (*niẓām al-ḥaqq*) of the subject of study. And if the peripatetics strive to achieve their aim, that is, "knowledge of the meanings of existence" (*maʿānī al-wujūd*), by means of logic, Ismāʿīli philosophers employ a different method.

Its basic premise can be expressed as follows: anything in the world belongs to some structure and may correctly be comprehended only within that structure, through its place in the overall framework and its structural role. Thus the preliminary step for cognition is to single out the universal structures that, being completely "balanced" (*mutawāzina*) and "isomorphic" (*mutashākila*), form the created world. In their mutual conformity universal harmony is embodied, expressing the highest wisdom of their creation and giving evidence to the perfection of our world, which is the best of all possible worlds.

The principle of hierarchical harmony, penetrating the Universe, can be traced on different levels. As Ismāʿīli works show, this can be done with great accuracy and amazing sophistication. There are four basic structures to be identified; the metaphysical world, the religious community, the natural world, and the human being. It is of fundamental importance that knowledge of any of these structures allows us to know all of the others with the help of special rules of interstructural translation of meaning, since corresponding elements of different structures have a similar structural place, function and essence.

Had all the structures of the Universe been manifest to us, no special cognitive procedures would be necessary. However, universal structures fall into two classes. Some of them are "obvious" (*ẓāhir*), while others are "latent" (*bāṭin*). Ismāʿīli theory of knowledge proceeds from the premise that "latent" structure (as a whole, as well as any of its separate elements) can be known only through the "obvious." Since it is the structure of Ismāʿīli community (or as al-Kirmānī prefers to say, the "world of religion") that is known to us in every detail, all new knowledge is acquired on this basis. This method is referred to as finding "balance" (*muwāzana*) and "correspondence" (*muṭābaqa*). Ismāʿīli community structure is harmoniously balanced with all other structures in the world (this is a postulate of Ismāʿīli philosophy, not a conclusion to be proved), and knowing it we can arrive at knowledge of anything. Besides, numeric structures are widely used in search of mutual structural correspondences. Using this method, al-Kirmānī consistently and in every detail describes the metaphysical world (the hierarchy of Cosmic Intellects) as well as the natural world and the microcosm.

Structural correspondence is for al-Kirmānī not only a method of finding new knowledge, but also a criterion for the verification of existing knowledge. Only that is valid which has a correct structure. "This criterion is such that what agrees with it, is true, and what disagrees, is false; it is this criterion that is so attractive for the intellect that seeks to know with its help what is given to it as well as what escapes it" (al-Kirmānī, 1983, p. 236). In cognitive procedures the structure of the "religious world" (which means the Ismāʿīli community) is taken as a paradigm, but that structure too is verified by correspondence to "God's creation." The perfection of the manifest structure and its undoubted validity is proved for al-Kirmānī by the fact that it disagrees with the Universe in no detail (al-Kirmānī, 1983, p. 237).

Certainly, the person who would endeavor to apply this method of cognition in his own research will hardly succeed. This method serves well in the exposition and structuring of already acquired knowledge, but in spite of what al-Kirmānī maintains, not in the search for new knowledge. The author of *Rāḥat al-ʿaql* leaves us ignorant of the most interesting and important detail of his method – those inter-structural semantic translation procedures that fill the unknown structure with *new meanings* so that it balances the structure manifest to us. In this respect what al-Farābī said on another occasion seems to be relevant. In this critique of astrologers, the "Second Teacher" argues that in the world one can single out diverse "sets" (*kathra*) of things, like animals' movements, the voices of birds, written signs, and so on, in order to put them in correspondence with the multitude of events that we experience; such a procedure, however, produces "only occasional, instead of necessary [truth] that reason should have accepted" (al-Farābī, 1890, p. 111).

Illuminative philosophy is another successor to peripatetism with respect to the theory of truth. It is no exaggeration to say that Ibn Sīnā is the greatest authority for the most prominent representative of this school, Shihāb al-Dīn Yaḥyā al-Suhrawardī. The affinity of these two thinkers is surprising, in view of the disagreements between their teachings caused by al-Suhrawardī's adherence to a metaphysics of light and darkness; on the subject of the theory of truth, however, the disagreements between them are minimal.

Like Ibn Sīnā, al-Suhrawardī speaks about two kinds of true knowledge: immediate intuitive knowledge and logical knowledge. The first he also calls "truthful witnessing" (*mushāhada ḥaqqiya*), and the second "research" (*baḥth*). Knowledge of the ego, or, as al-Suhrawardī himself calls it, ego-ness (*anā'iyya*), serves for him, as it did for Ibn Sīnā, as an archetype of the direct cognition of truth. But since the majority of people are unable to experience the completeness of truth immediately, they have to resort to indirect logical cognition, which starts with basic unquestionably valid premises and proceeds from them to the unknown (al-Suhrawardī, 1952, p. 18).

Al-Suhrawardī considers the elementary sensual perceptions "simple meanings," logical atoms from which the construction of concepts begins. These perceptions are simple, absolutely evident and self-identical; they are the principal elements known by anyone who has healthy organs of perception. Sensual perception is absolutely adequate, al-Suhrawardī argues: we perceive exactly what *is there* in the things perceived. Finally, basic sensual perceptions, being elements of knowledge, have no logical definition (al-Suhrawardī, 1952, p. 104). This sensualism of the celebrated mystic agrees well with his radical nominalism; according to al-Suhrawardī, no general concepts exist independently of our minds. On this basis he argues that quiddity is constituted not only by substantial features, as the peripatetics maintained, but also by accidental features. For the shape of a house, for example, is accidental with respect to the clay from which it is constructed, and nevertheless we say, in response to the question "what is it?" that it is a "house," rather than "clay" (al-Suhrawardī, 1952, pp. 85–6). Given Suhrawardī's metaphysics of light and darkness, he denies that the first matter is universal substance, and consequently is compelled to look for a different basis of individuation. For him it is not matter that is "responsible" for the multiplicity of individuals which all have the same quiddity and which therefore are, logically speaking, one and the same, but rather the degree of perfection (*kamāl*) or degree of completeness by which this or that "universal meaning" is represented in the individual (al-Suhrawardī, 1952,

p. 87). This concept of individuality as a degree of perfection will later be elaborated in Sufism by Ibn ʿArabī.

As for the syllogistic method, the importance that al-Suhrawardī attaches to it is testified to by the fact that the first half of his chef-d'oeuvre, *Ḥikmat al-ishrāq* (*Wisdom of Illumination*), is solely devoted to its exposition. Al-Suhrawardī points out that it is a necessary propaedeutic for the second, metaphysical and mystical, part of his book. In his analysis of syllogisms accompanied by a detailed study of possible errors and sophisms, al-Suhrawardī strives to prove that all modes of syllogism can be reduced to a single positive categorical mode, which, in his estimation, makes knowledge of all the subtleties of the other modes superfluous.

As for the complete and perfect witnessing of truth, it is reached, according to al-Suhrawardī, in the state of "illumination" (*ishrāq*). "Illumination" is the central concept of al-Suhrawardī's philosophy. It signifies direct irradiation of the soul by superior, metaphysical lights. The soul itself is a light that has descended from the "world of light" into the "world of darkness" and is yet impotent to return to its original abode. This congeneity of human soul and the highest principles of being constitutes the ontological foundation for the possibility of such irradiation. Illumination discloses the truth (*ḥaqq*) immediately and needs no verification (*taṣdīq*). Logical instruments that verify the correctness of "transition" procedures are of no use when no such transition takes place.

The Ṣūfī doctrine of the truth and the ways of acquiring it differs in its central point from any of the doctrines that we have hitherto discussed. No matter how truth is understood in Kalām, peripatetism, Ismāʿīlism, or the philosophy of illumination, all of these schools have in common an explicit or implicit understanding of true knowledge as something unhesitatingly established; the term "certainty" (*yaqīn*) generally serves to express this fixity. Such certainty is understood as "quiescence" (*iṭmi'nān*; the same idea of quietude reached through complete and true knowledge is expressed by the title of al-Kirmānī's magnum opus *Rāḥat al-ʿaql* – peace of mind) on the basis of the generally accepted notion of the "perfect" (*kāmil*) and "complete" (*tāmm*) as immobile. The true, by virtue of its completeness, needs nothing external to be accomplished and, consequently, no movement is necessary for it. Against this understanding of truth as a state of clear certainty, Sufism opposes the doctrine of the truth being witnessed in its completeness in a state of "abashment" and "confusion" (*ḥayra*) that presupposes constant restlessness.

Although in this respect Sufism stands in opposition to other trends of medieval Islamic philosophy, there is doubtless continuity in the way Ṣūfī theoreticians arrive at the above conclusion. Peripatetism, Ismāʿīlism and the philosophy of illumination understand the achievement of truth, at least in its logical form, as "transition" (*intiqāl*) from what a person possesses as established truth to what he or she currently does not possess; as for mystical revelation, it also provides a sort of finally established and unequivocally valid knowledge. "The unknown – against the known," Ibn Sīnā writes (Ibn Sīnā, 1960. Pt 1, p. 181): all things are divided into two classes that stand to each other in a relation of exact mutual correspondence; everything is truly known after it has been unknown. Dividing things into the "unseen" (*bāṭin*) and the "manifest" (*ẓāhir*) was commonplace in medieval Islamic thought, and these concepts remain fundamental in Sūfī epistemology as well, where cognition is often referred to as "making [the unseen] manifest" (*iẓhār*).

This substantial departure from traditional Islamic thinking in the final conclusion of Sūfī epistemology (that is, the cognition of truth as "confusion" instead of as "fixed certainty") in spite of common intention of finding the solution (truth as unseen made manifest) is explained by a basic feature of this philosophy that may be defined as interiorization. Both Sūfī ontology (see Article 37, CAUSALITY AND ISLAMIC THOUGHT) and epistemology are deeply marked by it. Just as the cause and effect relation is an inner division of the same essence rather than an external relation between two different essences, so the inner and the outside (the "hidden" and the "manifest") are not two different and *definite* aspects of things, but rather one and the same. What other schools of philosophy consider as occurring *between*, Sūfī philosophy regards as taking place *inside*.

However, Sūfī philosophy does not deny other points of view. As the doctrines of Ibn Sīnā and al-Suhrawardī demonstrated, logic may be regarded as an incomplete version of immediate and perfect truth-witnessing, rather than as its alternative. Ibn ʿArabī, the greatest of Sūfī philosophers, adopts the same position. In this sense his theory of truth is inclusive rather than exclusive, for he regards non-Sūfī ways of cognition as also true – within their limits, however, and not absolutely.

For example, the knowledge obtained through correct syllogisms is certainly true, and there is no doubt about its scientific results, like our knowledge of the sun's size or the rules of mathematics (Ibn ʿArabī, 1980, pp. 102–4). The intuitive "witnessing" (*mushāhada*) gives true knowledge as well: the "inner sight" (*baṣīra*) discovers immediately behind things their causes and thus discloses the inner essence of things hidden under their manifest outwardness. The cause of things and of their inner essence thus discovered is God, or The Truth (*al-Ḥaqq*) – each time seen in one of His infinite aspects. However, the "witnessing" first brings into sight the thing, and then behind it, or inside it, discovers God. The two are still divided and differentiated, and the all-encompassing Truth that constitutes the *core* of everything is not found as the thing's *outwardness*. The highest stage of truth is to see *things in God*, to notice the sameness and equality of the different, to be unable to differentiate. This is the ability of the "heart" (*qalb*). Intellect, inner sight, and heart form an ascending hierarchy of organs with their corresponding methods of cognition.

Rational knowledge is acquired by moving "from" premises "to" a conclusion, by going along "the stretched path," as Ibn ʿArabī puts it (Ibn ʿArabī, 1980, p. 73). The intuitive witnessing of God as the inner essence of things spheres this line. But only when the sphered line becomes equal to its center (see Article 37, CAUSALITY AND ISLAMIC THOUGHT) does "confusion" come, and the person sees the hidden as manifest and the manifest as hidden, sees God as His creation and the creation as God Himself. Total oneness and sameness, the transcendence of any differentiation and the non-fixity of any definiteness and any limit (the results of logical cognition included) – this is what such a way of seeing the truth boils down to. The Sūfī understanding of truth undermines well established stereotypes of dichotomizing divisions. The fundamental ontological sameness of God and His creation entails the sameness of any pair of opposed categories. The law of excluded middle is irrelevant for this point of view: what it points to is but a step that should inevitably be overcome. Truth turns out to be a transcendence of dichotomic divisions – a transcendence which, however, presupposes that each of them is fixed – but only as a step in an unceasing movement, equal to any other of its infinite steps.

Bibliography

Writings

Al-Ashʿarī, Abū al-Ḥasan 1980: *Maqalāt al-islāmiyyīn wa ikhtilāf al-muṣallīn* [Sayings of Muslims and Differences of Those Who Pray] 3rd edn (Wiesbaden: Franz Steinen).

Ibn ʿArabī 1980: *Fuṣūṣ al-ḥikam* [Gems of Wisdom] 2nd edn (Beirut: Dār al-kitāb al-ʿarabiyy).

Ibn Sīnā, Abū ʿAlī 1957–60: *Al-Ishārāt wa al-tanbīhāt, maʿa sharḥ Naṣīr al-Dīn al-Ṭūṣī* [Book of Remarks and Admonitions, with the commentary of Naṣīr al-Dīn al-Ṭūṣī] ed. Suleyman Dunya, 4 parts (Cairo: Dār al-maʿārīf).

Al-Kirmānī, Ḥamīd al-Dīn 1983: *Rāḥat al-ʿaql* [Peace of Mind] 2nd edn (Beirut: Dār al-andalus).

Al-Suhrawardī, Shihāb al-Dīn Yaḥyā 1952: "Ḥikmat al-ishrāq," in *Oeuvres philosophiques et mystiques de Shihabeddin Jahya Sohrawardi (1)*, ed. H. Corbin, Bibliothèque Iranienne, Vol. 2 (Teheran and Paris: Institut Franco-Iranien – Librairie d'Amèrique et d'Orient), pp. 2–260.

References and further reading

Badawi, A. 1972: *Histoire de la philsosphie en Islam*, 2 Vols (Paris: J. Vrin).

Al-Baghdādī, Abū Manṣūr 1981: *'Uṣūl al-dīn*, 3rd edn (Beirut: Dār al-kutub al-ʿilmiyya).

Chittick, W. C. 1989: *The Sufi Path of Knowledge: Ibn al-ʿArabi's Metaphysics of Imagination* (Albany: State University of New York Press).

Corbin, H. 1964: *Histoire de la philosophie islamique* (Paris: Gallimard).

Daftary, F. 1990: *The Ismaʿilis: Their History and Doctrines* (Cambridge: Cambridge University Press).

Dunlop, D. M. 1956a: "Al-Farabi's *Eisagoge*," *The Islamic Quarterly. A Review of Islamic Culture*, 3, pp. 115–27.

—— 1956b: "Al-Farabi's Introductory Risalah on Logic," *The Islamic Quarterly. A Review of Islamic Culture*, 3, pp. 224–30.

—— 1956, 1959: "Al-Farabi's Paraphrase of the Categories of Aristotle," *The Islamic Quarterly. A Review of Islamic Culture*, 4 (1957), pp. 168–83; 5 (1959), pp. 21–37.

Fakhry, M. 1983: *A History of Islamic Philosophy*, 2nd edn (New York: Columbia University Press).

Al-Fārābī, Abū Naṣr 1890a: "Fī-mā yaṣiḥḥ wa mā lā yaṣiḥḥ min aḥkām al-nujūm" [What Is Right and What Is Wrong in Astrology], in *Al-thamra al-marḍiyya fī baʿḍ al-risālāt al-farābiyya* [Longed-for Fruit of Some Treatises by al-Fārābī] (Leiden: E. J. Brill), pp. 104–14.

—— 1890b: "Maqāla fī maʿānī al-ʿaql" [On Meanings of "Intellect"], in *Al-thamra al-marḍiyya fī baʿḍ al-risālāt al-farābiyya* [Longed-for Fruit of Some Treatises by al-Fārābī] (Leiden: E. J. Brill), pp. 39–48.

—— 1968: *Kitāb al-milla wa nuṣūṣ ukhrā* [Book of Beliefs and Other Treatises], ed. M. Mahdi (Beyrouth: Dar al-mashriq).

Georr, Khalil 1948: *Les categories d'Aristote dans leurs versions syro-arabes* (Beyrouth).

Ibn ʿArabī 1859 and reprints: *Al-Futūḥāt al-Makkiya* [Revelations of Mecca], 4 Vols (Cairo: Dār al-kutub al-ʿarabiyya al-kubrā).

Ibn Sīnā, Abū ʿAlī 1954: *Al-Burhān min Kitāb al-Shifā'* [On Demonstration, from the Book of Healing] ed. Al-Badawi (Cairo: Maktabat al-nahda al-misriyya).

Ibn Rushd (Averroës) 1959: *Kitāb Faṣl al-Maqāl with its Appendix and an extract from Kitāb al-kashf ʿan manāhij al-adilla* (Leiden: E. J. Brill).

Ibn Ṭufayl 1954: *Qiṣṣat Ḥayy Ibn Yaqẓān* [Story of the Living, Son of the Wakeful] (Beirut: Dār al-Farābī).

Al-Kindī 1948: *Kitāb al-Kindī ila al-Muʿtaṣim bi-llāh fī al-falsafa al-ūla* [Epistle of al-Kindī to al-Muʿtaṣim bi-llāh in First Philosophy], ed. Ahmad al-Ahwani (Cairo).

Nasr, S. H. 1964: *Three Muslim Sages: Avicenna, Suhrawardi, Ibn ʿArabi* (Cambridge, Mass.: Harvard University Press).

Wolfson, H. A. 1976: *The Philosophy of the Kalam* (Cambridge, Mass.: Harvard University Press).

33

Islamic aesthetics

SEYYED HOSSEIN NASR

Aesthetics, as that branch of philosophy which deals with the meaning of beauty and various theories of art, has not been treated as a separate subject by the Islamic philosophers and one does not find separate treatises corresponding to the works on aesthetics by such Western philosophers as Hegel, Collingwood, and Croce among those Islamic thinkers who are called the *falāsifa* or *ḥukamāʾ*. In order to fully understand Islamic aesthetics, one has first of all to cull passages here and there from the Peripatetic (*mashshāʾī*) philosophers. But, in addition, one must turn to the works of the Illuminationist (*ishrāqī*) school and especially the Sufis for much greater elaboration of the subject. Furthermore, one must add to the written sources the oral tradition, the teachings transmitted from masters of various Islamic arts to their disciples from one generation to another, teachings which have underlined the actual production of Islamic works of art over the centuries and which have not died out to this day.

As far as Islamic Peripatetic philosophy, which has been mistakenly identified with Islamic philosophy, as such, until recently, is concerned, its major representatives have dealt formally with aesthetics only as it concerns poetry and in relation to commentaries upon the *Poetics* of Aristotle, which forms a part of his logical studies. (See, for example, S. Kamal, 1991, *The Poetics of Alfarabi and Avicenna.*) While the Islamic grammarians also dealt with various aesthetic questions in relation to poetry from the point of view of languages, the philosophers emphasized the logical framework of aesthetic validity.

Al-Fārābī mentions the logical nature of poetic discourse in several of his works, such as *al-Risāla fī qawānīn ṣināʿat al-shiʿr* ("Treatise on the Canons of the Art of Poetry") and his introductory treatise (*Risāla*) on logic, and sees poetry as "imaginative syllogistic proof by example" (see S. Kamal, "Aesthetics," in Nasr and Leaman, 1996, Vol. 2, p. 970). He considers the imaginative character of poetry to be in fact what distinguishes it from other forms of syllogism. Poetry brings to our mind an imaginary form which may not be true, but nevertheless affects us as a result of imaginative creation which takes place within our soul. This theory was to be criticized by later philosophers because the imaginative construct was subjective and psychological and not based on rational argument. Furthermore, poetic examples do not rely upon propositions which are applicable in general. Poetic syllogisms, therefore, become arbitrary and their legitimacy cannot be sustained. Finally, al-Fārābī was criticized for not explaining clearly the relation between the aesthetic aspect of poetry and the logical form of poetry when it is set in the form of a syllogism.

Ibn Sīnā tried to overcome what were seen as shortcomings in the aesthetic theory of al-Fārābī as it concerned poetry. Ibn Sīnā relied upon the conception of the demonstrative syllogism of Aristotle and "argued for the formal role of pleasure in constituting poetic syllogisms and for their moral value" (Kamal, "Aesthetics," p. 972). According to Ibn Sīnā, poetry and literary works in general have a logical form similar to what one finds in demonstrative reasoning. But in the case of sayings of a literary nature – including poetry – premises are used that derive from the emotions and not reason. Upon reading such works, we give imaginative assent to them because of the pleasure they give us and wonder at the harmony of their parts. The acceptance of poetic syllogisms depends on the psychology of the reader rather than the rules of rational thought. As for pleasure itself, it comes ultimately, according to Ibn Sīnā, from the harmonious relation of the parts with their given meaning.

Poetic discourse refers back to the subject rather than an object of thought, for it treats the subject as "the end process of production of aesthetic discourse because its experience forms the ultimate ground for appreciating a poem" (Kamal, "Aesthetics," pp. 973–4). Furthermore, since a particular human being has to give assent to the pleasure derived from poetry or other literary works, evil poetry cannot be aesthetically of any value. Such works, being devoid of virtue, lack balance, since virtue and goodness are based on balance and their absence marks the destruction of balance. Likewise, a good society in which good poetry is appreciated is one based on balance and harmonious interaction. The very act of giving assent to an evil poem would in fact destroy this balance for the subject giving the assent. Such poetry could not as a matter of fact provide pleasure if considered with sincerity.

Ibn Sīnā's aesthetic theory is therefore founded upon the significance of imagination and the principles of balance and harmony. Moreover, he seeks to relate aesthetics to ethics through the principle of balance as stated above. It is noteworthy that in those works of his concerned with what he called *al-ḥikma amashriqiyya* or oriental philosophy (which can also be read in Arabic orthography as *mushriqiyya*, meaning illuminative) and which he claimed to be the philosophy for the elite (*al-khawāṣṣ*), Ibn Sīnā chose a highly poetic medium to express his ideas. We find clear examples of this approach in his *Ḥayy ibn Yaqẓān* ("Living Son of the Awake"), for whose impact Ibn Sīnā relied not only on rational thought but also on the aesthetic factor, choosing a highly poetic and symbolic language for his discourse.

The concern of *mashshā'ī* philosophers with aesthetics continued with the last of the Andalusian members of this school, Ibn Rushd, who was fully aware of the significance of metaphors and allegories in cases in which ordinary language proved inadequate in one's attempt to express the truth. He considered metaphors to be valid in poetry, and also wrote a commentary upon Aristotle's *Poetics* in which he mentioned the basic principle that truth is vital to poetic validity. Aesthetic evaluation of a work of literature in reference to the presence of harmony and unity or lack thereof is determined by the element of truth contained in the literary work in question. A work is appreciated aesthetically to the degree that it is able to provide the reader or listener with a better understanding of the truths which it is seeking to convey. The more truths a literary work reveals, the more profound it is, and these truths are essential to the aesthetic character of the work.

A poem should seek to convey truths pertaining to its subject and it is these truths which determine its aesthetic value. The less truth conveyed by a poem, the less does it possess the inner unity and harmony so essential for the aesthetic appreciation of a work. Like Plato, Ibn Rushd emphasizes the relation between beauty and truth and states that since poetry combines beauty with truth, like philosophy, it is able to reveal to us what God demands of us. His aesthetic theory, based on those of his Peripatetic or *mashshāʾī* predecessors, takes a further step in its concern with beauty in relation to truth. (On the relation between truth and poetry in the thought of Ibn Rushd, see Mansour Ajami, 1988, pp. 57ff).

The treatment of beauty, and in fact other elements of a complete aesthetics, was to find its further elaboration during the later centuries of Islamic history with Suhrawardī, the founder of the School of Illumination (*al-ishrāq*) and to an even greater degree, the Sufis, who were always concerned with the question of beauty and the relation between terrestrial and celestial forms even before Suhrawardī (who died in the twelfth century CE) as seen in some of the writings of the two al-Ghazzālī's, Abū Ḥāmid and Aḥmad, who lived a century before the Master of *ishrāq*. But before turning to the Sufi tradition, it is important to deal with the aesthetic theories of the second major Islamic philosophical school after the *mashshāʾī* – that is, the School of *ishrāq*, and especially its founder Shihāb al-Dīn Suhrawardī.

Suhrawardī's metaphysics and cosmology provide the background for an aesthetics that identifies beauty with light and light with being itself. The universe is comprised first of all of a vertical hierarchy of light whose members are distinguished from each other by degrees of intensity of light and darkness, which are themselves nothing but light or the lack thereof. Second, there is a horizontal world of lights, identified with the archetypal realm. Each being in this world is a reflection of one of those archetypes which constitute also the angelic presence within the being in question. This truth holds true for natural forms as well as imaginal forms which are the origins of forms in art. While rejecting the Aristotelian theory of hylomorphism, Suhrawardī develops a theory of bodies as shadows imprisoning a light belonging ultimately to the angelic world and substitutes for Aristotle's theory of forms a theory which sees all forms as elements of light, which in the language of religion would be called angels.

Of special interest in Suhrawardī's theory is the role of the world of imagination (*ʿālam al-khayāl*), intermediary between the corporeal and purely intelligible realms. This world, treated explicitly for the first time by Suhrawardī, was also to be dealt with at length by Ibn ʿArabī, who spoke extensively of its creative powers, and it was given a clear status in the metaphysics and ontology of Mullā Ṣadrā. We shall therefore deal with it later when we turn to the seventeenth-century Safavid philosopher and theosopher.

(One can hardly over-emphasize in the context of this essay, the significance of the imaginal world, the modifier "imaginal" being used in the place of "imaginary" to avoid conveying any suggestion of its "unreality." The doctrine of the imaginal world is not only of the utmost significance in Ibn ʿArabī's analysis of the human macrocosm and its entelechy, but is also central for a total doctrine of form in art and artistic creativity in Islam and needs to be studied separately in light of this perspective. (On Ibn ʿArabī and the imaginal world, see Corbin, 1969, and Chittick, 1994.) There are some indications, in fact, of a direct relation between the imaginal world in its relation to eschatological realities as described by Ibn ʿArabī and certain major works of Islamic art, such as the Taj Mahal in India. See Morris, 1995.)

Suhrawardī also developed a most elaborate doctrine of beauty in his visionary recital *al-Risāla fī ḥaqīqa al-ʿishq* ("Treatise on the Reality of Love"), known also as *Muʾis al-ʿushshāq* ("The Vade-Mecum of the Fedeli d'Amore" to use the translation of Corbin), which is written in a Persian prose of exceptional beauty. In this treatise, Suhrawardī explains the mystery of beauty, both divine and human, in rapport with love and sorrow through a hermeneutic exegesis of the story of the prophet Joseph and Potipher's wife, Zulaykhā, in chapter 12 of the Quran. This story is in fact the longest continuous narrative in the Quran, which the Sacred Text itself refers to as the "best of stories" and which in Islamic eyes contains the supreme example of human love ensnared by a beauty of celestial origin and yet controlled by the gaze of God upon the human order. Although the story concerns the relation of human beauty to love, beauty is treated by Suhrawardī as a hypostatic reality independent of any particular human embodiment. His treatment, therefore, contains a philosophico-mystical discussion of beauty and its power – a discussion which is foundational to aesthetics and embraces human beauty as well as the beauty of works of art.

In the first chapter of this treatise, Suhrawardī establishes first of all the ontological status of beauty, for he tells us that the first thing that God created was a glowing pearl named the Intellect (*ʿaql*) that possessed three qualities: the ability to know God, the ability to know its own essence, and the ability to know the essence of things which had not existed but then came into existence. Of those three abilities, the highest was, of course, the first, from which appeared Beauty (*ḥusn*), while from the second there appeared Love, and from the third Sorrow. Beauty then issues from the highest ability of God's highest creation, the Intellect, that ability being to know the Divine Principle Itself. Beauty, through its very ontological status, is related to knowledge of the highest order and in its essence is inseparable from the knowledge of God by the Intellect, which we also contain at the center of our being. Moreover, Suhrawardī treats these three abilities of the First Intellect as brothers, of whom the eldest is Beauty. This hypostatic reality gazed upon himself and saw its own extreme goodness. This vision caused him to be illuminated and this luminosity in turn caused him to smile. From this smile thousands of cherubim were born.

As for Love, he was so intimate and close to Beauty, that he could not take his eyes away from Beauty for an instant. "When Beauty's smile appeared, a consternation befell Love, who was so agitated that he wanted to move. Sorrow, the youngest, clung to him, and from this clinging the heaven and earth appeared" (Thackston, 1982, pp. 62–3). Beauty, Love, and Sorrow thus have a central role in the cosmogonic process, and it might be said that Beauty and therefore traditional art, which is based upon the principle of expressing cosmic, and even ultimately metacosmic beauty, are keys to the understanding of the nature of the cosmos and provide another noetic possibility beyond the usual philosophical and scientific methods based upon concepts, rational demonstration and empirical experience divorced from aesthetic experience.

The creation of Adam was to be a new major event in cosmic history. God had created a perfect form on earth and news reached the heavenly hosts of the existence of this vicegerent of God on earth. Beauty decided to descend on earth to observe for himself this new creature and, having found Adam pleasing, disembarked from his steed and encompassed Adam completely. When Love arrived in pursuit of Beauty to the abode of Adam, he saw "Beauty crowned with the diadem of Absolute majesty and seated on the throne of Adamic existence" (Thackston, 1982, p. 63). The angels prostrated themselves before Adam, as stated in the Quran (15, 30). "So the angels fell prostrate, all of them together" not because of the clay from which Adam was kneaded, but because of the dazzling presence of Beauty which was at that moment dominating Adamic existence.

Adam, however, was a celestial being existing in that pre-eternal moment marking the archetypal reality of the human state. As Adam and consequently man fell and began his terrestrial life, Beauty gradually assembled its "belongings" and departed from the city of Adamic existence for its own original abode waiting to manifest itself once again on earth in a perfect being. And according to the Quran, this opportunity arose when Joseph was brought into the realm of existence. "When Joseph's turn came, Beauty was informed. Immediately he set out. Love took Sorrow by the sleeve and went in pursuit of Beauty. As he appeared, he saw Beauty so mingled with Joseph that there was no difference between the two" (Thackston, 1982, p. 64). The whole story of Joseph, involving the treachery of his brothers, the sorrow and blindness of his father Jacob, the love of Zulaykhā for Joseph, his refusal of this love, his imprisonment, his power of dream interpretation, his political and social prominence and finally forgiveness of his brothers and the cure of his father's blindness through the effect of the perfume of Joseph's shirt marking a final spiritual healing and redemption, is related to the descent of Divine Beauty into Joseph's very existence.

The inner meaning of the treatise of Suhrawardī is therefore not only to establish the ontological status of Beauty in relation to the Intellect and knowledge of God, but also Beauty's salvific power when it manifests itself, whether it be in art created by human artisans or the works of the Supreme Artisan whose greatest masterpiece is that vicegerent on earth who can share in divine creativity and produce works of art worthy of the descent of the rays of that celestial Beauty which, according to Suhrawardī, left the abode of Adamic existence long ago but which yet can descend on earth or at least cast a ray of its luminous being when a worthy receptacle appears upon the scene. No Islamic philosopher has written with greater profundity on beauty as the foundation of a metaphysically oriented aesthetics than has Suhrawardī.

It is well known that the task of developing fully the doctrine of the imaginal world and its significance was left to Mullā Ṣadrā, but little attention has been paid by scholars until now to the importance of this intermediate world for aesthetics (see Corbin, 1977, pp. 164ff). According to Mullā Ṣadrā, the levels of universal existence consist not only of the material world, in which form is united with matter, and the world of the purely intelligibles (*al-mujarradāt*), which can be identified with the Platonic archetypes. There is also a third world, itself consisting of many levels, situated between the two. This third world is none other than the imaginal world in which the archetypes (*al-aʿyān al-thābita*) become manifested as forms (*ṣuwar*), but forms which are not wed to matter. That is why this world is also referred to as the world of "hanging forms" (*al-ṣuwar al-muʿallaqa*).

As far as aesthetics is concerned, the significance of this world lies in that it is the immediate origin of artistic forms. Forms of art are not simply abstract ideas contained in the mind of the artist which are then produced externally. Rather, they are imaginal forms which appear in the imaginal faculty of the artist before becoming manifested in the material world. Artistic creativity is essentially related to the "creative imagination" and in the case of traditional art issue from the luminous levels of the imaginal world. Its products therefore clearly reflect the archetypes rather than veiling and hiding them. The imaginal world is sometimes called the *barzakh* or isthmus between the purely luminous archetypal realities and the material world.

Furthermore, this intermediate world consists of higher and lower levels (*al-barāzikh al-aʿlā* and *al-barāzikh al-asfal*). Traditional art, and especially its heart, which is sacred art, issues from the higher *barāzikh* and therefore possesses a revelatory aspect as far as manifesting the archetypal realities are concerned. In any case, the imaginative faculty (not to be confused with the usages of these terms by the Islamic Peripatetic philosophers) is not simply a subjective reality but a reality that has an objective and cosmic counterpart to which it is connected. The human imaginative faculty is like a tributary, which in a sense flows from and into that cosmic ocean that is the imaginal world.

Mullā Ṣadrā, himself, does not deal to any great extent with the artistic significance of the imaginal world and its role in the understanding of artistic creativity, but devotes himself mainly to the eschatological significance of this world. However, the doctrine of the imaginal world, as this is developed by Suhrawardī, Ibn ʿArabī, and Mullā Ṣadrā, contains one of the foundations for the understanding of the philosophy of Islamic art. It underlies the belief among so many Islamic artists, from poets to miniaturists, that traditional art involves an "alchemy" that transforms the corporeal into the spiritual and the spiritual into the corporeal. The alchemical process of spiritualizing the material and materializing the spiritual, with all of its significance for traditional art (see Burckhardt, 1986), can be fully understood in the context of Islamic thought only in the light of the metaphysics of the imaginal world which was to receive its final elaboration in the hands of Mullā Ṣadrā.

Nevertheless, it is in the writings of the Sufis rather than the Islamic philosophers that one can discover the most explicit development of Islamic aesthetics, especially the doctrines of form and beauty. From the earliest period, Sufis wrote of beauty and expressed themselves in a language impregnated with beauty, which in their estimation was inseparable from the Truth, as can be seen in the early Sufi poetry of Rābiʿa al-ʿAdawiyyah and Manṣūr al-Ḥallāj (see Schimmel, 1982). In the eleventh century (CE) the great Sufi theologian al-Ghazzālī turned to the discussion of beauty even amidst his discourse on the active life and argued against beauty being confined only to externality. Rather, he showed that God, being beautiful, according to the famous *ḥadīth* "God is beautiful and loves beauty", must of necessity be loved by the person who is able to behold this beauty with his inner eye (Ettinghausen, 1947, p. 162). According to al-Ghazzālī, there is a hierarchy of beauty leading from the outward to the inward, and at all stages beauty is the result of the perfection of a particular being or thing according to its nature. To perceive this beauty fully, there is need of inner vision – even where outward beauty is concerned. Al-Ghazzālī therefore associates the beauty of a work of art with the inner beauty of its creator, for he states, "The beautiful work of an author, the beautiful poem of a poet, the beautiful painting of a painter or the building of an architect reveal also the inner beauty of these men" (Ettinghausen, 1947, p. 164).

It was al-Ghazzālī's lesser known brother Aḥmad who was to write one of the most significant treatises on the relation between beauty and love in the annals of Sufi literature, *al-Sawāniḥ fi'l-ʿishq* ("Inspirations from the World of Pure Spirits"). This text, itself of great literary beauty, is devoted to the esoteric significance of love, but also deals with rarely equalled profundity with the meaning of beauty. At the deepest level, beauty, for Aḥmad Ghazzālī, is nothing but the imprint of the Divine upon the being whose beauty we behold. Beauty is, therefore, ultimately the ontological principle of existents, and what traditional art reveals is this ontological nexus that remains hidden from the eyes of those who are blind to beauty. To quote Aḥmad Ghazzālī himself,

> The secret face of everything is the point of its connection [with the Creator]. Moreover, there is a sign [of the Creator] concealed in the creation, and loveliness (*ḥusn*) is that sign. The secret face [of anything] is that which faces Him [the Creator]. Now, unless one sees that secret face [of a created thing], he will observe neither that sign in the creation, nor loveliness. That face is the beauty (*jamāl*) of the Lord's Face, reflected in the face of the created being, as it is expressed in the Quran, "and what remains is the Face of thy Lord" (Quran 50, 27). The other face [of a created being, that is the side which does not face the Creator] is not really a face, as it is said: "Everyone upon the earth perishes" (Quran 50, 26). Furthermore, you may know that the other face is ugliness. (*Sawāniḥ*, p. 23)

One may therefore say that the traditional artist is able to unveil the inner reality and meaning of things, carrying out esoteric hermeneutics (*kashf al-maḥjūb*) not upon texts but upon words, sounds and objects, which are thereby made to reveal the face they have turned to God and also the Face that God has turned towards them. Beauty is ultimately nothing other than the effulgence of that Face.

Following the two Ghazzālī's, many Sufis turned directly to the themes of beauty and its manifestation in forms. These included not only Sufi poets such as Awḥad al-Dīn Kirmānī, known especially for his contemplation of the Divine in the world of forms, but also those who wrote in prose. Of particular interest in the latter group are members of the Central Asian School of Sufism given especially to meditation upon the symbolism of color and apparitions of light in mystical contemplation. Najm al-Dīn Kubrā, the founder of the Kubrawiyyah Order, which was so important in Central Asia, is an outstanding representative of this perspective, as is his student Najm al-Dīn Dāyah Rāzī. Najm al-Dīn Kubrā entitled one of his major works *Fawā'iḥ al-jamāl wa fawātiḥ al-jalāl* ("Aromas of Beauty and Preambles of Majesty"), while Najm al-Dīn Rāzī's most famous opus is *Mirṣād al-ʿibād* ("The Path of God's Bondsmen"), which contains an elaborate account of the relation between the experience of colors and the psychological states of the mystic.

The foremost expositor of the metaphysics of beauty as well as integral aesthetics in this period (and perhaps all periods) of Islamic history was Jalāl al-Dīn Rūmī, for whom every expression of beauty was a direct gateway to the Divine Presence. This creator of the sacred dance of the Sufi order named after him, that is, the Mawlawiyyah, and one of the supreme poets of the Persian language expounded an elaborate doctrine of form and meaning, of beauty and its salvific power, not in organized essays, but in poems and as allusions interspersed in his vast corpus which includes the two monumental works of Sufi poetry – the *Mathnawī* and the *Dīwān-i Shams-i Tabrīzī*, constituting together some sixty thousand verses.

To understand Rūmī's aesthetics one must turn to the basic distinction made by him between outward form (*ṣūra*), which, however, must not be confused with Aristotelian form, and meaning (*maʿnā*), which is nothing other than the inner essence of a thing (see Nasr, 1987, pp. 129–30). In Peripatetic hylomorphism, form is the principle which at once existentiates an object and provides it with its intelligible reality. According to Rūmī, however, *ṣūra* means the outward aspect of any existent at once veiling and revealing the *maʿnā* wherein is to be discovered the intelligible principle and reality of the existent. All that exists possesses *ṣūrat* and *maʿnā*, and according to Rūmī, the role of the Sufi is to be able to journey from the *ṣūra* to the *maʿnā* and not to remain imprisoned in outward form.

As far as art is concerned, its function is precisely to facilitate this journey from the outward to the inward by revealing even in the outward form something of the beauty that belongs to the *maʿnā*. For Rūmī, all outward beauty is a gateway to the realm of spiritual beauty and even Beauty Itself. The beautiful dance of the Sufi order associated with his name – that is, the Mawlawiyya, a whirling dance which has also became known in the West – was created by Rūmī upon hearing the rhythmic sound of the hammer in the bazaar of the goldsmiths in Konya. This outward sound was to provide the occasion for the remembrance of the celestial world from which Rūmī received his inspiration for the most famous of all dances in Sufism.

Art for Rūmī was thus inseparable from recollection, because traditional art reflects on the plane of external form or *ṣūrat* realities which belong to the archetypal world. Nowhere is this truth better illustrated than in the story of the Greek (that is, Byzantine) and Chinese painters in the first Book of the *Mathnawī*. To quote Rūmī himself:

> The Chinese said, "We are the better artists"; the Greeks said, "The [superiority in] power and excellence belongs to us."
> "I will put you to the test in this matter," said the Sultan, "[and see] which of you are approved in your claim."
> The Chinese and the Greeks began to debate: the Greeks retired from the debate.
> [Then] the Chinese said, "Hand over to us a particular room, and [let there be] one for you [as well]."
> There were two rooms with door facing door: the Chinese took one, the Greeks the other.
> The Chinese requested the King to give them a hundred colours: the King opened his treasury that they might receive that [which they sought].
> Every morning, by [his] bounty, the colours were dispensed from the treasury to the Chinese.
> The Greeks said, "No tints and colours are proper for our work, [nothing is needed] except to remove the rust."
> They shut the door and went on burnishing: they became clear and pure like the sky.
> There is a way from many-colourdness to colourlessness: colour is like the clouds, and colourlessness is a moon.
> Whatsoever light and splendour you see in the clouds, know that it comes from the stars and the moon and the sun.
> When the Chinese had finished their work, they were beating drums for joy.
> The King entered and saw the pictures there: that [sight], as he encountered it, was robbing him of his wits.
> After that, he came towards the Greeks: they removed the intervening curtain.
> The reflexion of those [Chinese] pictures and works [of art] struck upon these walls which had been made pure [from stain].
> All that he had seen there [in the Chinese room] seemed more beautiful here: 'twas snatching the eye from the socket.
>
> (*Mathnawī*, Bk I, 3465–85)

From the point of view of spiritual realization, the mirror of the Greeks symbolizes the heart of the Sufis, as Rūmī himself asserts later in the poem. But the poem is also a metaphorical exposition of the *modus operandi* of traditional art. If the painting of the Chinese, so admired among the Muslims of Rūmī's day, represents celestial realities, the work of the Greeks, which must have certainly evoked for Rūmī's audience Byzantine icons with their supra-human origin and inspiration, represents what all authentic sacred art should be – a reflection of the celestial prototypes, which are more accessible to us here below than the celestial realities themselves. And it is precisely because traditional art forms reflect the celestial prototypes that they are the means to recollection or remembrance (*dhikr*) of the Friend or Beloved, to use the well known Sufi terminology. This is also why Rūmī insisted upon the significance of the Sufi concert (*samāʿ*) as an aid to spiritual realization. For him, hearing music brings forth ecstasy within the soul, for it causes the recollection of the celestial music that all human beings heard on the day when, according to the Quran, they made their pre-eternal covenant with God attesting to His Lordship. And so Rūmī chanted in these well known verses:

> 'Tis said, the pipe and lute that charm our ears
> Derive their melody from rolling spheres;
> But Faith, o'erpassing speculation's bound,
> Can see what sweetens every jangled sound.
> We, who are parts of Adam, heard with him
> The song of angels and of seraphim.
> Our memory, though dull and sad, retains
> Some echo still of those unearthly strains.
> (*Mathnawī*, Bk IV, 733)

Such is also the power of beauty in both life and art. The soul is in search of beauty in outward forms, usually not realizing that it is seeking the Divine Beauty.

> Kings lick the earth whereof the fair are made,
> For God hath mingled in the dusty earth
> A draught of Beauty from His choicest cup.
> 'Tis that, fond lover – not these lips of clay –
> Thou art kissing with a hundred ecstasies,
> Think, then, what must it be when undefined!
> (*Mathnawī*, Bk V, 372)

The beauty of art forms has the capacity of interiorizing the beholden and acting as a gate to the Throne of the One who is also the Beautiful as such. In fact, all beauty is but a reflection of Beauty and all beautiful forms so many reflections of the Face of the Beloved in the myriad mirrors of cosmic existence. Sufis are especially sensitive to beauty because in them the thirst for liberation from the confines of separative existence is particularly intense and they see in things beautiful a gate toward the illimitable world of Divine Beauty for which their souls yearn and which bestows upon them freedom from all separation and limitation. (Some two centuries after Rūmī, the Persian Sufi ʿAbd al-Raḥmān Jāmī wrote, "The Absolute Beauty is the Divine Majesty embued with [the attributes of] power and beauty. Every beauty and perfection manifested in the various grades of being is a ray of His perfect beauty reflected therein. It is from these rays that exalted souls have received their impress of beauty and their quality of perfection" (*Lawāʾiḥ*, pp. 6–7).) Among the

Sufis, no one emphasized more nor understood in greater depth the salvific power of beauty and therefore the profound nexus between art as traditionally understood and the spiritual life than did Rūmī.

The most evident document of Islamic aesthetics is, of course, the eloquent but usually outwardly silent presence of Islamic art itself. Over the centuries the aesthetics as well as the teaching of the techniques for the production of this art, from tile work to calligraphy, from architecture to music, have remained mostly in oral form and much of this tradition is still transmitted from master to disciple rather than through written documents. The products of Islamic art, whether visual or sonoral, themselves speak, however, of the philosophy upon which they are based, especially if we attune ourselves sufficiently to their message. These works reflect a philosophy of art that sees the origin of art forms in the imaginal and ultimately intelligible world beyond the whim and fancy of individual subjectivism, forms which, precisely because they descend from celestial archetypes, are able to carry us back to that realm. The function of Islamic art is therefore recollection in the Platonic sense – the recollection of spiritual realities which also reside at the center of our being. It is also a means of untying the psychological knots of the soul so as to enable the Spirit to breathe through the veils that stifle its presence within man. This art seeks to ennoble matter not by an idealism which would make matter appear to be something that it is not, but by revealing it to be what it *really* is – namely a mirror for the reflection of cosmic qualities which themselves reflect the Divine Qualities.

Islamic art is an art which dissolves the limitations of external form in the indefinite rhythms of form, space or sound, thereby opening the soul to the reception of the presence of the One who is not only absolute but also infinite. This art, issuing from the inner reality (*al-ḥaqīqa*) of the Quran, is an integral aspect of the Islamic revelation and plays a basic role not only in the beautification of everyday life, but also in the remembrance of God and the beauty of the Beloved for which our soul yearns here below, for we carry the imprint of the Divine at the center of our being even in the exile of our earthly existence and the confines of the world of forgetfulness.

Finally, it might be said that Islamic art is a demonstration of the truth of the Quranic verse, "Whithersoever ye turn, there is the Face of God" (2, 115), for in the ambience created by Islamic art over the centuries, and to the extent that that ambience still survives here and there in the Islamic world, wherever one turns one cannot but behold that beauty which is the radiance of the Face of the Beautiful.

Bibliography

Writings

Ghazzālī, Aḥmad 1986: *Sawāniḥ*, tr. Nasrollah Pourjavady (London: Kegan Paul International).

Jāmī, ʿAbd al-Raḥmān 1978: *Lawāʾiḥ – A Treatise on Sufism*, tr. E. H. Whinfield and Mīrzā Muḥammad Ḳazvīnī (London: Theosophical Publishing House).

Kirmānī, Awḥad al-Dīn 1978: *Heart's Witness*, tr. B. M. Weischer and P. Wilson (Tehran: Imperial Iranian Academy of Philosophy).
Rāzī, Najm al-Dīn 1982: *The Path of God's Bondsmen from Origin to Return*, tr. Hamid Algar (Delmar: Caravan Books).
Rūmī, Jalāl al-Dīn 1982: *The Mathnawī of Jalālu'ddīn Rūmī*, ed. and tr. Reynold A. Nicholson (London: Luzac and Co.)
Ṣadr al-Dīn Shīrāzī 1981: *Wisdom of the Throne*, tr. James Morris (Princeton: Princeton University Press).
Suhrawardī, Shihaboddin Yaḥyā 1977: *Oeuvres philosophiques et mystiques*, ed. S. H. Nasr, Vol. 3 (Paris: A. Maisonneuve).
—— 1982: *The Mystical and Visionary Treatise of Suhrawardī*, tr. Willard Thackston (London: Octagon Press).

References and further reading

Ajami, Mansour 1988: *The Alchemy of Glory: the Dialectic of Truthfulness and Untruthfulness in Medieval Arabic Literary Criticism* (Washington, DC: Three Continents Press).
Burckhardt, Titus 1976: *The Art of Islam*, tr. P. Hobson (London: Festival of the World of Islam).
—— 1986: *Alchemy – Science of the Soul, Science of the Cosmos*, tr. W. Stoddart (Shaftesbury: Element Books).
Chittick, William 1983: *The Sufi Path of Love* (Albany: State University of New York Press).
—— 1994: *Imaginal Worlds* (Albany: State University of New York Press).
Corbin, H. 1969: *Creative Imagination in the Sufism of Ibn ʿArabī*, tr. R. Mannheim (Princeton: Princeton University Press).
—— 1977: *Spiritual Body and Celestial Earth*, tr. N. Pearson (Princeton: Princeton University Press).
—— 1980: *Avicenna and The Visionary Recital*, tr. W. R. Trask (Irving: Spring Publications).
Corbin, H. in collaboration with Nasr, S. H. and Yahya, O. 1993: *A History of Islamic Philosophy*, tr. L. Sherrard (London: Kegan Paul International).
Ettinghausen, Richard 1947: "Al-Ghazzālī on Beauty," in *Art and Thought*, ed. K. Bharatha Iyer (London: Luzac and Co.).
Kamal, S. 1991: *The Poetics of Alfarabi and Avicenna* (Leiden: E. J. Brill).
Lings, M. 1976: *The Quranic Art of Calligraphy* (London: Festival of the World of Islam).
Morris, James 1995: "Divine 'Imagination' and the Intermediate World: Ibn ʿArabī on the Barzakh," *Postdata – Revista Trimestral de Arte, Letras y Pensamiento*, 15, June–August.
Nasr, S. H. 1977: *The Transcendent Theosophy of Ṣadr al-Dīn Shīrāzī* (Tehran: Imperial Academy of Philosophy).
—— 1987: *Islamic Art and Spirituality* (Ipswich: Golgonooza Press).
—— 1993: *An Introduction to Islamic Cosmological Doctrines* (Albany: State University of New York Press).
Nasr, S. H. and Leaman, O. (eds) 1996: *History of Islamic Philosophy*, 2 Vols (London: Routledge).
Nicholson, R. A. 1978: *Rūmī – Poet and Mystic* (London: Unwin).
Rahman, Fazlur 1976: *The Philosophy of Mullā Ṣadrā* (Albany: State University of New York Press).
Schimmel, Annemarie 1982: *As Through the Veil* (New York: Columbia University Press).
—— 1993: *The Triumphal Sun* (Albany: State University of New York Press).
Thackston 1982: *The Mystical and Visionary Treatise of Suhramardi*. London: Octagon.

34

Reality and divinity in Islamic philosophy

JOSEP PUIG MONTADA

A Philosophical theology

Because of the impact of Islam in the development of Arab culture, the first Arabic thinkers were theologians. Their main concern was not to prove God's existence or his creation of the world (both these facts being obvious in their view), but to solve questions related to human destiny. They argued about such questions as whether the Muslim who had committed a major sin had thereby lost his faith and deserted the community of believers, and about the exact status of human freedom. This second question was particularly perplexing since, if a person is the author of his own acts and therefore responsible for them, God's power would be curtailed, but on the other hand, if the person is not responsible, his freedom of action is suppressed and God would be unjust in punishing him for his bad deeds. (I make no distinction here between the terms "God" and "Allah," since for Muslim authors the God of Islam is also the God of Judaism and Christianity.)

Soon, however, the attention of Arabic theologians was drawn as well to the issue of the relationship between God and the world that He had created. Jahm Ibn Ṣafwān (d. 748) was probably the first thinker to have focused on God's almightiness and uniqueness (*tawḥīd*) in addressing this issue. According to Jahm, God ultimately creates all human acts, but He holds humans responsible for their deeds because He creates in them the capacity (*qūwa*) and the decision to act. In searching for a balance between God's uniqueness and His power, Jahm contended that originally God was alone and that in creating the world, which He maintains continuously in existence, He proves His almightiness. The world that God created, moreover, consists of Paradise and Hell as well as this material world. And when this material world reaches its end, as is announced in the Quran, Paradise and Hell will also be destroyed, Jahm maintained, so that God alone will remain.

Jahm Ibn Ṣafwān was one of a number of thinkers who contributed to the development of Islamic theology in the *Kalām*. The degree of influence of Christian theology, and especially its dialectical method, on the development of the *Kalām* remains a matter of discussion. Nonetheless, the whole remains an original Islamic product, the authorship of which has to be ascribed to the Muʿtazilites.

In spite of their diversity, the Muʿtazilites exhibited a common streak of independence, both in political affairs, such as the contest between the Calif ʿAlī (656–661) and his adversaries, and on religious issues, such as the debate over whether a major sinner continued to be a believer or not. They relied on human reason and on logical arguments to explain Islam, to clarify the relationship between God and His creation, and to defend Islam against other religions. Thus if Islam's basic tenet stresses that there is no other divinity than Allah, and therefore underlines the fact of His being unitary (*tawḥīd*), Muʿtazilism insists on the internal consistency of this unity. Everything is one in God and His attributes (*ṣifāt*), such as science and power, cannot be distinguished from His essence. God knows, wants, sees, speaks, and so on, because of His attributes. But these are identical to His essence. On the other hand, everything outside the Divinity has been created – even those divine actions that have an external projection. This is the case, for example, with respect to God's speech, which is eternal as residing in His essence, but is created as revealed in the form of the Quran.

Although all Muʿtazilites would agree with these general statements, they offered different interpretations in specifying the essence of God and the structure of the universe. Let us look first at the interpretation advanced by Abū al-Hudhayl al-ʿAllāf (d. 840 or 849), the founder of doctrinal Muʿtazilism. In his view, God's science or knowledge is God himself, as are His power, His hearing and seeing, and His wisdom:

> If someone says: "The Creator is able (*qādir*)" he asserts a power that is God, denies any incapacity in God and points out something decreed (*maqdūr*) to exist or not to exist. Similar was (Abū al-Hudhayl's) teaching about the essential attributes, following this order. (Al-Ashʿarī, 1985, Vol. 2, p. 157)

Consequently, Abū al-Hudhayl contended that these attributes are one in God, and that He is science, ability and life. Al-Ashʿarī remarks that Abū al-Hudhayl borrowed these concepts from Aristotle, but that he improved the expression of them with his contention that "His science is God himself (*huwa*) and His ability is God himself."

The created world, including humans, stands to this supreme reality in a relation of continuous dependency, and in the atomic doctrine Abū al-Hudhayl found the most adequate way to explain this dependency. The basic unit of beings in the created world is the body, which in turn is made of atoms – that is, "the one part that is not divisible." At least six atoms are needed to build a body, for there are six basic directions right–left, before–behind, above–below) of any body. One atom has no extension, but it can move or be at rest, come together with other atoms or move apart on its own and "become" at some place (*kawn*). Thus we find created reality divided into atoms and accidents, and the logical function of atoms is to serve as a substrate for the realization of accidents. Atoms, in other words, function as prime matter, while accidents constitute the actual being of all created reality, whether of atoms or of composite bodies, and can be understood as form. Accidents, however, do not result from essences, nor are they founded in the atoms. Abū al-Hudhayl did not conceive of becoming in quite the same sense that the philosophers did. As the latter saw it, becoming is a process in which something new comes out of something else, which itself had to have the capacity or potential of becoming this novelty. By contrast, Abū al-Hudhayl considered becoming to be an accident limited to space – that is, the accident of being temporally located in space.

Because of the volatility of this world, God needs to be active all the time, not only to bring all things into existence, but also to keep them existing, and eventually, to terminate their existence. Thus three distinct realities emerge in this picture: at one end of the spectrum, almighty God, at the other end, the insignificant thing "in itself," and between these two poles, the thing's existential dimension – either as beginning-to-exist, as enduring, or as being-annihilated.

> The act of creating (*khalq*) something is different from the thing itself, the endurance (*baqā'*) is different from the enduring thing, and the annihilation (*fanā'*) is different from the annihilated thing. The endurance is God's saying to the thing "endure," and the annihilation is God's saying "be annihilated." (Al-Ashʿarī, 1985, Vol. 2, p. 50)

The act of the Agent can be creation, endurance or annihilation of the object, and in all cases the act of the Agent is a voluntary act, which is manifested through the divine word. The word here unites will and intelligence, and acquires an essential role in God's activity with respect to the world.

Since God's activity is such that no event in the world occurs at random or by itself, the exercise of human freedom and responsibility would be impossible, were it not for the fact that humans have the kind of special status attributed to them by Abū al-Hudhayl. Like all created beings, a human being consists of a set of accidents – spirit, soul, life, senses – which inhere in a body, but unlike any other creature, a human has the power to implement his own acts. God has given him some share of power.

> Some people say: God has bestowed His servants with the ability to carry out movements, to rest, to utter sounds, to feel pain, and to all that the quality of which they know. As for those accidents whose quality men do not know, as [for example] colors, flavors, smells, life, death, ability (*qudra*) and lack of capacity, the Creator cannot be characterized with the power to endow them with the capacity of any of those accidents. This is the view of Abū al-Hudhayl. (Al-Ashʿarī, 1985, Vol. 2, p. 60)

Only if a person knows how to realize something does he have power over it, because, in general, there is no act or event that is not the direct result of an intentional choice. Abū al-Hudhayl links human choice to human knowledge of the means of achieving specific purposes. Human acts that are not produced in a deliberate and conscious way, are not human acts, but divine acts, like events in nature, and God is their intentional Agent. Human beings, therefore, have the power to act only insofar as they know *how* to act and consciously make the choice *to* act. Their action is not creation but innovation (*iḥdāth*) and their freedom is restricted to a choice between two alternatives. In spite of these limitations, humans escape the finiteness of all other created beings and transcend the limitations of their bodily substrate.

The Muʿtazilites, in fact, did not agree upon the extent of a human being's power to act, and Abū al-Hudhayl represents the middle position in their debates. Abū al-Hudhayl influenced Abū ʿAlī al-Jubbāʾī (d. 916) and his son Abū Hāshim [ibn] al-Jubbāʾī (d. 933), both of whom in turn influenced the Qāḍī ʿAbd al-Jabbār (d. 1025). While there are no extant original writings of the earlier Muʿtazilites, ʿAbd al-Jabbār's are numerous and give us a clear picture of the Muʿtazilite doctrine.

Abū l-Ḥasan ʿAbd al-Jabbār Ibn Aḥmad, who was born in Baghdad, was appointed chief judge of Rayy (Tehran) in 971 by aṣ-Ṣāḥib Ibn ʿAbbād, minister of the Būyid prince Muʾayyid ad-Dawla, who, as a Shīʿite, favored Muʿtazilite trends. Among the Qāḍī's many works, mention has to be made of *The Useful Text for the Sections of God's Unity and Justice*, the publication of which was encouraged by Ṭāḥā Husain. Although in ʿAbd al-Jabbār's system there is no section devoted exclusively to the sources and means of human knowledge, the issue preoccupies him, and he often discusses the nature of human knowledge. He distinguishes two kinds: necessary and acquired. Necessary knowledge is to be found in us, but is not from ourselves, whereas acquired knowledge is the result only of human reflection (*naẓar*).

Our knowledge of God, according to the Qāḍī, is only possible through reflection, as reality divides into two opposite categories: the visible and the hidden. The visible reality (*ash-shāhid*) is the whole of this world, with its substances and accidents, and the hidden reality (*al-ghāʾib*) is the other world, namely, God. We may have necessary knowledge of the visible reality, but not of the hidden. To acquire knowledge of God, we have to employ reflection, which, in relying on analogy (*qiyās*), enables us to infer something about the hidden reality on the basis of something in the visible reality.

The first element in our knowledge of the other world is a demonstration of God's existence. The Qāḍī's main argument, which he ascribes to Abū al-Hudhayl, is based on the fact that the bodies in our world are innovated (*muḥdath*, temporally produced). Bodies show four modes of being (*akwān*) – movement, rest, coming-together and going-apart – and no body can exist outside of these modes of being. These modes are themselves not eternal, because they may exist and may not exist. Since they are not eternal, they must be innovated. The bodies, in which these accidents inhere, must also be innovated, because the body does not exist before its accidents are produced. Everything that is innovated (*muḥdath*) needs someone who has brought it into existence (*muḥdith*). We can reach this conclusion by way of analogy: our own experience shows that whatever comes into existence through human effort needs a specific human being as the subject who brings it into existence. However, innovated beings do not have the power to produce bodies, because they act only according to a disposition that inheres in a substrate – for example, we can move only what is movable, and bodies can only be produced without using a substrate. Therefore, bodies must have a producer who is eternal.

Once ʿAbd al-Jabbār has provided us with a proof of God's existence, which recurs in the Kalām, we can address the issue of God's attributes. We may insist on the external and internal oneness of God, who, for ʿAbd al-Jabbār as for other Muʿtazilites, is an absolute and immaterial unity. This doctrine reduces God's attributes to pure names or, alternatively, we can say that the attributes are identical with God Himself, as we read in Abū l-Hudhayl. To mitigate this denial of the attributes, Abū Hāshim al-Jubbāʾī, the master of ʿAbd al-Jabbār, developed the theory of modes or states (*aḥwāl*). This was originally a general theory of predication, which he then applied to the issue of God's attributes. According to Abū Hāshim, one who is knowing differs from one who is ignorant by virtue of the state in which he is. "State" is thus a term predicated of a subject, and occupies a nebulous place between existence and non-existence.

For ʿAbd al-Jabbār, God is characterized by different states or modes. He is able (*qādir*) without limitations – that is, He is almighty, He is knowing (*ʿālim*), He always knows everything, and because He is knowing and able, He is living (*ḥayy*) and existent (*mawjūd*). These are the four essential qualities, but among His other qualities we may mention divinity. ʿAbd al-Jabbār, who again follows Abū Hāshim, considers divinity as one of God's states, and defines it by claiming that God alone deserves worship. By means of the theory of modes or states, the divine attributes gain a degree of reality (albeit slight) that does not affect God's unity and simplicity.

Recall that ʿAbd al-Jabbār's proof for God's existence was elaborated on the ground of a radical division between this perceptible world and the other, hidden world. With most Muʿtazilites, ʿAbd al-Jabbār agrees that the world is ultimately built from atoms. A body must be composed of at least eight atoms: two for its length, two for its breadth and four more for its depth. These eight points define the angles of a cube, which is the first body. The division between atoms and accidents becomes, for ʿAbd al-Jabbār, a division between substances and accidents. Substance is basically the substrate that bears the accident, so that substance and accident are often taken as synonyms. There are many kinds of accidents, and most of them can be brought into existence only by God. A human being, however, can produce these external accidents: being-in-space (*kawn*), pressure, composition, pain and sound (or speech); as well as these internal ones: conviction, will, aversion, opinion and reflection.

ʿAbd al-Jabbār contended that God, in spite of His absolute simplicity, exhibits states, and he claims that this is true as well of the created world. How are states related to substances and accidents? States are neither an additional category of being nor a pure abstraction: their reality lies between these. In contrast to substances, which only God can create, and to accidents, some of which human beings can produce too, states may be brought about by accidents inhering in the same substance that is to be characterized by these states. When an accident of this kind exists, the thing acquires the related state. In this way, ʿAbd al-Jabbār lets causes slip into the perceptible world.

The doctrine of states or modes derives originally from human self-experience: a person knows when he finds himself in a certain state, and says, for instance, "I am knowing," "I am able," "I am reflecting." The existence of states is made possible by that of related accidents or qualities, the most important of which are life, perception, ability, knowledge, and will. Endowed with these qualities, humans enjoy a privileged position among the beings of this world, although it implies a great degree of responsibility.

Human self-experience makes one aware that one is the agent of one's acts and that one is responsible for them. One's free act (*taṣarruf*) only results from one's will, and one knows as well that all of one's conscious acts have a moral value and that they deserve blame, if they are evil, and that they do not deserve it, but deserve praise, if they are good. Taking this as his starting point, ʿAbd al-Jabbār developed his ethical doctrine and established, by means of reason, the relative values of human acts. Here we face a problem, however. The Quran insists that all men will be punished or rewarded by God in the afterlife, and the Islamic legal tradition arranged its sanctions to correspond to those laid down by revelation for the future world. In contrast, ʿAbd al-Jabbār started from the rational standpoint and saw in human acts an objective value, causing them to be deserving of praise or blame, here as well as in the afterlife.

We might ask, then, whether ʿAbd al-Jabbār recognized any conflict between reason and the Quranic word? In fact, he did contemplate a few situations – as, for example, the offering of obligatory prayer – in which human reason may at first not find the same moral value that revelation does. He observed, however, that once the latter is known, we are able to uncover the rational justification of this value:

> Revelation only uncovers, about the character of these acts, aspects whose evilness or goodness we should recognize if we knew them by reason. For if we had known by reason that prayer is of great benefit to us, leading us to choose our duty and to earn reward thereby, we should have known its obligatoriness by reason. (ʿAbd al-Jabbār, 1962, Vol. 6, p. 64)

God's created speech, as the Muʿtazila defines the Quran, is the supreme manifestation of rational activity, and humans have no need to fear inquiring into this rationality. According to prevailing Muslim theology, however, humans should refrain from this adventure. According to Abū l-Ḥasan al-Ashʿarī (d. 935), the founder of "orthodox" Kalām, our human abilities in this respect are very limited and should be used for arguing in defense of the revealed dogmas.

It is true that Muʿtazilite Kalām does not constitute any close doctrinal *corpus*, but the foregoing exposition of two of its main representatives has outlined some basic features: (1) Divinity and worldly reality are radically distinct. God is not only one but His essence is pure unity, and His attributes are to be described in such a way that they do not affect this absolute simplicity. (2) God created this perceptible world, which remains in dependency upon Him. The evolution of the Kalām tends toward conferring upon this unstable reality some degree of internal causality, although all of its components are only temporally produced (*muḥdath* or "innovated"). (3) Human beings enjoy a special status within this worldly reality. They are able to listen to God's created speech, they are capable of rational activity and, above all, they are able to initiate their own acts and to bear moral responsibility for them. Moral behavior lifts humanity above material reality and brings it nearer to God, in spite of the insurmountable distance.

B Religious philosophy

Neoplatonism was the predominant philosophy in the geographic areas conquered by the Arabs and thus the philosophy cultivated by a group of Muslim thinkers who were attracted by "the sciences of the Ancients" was also Neoplatonic. It combined the doctrines of Plotinus (d. 270) with a significant amount of Aristotelian material, especially with regard to the philosophy of nature. The beginnings of philosophical work in the Arabic language (and still within the Greek tradition) can be traced to the reign of the Abbasid Caliph al-Ma'mūn (813–833), but the first philosopher who built up a representative system lived a century later. Abū Naṣr al-Fārābī (d. 950) was active in Baghdad and eventually at the court of Sayf ad-Dawla (945–967) in Aleppo.

Al-Fārābī accepted the Neoplatonic conception of the unity of all reality and the contention that there exists a primary Unity from which different manifestations emanate. His main work, the *Book on the Views of the Inhabitants of the Perfect State*, integrates this conception with the Aristotelian view of the world and nature in a somewhat naive way. In this book, al-Fārābī adopts an aprioristic method and begins with a description of God, as we see in his summary:

> First section. The thing that has to be asserted as Divinity in the perfect religion: Which kind of existent He is, what is His substance, with which attributes He must be described, how the existing beings derive from Him, on which aspect He is cause of their existence, by which names He must be called and invocated. (Al-Fārābī, 1972, p. 32)

God is the First Existent and His existence is the most excellent, since it is not stained by non-existence or by potential existence (and thus God is actuality). Al-Fārābī's description echoes Aristotle's in the *Metaphysics* (XII.6), but differs from Aristotle's in his use of the concept of existence, which is a Plotinian elaboration. For Aristotle, being is always used with reference to one principle, substance, and is always predicated of a subject. For al-Fārābī, existence is an autonomous entity and beings possess it as an attribute, so that God has "substance and existence." God's existence is different from that of all other beings because "it is that by which He is existing in Himself" (al-Fārābī, 1972, p. 46) – that is, it is an existence without external cause.

Unity is a divine characteristic as important as existence, and since being and oneness imply each other, God's unity and existence cannot be separated. Al-Fārābī argues that one of the meanings of unity is the particular existence that causes each existent to be different from all others. This is the main reason why the First Existent is called one: because of the existence He has and by virtue of which He is different from all others.

Intellect constitutes the substance of the Divinity. Aristotle had already established that God is pure self-thinking and Plotinus had made Intellect the second of the first three hypostases (after the One and before the Soul). Al-Fārābī follows this tradition and explains that, since the First Existent is not material and since only matter prevents form from being intellect, He is actual thinking (*ʿaql bi-l-fiʿl*). What He thinks is His own essence, and He becomes the thinking subject and the thought object. Al-Fārābī then goes on to describe God in terms of different attributes. The First Existent is "knowing," "wise," "true," and "living." He is perfect and possesses infinite majesty, greatness and glory. These attributes remind us of those listed by the Muʿtazilites, and like them, al-Fārābī maintains that attributes do not cause any multiplicity in God's essence.

Al-Fārābī often refers to the Divinity just as the First, and on other occasions as the First Cause, for he cannot isolate the concept of His from that of the universe which emanates from Him:

> The First is that from which existence is brought about. When the First exists with the kind of existence which He has, it follows that all existents come into existence but those that exist because of man's will and choice. (Al-Fārābī, 1973, p. 55)

Through emanation (*fayḍ*), the existence of one being comes out of the existence of another; at the beginning is the First and at the end, prime matter. In the process of emanation two stages can be distinguished: the superior comprises the heavenly spheres, each one endowed with soul and intellect, the inferior comprises the world below the sphere of the Moon. The sublunar reality is subject to life and death, to coming-to-be and passing-away. In spite of the striking difference of rank between the First Cause and the material world, the idea of unity prevails: the emanated existents constitute "one set and are like one thing" (al-Fārābī, 1973, p. 57).

The human situation in this system is two-sided: human beings obviously belong to the sublunar world, but their intellectual activity shows that they participate in the eternal world above. According to al-Fārābī, human intellect goes through three stages in the process of knowing. All humans have a natural disposition for intellectual knowledge, but they themselves cannot activate this potentiality. They need the intervention of the Active Intellect, to which Aristotle referred in *De Anima* III.5. The Active Intellect causes the natural disposition (passive intellect) to become active (actual intellect) – and makes out of this disposition something different (acquired intellect). The Active Intellect is also thought to be the source of the first universal principles of science and morality, which are innate to mankind.

Al-Fārābī identifies the Active Intellect with a hypostasis that emanates from the ninth celestial sphere – that of the moon – and is convinced that man can attain a permanent union with it. The way in which this conjunction is possible is similar to the way in which form is joined to matter: the acquired intellect becomes matter for the Active Intellect. This happens after the soul is free from bodily accidents, but only if the soul developed, during its bodily life, its rational faculties, both theoretical and practical. For this reason, we read in al-Fārābī that the souls of ignorant people will perish, since they have not built up the acquired intellect and need a material substrate to exist.

There are no signs at all that al-Fārābī sustained a Sufi or mystic doctrine with regard to the afterlife. The souls of the perfect community will survive and attain happiness, he contends, although he offers sometimes differing opinions and leaves certain questions unanswered concerning this. The souls of the perfect community, though, will not ascend to the First nor dissolve inside the Active Intellect; they will remain united to it.

God and His creation are two clearly distinguished parts of a unity: God is the First and all other existents come after Him by means of emanation. Now the question may be asked, of course, "How do we prove this?", and any such proof must define the nature of the dependency of this world on God, from a metaphysical point of view. Al-Fārābī did not answer the question, although he may have given some hint of an answer in stating that the First exists in Himself.

Abū ʿAlī Ibn Sīnā (or Avicenna, 980–1037) did answer it. He insisted on the distinction between essence and existence. In all created beings there is a gap between what they are and the fact that they exist. From what they are it does not follow that they exist. Their existence is possible and it becomes necessary once their cause acts. The idea of necessity is paramount in his system. Nothing can exist without necessity, but this necessity can be founded in the very subject or in another – that is, every actual existent is necessary either by virtue of itself or by virtue of another, the latter in turn possibly being existent by virtue of itself. From necessity we revert to causation: what is possibly existent needs a cause to exist actually and if the cause acts, it exists necessarily.

The beings we know through our experience are either innovated (they came to be and will pass away) or eternal (that is, the heavenly spheres), but in both cases they are not necessarily existent by virtue of themselves; they are necessitated by another. An endless chain – or even a circular one – of this kind cannot account for existence by virtue of itself, and so the chain must have a first link which is necessary by itself. This is a summary exposition of one of Avicenna's arguments, a cosmological one, for the existence of God as a being whose existence is necessary by itself.

Avicenna complemented Alfarabi's aprioristic doctrine with suitable proofs and endowed it with a metaphysical structure. Thus the distance between the First Cause and its chain of effects is deeper for him than for al-Fārābī, and the dependency of the created world on its efficient cause is stronger, since He is continuously adding existence to their essences, although not directly but through multiple intermediate causes. From this point of view, the differences between philosophy and Kalām, either Muʿtazilite or Ashʿarite, do not seem to be insurmountable. There is, however, an obstacle which orthodox Islam could not overcome – namely, the philosopher's belief in the eternity of the world.

In a chapter of his *Book of Directives and Admonitions* (1968, Vol. 3, pp. 65–71), Avicenna considers the two ways in which something can be necessary by virtue of another: always or at a certain moment. In the former case, the existence of the thing in question is not preceded by non-existence, as it is in the latter case. What always is necessary by virtue of another does not come in time after what necessitates it, although there is a priority in essence (*qabalīya bi-dh-dhāt*). As a consequence of this twofold distinction, Avicenna speaks of creation (*ibdāʿ*) and production (*ṣanʿ*). To create is to bring something into existence without an intermediate cause and without its non-existence preceding temporally. To produce is to bring into existence something that earlier did not exist in time by using an intermediate cause. The resulting being is innovated (*muḥdath*). According to Avicenna, the world exists through eternal creation and is not innovated. He explicitly attacks those who claim that God existed but the world did not until He decided, at a certain moment, to create it (Avicenna, 1968, Vol. 3, pp. 105–6).

(The conflict between Kalām and Falsafa was therefore obvious and Abū Ḥāmid al-Ghazzālī (1058–1111) undertook the systematic task of refuting the philosophers' views on the eternity of the world, but also their views that God only knows universals and that there is no resurrection of the body. To this purpose, he wrote the *Tahāfut al-Falāsifa*, or "Destruction – collapse – of the philosophers." Al-Ghazzālī's attack was countered by Ibn Rushd (Averroes, 1126–1198) in his *Tahāfut al-Tahāfut*, or "Destruction of the *Destruction*." Averroes did not just repeat Avicenna's arguments, but resorted to Aristotelian proofs based on the eternity of time and movement.)

For Avicenna, the relation between Divinity and reality is not limited to God's necessitating the existence of the latter, either directly or through intermediate causes. The place of human beings in the universe is a privileged one, since they have souls which can return to the Divinity. Still on earth, a person can become an *ʿārif*, one who enjoys an intuitive knowledge of the Divine. To reach the stage of the mystic *ʿārif*, one has to strain one's will towards the world of the intelligences, one has to practice severe auto-discipline and dominate one's passions. When the *ārif* reaches the final stage, he falls into ecstasis and takes immeasurable delight in knowing the eternal Truth. One's delectation of the Divine can be permanent once one's soul has left the body after death. The souls of those who did not cultivate their spiritual element during their earthly existence will survive in a state of "imaginary" reality comparable to that of dreams. Only the souls of the wise will be able to return to their source and will be eternally illuminated by the divine Light.

This Islamic interpretation of Divinity and reality under the influence of Greek philosophy exhibits certain distinctive features: (1) Divinity and reality are closely related. Hierarchic order and rational coherence unite the divine Cause with its effect, which is the universe. (2) As eternal as the Cause is, so eternal is the effect, the creation of which did not have a beginning and will not have an end. (3) The human dimension is not only moral, but intellectual as well. One's good deeds will save one, but the development of one's intellectual dimension will lead one back to God and allow one to enjoy the view of the Divinity.

Consequently, there is not just one conception of reality and Divinity in Islamic philosophy but two. For the Kalām, or philosophical theology, God is an absolutely unique Being who, in a conscious and voluntary way, created in time this perceptible world, and who is responsible for all of its events except for those that humans deliberately produce. For the Falsafa, or the philosophy inspired by the ancient Greeks, God is the First Cause of reality, which is its eternal effect (although this reality is also constituted by innovated beings that are not caused directly by God but by a chain of intermediate causes). While both Kalām and Falsafa place in our hands our future salvation, Falsafa reserves for the wise, for those who develop their intellectual capacities, the possibility of returning to the First Cause and enjoying perfect happiness in contemplation of the Divinity.

Bibliography

Writings

Abū l-Hasan Al-Ashʿarī 1985: *Maqālāt al-Islāmīyīn*, ed. M. M. ʿAbd al-Ḥamīd, 2nd edn, 2 Vols (Cairo: Dār al-Ḥadathā).

Abū l-Ḥasan ʿAbd al-Jabbār 1960–74: *Al-Mughnī fī Abwāb al-Tawḥīd wa-l-ʿAdal*, various eds, 16 Vols (Cairo: Ministry of Culture).

Abū Naṣr Al-Fārābī 1973: *Kitāb ārā' Ahl al-Madīna al-Fāḍila*, ed. A. N. Nādir, 3rd edn (Beirut: Dār al-Mashriq).

Abū l-Ḥusain Ibn Sīnā 1968: *Kitāb al-Ishārāt wa-t-Tanbīhāt*, ed. S. Dunyā, 4 Vols (Cairo: Dār al-Maʿārif).

Translations

Book on the Views of the Inhabitants of the Perfect State 1972: Abū Naṣr al-Fārābī's *Mabādi' ārā' Ahl al-Madīna al-Fāḍila*, tr. R. Walzer (Oxford: Oxford University Press).

Averroes 1954: *Tahāfut al-Tahāfut* [The Incoherence of the Incoherence], tr. S. van den Bergh, 2 Vols (London: Luzac).

Avicenna 1951: *Livre des directives et remarques* [Kitāb al-ishārāt wa l-tanbīhāt], French tr. A.-M. Goichon (Beirut and Paris: Vrin).

—— 1978–85: *La Métaphysique du Shifā'*, French tr. G. C. Anawati, 2 Vols (Paris: Vrin).

Further reading

Caspar, R. 1987: *Traité de théologie musulmane* (Rome: Pontificio ISAI).

Cook, M. 1981: *Early Muslim Dogma: a Source Critical Study* (Cambridge: Cambridge University Press).

Davidson, H. A. 1987: *Proofs for Eternity, Creation and the Existence of God in Medieval Islamic and Jewish Philosophy* (Oxford: Oxford University Press).

—— 1992: *Alfarabi, Avicenna and Averroes on Intellect* (Oxford: Oxford University Press).

Frank, R. M. 1966: *The Metaphysics of Created Being according to Abū l-Hudhayl al-ʿAllāf* (Istanbul: Netherlands Institute).

—— 1978: *Beings and their Attributes. The Teaching of the Basrian School of the Muʿtazila in the Classical Period* (Albany: State University of New York Press).

Galston, M. 1990: *Politics and Excellence. The Political Philosophy of Alfarabi* (Princeton: Princeton University Press).

Gardet, L. and Anawati, M. M. 1981: *Introduction à la théologie musulmane*, 3rd edn (Paris: Vrin).

Gimaret, D. 1980: *Théories de l'acte humain en théologie musulmane* (Paris-Leuven: Vrin-Peeters).

Hourani, G. F. 1971: *Islamic Rationalism. The Ethics of ʿAbd al-Jabbār* (Oxford: Oxford University Press).

Michot, J. R. 1986: *La destinée de l'homme selon Avicenne* (Leuven: Peeters).

Peters, J. R. T. M. 1976: *God's Created Speech* (Leiden: Brill).

Van Ess, Josef 1991–5: *Theologie und Gesellschaft im 2. und 3. Jahrhundert Hidschra*, 6 Vols (Berlin: W. de Gruyter).

Watt, W. Montgomery 1948: *Free Will and Predestination in Early Islam* (London: Oxford University Press).
Wensinck, A. J. 1965: *The Muslim Creed*, 2nd edn (Cambridge: Cambridge University Press).
Wolfson, H. A. 1976: *The Philosophy of the Kalam* (Cambridge: Harvard University Press).

35

Selfhood/personhood in Islamic philosophy

JOHN WALBRIDGE

I Introduction

The question of the self and person in Islamic philosophy can be considered from several different perspectives. The term "philosophy," *falsafa*, in Islam refers solely to the Greek tradition of thought represented by such thinkers as al-Fārābī, Avicenna, and Averroës. Even some of those who unquestionably belong to this tradition – Suhrawardī and Mullā Ṣadrā, for example – tend to avoid the term "*falsafa*" in favor of the Arabic synonym "*ḥikma*" (lit. wisdom). There are other Islamic intellectual traditions that are unquestionably philosophic in one sense or another or that have important implications even for thinkers working strictly within the Graeco-Islamic tradition of *falsafa*. The most basic tradition of thought about the self and person is Quranic Islam, which sets the fundamental terms of reference for moral and religious thought about the person in the Islamic world. (The Quran is always considered by Muslims to be the word of God, not of Muhammad.) The rich tradition of Islamic legal thought about the person may be considered an extension of Quranic thought on the subject. For convenience, in the present article this tradition will be referred to as "Quranic" or "Islamic," but it must be remembered that thinkers of other traditions in the Islamic world also considered themselves to be "Quranic" and "Islamic," though perhaps in different senses. The second tradition that I will discuss is Graeco-Islamic philosophy, which I will refer to as "philosophy." This represents the tradition of Plato and Aristotle, combined in various proportions and sometimes with conspicuous elements of Neoplatonism and Neopythagoreanism. The third tradition is Sufism, Islamic mysticism, which developed important and influential ideas about the self and person.

II Quranic Islam and the self and person

Is the Islamic conception of the person individualistic or communalist? It is both, each in an extreme sense, for the Islam of the Quran places the individual man, without friends or excuses, alone before God's awful throne of judgment, yet Islam identifies religion and community without separation or neutral ground. The second conception especially has proven deeply unsettling to modern Westerners accustomed to liberal notions of the separation of church and state.

It is difficult to avoid tracing the paradox of the Islamic notions of self and community to the primal Arabian experience of the desert. In pre-modern times the population of the Central Arabian desert must have been well below one person per square kilometer, much of which would have been huddled together in a handful of oasis communities. The deep-desert bedouin existed in tiny scattered kinship groups, constantly on the edge of starvation and ever on the move in search of pasture and water. They were a population too scattered and impoverished to support even the most rudimentary of governments. Such an environment produced individuals who were independent, quarrelsome, disdainful of law, proud to the point of braggadocio, utterly and unreasonably loyal to kinsmen and guest, yet in the end fatalistic. This is not the place for a study of the ethos of pre-Islamic Arabia; what is important is that the desert Arab combined two radically different attitudes towards the relation between himself and his community. On the one hand, he saw himself as utterly independent and self-reliant, owing allegiance to no other man and relying on no one else. The pre-Islamic poet Ta'abbata Sharran wrote of the bedouin outlaw:

> Through one desert in the sun's heat, through another in starlight,
> Lonely as the wild ass, rides he bare-backed Danger noon and night.
>
> (Nicholson, 1907, p. 81)

On the other hand, the bedouin's clan and tribe were of supreme importance to him, and so the poets constantly praised the nobility of their own tribes. Any injury done to a fellow tribesman had to be avenged, regardless of who was at fault. The poet Durayd b. Ṣimma, who had lost his brother in an ill-considered feud with another tribe, sang:

> I am of Ghaziyya: if she be in error, then I will err;
> And if Ghaziyya be guided right, I go right with her!
>
> (Nicholson, 1907, p. 83)

The Quran contemptuously dismisses the bedouin ethos with its bloody quarrels, its radical individualism, and its excessive pride in ancestry. While Islam and the Quran certainly do represent a fundamental ethical and religious change, they are not so much an utterly new and alien system as a transformation of the old attitudes, a deep and creative reinterpretation of the ethical ideals of the ancient life of the desert.

The fundamental religious and ethical premise of the Quran is the responsibility of the individual before God. The Arabs of Muhammad's day seem to have been less shocked by his condemnation of their gods than by his bald assertion that their noble ancestors were burning in hell. Whereas the bedouin outlaw had seen himself in a lonely struggle with the elements and all other men, the Muslim is engaged in an equally lonely struggle to prepare himself for the last judgment. When that dreadful day comes, he will stand alone before God and will be presented with a book recording all his deeds. If the good outweighs the bad, he will enter paradise. If not, he will be cast into eternal flames. That day – and, by extension, every day of his life in this world – his friends and relatives will be unable to help him. No excuses and no intercession will be accepted, only his good deeds. Though later Islamic thought sought to soften this doctrine by allowing the intercession of the Prophet and perhaps the saints, a radical sense of individual moral responsibility has remained at the heart of Islam, for no matter how close a Muslim's relations may be to family, friends, and fellow Muslims, he knows that he, and they, must each face God alone on the Last Day. The truest symbol of the spiritual life of Islam is thus the single Muslim kneeling in prayer while ordinary life goes on around him.

Paradoxically, this individualism is accompanied by an equally radical communitarianism. God says in the Quran, "Man has transgressed, for he thinks himself independent" (Quran 96, 6–7). In a sense, the senior member of a Muslim's community is God Himself, for the Quran lays constant stress on the mercy and bountifulness of God and His constant solicitude for man and especially the believers. The social expression of God's solicitude towards the believers is the *umma*, the community of the Muslims. Just as the bedouin poet found his only real security in the solidarity of his clan and took pride in the nobility and prowess of his tribe and its chiefs, so too the Muslim finds support, friendship, and security in the mercy of God and the brotherhood of the community of believers. By founding the Islamic community, Muhammad sought to destroy the old loyalties of the "Time of Ignorance" and replace them with a single loyalty to God, His Prophet, and the Muslim community. Muhammad was both prophet and ruler of this community, and so there was no distinction of church and state. Outside this community there can be no true Islam, thus the persistent discomfort Muslims feel in living outside of an Islamic state, whether as a minority in a non-Islamic land or under secular rulers with dubious claims to Islamic piety.

The combination of absolute individual moral responsibility and a demand for its expression within a community have produced an ideal of egalitarian theocracy. The individual's spiritual aspirations can only be fully realized within a community loyal to these aspirations and governing all aspects of life. Yet the moral and religious responsibility of the individual guarantee an ideal of religious egalitarianism, the fullest expression of which is the annual pilgrimage to Mecca, where Muslims of every degree, whether kings or slaves, don the same simple dress to visit the House of God.

The most widely accepted intellectual formulations of the Quranic intellectual tradition are religious law (*fiqh*) and dogmatic theology (*Kalām*, lit. speech [about religious subjects]). In Islamic law the person is defined by religious obligations acquired by a voluntary acceptance of a particular prophetic revelation, preferably Islam. First, a person must accept a prophetic religion, an obligation he acquired by his acceptance of the Covenant with God before the creation of the world (Quran 7, 172). Though to fail to do so was *kufr* (lit. "ingratitude" and thus "unbelief"), the acceptance of religious obligation must be a voluntary act, just as in Islamic political thought, where a king's sovereignty only became effective through the voluntary allegiance of the people through the pledge of allegiance made by their representatives. Within the Islamic system, all possible actions, however mundane, were governed by religious law, each being obligatory, desirable, indifferent, undesirable, or prohibited. Religious obligations could also be divided into those binding on each individual as an individual, such as the daily prayer, and those binding on some unspecified individual, such as ruling the state, fighting in the holy war or burying a dead person. In the latter case, someone arising to do the action meant that others were relieved of the obligation. Thus for the practitioners of Islamic law, individuals were defined primarily by their religious obligations. The whole structure of society is conceptualized in terms of individual religious obligations acquired by voluntary acceptance of the religion given by God through Muhammad.

Kalām, Islamic dogmatic theology, is a theological account of the universe. Unlike Graeco-Islamic philosophy, it was generally recognized by Muslims as a legitimate intellectual discipline. It predates the rise of Graeco-Islamic philosophy by about a century. *Kalām* arose from debates both within early Islam and between Muslims and non-Muslims. At its core were debates about the power, justice, and providence of God and the free will of human beings. In its mature formulation *Kalām* was generally atomist and occasionalist, rejecting all secondary causes in the universe in favor of God's unfettered power. Thus the *Kalām* discussions of persons as moral agents are an attempt to give a coherent account of how a just omniscient and omnipotent God and morally responsible human beings can coexist. The *Kalām* theologians saw that for human beings to be responsible, they must be able to act according to their free will, but if they did, they, like God, were creators. However, if God created the actions of human beings – in other words, if human beings are predestined to do what they do – then how can a just God hold them responsible for their actions? The difficulties of combining divine power and human free will were dramatized in a series of antinomies, the most famous of which concerned the fate of three people in the afterlife: a saint, a sinner, and one who died in infancy. To the infant's complaint that he had been denied the opportunity to do good works, God could reply that in His foreknowledge He knew that the infant would grow up to be a great sinner. But what answer could He then give to the sinner burning in Hell? The *Kalām* theologians offered a variety of answers to this and other dilemmas, ranging from firm affirmations of human freedom to radical predestination. The Quran supports both extremes. To the extent to which we can say there was an "orthodox," "official" answer, it was the doctrine of acquisition: that God in His omniscience knows what the moral decisions of individual human beings will be and creates their acts accordingly, which they "acquire" by their choices.

III Philosophical conceptions of the self and person

Whereas the Quranic conception of the self is grounded in religion and ethics, the conception of the self in Islamic philosophical psychology arises from epistemological concerns, in particular a set of problems arising from Aristotle's *De anima* and his view of the human soul and intellect. The most influential account of the soul and mind is that of Avicenna, as stated in his massive *Healing* and in shorter works, notably the *Salvation* and *Hints*. The self as an ethical and political entity is usually treated in Islamic philosophy from a point of view that combines Platonic and Aristotelian elements. The issue of consciousness becomes prominent in later Islamic philosophy, coming abruptly to the fore in the twelfth century with Suhrawardī's theory of mind as light.

Avicenna on the soul and intellect

For Avicenna "soul" was shared by human beings, animals, and plants. His views represent a systematization of those of Aristotle, influenced by Galenic medicine. In accordance with his Neoplatonic cosmology, the soul of each living thing is emanated whenever a suitable combination of matter comes into being. The lowest kind of soul is the vegetable soul, possessing only the faculties of nutrition, growth, and reproduction. To these the animal soul adds the faculties of voluntary motion and perception, including both external and internal senses. It is only the human soul, the "intellect" (*ʿaql*), that can think in terms of abstractions; animals can think, but only in terms of images. The human soul is a single substance, of which its vegetable, animal, and distinctively human portions are in some sense parts. The human soul, at least, is potentially an independent substance, for we can imagine a man created as an adult and suspended in air with all sensation cut off. He could not affirm the existence of his body, but he could affirm the existence of his mind. Thus the body and the mind are different entities.

Though Avicenna as a physician is well aware of the complexity of the vegetable and animal souls as they drive the various bodily functions, his chief philosophical interest is the intellect. He derives this theory from the murky hints of *De anima* III via an influential treatise on the subject by al-Fārābī. The underlying problem is how we can think universals – triangle in general, for example. It is not difficult to understand how an animal can think particulars, for the images of particulars can in a sense be projected in the eye and the brain. However, we can never form an *image* of triangle in general, since any image we form will be, for example, either a right triangle or not. No material organ, Avicenna concludes, can know universals, and no immaterial faculty can know particulars. The intellect, then, is an immaterial faculty that in use actually becomes the universal it contemplates. Following al-Fārābī, Avicenna identifies four (or five) stages in the development of intellect: the material intellect, which is the potential for knowing forms; (the habitual intellect, which is the intellect that has begun to contemplate the primary intelligibles;) the actual intellect, which is the intellect that has reached a level of actualization where it can contemplate these forms at will; the acquired intellect, which is the intellect in a higher degree of actualization where it can contemplate the forms, does so, and fully knows that it does so; and the active intellect, which is the intellect of the sphere of the moon and which emanates the forms onto the individual intellects of human beings.

This theory of Avicenna ran into difficulties with the problem of individuation and immortality. Islamic thinkers were naturally committed to the concept of the immortality of the human soul. While the vegetable and animal souls would presumably perish with the body, there seemed no reason why the immaterial intellect should not survive. But in what way was this intellect the same as the individual who had died? The accusation was sometimes made by critics of the philosophers that they could only prove the immortality of some sort of collective intellect, not of the individual; after all, those memories and experiences that distinguish the individual are experiences of the body, not of the immaterial intellect. Likewise, how could the philosophers explain the reward and punishment of the individual in the afterlife? Avicenna could only answer feebly that the immaterial intellect was in some way colored by its lifetime of association with the body, an answer that failed to reassure either the theologians of Islam or those of Latin Christendom. The identification of God as an immaterial intellect likewise raised questions about whether God could even know individuals. The definitive debate about these issues is found in al-Ghazzālī's *Incoherence of the Philosophers*, a text that identifies 20 philosophical propositions as either heretical or outright unbelief, and its refutation by Averroes, *The Incoherence of the Incoherence.*

Suhrawardī and the self as light

The most important alternative to the al-Fārābī/Avicenna theory of intellect was Suhrawardī's "illuminationist" theory of minds as immaterial lights. Suhrawardī (d. 1191), who considered himself to be in the tradition of Plato and the Sufis, identified the key problem of philosophical psychology and epistemology as consciousness. A mind is directly aware of itself and of the entities it experiences. Suhrawardī used the symbol of light to characterize mind: a light is manifest and makes other things manifest, in the words of an early commentator. A mind is an immaterial light, whose nature it is to be manifest to itself and to make other things manifest to itself – in other words, to know those things. Starting with the simplest case, Suhrawardī rejects both the intromission and intramission theories of vision, holding instead that vision is simply the unobstructed presence of a light or lighted thing before a sound eye. For him, the philosophically important aspect of vision is the conscious experience of seeing, not the intermediate conditions studied by the scholars of optics. Light does not travel from (or to) the lighted object; light simply makes the thing manifest to the eye. A similar explanation holds for the so-called inner senses. The forms of the imagination and memory cannot somehow be projected onto a bodily organ, since we imagine a mountain as far larger than the organ in which the image supposedly exists. The brain provides the locus wherein the image of the mountain is manifest, but it is the image of the *mountain* that is manifest to us, not some sort of picture of it. Intellectual knowledge and self-consciousness occur in the same way. The self is a light that is manifest to itself; the intelligibles are manifest to this light.

Though Suhrawardī's theory lacks the scientific complexity of Avicenna's, it does solve a number of difficulties. First, it explains the unity of the self. There is in a real sense only one mental faculty, the immaterial light/mind, which does all its knowing and perceiving in the same way, through presence. Suhrawardī also introduces a number of other questions, notably reincarnation and animal minds. Avicenna had been able make a clear distinction between animal and human minds by asserting that they knew in different ways: while animals know through the animal soul, a more-or-less physical entity, human beings know through the immaterial intellect. Suhrawardī erases this distinction and thus the distinction in kind between human beings and animals. The immaterial lights that are human minds are "brighter" than the lights of animal minds, but they are not different in kind. Suhrawardī, a self-identified platonist, knew of the platonic doctrine of reincarnation and rejected it, though with arguments so feeble as to cast doubt on his sincerity. His commentator, Quṭb al-Din Shirazi (1236–1311), accepted reincarnation as an explanation for animal minds: human beings were reborn as animals suitable to their character flaws, and went through many rebirths and were gradually purified until their souls could escape to the world of light.

The self in Islamic philosophical ethics and politics

The ethical and social self also appears in Islamic practical philosophy. Despite a promising start with the political works of al-Fārābī, ethics and political theory remained a relatively undeveloped area of Islamic philosophy, the subject being largely ceded by default to the religious lawyers. Ethics was most strongly influenced by the *Nicomachean Ethics*, though with a platonic cast. For Islamic philosophers, ethics is a natural outgrowth of psychology – moderation in the three faculties of anger, desire, and intellect, and also their proper balance, yielding the four cardinal virtues of courage, temperance, wisdom, and justice. Since the underlying temperaments of individuals differ, their respective virtues and vices may differ. A man with a strong tendency toward acquisitiveness, for example, may find its satisfaction in either greed or zealousness in the pursuit of virtue.

Since the *Politics* was not available in Arabic, Islamic thought on political philosophy was shaped by platonic sources, particularly epitomes of the *Republic* and the *Laws*. Al-Fārābī was the dominant figure in this branch of philosophy. He saw the function of the virtuous state as educational, with its laws and religion – the two are scarcely distinguished in Islamic thought – encouraging the moral development of the citizens. Imperfect states pursued lesser goals such as honor and wealth. Al-Fārābī and his followers, the most important of whom were in Spain, were troubled by the place of the philosopher in the imperfect city – the "weed" as he is sometimes called. Al-Fārābī and his followers saw religion, including Islam, as an imaginative representation of the truths of philosophy, designed to urge the ordinary man to do what is good for him – "the teachings of the theologian are based on fables," as the doctrine was indignantly rendered by the authors of the Paris Condemnation of 1277 (Hyman and Walsh, 1983, p. 591). The philosopher thus lived a life of semi-hypocrisy, urging others to follow to the letter a religion whose literal truth he did not accept, while he himself pursued a life dedicated to the acquisition of philosophical wisdom. This dilemma and its implications for the nature of the philosophical self is dramatized in the famous philosophical novel *Ḥayy ibn Yaqẓān*, by the twelfth century Spanish philosopher Ibn Ṭufayl.

Ḥayy, the hero, grows up all alone on an island, where he is raised by a doe. Through sheer intellectual power he is able to attain the heights of philosophical mysticism, discovering the various levels of scientific and philosophical truth until he finally learns to devote himself entirely to mystical contemplation. He is the philosophical self totally divorced from society. He does not even know language, only what pure reason can know. One day he discovers another human being, Āsāl, a pious and intelligent man who has come from a populated neighboring island to live as a religious hermit. Through him Ḥayy learns of the existence of society and of religion. Seeing in religion distorted versions of the truths he has discovered through reason, Ḥayy conceives that he has a duty to enlighten his fellow men. Despite the reservations of his new friend, the two sail for Āsāl's neighboring island. The missionary venture is a disaster, and just in time Ḥayy realizes that ordinary people are best left to follow their partial truths. Ḥayy and Āsāl return to the desert island and devote the rest of their days to lonely contemplation of the Infinite.

IV Sufism and the self

The subtlest discussion of psychological issues in Islamic thought occurs among the Sufis, the mystics of Islam, in the context of analysis of the stages on the mystical path. Three sets of issues are particularly relevant to the concepts of selfhood and personhood: the lower self and its control, the annihilation of the soul in God and its union with God, and the human being as a manifestation of the Godhead.

The lower self and its control

Sufis conceptualized the mystical enterprise as a journey. The seeker must travel a series of stages to reach his goal. Psychologically, this journey is understood as a process by which the self is gradually annihilated so that it can be restored in God. The Quran refers to the "commanding soul (or self)", the "blaming soul," and the "soul at peace." In the early stages of the mystical path, the seeker must repent and subdue his lower, "commanding self." This self is seen almost as a separate mind coexisting in the mystic's body, not unlike the Freudian unconscious. A Sufi talked of leading his self around on a leash like a little dog. The Sufi's decision to enter the mystical path must be followed by a determined effort to subdue this lower self through ascetic exercises, mortification of the self and the ego, and strict obedience to his Sufi master. Constant vigilance is required even by advanced mystics against the wiles of the lower self. The old Sufi who found himself regretting the fornication he had not gotten around to committing as a youth knew that this last minute fall from grace was due to the wiles of his lower self.

Annihilation

The next step in the control of the lower self involved love. Passionate, yearning, hopeless love burned away the attachments of the self to the flesh. It is for this reason that famous lovers have a central place in Sufi literature. The Sufi in love with God is compared with the poor man who falls in love with a rich and beautiful woman. She can care nothing for him, and he knows this very well, so he sits by her door in the alley. Gradually he wastes away from frustration and starvation, hoping only that she will notice him, if only to rebuke him. Since he cannot hope to win her, he can expect only self-destruction from his love. In the beginning of Rūmī's famous mystical epic, the *Mathnavī*, the reed flute's plaintive sound expresses its pain and yearning in its separation from the reed-bed.

Union

The annihilation of the self is not a goal but a means to union with God, or, to use the usual term, "abiding" or eternal life in God. The ontological nature of the state sought by the Sufi is a hotly debated question among Sufi theorists and Islamic theologians and philosophers, but the state certainly involves some sort of restoration of the self to wholeness and integrity. This insight led the Sufis on an increasingly sophisticated analysis of the relationships among God, the self, and the manifestations of the attributes of God in the world. The ecstatic or "drunken" mystics speak sometimes of becoming God, a formulation that is defended even by sober Sufis as appropriate to their psychological state. The early Sufi al-Ḥallāj had said, "Anā 'l-Ḥaqq," which means "I am the Truth" or "the Absolute" – in other words, "I am God." Al-Ḥallāj was crucified for his presumption, but his statement was defended even by Sufis who held that he ought not, out of prudence, to have said such a thing. Most Sufis would have denied that it was possible to become God, but that a mystic might feel himself to have become God was a perfectly normal expression of a certain stage of the mystical journey. Thus al-Ḥallāj came to be the martyr of ecstatic mysticism in Islam, the Sufi who could see no difference between his own self and God.

The most famous depiction of annihilation and union in Sufi literature is found in the mystical epic, *The Conference of the Birds*, by the Persian Sufi poet Farīd al-Dīn ʿAṭṭār. In this story, the birds of the world are told they must set out to find their king, the immortal phoenix who lived on the mountain at the end of the world. Various birds, each representing a character flaw, offer their excuses: the falcon cannot bear to leave the pomp of court, the duck cannot bear the loss of purity involved in a long journey across a waterless desert, and so on. Finally, the birds set out and cross the seven valleys representing the stages of the mystical path. When they finally reach the palace of the phoenix, they are turned away by the chamberlain, who points out that they are bedraggled, unimportant, and unworthy of the phoenix's attention. When the 30 surviving birds protest that they have journeyed very far, the herald admits them, only to present them with a document detailing their lives and their every sin and hypocrisy. With this final humiliation their last traces of self are burned away and they discover – to the frustration of the poem's translators – that they themselves are their king, for the 30 birds (Persian: *sī morgh*) are the immortal phoenix (*sīmorgh*). Thus the mystic will at the end find God within himself and find that God is his self.

The rational exposition of the ecstatic mysticism of al-Ḥallāj is found in the works of Ibn ʿArabī, the greatest theoretician of Sufism. For Ibn ʿArabī, the universe and everything in it, including the human self, are the self-manifestations of God. For him, God is both hidden and manifest. For Ibn ʿArabī – to oversimplify greatly his complex system – the things of the world are manifestations of the attributes of God, and the attributes of God are His relations with the world. The various things that are not God each manifest a different attribute or attributes of God. In a sense, says Ibn ʿArabī, every creature has a different God, the sum of the divine attributes that the creature manifests. Man occupies a unique place since he manifests – or rather, potentially manifests – all the attributes of God. The person in whom these attributes are fully manifested is the "Perfect Man," variously identified with the Sufi saint and the prophet, depending on the functions that he actually fulfills in the world. Ibn ʿArabī cites the Islamic tradition, "He who knows himself (or his self), knows his Lord," as evidence for the soundness of his view. Thus for Ibn ʿArabī and the innumerable Sufi thinkers influenced by him, the life of the spirit is a continual successions of meetings with the divine. As was the case for ʿAttar's birds, the most important such meeting is the one that takes place within one's own self.

V Modern thought

The challenges posed to the Islamic world by the West in the nineteenth and twentieth centuries have led to a thorough reappraisal of every aspect of Islamic thought. In particular, the challenge of Western ideologies of liberal capitalism and socialism have brought to the fore the tensions between the individualistic and communitarian aspects of Islam, leading important modern Islamic thinkers to attempt to articulate Islam as an ideology standing between the two great Western ideologies.

Theocracy

A number of important modern Islamic thinkers – notably Khomeini and Islamists like Sayyid Quṭb and the Muslim Brotherhood in the Arab world – have called for a theocratic state modeled on the Islamic state of Muhammad and the first caliphs. The separation of church and state, whether *de facto*, as in medieval and modern Islamic states, or *de jure*, as in the modern West, is un-Islamic in their view and prevents Islam from having its intended salutary effect on society. Only in a society in which Islamic law is enforced can the individual be molded to Islamic standards. Such a theory in fact justifies the informal theocracy of early Islam by an appeal to the theory of the state as educational institution as expressed by al-Fārābī. Less radical thinkers call for the enforcement of Islamic law by Islamic states or application of Islamic law in various areas of modern life, notably the so-called "Islamic economics," or advocate the spread of Islam in the West as a solution to its social problems. In a sense, such calls for reform may be seen as attempts to Islamize either socialism or liberal capitalism. Both approaches center on Islamic law and embody the old tension between the individual and the communal self.

Renewal of religion

A quite different approach to the reassertion of Islam in the modern world is found among a group of thinkers offering Islam as the solution to the spiritual aridity of modern life. Such thinkers usually draw inspiration from Sufism or esoteric Shiʿism and address themselves primarily to the West. These thinkers are highly intellectual as a rule and are concerned with mysticism and philosophy, usually giving little attention to the legal and communal aspects of Islam.

Bibliography

Writings

ʿAttar, Farid ud-Din 1984: *The Conference of the Birds* (Harmondsworth: Penguin).

Averroës 1954: *Tahāfut al-Tahāfut* [The Incoherence of the Incoherence], tr. S. van den Bergh, E. J. W. Gibb Memorial Series, n.s. 19, 2 Vols (London: Luzac).

Avicenna 1952: *Avicenna's Psychology: an English Translation of Kitāb al-Najāt*, Book II, Chapter VI, tr. F. Rahman (Oxford: Oxford University Press).

Ibn Tufayl 1972: *Ḥayy ibn Yaqẓān: a Philosophical Tale*, tr. Lenn Evan Goodman, Library of Classical Arabic Literature 1 (New York: Twayne).

Miskawayh 1968: *The Refinement of Character*, tr. Constantine K. Zurayk (Beirut: American University of Beirut).

Suhrawardī forthcoming: *The Philosophy of Illumination*, ed. and tr. John Walbridge and Hossein Ziai, Islamic Philosophy Translation Series (Provo: Brigham Young University Press).

References and further reading

Butterworth, Charles 1992: *Political Aspects of Islamic Philosophy: Essays in Honor of Muhsin S. Mahdi*, Harvard Middle Eastern Monographs 27 (Cambridge: Harvard Center for Middle Eastern Studies).

Chittick, William 1989: *The Sufi Path of Knowledge: Ibn al-ʿArabī's Metaphysics of Imagination* (Albany: State University of New York Press).

Corbin, Henry 1993: *History of Islamic Philosophy*, tr. Liadain Sherrard (London: Kegan Paul).

Dabashi, Hamid 1993: *Theology of Discontent: the Ideological Foundation of the Islamic Revolution in Iran* (New York: New York University Press).

Fakhry, Majid 1983: *A History of Islamic Philosophy*, 2nd edn (New York: Columbia University Press).

Ha'iri Yazdi, Mehdi 1992: *The Principles of Epistemology in Islamic Philosophy: Knowledge by Presence* (Albany: State University of New York Press).

Hyman, Arthur and Walsh, James J. (eds) 1983: *Philosophy in the Middle Ages*, 2nd edn (Indianapolis: Hackett), "Islamic Philosophy," pp. 203–335.

Kepel, Gilles 1993: *Muslim Extremism in Egypt: the Prophet and Pharaoh* (Berkeley: University of California Press).

Lerner, Ralph and Mahdi, Muhsin 1972: *Medieval Political Philosophy: a Sourcebook* (Ithaca: Cornell University Press), Pt 1, pp. 21–186.

Massignon, Louis 1982: *The Passion of al-Ḥallāj*, 4 Vols (Princeton: Bollingen).

Nasr, Seyyed Hossein 1964: *Three Muslim Sages: Avicenna – Suhrawardī – Ibn ʿArabī* (Cambridge: Harvard University Press).
—— 1978: *An Introduction to Islamic Cosmological Doctrines* (Boulder: Shambhala).
Nicholson, R. A. 1907: *A Literary History of the Arabs* (Cambridge: Cambridge University Press).
Rahman, Fazlur 1994: *Major Themes of the Qur'an* (Minneapolis: Bibliotheca Islamica).
Schimmel, Annemarie 1975: *Mystical Dimensions of Islam* (Chapel Hill: University of North Carolina Press).
Sivan, Emmanuel 1990: *Radical Islam: Medieval Theology and Modern Politics* (New Haven: Yale University Press).
Walbridge, John 1992: *The Science of Mystic Lights: Quṭb al-Din Shīrāzī and the Illuminationist Tradition in Islamic Philosophy*, Harvard Middle Eastern Monographs 26 (Cambridge: Harrard Center for Middle Eastern Studies).
Wolfson, Harry Austryn 1976: *The Philosophy of the Kalam*, Structure and Growth of Philosophic Systems from Plato to Spinoza IV (Cambridge: Harvard University Press).

36

The concept of the good in Islamic philosophy

MOURAD WAHBA

In his book, *Sufi Essays*, Nasr observes that:

> Islam presents a view of life which is completely sacred and a freedom which begins with submission [to] the Divine Will. . . . [I]n the language of Islamic peoples there is no distinction between the sacred and the profane or temporal realm. . . . Through the Divine Law, which encompasses all human life, every human activity is given a transcendental dimension: it is made sacred and therefore meaningful. (Nasr, 1972, p. 166)

Once the Divine Law is established, of course, theology must be based upon it. Consequently, the arguments of the theologians involve nothing but quotations from the sacred texts. And these quotations provide the main evidence, sufficient and final, in terms of which any question is to be settled. The pivotal belief of most Islamic theologians is that God's Unity necessitates the dependence upon Him of all beings. If this were not the case, there would be the possibility of transforming God into Gods. In ethics, for example, if man could judge what is good, he might overrule what God rightly prescribes for him, and this would be blasphemous. This view is theistic, then, in that the decider of all values is taken to be God.

In opposition to this generally held position stand the Muʿtazilites. Justice, according to them, is one of the attributes of God, but it is a negative attribute, in the sense that God does not commit acts that are evil and His acts cannot contradict human reason, which distinguishes between good and evil. Things, however, are either good or evil in themselves. Thus evil cannot be misidentified as the good, they contend, and the Divine Law cannot be against reason. It follows that reason is the basis of the idea of the good even prior to the Divine Law, and when the Divine Law appeared, it merely ensured what reason had said before. The Muʿtazilites also point out in this regard that, if reason were unable to distinguish between good and evil, then the prophets would not have asked people to use their reason in distinguishing between them. The Divine Law itself, moreover, does not speak about the fine details of good and evil. These issues are left to human beings to work out with the aid of their reason. Given that they believe that reason perceives the moral value of acts, the Muʿtazilites consider this value – that is, the goodness or badness of the acts themselves – to be absolute. Thus God does not determine, arbitrarily, the moral value of an act. On the contrary, this value is intrinsic in the act. All that God does is inform us of this value through the revelation of the Prophet, if He finds that this information is necessary.

The most expressive figure among the Muʿtazilites is ʿAbd al-Jabbār. In his book entitled *Summa on the Headings of God's Unity and Justice*, he states that good and evil are objective. In one sense, good is to be defined as nothing more than the negation of evil. But the absence of evil is still only a necessary, and not yet a sufficient, condition for good. This is evident from his classification of good acts. These are divided into three classes. The humblest class includes those acts for which the agent deserves neither blame nor praise for either doing them or not doing them. Among the examples he offers are breathing air and eating food. The next class of good acts includes those for which the agent deserves praise when he performs them, but for whose omission he does not yet deserve blame. Two kinds of acts fall into this class: those which do good directly to other people, and those which induce a state of mind in which such acts will subsequently be done. To this there corresponds yet another distinction – between acts known as good by reason and those known as good by revelation. The third and last class is that of the obligatory act. According to al-Jabbār, an obligatory act is one for which a person capable of doing it deserves blame if it is not done.

Al-Ashʿarī and al-Ghazzālī argue against this line. Al-Ashʿarī emphasizes that we cannot be satisfied with reason if we are to discover how we are to act, for our moral principles can only stem from God's commands. Our knowledge of good and evil and of our duty is obtainable only through our acceptance of revelation, in which God details the precise nature of his commands and prohibitions, in order that those who follow them may earn the enjoyment of rewards in the next life.

Al-Ghazzālī, on the other hand, objects to the idea of God's being confronted with human notions of good and evil which have been given the status of an extrinsic and independent law. In arguing against the objectivity of ethics, then, al-Ghazzālī presents an explanation of how religious references can be incorporated into the meaning of ethical terms. He does this by interpreting the key ethical concepts of good and evil theologically. God, he contends, has no ends. Thus it would be misleading to call any of His actions "good" in the normal sense. Consequently, His actions are not necessary but merely possible. He could have done otherwise. Al-Ghazzālī sums up his view as follows:

> We assert that it is admissible for God the exalted not to impose obligations on his servants, as well as to impose on them unachievable obligations to cause pain to his servants without compensation and without offense, that it is not necessary to Him to take notice of what is in their best interests, nor to reward obedience or punish disobedience and that it is not necessary for Him to send prophets, and if it is not necessary of God to send prophets and if He does not send them it is not evil or absurd, yet He is able to demonstrate their truthfulness by a miracle. (Sherif, 1975, p. 160)

This text implies that there is no point in arguing that God's actions are good since the notion of good is logically inappropriate as an attribute of divine action. Al-

Ghazzālī denies, then, that independent reason is a sufficient guide to ethical knowledge, while the Muʿtazilites distinguish between two kinds of obligations: those which are known by reason alone, and those which are known by revelation. By means of reason we can know the general direction in which moral activity must run, but by means of revelation we know the detailed rules that provide us with a practical guide to everyday actions. Against this claim, al-Ghazzālī argues as follows:

> In brief, whenever you wish to know the difference between those well-known judgments and the rational first principles, submit to your mind the statement "Killing a human being is bad and saving him from death is good" after imagining that you have come into existence all of a sudden mature and rational, having, however, received no instruction, been associated with to community, experienced no human hierarchy or polity, but having simply experienced sensible objects. You would then be able to doubt these premises or at least hesitate in assenting to them, whereas you would be unable to experience such hesitation [in assenting to such claims as] "our statement's negation and affirmation are not true in one and the same state" and "two is greater than one."

Al-Ghazzālī then applies this principle to the discussion of goodness and badness. Human beings can only be servants of God, he contends. Whether their service is good or bad depends upon the point of view adopted. From the viewpoint of God, all actions are necessary and therefore good. But from the human viewpoint, the good may be described as pleasant, useful, or beautiful. The pleasant is felt immediately; the useful is judged from the perspective of ultimate ends; and the beautiful is gratifying at all times and in all situations. Bad things, by contrast, are those that are harmful. Just as things are *absolutely good* when they involve the three qualities of goodness – that is, utility, pleasure and beauty – so things are *absolutely bad* when they involve all three qualities of evil – that is, harm, pain, and ugliness. In actuality, however, most things involve combinations of the above six qualities. Of the three qualities of the good, the most important is usefulness. And of those things that are useful, good deeds within faith are the most useful, for they serve the highest end of man – his happiness.

After usefulness comes pleasure, in order of importance. Pleasures are either spiritual or bodily, but the first of these two categories is peculiar to man. Accordingly, we can represent the hierarchy of the goodness of pleasures in the form of a pyramid. The base of this pyramid encompasses what all animals share, and as we move towards its apex, we focus in on what is peculiar to man – which is to say, wisdom. Wisdom, being the pleasure of the spirit, is, of all the pleasures, the highest in the quality of its goodness, and wisdom in this sense refers to fellowship with God.

The Islamic philosophers, however, were not all of one opinion concerning the nature of the good. According to Miskawa, the good is the realization of the perfection of human existence. But men differ in their disposition towards the realization of this end. Some are good by nature and, because their nature is unchangeable, they do not commit evil, but these are a minority. The majority are disposed towards evil. The third class is neither good nor evil and shifts from the evil to the good and vice versa through punishment or through accompanying the good men.

The good is either general or particular, and there is absolute good, which is the Supreme Being. Good men endeavor to grasp this Being. However, from the subjective viewpoint each individual has his own good and this is incarnated in his being conscious of happiness or pleasure. This particular good is nothing more than the emanation of acts from the individual in question, according to his essence. But as long as the individual is independent of others he is unable to realize these possible goods, and consequently individuals have to establish a community in which love for all men is the basis of all virtues and duties. Hence the fruits of love flourish within and only within community, and asceticism and solitude are forbidden.

After Miskawa comes al-Fārābī. At the beginning of his *Book of Letters*, al-Fārābī states that religion comes later in time than philosophy, since its aim is to teach the multitude theoretical and practical things that are deduced from philosophy in ways that facilitate the multitude's understanding. Theology and jurisprudence come later in time than religion, and consequently are subordinate to it. Thus, according to this hierarchy, reason comes before revelation. In this sense al-Fārābī declares that reason is able to judge whether an act is good or evil. On this point he differs from the Sunna, who declare that the good is what is ordered by God and the evil is what God has forbidden.

Al-Fārābī considers the good to be the perfection of Being, who at the same time is the Necessary Being. Evil, in turn, is the privation of this perfection. Given al-Fārābī's relating of the good to the Divine Being, so far as Providence encompasses all beings, it follows that they are all good. Therefore, the good is the substance of beings, and what seems to be evil in fact exists by accident. Thus it too can be considered good, even though it seems not to be. If you peer carefully into nature, you will find that many things which seem to be catastrophic and evil are, in reality, a means of destroying what is more evil and more dangerous. When human nature acts, however, good and evil definitely emerge. Thus al-Fārābī denies the reality of evil on the ontological level and affirms its existence on the moral level. And on this level, the exercise of will and choice determine one's orientation either towards good or towards evil, provided that the choice involved in the moral act is based on rational reasons. What are these rational reasons? They are derived from al-Fārābī's understanding of reason as being essentially political in nature. Thus he identifies the good with the political good, or justice, rather than the ethical good. The reasons underlying action within the moral realm, then, are political, which is why al-Fārābī is known primarily through his political writings – *The Virtuous City*, *The Political Regime*, and *The Attainment of Happiness*. From these books it is evident that political science does not depend on the results of the investigation of beings above and beyond nature; rather, it builds on the foundations provided by natural science. It investigates those things by means of which man reaches his perfection, and distinguishes them from the things that obstruct his progress. It is concerned, that is to say, with the moral virtues and vices. Political science then considers the structure of the city and compares this to the structure of the world (excluding from this comparison any consideration of metaphysical or divine beings).

Accordingly, although man is said to be a natural being and the science of man is said to belong to natural science rather than to metaphysics, political science is not reduced to natural science. Man is a natural being of a special kind, and the differences between man and all other kinds of natural beings result from the difference in the way that nature prepares man to achieve his perfection. It does not give man his perfection, but only the means for achieving it through will and choice. Unlike the other kinds of natural beings, man is able to know the end towards which he must work as well as the means with which he is to perform the actions that bring him to that end. This knowledge is prior to, and the indispensable condition for, good action.

Thus al-Fārābī states that reason alone can define what is good and what is evil, and the absolute good is the attainment of happiness. But this cannot be attained unless man lives in political communities. It is impossible, in other words, for the isolated individual to attain the virtues conducive to the good human life. At the same time al-Fārābī emphasizes the fact that not all men are capable of being virtuous. So a hierarchy is needed, because some individuals have no virtues, others have some virtues, and still others possess all virtues. These last are the philosophers, who must rule, while those without virtues or possessing only some virtues ought to be ruled and guided. For the rule of philosophy provides the only guarantee that those lacking in virtues may attain some semblance of well-being and happiness. In guiding them to happiness, the philosopher-ruler makes use of the Divine Law in order to promote in them virtues necessary for their happiness. He does this by means of a political act which is lower than philosophy in rank and dignity, but superior to the Divine Law. This act is the establishment of the virtuous city, the existence of which is necessary for the well-being of the masses, but not for that of the philosophers, who may lead happy lives in an imperfect regime. The best city, according to al-Fārābī, is that which has been ruled by a series of virtuous kings. In view of the impossibility of establishing a perfect political city, however, the masses do well to live according to the rules of the Divine Law. The question now is, how does one make a community happy?

According to Ibn Sīnā, there is a relation between God and goodness. God is a necessary Being in essence as well as in all other aspects. That is, He could not be a Necessary Being in one sense and a possible Being in another, because that would involve a contradiction. And if He is necessary and everything that is possible has become possible by virtue of its necessity in Him, there remains nothing incomplete or lacking in Him to be explained – not will, nor nature, nor knowledge, nor any of His attributes. Furthermore, He who is Necessary Being in his essence is pure good and pure perfection. Thus the good is what every being keenly desires in order to perfect its existence. It is a condition of perfection and evil does not exist in essence. That is why Ibn Sīnā says, "Existence is goodness, and the perfection of existence is the goodness of existence." Thus a being that does not suffer any evil in the form of the absence of a substance, or of any undesirable state of it, is pure good. This could not apply to what is in essence a possible being. As for goodness in the sense of the useful and profitable, this, of course, is only a matter of attaining perfection in things. God contemplates his essence as well as the order of the good pervading all things. By doing so, that order emanates from him to all existent things. We love and seek the good, but only for a purpose. God, on the other hand, entertains no such purpose, and he possesses this form of pure intellectual will with no specific aim in view.

Evil, according to Ibn Sīnā, takes various forms. It may be a defect stemming from ignorance or from the disfigurement of the body; it may be something that causes pain or sorrow as the result of some act; it may be just the lack of what brings happiness and provides for the good. In essence, it is the absence of something – a negative and not a positive element. It is not every form of negation, but the non-existence of what has been provided by nature for the perfection of things. Hence it is not something definite and determined in itself. If that were the case, there would exist what might be called "universal evil." As an accident, evil is the concomitant of matter and may come from outside and be an external factor, or from inside and be an internal factor.

To the question why God did not make the pure good always prevail unaffected by the presence of evil, the answer is that such a situation would not be suitable for our genre of being. If we were to suppose the absence of evil, the consequences would constitute a still greater evil. Our judgment of evil is always relative and in terms of human action. It is with reference to something. Burning is for fire a perfection, and for those who may lose something as a result of it, an evil.

It should be observed that Ibn Sīnā offers no classification for an entity that destroys the essence of other entities, such as a positive theory of evil. Underlying his classification is his aim to establish the sense in which the Necessary Existent is the absolutely perfect. He specifies this feature of absolute perfection so as to stave off the objection that the emanation aspect of the Necessary Existent may lead to deficiency on Its part – a deficiency or loss of substance caused by the emanation of other entities from It. Accordingly, the Necessary Existent is portrayed as generating or sustaining goodness by being essential to the realization of other entities without losing anything in this process.

Good and evil are distinguished in the following ways. (1) With respect to the intention of the terms, differences are recognized between intrinsic goodness and instrumental goodness. (a) For example, something having intrinsic goodness may be good in itself if it leads to the perfection of some entities which are imperfect, though these do not strive to accomplish such a good. (b) That which possesses instrumental goodness is a good by means of which other things become better. (2) Good and evil are further distinguished with respect to the extension of the terms. (a) We call that entity "totally good" from which nothing but good can come. (b) We call that entity "predominantly good" from which good may come even though evil exists within it. (c) Finally, we call that entity "predominantly evil" from which good may come even though evil is dominant within it. It is evident that in this context Ibn Sīnā wishes to identify the Necessary Existent with that which is intrinsically and predominantly good. It is also apparent that he has no classification covering totally evil entities.

Ibn Rushd (Averroës) follows al-Fārābī in focusing upon morality, not from the perspective of how it is to be acquired, but in terms of how it is to be used to attain happiness. The question, once again, is about happiness and not about the good. As happiness is the end of the political community, there is no good per se, but only the good of either justice or happiness within the human will, and not within the divine will. In this sense, Ibn Rushd is opposed to the theologians who declare that what God wills has no definite nature and merely turns on what the will of God lays down for it. According to this argument, there is nothing good except by fiat. And more specifically, there is no end of man other than by fiat. What brought them to this conclusion, of course, was a desire to defend the perfection of God's attributes, understood in terms of his capability of doing anything whatsoever. And by implication it follows that all things are in principle possible. Ibn Rushd observes that these opinions of the theologians reflect the opinions of the multitude concerning the nature of ethics and in particular of the good. In these opinions, however, they are very far from a true understanding of the nature of man and of the rational faculty which distinguishes him from other beings. Through this specific nature man is what he is, and from this result the actions that are specific to him. This having been laid down, the good and the bad of a man's action are necessarily to be found only in the action specific to him. And this being the case, a man's end is attained only if those of his actions that are specific to him are realized by him in the utmost goodness. The good, instead of being theologized, has been secularized by Ibn Rushd, and this secularization of the good conforms to his observation in *The Decisive Treatise* that the sacred texts can be interpreted by human reason in such a way as to grasp the true meaning symbolized, whereas the theologians, and with them the masses, rest content with the apparent meaning for fear of employing their reason.

In this context, that is, in relation to their approach to scripture, Ibn Rushd classifies people into three classes. The first class is comprised of those who are not people of interpretation at all. These are the rhetorical class, and they constitute the overwhelming mass. The second class is comprised of the dialecticians. The third, or demonstrative class is comprised of the people of certain interpretation. This interpretation, Ibn Rushd contends, is not to be expressed to the dialectical class, let alone to the masses. Accordingly, the concept of the good should be approached as it is understood by the third class, if we want to grasp its human character.

One can say, then, that the concept of the good in Islamic philosophy has been secularized through Ibn Rushd's distinction of the three classes and his insistence that the masses are deprived of the ability to interpret which is the basis of secularization. This is evident from Ibn Rushd's definition of interpretation in *The Decisive Treatise*. He writes, "If the apparent meaning of Scripture conflicts with demonstrative conclusions, it must be interpreted allegorically, that is, metaphorically." He then expounds his famous definition of allegorical interpretation as "the extension of the significance of an expression from real to metaphorical significance." Thus Ibn Rushd claims that the Scriptural texts have two meanings – an apparent meaning and a hidden one. The hidden meaning is disclosed by using human reason. Within this context the concept of the good can be conceived as a secular concept.

Having considered some of the ancient Islamic theologians and philosophers, we will now turn to the late nineteenth century and examine the thought of the most historical thinker, that is, Muhammad Abduh, who was interested in determining the relation between revelation and reason in order to define the true ethical norms. In his *Treatise*, Abduh writes:

> The obligation to perform actions that are commanded or simply recommended, and to avoid or disapprove actions that are forbidden, in the manner prescribed by the Divine Law, which determines the appropriate rewards and penalties – all this reason cannot attain by itself. The only way to know, then, is by revelation. This is not to deny that what is commanded is already good in the sense that it leads to worldly or other-worldly benefit.

Thus revelation does not endow actions with the quality of goodness or evil, but only defines the obligation. What is commanded is "already good" for reasons that man can understand. This means that reason can tell men what they should or should not do and revelation gives them the most compelling reason why they should or should not do it. But since reason is often distorted in its operation by other human qualities, it seldom proves adequate even for its own primary role, and therefore most men need the confirmation of revelation to help them decide what they should or should not do. Furthermore, although reason can provide reasons why one should behave in a certain way, these reasons lack compelling force, and therefore the religious imperative becomes necessary. This is evident from the following text:

> When have we ever heard that a class of people have made the good triumph in their actions solely on the grounds of the utility that this good offered for the masses or the elite, or that it prevented evil simply because it would have led to corruption and ruin? This has never occurred in human history and it is not in accord with human nature. The foundation of good habits rests only in dogmas and tradition, and these things themselves have no other basis than religion. Therefore, religion's power over men's minds is greater than the power of reason that is peculiar to them.

From this text we can conclude that the concept of the good has its roots in the Sacred Law and not in the secular law. In this sense, one could say that Abduh is the forerunner of the Muslim brotherhood that was formed in Egypt by Hasan Al-Banna in 1929. Its conception of goodness and evil was derived from Abduh's basic principle that the Quran is the only source to which one can go for an identification of the good.

Bibliography

Writings

Averroës 1974: *Averroës on Plato's Republic*, tr. R. Lerner (Ithaca: Cornell University Press).

Butterworth, C. E. 1986: *Philosophy, Ethics and Virtuous Rule: a Study of Averroës' Commentary on Plato's "Republic"* (Cairo: American University Press).

De Boer, T. J. 1984: *History of Philosophy in Islam*, tr. M. A. A. Ridah, 3rd edn (Cairo: Committee of Translation and Publishing Press).
Hourani, G. F. 1971: *Islamic Rationalism, The Ethics of ʿAbd Al-Jabbar* (Oxford: Clarendon Press).
Kerr, M. H. 1966: *Islamic Reform, the Political and Legal Theories of Mohammed Abduh and Rashid Rida* (Berkeley: University of California Press).
Sherif, M. A. 1975: *Ghazzali's Theory of Virtue* (Albany: State University of New York Press).

References & further reading

Afnan, S. M. 1958: *Avicenna, His Life and Works* (London: George Allen & Unwin).
Averroës 1960: *Averroës on the Harmony of Religion and Philosophy*, tr. G. F. Hourani (London: Luzac).
Frank, R. M. 1978: *Beings and their Attributes, the Teaching of the Basrian School of the Muʿtazila in the Classical Period* (Albany: State University of New York Press).
Hourani, G. F. 1975: *Essays on Islamic Philosophy and Science* (Albany: State University of New York Press).
Leaman, O. 1995: *An Introduction to Medieval Islamic Philosophy* (Cambridge: Cambridge University Press).
Lerner, R. and Mahdi, M. (eds) 1963: *Medieval Political Philosophy* (Ithaca: Cornell University Press).
Mahdi, M. (ed. and tr.) 1969: *Al-Fārābī's Philosophy of Plato and Aristotle* (Ithaca: Cornell University Press).
Nasr, S. H. 1972: Sufi Essays (London: George Allen and Unwin).
—— 1978: *An Introduction on Islamic Cosmological Doctrines* (London: Thames & Hudson).
Ridah, M. A. A. (ed.) 1978: *The Philosophical Treatises of Alkindi*, 3rd edn (Cairo: Dar Al Fikr Al Arabi).
Urvoy, Dominique 1991: *Ibn Rushd (Averroës)* (London: Routledge).

37

Causality and Islamic thought

ANDREY SMIRNOV

The great disputants within the Islamic tradition, the Mutakallimūn, laid down the basis for rational discussion of causality by affirming the right of reason to engage in independent research. This affirmation could not be absolute; it took the form of a division of the spheres of competence belonging, respectively, to reason and Law. Reason was declared to be the judge in ontological and epistemological questions, whereas the sphere of ethics and legislation were left subject to religious Law. Certainly, this division should not be understood too rigidly. The Mutakallimūn often remained loyal to the Law and did not permit reason to execute its rights to the full even when disputing ontological problems. On the other hand, in the sphere of legislation they asserted the rights of reason to define new norms, not established in Revelation, on the basis of rational analysis of revealed Law, thus defying the Ẓāhiriyya, "people of the manifest," who denied the legitimacy of rational procedures for determining new norms of law.

To inquire about causality is to ask whether a phenomenon is subject to logical analysis that discriminates in its structure cause, effect, and a necessary relation between them. The rights of reason asserted by the Mutakallimūn provided an opportunity for such analysis.

This does not mean, however, that the Mutakallimūn carried out the task to the full. The term "cause" (*ʿilla*, *sabab*), as well as its derivatives ("causality" – *ʿilliyya*, "to give reason" – *iʿtalla*), are too scarcely met in their writings. One would rather maintain that the Mutakallimūn strove to define the spheres in which the search for causality is relevant. Their basic method is negative, and its nature is best clarified through a comparison with the Qurānic idea of the absolute Divine will. Without denying the Divine will and creativity as the last foundation of existence, the Mutakallimūn nonetheless introduced *logical* restrictions on it. They did so while disputing the "permissibility" (*jiwāz*) and "impossibility" (*iḥāla*) or certain acts, including acts of God, and establishing these on logical grounds. The rational arguments here sometimes outweighed even Qurānic evidence.

According to the Mutakallimūn, the subject matter of rational discourse falls into two parts: God and the world. There is no similarity between them, so the world may be referred to as "non-God" (*ghayr allāh*) or "besides-God" (*mā siwā allāh*). Despite this ontological split, however, God and the world make up a field of uniform discourse, and the same logic applies to both of these ontologically different parts.

There are two general questions that the Mutakallimūn put concerning the relation between God and the world: is there any cause (*ʿilla*) for the Divine act of creation? and is there any cause for the Law given to the people?

One of the prominent Mutakallimūn, Abū al-Hudhail al-ʿAllāf, argued that any act – including Divine creation – must necessarily be based upon some reasonable foundation. People were created for their own "benefit" (*manfaʿa*); otherwise, for al-ʿAllāf, Divine creation makes no sense (al-Ashʿarī, 1980, p. 252). Another well known Mutakallim, Muʿtamar, argued that a creative act has its foundation; that that foundation must have its own foundation, and so on ad infinitum. Thus the recursive search for cause has no limit (*ghāya*). For al-Naẓẓām, "formation" (*takawwun*) itself serves as sufficient reason for creation. Thus he introduced, as al-Ashʿarī wrote, the concept of final cause (*gharaḍ*) (al-Ashʿarī, 1980, p. 470). Finally, some Mutakallimūn argued that the world was created for no reason at all.

Is there any rational basis, reason and cause (*ʿilla*) for what is prescribed and what is prohibited by Revealed Law? Radical rationalists among the Mutakallimūn argued that every prescription has its cause. Moreover, any new norm of law (*farʿ*) can be established only after it has been co-measured (*qiyās*; see also Article 32, TRUTH AND ISLAMIC THOUGHT) with these causes, so that the causes "are continuous" (*iṭṭirād*) and survive in the newly established legal norm. Thus the new norm of law, though adopted by people and not revealed by God, is nevertheless justified by the cause that necessitated one of the norms of Revealed Law. This view proceeded from the assumption that the human mind is capable of knowing the reasons that guided God's intentions. And, of course, some Mutakallimūn could not help saying the opposite, arguing that there is no cause besides God's will for any prescription of Revealed Law (al-Ashʿarī, 1980, p. 470).

Another question in connection with which causality was discussed in Kalām concerned the changes that occur in our world. Daily experience shows that bodies remain unchanged only for limited periods of time, after which alteration inevitably occurs. On what *basis* do these changes take place?

It might seem that the division of everything in the world into "substances" (*Jawāhir*) and "accidents" (*ʿawāriḍ*), which most Mutakallimūn eventually embraced, already answers the question. Accidents are attributes that bodies acquire, or of which they are deprived; as accidents replace each other, a body's "state" (*ḥāl*) changes. From this point of view, the instability of accidents is the cause of the world's transformation.

However, the question of change in the world may be rephrased in that case: what is the cause of the constant coming-and-going of accidents? Even those Mutakallimūn who argued that any body always exhibits all of the possible *classes* of accidents, had to provide an explanation for why the given – and not its opposite – accident is found in the body at a particular moment. This question was formulated with respect to the "priority" (*awlawiyya*) that the existence of one of the two opposite accidents has over the existence of the other. For example, "motion" and "rest" are opposite accidents that equally "deserve" or "have the right" (*istiḥqāq*) to be manifested in the body; why then is it one and not the other that gains existential preference at some moment, later giving way to its counterpart? It is hardly an exaggeration to say that the Mutakallimūn advanced almost every possible answer to this question. The variety of their theories is rivalled only by their incompatibility.

Some of them reproduced the scheme that explained changes in bodies, to supply a reason for the presence of accidents. There is something that accounts for the existence of the given, as opposed to its opposite, accident, they argued. This is called *maʿnā* ("meaning"; the term is sometimes translated as "nature" or "idea": see Chittick, 1983, pp. 15, 352; Wolfson, 1965). Motion outweighs rest and exists in the given body because there is the "meaning of motionability" (*maʿnā al-ḥarakiyya*) in that body. The Ashʿarite school later expressed this as a general rule: "Any change of attribute (*wasf*) in being is due to some meaning (*maʿnā*) that takes place in it" (al-Baghdādī, 1981, p. 55).

Certainly, this way of reasoning provides no final explanation, since it initiates an infinite regress. If any foundation, any "meaning," has to be justified by its own foundation, the resulting chain of principles is unending. But many Mutakallimūn maintained what was to become a generally accepted rule for medieval thinkers: an infinite cause-and-effect chain is absurd. The infinite regress must be interrupted at some stage. Where exactly? Perhaps the goal is achieved if a search for the explanation-of-an-explanation is forbidden. In fact, some Mutakallimūn argued that *maʿnā* explains the existence of an accident while itself existing for no reason. But the decision to half the regress at that stage is rather arbitrary; why not, then, give up looking for a justification at all? Accordingly, the view that an accident exists without any cause was expressed by some Mutakallimūn, although this admission certainly violated the principle of sufficient reason.

Another way to approach the problem is to explain the change of accidents in terms of their appearance, after pre-existing as hidden in the body, rather than in terms of their entering the body from outside. This theory is known as the "latency-and-manifestation" (*kumūn wa ẓuhūr*) doctrine. According to it, a body becomes heated, for example, not because the quality of heatedness is added to it, but because the latent corpuscles of fire appear on its surface. The doctrine's opponents argued – and with good reason – that there must nonetheless be a cause that accounts for an accident's "appearance" even if the accident does not enter the body from outside. Thus this theory still faces the objections discussed earlier.

The Ashʿarite school of late Kalām finally concluded that it is impossible to find a sufficient reason to account for the change of accidents, and thus gave up all attempts to find a rational explanation of the world's transformation. Instead of offering such an explanation, they spoke in terms of "origination" (*ḥudūth*), the nearest analogue of theological "creation" (*khalq*): "If there is no latency-and-manifestation, but bodies really undergo alterations of their states, and accidents cannot travel from body to body, then an accident's existence in substance is its origination in it" (al-Baghdādī, 1981, p. 56).

But what are cause (*ʿilla*) and effect (*maʿlūl*) as such? On the whole, the Mutakallimūn gave two contrary definitions of these concepts: first, a cause is a thing that *precedes* its effect (a cause never exists "together" (*maʿa*) with its effect);

and , second, a cause is always *together* (*maʿa*) with its effect, since nothing that can precede the thing may be its cause. Al-Naẓẓām acknowledged both possibilities, and added to the list the concept of a final cause (*gharaḍ*) that "exists after its effect, as when someone says: I have built this sunshade to find shelter from the sun – but shelter is found only after the sunshade is accomplished" (al-Ashʿarī, 1980, p. 391).

Furthermore, the Mutakallimūn distinguished causes of which the effects are "necessary" and "inevitable" (*ʿillat iḍṭirār, ʿījāb*) – what in modern terminology would be called "natural causes" like fire causing pain or the push that makes a stone fall down – and causes that act according to a person's choice (*ʿillat ikhtiyār*), like religious prescriptions that are observed or not according to one's will and which later cause one's punishment or reward (al-Ashʿarī, 1980, pp. 389–91).

Triumphant Aristotelianism did not silence altogether the free debates of the Mutakallimūn (which may well be compared in this respect to pre-Socratic philosophizing), but it provided unequivocal and indisputable answers to those questions that the Kalām so ardently and fruitfully discussed, having defined the unshakable patterns of wisdom for future generations.

The discussion of causality in Islamic peripatetism is directly connected with the problem of "ordering" (*tartīb*; *ḍabṭ*). All beings form a *sequence*; in other words, one exists always and only *after* another. No two things exist each owing to the other, Ibn Sīnā says, and no two things necessarily presuppose each other (Ibn Sīnā, 1957, Pt 2. pp. 200–13). The sequence of beings is understood in two ways – logically and chronologically. In any case, any given step – be it a step of the logical order of existence or of its chronological order – is represented by only one member of the sequence. It follows that cause-and-effect relations develop in only one direction and are irreversible. This means, first, that we can always distinguish a cause from its effect (the first always comes *before* the second either logically or chronologically), and, second, that an effect cannot influence its cause (what *follows* cannot influence what has *passed*). The general conclusion is thus formulated: "With the elimination of a cause its effect is eliminated too, but the elimination of an effect doesn't eliminate its cause" (Ibn Sīnā, 1957, Pt 2, p. 215). This applies to instances in which the cause and effect coincide in time, so that the absence of the effect gives the impression that the absence of the cause is produced by it, as in the case of a key's movement being caused by the movement of one's hand. In such cases the cause "precedes" the effect logically, or "by essence" (*taqaddum bi al-dhāt*). Logical precedence also takes place in the realm of the metaphysical principles of being that are not subject to temporal changes. Thus the concepts of "precedence" (*taqaddum*) and "retardation" (*taʾakhkhur*) lie at the core of the doctrine of strict linear causality.

It is most typical for Ibn Sīnā, both in logic and in metaphysics, to draw a distinction between essence (*dhāt*) and existence (*wujūd*). This distinction, of course, is paralleled, although not in every respect, by medieval Western philosophers. The chief aim of Ibn Sīnā is to distinguish two types of causes: causes of essence and causes of existence. The causes that he speaks of are the four well known causes introduced by Aristotle: material, formal, efficient, and final. For example, the causes of a chair are, accordingly, the material of which it was made, the way it was shaped, the carpenter who produced it, and our will to use it for sitting. Only some of these necessitate existence; accordingly, causes are subordinated so that the cause of existence appears to precede, logically or in time, causes of quiddity (Ibn Sīnā, 1958, Pt 3, p. 443). Such a cause turns out to be the efficient or final cause, the latter being reduced to the first, for the final cause is the "efficient cause for the causality of efficient cause" (Ibn Sīnā, 1958, Pt 3, pp. 441–2).

The peripatetics, as well as other thinkers, provided sophisticated proofs for the impossibility of an infinite sequence of essences that necessitate each other's existence (see, for example, Ibn Sīnā, 1958, Pt 3, pp. 449–55; al-Suhrawardī, 1952, pp. 63–4). Any cause-and-effect sequence is finite, and its final principle is the First Cause, or First Essence – the philosophical concept of Divinity. This First Cause is the "cause for all existence and for the cause of the essence of each being" (Ibn Sīnā, 1958, Pt 3, p. 446).

So the basis of the sequence is radically different from the sequence itself; what in the final analysis is the cause of everything has itself no cause. This means that there are two basically different types of relation of being to existence. "Each being in its self (*dhāt*), regardless of everything else, either necessarily possesses existence in itself, or does not. If it does, it is true by itself (*ḥaqq bi dhāti-hi*) and necessarily exists by itself; this is the Ever-existent" (Ibn Sīnā, Pt 3, 1958, p. 447). As for all other beings, they are neither necessary by themselves (for if they were, they would need no cause to exist), nor impossible (for then they would not exist at all). Considered as such, they are "possible" (*mumkin*) beings. This concept embraces beings for which neither of the alternatives of existence and non-existence has any preference. Neither of them can gain priority (*awlawiyya*) by itself. One of the two, "to exist," must become "prior" (*awlā*) to the other and outweigh its alternative in the scales of preference. It is precisely the cause that provides such priority. The "possible being," after it is "bound" (*mutaʿalliq*) to its cause, becomes "necessary" (*wājib*; also *wājib al-wujūd* – "necessarily-existent"). Since its necessity has an external source and is not derived from its essence, it is "necessarily-existent-by-the-other" (*wājib al-wujūd li-ghayri-hi*).

This line of reasoning seems to leave little room for non-determined events. All that exists (with the exception of the Divine essence) exists only due to its cause. On the other hand, when "cause, be it nature or determinant will, is there, effect takes place inevitably" (Ibn Sīnā, 1958, Pt 3, p. 522). But it should not escape our attention that Ibn Sīnā divides all causes (as did the Mutakallimūn) into the natural and the subjective, and the latter might well be viewed as acting "by choice," or freely. But even for natural events, determinism is not as straightforward as it might appear. As al-Fārābī maintains, not only necessary, but also contingent (*ittifāqiyya*) events take place in the natural world. The first have "proximate causes" (like the fire that causes heating), the second have "remote causes." However, al-Farābī's concept of contingency is subjective rather than objective, for contingent events are those for which the causes cannot "be put in order and known," so it might well be that they only *appear* contingent while having in fact a very long chain of causes necessitating them (al-Fārābī, 1890, p. 110). Ibn Sīnā argues that a cause has to be in an appropriate "state" (*ḥāl*) in order to become an "actual cause"; otherwise it does not bring about its effect. Thus Avicenna tries to explain the "delay" of effects and the very fact of the temporal development of the cause-and-effect sequence. This was not a problem for the Mutakallimūn, for whom it was the will of God that "originates" changes in the world, so that the world's temporal development seemed to need no special explanation. But for Ibn Sīnā, the First Cause cannot will anything, since otherwise it would not be perfect. (Accordingly, there is *no* final cause for the existence of the world – Ibn Sīnā, 1958, Pt 3, pp. 553–61.) Moreover, if the effect of the never-changing cause (which is the First Cause) "may be necessary and eternal" (Ibn Sīnā, Pt 3, 1958, p. 523), and this effect serves as the cause for the next being in the order of existence, and an effect inevitably exists if its cause exists, then it needs to be explained why not all possible events have yet occurred in our world, given the eternity of the First Cause and its effects. This is where the concept of "state" (*ḥāl*) comes in. The state of the First Cause never changes, but its remote effects – that is, the causes that act in our world – have yet to reach the state needed for their actual causality. The concept of "state" includes such things as the availability of instruments necessary for an action, tools, assistants, a suitable time, a stimulus, as well as the absence of an "obstacle" (*māniʿ*) to the fulfillment of the action (Ibn Sīnā, 1958, Pt 3, pp. 520–22). Any one of these is called a "condition" (*sharṭ*). Thus the efficiency of the cause is itself determined by positive (the availability of external factors) and negative (the absence of an obstacle) circumstances, and the determinism of peripatetic doctrine is considerably moderated.

So the order of existence is a cause-and-effect sequence. In this order, beings are ranked in many respects. First, there is a unity–multiplicity order. The foundation of the sequence, the First Necessary-by-Itself Essence is absolute unity devoid of all "aspects" (*ḥaythiyya*) (Ibn Sīnā, 1958, Pt 3, pp. 612–13). Since one cause brings about only one effect, while a multiplicity of effects is due to the diversity of a cause's "aspects," the Second being is also a unity. Multiplicity begins with the third member of the sequence and steadily increases further on. Causes are ranked logically and chronologically (as already mentioned), but also axiologically: what is placed "before," is more elevated and noble than what is "postponed." Thus effects are always inferior to their causes and deficient as compared to them. It is impossible to imagine, Ibn Sīnā writes, that the inferior might serve as the cause for that which is superior, better and more noble (Ibn Sīnā, 1958, Pt 3, p. 632).

The doctrine of the strict linear order of causes-and-effects, elaborated in Islamic peripatetism, became a sort of axiomatic teaching for Ismāʿīli thinkers and the philosophers of "illumination" (*ishrāq*). Ḥamīd al-Dīn al-Kirmānī, the most important of Ismāʿīli philosophers, considers it an unquestionable rule that needs no proof (al-Kirmānī, 1983, p. 130). Causality is universal: the "existence of any being is dependent on the fixity of the preceding cause: if it had not been established, its effect would not have existed." The cause-and-effect sequence ascends up to its foundation, for the existence of which the mere existence of its effects provides sufficient evidence (al-Kirmānī, 1983, pp. 158–9).

But unlike the Aristotelians (and, in this respect, the Mutakallimūn as well), al-Kirmānī sees no possibility of identifying the basis of the cause-and-effect sequence as the Divine essence. Any proposition about God, al-Kirmānī argues, implies the duality of His essence rather than its unity. For example, if we describe God as Perfect, we imply that His perfection is one thing, while the "bearer" (*ḥāmil*) of perfection has to be something else. The same line of reasoning, of course, applies to any other attribute of His that we may consider, including existence. But as an unshakable and *a priori* law suggests, duality is always preceded by unity. Thus any proposition about God (even a proposition of negative theology, since al-Kirmānī contends that the "particle 'no' has no power to deny His attributes") describes Him not only as cause, but as effect as well, which is absurd. It is noteworthy that al-Kirmānī, in contending that God *cannot* be the basis of universal cause-and-effect relations, employs the same terms that Ibn Sīnā uses to describe what *is* the First Cause in his doctrine (that is, that it has nothing equal to it (*nidd*), nothing opposite to it (*ḍidd*), no genus, no specific difference, and so on – see al-Kirmānī, 1983, pp. 135–54; Ibn Sīnā, 1958, Pt 3, pp. 480–1).

According to al-Kirmānī, then, the cause-and-effect sequence is opened not by the Divine essence, but by the First Intellect. The First Intellect is created by God from nothing and with the help of nothing, so that it is impossible to know *how* it was created. The First Intellect is "the first limit and the first cause to which the existence of all other beings is bound" (al-Kirmānī, 1983, p. 155). The creation of the first cause is the only irrational act of God that al-Kirmānī is compelled to admit, all further development of the cause-and-effect sequence being logically determined and explicable with the aid of Aristotelian terminology.

Since al-Kirmānī refuses to acknowledge that the foundation of the cause-and-effect sequence possesses in itself sufficient basis for its existence, he cannot make good use of the system of the classification of beings elaborated by the peripatetics. Since the existence of the First Intellect does not follow from its essence (its created character guarantees that), no being is necessary-by-itself, a fact which deprives the complementary concept of "possible being" of its efficiency as a philosophical concept. In fact, al-Kirmānī prefers to use the term *mutawallidāt* – or [beings] produced from [elements] – rather than *mumkināt* – or possible [beings].

Shihāb al-Dīn Yaḥyā al-Suhrawardī, the great philosopher of "illumination" (*ishrāq*), criticizes the peripatetic assertion that an effect may cease to be despite the continuation of its cause, which allowed them to explain why the sublunar world constantly changes although its celestial causes are everlasting, and argues that a cause must be understood as composite rather than simple, so that when some parts of it vanish (and those might well be of terrestrial, not celestial origin), its act ceases (al-Suhrawardī, 1952, p. 91). Since a cause is composite, the cause-and-effect sequence does not necessarily bring about a steadily increasing multiplicity of effects, as the peripatetics and Ismāʿīli theoreticians maintained. One part of a composite cause may bring about a simple effect, al-Suhrawardī argues (1952, pp. 94–5). What steadily increases is the meanness and degradation of beings. The cause-and-effect sequence, for al-Suhrawardī, is still linear and irreversible, and its foundation is the Everlasting Divine essence (al-Suhrawardī, 1952, pp. 91–2,

121–2). In his metaphysics of light and darkness, it is the living light, and not dead bodily substances, that serve as actual – that is, acting and creative – causes (al-Suhrawardī, 1952, pp. 109–10).

The teachings discussed so far all adhere to the linear conception of causality (with the exception, perhaps, of some of the Mutakallimūn). In Sūfī philosophical teachings this concept is abandoned altogether. These teachings incorporate some Kalāmic ideas and revive certain aspects of the peripatetic doctrines. The Sūfī concept of causality is rather singular and at the same time is immediately associated with the basic principles of Sūfī philosophy. We will outline it by contrasting it with the concept of linear causality.

The sequence of numbers provides a standard illustration of the concept of linear causality. Each number can exist only after the preceding number has gained existence, and all of them take root in the number "one," which is their foundation. One opens the sequence, regardless of whether it belongs to the sequence or not (this question was not agreed upon in medieval Islamic thought), and sets its direction: numbers increase as new ones are added to them.

This picture is transformed as follows in illustrating the Sūfī concept of causality. "From One appeared the numbers in known degrees. Thus the One gave birth to numbers, and numbers split and fractured the One," according to Ibn ʿArabī, the most outstanding Sūfī thinker (Ibn ʿArabī, 1980, p. 77). He positions the sequence of numbers *inside* its foundation – inside the One. Thus the foundation becomes all-encompassing and all-inclusive, as each member of the sequence is thoroughly contained within the One, and yet at the same time, as a sum of ones, transcends the One by virtue of its multiplicity. The foundation of the sequence, the One, is arithmetically speaking, equal to any of the ones from which the numbers are composed, so that the One is its own part, a "detail" (*faṣl*) of itself, and any number inside the One is thus identical to the One itself. The same idea of the created being included within the creator is expressed by the geometrical image of a central dot and a circle drawn around it. "The universe in itself is similar to the central dot, the circle and what is there between them. The dot is God, the emptiness outside the circle is non-existence, . . . and what is between the dot and the emptiness is possible being" (Ibn ʿArabī, 1859, Vol. 4, p. 275). Any dot of the circle belongs to the radius (the line connecting the circle and its center – God), and therefore is included in the center too, Ibn ʿArabī argues. Thus the circle (or image of the world) is drawn not outside, but inside its foundation (or God, First Principle), and each dot of the circle (each being of the world) is indistinguishable from its center – the circle's foundation.

As these images suggest, causality is not a relation *between* cause and effect, but an *inner* relation of an essence that may be considered, depending on the point of view, both cause and effect. The First Principle is the cause, but in one of its aspects (any number of the sequence, any dot of the circle) it is its own effect. "Reason judges that a cause cannot be the effect of what it is a cause for," but the one for whom truth is revealed in its totality sees that a cause is "effect of its own effect, and its effect is its cause" (Ibn ʿArabī, 1980, p. 185).

To provide a more theoretical exposition of the Sūfī doctrine of causality, at least two fundamental theses of Sūfī philosophy have to be mentioned – namely, the sameness of God and the world (or the sameness of unity and plurality) and the atomic concept of time.

According to Sūfī thinkers, the Divine essence is an absolute unity "necessarily-existing-by-itself." The world, or "non-God," is an *inner* multiplicity of this unity, and in itself this multiplicity is only "possible." The division of existence into necessary-by-itself and possible (which is absolutely correct, Ibn ʿArabī maintains) is an inner distinction of the Divine essence, not a fundamental external distinction between the foundation of a sequence and the rest of its members. Absolute unity *is* multiplicity by virtue of inner "relations" (*iḍāfa* – the Aristotelian category for such related concepts as "father" and "son" or "above" and "below"; the synonym *nisba* – or "correlation" – is also used). But what is related to what, if there is nothing outside the First Cause, and thus no external relation between it and anything else is possible? Paradoxically, "relation" (*iḍāfa*) provides not a description, but the basis, for the existence of related essences in Ibn ʿArabī's philosophy.

Unity and multiplicity are the same in the Divine essence, yet some distinctions between them may be outlined. Unity is associated with eternity (*qidam*), while multiplicity is temporal (*mu'aqqat*). Time consists of individual "moments" (*zamān fard, waqt fard*) deprived of duration. The atomic theory of not only time but space as well was outlined already by the Mutakallimūn who maintained that temporal duration and spatial extension are produced by combinations of atoms devoid of duration and extension. In Ibn ʿArabī's philosophy, at each moment of time, temporal essences of the world appear as some embodiment of unity's inner relations and then disappear, dissolving in absolute eternal unity; this "then" (*thumma*), Ibn ʿArabī argues, denotes only logical, not chronological sequence, for the appearance and disappearance of being are the same in a temporal atom. Each such act of existence and destruction is a certain "manifestation" (*tajallī*) of unity as plurality.

If follows from this theory, usually referred to by the Qur'ānic term "new creation" (*khalq jadīd*), that two consequent temporal states of the world are not related to each other as cause and effect. Each further state of the world is defined not by the preceding one, but by the way in which the inner relations of Divine unity will be embodied in the given moment. Cause-and-effect relations are *renewed* (they start *anew*) at each moment of time. They are in fact eternity-to-time relations: each essence, considered in its temporality, is effect, but regarded as an unmanifested inner correlation of Divinity, is cause. The situation can be described in terms of rigid determinism: There is no escape from the action of causes, Ibn ʿArabī writes, for what *is*, never exists *without* its cause – precisely because cause and effect are one. But this is only *a* description, for one can equally maintain that since a cause is nothing other than its effect, the latter completely determines itself and is consequently free. Furthermore, the concept of a temporal cause-and-effect sequence is denied altogether; what we take as development defined by a certain regularity, is no more than a semblance that may be violated at *any* moment of time. ("A miracle happened," people would then say.) A cause is never "the same," no cause-and-effect pattern can ever be reproduced, and thus no inquiry into causal laws as fixed and ever-repeated relations is possible.

This doctrine denies the possibility of influencing the future, and so it nullifies the grounds of ethical reasoning and of a person's responsibility. It is important, however, not to fall into the error of drawing this conclusion in its absolute form, which Ibn ʿArabī himself warns us against, for it is only *a* step to be followed by other steps, only a moment in the circular quest for truth. A person him- or herself is nothing less than an aspect of the Divine, being his or her own cause at any moment in time, and this means that the future, although not defined by a person's past, is nevertheless defined by no one other than him- or herself. Rigid determinism, as denied by Ibn ʿArabī, does not give way to indeterminism; it is replaced rather by an assertion of the impossibility of distinguishing between cause and effect.

Bibliography

Writings

Al-Ashʿarī, Abū al-Ḥasan 1980: *Maqalāt al-islāmiyyīn wa ikhtilāf al-muṣallīn* [Sayings of Muslims and Differences of Those Who Pray] 3rd edn (Wiesbaden: Franz Steiner, 1980).

Ibn ʿArabī 1859 and reprints: *Al-Futūḥāt al-Makkiya* [Revelations of Mecca], 4 Vols (Cairo: Dār al-kutub al-ʿarabiyya al-kubrā).

—— 1980: *Fuṣūṣ al-ḥikam* [Gems of Wisdom] 2nd edn (Beirut: Dār al-kitāb al-ʿarabiyy).

Ibn Sīnā, Abū ʿAlī 1957–60: *Al-Ishārāt wa al-tanbīhāt, maʿa sharḥ Naṣīr al-Dīn al-Ṭūṣī* [Book of Remarks and Admonitions, with the Commentary of Naṣīr al-Dīn al-Ṭūṣī] ed. Suleyman Dunya, 4 parts (Cairo: Dār al-maʿārīf).

Al-Kirmānī, Ḥamīd al-Dīn 1983: *Rāḥat al-ʿaql* [Peace of Mind] 2nd edn (Beirut: Dār al-andalus).

Al-Suhrawardī, Shihāb al-Dīn Yaḥyā 1952: "Ḥikmat al-ishrāq," in *Oeuvres philosophiques et mystiques de Shihabeddin Jahya Sohrawardi (1)*, ed. H. Corbin, Bibliothèque Iranienne, Vol. 2 (Téhéran and Paris: Institut Franco-Iranien – Librairie d'Amérique et d'Orient), pp. 2–260.

References and further reading

Badawi, A. 1972: *Histoire de la philosophie en Islam*, 2 Vols (Paris: J. Vrin).

Al-Baghdādī, Abū Manṣūr 1981: *'Uṣūl al-dīn*, 3rd edn (Beirut: Dār al-kutub al-ʿilmiyya).

Chittick, W. C. 1983: *The Sufi Path of Love: the Spiritual Teachings of Rumi* (Albany: State University of New York Press).

Corbin, H. 1964: *Histoire de la philosophie islamique* (Paris: Gallimard).

Fakhry, M. 1983: *A History of Islamic Philosophy*, 2nd edn (New York: Columbia University Press).

Al-Fārābī, Abū Naṣr 1890: "Fī-mā yaṣiḥḥ wa mā lā yaṣiḥḥ min aḥkām al-nujūm" [What is right and what is wrong in astrology], in *Al-thamra al-marḍiyya fī baʿḍ al-risālāt al-farābiyya* [Longed-for Fruit of Some Treatises by al-Farābī] (Leiden: E. J. Brill), pp. 104–14.

—— 1928: "Kitāb al-fuṣūṣ" [Book of Gems] in *Risāla fī ithbāt al-mufāriqāt wa nuṣūṣ ukhrā* [Treatise Establishing the Existence of Non-material Essences and Other Texts] (Hyderabad: Majlis dai'rat al-ʿulum at-ʿuthmaniyya), pp. 1–23.

Frank, R. M. 1966: *The Metaphysics of Created Being According to Abu-l-Hudhayl al-Allaf. A Philosophical Study of the Earliest Kalam* (Istanbul).

Goichon, A. M. 1938: *Lexique de la langue philosophique d'Ibn Sina (Avicenne)* (Paris: Desclee do Brower).

Ibn ʿArabī 1859: *Al-Futūḥāt al-Makkiya* [Revelations of Mecca], 4 Vols (Cairo: Dār al-kutub al-ʿarabiyya al-kubrā).

Ibn Rushd (Averroës) 1992: *Kitāb al-kawn wa al-fasād* [Book of Generation and Corruption], ed. J. P. Montada (Madrid: Consejo Superior de Investigationes Cientificas).

Al-Kindī 1948: *Kitāb al-Kindı ila al-Muʿtaṣim bi-llāh fī al-falsafa al-'ūla* [Epistle of al-Kindī to al-Muʿtaṣim bi-llāh in First Philosophy], ed. Ahmad al-Ahwani (Cairo).

Nasr, S. H. 1964: *Three Muslim Sages: Avicenna, Suhrawardi, Ibn ʿArabi* (Cambridge, Mass.: Harvard University Press).

Pines, S. 1954: "La longue recension de la Théologie d'Aristote dans ses rapports avec la doctrine ismaelienne," *Revue des Études Islamiques*, 22, pp. 7–20.

Tamir, A. 1991: *Ta'rīkh al-Ismāʿīliyya: al-daʿwa wa al-ʿaqīda* [History of al-Ismāʿīliyya: Appeal and Doctrine] (London, Cyprus: Riyad al-Rayyis li al-kutub wa al-nashr).

Walzer, R. 1962: "The Arabic Translation of Aristotle," in *Greek into Arabic* (Oxford), pp. 60–113.

Wolfson, H. A. 1965: "Muʿammar's theory of maʿna," in *Arabic and Islamic Studies in Honor of Hamilton A.R. Gibb* (Leiden: E. G. Brill), pp. 673–88.

38

Rationality in Islamic philosophy

MAJID FAKHRY

Introduction

The discussion of rationality can only be conducted today against the backdrop of the raging postmodernist and deconstructionist onslaught on the "citadel of reason," as one writer has put it recently. Although the current postmodernist skirmishes are launched against modernism as represented by Descartes and Kant, it is clear that the proclamation of the bankruptcy of reason or "the end of philosophy," as both Martin Heidegger and Richard Rorty have put it, goes well beyond the modernism of Descartes and Kant. It is part of the struggle between *logos* and anti-*logos* which is really perennial.

The greatest "misologist" of ancient times was probably the Sicilian sophist, Gorgias of Leontini (d. ca. 380 BC), who started by denying the "criterion" and published a book entitled *On Nature, or Concerning the Existing and the Nonexisting*, in which he argued that nothing exists at all; and even if it did, it could not be known, nor the knowledge thereof be communicated to others. Some of the present-day "misologists," like Rorty and Jacques Derrida, to whom I will be referring in this article, appear to espouse the same anti-metaphysical anti-epistemological cause, since the "mirror of nature," according to the former, does not mirror anything and even if it did, it could not he trusted to "mirror" accurately any external object or objects.

It should be noted at this point that "the end of philosophy" proclaimed with such assurance by the postmodernists is not altogether an end, since traditional philosophical aims can be achieved by recourse to other modes of discourse: hermeneutics, as recommended by Michel Foucault and Paul Ricoeur, narrative or conversation, as recommended by Rorty and Jean-François Lyotard, edification (*Bildung*), as recommended by Hans-Georg Gadamer, and even "nomadology," as recommended by Gilles Deleuze. The onslaught on reason or the *logos* has also taken the form of "deconstruction" or "grammatology" at the hands of Derrida, who argues that philosophical "writing" should be approached in an open-ended spirit which allows for a variety of meanings rather than a unique or privileged one.

The response to ancient misology came of course from Plato and Aristotle, who despite their fundamental differences, agreed that being exists, and is knowable and communicable. The prototypical mode of communicating the knowledge of being was dialectic or logic, which Plato practiced and Aristotle codified in an elegant syllogistic system. This logic exhibited the structure of language as well as that of human thought, and although it could be applied to the content of thought, it was really "formal" or independent of this content.

For two and a half millennia, rationality or the "cult of the *logos*" was unquestioned. Writing in 1781, Kant could still, in the *Critique of Pure Reason*, pay Aristotle the compliment of having codified logic in a definitive manner, so that "it has not been able to advance a single step" since. Nevertheless, Kant was compelled to go beyond Aristotle's "formal" logic in the direction of "transcendental" logic, in which the content of knowledge is not altogether ignored because of the organic connection between the knower who "creates" the cosmos and the sense-data or the "manifold of intuition" from which our representation of the world is constructed. Kant continued, however, to accord reason, in the form of the understanding (*Verstand*), a primordial role in the realm of nature (as in the science of physics), while denying it any legitimacy in the domain of supernature (or metaphysics). From that point on, the die was cast and modern philosophy became vulnerable to the onslaughts of the postmodernists and deconstructionists.

Conjunction with the active reason

Hegel in a sense restored to reason the dignity of which Kant had robbed it by "divinizing" it, so to speak – by identifying it with the *Weltgeist* or the Absolute of which it was, at the human level, an epiphany or manifestation. In Arabic–Islamic philosophy, the Neoplatonists, including al-Fārābi (d. 950) and Avicenna (d. 1037), had already "divinized" reason in the form of an agency called Active Reason or Intellect which was the "storehouse" of intelligibles, as both St Thomas Aquinas and Avicenna called it. According to this view, the acquisition of knowledge, or what we might call the human enterprise of cognition, consists ultimately in taking the final step of "conjunction" or contact with this supermundane agency which is the lowest of a series of ten "intelligences" or "separate substances," as Aristotle had called the series of 55 subordinate movers of the spheres in *Metaphysics* XII, 8. However, in Aristotelian cosmology, those subordinate movers perform a purely cosmic function, that of moving their corresponding spheres, whereas the ten "intelligences" or reasons perform additional functions – especially the tenth or Active Reason, which dominates the world of generation and corruption, otherwise called the sublunary world in the Arabic sources.

To understand this development, which does not appear to have a direct Greek predecessor, and is at the center of the Islamic view of rationality, it is necessary to review the stages through which the view of reason passed in the Arabic–Islamic philosophical tradition. As one would expect, it all started with Plato and Aristotle, or rather Plotinus, as he interpreted the two great masters. *Noūs* for Plotinus was the first emanation from the One or God and is referred to as the "second god." The life of reason had been defined by Plato in *Theaetetus* 176B as *homoiōsis tō Theō*, or the imitation of God, according to human capacity. Aristotle, on the other hand, had described, in *Nicomachean Ethics* X, 7, the activity of reason as the loftiest activity of which man is capable, and declared that "man more than anything else is reason." In *Metaphysics* XII, 1072b17, this activity is then identified with God or the Unmoved Mover, who is the actuality of thought thinking itself.

The Muslim philosophers, much as they were fascinated by this concept, were somewhat embarrassed by its elevation of reason to the rank of the Divinity. For this elevation clashed with the rigorous Quranic concept of the transcendence of God: "Unto Him nothing is Like" (Quran 42,9). Accordingly, they posited Active Reason as an intermediary between man and God, as indeed between the sublunary world and the intelligible world beyond. In that capacity, Active Reason played in Islamic philosophy three primary roles.

1 At the epistemological level, it played the role of repository of all intelligibles, which constituted the substance of all cognitions.
2 At the cosmic level, it performed the function of the mover of the sublunary world and the ultimate cause of all becoming or change in it.
3 At the biological level, it imparted the various "substantial forms" of life and growth (that is, souls) to living organisms, as soon as they become disposed for their reception.

The process whereby the Active Reason itself came into being was designated as emanation (*ṣudūr* or *fayḍ*), which the Muslim Neoplatonists following Plotinus and Proclus had introduced, in fact, as an alternative to the Quranic concept of creation *ex nihilo*. It was favoured by those philosophers because it appeared to bridge the gap between the intelligible and the material worlds, but was received with the utmost resistance by the theologians and the masses at large, because it appeared to rob God of the freedom of choosing to create or not to create the world at a point of His own choosing in time – the process of emanation being described as eternal by its Neoplatonic protagonists. Moreover, it appeared to contradict the concept of creation out of nothing, since the universe was supposed to emanate or overflow from the very essence of the One, according to them, in a progressive manner, generating first the series of intelligences, then the series of souls, followed by the series of heavenly spheres, and finally the material world of the elements.

The transition from potential to acquired reason

With respect to the cognitive or epistemological function of reason, the Neoplatonists, as already mentioned, regarded conjunction or contact with this semi-divine agency as the climactic point in a gradual process which consisted of four basic stages or steps. From the time of al-Kindī (d. ca. 866) almost all the major philosophers of Islam wrote treatises on reason or the intellect, modelled on the famous treatise of the great Aristotelian commentator, Alexander of Aphrodisias (d. ca. 205), entitled *Peri Noū*. Al-Fārābī, who wrote the most detailed treatise on this subject, begins by listing the different senses of the term reason (*ʿaql*):

1 Reason as predicated of the "reasonable" man in ordinary discourse and which Aristotle, according to al-Fārābī, calls *taʿaqqul* – that is, practical wisdom or prudence (*phronēsis*).

2 The reason that the theologians posit as the faculty which prescribes or prohibits certain actions on the ground that they are right or wrong, and which is synonymous with common sense or sound judgment.
3 The reason that Aristotle describes in *Analytica Posteriora* as the faculty that apprehends the first principles of demonstration instinctively or intuitively.
4 The reason referred to in *Nicomachean Ethics* VI as the faculty of apprehending the principles of right and wrong in an infallible way.
5 The reason referred to in *De anima* and to which Aristotle has assigned four distinct meanings, according to al-Fārābī. These are the epistemologically significant connotations of reason around which controversy raged in Arabic-Islamic philosophical, as well as Latin–Scholastic, circles in the Middle Ages.

(a) First comes reason *in potentia*, or potential reason, which Aristotle has defined as "a soul, a part of the soul or a faculty of the soul." This reason is capable of abstracting the forms of material entities with which it is subsequently identified. It was for this reason that potential reason is referred to in the Arabic sources as material or hylic (*hayūlāni*).
(b) Once potential reason has apprehended the above-mentioned forms and become identified with them, it is designated reason-in-act, or actual reason. At this level, the reason-in-act and the intelligible-in-act become one and the same.
(c) When actual reason has apprehended all the intelligibles, material and other, including the primary principles of demonstration, as well as itself, it is designated acquired reason (*mustafād*). This acquired reason marks for al-Fārābī and the Muslim Neoplatonists generally the culmination of the cognitive process at the human level.
(d) However, beyond this acquired reason, rises the Active Reason which al-Fārābī describes as "an immaterial form which neither inheres nor could inhere in matter," and is in fact a supermundane agency governing the sublunary world and serving as the "storehouse" of all intelligibles, as already mentioned. It is through conjunction or contact with it, as we have also mentioned, that the process of cognition is consummated.

Logic and rationality

The Muslim philosophers never questioned the certainty or finality of the cognitive process once it has received the imprint of conjunction with the Active Reason, reserved for the privileged class of metaphysical philosophers. In Aristotelian terms, the method leading up to this conjunction is demonstration (*burhān, apodeixis*), grounded in the intuition of the primary principles of demonstration. It was for this reason that Averroes (d. 1198) resorted, less than three centuries later, to a "sociological" interpretation of this cognitive or epistemological theory. Mankind is divided, according to him, into three classes: (1) the philosophers or "people of demonstration"; (2) the theologians or "people of dialectic" (*jadal*); and (3) the masses at large, or the rhetorical class (*khaṭābiyūn*).

The three classes, as well as their methods of cognition, are hierarchically ordered, according to Averroes. Neither the theologians nor the masses at large are able to attain the level of demonstrative certainty, because of the weakness of the premises upon which their arguments rest, and which are based on received opinions that are purely arbitrary. By demonstration, Averroes meant, following Aristotle, the process of syllogistic deduction, in so far as it rested upon primary premises which are both necessary and universal. Neither dialectic nor rhetoric can satisfy this condition. This was the consensus of Muslim logicians and philosophers from al-Fārābi, to Avicenna, Avempace (d. 1138) and beyond.

Moreover, demonstrative knowledge for those philosophers, contrary to the claims of present-day postmodernists, exhibited the knowledge of the being (*wujūd*) of the object, as well as the causes underlying this being or existence. It was for this reason that those philosophers and logicians placed the concept of causality at the center of their epistemological concerns and this concept became in due course a major bone of contention between them and the theologians (*mutakallimūn*), especially the Ashʿarites. The *locus classicus* of this contention is al-Ghazzālī's *Tahāfut al-Falāsifa* (Incoherence of the Philosophers) and its rebuttal by Averroes in *Tahāfut al-Tahāfut* (Incoherence of the Incoherence). For al-Ghazzālī (d. 1111), the alleged certainty of the cause–effect relationships is an illusion; it is reducible entirely to *habit*, which God could alter at any time. For Averroes, on the other hand, the concept of habit as applied to God or inanimate objects is meaningless. In addition, genuine knowledge is a matter of eliciting the causes underlying any occurrence in the world, so that the activity of reason itself may be described as "nothing more than its knowledge of existing entities through the knowledge of their causes, whereby it differs from other cognitive faculties. Thus whoever repudiates causes actually repudiates reason" (*Tahāfut*, 1930, p. 522). This repudiation will undermine the very foundation of the "art of logic," and having rendered genuine knowledge (*epistēmē*) impossible, will only leave us with opinion (*doxa*), concludes Averroes.

Rhetoric and poetics

What the function of the "art of logic" was for this Muslim philosopher is really more complex than this dogmatic statement appears to imply. The Muslim logicians tended to conceive of logic in much broader terms than Aristotle had conceived of it. Perhaps the best illustration of this point is the way in which those logicians had from the earliest times expanded the scope of Aristotle's *Organon* so as to include the two treatises of *Rhetoric* and *Poetics*, (as well as the *Isagoge* of Porphyry) in a manner which was probably no part of Aristotle's intent.

It is noteworthy, however, that the inclusion of the *Rhetoric* and *Poetics* in the logical corpus started much earlier than the tenth century, which witnessed the translation and diffusion of logical texts in the Muslim world. Classical scholars, including Richard Walzer, have shown as early as 1934 that the *Poetics* was already included in the *Organon* by Greek commentators of Alexandria who belonged to the School of Ammonius in the third century; whereas Simplicius

(d. ca. 532) grouped the *Rhetoric* with the logical treatises of Aristotle three centuries later.

If we take al-Fārābī and Averroes as representatives of the Arab–Muslim logical tradition, it will be appropriate to discuss their reasons for this inclusion. Al-Fārābī, to whom Averroes refers often in this connection, begins by defining rhetoric as a "syllogistic art," the aim of which is persuasion (*iqnā'*), possible through rhetorical and dialectical, as well as demonstrative, means. In fact, he argues in a historical note, that rhetorical and dialectical methods of "persuasion" actually preceded the demonstrative, in point of time, as did the sophistical. It was not until Plato's time that dialectical, sophistical, rhetorical and poetical methods of discourse were clearly demarcated, although it was Aristotle who formulated the rules governing those different modes of discourse (al-Fārābī, 1970, p. 132).

As for poetry, al-Fārābī argues that the essence of this art for the "ancients" (meaning Aristotle and his followers) "consisted in being a discourse made up of what involves the imitation of the object," either through action or speaking, wherein the imaginative representation (*mimēsis*) of the object is sought, as is the case with scientific and logical statements. That is why imagining is analogous to scientific knowledge (*epistēmē*) in demonstration, opinion (*doxa*) in dialectic, and persuasion in rhetoric. For this reason, al-Fārābī contends, poetics can be regarded as part of logic. Both Avicenna and Averroes follow al-Fārābī's lead in this regard.

Despite its ingenious character, al-Fārābī's argument does not justify, we believe, the inclusion of poetics in the logical corpus, and this inclusion at any rate appears alien to Aristotle's purpose. Poetic discourse, according to him, is not liable to truth or falsity and "the poet's function is to describe, not the thing that has happened, but a kind of thing that might happen; that is what is possible as probable or necessary," in Aristotle's own words. The case of rhetoric, however, is different, and it is significant that a whole class of philosophically inclined writers, such as Abū Ḥayyān al-Tawḥīdi (d. 1024) and Ibn Ṭufayl (d. 1185) were able to express themselves in a more rhetorical or literary idiom than the professional philosophers, even when they were conveying a strictly philosophical message.

The uses of the hermeneutic method

As we have seen, some postmodernists, in their attempt to exorcise philosophy altogether, because of its preoccupation with certainty, objectivity, and universality, have proposed hermeneutics as a substitute. For Muslim philosophers, hermeneutics or its Arabic equivalent, *ta'wīl*, was welcomed from the earliest times as a complement, rather than a substitute, for philosophy. Even the theologians who tended to be suspicious of the whole method of interpretation, fell nevertheless into two groups:

1 the literalists, like Ibn Ḥanbal (d. 855) and Ibn Ḥazm (d. 1064), who repudiated the application of the hermeneutic method of interpretation to the sacred text of the Quran; and

2 the rationalists, or semi-rationalists, like the Muʿtazilites and the Ashʿarites, who allowed for such application, and may therefore be described as pro-philosophical.

Of the philosophers, Averroes was perhaps the most explicit in his advocacy of the application of the method of interpretation to the Quranic texts. Schooled in Aristotelianism, of which he was one of the greatest champions in the Middle Ages, both in the East and the West, he begins in one of his major theological treatises, entitled "The Decisive Treatise concerning the Relation of Philosophy and Religion" (*Faṣl al-Maqāl*), by giving a definition of philosophy that accords with the Quranic exhortation to "reflect" upon God's creation (Quran 29,2 and 7,184), as well as with St Paul's assertion, in Romans I, 20, that God's "everlasting power and deity, however invisible, have been there for the mind to see in the things He has made."

This definition of philosophy, which is clearly un-Aristotelian, states that "the examination of existing entities and their consideration in so far as they exhibit the Creator – I mean, in so far as they are created," implies that religion (*sharʿ*) exhorts us to reflect upon existing entities in a rational manner. Such reflection, argues Averroes, is nothing more than "extracting the unknown from the known and deducing it from it," which is precisely what the logicians designate as syllogistic reasoning (*qiyās*).

If it is objected that the use of syllogistic reasoning is an innovation or heresy (*bidʿa*), we would retort, says Averroes, that "juridical reasoning" introduced during the early part of Muslim history is not regarded as an innovation or heresy by the opponent. Accordingly, we should be willing to apply the syllogistic methods of proof, of which demonstration is the highest form, to the interpretation of the sacred texts, when they appear to be in conflict with demonstratively warranted principles or cognitions. By interpretation, Averroes then explains, we should understand: "Extending the connotation of the term from its real to its figurative meaning, without violating the linguistic usage of the Arabs, which allows for giving a thing the name proper to its equal, its cause, its accident or its concomitant." If the use of this method by legal scholars or jurists is allowed in legal decisions, the philosophers, or "masters of demonstration," who investigate the nature of reality, should *a fortiori* be allowed to use it also.

At the social level, as we mentioned earlier, Averroes recognizes that the method of demonstrative interpretation should be reserved to the philosophers and is not open to the common run of men, because of the diversity of their intellectual aptitudes. He even finds in the Quran a confirmation of this thesis in verse 3,5 which states in Arberry's translation:

> It is He who sent down upon thee the Book, wherein are verses clear which are the Essence of the Book and others ambiguous. As for those in whose hearts is swerving, they follow the ambiguous part desiring dissension and desiring its interpretation; and none knows its interpretation save only God. And those firmly rooted in knowledge say: "we believe in it; it is all from our Lord."

By those firmly rooted in knowledge, Averroes claims that the philosophers or "people of demonstration" are actually meant; and to substantiate this claim, he resorts to an ingenious expedient: he removes the period after God and reads the latter part as follows: "And none knows its interpretation, save only God and those firmly rooted in knowledge," that is, the philosophers.

Be this as it may, perhaps the most interesting application of the hermeneutic method as recommended by Averroes is the way in which he rebuts the three charges which al-Ghazzālī had levelled against the philosophers: namely, their denial of God's knowledge of universals, their assertion of the eternity of the world, and their denial of personal immortality. In none of these cases, says Averroes, can al-Ghazzālī produce a single explicit and unambiguous Quranic text supporting his view.

Take the eternity of the world as an example. Al-Ghazzālī and the Muslim theologians generally contended that the creation of the world in time (*ḥudūth*) and out of nothing is explicitly enunciated in the Quran, whereas a careful examination of relevant Quranic texts simply proves that the "form" of the world is created, whereas its existence is continuous *a parte ante* and *a parte post*. Thus verse 11,9, which states that "it is He (that is, God) who created the heavens and the earth in six days, while His throne was upon the water," appears to imply that the water, the Throne and the time measuring their duration are all eternal. Similarly, verse 41,10 which states, "Then He arose unto heaven which was smoke", appears to imply that the heavens were created from pre-existing matter, that is, smoke. This interpretation of these two verses is clearly antithetic to the theologians' thesis of creation in time and out of nothing, but is perfectly acceptable.

Hermeneutics and the method of commentary or exegesis

If the aim of hermeneutics is to probe the meaning(s) of the text – the relation of sentences or words to other sentences or words, as Rorty has put it, then the method of commentary or exegesis should be regarded as a privileged one. This method is in fact a distinctive feature of the Islamic tradition, the prototype of which is Quranic exegesis (*tafsīr*). Together with the Talmudic tradition, Quranic exegesis is not too far removed from the new mode of discourse labelled "grammatology" by Jacques Derrida and his followers. Derrida appears from his earlier writings to have been drawn to the view that writing (*écriture*) is superior to speaking, as a reaction to Plato's argument in the *Phaedrus* that writing is a debased way of expressing the truth because it reduces the spoken word to a lifeless inscription and serves simply as the basis of an apparent or false wisdom.

The exegesis of the Quran which, according to Muslim believers, is the direct revelation of the "Mother of the Book" or "Preserved Tablet," existing eternally in heaven, took in general two contrasting forms. Some commentaries like *al-Kashshāf* of al-Zamakhshari (d. 1144) tended to be grammatical or linguistic, whereas others, such as *al-Bayān* of al-Ṭabarī (d. 925) tended to be more theological or discursive. However, in almost all cases, the commentators tended to sprinkle their commentaries with biographical, historical and other circumstantial information drawn from the Prophetic biographical tradition (*al-Sīrah*) or other sources. In this respect, Quranic commentators may be regarded as genuine forerunners of modern hermeneutics.

The philosophers, on the other hand, adopted as early as the tenth century a more literal approach to philosophical texts, which were almost exclusively Aristotelian. Al-Fārābī, who was the first commentator on Aristotelian logic, as appears, from his extant commentary on *Peri Hermeneias* (*Kitāb al-ʿIbārah*), has Arabicized Aristotle, without departing very much from the Aristotelian text. In addition, he wrote paraphrases of all the parts of the *Organon*, which included the *Rhetoric* and the *Poetics*, as well as the *Isagoge* of Porphyry, as mentioned above. He has also made a valuable contribution, unmatched before modern times, to the analysis of logical terms in two major treatises, the *Terms Used in Logic* and the *Book of Letters*, as well as other minor logical tracts.

Averroes, who has also covered the whole range of Aristotelian logical texts, wrote extensive (or "large") commentaries, middle commentaries, as well as paraphrases or epitomes which have survived either in Arabic or in Latin. On the whole, Averroes tends to be more slavish or literal in his commentaries, and often criticizes al-Fārābī, either for unwarranted additions to or departures from the Aristotelian texts.

Conclusion

If philosophy is to be replaced by hermeneutics, rhetoric, conversation, or poetry, as some postmodernists have suggested, the question arises as to whether there is an irresolvable conflict between the philosophical method, especially epistemology, and these alternative methods proposed as substitutes, or whether they cannot all be enlisted in the service and support of philosophy. After all, some of the greatest philosophers, of whom I might mention Plato, Nietzsche, Kierkegaard, and Sartre, have tended to use more literary and even rhetorical modes of discourse than others, without jeopardizing their status as genuine philosophers.

On the whole, the alleged conflict between the various modes of discourse mentioned above did not present serious difficulties to the Arab–Muslim philosophers who were willing to exploit them to the full.

Second, it is not clear from the postmodernists' revolt what the aim of philosophy or its successor modes of discourse which they favor really is. In fact, it is not clear what the positive aim of the whole movement really is. If this aim is conversation or edification (*Bildung*), as Rorty and Gadamer contend, we need not quarrel with them, first, because conversation (or dialogue), as a method of eliciting truth, was one of the earliest methods used by some of the earliest philosophers, Socrates, and his disciple, Plato, for instance, as well as many later thinkers, such as David Hume and A. E. Ritchie. However, Socrates avoided making dogmatic or uncritical assertions and claimed to practice his mother's art of midwifery, delivering his interlocutors or disciples of ideas with which they were pregnant. He used conversation or dialogue as a means of leading those interlocutors or disciples to recognize the superiority of certain assertions over others, after first having recognized the incoherence of their initial positions. In other words, his aim was construction, not deconstruction.

Third, edification, including self-edification, is surely possible only on the assumption that the speaker has a message to convey, whether to instruct, to inform, or to reform. If, however, the conversation is allowed to drag on without any visible goal in sight, then edification will not be possible and no purpose, except possible esthetic enjoyment or entertainment, will be served. The question would then arise as to how philosophy can differ from comedy, drama, poetry or other artistic or literary genres intended to please or entertain.

The Arab–Muslim philosophers were not disturbed by these methodological squabbles. Avicenna, for example, wrote a medical poem which was translated into Latin as the *Cantica* in the Middle Ages; Ibn Ṭufayl (d. 1185) wrote a philosophical novel, *Ḥayy Ibn Yaqẓān*, believed to have influenced Daniel Defoe, the author of *Robinson Crusoe*; and the versification of logic and grammar was undertaken by less renowned writers. The point is that poetical, rhetorical, and other literary modes of discourse were not considered inimical to philosophical discourse, which allows for the greatest measure of diversity and inventiveness. Hermeneutics itself should be welcomed by philosophers, not as a threat, but rather as a means of expanding the scope of philosophical discourse, by tapping biographical, social and cultural sources of information intended to make philosphical texts more reality anchored.

Today, the battle is joined in the Arab–Muslim world on two fronts: (1) the fundamentalists who are pitted against liberals and modernists; and (2) the neo-positivists pitted against the protagonists of classical metaphysics and theology. Deconstruction and postmodernism have not made serious inroads into the Muslim cultural arena; a noteworthy and perceptive recent publication on *Postmodernism and Islam* (1992) by Akbar S. Ahmed, highlights the major responses of Islam to these two contemporary movements. However, Ahmed's analysis is essentially sociological and cultural, rather than philosophical. In a more philosophical work, *Postmodernism, Reason and Religion* (1992), Ernest Gellner argues that postmodernism and deconstruction amount to the contention "*Relativismus über Alles*" and cannot possibly be reconciled for that reason with the Islamic worldview. I agree that this worldview, which is still predominant, either in a liberal or radical form, is predicated on the thesis that the Islamic revelation is final and definitive and that truth, religious or other, can be known by a variety of means, linguistic, literary, philosophical, theological or other, but cannot be questioned or "deconstructed."

Bibliography

References

Ahmed, Akbar S. 1992: *Postmodernism and Islam* (London: Routledge).
Aristotle 1941a: *Analytica Posteriora*, ed. Richard McKeon (New York: Random House).
Aristotle 1941b: *De anima*, ed. Richard McKeon (New York: Random House).
—— 1941c: *Metaphysics*, ed. Richard McKeon (New York: Random House).
—— 1941d: *Nicomachean Ethics*, ed. Richard McKeon (New York: Random House).

Al-Fārābī 1932: *Risāla fī l'Aql* [Epistle on Reason] (Beirut: Catholic Press).
—— 1970: *Kitāb al Ḥurūf* [Book of Letters] (Beirut: Dar al-Mashriq).
Gellner, Ernest 1992: *Postmodernism, Reason and Religion* (London: Routledge).
Ibn Rushd (Averroes) 1930: *Tahāfut al-Tahāfut* [Incoherence of the Incoherence] (Beirut: Catholic Press).
—— 1954: *Faṣl al-Maqāl* [The Harmony of Religion and Philosophy], tr. G. Hourani (London: Luzac).
Norris, Christopher 1987: *Derrida* (Cambridge: Harvard University Press).
Ricoeur, Paul 1969: *Le Conflit des Interprétations* (Paris: Éditions du Seuil).

Further readings

Black, Deborah L. 1990: *Logic and Aristotle's Rhetoric and Poetics in Medieval Arabic Philosophy* (Leiden: E. J. Brill).
Derrida, Jacques 1967: *De la Grammatologie* (Paris: Éditions de Minuit).
Fakhry, Majid 1983: *A History of Islamic Philosophy* (New York: Columbia University Press).
Rorty, Richard 1979: *Philosophy and the Mirror of Nature* (Princeton: Princeton University Press).
Taylor, Mark C. (ed.) 1986: *Deconstruction in Context* (Chicago: University of Chicago Press).

PART III

THE CONTEMPORARY SITUATION

39

Contemporary Chinese philosophy

ROGER T. AMES

Contexts and continuities

> Confucius, standing on the riverbank, remarked: "So it passes, never ceasing day or night."
>
> Confucius, *Analects*

Philosophy, like most things Chinese, must be understood in terms of continuities. And any discussion of the cultural interests of contemporary China must begin from context: the "where" and the "when" of things. In contrast to Western philosophy, which began from the decontextualizing metaphysical sensibilities of the classical Greeks, the Chinese tradition is resolutely historicist. Reason is a series of historical instances of reasonableness; culture is a specific historical pattern of human flourishing; logic is the internal coherence of this particular human narrative; knowledge modestly is local and site-specific – making one's way smoothly and without obstruction; truth is proximate – the capacity to foster productive relationships that begin with the maintenance of one's own integrity and extend to the enhancement of one's own natural, social and cultural contexts.

The specific character of Chinese philosophy is such because a cultural dominant in the tradition, now and then, has been the priority of process and change over form and stasis which can be expressed as a privileging of cosmology over ontology. That the *Book of Changes* (*Yijing*) is the first among the Chinese classics in every sense, bears witness to the priority of cosmological questions: "*how* should the world hang together?" over ontological questions: "*what* is the reality behind appearance, the Being behind the beings, the One behind the many?" In Chinese, "the world" is *shijie*, literally "generational boundaries" which conjoin one's own generation to those who have come before, and to the generation that will follow this one; "the cosmos" is *yuzhou*, "the turning canopy of the heavens under which we live." And the pursuit of wisdom has, from classical times, centered on finding a way to stabilize, to discipline, and to direct the unstoppable stream of change in which the human experience is played out.

This "way" or *dao* for the Confucian tradition has been constituted by bringing a framework of formal roles, relationships, and institutions (*li*) to regulate the process of communal living. *Li*, often translated as "rites" or "propriety" is an enduring yet always malleable infrastructure through which the human being can pursue refined and appropriate relationships. For the Daoist tradition, the net of relevant circumstances is cast beyond human community, sacrificing a degree of focused human intensity for an increase in width and diversity. The regularities observable in nature – the cycle of the seasons, the growth and decay of every form of life, the turning of the heavens, the weathered striations on a piece of stone – are a synergistic model on which human beings can construct their path through life, walking in rhythm with the cadence of the cosmos.

Although this way of living, this *dao*, has historical antecedents, it is not simply to be discovered and walked. As the *Zhuangzi* says, "The path is made in the walking of it." *Dao* means both to lead along a path, and to be led along it. In the *Analects* 15:29 we read, "It is the human being that can broaden the way (*dao*), not the way that broadens the human being." The human being must be a roadbuilder because human culture is always under construction. But this passage has to be read together with *Analects* 8:9: "The people can be made to travel along the path, but they cannot be made to realize it." That is, "making a roadway real" must be distinguished from simply walking along it; some human beings build roads and others travel behind. In lieu of gods, the Chinese tradition has celebrated cultural heroes and supreme personalities over its long career. This need for models to emulate, then, late and soon, has required the philosopher to be a paradigmatic individual and a scout to recommend a "way" for the generations to come. (See Article 14, THE WAY AND THE TRUTH.)

With this contextualization of the Chinese philosophical tradition in place, we can now consider the contemporary status of Chinese philosophy as it is unfolds within the Chinese world itself.

As a footnote, the value of "Chinese philosophy" within the contemporary Western academy is an entirely different story. In fact, the field of "Chinese philosophy" has been rendered oxymoronic by having been largely excluded from the discipline of professional philosophy. Hence any discussion of Chinese philosophy within the context of Western culture, while taking account of the work of a small, marginalized community of comparative philosophers, will contrast starkly with the practical Chinese narrative by having to address a theoretical issue: Why has Chinese philosophy *not* been included in Western philosophical discourse?

On the other hand, in recounting the life of Chinese *philosophes* – a survey of often passionate, sometimes courageous intellectuals advancing their own program of human values and social order – we will be immediately aware that a record of the existential, practical, and resolutely historical nature of this tradition stretches it beyond the boundaries of what would be defined as "philosophy" within the contemporary Western context. Here we will find a partial answer to why Chinese philosophy has not been perceived as a legitimate area of philosophical inquiry – the difference between a Western search for truth, and a Chinese need to find a better way.

"Philosophy" in contemporary China

Within China today, philosophy is much more than a professional discipline. Chinese philosophers – traditionally scholar-officials – continue to be institutionalized intellectuals who have the practical responsibility to forge a "way" for the daily workings of government and society. "Philosophy" in the contemporary Chinese context continues to range over the relationship between prevailing cultural values, and the social and political life of the people. Philosophers have been and still are the intellectual leaders of society. Hence a reflection on Chinese philosophy from an internal and contemporary Chinese perspective must be primarily practical: a survey of the intellectual discourse as it has driven and shaped recent social, political, and cultural developments. Given the avowedly Marxist orientation of the state, then, how much has contemporary Chinese thinking been shaped by outside forces?

A compelling argument can be made that China has been doing comparative philosophy since the introduction of Buddhism into China in the second century. Another wave of Indo-European ideas entered China with the Jesuits in the late fifteenth century, armed as they were with religious convictions fortified by the best of classical Western philosophy. More recently, Yan Fu (1853–1921) stands out at the beginning of an ambitious project to translate recent Western philosophical classics into Chinese in the late Qing dynasty. Soon after, the Marxist heresy was appropriated by iconoclastic modernizers as a foundation for Chinese socialism. We must ask the question, then: what relevance has *Western* philosophy had in recent Chinese philosophical debates? In fact, there are some more cynical interpreters of recent Chinese intellectual trends who, viewing the present struggle between seemingly Marxist and Western liberal democratic ideals, might turn the question around, and ask: what relevance has *traditional Chinese* philosophy had in recent Chinese philosophic reflection?

Still, the resilience of grounding values has caused history to repeat itself. When Buddhism was introduced into China through a largely Daoist vocabulary, the foreign ideas were, in due course, overwhelmed by the vitality of the indigenous impulse, and Buddhism was effectively sinocized. Pervasively, but perhaps most clearly in its Sanlun, Huayan, and Chan incarnations, Chinese Buddhism has a closer correlation to the early Daoist classics than it does to its South Asian origins. Christianity melded with popular religions to spawn one of the largest uprisings in human history – the Taiping rebellion. And with Yan Fu's penchant for the arcane, evocative language of China's own philosophic tradition, the foreign ideas of modern Western thought were largely overwritten with traditional Chinese values and sensibilities. In this pattern of assimilation and ingestion, China's Marxist experience has certainly been no exception.

Chinese Marxism – most recently, Maoism – is a peculiarly Chinese run on Marx that has redefined a doctrine which, on most interpretations, owned universalistic aspirations, into a kind of "neo" neo-Confucianism by historicizing, particularizing, and depsychologizing it. On the other hand, any reference to Chinese "democratic" ideals introduces terrible equivocations: the promotion of seemingly individualistic values in the absence of Western notions of the individual, autonomy, independence, human rights, and so on. As soon as we get beneath surface impressions, we realize that contemporary Chinese philosophic developments are deeply embedded within traditional values and Chinese methods of philosophizing. By and large, they continue to be concerned with a creative appropriation of China's own cultural tradition. Marxian rhetoric and liberal democratic values are largely heuristic structures through which more fundamental traditional Chinese values are revisited, reconfigured, and sometimes, revitalized.

The recent narrative: a choice among "ways"

A new intellectual discourse has emerged in contemporary China since 1978 that has attended the rebirth of China's spiritual identity. This conversation has moved from the discussions on the criteria for "truth" (as we might expect, "practice is the sole criterion of truth") in the late seventies, to the great debate on China's cultural construction (whence and whither Chinese culture?) which began in the early 1980s and has continued with varying degrees of intensity down to the present historical moment. In the gradual awakening of a humanistic self-consciousness and the cultural consciousness which has attended it, several sometimes overlapping yet clearly discernible "ways" can be mapped.

The 1980s in China were, until late in the decade, defined philosophically by a healthy climate of debate unprecedented since the founding of the People's Republic in 1949. Far-ranging cultural discussions, often appealing to Western vocabularies, methodologies, and philosophies as their frame of reference, revealed many differences of opinion on the spirit and values of traditional culture. In retrospect, there have been several discernible postures.

First, one extreme position was occupied by those ageing political leaders who, in spite of the proliferation of faxes and satellite dishes throughout the country, still believed that China is self-sufficient, and can remain isolated and insulated from Western culture. The Great Wall can preserve China as the Chinatown of the world.

A second "way," with a future for China only slightly less naive and unlikely than the first, were the iconoclasts whose concerns culminated in Tiananmen. Led by Gan Yang and others, they have expressed profound reservations about the viability of the Chinese cultural legacy, and in many ways have reiterated the critical posture of anti-traditionalism in which the irony of "patriotic iconoclasm" prevails. Gan Yang, Huang Kejian and others have rejected established values as being unsuited to the realities of modern Chinese society, and have advocated "countering the tradition" as a means of advancing the tradition. Bao Zunxin has also asserted that traditional Chinese culture is self-sufficient, but has taken the opposite position of the guardians of the Great Wall: China cannot achieve renewal through self-criticism. This radical "anti-traditionalism" led to "The River Elegy" (*Heshang*) television series and its bitter attack on the perceived negativity and inertia of the tradition. The most extreme statement of this position, often posited by idealists such as Liu Shaobo who have a jaundiced appreciation of the Chinese tradition and a rather romantic perspective on Western society and institutions, rejects "Chineseness" utterly, and recommends the wholesale importation of another culture's future. Jin Guantao and Liu Qingfeng, although less strident, have also seen the tradition as largely unadaptable, describing

Confucian culture in terms of "structural stagnation" and "conservatism strangling individuality."

Advocates of a third "way," called "creative synthesis and synthetic creation," have promoted a "creative transformation of Chinese culture" through a full and thoroughgoing convergence of Chinese and Western cultures. Rejecting the assumed antagonism between Chinese and Western thinking, Zhang Dainian, a leading exponent of this trend, encouraged a scientific analysis of theory and practice to identify and assimilate all advanced and outstanding cultural achievements into a new tradition. The American scholar, Lin Yusheng [Lin Yü-sheng], has been prominent in this group, as has Zhang Liwen.

A fourth identifiable "way" has been "selective inheritance," a less radical, more academic trend which affirms the spiritual values of traditional culture. This group has opposed the more popular "introspective criticism" and "thoroughgoing reconstruction," and has sought to make a positive appraisal of the tradition so as to identify, select from, and carry over, the cultural wealth of the past. These scholars are committed to a tradition-based scenario for China's cultural reconstruction. A leading voice in this movement, defining itself as a "revival of Confucianism (*xinruxue*)," was the late Liang Shuming. As this impulse took hold, it was joined by many representatives of the Western-based diaspora on China's periphery – Yu Yingshi [Yü Ying-shih], Du Weiming [Tu Wei-ming], Zhang Hao [Chang Hao], Lin Yusheng, Liu Shuxian [Liu Shu-hsien], Jin Yaoji [Ambrose King] – who had themselves been trained by a generation of often self-exiled intellectuals: Tang Junyi, Mou Zongsan, Xu Fuguan, Fang Dongmei, Qian Mu. It is this "way" with its strong ties to Western society that has in some degree rekindled the long-stalled process of trying to reconcile the Chinese tradition with global culture.

Other scholars associated with this group such as Mou Zhongjian and Tang Yijie have championed a syncretic "selective inheritance" which goes beyond simply Confucianism, looking for a broader and deeper philosophical base for cultural renewal. These more pluralistic thinkers have been advocates of traditional values which extended well beyond the confines of Confucianism per se, invoking an eclectic "Chineseness" rather than just "Confucianism" and giving rise to notions such as "cultural China" (as opposed to geographical China) with its "Chinese" citizenry determined by cultural sensibilities rather than political allegiance or even sympathy.

A fifth "way" is really the more radical extreme of the last in that it too is tradition affirming. It is perhaps best represented by Li Ẓehou and the re-exploration of China's rediscovered humanity – "the subjectivity trend." What distinguishes this track most clearly from the fourth is the radical degree of transformation not only anticipated but readily embraced in the convergence of Chinese and Western culture. Li Zehou's quasi-Marxist revision of the familiar "Chinese body and Western function" to "Western body (read 'modern industrialized materialism') and Chinese function" as the model for China's cultural future, acknowledges (perhaps naively) the overwhelmingly positive value of Western-born ideological drives such as practical rationality, personal autonomy, and modern science, and the social, economic, and administrative institutions which issue from them.

In response to the obvious question, beyond the institutions of Western liberalism, "what else is there?", Li Zehou might well reply that while the contribution of Western cultures tends to be formal in structure, and hence is articulated and more readily discernible, the contribution on the Chinese side is more fluid, more particularistic, and more easily undervalued. At the same time, it is of enormous importance. For example, one might celebrate the centrality of rights in pursuing the goals of human dignity and personal realization. But rights-talk without appeal to *li* ("rites") – the concrete and specific roles and relationships which constitute the fabric of community and which generate the sense of shame necessary for social living – is hollow and meaningless. Laws are not more real than ritual practices, and both are necessary for effectively realizing a healthy, functioning society. It is the tension and the achieved balance between formal and informal procedures which is difficult to sustain. Perhaps the critical question which must be asked as China, willy-nilly, like-it-or-not, moves along this fifth track, is: "will China be able to remain culturally *Chinese* under the erosive conditions of modernization?"

Bibliography

Hall, David L. and Ames, Roger T. 1993: "Culture and the Limits of Catholicism: a Chinese Response to *Centesimus Annus*", *Journal of Business Ethics*, 12, pp. 955–63.

Hansen, Chad 1985: "Chinese Language, Chinese Philosophy, and 'Truth,'" *Journal of Asian Studies*, 44, pp. 491–517.

Hua Shiping 1995: *Scientism and Humanism: Two Cultures in Post-Mao China (1978–1989)* (Albany, NY: State University of New York Press).

Kelly, David 1990: "Representative Culture: Official and Unofficial Values in Tension," *China Review* (Hong Kong: Chinese University Press).

Lin Tongqi and Li Minghua 1994: "Subjectivity: Marxism and 'The Spiritual' in China since Mao," *Philosophy East & West*, 44, 4, pp. 609–46.

Lin Tongqi, Rosemont, Henry Jr and Ames, Roger T. 1995: "Chinese Philosophy: a Philosophical Essay on the State-of-the-Art," *Journal of Asian Studies*, 54, 3, pp. 727–58.

Mao Zedong 1952: "Maodunlun [On Contradictions]," *Mao Zedong xuanji* [Selected Works of Mao Zedong], Vol. 1 (Peking: Peoples Press).

Munro, Donald J. 1979: *Concept of Man in Contemporary China* (Ann Arbor: University of Michigan Press).

Shi Yanping 1993: "Developments in Chinese Philosophy Over the Last Ten Years," *Philosophy East and West*, 43, 1, pp. 113–25.

40

Contemporary Japanese philosophy

SHIGENORI NAGATOMO

1 Introduction

Although it seems natural to consider the last fifty years the contemporary period, because this year (1995) punctuates a historical period celebrating the fiftieth anniversary of the end of the Pacific War, this essay will limit the term "contemporary" roughly to the last twenty-five years. The reason for this demarcation is that at the beginning of the 1970s, we witnessed a new philosophical mood emerging in Japan. Prior to that period, the Japanese philosophical scene was dominated by the study of European thinkers, such as Husserl, Heiddeger, Sartre, and Merleau-Ponty. The end of the students' movement in the early 1970s also marked the end of the ideological disputes launched by Marxism since the early 1930s. Instead, it appears that the Japanese intelligentsia in the early 1970s began to acutely sense problems inherent in the Eurocentric philosophy which had served as a foundation for Western science and technology. This occurred largely through a recognition that scientific technology had yielded, as its unexpected byproduct, a "mind/heartless" society, pollution, and global ecological crises, which had permeated almost all parts of the Japanese archipelago to threaten the psyche of the Japanese people and their mode of living. In this essay, I should like to briefly introduce three representative contemporary Japanese thinkers who have addressed some aspects of these problems in their writings. They are Nakamura Yūjirō, Sakabe Megumi, and Yuasa Yasuo. (Because of the limitations of space, this article will restrict itself to these three thinkers, but this should not suggest that there are no other representative thinkers in Japan. Consider particularly those belonging to the neo-Kyoto school, such as Nishitani Keiji, Kōsaka Masaki, Kōyama Iwao, Umehara Takeshi and Ueda Shizuteru. Nishitani's works are well known in the English-speaking world, along with those of Abe Masao. Outside of the Kyoto school, we can also mention other thinkers, such as Matsumoto Masao, Hiromatsu Wataru and Ichikawa Hiroshi.)

2 Nakamura Yūjirō

Among the many books Nakamura Yūjirō has so far published, his *Kyōtsūkankakuron: chinokumikae no tameni* (A Discourse on *Sensus Communis*: For the Sake of Recomposing Knowledge, 1979) deserves special attention, because it is framed as a philosophical response to the crises he feels threatening our contemporary period. By examining the concept of *sensus communis*, he wants to argue for a replacement of the paradigm of knowledge based on visual perception with one based on tactile perception. He critiques the former's despotic predominance, which has been extolled in modern civilization, because it has effected "a separation of subject from object, and . . . all that is seen and known is turned into a (material) object by means of intellectual abstraction, rendering the subject into an indifferent, cold 'glance' that controls the object," as is symbolically exemplified in Bacon's "panopticon" (*Kyōtsū*, pp. 53–4).

To break this predominance, Nakamura questions the self-evident horizon presupposed in common sense – that stable, "self-evident" knowledge within the meaning-field of a given society and culture, based on the everyday experience common to the members of that community. Historically, he traces it from Cicero to its use in eighteenth-century Britain as a common power of making judgments, but turns back to its original meaning in Aristotle's *sensus communis*. Following Aristotle, Nakamura interprets the tactile as the basic sense among the five, and defines *sensus communis* as a synthetic power bringing together the five senses. With this understanding he critiques the superiority of visual perception advocated in paleontology, zoology and neuro-physiology, by focusing his analysis on the deconstruction of the myth of visual perception, the analysis of inverted vision, and the pathology of common sense. Philosophically, he draws on Aristotle, Berkeley, and Condillac to restore the tactile, and argues, in summation, that "the idea of space and a position in it cannot be obtained unless one appeals to the tactile" (*Kyōtsū*, p. 104). Nakamura affirms the tactile as the fundamental synthetic sense for living our concrete life, and links it to coenesthesia, including motor sensation and sensation in the muscles (awareness of one's body). He contends that since coenesthesia is an elemental synthesis, it is fundamentally grounded in the predicate-synthesis (*jutsugoteki tōgō*) as opposed to the subject-synthesis (*shutaiteki/shugoteki tōgō*). This distinction is derived from Nishida, but in Nakamura the former designates a mode of activities that enables the human to take root in the world, which the linguistic act realizes in predication, whereas the latter refers to a self-reflective, conscious mode of being, detached from the world, appearing as the subject of a sentence as well as an epistemological subject whose representative mode is visual perception (*Kyōtsū*, p. 284). The predicate-synthesis is un- or pre-conscious in its ontogenesis, and therefore is difficult to grasp, but when it is grasped, Nakamura points out, it is unfortunately grasped vis-à-vis the subject-synthesis. For this reason, people mistakenly think that the subject-synthesis has a priority and predominance. However, the phenomenological fact is that the subject-synthesis is a derivation from coenesthesia, the synthetic activity of which is pre-predicative in nature and upon which visual perception rests (*Kyōtsū*, pp. 284–5). Nakamura concludes that through the synthesis of the various senses with coenesthesia as its foundation, it is possible "for each of us to sympathize with others and nature, and become one with them" (*Kyōtsū*, p. 110). His conclusion is in accord with Bergson's "motor scheme," Merleau-Ponty's "body-scheme" and Husserl's "kinesthesis," as these all pertain to aspects of the coenesthesia through which we live our concrete life as incarnate beings.

Nakamura's analysis extends to cover such topics as language, memory, time and *topos* as they bear on *sensus communis*. Concerning language, Nakamura maintains that the rehabilitation of coenesthesia in the use of language lies above all in restoring the positive significance of image, because image enables us to participate directly in the world, owing to its imaginary character and somaticity. The restoration of image in language counters the logos of analytical rationality in favor of the logos of coenesthesia (*Kyōtsū*, p. 286). This is a criticism of Cartesian linguistics (for example, Descartes and Chomsky), which has one-sidedly emphasized the syntax of sentence over against the paradigm of sentence (*Kyōtsū*, p. 290), insofar as the force of his criticism falls on the unnecessary division between rationality and sensibility.

3 Sakabe Megumi

Sakabe's major efforts have been to articulate the features of Japanese language, through which he wants to grope for a possibility of doing philosophy in Japanese. He acknowledges Watsuji Tetsurō and Kuki Shūzō as his immediate predecessors in this endeavor. A primary reason that he feels compelled to pursue language analysis is that when Western philosophies are translated into Japanese, key terminologies have been rendered into Chinese compounds, thus making philosophy less congenial to the Japanese. For this reason, he consciously focuses in all of his linguistic analyses on indigenous Japanese words (*yamato kotoba*). In this respect, his work has also been stimulated by Anglo-American linguistic analysis, particularly after the 1960s. Sakabe's hermeneutical analysis of language encompasses various levels, such as the lexicographical, syntactic, semantic, and narratological dimensions. Here I shall present his philosophy by taking up his lexical, syntactic and semantic analyses, as these are found in *Perusona no shigaku* (The Poetics of Persona, 1989) and *Kagami no naka no Nihongo* (The Japanese Language in the Mirror, 1989).

To give an example of lexical analysis as a way of illustrating the Japanese understanding of the relationship between one's self and the other, Sakabe examines the Japanese term "*omote*," which means both mask and face. His analysis starts with a derivative word, "*omo-zashi*," meaning facial look or facial figure, which is a compound of *omote* and *zashi*, and *zashi* he takes as corresponding to Husserl's notion of intentionality. By comparing *omo-zashi* and *mana-zashi* (or Sartrean *regard*), he points out that whereas *mana-zashi* is of the nature of unidirectional intentionality, *omo-zashi* reveals a multi-layered intentionality and has a mutual reversibility of intentionality in the intersubjective space. Accordingly, *omo-zashi* should be understood as "that which is seen by the other, as well as that which sees itself, and furthermore as that which sees itself as the other" (*Kagami*, p. 43), where *omote* is the ground of *omo-zashi*. This is the structure of the face as well as of the mask, which discloses a unique feature of (Japanese) interpersonal relationships.

Sakabe connects this structure of *omote* as mask or face to the homophonous word "*omote*," meaning a surface or the front side of a thing. Cautioning us that this word "*omote*" never means in Japanese that which opposes Kant's thing-in-itself or Plato's *eidos*, he says that there is rather a reversibility, a mutuality between the visible front (*omo-te*) and the invisible back (*ura-te*) (*Kagami*, p. 47). That is, the visible and the invisible, depending on the perspective, are in principle reversible, as is exemplified in Zeami's experiential account of "seeing via the detached seeing" (*riken no ken*). (Compare this, for example, with Merleau-Ponty's *The Visible and the Invisible*.) This reversibility suggests to Sakabe that what there is is only *omote* as a visible surface or the front side of a thing, not a substantial being, nor a self-identically fixed being. Accordingly, "no-thing exists except the world of multifarious and infinite metamorphoses" (*Kagami*, p. 51). Based on this observation, Sakabe concludes that there is no need to advocate reversing Platonism or re-evaluating onto-theo-teleo-logical metaphysics (*Kagami*, p. 49).

An example of Sakabe's syntactic and semantic analysis may be found in the following construction, in which the intransitive verb "*fureru*" (to touch) occurs: (*watashi ga*) *tsukue ni fureru*. This sentence is syntactically constructed as a subject-less sentence, the absence of the subject "*watashi*" being indicated by the parentheses. It has the noun "*tsukue*" (desk) marked by the locative "*ni*," and followed by the verb "*fureru*." Since this verb is intransitive, it becomes ungrammatical if it takes the direct object marker, "*o*." In Western languages, in which "to touch" is a transitive verb, the above Japanese sentence would be translated as "(I) touch the desk." Sakabe makes clear, however, that the sentence means in Japanese that "a touching takes place at the desk." The use of the locative marker "*ni*" as it accompanies "*fureru*" indicates a place (*basho*) in which "a person encounters an emergence of a segmenting world prior to a decisive, dualistic separation between subject and object, activity and passivity, the self and the other," where there is a mutual reversibility between these polar terms (*Kagami*, p. 66). (This is in sharp contrast to the dualities that are expressed and thematized in the Western languages in terms of "the extensional/exclusive layers of lived experience" (*Perusona to shigaku*, p. 91).) The peculiarity of the intransitive verb "*fureru*" is even more striking when it is contrasted with other verbs of sensory experience, such as "*miru*" (to see), "*kiku*" (to hear), "*ajiwau*" (to taste), "*kagu*" (to smell). In all of these cases, the object maker "*o*" appears, indicating that these verbs are all transitive. Moreover, we find that the verb "*fureru*" also refers to visual and auditory experience, as in "*me ni fureru*" (literally, "touching takes place in the eye"; or "something comes into vision") or "*mimi ni fureru*" (literally, "touching takes place in the ear'; or "something is heard") (*Kagami*, pp. 75–6). Accordingly, like Nakamura, Sakabe advocates the primacy of the tactile and concludes that it is more basic than other forms of sensory experience. For this reason, the tactile discloses "a vivid 'touch' with the cosmos, and is nothing but a primal experience that is the foundation for all the other succeeding experiences" (*Kagami*, p. 77). To interpret it *à la* Nishida, "the verb '*fureru*' is the most fundamental predicate that characterizes an aspect of the transcendental predicate where the self-awareness comes to an awakening as a cosmic awareness" (*Kagami*, p. 77). Nishida's "transcendental predicate" is proposed in opposition to the (transcendental) subject, which has been cherished by substantialistic ontologists starting with Aristotle and proceeding all the way to

Husserl, in order to disclose the primordial life-energy of the cosmos, as is illustrated in some experiences of Zen *satori* or the *dao*.

Sakabe observes that the subjectless sentence often used in Japanese points to a layer of experience, as is exemplified above, of what he calls proto-personal reference – that is, where there is no clear-cut demarcation between the first, second and third person pronouns (*Shigaku*, pp. 30, 115–24; *Kagami*, p. 155). A subject in this dimension is neither the transcendental subject nor the grammatical subject (*Kagami*, p. 142), but if and when it is thematized as an object, all one can say is that it is nothing (*rien*). The subjectless construction in Japanese is not, therefore, a simple elimination or suppression of the subject, but rather a result of the operation of ambiguity lived at the level of proto-personal reference. However, out of this level of experience, Sakabe points out, the philosophers of the past have created their own systems: emphasis on the first person pronoun yielded Descartes' *cogito* and Fichte's *Ich*; emphasis on the second person pronoun, the Judeo-Christian tradition; emphasis on the third person pronoun, the Islamic tradition, Schelling's philosophy and Jung's role-playing *persona* (*Shigaku*, p. 117).

4 Yuasa Yasuo

Among over thirty books Yuasa has published so far, I should like to focus on two of his recent publications: *Shintai no uchūsei: tōyō to seiyō* (The Cosmic Nature of the Body: The East and the West, 1994) and *Kyōjisei no uchūkan: jikan, seimei to shizen* (The Synchronistic View of the Cosmos: Time, Life and Nature, 1995). Both of these works were written in search of an alternative paradigm of thinking that could overcome that of the contemporary period. Yuasa identifies four points which need to be addressed in tackling contemporary problems, and he wants to present them as sign-posts for future philosophical tasks.

(1) In his historical research on world mythology, a womb out of which philosophy has emerged, Yuasa finds a pattern of thinking universal to humans, namely the pattern that the human and the cosmos are correlative with each other. Contemporary depth psychology concurs with this observation through its analysis of the symbolic image-experience appearing out of the psyche. While the East has inherited and nurtured the idea of the human-cosmos inter-resonance through its technical thinking on meditational cultivation, Yuasa discovers that the parallel idea in the West, as Christianity spread, disappeared out of mainstream philosophy and sank into an intellectual undercurrent. However, we need to investigate this correlative relationship between microcosm *qua* the human and macrocosm *qua* physical nature based on the concept of the body.

(2) Through the examination of the East Asian view of nature, Yuasa has come to the conclusion that it can provide us with many suggestions and clues to think through the ecological crises which modern scientific technology has produced. That is, through its oppositional thinking between subject and object, today's science is confronted with the problem of how to discover nature as life phenomena,

and how to restore it. Yuasa develops this point by observing that the East Asian view holds nature to be a great body of life, and the human as a receptive being made to live within this nature together with the other living beings, while receiving nature's activity. Nature conceals a holistic, synchronistic, and teleological activity for the human. This provides a possibility of understanding the relationship between nature and the human from a fresh perspective – one not based upon the modern principle of scientific (mechanical) causality. Here Yuasa proposes to understand time as a qualitative timing in attunement with the activity of nature that has bearing on the existential, ethical course of one's life, and in contrast to the idea of time as a homogeneous, measurable dimensionality.

(3) Yuasa connects this idea of nature to a re-examination of human nature. He defines the human being as an integrated, inseparable mind-body unity, insofar as the human lives in this world, suggesting an overcoming of the mind-body dualism that modern philosophy has postulated. Yuasa bases his position on the concept of the body espoused by Eastern medicine. It has understood the human body from the viewpoint of *ki*-energy, which is an invisible psycho-physical energy, and it maintains that the human body functions as an open-system in communication with the environmental world (that is, nature) while the activity of *ki*-energy penetrates the three dimensions of mind, body and matter (psychology, physiology, and physics), and originates in an area of activity unique to the living organism that can be intuitively observed through a cultivated awareness. In this connection, Yuasa also notes that the activity of *ki*-energy is in some way linked to the experience of the psyche which religious thought – both Eastern and Western – has long pursued. Accordingly, he concludes that the research in *ki*-energy opens up a way of going beyond the modern view of human nature. (For a more extensive discussion of *ki*-energy, see Yuasa Yasuo, *The Body, Self-Cultivation and Ki-Energy*, 1993.)

(4) The last issues for our future philosophical task are the problems of death and eternity. Yuasa reminds us that the Western tradition, unlike the Eastern tradition, has persistently pursued this topic, beginning with the deaths of Socrates and Jesus. Plato had Socrates in his death chamber speak of the immortality of the soul and reincarnation, while teaching the recollection of eternal ideas as the foundation for philosophy. Christianity is founded upon the crucifixion and resurrection of Jesus. The deaths of both of these men, though occurring in conditions of disgrace insofar as the standard of worldly values is applied, have taught us the value of eternity.

Yuasa notes that once we take the problem of death into our purview, the distinction between the body and the spirit will begin to take on a different meaning. Given the undeniable fact of mind-body inseparability which is a feature of life in this world, it may appear that there is a contradiction here with the fact of death. Yet Yuasa calls to our attention that this sense of contradiction arises from the modern view of the human. The modern scientific view of the world has tended to deny the existence of a world after death, and what is left to the human is flesh and material substance. Consequently, modern human beings have placed the fundamental value of life in the pursuit of the eternity of the flesh (in youth and sex) and material affluence. Modern medicine, coming from such a background, has examined the human only with respect to its somaticity, abandoning questions of death and mind (psyche). A questioning of this dualism has emerged, however, from reflection on the one-sidedness of this view. Now various issues relating to bioethics and research on near-death experiences are demanding reflection concerning death and eternity. This will, as Yuasa envisions, invite us to an investigation into religiosity, where I surmise mind-body inseparability will be scrutinized from a heightened awareness of subtle energy, persisting even after physical death.

5 Concluding remarks

In the foregoing, I have given a cursory presentation of the three most prominent contemporary Japanese thinkers, with a view to introducing the reader to how they conceive of overcoming the contemporary period, while at the same time providing a few features of Japanese philosophy to compare with certain aspects of Western philosophy. In so doing, I have touched upon: (1) an urgent need to think of a reconfiguration of knowledge by way of introducing Nakamura's understanding of coenesthesia; (2) the nature of the (Japanese) understanding of interpersonal relationships vis-à-vis Sakabe's skillful analysis of the Japanese language; and (3) the four areas of global philosophical concern, as Yuasa envisions them. These last are: (a) the commonality of understanding concerning the human's relation to nature exemplified in mythology and today's depth-psychology; (b) a proposal to understand nature as a holistic, synchronistic, and teleological activity; (c) a view of the human being as an integrated, inseparable unity while living in this world, with *ki*-energy activating the three domains of mind, body and matter; and (d) the problem of death, which leads into the investigation of religiosity.

There are, of course, other views to be found among Japanese intellectuals concerning the issue of overcoming the contemporary period. Some believe that the twenty-first century will belong to Asia, others think that scientific technology will permit us to solve the problems of the twentieth century, and still others hold the view that one-third of the world's cultural and economic activity will center on the East in the next century. (See, for example, *Nihonjin wa shisōshitaka* [Have the Japanese Philosophized?, 1995] in which Yoshimoto Takaaki, Umehara Takeshi and Nakazawa Shinichi discuss the issue of overcoming the contemporary period.) Yet still others close their lips tightly on this issue. Whatever the future may hold, we will be welcoming in a few years the dawn of a new century, and we are now in a transitional period in which we must envision a new paradigm of knowledge valid for all of the peoples living on this planet. It is a time in which we must strive for a deeper understanding of what it means to be human, beyond ethnic/cultural differences, and incorporate a holistic understanding of the human, rather than persist in a one-sided emphasis on human rationality. In this global endeavor we need to transcend our national/ethnic karma for the sake of the countless generations yet to come.

Bibliography

Nakamura Yūjirō 1975: *Kansei no kakusei* [The Awakening of Sensibility] (Tokyo: Iwanami shoten).

—— 1977: *Tetsugaku no genzai* [Philosophy in the Present] (Tokyo: Iwanami shoten).

—— 1979: *Kyōtsūkankakuron: chinokumikae no tameni* [A Discourse on *Sensus Communis*: For the Sake of Recomposing Knowledge] (Tokyo: Iwanami shoten).

—— 1994: *Gendai no jōnenron* [On Contemporary Passions] (Tokyo: Kodansha).

Sakabe Megumi 1984: *Risei no fuan* [The Anxiety of Reason] (Tokyo: Keisōsha).

—— 1985: *Kamen no kaishakugaku* [The Hermeneutics of the Mask] (Tokyo: Tokyo Daigaku shuppankai).

—— 1989a: *Kagami no naka no Nihongo* [The Japanese Language in the Mirror] (Tokyo: Chikumashobō).

—— 1989b: *Perusona to shigaku* [The Poetics of Persona] (Tokyo: Iwanami shoten).

Yuasa Yasuo 1987: *The Body: Toward an Eastern Mind-Body Theory* (Albany: State University of New York Press).

—— 1993: *The Body, Self-Cultivation and Ki-Energy* (Albany: State University of New York Press).

—— 1994: *Shintai no uchūsei: tōyō to seiyō* [The Cosmic Nature of the Body: the East and the West] (Tokyo: Iwanami shoten).

—— 1995: *Kyōjisei no uchūkan: jikan, seimei to shizen* [The Synchronistic View of the Cosmos: Time, Life and Nature] (Kyoto: Jinmonshoin).

41

The contemporary Indian situation

BINA GUPTA

In order to appreciate the content and structure of this article, one must first distinguish between Indian philosophy, even in its modern form, and philosophy which is done by Indians. When a philosopher of Indian heritage writes on modern Western logic or on phenomenology, he/she is not doing Indian philosophy. Such philosophers have not been included in this essay. According to my understanding of the term, their work would be Indian philosophy only if these Western ideas have some impact on their study of Indian philosophy, or if they use Indian philosophical ideas to interpret Western philosophy, or if their work is aimed at preserving and/or extending traditional Indian philosophical pursuits. Similarly, Indian philosophy is not restricted to philosophy written by Indians; it includes philosophy written by anyone, regardless of national origin, who develops, interprets, or reinterprets the themes of classical Indian philosophy. There are many excellent Western scholars of Indian philosophy, such as Eric Frauwallner, Eliot Deutsch, Daniel Ingalls, and Karl Potter. However, because of the limitations of space, I have not discussed their work in this article. I have selected only contemporary philosophers of Indian heritage whose work coherently fits into a narrative account of recent developments in Indian philosophy that reflects the continuation and enrichment of the Indian tradition.

In reviewing the works on Indian philosophy written in the past fifty or sixty years, one comes across divergent characterizations of Indian philosophy. A majority of scholars perceive philosophy in India as essentially spiritual. This characterization of Indian thought has been widely accepted since the publication of Radhakrishnan's *Indian Philosophy* and continues to be widely entertained today. P. T. Raju, for example, notes that "Indian philosophy is *Ātman*-centric. Both the starting point and end of philosophy are the *Ātman*" (Raju, 1982 p. 88). B. K. Matilal, by contrast, contends that "verification and rational procedure are as much part of Indian philosophical thinking as they are in western philosophical thinking" (Matilal, 1971, p. 11). And bearing such divergent characterizations in mind, Narayana Moorty concludes that "Indian philosophy is at the crossroads. . . . [T]he contemporary Indian philosopher . . . has a choice. He can embrace the analytical and verificationist approach of the west . . . or can choose to rejuvenate the tradition of Indian philosophy. . . ." (Moorty, 1982, pp. 260–72). Debabrata Sinha asks,

> [In the Indian philosopher's] effort to move forward in the current of creative thinking in response to [the] contemporary philosophic situation, is he expected to forgo the

> burden of traditional thinking? Or should he rather reinforce the strengths and foundations of his thinking by creative appropriation of the on-coming movement of philosophic tradition? (Sinha, 1982, p. 277)

Let us briefly review, then, the important themes of the contemporary Indian philosophical scene in order to assess the current status of Indian philosophy.

Philosophy in contemporary India may be divided into two periods: that before and that after the achievement of India's independence in 1947. To the first belong such well known figures as Aurobindo Ghosh, K. C. Bhattacharyya, Rabindranath Tagore, Mohandas K. Gandhi, S. Radhakrishnan, B. Seal, H. Haldar, R. D. Ranade, D. M. Datta, N. V. Banerjee, R. Das, and A. C. Mukherjee. Some of these figures were not professional philosophers, but educated, literate, action-oriented, public figures. Nevertheless, their ideas are of great significance even for academic philosophy. The fact that Tagore, a poet and a non-academic figure, was elected as the President of the first Indian Philosophical Congress in 1925 testifies to the importance and impact of such figures in India. These figures, with the exception of R. Das and N. V. Banerjee, were idealist metaphysicians in that they believed that reality is spiritual. Their mode of thinking was influenced by Western philosophers such as Hegel, on the one hand, and Indian philosophers such as Śaṃkara, on the other. In the second group, P. J. Chaudhury, K. D. Bhattacharyya, and A. S. Ayyub are most noteworthy. To a still younger generation belong M. Chatterjee, N. K. Devaraja, Daya Krishna, Bimal Matilal, J. N. Mohanty, Rajendra Prasad, and P. K. Sen. These philosophers, perhaps with the exception of Kalidas Bhattacharyya, were influenced by analytic philosophy, modern logic, phenomenology and/or Navya-Nyāya – the logical–epistemological school of Indian philosophy.

It will not be possible to discuss all of these figures here. Instead, I will outline only the most significant contributions of a selected few of them on certain important themes in four sections, dealing respectively with Epistemology and Logic, Metaphysics, Ethics, and Social and Political Philosophy, followed by some concluding general remarks.

I

In epistemology, issues such as the relationship between intuition and intellect, between knowledge and its object, and the distinction between knowledge by identity and by difference, preoccupy Indian thinkers. Aurobindo, for example, makes a distinction between knowledge by identity and separative knowledge – that is, knowledge by difference. He contends that the direct, non-sensuous experience of reality is actually present in all of us – that is, we are all immediately aware of our own existence. This is knowledge by identity or what Aurobindo calls "intuition."

Separative knowledge, or knowledge by difference, is discursive. The distinction between the subject and the object is always present in it. Separative knowledge, though not perfect like intuitive knowledge, is not useless; it guides us toward integral knowledge – a synthesis of knowledge by identity and difference. Descent from knowledge by identity to separative knowledge, and ascent back to knowledge by identity are both possible. This ascent is integral knowledge. It culminates in integral transformation – the unity of our being with Reality. Radhakrishnan, like Aurobindo, argues for the supremacy of intuition. Among the various forms of knowledge – for example, intellect, intuition, faith, or testimony of the scriptures – intuition is the highest. Whereas intuition is integral experience, intellect is discursive, involving a duality of subject and object. This does not mean, however, that intellect and intuition are discontinuous and separate. Nor does it imply that the passage from intellect to intuition involves a move from reason to unreason. This move implies a passage in the direction of the deepest content of rationality. Intuititive knowledge is not non-rational; rather it is non-conceptual. Thus the highest knowledge is attainable only via intuition. It is direct experience of reality (*aparokṣānubhūti*).

Whereas Aurobindo and Radhakrishnan make a case for considering knowledge by identity or intuition as the highest form of knowledge, K. C. Bhattacharyya, basing his argument upon the Jaina theory of "many-ended-ism" (*anekāntavāda*), demonstrates that neither the category of difference nor that of identity is by itself indispensable to philosophy. He argues for an alternation of the two. According to Jainism, in a given case the seven predicates (is, is not, is and is not, is indeterminate, is and is indeterminate, is not and is indeterminate, is and is not and is indeterminate) may be asserted only relatively, but not absolutely. For K. C. Bhattacharyya, the Jaina theory not only asserts a plurality of determinate truths, but also takes each truth to be an indetermination of *alternative* truths. By contrasting the definite and the indefinite, he deduces seven modes of truth. To claim that a determinate existent, an *X*, *is* in one respect and *is not* in another, does not point to their identity – that is, that *X* is *X* and is not *Y*; but rather asserts that *X*, as an existent universal, is different from itself as a particular. Accordingly, every mode of truth is at once a determinate truth and an indetermination of other possibilities or alternative modes of truth. There are "not merely many truths but alternative truths" (Gopinath Bhattacharyya, 1983b, p. 342).

This logic of alternation finds further expression in the writings of Kalidas Bhattacharyya, the son of K. C. Bhattacharyya. He articulates the central problem of epistemology in the question "How is knowledge of an object possible, since knowledge and its object are inherently opposed to each other?" One may adopt either an outward objective attitude to apprehend an object or an inward subjective attitude to apprehend knowledge. If we assume a dialectical attitude, we have willing – that is, a dialectical unity of the two. These three alternative attitudes, again as with K. C. Bhattacharyya, lead to three alternative absolutes. In his later writings, Kalidas Bhattacharyya did not return to this thesis of alteration, but focused on the relation between pre-reflective experience and reflective, metaphysical thinking, seeking to preserve the autonomy of each.

Younger philosophers in India today are trying to translate their thoughts into the language of modern Western epistemology and logic. The work of these Indian philosophers is primarily interpretive. In recent years, there has been a growth of interest in *śabdapramāṇa*, which can be traced back to J. N. Mohanty's

Presidential Address to the Indian Philosophical Congress in 1986, in which he presented a reconstructed theory of *śabdapramāṇa*. In *Gaṅgeśa's Theory of Truth*, Mohanty (1966) demonstrates that the theories of *svataḥprāmāṇya* and *parataḥprāmāṇya* are not really incompatible, because they operate on two different conceptions of knowledge and truth. He provides a kind of compatibilist view. Mohanty also interprets the two classical theories of *anvitābhidānvāda* and *abhihitānvayavāda* in terms of Frege's composition and context principles: in the former the meaning of a sentence is composed of the meaning of the words; in the latter the meaning of a word depends on the meaning of the sentence. Mohanty's work inspired Bimal Matilal and P. K. Sen to further examine the issue in an important paper in *Mind* (Matilal and Sen, 1988, pp. 73–97). The discussion culminated in Matilal and Chakrabarty's edited epistemological work entitled *Knowing from Words* (1994). Additionally, some of these younger philosophers argue that formal logic can be conceived as a part of philosophy. Matilal's *The Navya-Nyāya Doctrine of Negation* (1968) and Sibajiban's *Gadhādhar's Theory of Objectivity* (1990) are two excellent examples of this sort of enterprise. Employing a method that combines philology and philosophy, both attempt to render the Navya-Nyāya logic into the extensional language of modern Western logic.

II

In metaphysics, questions regarding the nature and relevance of the absolute, and the distinction between idealism and realism dominate the philosophical scene. There is a persistent tendency to either reject, reinterpret, or defend Śaṃkara's Absolute. An attempt is made to come to terms with questions such as: How can the transcendence of the Absolute be reconciled with its immanence? Or, in what sense, if any, can the Absolute be said to be the creator of the world?

For example, recognizing matter and spirit as equally real, Aurobindo rejects Śaṃkara's non-dualism in favor of his own integral monism. Aurobindo holds that nature evolves on several levels because Brahman has already involved itself at each level. Evolution, on the other hand, is the inverse of involution; it is the unfolding of consciousness in matter, whereby the unmanifested becomes manifest. Spirit's prior involvement in matter and its manifestation in grades of consciousness, is the significance of evolution. Evolution transforms ignorance into knowledge. There is an emergence of a gnostic being, of a completely divinized Spirit. For Aurobindo, unlike Śaṃkara, *māyā* is the real power of Brahman and possesses the characteristics of infinite self-variation, self-limitation, and self-absorption. Thus supramental transformation does not mean a rejection of the world, but rather implies a gnostic personality that has realized that matter is also Brahman; it is a unique experience of oneness, of the many-in-one, of supramental consciousness.

Whereas Aurobindo placed the many and the becoming in Brahman, the Absolute, K. C. Bhattacharyya articulates the absolute as alternation. He makes consciousness his point of departure – a consciousness which cannot be defined in terms of either the objective or the subjective, because it transcends both. Such a transcendence is "indefinite," the definite being the realm of the subject and the object. Philosophy, for him, is the natural activity of human beings. It begins in a state of reflective consciousness which contains an awareness of an indefinite relation between a content and consciousness. Reflection does not simply stop at this indefinite relation; there is a demand for it to be defined, that it be rendered definite depending upon whether consciousness is consciousness of knowing, or of willing, or of feeling. Accordingly, the relation between consciousness and its content varies. In knowing, the content is not constituted by consciousness; in willing, it is constituted by consciousness; and in feeling there is a kind of unity between content and consciousness. When the dualism between content and consciousness is overcome, each of these three functions of consciousness has its own formulation of the absolute. When the content is ultimately freed from consciousness in knowing, the absolute is truth, it simply *is* – the sort of formulation we find in Advaita Vedānta. When consciousness is freed from the willed content in willing, the Absolute is freedom – the type we find in Mādhyamika Buddhism. When the implicative dualism between content and consciousness is itself freed in feeling, the absolute is unity – the kind we find in Hegel. Thus we find in K. C. Bhattacharyya's writings an absolute for knowing, an absolute for willing, and an absolute for feeling. To question whether there is one absolute or three is meaningless, he notes, because such a question arises only in the context of a known content. The absolute of knowing, insofar as it is self-evident, is not a known content. Similarly, the remaining two absolutes, given the absence of cognitive consciousness, cannot be characterized as known contents. "Each is an absolute . . . but what are here understood as three are only their verbal symbols, they themselves being understood together, but not as together" (Gopinath Bhattacharyya, 1983a, p. 504). They are genuine absolutes in that from one perspective the question of their identity and difference is meaningless, while from another their identity, though meaningful, is not assertible. These three verbal symbols are incommensurable: a synthesis of the three is not possible.

Kalidas Bhattacharyya, following the footsteps of his father, K. C. Bhattacharyya, develops the concept of alternation. Construing alternation as disjunction, the younger Bhattacharyya argues that one cannot decide between idealism and realism from a purely theoretical point of view. The decision depends on other kinds of commitments: the "object is that which is felt as over against consciousness." In this statement, the "object is that" indicates the independent character of the object and "over against consciousness" indicates the dependence of the object on consciousness. The realists emphasize the first half of this expression and the idealists the second half. Hence the conclusion that there is necessarily an alternation between Idealism and Realism. "Which half one will prefer depends on temperament and tradition" (K. D. Bhattacharyya, 1951, p. 18). Alternation, according to Bhattacharyya, is not simply confined to the phenomenal world, where knowing, feeling, and willing are confused. Reflection demands subordination, rejection, and incorporation. Accordingly, alternation yields three possibilities: pure subjectivity (absolute knowing), pure objectivity (absolute feeling), and a synthesis of the two (absolute willing), each of which is absolute alternatively, not simultaneously.

T. R. V. Murti, like K. C. and K. D. Bhattacharyya, argues that the relation between consciousness and object may be conceived in three possible ways, corresponding to these three conscious functions. In knowing, content may determine consciousness; in willing, consciousness may determine content; and in feeling, both consciousness and content may determine each other. Although the three are confused in our everyday experience, it is possible to arrive progressively at pure knowing, pure willing, or pure feeling by purifying any one of the three from the influences of the other two. Pure knowing is absolute truth when freed from all subjectivity; pure willing is absolute freedom when freed from all objectivity; and pure feeling is absolute bliss when freed from all distinctions. Each absolute is incommensurable, in that the absolutes cannot be reduced to each other; they are alternative absolutes (Murti, 1983, p. 27).

It is interesting to note that although all three of these philosophers make a case for three alternative absolutes, they relate these absolutes to the three conscious functions differently. Knowing, willing, and feeling, respectively lead to absolute subjectivity, objectivity, and unity, for K. C. Bhattacharyya; to absolute subjectivity, unity, and objectivity, for K. D. Bhattacharyya; and to absolute objectivity, subjectivity, and unity, for Murti.

N. V. Banerjee, by contrast, contends that any inquiry regarding the absolute is futile. The absolute does not, and should not, have a place in philosophy. Reality, as he sees it, is an existential, and not an evaluative, concept. Whereas it makes perfect sense to talk of distinctions, of kind as well as of degree, in the context of evaluative concepts, the concept of reality does not admit of any such distinctions. One can make a distinction between reality and unreality, but as contradictories they are exclusive of each other. So "the admission of kinds or else degrees of reality is, in either case, tantamount to the arbitrary elimination of the ineliminable relation of disjunction between reality and unreality" (Banerjee, 1974, p. 227). Hence he concludes that absolutism as a metaphysical theory is "a failure." According to Banerjee, the most fundamental concept is "I with others," so that he construes liberation as "the actualization of the transcendental 'I with others.'"

III

In ethics, the distinction between fact and value, between the objective and the subjective, preoccupies the minds of Indian philosophers. Devaraja, for example, questions the dichotomy between factual and evaluative statements. Construing evaluative statements as preferential statements, rejecting the correspondence theory of truth, and basing a statement's truth or falsity on the subjective intention and purpose of the speaker, he attempts to demonstrate the parallels between factual and evaluative statements. Rajendra Prasad argues that ethics cannot be deduced from metaphysics. Construing philosophy as a "conceptual analysis," Prasad does a conceptual study of *mokṣa*, in order to assess its "logical status . . . *vis-à-vis* some other related Indian value-concepts" (Prasad, 1971, p. 381). He maintains that "regardless of how one articulates *mokṣa*, it remains a factual or ontological state . . . and so it is a descriptive term" (Prasad, 1971, p. 390). Daya Krishna attacks the rejection of the notion of objectivity and observes that without it, "human seeking will not make sense in any realm whatsoever" (Krishna, 1972, p. 168), since the tension between the subjective and the objective motivates all human pursuits. "The necessity of resolution, however, is felt only because it is assumed that a pair of contradictories cannot characterise a real situation" (Krishna, 1972, p. 177). Daya Krishna extends this reasoning to the Hindu concept of *mokṣa* which, in his estimation, is a state of consciousness in which the "other" is either sublated or bracketed.

Gandhi, on the other hand, argues that principles of ethics must be translated into actions, which result in our taking sides on concrete issues. These actions must be based on love and self-sacrifice. He finds some of his deepest convictions reflected in Ruskin's *Unto This Last*, which he personally translated into Gujarati, entitling it *Sarvodaya* (The Welfare of All). Gandhi explicitly rejects the utilitarian doctrine of the pursuit of the greatest good for the greatest number. In cases of rule by majority, the interests of minorities are often neglected. Therefore, the only real, dignified ethical doctrine must be the pursuit of the greatest-good-of-all. Gandhi himself observes that the greatest-good-of-all includes the greatest good of the greatest number. His ethics, therefore, is far more comprehensive than any based on the utilitarian principle, although he never systematically develops the ramifications of his ethical theory.

IV

In social and political philosophy, fundamental questions regarding the basis upon which political structures should be founded were raised by Indian thinkers. Tagore, for example, in his social and political philosophy rejects geographical patriotism, puritanism, asceticism, and absolutism. Taking his point of departure from the Upaniṣadic texts that reinforced the creation of the finite out of the infinite, Tagore contends that the finite is not illusory; it is real. He argues for an immanent God rather than a transcendent One: God is not beyond the universe, he claims, but is a synthesis of goodness, beauty, truth, and love. The ideal of universal brotherhood permeates all of Tagore's writings. He repeatedly emphasizes that the idea of a nation-state is Western in origin, whereas the idea of community is central to the Eastern mode of thinking. In his lectures in Japan, he urged the Japanese to go back to the fundamental notions of community or society, rather than glorifying the nation. The wisdom of this advice has been well borne out by subsequent history. Tagore concedes that each nation reaches its goal by a different path and the significance of that path must not be minimized. But, notwithstanding the fact that there are accidental differences between us, our education must instill in us a sense of our essential unity.

Writing under the influence of Hegelian thought, Aurobindo Ghosh disagreed with Tagore. Aurobindo held that the idea of the state is historically a higher development which emerged out of the idea of society. What Aurobindo had in mind was a world government which would supersede the nation-state. Contending that only through the attainment of inner freedom on the part of individuals was it possible for society to be saved, he made the spirit the basis of India's struggle for freedom. To explore and realize the spiritual was, in his opinion, the calling of humanity. Spirituality, he adds, is not the monopoly of the Hindus, because "each nation is a Shakti or power of the evolving spirit in humanity" (Aurobindo, 1959, p. 3). The different nations approach and formulate this spirit differently. They do not recognize the underlying unity of this human spirit, but reinforce the differences. He describes the twentieth century as the "shadow of a spirit that is unborn" but which is "preparing for its birth."

> A Spiritual religion of humanity is the hope of the future. . . . A religion of humanity means the growing realisation that there is a secret Spirit, a divine Reality, in which we are all one. (Aurobindo, 1971, p. 554)

His goal was the spiritualization of the entire human race, not merely of the souls of individuals, but of nations as well.

The ideal of human unity envisaged by Tagore and Aurobindo was translated into practical politics by Mahatma Gandhi. He emphasized that India's freedom would mean little if the people lost their souls in the process. The method used to achieve independence had to be such that it would take India and the world closer to the spiritual goal of humankind – the unity of individual with individual and finally with all of humanity. Gandhi tried to find common themes between the mainstream of Western philosophy and the Hindu philosophico-religious tradition upon which to ground and develop the process of *satyāgraha*, "the truth-force," a process which is comprised of three essential elements: *satya* (truth), *ahiṃsa* (non-violence), and *tapasya* (the willingness to endure suffering to demonstrate the truth of one's principles). He advocated *Rāmrājya* – government based on service, kindness, justice, and morality – as the foundation of the ideal state. By pointing out a close connection between *swaraj* (self-rule) and *swadeshi* (self-reliance), he demonstrated that the pursuit of *swaraj* entails the acceptance of *swadeshi*, that the former is logically and morally prior to the latter. The relationship between *swaraj* and *swadeshi* corresponds to the relationship between *satya* and *ahiṃsa*. *Satya* is prior to *ahiṃsa* in theory; in practice, however, the pursuit of *satya* amounts to the practice of *ahiṃsa*. Similarly, *swaraj* is of a higher order from a theoretical perspective; however, in practice *swadeshi* has greater urgency and significance than *swaraj*.

Gandhi endorsed a view (like Hannah Arendt's) whereby "power corresponds to the human ability not just to act, but to act in concert" (Habermas, 1990, p. 174). Non-violence thus entails not only refraining from physical or psychological coercion of others but also listening to the views of others in an attitude of humility and openness. *Satyāgraha*'s goal is an adjustment in the belief and opinion of all parties to a dialogue in which truth develops dialectically. Gandhi demonstrated the truth of the maxim that "if one would rule, he must first learn to serve" (*I Ching*,

17). His life exemplifies the willingness to live simply, so that others could simply live.

V

In conclusion, a review of Indian philosophy dispels the common characterization of it as spiritualistic. Philosophy in India is not simply a search for spirit, it is also a critical analysis (*ānvīkṣikī*) of the data provided by perception. This, however, is not to suggest, as Matilal argues, that verification and rational procedure are as much a part of the Indian tradition as they are in the West. According to the fundamental framework of the Indian tradition, logical and epistemological studies, though an integral part, are ancillary to the study and interpretation of scriptures.

We live in a transitional era. No philosophy exists *in vacuo*; it neither originates nor develops without some undergirding context. Although shaped by culture, it has meaning and relevance beyond the given culture. British rule opened the door to Western philosophy. Thus it should come as no surprise that the younger generation of Indian philosophers use the conceptual apparatus of Western logic to explain and expound Indian philosophy. It is generally assumed that tradition is to be juxtaposed against, or exists in tension with, modernity. A review of the concrete situation suggests otherwise. Worse yet is the implicit assumption that the traditional is bad while that which is modern is laudable. A tradition is not something that is static and unchanging; it too evolves, grows, expands. Some traditions change naturally, some as a result of conscious effort by those who are its adherents. Modernity, on the other hand, is not marked by a total rejection of the past; it implies an element of self-consciousness, of choice, of selection. One can begin to speak of modernity within a traditionalist context only when one becomes self-consciously aware of one's place in the tradition. Modernity implies assuming a critical spirit, becoming self-critically aware. One enters into a dialogue with the past, in which there is an active interaction between one's own consciousness and the consciousness of one's predecessors in the tradition.

There does not seem to me to be an exclusive either–or choice between tradition and modernity. Likewise, for Indian philosophers, it is not a choice between "rejuvenating" the Indian philosophical tradition or embracing the analytical and/or phenomenological traditions of the West. It is not a matter of either wholesale acceptance or rejection of the past, but a reappraisal of the traditional to see what is viable in it. So the basic issue in the maintenance of a tradition, regardless of whether one is talking about the East or the West, is bringing out its creative potential to meet the demands of the time. In the Indian context, reinterpretation of the old keeps the tradition alive. Aurobindo and Radhakrishnan have rejected the Śaṃkarite interpretation of the world as an appearance in favor of the world as real; there is an emphasis on the *mokṣa* of humankind rather than that of one individual person. Along with these, there is a reinterpretation of Indian philosophy using the philosophical tools, the conceptual apparatus of Western philosophy. If in the process one becomes critically aware of new issues and themes within the Indian tradition, there is nothing wrong in this – as long as one does not conflate the two traditions. Moving forward in an attitude of objective, critical understanding and making an assessment of one's tradition using the tools of Western philosophy is to make the most profitable use of available resources. In the final analysis, one has to come to terms with what is personally philosophically challenging and rewarding. Creativity thrives in an atmosphere of freedom and openness. Dogmatic adherence to any tradition, whether indigenous or foreign, amounts to philosophic suicide.

Bibliography

Śri Aurobindo 1959: *The Foundations of Indian Culture, Sri Aurobindo Birth Centenary Library*, ed. A. Ghosh, Vol. 14 (Pondicherry: Śri Aurobindo Ashram).

—— 1971: *The Ideal of Human Unity, Sri Aurobindo Birth Centenary Library*, ed. A. Ghosh, Vol. 15 (Pondicherry: Śri Aurobindo Ashram).

Banerjee, N. V. 1974: *The Spirit of Philosophy* (New Delhi: Arnold-Heinemann Publishers).

Bhattacharyya, K. C. 1983a: "The Concept of the Absolute and its Alternative Forms," in *Studies in Philosophy*, ed. Gopinath Bhattacharyya (Delhi: Motilal Banarsidass), pp. 487–508.

—— 1983b: "The Jaina Theory of Anekānta," in *Studies in Philosophy*, ed. Gopinath Bhattacharyya (Delhi: Motilal Banarsidass), pp. 329–47.

Bhattacharyya, K. D. 1951: *Object and Content and Relation* (Calcutta: Dasgupta).

Bhattacharyya, S. 1990: *Gadādhara's Theory of Objectivity* (New Delhi: Indian Council of Philosophical Research).

Devaraja, N. K. 1972: "Nature and Validity of Value Statements," in *Current Trends in Indian Philosophy*, ed. K. S. Murty and K. R. Rao (Waltair: Andhra University Press), pp. 122–38.

Gandhi, M. K. 1926: "The-Greatest-Good-of-all," *Young India*, December 9.

Habermas, J. 1990: *Philosophical–Political Profiles*, ed. F. G. Lawrence (Cambridge: MIT Press).

Krishna, D. 1972: "Appearance and Reality," *Current Trends in Indian Philosophy*, eds K. S. Murty and K. R. Rao (Waltair: Andhra University Press), pp. 122–38.

Matilal, Bimal K. 1971: *Epistemology, Logic and Grammar in Indian Philosophical Analysis* (The Hague: Mouton).

Matilal, B. K. 1968: *The Navya-Nyāya Doctrine of Negation* (Cambridge: Harvard University Press).

Matilal, Bimal K. and Chakrabarty, A. (eds) 1994: *Knowing from Words* (Dordrecht: Kluwer).

Matilal, Bimal K. and Sen, P. K. 1988: "The Context Principle and Some Indian Theories of Meaning," *Mind*, Jan., pp. 73–97.

Mohanty, J. N. 1966: *Gaṅgeśa's Theory of Truth* (Santiniketan: Center of Advanced Study in Philosophy).

—— 1974: "Philosophy in India, 1967–73," *Review of Metaphysics*, 28, 1, pp. 54–84.

Moorty, Narayana, J. S. R. L. 1982: "Indian Philosophy at the Crossroads," in *Indian Philosophy: Past and Future*, ed. S. S. Rama Rao Pappu and R. Puligandla (Delhi: Motilal Banarsidass), pp. 260–90.

Murti, T. R. V. 1983: "Knowing, Feeling, and Willing as Functions of Consciousness," in *Studies in Indian Thought*, ed. Harold G. Coward (Delhi: Motilal Banarsidass), pp. 17–32.

Prasad, Rajendra 1971: "The Concept of *Mokṣa*," *Philosophy and Phenomenological Research*, Vol. 31, pp. 381–93.

Raju, P. T. 1982: "The Western and the Indian Philosophical Traditions," in *Indian Philosophy: Past and Future*, eds S. S. Rama Rao Pappu and R. Puligandla (Delhi: Motilal Banarsidass), pp. 61–100.
Sinha, Debabrata 1982: "Indian Philosophy at the Crossroads of Self-Understanding," in *Indian Philosophy: Past and Future*, eds S. S. Rama Rao Pappu and R. Puligandla (Delhi: Motilal Banarsidass), pp. 273–90.

42

Contemporary Polynesian thinking

JOHN CHARLOT

Many Polynesian cultures experienced a flowering in the early contact period, taking advantage of the new knowledge and technology and inspired by the opening of a wider world. Through the nineteenth century, traditional and introduced elements were synthesized to produce distinctive cultural achievements, such as Hawaiian music and the elaboration of Māori wood sculpture made possible by the introduction of metal tools.

This positive mood was, however, increasingly depressed by population decline, political and economic problems, and in places even the loss of the native language as the normal means of communication. Most important for our subject, many higher educational institutions were abandoned in favor of Western schooling. In Hawaiʻi, the temples with their schools were destroyed, and the new, centralized court – unlike the courts of old – did not function as an educational institution. Important efforts were made, however, to perpetuate the old learning. The Māori established an innovative inter-tribal educational center. Samoan Christian pastors' schools assumed many of the tasks of traditional instruction. Various crafts schools and arts academies continued to operate.

Nevertheless, the decrease in higher speculation was especially harmful because Polynesians needed to solve the intellectual and emotional problems of contact. Western influences were indeed intensifying, but contrary to general expectation, the old culture was not disappearing under its impact. Polynesians became bicultural in most fields, such as religion, medicine, the arts, and education.

The post-contact history of Polynesia is therefore potentially helpful in understanding the increasing multiculturalism of the contemporary world. We can see that cultures – even minority ones seemingly overwhelmed by larger cultures – endure, not just superficially in costumes and folk customs, but down to the level of experience. Polynesians continued to have Polynesian experiences even when missionaries and others assured them they were imaginary. The gods continued to appear, prayers and curses continued to work, and native medicine still cured.

In what mental framework could this bicultural situation be understood? The introduced views of the world – such as missionary Christianity – offered no satisfactory explanation. Polynesians were therefore left to their own resources. The author of "A Story from 1890," probably the great Orator Chief Lauaki Namulauʻulu, depicts the Samoan gods fighting among themselves and their wounded applying for help at the home of a Christian missionary. When he sees the horribly mutilated but still living gods at his door, he flees terrified. Disgusted, one of the gods states, "*ʻana ʻua tonu ifo i luga mātou te pule iā teʻoe po ʻua ʻoti*" ("Had it been ordained down from above that we should have power over you, you would die"). That is, both religions exist side-by-side in Sāmoa, but under a higher, unidentified power that regulates them both. Similarly, Tauanuʻu, the author of a late nineteenth-century text on Tangaloa's extensive creation of the world, combined an astonishing number of Samoan traditions into an original scheme that continued the classical direction of Samoan cosmology while alluding to the confrontation with the foreign Bible. The highest Samoan speculation was thus perpetuated for another generation alongside Christian education.

Many problems of the bicultural situation were both practical and crucial to survival, such as the development of forms and procedures of government that would be viable in the modern world. Samoan chiefs have coordinated the chiefly and democratic elements already present in their culture to construct polities that appear to be both effective and emotionally satisfying. In the 1830s, the Hawaiian ruling chiefs commissioned a missionary teacher to lecture to them on political economy or science; they then established a form of constitutional monarchy that, with amendments, enabled them to preserve Hawaiʻi's sovereignty through most of the nineteenth century. The chiefs were following the classical method of discussing all possible historical models before choosing a course of action. However, the contemporary Hawaiian sovereignty movement appears to be carrying on its discussions in a historical vacuum with no conscious or affective ties to the polities of the past. More successfully, the Māori have been able to use their tribal identities as a powerful political base for regaining treaty rights. Moreover, their tribal system is being extended creatively to cover those who, through the dislocations of nineteenth-century history, have lost their original tribal roots.

Faced with such problems of contact, Polynesians have steadfastly affirmed the value of their traditional culture and attempted to explain it to the upcoming generations and foreigners. Often, however, much of the richness and complexity of the older cultures has been lost. Simplistic criticisms of Western culture accompany oversimplified descriptions of the native. Studies of religion identify "the four great gods of Polynesia": Tū, Tāne, Tangaloa, and Lono; but of these four, only Tangaloa is found in Western Polynesia! In Hawaiʻi, God, Man, and Nature are pictured as the points of a triangle in an attempt to do justice to the importance of the environment in Hawaiian thinking. But in classical thought, both gods and human beings were contained within the framework of sky and earth. In New Zealand, the classical culture is often simplified into a diminution of *mana* by gradations as it distances itself from its supposed source. This curiously Neoplatonist scheme cannot be found in classical Māori texts or in the early discussions of foreigners. It seems, as do so many modern descriptions of Polynesian culture, to be a combination of half-remembered tradition and half-understood anthropology.

In all such descriptions, however, can be appreciated the effort to articulate cultural values that are still deeply felt – such as the close relation to the environment, the importance of the family, and the positive appreciation of human capabilities – and to find a way to express them in the contemporary world. Because classical Polynesian thinking is deeply religious, the forum for much of the modern discussion is Polynesian Christianity.

Today, as during the contact period, the Polynesian response to Christianity can be described as covering a spectrum. At one extreme are those who reject Christianity totally. Some Māori religious leaders call for the abandonment of Christianity as a foreign, imperialist tool. The Hawaiian religious leader Sam Lono ordered applicants to his school to step on a crucifix – the same symbolic gesture employed in Tokugawa Japan.

At the other extreme are Polynesians who attempt to abandon their Polynesian cultural heritage in order to conform completely to the Western form of Christianity with which they are familiar. For instance, one Hawaiian Christian church practices a ceremony called *ʻoki ʻao ʻao* (cutting off the [Hawaiian] side), a sort of spiritual lobotomy.

Most Polynesians, however, can be found somewhere between these extremes, joining elements of their classical culture with elements of the new religion. They are aided in this process by the emphasis in Polynesian thought on similarities over differences – by the tendency to harmonize elements rather than oppose them to each other. Again a spectrum can be found, from those who conform to the current political–economic situation to those who want to use a native Christianity for liberation purposes, such as a new school of Tahitian Protestants.

No generally accepted theology has been formulated that reconciles Christianity and native religions. Nonetheless, various accommodations, from syncretism to genuine synthesis, have been achieved and reveal much about Polynesian thinking and culture at particular historical moments. Most obviously, many traditional practices continue in baptized form. On one island in precontact times, a divination ceremony was conducted before important initiatives: a priest blessed a large rock, and a strong youth attempted to lift it. The local minister officiates at the ceremony today. Many burial practices and ceremonies to reconcile the soul of the recently deceased are maintained under such shallow Christian covering.

Other developments are more conscious and intellectual and involve basic areas of Polynesian thinking. One of the most obvious areas of friction is the opposition between Christian monotheism and Polynesian polytheism. Missionaries denounced the Polynesian gods as fictions, but Polynesians have continued to experience them as real and powerful. Indeed, gods are often deified ancestors with a long history of benevolent interaction with family members. Many Polynesians began to interpret these family gods according to the Christian idea of guardian angels. Moreover, the Biblical world with its acknowledged multitudes of spirits – from poltergeists, to ghosts, to ranks of devils and angels (see, for example, I Corinthians 8:5; Philippians 2:6–11) – has more in common with the Polynesian world than with the secularized homelands of the missionaries.

One of the most basic subjects of dialogue with Christianity is the Polynesians' positive view of the universe and of the relation of human beings to it; this view is opposed to Christian ideas of our fallen nature and of heaven as our true home. Moreover, for classical Polynesians the universe was the ultimate reality to be studied and revered. Many Polynesian Christians have been able to join their classical view to Christianity by emphasizing God the Father, the creator of the universe, rather than God the Son, the Savior Jesus Christ. They can thus emphasize the goodness of God's creation rather than the Fall that necessitated Salvation.

The Polynesian emphasis on the positive in the universe is reflected in the same emphasis in their view of human nature: human beings are initially good and potentially powerful rather than basically evil and powerless to achieve their own salvation. An important consequence of this view has been developed by the Hawaiian theologian David Kaʻupu (born 1934): the appreciation of cultural achievements, considered religious in themselves in the classical culture. Net-making, fishing, farming, chanting, and dancing are filled with religious values and form an important part of *ka ʻimi loa*, the study of the universe in order better to love and appreciate it. Religion therefore permeates the whole of culture, and the activities of that culture are themselves a form of prayer. That is, just as God creates the natural world, human beings create the cultural one, and their creativity is another sign of their having been created in the image and likeness of God. Moreover, the cultural world should not be evaluated wholly in terms of the Fall, as a distraction or an estrangement from God, but should be seen as proclaiming His glory through the achievements of His creatures. The Polynesian emphasis on family, sexuality, and beauty is in accord with the above points; they are also areas in which Polynesian thinking can contribute to contemporary Christian teaching.

Discussions of values are, of course, conducted in non-theological contexts as well. For instance, development projects almost inevitably raise questions of proper land use, which must ultimately be referred to one's view of the universe and the place of human beings within it. Western environmentalism is often based on arguments from logic and from the broader, long-term self-interest of human beings; it therefore lacks the emotional power to counter more focused selfish interests. In contrast, Polynesian thinking and literature are inspired by – and stimulate in turn – a deep emotional commitment to the land and to its care. Thus they can help non-Polynesians achieve the emotional restructuring needed for a successful reform of world environmental practices. In this area, ancient worldviews often prove more effective than post-Enlightenment Western thinking.

In fact, the difference between Western and Polynesian thinking is often identified as the foundation of all cultural differences and frictions. Again, in these discussions the descriptions of each type of thinking are often oversimplified, one-dimensional, and even incorrect – for example, in the contrast of a linear Western mode of thinking with a circular Polynesian mode. One political activist even proposed recovering Hawaiian thinking by emptying her head of all traces of Western thinking! Nevertheless, Polynesians are directed by such discussions to a renewed study of their intellectual heritage, which involves a determined educational effort. Such an effort is in accord with classical Polynesian culture even if it clashes with the modern stereotype of the unthinking native, based on the difficulties Polynesian students have had in Western schools.

In some places, such as Hawaiʻi and New Zealand, this educational effort must begin at the basic level of language recovery. The Māori *kohanga reo* (language nests) – and the Hawaiian *pūnana leo* based on them – start their students at a sufficiently early age that the native language will be their mother tongue. For places like Sāmoa and Tonga, where language knowledge is stronger, training must still be offered in correct, polite, and classical usage.

For most Polynesians, if not for most Western academics, knowledge of the language is a prerequisite for any authentic knowledge of the culture and ways of thinking. Language must not, however, become a veneer for Western thinking. The student must also be familiar with the riches of the literary tradition. Thus language and literature are taught inseparably in Sāmoa; and through the nineteenth century, Hawaiian writers constantly stressed the need to record and teach the classical literature as the main communicator of their cultural ideals: love of the land, respect for chiefs, pride in accomplishments, piety, and hospitality. Without such a background, youngsters were beginning to talk and even to think like foreigners. Unfortunately, opportunities to study Polynesian literature academically are rare, and the creation of appropriate courses and the development of faculty to teach them are urgent tasks.

Finally, renewed appreciation of Polynesian culture must be coordinated with knowledge of world cultures, just as the Polynesians of the early contact period found their islands on the map. This coordination is often done superficially, with slogans and slaps. But the task itself is mentally and emotionally important; it is a task imposed on everyone in this multicultural world.

One who addresses the problem of cultural understanding at its deepest level is the modern Tongan educator Futa Helu (born 1934). In his view, our contemporary world is the result of millennia of increasing and intensifying intercultural contact, the problems of which have been felt more keenly than the opportunities for greater knowledge and communication. Education and the arts are the means to seize those opportunities and need, therefore, to be developed for their multicultural purpose. At the ʻAtenisi (Athens) Institute, which he founded, Helu has been a pioneer in the academic study of Tongan literature and in its incorporation into the curriculum. His curriculum includes also Greek and Latin, so that students can compare, in the original languages, Western and Tongan classics. In his view, true education must be based on the classics, and the classics of all cultures are mutually reinforcing. Moreover, as does any learned Polynesian, he realizes that the classics must be studied in their original languages. Similarly, in the 1830s, an experimental course in Greek was taught at the only high school in Hawaiʻi in order to equip the students for Bible translation, but also to train their minds. That is, they would be taught Western thought from its very roots rather than superficially.

The best Polynesian thinkers clearly have a good comprehension of and much respect for Western culture and thinking. Their continued appreciation of their native heritage as more than folklore or an inducement to nostalgia invites the foreign thinker to treat Polynesian intellectual culture with equal respect; to consider Polynesian thinkers, not objects of ethnographic investigation, but peers in the worldwide quest for knowledge and understanding.

Indeed classical Polynesian literature – like that of Japanese Shintō – can take us back to the youth of human thinking, when ideas like the mating of sky and earth were fresh and inspired intense reflection. We can observe how those ideas work in people's lives rather than having to excavate them imaginatively from artifacts and texts. Moreover, seeing how those ideas enable people to confront modern problems and devise novel solutions, we can retrace the long history of our Western thinking back to its foundations, gaining some further perspective on our own intellectual stage. Perhaps we will find – as Polynesians have – that our ancestral ideas can help us understand ourselves and our place in the world and rejoin much that has been alienated. Classical Polynesian thinking has not lost its connection to the primary sense of awe and wonder that inspires its vision of life as an appreciative quest for understanding. Polynesian culture is the creative response to the discoveries of that life-long search.

43

Current trends and perspectives in African philosophy

SEGUN GBADEGESIN

Introduction

In the last four decades, there has been a lively debate regarding the nature and status of African philosophy. While some Western-trained African philosophers maintained that African philosophy is just in the making, and that it can only emerge out of the current works of professional philosophers, others insisted that it has always been with us. This debate engaged the attention of philosophers for such a long time that it appeared there can be no substantive African philosophy beyond the debate on its nature. But there has been a change of focus in the last few years. My interest in what follows is to discuss the contemporary situation as revealed in research publications on substantive issues. I hope to show through a few snapshots of current research that despite the controversy, much has been done on substantive African philosophy.

The reality of African philosophy: Lévy-Bruhl's challenge

It is common knowledge that ancient Egyptians engaged in serious philosophical discourse, preserved in hieroglyphic writings and now available in modern English translations. As we all know, however, in pre-colonical sub-saharan Africa there was no well recognized tradition of writing. Although some forms of writing existed (for example, among the Yoruba and Akan people of West Africa), these were not generalized, and were mostly used to convey information of a practical nature rather than to *preserve* discussions on the fundamental questions of meaning and existence.

Of course, there was a tradition of oral discourse, and it has not been doubted that the sages of the various communities held rational philosophical discussions. The question is "how do we know?" For whatever those wise persons thought and discussed orally among themselves, or in individual meditations, were largely unknown to us. We now have access to only their central points of agreement, which may have been distorted in their transmission from one generation to another. Furthermore, we are also not in a position to know the points of disagreement among these sages, and it is hard for a tradition of philosophy to be sustained in such situation. This is one basic issue in the controversy: though philosophy without writing is possible, a tradition of philosophical discourse cannot be established without writing. From this, the argument concludes that there could not have been African philosophy prior to the beginning of the development of a writing tradition. At the same time, the critics concede that there may have been African philosophers. This insistence on the notion of a strict *written* philosophy or nothing then leads us to the conclusion that there might have been African philosophers but no African philosophy.

The position of professional philosophers on what is or is not to count as philosophy had a historical basis in the earliest anthropological studies of African thought systems which had characterized African thought as primitive and non-philosophical. In 1923, Lévy-Bruhl published his *Primitive Mentality* as a report of research on African thought systems which, in his view, were pre-scientific and pre-logical, ignorant of the principles of non-contradiction, identity, and excluded middle. There is, according to Lévy-Bruhl, a difference in kind between the African mind and European mentality. Though he later abandoned this position in his *Notebook on Primitive Mentality* published posthumously in 1975, the controversy it generated has had a great impact on discussions in and about African philosophy. Before Lévy-Bruhl, some anthropologists had based the difference (between African and European thought) on philosophical orientations. Tylor, for instance, had argued that scholars should explain "primitive" thought by appeal to their distinctive theoretical presuppositions, since human nature, according to him, was the same everywhere. Lévy-Bruhl apparently rejected this position. For him, if there was such a thing as the African theoretical presupposition, it was different from the European's and it did not belong to any category of rational thought. It was pre-rational. The wedge thus driven between European and African mentality had the effect of putting Africans on the defensive. In their response to this situation, the works of a new generation of Western anthropologists and theologians supported and inspired them.

Placide Tempels's response

One member of this new generation was Father Placide Tempels, a Belgian theologian whose work, *Bantu Philosophy*, provided another landmark in the history of African philosophy. Tempels's work is significant for the history of African philosophy because it was the first attempt to apply the term "philosophy" to an African thought system. Tempels undertook an interpretation of Bantu beliefs and values with the objective of showing that Africans have a systematic philosophy. The result is an elaborate exposition of the worldview of the Bantu people as a philosophical system. According to Tempels's exposition of this philosophy, what is known as *being* in Western philosophy is understood as *force* in Bantu philosophy. *Being* is *force*. However,

> *force* is not an accident; it is more even than a necessary accident, it is the very essence of *being*. . . . Our notion of *being* is "*that which is*"; theirs is "*the force that is*." Where we

> think the concept "*to be*," they make use of the concept "*force*." Where we see concrete *beings*, they see concrete *forces*. Where we would say that *beings* are distinguished by their essence or nature, Bantus would say that *forces* differ by their essence or nature.

Tempels thus attempted to rescue African thought from the Lévy-Bruhlian axe by forcing on it an invented discourse of alterity.

Tempels's efforts inspired some African scholars and provided them with the ammunition to counter what they believed to be a racially motivated devaluation of their culture and thought system. In this group were the negritude theorists, including the poet-statesman, Leopold Senghor. Although they took issue with some specific details in Tempels's assumptions, they built on the foundation he had laid, and took over some of his main conceptual categories, including the attribution of philosophy to a whole people. This latter position, that philosophy could be attributed to whole peoples, was to be rigorously defended by a professional philosopher and pro-Tempelsian, Alexis Kagame.

However, while some African philosophers took a cue from Tempels's initiative and directed their efforts toward building on it, many leading professionals rejected this attempt as unphilosophical. Thus attempts to construct a philosophy out of the collective worldview of a people, such as that by Tempels, have been described as ethnophilosophy by Paulin Hountondji, the Beninese philosopher whose *African Philosophy: Myth and Reality* has become a classic of African neo-positivists. Peter Bodunrin's "The Question of African Philosophy" and Odera Oruka's "Fundamental Principles in the Question of African Philosophy" belong to the same class. The distinctive feature of ethnophilosophy, they hold, is that we come to know it as a collective possession of a group. As collective thought, it can hardly pass as philosophy because, on this view, philosophy is necessarily individualized thought. Second, since such a group thought does not exist in written form, it cannot qualify as philosophy because, for Hountondji, philosophy necessarily exists in written texts. Bodunrin supports this view while Oruka rejects it. The latter has since undertaken to investigate the philosophical ideas of indigenous Africans who are not literate in Western scripts.

African philosophers and the critique of ethnophilosophy

As observed above, there are two main objections to ethnophilosophy: first, that in looking for philosophy in the communalized thought of a people, it is based on an assumption of the unanimity of views, and therefore is not philosophy; second, that its object exists in an unwritten form, which therefore cannot serve as a basis for developing a philosophical tradition. Some African philosophers have expressed doubt about the import of these objections. A major problem is that it is not clear whether the objection to "ethnophilosophy" is that it focuses on "communal" thought, or that it has not engaged in critical analysis of "communal" thought as its object of focus. One gets the impression that "communal" thought, simply in virtue of its being "communal" cannot be philosophy. Yet it is not self-evident that philosophy is (or ought to be) an individualistic activity, except that it appears to have been so at some point in some space. A more effective critique of "ethnophilosophy" must focus on its orientation as a descriptive account of a people's worldview instead of as a critical analysis of such views.

The second objection raised against the idea of a traditional African philosophy is the absence of written texts. Critics argue that there can be no philosophical tradition without a tradition of writing. This is, of course, true. But it does not then follow that people cannot engage in philosophical discourse without writing. Indeed, as Kwasi Wiredu has rightly observed, writing cannot be a precondition for philosophy because we have to think a thought before it is written down (1991, pp. 94–5). So there could have been philosophical reflections, and thus philosophers, in traditional African societies. The problem raised here is how to identify them, and it seems to me that this is no longer an insurmountable problem in view of the development of such new approaches as philosophic sagacity. Besides, the results of such reflections are contained in the "books of life" in various societies.

The challenge posed by anthropologists and the response of African philosophers have led to the heightening of interest in substantive African philosophy (as opposed to meta-African philosophy) and to the development of some identifiable trends and perspectives. I would like to identify and discuss four such perspectives: critical cultural philosophy, sage philosophy, political–ideological philosophy, and critical philosophy of Africa.

Critical cultural philosophy

In recent times, a good number of African philosophers have turned their attention from the debate over method to the investigation of concepts in traditional African philosophy. The underlying motive for this school is that philosophy is critical reflection on fundamental issues, and that such issues exist in all cultures, including the traditional cultures of Africa. This should therefore inspire a program of research for academic philosophy in Africa. As Kwasi Wiredu puts it, "the agenda for contemporary African philosophy must include the critical and reconstructive treatment of the oral tradition and the exploitation of the literary and scientific resources of the modern world in pursuit of a synthesis" (1992, p. 35). Wiredu believes that since modern African culture has been produced from an interplay between the traditional, the Christian, and Islamic ideas, and the impact of science and modernization, a philosophical approach which takes "cognizance of all these strands of the African experience" should yield a modern African philosophy that should be rich in its variety and vital in its relevance to contemporary experience (1992, p. 36).

Wiredu himself has been in the forefront of this effort to fashion a tradition of modern African philosophy through a critical and reconstructive treatment of the oral tradition. Thus in several papers he has made path-breaking efforts to reconstruct the Akan philosophical worldview. Wiredu recognizes the weaknesses of an oral tradition of philosophy: the tendency for it not to develop a sustained and readily accessible exposition of speculative thought; the relative absence of diverging schools of thought, and the brevity and sparseness of the thought forms as opposed to the elaborate explanation and analyses found in written philosophy. Yet this does not mean that oral philosophy is therefore bound to indulge in superficiality. There are deep and profound thought forms in traditional philosophy, if only we have the patience to explore it and understand it. In his "African Philosophical Tradition," Wiredu (1992) explores two themes in Akan traditional philosophy: the concept of God and the concept of a person.

Wiredu argues that the idea of God as a supreme being is not commonly held among the Akans – that the Akan God is omnipotent only in the qualified sense that he can accomplish any well defined task. For instance, it is not possible for the Akan God to reverse the lawlikeness of phenomena that defines the cosmic order as we know it. This is illustrated with the example of the message of the talking drum: the creator created death and death killed him. The Akan sense of the universality of law and its indefeasibility is so strong that they view the process of creation itself, not as the outcome of a motivated decision-making by the supreme being, but as the necessary result of his nature. To illustrate this point, Wiredu turns again to an Akan metaphysical drum text:

> Who gave the word
> Who gave the word
> Who gave the word
> Who gave the word to Hearing
> For Hearing to have told the Spider
> For the Spider to have told the Creator
> For the Creator to have created things?
> (1992, p. 42)

The interpretation of this is that, not only must we not look for reasons beyond the creator for creation, but also we must not look for God's reasons for creation, for there can be no such reasons. To ask for a reason for God's creative activity is to open a chain of reasons that cannot possibly end. The Akan concept of creation also differs from the Judeo-Christian concept in the sense that, for the Akan, creation is a demiurgic fashioning of order from pre-existing stuff rather than creation out of nothing. This, incidentally, is the Yoruba concept of creation too. An Akan riddle provides the argument for this conception. Likening the supreme being to a bagworm, "the question is raised as to how the bagworm got into its case. Did it weave it before getting into it or did it get into it before weaving it?" If the former, then there was no bagworm, because a bagworm does not exist without a bag. But if the latter, then the bagworm would have to get into a non-existent bag. Therefore, God's creation can only have been a process of transformation and to explain it is to explicate the internal structure of the universe. Suppose we now raise the question of whether the Akan are capable of thinking in this way. The answer must be "yes," because the illustrations interpreted here come from the Akan traditional conceptual system.

From his reconstruction of the Akan conception of existence and creation, Wiredu further argues that the distinctions between the spiritual and the material, the natural and the supernatural, do not exist in Akan philosophy. This is because, according to him, the Akan view reality as one, and though they give explanations that refer to the causal agency of ancestors and a variety of other extra-human beings and forces, this is not supernatural explanation. They rely on the principle of sufficient reason and therefore they find it natural to "seek the explanation for a given phenomenon apparently inexplicable in terms of the factors of one part of the world from another regular part" (1992, p. 46). But while Wiredu argues for a monist position regarding traditional Akan ontology, Kwame Gyekye, another Akan philosopher, argues for a dualist position. For Gyekye, the Akan affirm a belief in a supernatural realm and their causal explanations refer to this realm (Gyekye, 1987). I have also argued that the reference to the absence of a spiritual material distinction or nature/supernature distinction may not be a correct interpretation of the traditional philosophers' position (Gbadegesin, 1991).

Wiredu argues for monism because he finds Cartesian dualism to be incoherent. For, according to him, the idea of a spiritual or mental existence without a spatial location is incoherent. At the same time, he concedes that traditional thinkers do not accept the view that human laws of motion can control ancestors and extra-human beings or that they can be perceived by the senses. But this is all that is meant by referring to such forces as supernatural. A supernatural power is one that exceeds the normal or natural capability of human beings. Busia's claim that there is an apparent absence of a conceptual cleavage between the natural and the supernatural in the conceptual scheme of the people, which supports Wiredu, is meant to suggest that: (1) the people understand that, if everyone had the knowledge of the web of nature that the medicine person has, they could prepare similar charms and get similar results; and (2) the results thus derived are still understood to belie the known laws of nature and are, to that extent, supernatural (Busia, 1962, p. 36). There is, therefore, no sharp demarcation, no unbridgeable gulf between the natural and the supernatural in the thought system. However, to infer from this that there is no belief in a supernatural realm seems to me to miss the point.

Critical cultural philosophy has also focused on the very important topic of African concepts of personhood. With respect to traditional Yoruba philosophy, I have argued that the concept of person, *eniyan*, has a dual meaning: normative and descriptive, the former being the more important of the two because it determines the foundation of the community. Descriptively, a person is made up of body, called *ara*, a life principle, called *emi*, the locus of thought, called *okan*, and a personality principle, called *ori*. As the active element of life, *emi* is a spiritual component common to all human beings. Unlike *emi*, *okan* has a dual status. It is the name of a physical organ responsible for blood circulation. It is also the name for the seat of thought, and thus the equivalent of the English concept of mind. *Ori* is also construed in two senses: as the physical head, and as the spiritual bearer of a person's destiny. "Destiny" refers to the preordained portion of life, believed to be chosen in the primordial existence and, to a large extent, responsible for the general course of a person's life. The concept raises a number of philosophical problems, of course, but the most serious of these is the question of the *extent* to which destiny can be said to be chosen. On one account, individuals choose their destiny but the choice is blind and uninformed, since one is wholly ignorant of what is included in the portion. (Can one be said to make a choice of *X* without knowing anything about *X*?) Furthermore, since destiny imposes a personality on one, and since one needs a personality in order to make choices, how can one choose one's destiny prior to having a personality?

With regard to the normative concept of *eniyan*, it is not unusual, referring to a human being, for an observer to say "*Ki i se eniyan*" (he/she is not an *eniyan*), meaning that, with regard to moral standing, he/she falls short of what it takes to be a person. The observer's point is that this individual is either an *eniyan lasan* (a good-for-nothing being) or *eniyan bee bee* (a human being in name only) or *omolangidi eniyan* (a mere bone and flesh). On the other hand, a human being described as a person is *eniyan gidi* (a genuine *eniyan*) or *omoluabi* (an offspring of *iwa*). This last description is what ties up the Yoruba concept of person with its moral requirement. A genuine *eniyan* is an offspring of *iwa*, and *iwa*, in this context, means character; thus the offspring of *iwa* is the offspring of character, or simply, a being of good character.

From the foregoing, it would appear that personhood is an achievement: it is something achieved over and above the given status of being a human being with flesh, bones, and divine breath. A docile life is therefore discouraged, because it is not the path to achieving personhood status. One has to be an achiever in moral behavior, in contributions to the community and in living a productive life – a life of work, service and commitment to a regeneration of the ancestral spirits through offspring. An *omoluabi eniyan* is one who is steadfast in moral behavior. However, there are no rigid rules of morality and, contrary to some interpretations, the Yoruba moral universe is not grounded on religion.

The *omoluabi eniyan* is expected to contribute to the development of the community. This is in virtue of the fact that it is the community that grounds his/her existence. Personal existence is appreciated, but it is not severed from social existence. Destiny is the meaning of a person, the purpose for which an individual exists. However, though this is a personal purpose, realizable through the individual's will to achieve, it cannot be separated from the communal reality of existence. Here is the limit of individualism. The purpose of individual existence is intricately linked with the purpose of social existence, and cannot be adequately grasped outside of that existence. Therefore, while the concept of destiny confirms the individual's personality, it also joins it to the community, and individuality and community are intertwined. Personhood, then, takes on its full meaning by appeal to destiny and community. Nurtured by the community, the individual cannot achieve, outside of it. Destiny itself is a community concept. It is the combination of destiny, character, and community that make a genuine person. The "I" is just a "we" from another perspective. And by simple logic, individuals whose existence is dependent upon the community are expected in turn to contribute their own quota to the continued existence of the community which nurtures them. The crown of personal life is to bear fruits (to have offspring – this is also a community requirement); the crown of communal life is to be useful to the community. Therefore, one must be committed to the pursuit of social ideals. The question "*Kini o wa fun?*" (What is your life for?) is posed when a person is judged inadequate in respect to their communal obligations. An *omoluabi eniyan* can develop to his/her fullest capacity, then, only by full membership in the life of the group.

Critical cultural philosophy recognizes the fact that the philosophy embodied in communal oral tradition is practical. Thought here is at the service of practice and there is limited attention paid to the niceties of argument and analysis. The point worth emphasizing is that the views, arguments and analyses of indigenous philosophers are taken to have instrumental value only, for the benefit of their community. The emphasis is on wisdom for communal survival, not for the boosting of an individual's ego. This is not to suggest that indigenous philosophers cannot be critical and analytical. Thus in recent times there have been remarkable efforts to identify individual philosophical sages, in order to demonstrate that individualized philosophical activity is not foreign to Africa. This is the preoccupation of the school of sage philosophy.

Sage philosophy

Odera Oruka, a Kenyan philosopher, is the founder of the school of sage philosophy. His major objective is "to introduce the issue of research about the sagacious and philosophical thinking of the indigenous native Africans whose lives are rooted in the cultural milieu of traditional Africa" (Oruka, 1990, p. xv). He distinguishes his approach from that of ethnophilosophy, which he accuses of assuming that "traditional Africa is a place of philosophical unanimity allowing no room whatsoever for a Socrates or Descartes" (1990, p. xv). He also distances himself from the position of his fellow professional philosophers who insist on writing as a precondition for philosophy. Finally, he disagrees with the view that philosophy is only "Greek" or "European." Sage philosophy is based on the belief that there are traditional philosophical sages with independent and critically arrived at knowledge of fundamental moral and metaphysical questions which are of assistance to the folk. It can also serve as a raw material for technical philosophical reflections. Since folk philosophy, which is the basic raw data for the philosophical sage is, in its own right, a reflection of the lived experiences of the folk, it follows that technical philosophy is second order in a double sense. First, it is the critical reflection of the professional philosopher on the reflections of the philosophical sage. Second, since the philosophical sage is also reflecting on the reflections of the folk sage, technical philosophy is indirectly a critical reflection on the folk sage's reflection on live experience. "A person is a sage in the philosophical sense only to the extent that he is concerned with the fundamental ethical and empirical issues and questions relevant to the society and his ability to offer insightful solution to some of those issues" (1990, p. xviii). The essential difference between sage philosophy and critical cultural philosophy is that the former deliberately looks for individual sages whose views diverge from one another and from the communal view, and then shows this as an example of genuine philosophical thinking. Critical cultural philosophy, on the other hand, focuses on the conceptual scheme of Africans and attempts its critical reconstruction. Of course, some sages also express traditional cultural views.

Oruka rejects what he calls "culture philosophy" which consists of the beliefs, practices, myths, taboos, and general values of a people, which govern their everyday life and are usually expressed and stored in the oral vocabulary of the people (1990, p. xviii). Yet he considers it raw material for sage philosophy. Thus philosophical sagacity antedates ethnophilosophy but is second order to culture philosophy. This assumes that culture philosophy is also not a critical reflection on people's experience. On this, I think he is wrong. Culture philosophy is also a product of reflection on experience. Oruka himself defines philosophy as "a human reflection on life, nature and on what there is and what could be" and argues that such "a reflection takes place in every human society" (1990, p. xxv). In Africa, culture philosophy is the product of such reflection and the fact that it is not identified with specific individuals should not negate its philosophical status. Oruka also recognizes that "there can be many ways to [do] philosophy. Some employ stories, poetry or oracle to philosophize" (1990, p. xxv). If so, then the traditional sacred tales, proverbs, and poetry should be recognized as means of philosophizing and it is inconsistent to deny this while approving as philosophy the "oracular epigrams, epic poems and story telling of Heraclitus and Parmenides." It appears that Oruka's only quarrel with critical cultural philosophy is that the latter takes seriously the philosophical contents of language, poems, stories, and other thought forms in African conceptual systems and tries to critically reconstruct and explicate them. To Oruka, this is unacceptable because philosophy cannot be communal; it has to be an individual enterprise. The problem with this is that it takes a given paradigm of philosophy as a divine model to which every sample must conform.

Sage philosophy has a positive contribution to make. As "the expressed thoughts of wise men and women in a given community," it is a means of identifying individualized forms of philosophy along with their authors. This may then be presented by the professional philosopher in a form that is accessible to others for further explication and reconstruction. This will contribute to the furtherance of an African philosophical tradition. It is in this spirit that one can understand the examples of sagacious reasoning presented by Oruka, three of which are given here:

> Mzee Oruka Ranginya reasons that "God has no likeness of a man. God is like air or wind. . . . He can be anywhere. . . . God is the idea of goodness or power that man wishes or seeks to attain."
>
> Nyaga Wa Mauch thinks that "God is not part of man or nature. It is mystery and man cannot know the exact nature of this mystery."
>
> Njeru Wa Kanyenge remarks that "Religion is witchcraft. I do not pray to God nor do I consult witchdoctors. Both religion and witchcraft are bluffs. They have no truth in them." (Oruka, 1990, pp. 32–4)

There is, of course, a problem regarding the methodology for identifying genuine philosophical sages. It seems that the criterion is the ability and willingness of a sage to criticize the belief system of his or her people. But this rests on the implied assumption that the cultural beliefs of the people must be defective. Yet a sage can provide philosophical justification for the belief of his or her people; and, of course, the question of what constitutes a philosophical justification has to be addressed. We have to avoid the temptation to beg that question. To determine that popular wisdom is wrong or inadequate, we have to appeal to an acceptable criterion of adequacy. It cannot be simply dismissed because it is popular or common. For folk wisdom can also arise from didactic wisdom. Thus I once had a conversation with a traditional priest of Ifa who was determined to defend the common cultural belief of the Yoruba that work is noble and a cure for poverty. I suggested to him the idea that work is a curse, following the Biblical story of the Fall of Humanity. This man paused for a while and then said to me, "You really believe that? But does the Bible not tell you that God worked for six days and rested on the seventh? Did God cause God, then?"

My point is that we must not start with the assumption that a cultural worldview does not arise from serious reasoning. Sage philosophy starts with individuals, considered to be wise, because of their philosophical critique of cultural beliefs, which are themselves considered to be unphilosophical. Yet it moves on to totalize the responses as a belief system. This means that, in the final analysis, sage philosophy comes back to the idea of cultural philosophy. Oruka puts it thus:

> given the method for a research into sage philosophy, we should be capable of totalizing what the belief system of the community is, because some of the sages we interviewed begin by stating or assuming the given beliefs of their people. We should also be able to design the common views and beliefs on the various cultural topics discussed by the sages. (1990, p. 57)

Of course, the answers adopted by Oruka to the various questions posed to the sages are "a summary of the views common to the informants." We have, then, come back full circle to cultural philosophy. It cannot be otherwise. Indeed, the reference to the "philosophical sage" as an "informant" is instructive. In a footnote, Oruka makes a point that seems to me to undermine the project of sage philosophy: "Since these findings are a summary of the common points made by the informants, they are not to be treated as ideas of individual sages, but as the beliefs of the community as revealed by the various sayings of its sages" (1990, p. 58). So much, then, for the myth of individualized philosophy.

Contemporary African political philosophy

Contemporary African philosophical thought has a rich resource in the works of political thinkers who have confronted the heritage of servitude and dependency with their incisive analysis and critique of racism, colonialism, and neocolonialism. But they have not been spared by critics. Bodunrin has argued that these political thinkers are guilty of romanticizing the African past and that they do not provide rigorous analyses of their positions. Comparing them with Locke, Rousseau, and Mill, he finds them wanting. There is a problem with such comparison. African political thinkers confronted a different kind of experience than did Western political thinkers, and consequently their proposed solutions had to be different. We find hardly any of the classical political thinkers addressing problems relevant to Africa. Take the question of ethnicity in the wake of colonization, for instance, or the question of development, or of military rule. When they do discuss some issues that affect Africa, as Mill does regarding colonialism, it is to defend the status quo through rationalization. Thus even while a liberal like Mill argues for liberty, he contends that it is not to be extended to those who "cannot govern themselves." That, of course, was during the era of colonization. African political thinkers blazed the trail of independent thinking, the kind that Oruka is looking for, and it is not clear why they should be devalued. Kwame Nkrumah, Julius Nyerere, Obafemi Awolowo, Sekou Toure, Leopold Senghor, Nnamdi Azikwe, Amilcar Cabral, and Frantz Fanon, in various ways, passed on a heritage of political philosophizing that should serve as a basis for the development of a tradition. Second, the idea that they do not develop rigorous analyses cannot be a ground for denying their philosophical status. After all, rigor is a matter of degree, and whatever problems they have can be pointed out in further studies. This is how a tradition of philosophy develops. Dismissing their writings as non-philosophy because they are not rigorous works does not help the cause of contemporary African philosophy. It is in this spirit that I discussed Nyerere's account of democracy in Africa (Gbadegesin, 1994).

Nyerere's defence of democracy as the only viable principle of political participation follows from his rejection of colonialism and the principle of a divine right to rule. Colonialism is rejected because it violates the principle of equality. In a legislative debate in 1959, Nyerere had observed that the opposition of Tangayika African National Union (TANU) to colonialism is "based on the belief in the equality of human beings, in their rights and duties as human beings, and in the equality of citizens, in their rights and duties as citizens" (1966, p. 76). To the suggestion that Africans need to learn the art of democracy, Nyerere replies with resentment. "We in Africa have no more need of being 'converted' to socialism than we have of being taught democracy. Both are rooted in our own past – in the traditional society which produced us" (1968, p. 12). Later on, however, he finds it necessary to consider the essence of democracy in order to make room for the idea of a single-party democracy.

The essence of democracy and the African democratic tradition

Nyerere's first attempt to reject a Western model of democracy was in an article published in 1961. In it he identifies three features that he considers essential to democracy. These are "discussion, equality and freedom" (1966, p. 103). A democracy is, in his estimation, a means of carrying out community tasks by agreement, and agreement can only be reached through discussion. So whether we talk of a small village community or a complex political system, discussion is an essential feature of democracy.

Discussion, equality and freedom are thus the essential conditions of democracy. Where they constitute features of a political arrangement, that arrangement cannot be described as undemocratic. Yet these are important features of traditional African political arrangements even before colonial imposition. Therefore, traditional Africans are democratic and do not have to be taught democracy. From this it follows that an organized party system with an institutionalized opposition is not essential for a democracy. Therefore, a single-party system can be a democracy.

Nyerere's argument for the one-party system is as follows:

1 New nations of Africa emerged from the nationalist struggles for independence.
2 These struggles were patriotic ones, which necessarily leaves no room for differences.
3 These struggles were led by nationalist movements in particular countries.
4 The nationalist movement unites all the elements in a country together, and thus instead of several political parties, there is only the nationalist movement.
5 The nationalist movement that led a country to independence must inevitably form the first government.
6 Therefore, in such a situation there is no place for opposition.

It is obvious that this argument will not convince opponents of the one-party system. For one thing, it is not clear what the dispensability of opposition involves here. It is neither logical nor physical. Second, even if the first government is formed by the nationalist party, it cannot be expected that the people will always be in support of that party. Third, as the society grows more complex, there are always bases for fundamental disagreements, if not about ends, at least about the means of achieving those ends. Thus even if "it could hardly be expected that a united country should halt in mid-stream and voluntarily divide itself into opposing political groups just for the sake of conforming to . . . the Anglo-Saxon form of democracy" (1966, p. 106), it should be expected that as society progresses there would develop differing viewpoints on solutions to problems and these may become fundamental enough to warrant breaking into camps. This happens among groups of friends, so clearly it is reasonable to expect it of a nation. And in any case, if it is not expected that such fractures will tend to occur, what need is there for legislation to prohibit them? That is, if it is true that every citizen voluntarily agrees to remain within the nationalist party and not to form opposing parties, why would it be necessary for the nationalist party to legally proclaim itself as the only recognized party and ban the existence of others? Such a move itself suggests that there are other viewpoints which are thereby silenced.

Nyerere may argue that those who are thus silenced represent a fraction of the entire population and that they are agents of imperialism who want to maintain the status quo. This is in fact the usual way some advocates of the single-party system have argued. But this is not a good argument. For one thing, it assumes that the majority knows better, which is not always so. Besides, it negates the principle of discussion inherent in the democratic principle as enunciated by Nyerere. Finally, it presumes that what the minority represents is necessarily antithetical to the interests of the community.

There is, however, a way in which Nyerere's point may be understood. If there is a general agreement about what the goal of society is, then there is a basis for unity. The only differences would concern the means to be employed. In that case, there is no need for division into political parties. Three points may be made here. First, it is an empirical matter whether there is such a general agreement among citizens. Given the various mutinies and coup attempts even in Tanzania, it is not clear that everyone accepts a socialist ordering. (See Smith, 1973, pp. 191–2.) Second, finding the means is sometimes more problematic than agreement on the goal. Disagreement may also be sufficiently fundamental at that level to warrant divisions. Finally, suppose it is true that there is a general agreement and that all that is required is discussion about means. In that case, what is required politically is not a single-party system, but a no-party system. In other words, there should be no constraint on people to belong to a party. Just as traditionally, there were no political parties, so too, if that kind of agreement is presumed, people should be allowed to represent themselves rather than any political party. Whereas Nyerere claims that an organized opposition is not an essential element for representative democracy, my point is that any organized political party is not an essential element. Surely, "the choice of the best individual for the job" does not require the organization of even a single political party! So if a two-party system is unnecessary where there is a broad agreement over goals, a one-party system is equally unnecessary.

Critical philosophy of Africa

In recent times, there have been efforts on the part of some African and non-African philosophers to introduce a new research agenda in African philosophy. This effort rests on the important observation that the whole debate over the status of African philosophy presupposes a resolution of the question "What is Africa?" However, this question has yet to be addressed, much less resolved. Therefore there is a need for "a problematization of the idea of Africa itself" (Moore, 1992). This is a metaphilosophical agenda, and perhaps it is one that should be encouraged. In any case, we know that it is already receiving serious attention in the writings of Antony Appiah, V. Y. Mudimbe and a few others. What is its rationale and what prospects does it have?

Its main rationale seems to me to be historical, having to do with the way African identity came to be created. On this perspective, Africa is an invention, the identity of which is based on its difference, rather than on a distinctive essence. As David Moore puts it, "'Africa,' as both word and identity comes not from its own center but from its northeastern periphery: it is a term not of interiority but of contact, an appelation not of essence but of difference. 'Africa' has historically been, in the final analysis, that which Europe is not" (1992, p. 8). In the first stage of its invention, African identity was an external imposition – a mere geographical expression. In the latter stage, the horror of enslavement and the injustice of colonial exploitation contributed to the internal creation of an African identity. So the story of Africa as an externally created entity is posed as a rationale for the idea of a philosophical problematization of Africa as an idea. But this is not enough. Such an agenda has to derive from a more current problem. After all, Europe's identity has a similar historical foundation in otherness. To identify is to differentiate. Why does the case of Africa justify a problematization of its existence and that of Europe does not? One answer is that Africa "is still fraught with uncertainty. The continent itself has no particular linguistic, religious, climatic, agricultural, 'racial,' cultural, or indeed philosophical unity, and its principal historical justification comes mainly out of confrontation with the West" (Moore, 1992, p. 10). But as Moore goes on to say, this statement "should apply to Europe as well." So are we to have a philosophy of Europe too? We do not have an adequate answer yet.

As conceived by its advocates, the school of philosophy of Africa will serve others as "the rigorous theoretician, the moral watchdog, and the intellectual cheerleader for the important project of Africa: 'constantly to maintain,' to paraphrase Jacques Derrida, 'an interrogation of the origin, grounds, and limits of our conceptual, theoretical or normative apparatus' surrounding Africa" (Moore, 1992, p. 10). This is certainly ambitious, but that is not the problem. This way of characterizing the project seems to rest on the unproved assumption that the other "schools" are short of rigor, moral resources and ideas.

I do not raise these issues to belittle the importance of the considerations that seem to inspire the school of philosophy of Africa. Indeed, those considerations have always been with us and they have been the subject of philosophical discussions since the African confrontation with Europe, as a result of nationalist worries about the loss of identity. Their intellectual efforts resulted in theories of negritude, African personality and authenticity. The difference is that earlier nationalist writers did not raise these issues from a position of doubt concerning what African identity is. They discussed the issues to reinforce that identity as they understood it, in the face of its invasion and erosion by Europe. Contemporary theorists, however, start from a different ground. For them, the very idea of African identity is a problem. As Appiah puts it, "Every human identity is constructed. . . . [I]nvented histories, invented biologies, invented cultural affinities come with every identity; each is a kind of role that has to be scripted, structured by conventions of narrative to which the world never quite manages to conform" (1992, p. 174). And Mudimbe, paraphrasing Eboussi-Boulaga, posed the searching questions: What is an African and how does one speak for him or her and for what purpose? Where and how can one gain the knowledge of his or her being? How does one define this very being, and to what authority does one turn for possible answers? (Mudimbe, 1988, p. 153) If there is a warrant for raising these questions, it can only be in the understanding that the European confrontation with Africa has created a problem of identity for the African, and this cannot be said in the case of Europe. After all, if the absence of a continental unity in religion, language, and culture does not demand the posing of these questions in the case of Europe, it should not be a rationale for posing them in the case of Africa. The prospect of a philosophy of Africa as a research program in African philosophy depends on how it is able to reconcile itself to these points and strike a balance between negative critique and positive reconstruction.

Conclusion

This has been a brief survey of the map of African philosophy. I have tried to present its current trends and perspectives. Starting with its foundations in the works of ethnological precursors and African reactions, I moved on to discuss four major trends: critical cultural philosophy, sage philosophy, political philosophy, and critical philosophy of Africa. Obviously, this kind of survey cannot cover all of the current interests, given space limitations. Regarding the present scholarly interest in African philosophical research, however, the advice would be well taken to "let a hundred flowers bloom." For this can only lead to the cultivation of a richer and more beautiful field of philosophical scholarship in Africa and the world.

Bibliography

Appiah, K. A. 1992: *In My Father's House: Africa in the Philosophy of Culture* (New York: Oxford University Press).

Bodunrin, P. O. 1984: "*The Question of African Philosophy,*" in *African Philosophy: an Introduction*, ed. Richard Wright (Lanham: University Press of America), pp. 1–25.

Busia, K. A. 1962: *The Challenge of Africa* (New York: Frederick A. Praeger).

Gbadegesin, Segun 1991: *African Philosophy: Traditional Yoruba Philosophy and Contemporary African Realities* (New York: Lang).

—— 1994: "*Ujamaa*: Julius Nyerere on the Meaning of Human Existence," *Ultimate Reality and Meaning*, 17, 1, pp. 50–69.

Gyekye, K. 1995 [1987]: *An Essay on African Philosophical Thought: the Akan Conceptual Scheme* (London: Cambridge University Press, 1987; rev. 2nd edn, Temple University Press, 1995).

Hountondji, Paulin 1983: *African Philosophy: Myth and Reality* (Bloomington: Indiana University Press).

Kagame, Alexis 1956: *La philosophie bantu-rwandaise de l'être* (Brussels: Académie royale des sciences coloniales).

Lévy-Bruhl, L. 1923: *Primitive Mentality* (New York: Macmillan).

—— 1975: *The Notebooks of Lucien Lévy-Bruhl*, tr. P. Rivière Blackwell.

Moore, David C. 1992: "African Philosophy vs. Philosophy of Africa," paper presented at the eleventh annual SSIPS/SAGP conference on Ethics, Aesthetics and Ontology in Antiquity and in Greek, Jewish, Christian, Islamic, Sikh, and African Philosophy, Columbia University, New York, October 23–5.

Mudimbe, V. Y. 1988: *The Invention of Africa: Gnosis, Philosophy and the Order of Knowledge* (Bloomington: Indiana University Press).

Nyerere, Julius 1966: *Freedom and Unity* (Dar es Salaam: Oxford University Press).

—— 1968: *Ujamaa: the Basis of African Socialism* (Dar es Salaam: Oxford University Press).

Oruka, Odera 1975: "Fundamental Principles in the Question of African Philosophy," *Second Order*, 4, pp. 44–55.

—— 1990: *Sage Philosophy: Indigenous Thinkers and Modern Debate on African Philosophy* (Leiden: E. J. Brill).

Senghor, Leopold 1956: "The Spirit of Civilisation or the Laws of African Negro Culture," *Présence Africaine*, 8–10, June–Dec., pp. 51–64.

—— 1971: *The Foundations of "Africanité" or "Negritude" and "Arabité"* (Paris: Présence Africaine).

Smith, William E. 1973: *Nyerere of Tanzania* (London: Victor Gollancz).

Tempels, P. 1959: *Bantu Philosophy* (Paris: Presence Africaine).

Wiredu, Kwasi 1991: "On Defining African Philosophy," in *African Philosophy: the Essential Readings*, ed. Tsenay Serequeberhan (New York: Paragon House) pp. 87–110.

—— 1992: "African Philosophical Tradition: the Case of the Akan," *Philosophical Forum*, spring, pp. 35–62.

44

Contemporary Buddhist philosophy

MICHIKO YUSA

"Buddhist philosophy" or Buddhist philosophies may be roughly grouped into two types: those philosophies "influenced" or "inspired" by Buddhist teaching, and those comprising philosophical activities carried out by Buddhist scholars. Due to space constraints, predominant attention will be given in this article to the first type.

The most significant contemporary philosophical endeavor carried out under the influence of the Buddhist worldview was that of Nishida Kitarō (1870–1945), professor of philosophy at the Imperial University of Kyoto. Nishida's thought served as the cornerstone of those further developments in Buddhism-inspired philosophy that came to be known as the Kyoto School of philosophy. Because the philosophies of the Kyoto School have been the subject of lively debates in recent years, both in Japan and abroad, and because much of this discussion is pursued without a proper recourse to Nishida's thought (involving merely an empty citing of terminology that he developed), it will be worthwhile to focus on the essentials of Nishida's thought – specifically on the notions of "*topos*" (*basho* in Japanese) and "absolute nothingness" (*zettai mu*). An adequate grasp of these basic concepts is needed if we are to avoid degenerating into mere "empty" talk.

Nishida practiced Zen Buddhism for a decade. He was always pulled toward philosophy, but after his *kenshō* experience (or "comprehension of what one's true self is"), he came to see clearly that philosophy was his vocation. The influence of Zen Buddhism is evident in his epistemological conviction that "the separation and independent existence of subject and object is but a dogmatism deeply ingrained in our thought" (*NKZ* 2.53). The following letter of Nishida to Nishitani Keiji, one of his most distinguished students, reveals Nishida's stance on philosophy and Zen:

> You are absolutely right that something of Zen is at the background of my thought. I am not an expert on Zen, but I think that people generally misunderstand what Zen is all about. I think the life of Zen consists in "getting at reality." Since my thirties it has been my dearest wish to unite Zen and philosophy, even though this is impossible. Certainly, it is alright if *you* say [that Zen elements are present in my thought], but if ordinary uninformed people call my thought "Zen," I would strongly object to it, because they do not know either Zen or my thought; they simply say that *X* and *Y* are the same thing, which is to misunderstand both my thought and Zen. (*NKZ* 19.224–5; February 19, 1943)

Nishida's task was to bring a worldview fostered by his Zen practice into the domain of philosophical discourse, a scientific discipline developed in the West. Ueda Shizuteru, the leading thinker of the Kyoto School tradition, says Nishida thereby transformed philosophy just as much as the Christian worldview transformed Greek philosophy (Ueda, 1994, p. 166). Thomas Merton's remark is well taken: "Dr. Daisetz Suzuki rightly said that it is difficult to understand Nishida unless one has some acquaintance with Zen. On the other hand, some knowledge of existential phenomenology may serve as a preparation for understanding [Nishida's works]" (Merton, 1968, p. 67). Knowledge of Western philosophy is indispensable for appreciating the full scope of Nishida's thought, but the Zen worldview is its fountainhead and unifying force. D. T. Suzuki and Nishida were life-long friends, and Nishida, in his preface to the Japanese translation of Suzuki's *Zen and Japanese Culture* (1940), wrote: "In terms of my philosophical ideas, I owe much to you, my friend" (*NKZ* 12.225). Nishida and Suzuki worked in tandem, as it were. The former philosophized by drawing from the well of religious and cultural traditions, while the latter engaged in scholarship to explain the wealth of religious traditions to his contemporaries. The relationship between Nishida and Suzuki was something comparable to that between Jacques Maritain and Etienne Gilson.

1 Nishida's "Logic of *Topos*"

The starting point of Nishida's philosophical endeavors was always to "begin from the most immediate and fundamental standpoint" (*NKZ* 9.3). This approach was first employed in his work on "pure experience" (published in 1911). He believed the primordial form of experience consisted in the unity of subject and object. (It is no coincidence that the cultivation of this unitive awareness is the basis of any Zen student's practice.) This unity only later gets split up into subject and object in our thought. *At the very moment when* (*setsuna* in Japanese, *Kṣaṇa* in Sanskrit) there is the rustling of leaves, we and the rustling noise *are* an unbroken whole. Only later, in the reflexive moment do we say, "Ha, the wind is up" or "Leaves are agitated" or "I hear a rustling noise out there." Nishida attempted to explain reality (*tathātā*) as the unfolding of a series of pure experiences, which of themselves undergo moments of unity and differentiation that inform and form each individual person.

Nishida knew, however, that this way of approaching "reality" was much too psychologistic. He thus turned to the study of self-consciousness, finding a hint in Fichte's notion of *Tathandlung*. That is, in self-consciousness, "I" means that "I act on myself." Nishida also found Royce's observation of the infinite self-representative system of consciousness to support his view. Nishida's untiring philosophical meditation on "the most immediate" bore fruit in his 1926 essay on "*Topos*" or "Field."

For about fifteen years, until 1926, Nishida's philosophical attention focused on one single point: how *logically* to account for how we exist in the world. He pondered the question of how to form a logic that embraces subjectivity, the thinker him- or herself. Eventually the Aristotelian definition of *hypokeimenon* (substratum)

– that which becomes the subject but not the predicate ("that of which the others are predicated, while it is itself not predicated of anything else") (*NKZ* 4.95) – provided him with a breakthrough. Nishida found in this a clear definition of the unique and irreducible individual. It dawned on him that he could bridge the gap between logic and being (that is, life) by incorporating this definition of the individual into the form of judgment, more specifically, into the form of the logic of subsumption, *S* is *P*, which says that the particular exists in the universal. Nishida's basic point is that the individual must exist "at some place." That is to say, "*S* is *P*" always implies that *P* subsumes *S*, or "*S* is *in P*." In terms of judgment, he identified *P* with the field of consciousness. Whatever we know (*S*) is in our consciousness (*P*). The field of consciousness is the *topos* of intellectual judgment; as such, subjectivity qua undistorted field of consciousness (*P*) is retained together with its intellectual object (*S*). This undistorted field of consciousness, he suggested, is none other than the "original face" or the "real self" that Zen Buddhism speaks of.

How does Nishida's logic of *topos* differ from traditionally developed logic or epistemological theories? His criticism of Aristotelian logic was that in its emphasis on the individual aspect of being, it failed to account for its universality. Plato's philosophy, on the other hand, emphasized the universal (form), but this approach cannot pinpoint the particularity of a living individual and hence remains on the level of abstraction. Kant's critique of knowledge left open the problem of the thing-in-itself because Kant was not able to free himself from the haunting yoke of the subject–object dichotomy, and implicitly started out from that opposition. Nishida agreed with Fichte's solution of the thing-in-itself problem by identifying it as the dynamic operation of self-consciousness, but Nishida did not give a wholesale stamp of approval to Fichte's idea of the absolute ego, because of its substantial residue. Hegel's dialectic unfolds as the universal differentiates itself into an individual, so it is clear that the universal is the individual, but "it is not clear as to how an infinite number of individuals are contained in the universal," and "in order to give expression to that how," Nishida developed his idea of *topos* (*NKZ* 14.334).

The logic of *topos* works on various levels, from our intellectual activities to our volitional activities. In terms of judgment, let us take a statement, "This flower is red," as an example. When I say, "This flower is red," I am already looking at this flower. The flower (*S*) is already in my consciousness (*P*). My consciousness predicates on the flower as red. From the point of view of the field of consciousness, it *mediates* the judging-I and "this [particular] flower'. The *topos* of judgment is where this flower and the judging-I both exist. We are self-objectifying beings, however, and we submit ourselves as the subject of our own scrutiny, self-reflection, and so forth. In this way, the subject (*S*) is an objectified subjectivity, and as such a shadow of the field of consciousness (*P*). Nishida observes that in reality, *S* and *P* are intricately intertwined and form innumerable layers.

Nishida contends that the truest mode of self-consciousness is found in our *action*. In action, the objectified self (*S*) "sinks" or "submerges" deep into the field of consciousness (*P*) and becomes that which acts. The field of consciousness, the *topos*, becomes the vessel of action as well as that which sees. In action we externalize what is inside (that is, our will) and we internalize what is outside. Take, for example, the act of drinking water. My thought of wanting to drink the water is "expressed" in my action of drinking water. And the water drunk by me becomes one with me.

The *topos* is infinitely open and connected to the *topos* of the other. In response to materialist dialectics, Nishida offers his observation that "I see the other at the depths of myself," and that "I see myself over against this absolute other; that is, the other is myself!" If I only see others in myself, I fall into subjective idealism and spiritual monism. If I only see myself in the absolute other, I fall into materialism. The real self exists where these two directions are united: "I see the other in myself and I see myself in the other" (*NKZ* 14.152–7).

In the later Nishida, his logic of *topos* becomes the world in which we live. It is eminently historical and social, and individuals are creative constituents of the world. Theoretically, there are as many *topoi* as there are individuals within the world, which is the *Topos* par excellence. The *Topos* (that is, the world itself) is the dialectical universal, in which the one (world) and the many (individuals) stand in a dialectical relationship. Nishida calls this *Topos* "absolutely contradictory self-identity."

2 "Absolute nothingness"

The term that came to be most conspicuously associated with Nishida's thought and the rest of the Kyoto School thinkers is "absolute nothingness" (*zettai mu*). Nishida coined this term in connection with his logic of *topos*. Absolute nothingness is the very mode of *topos*. Nishida starts out by observing that things may be said to exist either in relation to other things or in relation to our consciousness. In the case of "the glass existing on top of the table," the glass exists in relation to the table, and understood as such, the glass is in "relative" existence. However, the "glass on top of the table" that exists in my consciousness is in "absolute" existence, because it is in "absolute nothingness," and there exists for it the freedom to be or not to be. The notion of "absolute nothingness" is "the essence of the mind, which is absolutely nothing and yet absolutely being [or real], and which transcends the realm of our intellectual knowledge. Rather, our intellectual knowledge arises from there" (*NKZ* 5.451). One attains this awareness of absolute nothingness, in the "the religious experience of 'phenomena-qua-emptiness and emptiness-qua-phenomena' (*shiki soku ze kū, kū soku ze shiki*), wherein there is neither the seer nor the seen" (*NKZ* 5.451). That Nishida is referring to a line from the *Heart Sutra* and is alluding to the Buddhist worldview is almost too obvious to mention.

In order to have a more concrete understanding of what Nishida means by "absolute nothingness," we need to turn to his mediation on time:

> Time disappears in a moment, but it exists in the next moment. That which absolutely does not exist comes into being. From absolute nothingness absolute being is born. Should we consider the present moment as that which exists and something that we can hold onto, we cannot think of "time." Again, if the present is simply nothing, then

> there is no time. If time is being, it makes no sense that it disappears in the next moment. On the other hand, if time is "absolutely nothing," it disappears at every moment. Time is absolutely nothing and yet exists at every moment. That is to say, we can think of time as "that which absolutely exists not" (*zettai mu*) comes into "existence" (*u*). This is why we can think of time only at the *present* moment. The present moment is the point at which nothingness is being. Whenever being and nothingness form one point, it is the present. (*NKZ* 14.140–1)

This reflection on time is at the heart of Nishida's philosophical vision. Nishida considers this "form" of time as the form of reality and of our self-consciousness. "Absolute nothingness" is the mode of the dynamic arising and disappearance of the "moment" at every instant. It was no accident that Nishida contemplated the meaning of time. Between 1918 and 1925, his life was plagued by illnesses and deaths of his loved ones. A year after his mother's passing away in 1918, his wife was struck by a brain hemorrhage and became bed-ridden until her death in 1925; his eldest son died in 1920 at the young and promising age of 23. As he contemplated this brutal reality, Nishida confided to his friend:

> Human beings exist in time. Precisely because there is the past, such a thing as "I" exists. That the past is present in the present moment simultaneously constitutes that person's future. When my wife was suddenly paralyzed because of illness, I was overcome by this thought. It felt to me as if the important part that constituted my past had disappeared all at once, and it was also as if my future also disappeared with it. Even if there is a merry occasion, there is no one to rejoice with. Even if there is a sad moment, there is no one to commiserate with. (*NKZ* 18.321; February 9, 1927)

Despite this personal suffering Nishida continued to push past the limits of his philosophical frontier. In 1930 he wrote that "the moving force of philosophy is not 'surprise' but the profound pathos of life" (*NKZ* 6.116). This makes sense only when we look at Nishida the man behind or "prior to" his thinking.

A moment disappears but a new moment arises. Absolute nothingness, the *topos* of moments, is not a sheer negation but is the vital source that gives birth. Nishida indefatigably emphasizes this *creative* aspect of absolute nothingness, for the term tends to be interpreted to mean sheer negativity. Absolute nothingness constantly rejuvenates life. Nishida underwent an experience of rebirth on July 3, 1927. His diary of this day reads: "As if awakened from a bad dream. Even the old dried up tree can bear new buds; I'm feeling the happiest today" (*NKZ* 17.438). Nishida identifies a personalistic aspect of absolute nothingness as compassion (*karuṇā*) – absolute nothingness is the very working of love. In 1933, he was introduced to an ideal woman with whom to share the rest of his life and married her. In Nishida's life and thought, the Buddhist understanding of *mujō* or *anityā* (impermanence) was given a positive meaning as not just the source of death but also of life. Some may wonder why Nishida chose to call the source of reality absolute nothingness rather than absolute being, but for absolute *being* changes are impossible. It was therefore fortunate that the Buddhist worldview of impermanence, or constant change, was fundamental in Nishida's choice of the expression absolute nothingness.

3 Formation and development of the Kyoto School

Tanabe Hajime (1895–1962) was the next holder of Nishida's chair at the Imperial University of Kyoto, and the one who contributed most to forming the Kyoto School as such. Tanabe was under Nishida's guidance and influence until Nishida turned to his logic of *topos*, the significance of which eluded Tanabe's comprehension. Instead, he criticized Nishida's philosophy for being based on religion, and that as such it could no longer properly be called philosophy. Sensitive to the needs of the day, Tanabe developed his logic of "species" in order to give a moral underpinning to the Japanese identity as a people and as a nation. In the end, this attempt failed because Tanabe refused to see the evil of actual Japanese nationalism, which took the form of imperialism abroad and censorship at home. In the fall of 1941, when Tanabe came to see the monster behind the state machinery, he stopped writing for three years. He suffered from indecision as to whether or not to voice criticism of the government. When the university students were summarily drafted into the ever-escalating war in 1943, Tanabe's agony heightened. He let go of himself in the face of his own inability and helplessness. To his own amazement, a new philosophical direction emerged from this posture of surrender and humility: a philosophy of conversion, or "metanoetics." Tanabe abandoned his intellectualism and moralism, and acceded to the grace of absolute Other. In implicitly Buddhist terms, he took compassion as the basis of society. In his "conversion," he at last adopted Nishida's term, "absolute nothingness," but with one qualification: "absolute nothingness-qua-love" (*zettai mu soku ai*). For Tanabe, the process of rebuilding the post-1945 Japan as a nation had to be mediated by compassion (*karuṇā*).

While Tanabe underwent this conversion of his stance from "self-reliance" to that of the Other-power (*tariki*), he found a funny paradox:

> once I had arrived at belief in Other-power [that is, *tariki*], I found myself feeling still closer to the spirit of Zen, whose emphasis on self-power [*jiriki*] is generally considered opposed to Pure Land doctrine. Nor was this the last of my surprise. A key to solving a problem in mathematical philosophy, which would at first glance seem to be rather far removed from religious concerns, also emerged at this time. I refer to the puzzle of infinite-set theory. (Tanabe, 1986, p. liv).

Tanabe's logic of "species, individual, and the universal" was transformed into one of "brotherly love, repentance, and nothingness-qua-love," and finally into "the existential cooperation, practice of death-resurrection, and absolute nothingness-qua-love." Tanabe's philosophical stance evolved into "death as rebirth" (*shi-fukkatsu*), which came from a profound personal experience in September, 1951 – the death of his indispensable wife, who had devoted her life to him: though she died, she lived on in Tanabe! The pull towards Zen Buddhism grew stronger during the last decade of his life. Tanabe underwent a philosophical and religious odyssey covering considerable ground. Ironically, his final destination was the world of Zen, and more specifically, the practice of a Bodhisattva motivated by altruism. The insight of absolute nothingness presented by Nishida, which Tanabe had once criticized harshly, in the end got the better of him.

Nishitani Keiji (1900–1990) walked onto the ground already cleared by Nishida and tilled by Tanabe; such ideas as the logic of *topos* or absolute nothingness had become established concepts which he could freely use. He took *śūnyatā* (*kū*; emptiness) as the standpoint of his philosophy, and set it over against the standpoint of being. This juxtaposition became the cause of uneasiness among some of the Westerners who engaged in dialogue with Nishitani, for Nishitani's argument seemed to be coming from the "other shore," the "shore of enlightenment," and did not sufficiently explain the logic, if this is at all possible, of *śūnyatā*. In his elaborate critique of Hegel's dialectic, Nishitani simply said, "it is possible to start out from nothingness rather than from being" (Nishitani, 1987). If Nishida's "religion" was the source of human reality and he himself was a Zen practitioner who was also a philosopher, and Tanabe's religion was eclectic but also eventually linked to his work as a philosopher, Nishitani's religion was clearly Zen and one which he practiced.

Nishitani's personal experience determined the course of his thought: he felt the salvific power of absolute nothingness, or *śūnyatā*. At the age of 16 Nishitani experienced the death of his father, and around that time he was also struck by a lung disease, which delayed him from entering the elite First High School for a year. These experiences were enough to make this tender youth nihilistic. He found solace in Nishida's *Philosophical Contemplation and Personal Experience* (*Shisaku to taiken*), a copy of which he picked up by accident. He became Nishida's student, and eventually occupied a chair of religion at the university. Nishitani went to Germany to study with Heidegger in the 1930s, and he witnessed there the *Zeitgeist* of "*Angst*" (anxiety). In response to existential anxiety and nihility, Nishitani, out of his own experience, offered an alternative "existential stance" – that of *śūnyatā*. The problem of science, for instance, is viewed entirely differently if one first transforms one's standpoint. We may characterize Nishitani's philosophical attempt as an invitation for us to go through an existential transformation by opening up our consciousness to absolute nothingness (Nishitani, 1961).

Ueda Shizuteru, born in 1926, is presently the torchbearer of the Kyoto School. A one-time student of Nishitani Keiji, and now professor emeritus of the University of Kyoto, Ueda is the foremost interpreter of Nishida's thought. Ueda muses on the theme of Nishida's *topos* of "absolute nothingness" in terms of the "double structure" of reality itself (Ueda, 1994). That is, we view the world from our subjectivity, but also we go out of our subjectivity and view the world from within the world's utter openness. This we do constantly, whether knowingly or unknowingly. Ueda interprets absolute nothingness as infinite "openness" and hence as the source of "freedom." In German, when one wants to find out whether or not a given seat is occupied, one asks: "Is that seat *frei* [lit., free]?" Ueda finds a positive meaning of openness in this locution. Ueda, very much a man of Zen practice, continues to hold his dialogues with Heidegger, Eliade, Jaspers, Bergson, Meister Eckhardt, et al., while still carefully tending the ground cleared and cultivated by Nishida and his company.

The philosophical tradition stemming from the work of Nishida is an influential one within contemporary intellectual discourse. Christian thinkers have found a promising dialogical partner in the Kyoto School. But it is also true that scholars have found the Kyoto School a perfect target of deconstructionism and postmodernist critique. One thing is certain: the ideas developed by the Kyoto School thinkers continue to generate heated discussions around the world.

While Buddhologists are breaking away from the traditional philological role to voice their concerns regarding pressing contemporary issues, such as ecology, and feminism, or to offer solace to people cut off from their traditional roots and suffering from profound loneliness, we scholars of Buddhism must remember that Buddhist philosophies are meaningful only if there is authentic Buddhist practice, generously carried out by nuns and monks. At the same time, the Buddhist tradition as a whole will do well if it can remain responsive to the need for transformation, lest the institution becomes a mere handing down of the old cloak.

Bibliography

Note: in this article, references to Nishida Kitarō's words were cited by the volume number and page number(s) following the abbreviation of *Nishida Kitarō Zenshū* [Collected Works of Nishida Kitarō] – *NKZ*. Japanese names are given according to the Japanese order: family name first, and given name second.

Writings

Nishida Kitarō 1979–80: *Nishida Kitarō Zenshū*, ed. Shimomura Toratarō et al., 3rd edn, 19 Vols (Tokyo: Iwanami Shoten).

Nishitani Keiji 1982 [1961]: *Shūkyō to wa nanika* (Tokyo: Sōbunsha, 1961); tr. J. van Bragt, *Religion and Nothingness* (Berkeley: University of California Press, 1982).

Tanabe Hajime 1986 [1946]: *Zangedō to shite no tetsugaku* (Tokyo: Iwanami Shoten, 1946); tr. Takeuchi Y., *Philosophy as Metanoetics* (Berkeley: University of California Press, 1986).

References and further reading

Heisig, J. and Maraldo, J. (eds) 1995: *Rude Awakenings: Zen, the Kyoto School, and the Question of Nationalism* (Honolulu: University of Hawaii Press).

Merton, Thomas 1968: *Zen and the Birds of Appetite* (New York: New Directions).

Nishida Kitarō 1990 [1911]: *Zen no kenkyū* (Tokyo: Kōdōkan, 1911); tr. Abe Masao and C. Ives, *An Inquiry into the Good* (New Haven: Yale University Press, 1990).

—— 1987 [1917]: *Jikaku ni okeru chokkan to hansei* (Tokyo: Iwanami, 1917); tr. V. Viglielmo with Takeuchi Y. and J. S. O'Leary, *Intuition and Reflection in Self-Consciousness* (Albany: State University of New York Press, 1987).

—— 1970 [1933–4]: *Tetsugaku no konpon mondai* (Tokyo: Iwanami Shoten, 1933–4); tr. D. Dilworth, *Fundamental Problems of Philosophy* (Tokyo: Sophia University, 1970).

—— *Bashoteki ronri to shūkyōteki sekaikan* [The Logic of *Topos* and the Religious Worldview], 1945, Yusa, M. tr.; *Eastern Buddhist* (19,2, 1986, pp. 1–29; 20,1, 1987, pp. 81–119).

Nishitani Keiji 1987: *Hannya to risei* [*Prajñā* and reason] in *Nishitani Keiji Chosakushū* [Works of Nishitani Keiji], Vol. 13 (Tokyo: Sōbunsha), pp. 31–96.
Tanabe Hajime 1947: *Shu no ronri no benshōhō* [Dialectics of the Logic of Species], (Osaka: Akitaya).]
—— 1965: *Tanabe Hajime* [Selected Works of Tanabe Hajime], ed. Tsujimura K., (Tokyo: Chikuma Shobō).
Ueda Shizuteru 1992: *Basho* [*Topos*], (Tokyo: Kōbundō).
—— 1994: *Keiken to jikaku* [Experience and Self-Consciousness], (Tokyo: Iwanami Shoten).

45

Contemporary Islamic thought

MARIETTA STEPANIANTS

The modern era has been a time of awakening on the part of the Muslim world in response to challenges from the West. The deeply rooted foundations of political and socio-economic organization in Muslim societies have been shattered, and the traditional ideals and values of their culture have been challenged. At the same time, however, these challenges aroused national self-awareness, and provoked a search for ways to escape from economic backwardness and spiritual stagnation.

The initial response to this Western influence manifested itself in vigorous criticism – to the point of rejection – of the national cultural and philosophical traditions, which were seen as chiefly responsible for the social backwardness of the Islamic world, owing to their failure to provide ethical motivations for progress. This negative attitude toward tradition among Muslim intellectuals contributed to their unreserved pursuit of Western values and institutions as the sole antidote to decline and stagnation. Modernism in the Islamic world expressed itself simultaneously in theologico-legal reinterpretation, literary–intellectual renaissance, and rationalist–ideological *aggiornamento* (see Sadiq J. Al-Azm, 1993).

Usually, however, this modernism expressed itself in an orientation to a *particular* trend in Western thought. In some cases, Muslim thinkers were drawn to the idea of law-governed regularities in the evolutionary process unfolding in nature and society. Hence the immense interest in Charles Darwin and the social Darwinism of Herbert Spencer exhibited by thinkers like I. Mazhar. The notion that progress is possible only through the overcoming of inert dogmatism (primarily religious) enhanced the appeal of Cartesian and positivistic ideas. The positivist outlook was thus championed by the Lebanese Shibli Shmayyel, the Egyptian Zaki Nagib Mahmud, and the Pakistani C. A. Qadir. The image of man as the subject of social transformation was confirmed by those philosophers who emphasized the creative and volitional principles of man-the-doer (as expressed in the works of Arthur Schopenhauer and Friedrich Nietzsche). Existentialism caught the attention of such Muslim thinkers as A. R. Badawi in Egypt and Rene Habashi in Lebanon because of the importance it attaches to the problem of the individual and human freedom.

Even today a number of these approaches persist, although mainly among professors of philosophy in the universities. Among those still pursuing philosophy along Western lines are the Egyptian existentialist Ahmad Abd al-Hakim Atiya, the Moroccan structuralist Abd al-Raziq ad-Dawai, the Egyptian Marxist Mahmud

Amin al-Amin, the Jordanian Marxist Ahmad Madhi, and the Moroccan postmodernist Salam Yafut.

This negative attitude toward their own national philosophical traditions, which was characteristic of the first half of the twentieth century, and which gave rise to schools of Arabian social Darwinism, Muslim existentialism, Islamic Marxism, and the like, turned out to be of limited duration. The exclusive orientation toward Western ideas eventually raised sharp public criticism and was opposed by those who believed that it was more reasonable and worthwhile to build on the foundations of national culture – which did not exclude but, on the contrary, necessarily implied the assimilation of the most valuable elements of other cultures.

This assimilation takes place in a number of ways. In some cases, it is realized through a synthesis of Western and Eastern ideas. Muhammad Mayan Sharif, for example, one of the most authoritative Muslim thinkers of the twentieth century (he died in 1965), founder of the Pakistani Philosophical Congress, and the editor of such fundamental work as *A History of Muslim Philosophy*, devised an ontological theory which he called "dialectical monadism" and which is based on the atomistic thought of Muslim scholastic theology. Following in the footsteps of the Mutakallims, Sharif asserts that the entire universe and each body is composed of the tiniest indivisible substances which he calls "monads." He assumes that there are three types of beings: the ultimate being or reality – God; the spiritual essences – monads; and the world of sensations in time and space. From electron to human being, all things in the world are spiritual monads. In as much as God is immanent in every monad, the monad is eternal, deathless, invisible, indivisible and unlimited in time and space. Its existence is determined by the divine will, though the latter permits the monad an appropriate degree of freedom.

In many respects, Sharif's monadology is reminiscent of Leibniz's. However, he rejects the principle of the monads' impenetrability. He also "complements" Leibniz by introducing dialectics (obviously under the influence of Hegel). The monads are of a dialectical nature. Within them the process of development occurs through triads – "from self through the complementary not-self or rather not-yet self to the synthesis of both in a more developed self."

Just as the transition to capitalism in Europe in the sixteenth century was impossible without the Reformation, or "the bourgeois religious revolution," traditional social structures in the Muslim world could be broken down only through a radical change in the role played by Islam, and therefore through a reappraisal of the entire set of its tenets. Similarly, just as the Reformation strove to overcome religious estrangement, to set Christians free from the mediation of the church and clergy, so were the reformers of Islam trying to reappraise the relation of God and man, with a view to bringing the believer "nearer" to God and thereby fostering his "emancipation."

One such reformer, the poet-philosopher Muhammad Iqbal (1877–1938), wrote: "The world, in all its details, from the mechanical movement of what we call the atom of matter to the free movement of thought in the human ego, is the self-revelation of the 'Great I am'" (*The Reconstruction of Religious Thought in Islam*, p. 71). It achieves its highest level in man alone and so, according to Iqbal, "that is why the Quran declares the Ultimate Ego to be nearer to man than his own jugular vein." Further on he stresses that man "possesses a much higher degree of reality than the things around him. Of all the creations of God, he alone is capable of consciously participating in the creative life of his Maker."

The reformist interpretation provides grounds for a novel treatment of man's role in the universe. The recognition of man's possession of some degree of free will not only justifies human self-reliance in attempting to transform the quality of earthly life, but also elevates such efforts to the level of a moral and religious duty. Not detachment, or the search for individual salvation, but active and effective personal involvement in the reconstruction of society in accordance with new humanistic values is the modern reformers' governing principle.

The emancipation of thought is indispensable to the individual's creative activity. Justification and articulation of the right to independent judgment is thus the leading subject of reformist Muslim thought. The vital importance attached to the problem of harmonizing belief and reason, religion and science, is entirely justifiable, given that the backwardness of the countries in this region was due in large measure to the negative attitude of the dominant religious dogmatism towards rational knowledge, the development of the natural sciences, and technological progress. As Jamal al-Din Afghani (1839–1909), the ideologist of Pan-Islamism, acknowledged, for the decline of Arab civilization Islam "bears all the blame. Wherever it penetrated, it sought to choke science, and was assiduously encouraged in this by despotism" (*Réfutation des Matérialistes*, p. 184). Such admissions were also made by other Muslim reformers inclined to place the entire blame for backwardness not on the traditional religion as such but on its dogmatic interpretation. Hence their task was to demonstrate the compatibility of faith and rational knowledge, to show that "true" religion was not an enemy but an ally of scientific progress.

Muhammad Abduh (1834–1905), the Grand Mufti of Egypt and disciple of al-Afghani, in his famous treatise *The Theology of Unity*, maintained that "there is nothing impossible for reason to tackle" (p. 31) and that, moreover, the "Supreme Being and its perfect attributes are rationally cognizable" (p. 71). Elsewhere in the same treatise, however, he contended that "the most that our reason can achieve is a knowledge of the accidents, but not the essence of things" (p. 54). Generally speaking, according to Abduh, the human mind is not competent to know God or the life to come, or to comprehend the requital which every sort of action will receive in that world. Conscious of the inconsistent nature of his rationalist outlook, Abduh averred the existence of different levels of intellect. Potentially at least, the mind is unlimited, and for those who possess a more perfect intellect (for example, the prophets) there is no limit to cognition. The ordinary mind, by contrast, is subject to all sorts of intellectual limitations.

Abduh's interpretation of prophecy was in no way supernatural. He portrayed the prophets without haloes. As Abduh saw them, they differ from other people merely by virtue of their more highly developed intellectual ability. He allowed that they too are liable to make incorrect judgments, although far less frequently than other mortals.

In contrast to the traditionalists, who advocated the adoption of religious faith prior to any offering of proofs for the truth of one's religious beliefs, Abduh embraced the opposite principle of "first prove, then believe." He denounced belief based on the blind uncritical acceptance of authority, and called on the faithful to have knowledge and proofs of the verity of their faith. For Abduh, the *ayat* "And guard yourselves against a day when no soul will in aught avail another, nor will intercession be accepted from it" (II:48) was a warning to believers that on the Day of Judgment they would not be allowed to justify their departures from the Quran by claiming to have followed the example of their ancestors. Abduh's views were directed against inert traditional thinking. At the same time, however, they were intended to vindicate and defend religion, to adapt it to the new times, and to reconcile it with science.

The task of dividing the spheres of influence belonging to science and religion, and thus of reconciling them, is pursued as well in the work of Seyyed Hossein Nasr (born 1933), the leading Muslim philosopher of today. A physics graduate of Harvard and the Massachusetts Institute of Technology, Nasr held the posts of Rector of Tehran University and Director of the Shah Academy of Sciences on the eve of the anti-Shah revolution in Iran. Nasr's attempt to reconcile science and religion was rooted in immediate pragmatic considerations. The Shah's regime, as is well known, was vigorously carrying out reforms designed to streamline the Iranian national economy. This necessarily involved the widespread introduction and application of technological expertise and theoretical knowledge. At the same time, the Shah and his supporters were aware of the need to retain the religious foundations of the monarchy. The task, then, was to dramatically improve Iranian economic performance while preserving the traditional underpinnings of society.

In his attempt to reconcile science and religion, Nasr is also governed by a desire to appropriate what is of value in technological progress while avoiding its adverse side-effects. He accuses modern man (by which he means the Westerner) of adopting a thoughtless attitude toward nature in his worship of rationalism. According to Nasr, rationalism implies "a secular vision of nature in which there is no place left for God." It fails to take into consideration the sacred aspect of nature – that is, its dependence on the Almighty – and orients man to the utilization and exploitation of nature for his own selfish interests.

In his efforts to work out a synthesis of science and religion, Nasr appeals to Sufism, deducing the ontological grounds for the existence of science and religion from man's occupation of a middle position between heaven and earth, between the absolute and relative realities. Given his current state of "detachment from God," man strives to return to the state of being near Him, which manifests itself in the search for the eternal and the absolute. This search is undertaken by means of "intellectual intuition" or the faculty of insight, instantaneous and immediate perception of transcendental knowledge in one's soul. Intellectual intuition is inherent potentially in everyone, but it is fully actualized only by prophets and mystics. Though intellect is a natural human faculty, it can achieve its full potential only when it is properly oriented through religious revelation.

Man's residence in the empirical world gives rise in him to needs that can only be satisfied through knowledge of this world. As a result, certain cognitive faculties are set into action – specifically, sensation and mind. In Nasr's opinion, mind can interpret the data of sensory experience in two possible ways – either as factual and naturalistic or as symbolic visualizations of reality. Hence there are two different types of science: natural science and cosmology. The natural sciences deal with the empirical nature of things, which is characterized by multiple and eternally changing materiality. Cosmology addresses the supernatural, the immortal and the immutable. According to Nasr's classification of the types of knowledge, metaphysics belongs to the highest category, the cosmological sciences make up the intermediary level, and the natural sciences are reduced to the lowest category. The last type of science studies things in their own material relationships; being metaphysically limited, it is not concerned with the elucidation of the profound extramaterial causes underlying the origin and existence of the natural world. Just as the object of the natural sciences – the phenomenal world – represents the reflected image of God, so too any natural science is nothing but a reflection of metaphysics, or the knowledge of the Divine reality.

For their content, the cosmological sciences draw on the same sensory experiences as do the natural sciences. But through the superimposition of the metaphysical coordinates upon the data supplied by the senses, they permit disclosure of the hidden inner meaning of natural phenomena. Making use of the allegorical *ta'awil* method applied by the Sufis to the interpretation of the Quran, Nasr tries to translate the vocabulary of science into the language of religious symbols.

In the final analysis Nasr fails to overcome the dichotomy of science and religion, but his system nonetheless validates the autonomy of scientific knowledge in a society regulated by religious principles. Such a reformist approach answers to the social need to employ the products of modern science, even though this employment remains essentially utilitarian, and is confined exclusively to the sphere of material production.

The reappraisal of ontological, epistemological and ethical ideas in the reformative spirit was affected, of course, by changing social conditions. Though up to the winning of political sovereignty there was virtually no clear-cut idea in the Islamic world about what kind of social structure was most desirable, it was obvious that the stagnant economic and political organization of traditional society had to be radically changed. But in what direction was one to move? This difficult question confronted all of the newly independent Islamic nations, which seemed compelled to make a choice between the two most influential models – the capitalist and the socialist – currently in force on the international scene. Many of them, however, opted for a third model, combining some elements of capitalism and socialism. Thus there appeared theories of a "third way of development," involving various kinds of religious socialism. The theoretical justification of these is based on the alleged similiarity of Marxism and Islam. As Hassan Hanafi, one of Egypt's most prominent philosophers, observes, "Islam is the implementation of the Marxist ideals of socialism, freedom and justice. . . . Marxism is an Islamic ideology just as Islam is a Marxist religion. . . . Marxism as an ideal motivation in Western experience in the nineteenth century is almost identical to Islam, which exhibits the same ideal motivation in Arabian experience" (*Islam in the Modern World*, Vol. 2, p. 417).

Even in those cases in which one of the models – either capitalism or socialism – seemed to be unconditionally preferred, however, that model inevitably received the imprint of the relevant national culture, so that the chosen ideal was often radically transformed and distorted. There have been many illustrations of how the application of one or the other of these "alien" models of development arouses resistance on behalf of the "Islamic realities" – resistance which is often temporarily overcome by the establishment of political dictatorship. But even this concentration of power eventually proves unable to secure the successful "transplantation" of Western ideology. And so the postwar history of Muslim countries provides a number of examples of the rejection of these "alien" models, the most illustrative being the anti-Shah revolution in Iran.

The efforts at reform have repeatedly come under attack from what are conventionally called "fundamentalists" and "revivalists." The social basis of this movement is quite wide, ranging from the middle classes, the petty bourgeoisie, workers, tradesmen, and students, to the youth in general. The emergence of Islamic fundamentalism has been caused by the failure of all the efforts to rehabilitate the system by borrowing from the West, by the realization that "there is no solution from without."

Fundamentalism, associated as it is with militant nationalism, is implacably hostile to cultural nihilism and all attempts to adopt foreign social or political models. Revivalism, on the other hand, gives concrete substance to the idea of "salvation" through the nostalgic pursuit of a return to the "golden age" in which Islam manifested itself in its "pure" form. The Islamists insist on the primacy of the Quran and the necessity that everything, both historical and contemporary, should be tested against it. As the Egyptian Saleh Sirriya (1991) affirms in his *Epistle of the Faith*, "there should be no barrier of any kind between the faithful and the Quran." The "direct relationship of the faithful to the Quran, unmediated by any agency, obliterates the inherited distinction between 'the men of religion' and ordinary Muslims." The Tunisian Shukri Mustafa thinks the same: Islamic history went awry when Muslims "abondoned the reception of their religion from the Quran and Sunna, confining themselves instead to the imitation [*taqlid*] of men known as the Imams and their opinions."

Still the range of opinion among the advocates of revivalism is as great as the amplitude of ideological oscillations intrinsic to the petty bourgeois masses and the middle classes, ranging from the most conservative (oriented to a return to the Middle Ages – that is, to the spirit and institutions of the time of the Prophet and the first four pious Caliphs) to extreme leftist views (compare the views, for example, of Abu'l-Aʿla Mawdudi, the Jamaʿat-i-Islami's founder, and of Gulam Parwez in Pakistan, of Sayyid Qutb, the Muslim Brotherhood's leading ideologue, and of Muammar Qaddafi, the leader of Libyan Jamahiriya, of Ayatollah Homeini, and of ʿAli Shariʿati in Iran).

The complex phenomenon of fundamentalism cannot be represented by its anti-reformist variety alone. The expansion of revivalism testifies, not to the end of the reformational process, but on the contrary, to its beginning, this time not as the élitist undertaking it has so far been, but as a large-scale popular movement for radical transformation of the traditional society. In his *Islamic Fundamentalism Reconsidered* (p. 52), Sadik L. Al-Azm, a leading contemporary Arab philosopher, concludes that Islamic fundamentalists

> may still show themselves to be the bearers of an "Islamic" movement bent on more industrialism, technologism, developmentalism, capitalism, nation-state building, empowerment and catching up with the developed world, all to be implemented under the guise of an ideology which makes the very fulfillment of this eminently modern, secular, bourgeois and originally European historical project look like a movement towards Allah's goals and a working out of His will in history instead of the opposite.

The failure of the experiments with capitalism and "installed socialism" have demonstrated that any socio-political model, no matter what its advantages, will be distorted and prove unworkable if it is transplanted onto unprepared and vulnerable soil. Though in many of their conceptions, goals and even conclusions the ideological processes at work in the Muslim world are in some sense reminiscent of those occurring in Europe during the Renaissance and Reformation, essentially these processes should not be viewed as reformational in the *full* sense of the word. To make the reforms workable, it is necessary to specify the inner impulses of development and set them into action.

Bibliography

Writings

Abduh, Muhammad 1966: *The Theology of Unity*, tr. I. Musaʿad and K. Cragg (London: Allen & Unwin).

Iqbal, Muhammad 1962: *The Reconstruction of Religious Thought in Islam* (Lahore: Ashraf Press).

Hanafi, Hassan 1995: *Islam in the Modern World*, 2 Vols (Cairo: Anglo-Egyptian Bookshop).

Nasr, Seyyed Hossein 1981: *Knowledge and the Sacred* (New York: Crossroad).

Sharif, M. M. 1952: "Dialectical Monadism," in *Contemporary Indian Philosophy*, ed. S. Radhakrishnan (London: Allen & Unwin).

References and further reading

Adams, Charles C. 1968: *Islam and Modernism in Egypt* (New York: Russell & Russell).

Afghani, J. 1942: *Réfutation des Matérialistes* (Paris: Librairie Orientaliste).

Al-Azm, Sadiq J. 1993: "Islamic fundamentalism reconsidered: a critical outline of problems, ideas and approaches," *South Asian Bulletin, Comparative Studies of South Asia and the Middle East*, 13, 1 and 2.

Cragg, K. 1965: *Counsels in Contemporary Islam*, Islamic Surveys 3 (Edinburgh: University Press).

Enayat, H. 1982: *Modern Islamic Political Thought* (London: Macmillan).
Fakhry, M. 1983: *A History of Islamic Philosophy* (New York: Columbia University Press).
Grunebaum, V. G. 1962: *Modern Islam, the Search for Cultural Identity* (Berkeley: University of California Press).
Keddie, N. R. 1968: *An Islamic Response to Imperialism* (Berkeley: University of California Press).
Maududi, A. A. 1961: *Towards Understanding Islam* (Delhi: Makazi Maktaba Jamaat-e-Islami Hind).
Nasr, S. H. 1987: *Traditional Islam in the Modern World* (London and New York: Kegan Paul International).
Qutb, M. 1968: *Islam, the Misunderstood Religion* (Delhi: Board of Islamic Publications).
Rahman, F. 1982: *Islam and Modernity. Transformation of an Intellectual Tradition* (Chicago: University of Chicago Press).
Shariati, A. 1980: *Marxism and Other Western Fallacies: an Islamic Critique* (Berkeley: University of California Press).
Sharif, M. M. (ed.) 1963–6: *A History of Islamic Philosophy*, 2 Vols (Wiesbaden: Pakistan Philosophical Congress).
Sirriya, S. 1991: *The Armed Prophet: the Rejectionists* (London: Riad al-Rayyes Books), p. 35.
Smith, W. C. 1957: *Islam in Modern History* (Princeton: Princeton University Press).
Stepaniants, M. T. 1989: *Islamic Philosophy and Social Thought (19th–20th Centuries)* (Lahore: People's Publishing House).

Index